"In *Thousands and Thousands of L* [illegible] the most engaging aspect of Helfta's spirituality: the nuns' powerful sense of community. In a period of just fifteen years, these nuns produced a treasure trove of Latin mystical literature, creating a utopian vision of their monastic life as an icon of the kingdom of heaven. Exploring the sisters' loving relationships with one another, with clergy and laity, with the dead in purgatory and the saints in heaven, Harrison shows that mysticism is not just a pursuit for the lonely soul in its solitude. It can be—and at Helfta it is—the most profoundly social of all human activities."

— Barbara Newman, Northwestern University

"In *Thousands and Thousands of Lovers,* Anna Harrison offers a rich and engaging account of women's religious community during the thirteenth century, focusing on the German monastery at Helfta—the period's most important and prolific center of women's religious writing. Considering the Helfta women as part of a community animated by a daily sense of Christ's presence and by the rhythm of the liturgy, but also by quotidian preoccupations—the presence of illness and death, friendships with each other, and relations beyond the cloister—Professor Harrison places the women's writings alongside their shared monastic and spiritual experience, bringing vividly to life their communal commitments, concerns, and sometimes annoyances. Brimming with fascinating observations about life at Helfta—from the nun who was excessively pleased with her golden bedspread, to the Christ-given power of Gertrude to hear confession, absolve, and assign penance—*Thousands and Thousands of Lovers* is a learned and delightful book that will be warmly welcomed by scholars and students concerned with questions relating to monastic community, spirituality, authorship, and gender."

— Fiona Griffiths, Stanford University

"This book offers an astonishingly rich reconstruction of the visionary, communal, personal, and literary lives of the nuns of Helfta. It rests on a rich knowledge of their teachings and writings but understands these as born as much from communal experience and insight as the visions or writings of unusually graced individuals. Amidst a larger interpretive literature, much of it not in English, this book follows upon Caroline Walker Bynum's pioneering introduction of these materials to English-speaking readers a generation ago. It is an attractive and compelling general reflection on the lives and writings of these women, yet thoughtfully focused. Readers will find themselves immersed in its narrative flow as well as its host of illuming and learned notes."

— John H. Van Engen, Andrew V. Tackes Professor of Medieval History, Emeritus, University of Notre Dame

"The nuns of medieval Helfta occupy a special place in the history of spirituality, both as individuals and as members of their community. Anna Harrison has given us a much-needed book on the writings associated with Mechtild of Hackeborn and Gertrude the Great. She shows how these nuns flourished in their monastic community. Her work is deeply grounded in scholarship, thoughtful, gracefully formulated, and accessible. It will be read for many years to come as a landmark in the study of spirituality."

— Richard Kieckhefer, Emeritus Professor of Religious Studies and History, Northwestern University

CISTERCIAN STUDIES SERIES:
NUMBER TWO HUNDRED EIGHTY-NINE

Thousands and Thousands of Lovers

Sense of Community among the Nuns of Helfta

Anna Harrison

Cistercian Publications
www.cistercianpublications.org

LITURGICAL PRESS
Collegeville, Minnesota
www.litpress.org

A Cistercian Publications title published by Liturgical Press

Cistercian Publications
Editorial Offices
161 Grosvenor Street
Athens, Ohio 45701
www.cistercianpublications.org

Cover design by Monica Bokinskie. Jean Colombe's *Hours of Louis de Laval*, Bibliothèque nationale de France.

1 2 3 4 5 6 7 8 9

Library of Congress Cataloging-in-Publication Data

Names: Harrison, Anna (Associate professor), author.
Title: Thousands and thousands of lovers : sense of community among the Nuns of Helfta / Anna Harrison.
Description: Collegeville, MN : Cistercian Publications, [2022] | Series: Cistercian studies ; two hundred eighty-nine | Includes bibliographical references and indexes. | Summary: "Thousands and Thousands of Lovers examines the spiritual significance of community to the Cistercian nuns of Helfta"— Provided by publisher.
Identifiers: LCCN 2021048997 (print) | LCCN 2021048998 (ebook) | ISBN 9780879072896 (paperback) | ISBN 9780879071899 (epub) | ISBN 9780879071899 (pdf)
Subjects: LCSH: Cistercian nuns—Germany—Eisleben. | Helfta (Convent : Eisleben, Germany) | Communities—Religious aspects—Christianity. | Cistercian nuns—Spiritual life.
Classification: LCC BX4328.Z5 G3385 2022 (print) | LCC BX4328.Z5 (ebook) | DDC 271/.97—dc23/eng/20211227
LC record available at https://lccn.loc.gov/2021048997
LC ebook record available at https://lccn.loc.gov/2021048998

A l'alta fantasia qui mancò possa;
ma già volgeva il mio disio e 'l *velle*,
sì come rota ch'igualmente è mossa,
l'amor che move il sole e l'altre stelle.
Dante, *Paradiso*

For
Hilary Cousins,
Eve Harrison,
Barbara Grizzuti Harrison,
and Caroline Walker Bynum

Contents

PART TWO
Within and Beyond the Cloister

PART THREE
The Living and the Dead

Abbreviations

ABR	American Benedictine Review
Analecta	*Analecta Cisterciensia*
CF	Cistercian Fathers series
Cîteaux	*Cîteaux: commentarii cistercienses*
Collectanea	*Collectanea Cisterciensia*
CS	Cistercian Studies series
CSQ	*Cistercian Studies Quarterly*
DSAM	*Dictionnaire de spiritualité ascétique et mystique, doctrine et histoire*. Ed. M. Viller, et al. Paris: G. Beauchesne et ses fils, 1980.
New Catholic	*The New Catholic Encyclopedia*. 2nd ed. Ed. Berard L. Marthaler, et al. Detroit: Gale, 2003.
RB	*The Rule of St. Benedict*. Trans. Carolinne White. London: Penguin Books, 2008.
SBOp	Sancti Bernardi opera. Ed. Jean Leclercq, C. H. Talbot, and H. M. Rochais. 8 vols. in 9. Rome: Editiones Cistercienses, 1957–1977.
SCh	Sources Chrétiennes. Paris: Les Éditions de Cerf.
Tjurunga	*Tjurunga: Australasian Benedictine Review*

The Works of Gertrude of Helfta and Mechtild of Hackeborn

CF 35	Gertrud of Helfta. *The Herald of God's Loving-Kindness, Books One and Two*. Trans. Alexandra Barratt. Kalamazoo, MI: Cistercian Publications, 1991.

CF 49 Gertrud the Great of Helfta. *Spiritual Exercises*. Trans. Gertrud Jaron Lewis and Jack Lewis. Kalamazoo, MI: Cistercian Publications, 1989.

CF 63 Gertrud the Great of Helfta. *The Herald of God's Loving-Kindness, Book Three*. Trans. Alexandra Barratt. Kalamazoo, MI: Cistercian Publications, 1999.

CF 85 Gertrud the Great of Helfta. *The Herald of God's Loving-Kindness, Book Four.* Trans. Alexandra Barratt. Collegeville, MN: Cistercian Publications, 2018.

Legatus Gertrude of Helfta. *Sanctae Gertrudis Magnae virginis ordinis sancti Benedicti: Legatus divinae pietatis accedunt ejusdem Exercitia spiritualia*. Vol. 1 of *Revelationes Gertrudianae ac Mechtildianae*. Ed. the monks of Solesmes [Louis Paquelin]. Paris: H. Oudin, 1875.

Liber Mechtild of Hackeborn. *Liber specialis gratiae*. In *Sanctae Mechtildis virginis ordinis sancti Benedicti: Liber specialis gratiae accedit sororis Mechtildis ejusdem ordinis Lux divinitatis*, edited by the monks of Solesmes [Louis Paquelin]. Vol. 2 of *Revelationes Gertrudianae ac Mechtildianae*. Paris: H. Oudin, 1877.

SCh 127 Gertrude of Helfta. *Oeuvres spirituelles I: Les Exercices*. Trans. Jacques Hourlier and Albert Schmitt. Paris: Les Éditions du Cerf, 1967.

SCh 139 Gertrude of Helfta. *Oeuvres spirituelles II: Le Héraut, Livres I et II*. Trans. Pierre Doyère. Paris: Les Éditions du Cerf, 1968.

SCh 143 Gertrude of Helfta. *Oeuvres spirituelles III: Le Héraut, Livre III*. Trans. Pierre Doyère. Paris: Les Éditions du Cerf, 1968.

SCh 255 Gertrude of Helfta. *Oeuvres spirituelles IV: Le Héraut, Livre IV*. Trans. Jean-Marie Clément, the nuns of Wisques, and Bernard de Vregille. Paris: Les Éditions du Cerf, 1978.

SCh 331 Gertrude of Helfta. *Oeuvres spirituelles V: Le Héraut, Livre V*. Trans. Jean-Marie Clément, the nuns of Wisques, and Bernard de Vregille. Paris: Les Éditions du Cerf, 1986.

I have benefited from English and French translations of the Helfta books by Alexandra Barratt; Pierre Doyère, Jean-Marie Clément, the nuns of Wisques, and Bernard de Vregille; Jacques Hourlier and Albert Schmitt; Gertrud Jaron Lewis and Jack Lewis; Barbara Newman; the nuns of Dordogne; and Margaret Winkworth. All these works are cited in the bibliography.

Acknowledgments

My interest in the topic of community owes much to my neighbors at 401 8th Avenue, my Brooklyn apartment building, and especially to Kyle Gordon, Barbara O'Toole, and Amalia Miro, among my most important teachers in the meaning of community. Special thanks go to Patricia Llosa for her unflagging enthusiasm for this project and to Laura Boylan, who gave me a place to write. I am indebted to Roberto Dell'Oro, who helped me better understand the Helfta literature. I thank Catherine Osbourne for her careful reading and Jack McCambrige for his grappling with the nineteenth-century German.

A National Endowment for the Humanities Fellowship and Summer Stipend provided support for my research, as did the labor of many faculty colleagues off the tenure-track, whose own scholarship might have flourished under more just working conditions; I acknowledge especially Sheila Jones and Arik Greenberg of the Department of Theological Studies at Loyola Marymount University. The contribution of Senior Administrative Coordinator Faith Sovilla to fashioning a department workplace conducive to faculty research has been vital.

My warmest appreciation goes to Carmela Vircillo Franklin, Joel Kaye, Wayne Proudfoot, and Robert Somerville at Columbia University, where I was a graduate student long ago. Many readers will be familiar with the dazzling scholarship of Caroline Walker Bynum; far fewer will be aware of her unmatched generosity as a teacher, which is the bedrock of this book. A supportive community of fellow graduate students reverberates throughout these pages and includes Donna Alfonso Bussell, Leah DeVun, Mary Doyno, Anna Trumbore Jones, and Nicole Randolph Rice.

The last half century has seen a surge of scholarship in the religiosity of the women of the Latin Christian Middle Ages, invigorated by 1970s feminism and the increased attention to the history of women; like so many others, I owe an enormous debt to the women's movement of the previous century and particularly to one of its more contrarian contributors, Barbara Grizzuti Harrison, my mother, who took up the presumptuous proposition that a single mother of two, high school graduate, and first-generation Italian American had something of value to offer the literary world. I offer this book to her. I thank my husband and my daughter for everything.

Preface

Suffused with communitarian and corporate imagery, laced with other-directed prayers as well as instructions for the strengthening of conventual ties, and crowded with visions asserting solidarity between the living and the dead, the writings of the thirteenth-century Cistercian nuns of Helfta attest to their wholehearted investment in the topic of community. They shine a spotlight on an intricate web of thought concerning social commitments and relationships both within the monastery and beyond its walls. This is a complex account. Bursting with emphatic optimism about what community offers for individual and group spiritual progress,[1] the Helfta literature also exposes tensions in the nuns' notions of the reach of the community—and of the women's associated obligations. Buoyed by a vibrant and growing body of scholarship on Helfta, in this book I examine the nuns' sense of community more deliberately than have previous studies.

Among a wealth of compositions that thirteenth-century women wrote, three surviving works produced at Helfta and associated with Mechtild of Hackeborn (1241–ca. 1298/99) and Gertrude of Helfta (1256–ca. 1301/2) stand out as exceptional in several ways. Gertrude's *Spiritual Exercises* is a series of loosely organized prayers, chants, and litanies based chiefly

[1] For the optimism of the Helfta literature, see for example Philibert Schmitz, *Les Moniales, Histoire de l'Ordre de Saint-Benoît*, vol. 7 (Liège: Les Éditions de Maredsous, 1956), 299; and Caroline Walker Bynum, "Women Mystics in the Thirteenth Century: The Case of the Nuns of Helfta," in *Jesus as Mother: Studies in the Spirituality of the High Middle Ages* (Berkeley: University of California Press, 1982), esp. 193–94.

on the liturgy. The *Herald* and the *Book of Special Grace* are composite, hybrid creations, weaving together accounts of revelations and ecstasies, spiritual teachings, prayers, and a variety of testimonies to the exemplary devotion of Gertrude and Mechtild as well as that of Abbess Gertrude of Hackeborn (1223–1292)—and to the piety of the monastery's female inhabitants considered collectively. Together, these texts run close to 1,250 printed pages, making this the century's largest body of religious writing by women. The monastery's concern with the community—unyielding, nuanced, wide-ranging—is evident in virtually every nook and cranny of this literature. Its centrality to the women's religiosity is exemplified in the multi-decade enterprise that gave birth to the *Herald* and the *Book of Special Grace*, a collaborative process that called on the varied contributions of an indeterminate number of nuns, with almost no discernible male involvement.[2] These all-female compositions offer insight into the emotions, thoughts, and experiences of a remarkable monastic family, a group of highly educated, theologically sophisticated, and self-consciously literary women, and they are among our richest resources for understanding the spiritual significance of community to late medieval people.

Scholars have long identified the thirteenth century as central in the elaboration of western European notions of community. There has been a tendency, however, to see late medieval religiosity as centering on individual, inner experience rather than on group practice or on communal response, even when the context is religious or monastic community. And though the view is now much contested, some scholars

[2] See especially Kurt Ruh, "Gertrud von Helfta: Ein neues Gertrud-Bild," *Zeitschrift für deutsches Altertum und deutsche Literatur* 121 (1992): 1–20; Margarete Hubrath, *Schreiben und Erinnern: Zur "memoria" im* Liber specialis gratiae *Mechthilds von Hakeborn* (Paderborn: Ferdinand Schöningh, 1996), 37, 51; Laura M. Grimes, "Writing as Birth: The Composition of Gertrud of Helfta's *Herald of God's Loving-Kindness*," CSQ 42, no. 3 (2007): 329–45.

have argued that the surge during the late Middle Ages in subjective spirituality—characterized, in part, by a deliberate curling inward of attention to the self in relation to God—drained enthusiasm for the common life. In spite of a sustained interest in female spirituality and collective institutions, medievalists have paid little attention to women's voices in fashioning this account. Focusing on writing from Helfta—a woefully underused resource for major areas of medieval religious thought—this book explores a more subtle interplay between communal practice and private piety, other-directed focus and inward-religious impulse, than is often allowed.

I cast a wide net in this book, following the nuns' lead as they wrote about a broad spectrum of matters related to community that captured their imagination and pulled on their conscience. It is arranged in three parts. The first part concentrates on the nuns' sense of community among themselves. In chapter one, I examine the collaborative process of the composition of the *Herald* and the *Book of Special Grace*, asking what this process tells about writing as a sustained spiritual practice that depended upon and contributed to building a sense of community among the sisters. In chapter two, I explore friendship and spiritual guidance at Helfta, and I consider the meaning of the nuns' relationships with one another for their sense of community. In chapter three, I take a close look at attitudes toward relationality that come to the fore in the nuns' experiences of illness, dying, and bereavement, to which the literature devotes considerable attention. The Helfta writings contain numerous reports of revelations that came to the sisters in Office and in Mass. In chapter four, I study these for the women's sense of relatedness to and responsibility for one another during public communal worship—as well as their sense of separateness from one another.

In the book's second part, I widen the scope of my investigation. In chapter five, I consider the place of clergy in the women's perceptions of community, including those priests who tended to their pastoral needs (or neglected to do so), and to whom the nuns sometimes served as confidants and counselors. In chapter six, I examine the nuns' sense of community with members of their household who are neither nuns nor clergy, such as *conversi* and convent administrators. I consider in addition how the nuns related to the laity who attended the monastery's chapel as well as to armed aggressors who periodically threatened the monastery's integrity. In the book's final part, I turn to visions of departed souls for what they convey about the ties that bound the sisters to the population of purgatory, the subject of chapter seven, and the inhabitants of heaven, the focus of chapter eight.

I intend this book as a history of the Helfta nuns' thoughts about and attitudes toward community. The considerations of community that the women offered were never fully free from the scrim their interpretative gaze created, a gaze harnessed to a desire to shape what they saw.[3] They thus portrayed their monastic household both as it was and as they wished it to be, braiding an idealized version of the common life with frank accounts of what was, here and there conceding that the community they conjured through literary creativity was openly different from and sometimes at odds with the reality they knew themselves to live. Because the boundary between the sisters' sense of community and their experience of community was not absolute, the reader may notice a degree of slippage between the two in my own writing.

The convent's compositions—joyous, solemn, and ribboned with praise for God—are a synesthetic explosion of images for the edification and entertainment of the reader. Liquid and light, feasting and dancing, ornate vestments and brilliant

[3] Barbara Newman has characterized the *Book of Special Grace* as a type of "utopian genre," offering its readers an ideal community "in action" (introduction to *Mechthild of Hackeborn and the Nuns of Helfta: The Book of Special Grace*, trans. Barbara Newman [New York: Paulist Press, 2017], 8).

jewels, foliage and flowers adorn pages drenched in a kaleidoscope of colors and punctuated with sighs, whispers, and song, offering sometimes chummy, sometimes erotic, now regal, now homey delights. Their extravagantly cataphatic quality, long regarded by scholars as second rate in comparison to a more sober, speculative (often presumed to be mostly male) apophatic mystical orientation,[4] complements a celebration of the loyal love relationship between Christ and the visionary nuns, Gertrude and Mechtild, as well as their sisters. These qualities have not failed to elicit the squeamishness of some modern readers, including William James, who dismissed the whole of the *Herald* as the musings of a personality so absorbed in love of God and so narrowly fixed on securing demonstrations of his love for her as to push from her purview "all human loves" and all "practical human interests."[5] In fact, the Helfta authors join sumptuous descriptions of mystical flight and evocations of affective response with delicate meditations and razor-sharp insights that betray seasoned sensitivity to questions of community; their intellectual acuity is less obvious, perhaps, to the reader unaccustomed to their peculiarly poetic (to some, fussy and ponderous) literary leanings, including, especially, their heavy borrowings from the language of the liturgy.

These writings signal a surge of female confidence in a century that saw the growing clericalization of the church and the rise of the university as a center of theological reflection, a world in which almost all the writers the nuns knew were male—with the exception of their late-in-life cloister companion, the literary giant and Beguine Mechtild of Magdeburg (1207–1282), and, probably, the Benedictine Elisabeth of Schönau (1129–1164), whose liturgically inflected visionary

[4] On the relation of gender to the categories of cataphatic and apophatic, see Barbara Newman, "Gender," in *The Blackwell Companion to Mysticism*, ed. Julia A. Lamm (London: Blackwell Publishing, 2013), 41–55, esp. 53.

[5] William James, *Varieties of Religious Experience* (1902; repr. New York: Image Books, 1978), 335–36.

compositions may have been influential at Helfta.[6] Giving virtually no thought to their femaleness, the nuns launched themselves into a larger elite Latin textual culture, filled with trust in the worth for themselves of their bookish endeavors and sure that the fruit of their labors would be meaningful to audiences stretching out into the far future.

I take as my central concern what the women of Helfta themselves wished to communicate. Thus, when I write, for example, that this or that sister heard a heavenly harmony accompany the nuns in communal song, felt God's grace coursing like liquid through her body, or witnessed Christ comfort a dying sister with a kiss, I do so because this is what the authors tell us, and I try to understand what they seem to want to say. I deliberately do not adduce whether events such as these "really happened." Never casting doubt on the divine origin of the visions, auditions, and ecstasies they record, the Helfta compositions themselves suggest that such sleuthing misses a larger point. About the visions the *Book of Special Grace* attributes to Mechtild, we read that she received them not only for herself but for *us*,[7] an interpretive framework instructing the reader to appropriate what these revelations convey. We also learn that when Christ flooded Gertrude with his grace, he sometimes did so by means of images that would make his presence to her comprehensible to others.[8]

Threaded through the phenomena the *Herald* and *Book of Special Grace* chronicle, therefore, is a candid missionary impulse, molding (so we read) what the visionary undergoes so as to make the experience of one (often but not always Mechtild

[6] Newman, introduction to *Mechthild of Hackborn*, 8, 10.

[7] *Liber specialis gratiae*, in *Sanctae Mechtildis, virginis ordinis sancti Benedicti: Liber specialis gratiae accedit sororis Mechtildis ejusdem ordinis Lux divinitatis*, ed. the monks of Solesmes [Louis Paquelin] (Paris: H. Oudin, 1877), 5:30, 363; hereafter *Liber*.

[8] *Le Héraut*, ed. and trans. Pierre Doyère, et al., *Gertrude d'Helfta: Oeuvres spirituelles*, 4 vols., SCh 139, 143, 255, 331 (Paris: Éditions du Cerf, 1968–86); 1 Prol. 6 (SCh 139:114); hereafter *Le Héraut*.

or Gertrude) accessible to another (the sisters themselves as well as the texts' broader audience). Thus the nuns crafted into a stylized whole an abundance of discrete experiences and insights that they attributed to a number of women, putting into play the gospel's command: "what you hear whispered, proclaim from the rooftops" (Matt 10:27).[9] Keeping motive in mind and convinced of the value of attunement to the nuns' thought, I attempt a way of reading that Caroline Walker Bynum has modeled in her many works: I believe that a careful study of particular images in the context of other images, of theological teachings as well as of religious practices and social behavior, can yield insights into the assumptions of medieval people and thus offer entry into their experience.

I hope my work will contribute to the history of ideas about the function of the collective in forming the self, to the study of female authorship and intellectual achievement, and to investigations into monastic spirituality of the later Middle Ages. I write for medievalists as well as for readers with general interest in the history of women and in the history of Christianity. Although the book's chapters build sequentially, each can stand independently of the others. Those interested in delving into an expression of the medieval experience of liturgy can jump directly to chapter four, for instance, while readers whose curiosity lodges in the role of the saints in the lives of the faithful can skip over the others to the book's last chapter.

The *Book of Special Grace* circulated widely in the late Middle Ages, in both lay and monastic circles.[10] Over a hundred manuscripts in Latin contain either the bulk or portions of the book.

[9] *Liber* 7.7 (399).

[10] For the manuscript history of the *Book of Special Grace* and patterns of circulation, see Louis Paquelin, Praefatio to *Liber*; Margot Schmidt, "Mechtilde de Hackeborn," DSAM 10:873–77; Ernst Hellgardt, "Latin and the Vernacular: Mechthild of Magdeburg—Mechthild of Hackeborn—Gertrude of Helfta,"

One manuscript, the second oldest, written in 1370, contains the entirety of the *Book of Special Grace's* seven parts. It is probably a reliable descendant of an original Helfta composition. The *Herald* achieved a far smaller circulation in any form in the first several centuries after its creation. There are seven known manuscripts, two of which contain incomplete versions of the text as it survives in the other five.[11] There are no known manuscripts of the *Spiritual Exercises*.[12] In spite of the absence of a manuscript, and of a manuscript tradition, scholars who have closely studied the *Exercises* have for the most part not raised concerns about its authenticity or authorship.[13] Scholars have been divided as to the language in which the *Book of Special Grace* was first written, with the majority considering the original a Latin composition; both the *Herald* and the *Exercises* were probably composed in Latin.[14]

---

in *A Companion to Mysticism and Devotion in Northern Germany in the Late Middle Ages*, ed. Elizabeth Andersen, et al. (Leiden: Brill, 2014).

[11] For the *Herald's* manuscript tradition, see *Le Héraut*, Appendix (SCh 143:345–50); Balázs J. Nemes, "Text Production and Authorship: Gertrude of Helfta's *Legatus Divinae Pietatis*," in Andersen, et al., *Companion to Mysticism and Devotion*, 103–30.

[12] John Lansberg, the text's first editor, neither mentions any manuscript nor reviews the process by which he prepared his edition, a surprising omission since he does indicate his source for the *Herald* in a preface to that work (*Les Exercices*, ed. and trans. Jacques Hourlier and Albert Schmitt, in *Gertrude d'Helfta*, SCh 127 [Paris: Éditions du Cerf, 1967)], 40–43; Balázs J. Nemes, "Die 'Geistlichen Übungen' Gertruds von Helfta: Ein vergessenes Zeugnis mittelaltlicher Mystik," review of *Gertrud von Helfta: Exercitia spiritualia. Geistliche Übungen. Lateinisch und deutsch*, ed. Siegfried Ringler [Elberfeld: Humberg, 2001]; Marie-Hélène Deloffre, "Les Exercices sont-ils l'oeuvre de Sainte Gertrude d'Helfta? Approche Stylistique," *Cîteaux* 68, nos. 1–4 [2017]: 121–91).

[13] Gertrud Jaron Lewis and Jack Lewis (introduction to *Spiritual Exercises*, ed. and intro. Gertrud Jaron Lewis and Jack Lewis, CF 49 [Kalamazoo, MI: Cistercian Publications, 1989], 2); and Kurt Ruh (*Frauenmystik and Franziskanische Mystik der Frühheit* [Munich: C. H. Beck, 1993], 318; Ruh, "Gertrud von Helfta"), believe Gertrude wrote this work. Nemes does not regard as credible Lansberg's ascription of the *Exercises* to Gertrude (Nemes, "Die 'Geistlichen Übungen'"; Nemes, "Text Production and Authorship," 105).

[14] Ruh, *Frauenmystik*, 301–2, reviews scholarly opinions with regard to the original language of the *Book of Special Grace*. For a discussion of the language

It was not until the 1536 edition of John Lansberg (1490–1539) of the Charterhouse of Saint Barbara in Cologne that the *Spiritual Exercises* and the *Herald* began to achieve the renown that had long belonged to the *Book of Special Grace*, in fact coming to overshadow it in popularity. The first printing of the *Book of Special Grace* seems to have been the 1503 German-language edition of Paul Weida, who translated a Latin manuscript,[15] and in 1536, Lansberg edited what has come to be regarded as the complete version of the Latin text. Numerous printings of the three works followed,[16] a rush of sixteenth-century editions and translations augmenting readership for versions of the Helfta writings, many with content at a distance from the medieval texts themselves.[17] There is no critical edition of the *Book of Special Grace*. Modern studies that rely on the Latin transmission depend on the late-nineteenth-century edition based exclusively on the 1370 manuscript, which the monks of Solesmes prepared under the direction of Louis Paquelin. Pierre Doyère, Jean-Marie Clément, and Bernard Vregille prepared the definitive critical Latin edition of the *Herald*.[18]

---

in which the *Herald* was composed, see Doyère, introduction to *Le Héraut*, 25; Hourlier and Schmitt, introduction to *Gertrude d'Helfta*, 42–44; Siegfried Ringler, "Die Rezeption Gertruds von Helfta im Bereich süddeutschen Frauenklöster," in *"Vor dir steht die leere Schale meiner Sehnsucht": Die Mystik der Frauen von Helfta*, ed. Michael Bangert and Hildegund Keul (Leipzig: St. Benno Buch- und Zeitschriftenverlagsgesellschaft, 1998), 136–37.

15 Paquelin, Praefatio to *Liber*, xi; Paquelin, Praefatio to *Sanctae Gertrudis Magnae, virginis ordinis sancti Benedicti: Legatus divinae pietatis, accedunt ejusdem Exercitia spiritualia*, ed. the monks of Solesmes [Louis Paquelin] (Paris: H. Oudin, 1875), iii and xlvi (hereafter *Legatus*); Hourlier and Schmitt, introduction to *Gertrude d'Helfta*, 42.

16 Ursmer D. Berlière, "Sainte Mech[t]ilde et sainte Gertrude la grande, furent-elles Bénédictines?" *Revue Bénédictine* 6 (1899): 42–52; Paquelin, Praefatio to *Liber*, x–xiii; Wilhelm Preger, *Geschichte der deutschen Mystik bis zum Tode Meister Eckharts* (Leipzig: Dörffling und Franke, 1874), 79–82; Ruh, *Frauenmystik*, 296–97.

17 Hellgardt, "Latin," 144.

18 For the edition's preparation, see Doyère, introduction to *Le Héraut*, 63–64, 77–83.

In comparison with other medieval women who composed religious literature, the Helfta nuns have sparked relatively little modern scholarly interest. There are multiple reasons for this neglect, including a reluctance among American medievalists to grapple with German religious culture and the relative lack of interest among Germanists in studying works that have been transmitted largely in Latin.[19] Anglophone scholars' concentration on the new (formal and informal) religious roles for women that emerged during the later Middle Ages may have contributed to dulling interest in a spirituality anchored firmly in the cloister, the Helfta literature's rootedness in liturgical practices and texts probably being alienating to some tastes. The fact that neither Gertrude nor Mechtild was a reformer or sharp critic of the church has perhaps rendered their contributions less relevant to a contingent of readers. The virtual absence of male involvement in the creation of the Helfta writings may have made them less compelling to those whose interest fixes on the interaction between women and men, and since Bynum's groundbreaking 1982 article on Helfta, relatively few historians of gender have looked to this literature.[20] There are signs that the pull of the Helfta nuns has, however, begun to increase. We have seen, for example, the first translation into English in over five hundred years of the Latin-language version of the *Book of Special Grace*,[21] renewed engagement with the works' liturgical significance[22] and mysticism,[23] and an

[19] For the reception of the *Book of Special Grace*, see Hans Urs von Balthasar, Einführung to *Das Buch vom strömenden Lob*, ed. Hans Urs von Balthasar (Einsiedeln: Johannes Verlag, 1955), 7–8.

[20] Bynum, "Women Mystics."

[21] Barbara Newman, trans., *Mechthild of Hackeborn and the Nuns of Helfta: The Book of Special Grace* (New York: Paulist Press, 2017).

[22] See, for example, Helga Unger, "Interaktion von Gott und Mensch im *Legatus divinae pietatis* (Buch II) Gertruds der Großen von Helfta. Liturgie—mystische Erfahrung—Seelsorge," in *Liturgie und Literatur: Historische Fallstudien*, ed. Cornelia Herberichs, et al. (Berlin: De Gruyter, 2015), 133–65.

[23] See for example Beate Korntner, *Mystikerinnen im Mittelalter: die drei Frauen von Helfta und Marguerite Porete—zwischen Anerkennung und Verfolgung* (Munich: Akademische Verlagsgemeinschaft München, 2012).

invigorated exploration of the nuns' writings for what they might contribute to modern Christian worship.[24] All these areas of inquiry—and others still—are likely to gain momentum as word spreads of efforts currently afoot to proclaim Gertrude a Doctor of the Church.[25]

Over seven hundred years separate us from the golden age of Helfta; aspects of the nuns' notions of community will probably appear to many of us as frankly odd. Yet their preoccupation remains familiar. If in 1988 medieval historian Miri Rubin could remark that the word *community* was so much in vogue that any category of people could be called a "community,"[26] its application is even more promiscuous today, sometimes employed to summon up what it describes, promoting a sense of affinity, solidity, and homogeneity that may mask unspoken complexity or whispered antipathies, or live side by side with them. It is certain that attitudes about community continue to be of utmost relevance to the ways in which we experience and organize our world, think about self in relation to others, and make decisions about affairs clearly political, patently personal, and obviously religious. Our modern sensibilities are informed by a long history of notions about community. It seems worthwhile to consider what the Helfta nuns expressed about a subject of singular meaningfulness to them that still stirs our imagination.

[24] See for example Michael Anthony Abril, "Gertrude of Helfta's Liturgical-Mystical Union," CSQ 43, no. 1 (2008): 77.

[25] Ana Laura Forastieri, "Saint Gertrude's Postulation for Doctor of the Church," *Magistra* 24, no. 2 (Winter 2018): 42–45.

[26] Miri Rubin, "Small Groups: Identity and Solidarity in the Late Middle Ages," in *Enterprise and Individuals in Fifteenth-Century England* (Stroud, UK: Alan Sutton Publishers, 1991), 133.

Introduction

Because God, being merciful and clement, wishes no one to be lost and desires all people to be saved, he frightened [Count Burchard] for his soul's health, and mercifully warned him on a certain night by means of a dream in order that [Burchard] might care for his soul—since with so much wealth, he would not be saved unless he were to construct a monastery of women in honor of the most glorious Mother of God, and thus reconciled through the Mother of Mercy, be able to obtain the true salvation of his soul. Concerned beyond measure for his soul, he prudently did not delay in the least to complete the counsel with salubrious work. . . . With the help of divine grace . . ., the illustrious Count Burchard of pious memory, in the fifth week of the Easter feast, began to build the women's cloister, close to the castle of Mansfeld. . . .[1]

Abbess Sophia of Stolberg, *Narratio* (1451)

On the feast of Saint Peter and Saint Paul, 1229, Countess Elizabeth Mansfeld (d. 1240) and her husband, Count Burchard (d. 1229), founded a monastery dedicated to Mary, Mother of God, in the vicinity of their castle at Mansfeld, in Saxony. Later the same year, the monastery's first inhabitants, seven nuns led by Cunegund—the woman who would become their abbess—arrived at the foundation from the Cistercian monastery of Saint John and Saint Burchard in the city of Halberstadt,

[1] Max Krüne, ed., *Urkundenbuch der Klöster der Grafschaft Mansfeld* (Halle: Otto Hendel, 1888), no. 148, 223.

approximately forty-five kilometers northwest of Mansfeld.[2] Elizabeth and Burchard donated several additional possessions, including land and buildings. It was their expectation that the nuns might thus engage undisturbed in "pious leisure" and "knock on the door of divine mercy, for us and for our progenitors and successors, without intermission."[3] The monastery remained at its original foundation for five years. It was transferred to Rodarsdorf, only a few kilometers from Mansfeld, in about 1234, and in 1258 or 1259, the house was translated to Helfta, two or three kilometers southeast of the village of Eisleben, where it remained for close to a hundred years.[4]

The monastery, in its various locations, was a center of sustained engagement for its founders' family over the course of several generations. In 1230, the newly widowed Elizabeth

[2] The circumstances of their arrival go unspecified. For the foundation of the monastery and its institutional history, see, in addition to the medieval and early modern documents, see Wilhelm Preger, *Geschichte der deutschen Mystik bis zum Tode Meister Eckharts* (Leipzig: Dörffling und Franke, 1874), 113–16; Louis Paquelin, Praefatio to *Liber*, xi, and Louis Paquelin, Praefatio to *Legatus*, v–ix, xxv–xxvii; A. Mary F. Robinson, "The Convent of Helfta," *Fortnightly Review* 40 (1886): 641–58; Herman Grössler, "Die Blützeit des Klosters Helfta bei Eisleben," in *Jahres-Bericht über das königliche Gymnasium zu Eisleben* (Easter 1886–Easter 1887), 1–38; Krüne, Foreword to Krüne, *Urkundenbuch*, xv–xviii; Lina Eckenstein, *Women under Monasticism: Chapters on Saint-Lore and Convent Life Between A.D. 500 and A.D. 1500* (1896; repr. New York: Russell and Russell, 1963), 328–53; R. P. Émil Michael, "Die hl. Mechtild und die hl. Gertrud die Grosse Benedictinerinnen?" *Zeitschrift für katholisches Theologie* 23 (1899): 448–552; Joseph Gottschalk, "Kloster Helfta und Schlesien," *Archiv für schlesische Kirchengeschichte* 13 (1955): 63–82.

[3] Krüne, *Urkundenbuch*, no. 1, 129; see also Krüne, *Urkundenbuch*, no. 148, 224.

[4] Krüne, *Urkundenbuch*, no. 148, 225. The reasons for these translations are unclear; proximity to the castle at Mansfeld may have cast a protective shadow over the monastery; it may, on the other hand, have endangered the nuns' welfare by placing them within an orbit of feuding nobility, and a water shortage may have precipitated the move from Rodarsdorf. Eisleben was under the control of the Mansfeld family through the end of the eighteenth century. It is located in the eastern foothills of the Harz mountains, Germany's most northerly mountain ranges.

further enriched the foundation.[5] She may have championed transferring the monastery to Rodarsdorf, accompanying the nuns on their move and remaining with them until her death in 1240. Two of her granddaughters, Sophia (fl. 13th c.) and Elizabeth (fl. 13th c.), entered the monastery at Helfta. The monastery's third abbess, Sophie of Querfort, who ruled from 1291 to 1298 or 1301, was a great-granddaughter. The sixth abbess, Lutgard (1337–1347), also stemmed from the house of Mansfeld, and Oda von Hamersleben, another relative, followed, ruling the monastery from 1348–1351. Soon after its establishment, Elizabeth's and Burchard's sons-in-law agreed to protect it. The land on which the new monastery at Helfta was erected was a gift of Archbishop Rupert of Magdeburg (r. 1260–1266), a grandson of the founders and the brother of Burchard III (1229–a. 1274). In 1265 Burchard erected a chapel at Helfta in honor of John the Baptist and John the Evangelist, which became the family burial ground. In the thirteenth century, therefore, the Mansfeld women played the part of benefactors at the monastery; they retired there and took final vows at the monastery, and several held a position of highest distinction as abbess. The men—laity and ecclesiastics—contributed as protectors and patrons.

Together with the Mansfelds, the Hackeborn family figures prominently among those closely associated with the monastery, the two families helping to shape a common history.[6]

[5] For female patronage of women's houses, see Sharon A. Farmer, *Communities of St. Martin: Legend and Ritual in Medieval Tours* (Ithaca, NY: Cornell University Press, 1991), esp. 99, 102, 109, 114–16; Jeffrey F. Hamburger, "Art, Enclosure, and the Pastoral Care of Nuns," in *The Visual and the Visionary: Art and Female Spirituality in Late Medieval Germany* (New York: Zone Books, 1992), 58–71; Jo Ann McNamara, "The Need to Give: Suffering and Female Sanctity in the Middle Ages," in *Images of Sainthood in Medieval Europe*, ed. Renate Blumenfeld-Kosinski and Timea Szell (Ithaca, NY: Cornell University Press, 1991), 199–221.

[6] The literature also attests to the continuing presence in the life of the monastery of several other families—the Querforts, Stolbergs, Wippras, and Friedeburgs (all of whom intermarried).

The Hackeborns, whom the oldest documents from Helfta mention more often than they do the Mansfelds, were wealthy nobles, with possessions in northern Thuringia and the Harz. Albert II of Hackeborn (1209–ca. 1250) signed the monastery's foundation charter in 1229, and from its early days, Hackeborn women populated the monastery side by side with women from the Mansfeld family. Of Albert's four known daughters, two, Mechtild and Gertrude, became nuns, renowned visionary and abbess respectively. Both of Albert's sons contributed to the monastery. Ludwig I (d. ca. 1301) donated repeatedly, as did his brother, Albert III (d. 1304), two of whose daughters took the veil at Helfta. Throughout the thirteenth century, the Hackeborn men pledged to defend the monastery's nuns.

Under Abbess Gertrude of Hackeborn, the monastery amassed multiple gifts from the Hackeborns and negotiated the exchange of material assets, further cementing a productive relationship between the monastery and Abbess Gertrude's family and widening the monastery's economic support. The monastery appears to have been well-endowed and to have prospered throughout Gertrude's tenure; while there are indications that in the second half of the thirteenth century Helfta labored under the burden of debt,[7] Abbess Gertrude oversaw

[7] The *Book of Special Grace* reports that during an episcopal vacancy in the see of Halberstadt, the canons placed an interdict on the community on account of unspecified financial matters; the *Herald* testifies to the suspension of divine rites as well and refers to a year in which the monastery strained under debt (*Liber* 1.27 [95], and *Le Héraut* 3.16; 3.17; 3.68 [SCh 143:66, 74, 274]). The vacancy during which the interdict was issued refers to a brief period that elapsed between the death of Bishop Vulrad and assumption of the bishopric by Herman of Blankenberg (1296–1303); see Paquelin, Praefatio to *Legatus*, xv; and Raphaela Averkorn, "Die Bischöfe von Halberstadt in ihren kirchlichen und politischen Wirken und in ihren Beziehungen zur Stadt von den Anfängen bis zur Reformation," in *Bürger, Bettelmönche und Bischöfe*, 25. For the monastery's prosperity, see Eckenstein, *Women under Monasticism*, 329; Jeanne Ancelet-Hustache, *Mechtilde de Magdebourg (1207–1282): Étude de psychologie religieuse* (Paris: Librairie Ancienne Honoré Champion, 1926), 61; Margarete Hubrath, *Schreiben und Erinnern: Zur "memoria" im* Liber specialis

a significant building program, and the monastery continued to attract noble entrants. The nuns, where we can identify their social background, were primarily daughters of nobles of the area, and it is likely that the majority came from Saxon and Thuringian families of wealth and nobility.[8]

Helfta declared itself Cistercian from its foundation,[9] one of many unincorporated women's houses that followed some Cistercian customs, tailoring them to their particular needs and circumstances. The seven nuns who arrived at Mansfeld in 1229 came from a Cistercian monastery in Halberstadt, and in 1262, Abbess Gertrude dispatched twelve of Helfta's daughters to a Cistercian house founded by her brothers at Hedersleben, in the Harz, suggesting a continuing identification with aspects

---

gratiae *Mechthilds von Hakeborn* (Paderborn: Ferdinand Schöningh, 1996); Sabine Spitzlei, *Erfahrungsraum Herz: Zur Mystik des Zisterzienserinnenklosters Helfta im 13 Jahrhundert* (Stuttgart-Bad Cannstatt: Frommann-Holzboog, 1991), 28.

[8] Noblewomen monopolized places in the more prestigious monasteries; women's houses in Germany were especially restrictive with regard to their entrants' social status, and taking full vows was still largely confined in the thirteenth century to members of the nobility. For the social background of nuns, see for example Power, *English Nunneries*, 4–9; Herbert Grundmann, *Religious Movements in the Middle Ages: The Historical Link Between Heresy, the Mendicant Orders, and the Women's Religious Movement in the Thirteenth Century, with the Historical Foundations of German Mysticism*, trans. Steven Rowan (Notre Dame, IN: University of Notre Dame Press, 1995), 82–85; Philibert Schmitz, *Les Moniales* (Liège: Les Éditions de Maredsous, 1956), 248; Maren Kuhn-Rehfus, "Zisterzienserinnen in Deutschland," *Die Zisterzienser: Ordensleben zwischen Ideal und Wirklichkeit*, ed. K. [Kaspar] Elm, et al. (Bonn: Rheinland-Verlag, 1980), 131. The parentage and family name of the visionary Gertrude of Helfta goes unmentioned in the Helfta revelation literature, contemporary charters, and later chronicles. There is a range of scholarly suppositions regarding Gertrude's background and little strong evidence for any particular claim: see Preger, *Geschichte*, 123; Gilbert Dolan, *St. Gertrude the Great* (London: Sands, 1913), 9; Finnegan, *Women of Helfta*, 110; Ruh, *Frauenmystik*, 298.

[9] See the charters originating with the founders and a charter associated with Abbess Gertrude of Hackeborn in Krüne, *Urkundenbuch*, no. 1, 39; no. 2, 130; no. 5, 132; no. 17, 138; no. 20, 140; no. 45, 152–53.

of a Cistercian way of life. In addition, charters suggest that through the thirteenth century, the nuns and lay people associated with the monastery regarded it as Cistercian. In her fifteenth-century *Narratio*, furthermore, Abbess Sophia refers to the women as "nuns of the gray order."[10] There is no indication that it was under the jurisdiction of the general chapter or received the visitation of any abbot of the Order.

The convent at Helfta was in the diocese of Halberstadt and under the authority of the diocesan bishop. We have little documentation about the bishops' relationship with the monastery; we do know that, according to the *Narratio*, the then-bishop of Halberstadt, Vulrad of Kranichfeld (1255–1296), laid the foundation stone at Helfta and celebrated Mass on the occasion of

[10] Krüne, *Urkundenbuch*, no. 148, 224; and see no. 38, 149. For all this, it is not clear what exactly "being Cistercian" might have meant to the nuns. Thus, for example, there has been no careful analysis to determine whether the nuns themselves characterized their attitude toward liturgy as distinctly Cistercian as opposed to more generally Benedictine. Passages concerning Bernard of Clairvaux appear in the writings of Gertrude and Mechtild, which some scholars marshal as evidence that the women conceived of themselves as Cistercians; see for example Michael, "Die hl. Mechtild und die hl. Gertrud," 551; and Johanna Lanczkowsi, "Einfluss der hohe-lied Bernhards auf die drei Helfta Mystikerinnen," *Benediktinishe Monatsschrift, Erbe und Auftrag* 66 (1990): 17–28. With the exception of Bernard, however, there appears to be no identifiably Cistercian men mentioned in the Helfta literature. Studies that insist on a quintessentially Benedictine (as opposed to Cistercian) quality of the nuns' attitudes toward liturgy and of broader currents of spirituality at the convent are unconvincing. For the nuns as Benedictines, see Schmitz, *Les Moniales*, 293; Pia Schindele, "Elemente der Benediktinerregel in den Offenbarungen der heiligen Gertrud von Helfta," in *Und sie folgten der Regel St. Benedikts: die Cistercienser und das benediktinische Monchtum*, ed. Ambrosius Schneider with Adam Wienand (Cologne: Wienand, 1981), 156–68. The adoption of Cistercian customs by unincorporated monasteries had been occurring since the administrative framework of the Order began to take shape in the second half of the twelfth century, and these houses continued to multiply even after the restrictive promulgations of the first half of the thirteenth century. See for example Simone Roisin, "L'Efflorescence cistercienne et le courant féminin de piété au xiiie siècle," *Revue d'histoire ecclésiastique* 39 (1943): 351–59; Kuhn-Rehfus, "Zisterzienserinnen," esp. 125–26, 136.

the community's transfer there. In the presence of Archbishop Rupert of Mansfeld, Bishop Vulrad consecrated several young women, including Sophia and Elizabeth, granddaughters of the founders. The nuns would have employed a priest for the celebration of daily Mass and for the proliferating Masses offered for the dead, as well as for the ceremonies of Holy Week. A confessor's regular services were also essential. The sisters would have heard preaching at Mass, and clergy would have provided formal spiritual direction. One person or several might have fulfilled these sacerdotal responsibilities. Neither the charters, the chronicles, nor the visionary literature states explicitly who provided for the women's pastoral care.[11] Dominicans may have assumed this responsibility, and Franciscans may have also participated in the women's care,[12] as may

[11] The literature does little to illuminate the contours of priestly guidance at Helfta or other contributions priests may have lent the nuns. Scholars have noticed this silence. See Ursula Peters, *Religiöse Erfahrung als literarisches Faktum: Zur Vorgeschichte und Genese frauenmystischer Texte des 13. und 14. Jahrhunderts* (Tübingen: Max Niemeyer Verlag, 1988), esp. 127.

[12] For the presence of friars at Helfta, see, for example *Liber* 4.38; 4.40–42; 5.7; 5.8; 5.25 (298, 298–300, 329, 331–32, 359). The approbation that accompanies the *Herald* indicates the involvement in the life of the convent of Dominican and Franciscan brothers (*Le Héraut*, "Approbations des docteurs," SCh 139:104). Dominican men informed Mechtild of Magdeburg's religiosity, and some have concluded that her entry encouraged a deepening of communication between them and the nuns (Frank Tobin, *Mechthild von Magdeburg: A Medieval Mystic in Modern Eyes* [Columbia, SC: Camden House, 1995], 128–31). Proximity to Helfta by 1250 of Franciscan and Dominican houses in Halberstadt, Halle, and Magdeburg increases the probability that both orders had a presence at Helfta. See John B. Freed, "The Friars and the Delineation of State Boundaries in the Thirteenth Century," in *Order and Innovation in the Middle Ages: Essays in Honor of Joseph R. Strayer*, ed. Bruce McNab, et al. (Princeton, NJ: Princeton University Press, 1976), 31, 33, and see 14; Heinrich Denifle, "Uber die Anfänge der Predigtweise der deutschen Mystiker," in *Archiv für Literatur- und Kirchen- Geschichte des Mittelalters*, ed. Heinrich Denifle and Franz Ehrle (Berlin: Weidmannsche Buchhandlung, 1886), 641–48; Angela Koch, "Mendikanten in Halberstadt: Ein Beitrag zur Gründung, Etablierung und Auflösung von Bettelordenskonventen im mittelalterlichen und frühneuzeitlichen Halberstadt," in *Bürger, Bettelmönche und Bischöfe*, 143;

have secular priests, appointed by the bishop of Halberstadt.[13] Whoever was responsible for providing for the nuns' sacramental and pastoral needs, we would be wrong to imagine that a spirituality specific to any order or orders dominated the nuns' religiosity. The documents associated with Helfta, taken together, hint at the complex means by which the nuns' cloistered piety was fed by the world outside its walls.

The monastery's principal benefactors forged connections with other religious institutions in the surrounding areas, forming a religious network that overlapped at least occasionally with Helfta's. They extended their patronage to other monasteries (Cistercian, Dominican, and Franciscan) and sometimes facilitated transactions between houses. The Mansfelds counted among their ranks an archbishop and several cathedral canons at Halberstadt and Magdeburg, as well as a cathedral dean at Hildesheim. Women from both families embraced the religious life at a number of other monasteries. The Hackeborns were already donors to the nearby Cistercian convent of Hedersleben in Harz, and Abbess Gertrude had already sent twelve nuns there over twenty-five years earlier, when in 1262 two of her nieces entered there. One of these, Katherine Elizabeth (d. ca. 1301), would become its prioress in 1299. Gertrude and Mechtild's brother Ludwig I married Elizabeth, the biological sister of Anna (ca. 1298–1309), abbess of the imperial convent at Trebnitz, near Breslau. As bishops, canons, patrons, and nuns, as well as through marriage, the female and male relatives of the nuns were thus involved with a host of key religious institutions.

The case of the nuns' devotion to Elisabeth of Hungary (1207–1231) offers one example of the way the monastery's

---

Ingo Ulpts, "Geschichte des Franziskanerkonvents in Halberstadt vom 13. bis zum 16. Jahrhundert," in *Bürger, Bettelmönche und Bischöfe*, 213–16.

[13] Spitzlei, *Erfahrungsraum Herz*, 33–36; Balázs J. Nemes, "Text Production and Authorship: Gertrude of Helfta's *Legatus Divinae Pietatis*," in *A Companion to Mysticism and Devotion in Northern Germany in the Late Middle Ages*, ed. Elizabeth Andersen, et al. (Leiden: Brill, 2014), 112.

larger environment may have excited fervor within the cloister.[14] Elisabeth of Hungary, wife of Louis of Thuringia, was a contemporary of Elizabeth Mansfeld and lived in a region contiguous with Saxony. Abbess Sophia of Stolberg describes an encounter in which Elizabeth Mansfeld holding in her arms a boy deaf and blind from birth, came before the other Elisabeth, in whose presence the child heard and saw for the first time. Although the *Narratio* is at great chronological distance from the incident it describes, it is entirely possible that (as Sophia's work relates) the monastery's founding patron lavished special devotion on the wonder-worker, who was revered even during her short life and canonized less than five years after her death and during the lifetime of Gertrude and Mechtild of Hackeborn and Gertrude of Helfta.[15] It seems reasonable to suppose that when Elizabeth Mansfeld entered the monastery (or even before this), she might have communicated to the sisters her own special affection for Elisabeth of Hungary. Her granddaughters, also nuns at the monastery, may also have learned from Elizabeth herself, or from other family members, of the saint's importance to their grandmother.

There may have been additional sources for the nuns' devotion to Elisabeth. Among the brothers who approved the *Herald* was the Dominican Theodore of Apolda (1220/30–1302/3), author of a *Life* of Elisabeth (in addition to a *Life* of Dominic

[14] Elisabeth is among the few identified saints to appear to Gertrude; most remain anonymous, and a vision in which Elisabeth comes to her is assigned a discrete chapter, a privilege accorded few of the holy dead in Gertrude's revelations (*Le Héraut* 4.56 [SCh 255:462]).

[15] Krüne, *Urkundenbuch*, no. 148, 224; Michael Bihl, "St. Elizabeth of Hungary," in *The Catholic Encyclopedia*, ed. Charles G. Herbermann, et al. (New York: Robert Appleton Company, 1907), 5:389–91; M. Werner, "E. v. Thüringen, hl.," in *Lexikon des Mittelalters*, ed. Robert Auty, et al. (Munich: Artemis Verlag, 1977–1998), 3:1838–42; Ulrike Wiethaus, review of *Die Vita der Heiligen Elisabeth des Dietrich von Apolda*, ed. Monika Rener, *Speculum* 71, no. 1 (January 1996): 152–53.

Guzman [1170–1221]).[16] It is possible that during the frequent conversations between Theodore and Gertrude, to which the approbation attests, the two may have spoken about Elisabeth.[17] Gertrude's and Mechtild's two brothers were linked to Trebnitz, the Cistercian monastery founded in 1202 by Elisabeth of Hungary's aunt, Hedwig of Silesia (ca. 1174–1243). Ludwig I of Hackeborn married the sister of the abbess, and both he and Albert III were patrons of the convent. Through the Hackeborns and perhaps the Mansfelds as well, the sisters were thus fairly closely connected to Elisabeth and drawn into a circle of royal religious women who were influential and well-regarded among their contemporaries. Elisabeth and Hedwig played an important part in fashioning late medieval expressions of lay piety, and Agnes of Prague (1203–1282), who was educated at Trebnitz and betrothed to Hedwig's son, was instrumental in furthering the growth of the Franciscans.[18] We also know that Vulrad, the bishop responsible for Helfta, promoted Elisabeth's cult, offering a forty-day indulgence to those who took part in translating the saint's relics to the cathedral at Halberstadt, and he promised the same indulgence to all who commemorated her feast day.[19] Finally, Mechtild of Magdeburg, who expresses her high regard for Elisabeth in a section of the *Flowing Light of the Divinity* that she is thought

[16] Renate Kroos, "Zu frühen Schrift- und Bildzeugnissen über die heilige Elisabeth als Quellen zur Kunst- und Kulturgeschichte," in *Sankt Elisabeth: Fürstin Dienerin Heilige* (Sigmaringen: Jan Thorbecke Verlag, 1982), 215–16; M. Werner, "D. v. Apolda," in *Lexikon des Mittelalters*, 3:1032–33.

[17] *Le Héraut*, "Approbations des docteurs," SCh 139:104.

[18] Hamburger, "Art, Enclosure," 58–61; J. J. Menzel, "Trebnitz," in *Lexikon des Mittelalters*, 8:967; Gábor Klaniczay, *Holy Rulers and Blessed Princesses: Dynastic Cults in Medieval Central Europe*, trans. Éva Pálmai (Cambridge: Cambridge University Press, 2002), esp. 202–43.

[19] Thomas Franke, "Zur Geschichte der Elisabethreliquien im Mittelalter und in der frühen Neuzeit," in *Sankt Elisabeth*, 168–69.

to have composed before retreating to Helfta, may have communicated her admiration to the nuns.[20]

Immediately surrounding the cloister was a world bustling with expressions of personal piety and with public rituals, some of which fastened onto Saint Elisabeth. It is doubtful that the nuns would have been unaware of all this or of the dynastic alliances by which their monastery could claim a connection, however circuitous, with a company of prestigious and powerful holy women. The cult of Elisabeth at Helfta may have received encouragement, perhaps indirectly, from a Dominican friar and a bishop, female as well as male lay patrons and family members, and an elderly Beguine. In its layered juridical, liturgical, and pastoral associations, Helfta was typical of many women's houses in the late Middle Ages, fitting neatly into no one institutional category.[21] It is clear that the sisters identified themselves as Cistercian, although the Beguine Mechtild of Magdeburg found a place among them, and the monastery was under the jurisdiction of the diocesan bishop. While the literature attests more persuasively to a Dominican than to a Franciscan presence at the convent, we cannot conclude that the women's direction and discipline was the exclusive purview of Dominicans, and members of both orders probably served at the monastery. Brief consideration of the wider context of the sisters' devotion to Elisabeth of Hungary points to ways in which the religious preoccupations and familial alliances of their contemporaries and near contemporaries may have had a hand in shaping the spirituality of the Helfta nuns.

[20] *Mechthild of Magdeburg: The Flowing Light of the Godhead*, trans. Frank Tobin (New York: Paulist Press, 1998), 5:34, 215.

[21] Barbara Newman, review of *The Women of Helfta: Scholars and Mystics*, by Mary Jeremy Finnegan, *Speculum* 63, no. 1 (January 1993): 505–6.

PART ONE

The Nuns

Chapter 1

"Oh! What Treasure Is in this Book?"

Writing, Reading, and Community

Whoever reads or listens to this, all these consolations that God made to people through his lover, [Mechtild,] I counsel you to make them your own as well.[1]

The Literature of Helfta

The last decades of the thirteenth century through the first years of the fourteenth century were busy with literary activity at the monastery of Helfta, and the monastery's writings attest to numerous individuals who participated in this burst of creativity. We can identify only a few of these people by name. The celebrated and persecuted Beguine Mechtild of Magdeburg sought refuge at Helfta sometime around 1270. She remained at the monastery for perhaps twelve years, until her death, and it is likely that she there composed and dictated to the nuns the final portion of her vernacular mystical masterpiece, *Flowing Light of the Divinity*,[2] a work containing poems, instructions,

[1] *Liber* 4.38 (297). See the list of abbreviations (pp. ix–x) for editions of the Helfta works and for their translation into English and French.

[2] Frank Tobin reviews what most scholars continue to accept as the skeletal outlines of Mechtild's life; Frank Tobin, *Mechthild von Magdeburg: A Medieval Mystic in Modern Eyes* (Columbia, SC: Camden House, 1995), 128–31.

admonitions, and revelations. It was probably in the 1280s and 1290s that Gertrude of Helfta wrote the *Spiritual Exercises* and book two of what would become the five books (or sections) of the *Herald*.[3] She also produced other original writings, including an uncertain number of prayers and letters as well as a song commemorating Christ's passion, and she may have written a collection of daily meditations meant to help readers prepare for death.[4] Gertrude also tended to an array of editorial tasks: she compiled a book of sayings of the saints, elucidated them, and drew on them to produce songs in praise of God. We also know that she cast portions of the Bible into simpler language, abridged lengthy scriptural passages, and explained difficult ones.[5] With the exception of the *Exercises* and the *Herald*, none of these writings survives as a discrete work. Some of the prayers became part of the *Herald*, and there may be other portions of that work that originated as independent pieces of writing.

According to her sisters, Mechtild of Hackeborn wrote so many prayers that if they were gathered together, there would be more than all the psalms. No individual prayer exists independently of the *Book of Special Grace*,[6] and it is possible that portions of Mechtild's prayers were woven into this work. Book five of the *Book of Special Grace* contains epistolary extracts written by Mechtild and addressed to a laywoman.[7] Both the

[3] For a chronology of events in Gertrude's life, see Herman Grössler, "Die Blützeit des Klosters Helfta bei Eisleben," *Jahres-Bericht über das königliche Gymnasium zu Eisleben* (Easter 1886–Easter 1887), 30; Doyère, introduction to *Le Héraut*, SCh 139:22; Kurt Ruh, *Frauenmystik und Franziskanische Mystik der Frühzeit* (Munich: Verlag C. H. Beck, 1993), 317.

[4] See *Le Héraut* 3.54.2; 2.23 (SCh 143:234; SCh 331:210–22, n. 1); and Columba Hart, introduction to *The Exercises of Saint Gertrude*, trans. a Benedictine nun of Regina Laudis [Columba Hart] (Westminster, MD: The Newman Press, 1956), xvi. Letter writing was a means by which Gertrude helped to soothe the distress of others at a distance from herself (*Le Héraut* 1.8 [SCh 139:158]).

[5] *Le Héraut* 1.1; 3.54 (SCh 139:120–22; 143:234).

[6] *Liber* 5.30 (365).

[7] *Liber* 5.30; 4.59 (365, 310–15). For Mechtild's letters, see Lucie Félix-Faure Goyau, *Christianisme et culture féminine* (Paris: Librairie Académique, 1914),

Herald and the *Book of Special Grace* are a jumble of genres, containing treatises on Mary and John the Evangelist, accounts of visions and ecstasies, discourses on the religious life and related instructions, liturgical commentary, spiritual confessions, deathbed narratives, prayers, and hagiographical accounts of contemporary nuns.

Working with Gertrude, one or several unknown nuns were principally responsible for writing portions of the *Herald* and fixing it in its final form.[8] When this work was completed we do not know, although it probably took place after Gertrude's death in 1301 or 1302.[9] Nuns whose names are lost to us were also responsible for the *Book of Special Grace*, work on which may have begun in 1291 (or perhaps the later years of the 1280s) and seems to have continued throughout the decade.[10] We do not know whether the same persons participated in developing each of the several sections that make up the *Herald* and the *Book of Special Grace*, or whether the sisters who worked

193; and Margot King, "Letters from Mechthild of Hackeborn to a Friend, A Laywoman in the World, Taken from the *Book of Special Grace*, Book IV, Chapter 59," Vox mystica: *Essays on Medieval Mysticism in Honor of Professor Valerie M. Lagorio*, ed. Anne Clark Bartlett, et al. (Cambridge: D. S. Brewer, 1995), 173.

[8] See, for example, *Le Héraut* (SCh 139:25); Ruh, *Frauenmystik*, 301–2.

[9] Most scholars concur with Grössler's assessment ("Die Blützeit," 30) that books 3–5 were completed during Gertrude's lifetime. The majority think that the addition of book 1 to the corpus took place after Gertrude's death. See Wilhelm Preger, *Geschichte der deutschen Mystik bis zum Tode Meister Eckharts* (Leipzig: Dörffling und Franke, 1874), 78; Kurt Ruh, "Gertrud von Helfta: Ein neues Gertrud-Bild," *Zeitschrift für deutsches Altertum und deutsche Literatur* 121 (1992): 3.

[10] *Liber* 1, *caput praevium*; 2.26 (6; 169). The majority of scholars assume that the women who wrote the *Book of Special Grace* worked on it through Mechtild's death and beyond. See Preger, *Geschichte*, 117; Paquelin, Praefatio to *Legatus*, iii; Theresa A. Halligan, introduction to *The Booke of Gostlye Grace of Mechtild of Hackeborn*, trans. Theresa A. Halligan (Toronto: Pontifical Institute of Mediaeval Studies, 1979), 7; Susanne Köbele, *Bilder der Unbegriffenen Wahrheit: Zur Struktur mystischer Rede im Spannungsfeld von Latein und Volkssprache* (Tübingen: Francke, 1993), 105; Margarete Hubrath, *Schreiben und Erinnern: Zur "memoria" im* Liber specialis gratiae *Mechtilds von Hakeborn* (Paderborn: Ferdinand Schöningh, 1996), 37, 51.

on one book also fashioned the other. While scholars have long pointed to a range of similarities in the content, language, and imagery of the *Herald* and the *Book of Special Grace* as indications that Gertrude had a hand in composing the latter, the case for her as one of its unnamed authors is less secure than has usually been supposed.[11] While it appears that at some point a two-woman team took the lead in its writing, inconsistencies in the text's own communications about its authorship suggest that this was not always so. Although there is strong evidence to suggest that a single *compilatrix*—together with Gertrude—was primarily responsible for the *Herald*, this work is also not consistent about the number of its principal authors.[12] For both, I therefore generally use the plural *authors*. Some sisters also seem to have assisted Mechtild of Magdeburg in completing the *Flowing Light of the Divinity*, perhaps taking dictation when old age weakened her eyesight and limited her use of her hands.[13]

The creation of the Helfta literature was an all-female endeavor. The absence of the participation of a male confessor or other male superior as overseer, advisor, or redactor of the

[11] Ursula Peters, *Religiöse Erfahrung als literarisches Faktum* (Tübingen: Max Niemeyer Verlag, 1988), 53–67, 116–29, esp. 126. Ruh has concluded that parallels in the substance of the *Herald* and the *Book of Special Grace* derive from Mechtild's spirituality ("Gertrud von Helfta," 317–20). Among those who have argued for Gertrude's authorship of the *Book of Special Grace* are Paquelin, Praefatio to *Legatus*, ii–iii; Hans Urs von Balthasar, Einführung to *Das Buch vom strömenden Lob*, ed. Hans Urs von Balthasar (Einsiedeln: Johannes Verlag, 1955), esp. 12 and 17; and Pierre Doyère, introduction to *Le Héraut*, SCh 139:21.

[12] See, for example, *Liber* 2.43; 5.24; 5.31 (356–57, 370); *Le Héraut* 3 Prol. 1.8–9; 5.1; 16.8–13; 5.34.1; 5.35.1 (SCh 139:108–17; SCh 143:3, 12; SCh 331:36, 266, 268–72). Among the most important considerations of the *Herald's* authorship is Laura Grimes, *Wisdom's Friends: Gertrude of Helfta's Conversational Theology* (Saarbrücken: VDM Verlag Dr. Müller, 2009), esp. 23–43; she argues convincingly for the centrality of communal authorship to the text's preoccupation with community.

[13] *Mechthild of Magdeburg: The Flowing Light of the Godhead*, trans. Frank Tobin (New York: Paulist Press, 1998), 7.64, 334.

works is conspicuous. Moreover, there is no formidable presence of a confessor or other priest who might have assumed a consequential role in the intellectual life of the sisters and in this way influenced the books' composition.[14] No male patron is associated with their production. Freedom from male participation in the monastery's literary projects may have embedded these works, and their authors, more firmly in their community. Neither Gertrude nor Mechtild nor the anonymous women who joined in this work were burdened with worries about writing because of their gender.[15] They demonstrate an unflagging sureness in the value of their endeavor.

Writing in Need of Community

A sense of God's condescension toward her fuels Gertrude's writing and drives her participation in the whole of the *Herald*.[16] Not only has Christ, by his death, freely paid Gertrude's debt,

[14] This is especially noteworthy in light of the probable presence at Helfta of the Dominican Henry of Halle, Mechtild of Magdeburg's confessor and spiritual advisor, whose involvement in crafting Mechtild's *Flowing Light of the Divinity* would have provided precedent for clerical involvement in women's writing at the monastery (Tobin, introduction to *Flowing Light*, 6–7).

[15] Gertrud Lewis and Jack Lewis, introduction to *Spiritual Exercises*, CF 49:5–7; Anna Harrison and Caroline Walker Bynum, "Gertrude, Gender, and the Composition of the *Herald of Divine Love*," in *Freiheit des Herzens: Mystik bei Gertrud von He[l]fta*, ed. Michael Bangert (Münster: Lit Verlag, 2004), 60–66.

[16] A variety of motives appear to have propelled Gertrude to participate in the *Herald*. Her superiors insisted that Gertrude write what is now its second book. We read, furthermore, of the impulse that overcame her when, moved by the Holy Spirit, she snatched up the writing tablet at her side and began to write: *Le Héraut* 1 Prol. 4 (SCh 139:112); and see *Le Héraut* 1.15.2 (SCh 139:206). Elsewhere, Gertrude confesses to a pressing need to write, although she sometimes tries to dodge the prodding of her conscience to do so: *Le Héraut* 2.10.1; 2.22.1; 2.21.2 (SCh 139:272, 328, 322–24). She wishes to counter the frailty of memory in order to be able at some future time to recall the gifts God has poured into her and in this way to secure her own continuous praise of God: *Le Héraut* 2.21.2 (SCh 139:322–24). All of these concerns pale as motivating forces before a divine command to write, which finds a receptive response in Gertrude.

but he continues ceaselessly to make up for her ever-renewed deficiencies,[17] and he offers tender intimacy, indulgent correction, and inclusion in the circle of his friends, the saints and angels.[18] Although Christ's mercy is unmerited—a gift no human being can ever repay—he does demand something in return. For Gertrude's redeemer, having assumed Gertrude's debt (as he has that of the whole human race), takes delight in each pittance he can extract from her:

> Just as an avaricious usurer would not willingly neglect to earn even a single penny, in this way, I, who have decided to have my pleasure in you, would much more unwillingly permit a single thought or movement of your little finger, done on my account, to come to nothing, because I did not turn it to the advantage of my great praise and your eternal salvation.[19]

Christ yearns for Gertrude's glory, but justice does not permit mercy to overlook her faults. For Gertrude (as for everyone) redemption is a matter of sharing in Christ's perfect satisfaction by attaching herself to good works and uniting these to her Savior.[20] As Gertrude understands it, she is unworthy of the gifts God has given her, so he cannot have intended them exclusively for her.[21] Caught between Christ's

[17] *Le Héraut* 2.19.1 (SCh 139:302–4). The theology of the atonement is the implicit context for Gertrude's formulation of her relationship with God and the background against which her involvement in the *Herald* gains coherence.

[18] See *Le Héraut* 2.21.4; 2.23.9; 4.4.10 (SCh 139:326, 338; SCh 255:76–78).

[19] *Le Héraut* 3.54.2 (SCh 143:234).

[20] See *Le Héraut* 4.21.2 (SCh 255:202).

[21] *Le Héraut* 2.21.2 (SCh 139:322–24). For Gertrude's sense of herself as a vile woman, grateful for God's condescension, see *Les Exercices* 3.52–56 (SCh 127:96). For Gertrude's humility, see *Le Héraut* 3.88 (SCh 143:98); for Gertrude as unworthy servant, see *Le Héraut* 3.308–9 (SCh 143:116). This theme has been pointed out: Doyère, introduction to *Le Héraut*, 17–18; Mary Jeremy Finnegan, *The Women of Helfta: Scholars and Mystics* (1962; repr., with additions from author, Athens, GA: University of Georgia Press, 1991), esp. 96; Jane Klimisch, "Gertrude of Helfta: Woman God-Filled and Free," in *Medieval Women Monastics: Wisdom's Wellsprings*, ed. Miriam Schmitt and Linda Kulzer

justice and his mercy, Gertrude is at an impasse that (she understands from Christ) only her participation in the spiritual gains of others can break: "In your merciful love, you do not want me to perish, and yet, in your excellent justice you could not allow me to be saved with so many imperfections. At least you have provided for me that, from the participation of many, the gain of each might increase."[22] When Gertrude reveals God's nearness and accessibility to others, as well as her own devotion to him, she assists them in achieving spiritual gains and thereby has a share in them.

When Gertrude resisted putting into writing the story of the graces she received[23]—sure that she had paid restitution to God by communicating them verbally to her neighbors—Christ was unwavering in his demand that she write. "Know

---

(Collegeville, MN: Liturgical Press, 1996), 250; Lillian Thomas Shank, "The God of My Life: St. Gertrude, A Monastic Woman," in *Medieval Religious Women: Peaceweavers*, ed. John A. Nichols and Lillian Thomas Shank, CS 72 (Kalamazoo, MI: Cistercian Publications, 1987), esp. 243. It was often the case that when Gertrude enjoyed an experience of God too wondrous for her to recount, she was nonetheless moved to speak and to write and thus composed new devotions on such occasions. She did so, we read, as payment for debt acquired for saying the hours tepidly, including the hours of the Virgin, Vigils for the dead, and other offices, and in reparation for not having sufficiently loved her God and her neighbor: *Le Héraut* 5.30.5 (SCh 331:244).

[22] *Le Héraut* 2.20.6 (SCh 139:314).

[23] Gertrude expresses various reservations about writing: she thinks readers will derive no profit from her work, she worries that her writings may give others license to claim God's authority for the introduction of false teachings, and she is concerned that the dissemination of her writings may prompt some to slander her: *Le Héraut* 1.15.1; 2.10.2 (SCh 139:204, 274). Both the *Herald* and the *Book of Special Grace* employ the humility topos so common in monastic circles; see Harrison and Bynum, "Gertrude, Gender," esp. 61–62, 72–76. And in a topos equally familiar in the mystical tradition, Gertrude insists on the irreducibility of her divine experiences to words (see *Le Héraut* 2.8.5; 2.21.4; 2.10.2 [SCh 139:266, 324, 274]). On the ineffability topos, see Michael Bangert, *Demut in Freiheit* (Würzburg: Echter, 1997), 252, for the *Herald*; and for the *Book of Special Grace*, see Hubrath, *Schreiben*, 50–51; Alois Maria Haas, "Die Problematik von Sprache und Erfahrung in der Deutschen Mystik," in *Grundfragen der Mystik*, ed. Werner Beierwaltes (Einsiedeln: Johannes Verlag, 1974), 73–104; Ernst Robert Curtius, *European Literature and the Latin Middle Ages* (London: Routledge & Keegan Paul, 1973), 159–62.

for sure: you will never leave the prison of your flesh until you have paid that coin that you are still holding back," Christ insisted to her.[24] Referring to the most holy of books, he illustrated for her the peculiar capacity of the written word to stretch out into the future and affect lives to which the spoken word has no access: "If the Lord had only spoken his teaching for those who were [then] living, his words would not have been written. But now they have been written for the salvation of many."[25]

The parable of the talents, a biblical lesson from Matt 25:14-30 to which the above quotation alludes, tells of a nobleman who, before setting out on a journey, deposits coins with each of his servants. Upon his master's return, the servant to whom the master had given two coins, and who had invested them, extended him four, while the five coins the nobleman had given another servant doubled in number, extracting praise from the master and a promise of future reward. A third servant, however, hoarded the talent that his lord entrusted to him and received his master's condemnation. Gertrude and the authors of the *Herald* take up this parable to elaborate on the reason that Gertrude must write. As the *Herald* makes clear, this book is the last coin to be paid before release. Gertrude owes God everything. Writing is a means by which Gertrude returns to God some of what she owes him: "Behold, most loving Lord, the talent of your most condescending familiarity with me . . .; and it is for love of your love and for the increase of your praise that I disclose this in this writing and in those that follow."[26]

Christ's gifts to Gertrude are his investment, whose multiplication she brings about by sharing them with others.[27] In

[24] *Le Héraut* 2.10.1 (SCh 139:272).

[25] *Le Héraut* 2.10.1 (SCh 139:272–74).

[26] *Le Héraut* 2.24.1 (SC 139:350).

[27] *Le Héraut* 1.15.2 (SCh 139:206). See also *Le Héraut* 5.36 (SCh 331:268–72). For a fuller discussion of the role of the nuns' notion of gift-giving in creating

Matthew's version of the parable, the anxious servant dug into the earth and hid his master's coin there. When Gertrude divulged her experience to others, it was as if she lifted a gem out of the dung, out of the slime of her heart, and encased it in gold.[28] Gertrude is bound to others by a common need: she requires a portion of the spoils of their victory, while they will emerge triumphant in part through Gertrude's travail, which includes her written self-disclosures. This logic links self and other in a reciprocal movement toward redemption.[29]

While the *Herald* pictures Gertrude as enjoying an enviable closeness with God, such familiarity does not replace Gertrude's reliance on others. On the contrary, because they augment her indebtedness to Christ beyond the common debt of all, she is constrained to share her gifts with others. Thus Gertrude's acknowledgment of her unworthiness before God's never-ending flow of grace is fundamental to the mutuality she enjoys with God, which in turn drives her writing. This is the larger context within which Gertrude and her anonymous co-authors situate her written self-disclosures, and it is in this context that we should understand Gertrude's eagerness to confide in someone about those graces she did not reveal in her own writings.[30]

---

community, see chap. 8 below. Clark emphasizes gift-giving in all directions in the *Herald*; see Anne L. Clark, "An Uneasy Triangle: Jesus, Mary, and Gertrude of Helfta," *Maria: A Journal of Marian Studies* 1 (August 2000): 51; see also Hugues Minguet, "Théologie spirituelle de sainte Gertrude: le Livre II du *Le Héraut* (III)," *Collectanea* 51 (1989): 317–28.

[28] *Le Héraut* 2.5.5 (SCh 139:252).

[29] On the theology of co-redemption, see Barbara Newman, "On the Threshold of the Dead: Purgatory, Hell, and Religious Women," in *From Virile Woman to WomanChrist: Studies in Medieval Religion and Literature* (Philadelphia: University of Pennsylvania Press, 1995), esp. 119–22; Caroline Walker Bynum, *Holy Feast and Holy Fast: The Religious Significance of Food to Medieval Women* (Berkeley: University of California Press, 1987).

[30] *Le Héraut* 1.11.1; 3.1.2 (SCh 139:170–72; SCh 143:14–16). See also *Le Héraut* 4.2.3 (SCh 255:24–26).

Writing in Community

When the reference to the parable of the talents surfaces in the *Book of Special Grace*, it commands none of the sustained reflection it receives in the *Herald*; it calls attention to community in a different way:

> "Who would like honey from the heavenly Jerusalem?" Then when all the sisters who were in the choir were approaching her, she brought to each honey from the vial of honey. This person, however, who saw these things in sight, approached, and she gave to her a piece of bread infused with this honey; when she held this in her hands, the piece of bread together with the honey began to grow in a wondrous way, so that the piece grew into a whole bread, soft and warm, and the honey, penetrating the bread inside and out, dripped so copiously that it rained like oil through her outstretched hands, flowing onto her clothes and then onto the floor.[31]

Although Mechtild herself distributes the honey that is the *Book of Special Grace* to her sisters, the honey increases in the hands of the writer. This reference to the parable occurs, furthermore, in a dream vision that comes not to Mechtild but to one of the unknown authors of this work, who, through the vision, was plucked out of the solitude of sleep and landed in the midst of the chapel. In this account, the parable evokes a running theme in the *Book of Special Grace*: the importance of both specific sisters and the wider cloistered community to the work's genesis and advancement.[32]

[31] *Liber* 5:24 (356–57).

[32] As Rosalynn Voaden has noticed, the *Book of Special Grace* contains neither a divine command directed to Mechtild nor an expression of Mechtild's conviction that she ought to write. The text instead highlights the role of her sisters in spearheading and superintending the book's creation (Rosalynn Voaden, "Mechtild of Hackeborn," in *Medieval Holy Women in the Christian Tradition c. 1100–c. 1500*, ed. Alastair Minnis and Rosalynn Voaden [Turnhout, Belgium: Brepols, 2010], 435).

In the winter of 1290–1291, severely ill and bedridden for a prolonged period, the fifty-year-old Mechtild began to divulge the contents of her revelations and to channel to others her access to God in a manner that the authors of the *Book of Special Grace* mark as a departure in conduct for her:

> During this time, the merciful Lord revealed to her the wonder of his secrets, and she rejoiced in the sweetness of his presence to such an extent that, as if she were drunk, she could not contain herself and poured out to guests and to strangers that interior grace that she had hidden for so many years. In consequence, many people communicated their affairs through her to God, to each of whom, as God deigned to show her, she made known the desires of their hearts, and they, extraordinarily joyful on this account, returned thanks to God.[33]

The writers of the *Book of Special Grace* may have been among those drawn to Mechtild, and they may have begun composition of the book at the beginning of the last decade of the thirteenth century. Mechtild, however, may not have known about her sisters' decision to record her utterances until the writers were about six or seven years into the process.[34]

[33] *Liber* 2.26 (169).

[34] *Liber* 2.31 (176). Its authors do not explicitly connect Mechtild's "drunken speech" with the period at which they began to write the *Book of Special Grace*, although the evidence for this chronology is suggestive; see *Liber* 1, *caput praevium*; 2.26 (6, 169). Whether the words Mechtild uttered in this state continued to cascade unreservedly, whether she from this point forward took sober determination to communicate to others the workings of her spiritual life, or whether she at some subsequent moment descended anew into a semblance of silence is also not evident, although we are told that her sisters continued surreptitiously to record parts of their conversations with her for more than half a dozen years. On these and related matters, see: Doyère, introduction to *Le Héraut*, 21; *Liber* 177, n. 1; Preger, *Geschichte*, 117; Von Balthasar, Einführung to *Das Buch*, 12; Halligan, trans., *The Booke*, 37; Margot Schmidt, "Mechtilde de Hackeborn," DSAM 10:874; Köbele, *Bilder*, 105.

What Mechtild seems to have lamented especially about her illness was that it rendered her unable to serve the household's members, and she confessed to feeling useless.[35] Although her ecstatic loquacity may have been a means of service during her sickness, and although, in common with Gertrude, Mechtild is perplexed that God chose to offer her a profusion of gifts, her notion of herself as undeserving does not appear to find resolution in confiding to others about God's gifts to her. The authors make little immediate use of their assertion that Mechtild received her revelations "not for herself but for us and for those in the future."[36] We may suppose, nonetheless, that Mechtild or the anonymous writers understood that benefits would accrue to Mechtild in consequence of the dissemination of the *Book of Special Grace*. Although the writers report Mechtild's sadness and worry upon learning of their work,[37] when God explained to Mechtild that she was discomfited because she lacked gratitude for the gifts he had given her, she expressed the hope that gratitude to God might be awakened in those who read the *Book of Special Grace* and that the audience would in this way supplement her meager thankfulness.[38] By setting side by side passages that appear here and there in the *Book of Special Grace*, we may surmise that the women expected that readers' gratitude would compensate for Mechtild's lack. Such expectation brings to mind a notion that we find throughout the *Herald* and elaborated explicitly there: that one person can make up for the deficiencies of another.

The *Herald* underscores Gertrude's need for others to make right her relationship with God; the *Book of Special Grace* implies this fact about Mechtild but does not emphasize it or work it

[35] *Liber* 2.36 (183). Mechtild's infirmity kept her from regular participation in choir, the communal hub of the cloister day.

[36] *Liber* 5.30 (363).

[37] *Liber* 5.31; 2.42 (370 and 191).

[38] *Liber* 5.22 (354–55). The authors of the *Herald* also identify Gertrude as ungrateful for the favors she has received (*Le Héraut* 13 Prol. 12 [SCh 139:312]).

out in detail. In the *Herald*, the gifts God gives Gertrude (which she is obliged to distribute to others) assume prominence. The language of gift-giving, although present in the *Book of Special Grace*—God tells Mechtild that he wants a little house with one window through which he can distribute gifts; this window is Mechtild's mouth[39]—is not developed in connection with the book's creation. It is Mechtild's and the audience's attitudes (her sense of uselessness and ingratitude, their thankfulness) toward these gifts that come to the fore, not the gifts per se or the mutuality of the exchange.[40] Mechtild's role in securing the compensation the audience provides is muted in comparison with Gertrude's. The *Herald* highlights the reciprocity that inheres in Gertrude's relationship with the reading audience and accentuates her function in forging that relationship.

Accounting for Differences

Mechtild seems to have been pulled between a yearning to closet herself in seclusion with Christ and the desire to communicate to others her encounters with her Lord, his holy and angelic friends, and the needy dead. Passages scattered throughout the *Book of Special Grace* indicate that she harbored misgivings about speaking about her visions and insights—and that she held them back even before she knew that others were recording her words.[41] Fear that her visions might have a demonic source hovered in her consciousness, a concern that they might be riddled with error clouded her conscience, and she was troubled that the words she thought came from Christ

[39] *Liber* 2.33 (178).

[40] The gifts God has lavished on her are, he explains, for Mechtild. If he had not attracted her to himself, she would have sought consolation in things terrestrial (*Liber* 5.22 [354]).

[41] For Mechtild's doubts about sharing her revelations, see Caroline Walker Bynum, "Women Mystics in the Thirteenth Century: The Case of the Nuns of Helfta," in *Jesus as Mother: Studies in the Spirituality of the High Middle Ages* (Berkeley: University of California Press, 1984), 223–24.

might be instead of her own making.[42] Mechtild sometimes perceived God to be abetting her longing to keep her thoughts to herself. Yet her sisters are said to have flocked to her side as if to a preacher to hear her proclaim God's word, and Mechtild offered them her teachings and consolation.[43] Moreover, in the face of clerical objection, she strove to give voice to a cluster of visions that granted her knowledge of certain souls in purgatory.[44] Mechtild's general disposition with regard to speaking about her revelations, ecstasies, and perceptions is elusive.[45]

Gertrude seems more confident than Mechtild in the divine source of her visions and less anxious about determining their origins when they are not immediately apparent to her, her assurance perhaps fueled by the presence in the house of older visionary women, including Mechtild herself.[46] Gertrude's relative ease with her revelations probably contributed to her apparently lesser hesitation about sharing her experiences and teachings with others. Both aware of the problems that might

[42] *Liber* 1.9; 2.12; 1.23 (29, 146, 82). See also *Liber* 5.22 (54). On Mechtild's concern for the truth and on Christ's keeping the *Book of Special Grace* from error, see *Liber* 5.31; 5.22 (370, 354). For Mechtild's fear of the devil's deceptions and desire to receive God's confirmation of the divine origins of her visions, see Rosalynn Jean Voaden, "Women's Words, Men's Language: *Discretio Spirituum* as Discourse in the Writing of Medieval Women Visionaries," in *Proceedings of the International Conference of Conques, 26–29 July 1993*, ed. Roger Ellis and René Tixier (Turnhout: Brepols, 1996), 77.

[43] *Liber* 5.30 (365).

[44] *Liber* 5.18 (347).

[45] It is not possible, for instance, to discern whether Mechtild may have shaken off, once and for all, a hesitancy to give voice to her inner life or whether she may have ricocheted between the impulse to shroud herself in silence and the desire to speak. I agree with Bynum, "Women Mystics," 223, that Mechtild had more ambivalence than Gertrude about confiding in her sisters. Laurie Finke, *Women's Writing in English: Medieval England* (London: Longman, 1999), 127, contends that Mechtild was not hesitant about speaking of her visionary life but that the recording of her visions, a fear of losing control over the text, was what perturbed her.

[46] *Le Héraut* 2.4.2 (SCh 139:244).

develop and certain of the gains that would be reaped with the dissemination of the *Herald*, Gertrude was more attuned than Mechtild to the possible ramifications of this public work.[47] This awareness may be related to the recognition of Gertrude's literary aptitude by others (which seems to have preceded her writing book two of the *Herald*) as well as to her history of using her scholarly pursuits to improve the spiritual well-being of others[48]—and to further her own devotion. Mechtild's writings were less extensive than Gertrude's: Mechtild was chantress, in which capacity she directed the sisters in song and taught the novices, and she may have been especially disposed to verbal expression,[49] more a preacher than a writer.[50] Her participation in the *Book of Special Grace* was primarily oral. Furthermore, because Mechtild may not have known about the book until the last year of her life, she did not have the same opportunity as Gertrude to reflect on

[47] See *Le Héraut* 1 Prol. 1.12 (SCh 143:3). For the variety of apprehensions women express about exercising visionary authority, see Sara S. Poor, "Cloaking the Body in Text: The Question of Female Authorship in the Writings of Mechthild von Magdeburg," *Exemplaria* 12, no. 2 (Fall 2000): 419; Sara Beckwith, "Problems with Authority in Late Medieval English Mysticism: Language, Agency, and Authority in the *Book* of Margery Kempe," *Exemplaria* 4, no. 1 (1992): 171–99; Barbara Newman, *Sister of Wisdom: Hildegard's Theology of the Feminine* (Berkeley: University of California Press, 1987), 34–41; Bynum, "Women Mystics."

[48] On the acclaim Gertrude received for her written work, see *Le Héraut* 1.1.1–2 (SCh 139:118–22). On her zeal for the salvation of souls finding expression in her literary activities, see *Le Héraut* 1.4.2; 1.6.1; 1.7.1–2 (SCh 139:142–44, 150, 152–54).

[49] *Liber 1, caput praevium* 6; and see 6, n. 1. In this role, Mechtild would also have been charged with oversight of the library and scriptorium (Newman, introduction to *Mechthild of Hackeborn and the Nuns of Helfta: The Book of Special Grace*, trans. Barbara Newman [New York: Paulist Press, 2017], 4). For vocal leadership in women's houses and Mechtild as chantress, see Anne Bagnall Yardley, *Performing Piety: Musical Culture in Medieval English Nunneries* (New York: Palgrave, 2006), 64–66.

[50] *Liber* 5.30 (365).

the meaning for herself and her audience of its dissemination.[51] It thus makes sense that she did not invest the written expression of her words with the same force that Gertrude attributed to her own. This possibility seems to be why the parable of the talents, as the *Book of Special Grace* employs it, does not depict the written disclosure to others of the gifts Mechtild has received as being crucial to Mechtild's relationship with God. For the women involved in this book's composition, the parable instead draws attention to the collaborative aspect of the compositional undertaking and to the larger community within which this took place.[52]

Visionary Writers: Authors and Subjects

From certain perspectives, neither the *Herald* nor the *Book of Special Grace* is obviously concerned with the communal aspect of its production. Neither offers explicit, extended discussion of collaborative authorship. Throughout both works, the writers, following monastic convention, remain anonymous.[53] Furthermore, the exact nature of their authors' varying

[51] Because of the absence of coherent chronology, it is not possible to gauge precisely Mechtild's attitude toward the *Book of Special Grace*.

[52] Gertrude, like Mechtild, relied on others to help broadcast her ecstasies and devotion. She, however, elaborates on the parable of the talents even in her own book two, where she accomplishes by herself that for which Mechtild requires the mediation of another.

[53] Placed in a larger context, these omissions are less exceptional. The *Book of Special Grace* and the *Herald* refer to a few of the women who pass through their pages by the title of the office they hold. They sometimes characterize a woman as an older sister or novice or laywoman, and sometimes they attach a nun to her initial; only rarely do they provide anyone—including Mechtild or Gertrude—with a name: *Le Héraut* 5.6.1; 5.7.1; 5.15.1 (SCh 331:116, 122, 166); *Liber* 5.5; 5.4 (322, 321). Only once does the *Herald* refer to Gertrude by name: *Le Héraut* 4.17 (SCh 331:184). Usually the women are simply "sisters": *Le Héraut* 3.81.1; 5.4.11 (SCh 143:332; SCh 331:78); *Liber* 4.14; 65.1, 6, 9 (270–71, 335, 389). Ruh, "Gertrud von Helfta," accounts for the authors' absence of self-identification as an instance of the monastic custom to wrap oneself in anonymity. The Sister Books, collective accounts of religious life

contributions to the *Herald* and the *Book of Special Grace* is far from obvious. The anonymous writers acknowledge having exercised a degree of editorial control.[54] They sifted through visions, electing to record only those they deemed useful for the reader.[55] They have sometimes lifted a broadly applicable instruction out of an incident or series of events in which the visionaries figure.[56] Although occasionally remarks break through as unambiguously their own, the instances in which the writers lay claim to a particular comment do not elucidate the full extent of their involvement in either book.[57]

---

associated with fourteenth- and fifteenth-century German women's houses, provide examples of the author's personality coming to the fore while she continues to maintain her anonymity (Gertrud Jaron Lewis, *By Women, for Women, about Women: The Sister-Books of Fourteenth-Century Germany* [Toronto: Pontifical Institute of Mediaeval Studies, 1996], 33).

[54] *Liber* Prol. 2; 2.31 (2, 177). Laura Grimes calls the anonymous contributors to the *Herald* "active authors"; they are not "simply taking her [Gertrude's] dictation" (*Wisdom's Friends*, 36). The authors of the *Book of Special Grace* admit of a distance between that book and what Mechtild sought to express: the words she spoke to them were sometimes so obscure that they could not understand her and so abstained from writing them down (*Liber* 2.31 [177]). The claim of Mechtild's incomprehensibility may be indicative of actual circumstances, or it may be a literary convention; it may be both. It is possible that the language in which the visionaries spoke and that in which the authors composed were not the same, which would mean that the works were at a farther remove from their central subjects than has been thought. For the distance between the vision and the writing of the Helfta literature, see Finke, *Women's Writing*, 127–28.

[55] This is a criterion Gertrude herself employs in book two, but which the nameless nuns nowhere claim to have exercised in consultation with either her or Mechtild. For example, *Liber* Prol.; 2.31; 2.43 (2, 177, 192–93); *Le Héraut*, between chaps. 65 and 66 of book three: 1.4.2; 3.40 (SCh 139:170; SCh 143:142–44; SCh 143:186–88). See also *Le Héraut* 2.10.1; 1.15 (SCh 139:272, 204). For the emphasis on the works' utility, see Alois Maria Haas, "Mechthild von Hackeborn: Eine Form zisterziensischer Frauenfrömmigkeit," in *Geistliches Mittelalter* (Freiburg: Universitätsverlag, 1984), 222; Hubrath, *Schreiben*.

[56] For example, *Le Héraut* 3.41 (SCh 143:190); *Liber* 5:22 (355).

[57] For example, a *compilatrix* instructs her readers in the disposition required of them to profit from the *Herald*, expresses hope for their well-being, and beseeches God on their behalf; the authors of the *Book of Special Grace* also

Images of the collaborative pursuit pepper both books, and the anonymous writers cast themselves as prominent players in the experiences they relate, lavishing attention on several facets of their work's conception and unfolding. Their authors disavow responsibility for initiating the *Book of Special Grace* and the *Herald*: the women heeded their superiors' call to obedience, and God compelled them to write.[58] They took to their task with industrious zeal, regarding it as privileged participation in a divinely ordained enterprise, and from time to time their voices sweep in to accentuate and celebrate their part in these literary creations. "Me," exclaims one of the *Herald's* unnamed writers: God has chosen "to make me the minister of the disposition of these most holy revelations."[59]

The authors express admiration for their subjects, counting themselves among the beneficiaries of their sisters' exemplary piety.[60] Enthusiasm for their mandate infuses the nuns' writings, which are redolent with their own sense of mission. The authors proclaim their determination to write for the profit of

pray for their readers; a narrator tells the reader how she should respond to a particular vision about which she has just read and instructs the reader on how to greet the day, offer her heart to God, make the sign of the cross, and so on; *Le Héraut* 3.18; 5.35 (SCh 143:88; SCh 331:268–72); *Liber* Prol. (3). Hubrath, *Schreiben*, 48–52, discusses the relationship the anonymous authors establish with the readers.

[58] *Liber* 5:31 (369); *Le Héraut* 1 Prol. 1–8 (SCh 139:110–16).

[59] *Le Héraut* 5.35.2 (SCh 331:272). The participation of women other than Mechtild and Gertrude in composing the *Book of Special Grace* and the *Herald* is almost always remarked upon in studies of these works. Their all-female authorship has occasioned some celebratory cries: see Rosalynn Jean Voaden, "All Girls Together: Community, Gender, and Vision at Helfta," in *Medieval Women in Their Communities*, ed. Diane Watt (Buffalo, NY: University of Toronto Press, 1997), esp. 80; Hubrath's *Schreiben* is the most thorough consideration of the circumstances of the *Book of Special Grace*, but Hubrath does not closely consider the authors' descriptions of the importance of their work for themselves. Grimes's *Wisdom's Friends* notes the significance to one of the anonymous authors of the *Herald* of her literary labor (36–37).

[60] See *Liber* 5:30 (363); *Le Héraut* 5.33–36 (SCh 331:264–74). See Grimes, *Wisdom's Friends*, 30.

their neighbors and confess that their efforts are laden with consequences for their own salvation.[61] Their labor moves them even now. The very physical presence of the *Book of Special Grace* floods its authors with wonder: "One feast day, when one of them [the writers], wishing to read it, opened the book, the other one said to her fervently, 'Oh! What treasure is in this book? As soon as I saw it, my heart was filled with wonder and strong emotion ran through my whole body.'"[62]

The authors of neither work vanish for long from the readers' purview; indeed, it is sometimes Gertrude and Mechtild who fade from sight.[63] Thus, for example, the commendation of the *Herald* refers to the *compilatrix*, God, and the reader, but is empty of reference to the visionary woman who occasions the work.[64] As the anonymous authors tell it, they proceed under the cloak of God's pleasure in their labors. Christ recognizes the good will animating one of these women, which is to him as a delicious scent that appears on each page of the book: it is as if she traced each letter with perfume.[65] He proclaims that he has nourished the anonymous author with the same love with which he fed Gertrude and shepherded all her endeavors.[66] In dulcet expressions that here and there reiterate Christ's satisfaction with the anonymous nuns and their work, the nameless writers draw attention to their own roles in the creation of the *Book of Special Grace* and the *Herald*, and the familiarity with God that their work opens up for them.

[61] *Le Héraut* 5.27; 5.35 (SCh 331:210, 268–72); *Liber* 2:31; 5.22; 5.30 (176–77, 353–55, 363–69).

[62] *Liber* 5:24 (357). Mary Carruthers remarks on the "intensely emotional" response that the physical presence of a book sometimes occasioned ("Reading with Attitude, Remembering the Book," in *The Book and the Body*, ed. Dolores Warwick Frese and Katherine O'Brien O'Keefe [South Bend, IN: University of Notre Dame Press, 1997], 37).

[63] Hubrath, *Schreiben*, 37, makes this point.

[64] *Le Héraut* 5.35 (SCh 331:268–72). And see *Liber* 5:31 (369).

[65] *Le Héraut* 5.33 (SCh 331:265).

[66] *Le Héraut* 5.33 (SCh 331:266).

The anonymous nuns find themselves a topic of discussion between their esteemed sisters and Christ. Speaking with Gertrude, Christ declares the delight he takes in the *Herald*'s second part (which Gertrude did not compose by herself) and announces to her the merit its writer will receive.[67] The *Book of Special Grace* records a vision in which, at some late stage in the process of composition, God urged Mechtild to cooperate with the authors.[68] Mechtild sees "three rays reaching from the heart of God into the hearts of the two people who wrote this book, by which she understood that these women accomplished this work with divine inspiration and with grace strengthening them."[69] As God's instructions to Mechtild and Gertrude about the anonymous authors find a place in the very work about which Mechtild and Gertrude speak with God, the anonymous authors write about themselves. Moreover, the authors of the *Book of Special Grace* and the *Herald* claim to have received revelations that center on their literary pursuits, and in the visions to which they are privy, they encounter God and their subjects, Mechtild and Gertrude. Thus the anonymous nuns and their sister subjects become the stuff of each other's visions, the boundary between subject and recorder blurs, and hard edges distinguishing holy women from their scribe confidantes dissolve.[70]

In visions that come to them and in those that come to the writers, Christ encourages Gertrude and Mechtild to work with the nameless nuns. Championing the collaborative venture and insisting that the women write at his bidding, he advocates for them and assures Mechtild and Gertrude that he sustains the works in progress. Soothing the anxious chant-

[67] *Le Héraut* 5.33 (SCh 331:266). And see *Liber* 5:42 (190).

[68] *Liber* 5:22 (355).

[69] *Liber* 5:22 (355).

[70] For example, *Le Héraut* 5.24 (SCh 331:357–58). Barbara Newman, review of Mary Jeremy Finnegan, *The Women of Helfta: Scholars and Mystics*, in *Speculum* 63 (1993): 506, observed the "extraordinary fluidity surrounding the roles of . . . author and subject" in the literature associated with Mechtild and Gertrude.

rix, Christ corrals her into cooperation with a writer of the *Book of Special Grace*: "Allow her to do what she does," he appeals, coaxing Mechtild into speech.[71] The resulting works incorporate revelations in which Christ's command that the sisters work collaboratively is effectively realized. The vision of the overflowing honey, for instance, does more than make plain a collaborative process at work; it decrees the fruitfulness of the cooperation that Christ superintends. In the *Book of Special Grace*, the talent is the honey, and the honey, as the narrator explains, prefigures the book.[72] Honey is, in addition, Christ's love: in heaven, he touches his heart to the heart of his elect, flooding it with this sweet substance, liquefying it and joining a soul to himself.[73] In the hands of the anonymous writer, the honey increases and causes Christ's incorporative love to flow in abundance far beyond either the original woman who received the gift of honey, Mechtild, or its immediate beneficiary, the writer sister herself. Working together, she and Mechtild each play a part in making available to others a foretaste of heaven on earth.

The cooperative nature of the creation of the *Book of Special Grace* is further emphasized when focus shifts to the supreme artist at its center. Both speaker and writer come before God as his attendants, and he enables the work that follows. As Christ explains to Mechtild,

> I am . . . in the mouth of those speaking; I am in the hand of those writing; in all these matters, I am a cooperator for those people and an assistant; and thus, everything they speak and write is true because [they speak and write] in me and through me. And just like an artist who has many assistants helping him in his work, who (although they cannot bring the work to perfection) each help him in accordance with his ability, in such a way that all actually cooperate to produce the work, in this way, although those women who

[71] *Liber* 2.24 (191).
[72] *Liber* 5.24 (357–58).
[73] *Liber* 1.1 (8–9). And see *Le Hérault Missa* 3, 11–15 (SCh 331:288).

> write these things do not communicate as elegantly as I communicated to you, with my grace cooperating and assisting, the work is approved and confirmed in my truth.[74]

Thus the making of the *Herald*, and even more obviously the *Book of Special Grace*, was infused with a sense of the affinity between writers and speakers as well as between God and his creatures. Nevertheless, the *Book of Special Grace* insists that Mechtild and the visionary writers alike are *Christ's* assistants, and Christ likewise takes credit for the *Herald*. Coming before the *compilatrix* after the *Herald* was completed, Christ said to her, "With the sweetness of my divine love, I shall penetrate, and by penetrating I shall make fecund all the words of this, my book . . ., [which words] were truly written by the impulse of my spirit."[75] The *Herald* and the *Book of Special Grace* are God's books. He maintains a continual engagement with his participating co-workers: soothing, explaining, cajoling, praising. In both books, the difference between Creator and creature overwhelms the distinction between Mechtild and Gertrude, on the one hand, and, on the other, the anonymous writers.[76] The writers do not therefore present the multiplication and confusion of the works' main human subjects and authors as a matter for untangling: each cooperates with God, through whose grace each speaks and writes his words, not her own. From this perspective, attempting to attribute authorship to any particular person or to separate out strands of writing specific to any one woman—in the manner of some recent scholarship[77]—is beside the point. At least this is the story the

[74] *Liber* 5.22 (354–55). See also *Liber* 5.22; 2.42 (354; 191). See Rosalynn Voaden, "Mechtild of Hackeborn," 435, for God's authorization of the *Book of Special Grace*.

[75] *Le Héraut* 5.34 (SCh 331:268).

[76] God expresses a blanket enthusiasm for the joint accomplishments. For example, *Le Héraut* 5.33.1 (SCh 331:264, 266); *Liber* 2:43; 5.31 (193, 369).

[77] In a careful and provocative analysis, Ruh has argued that a contemporary nun, whom he names "Sister N.," played a prominent role in the com-

writers of the *Book of Special Grace* and the *Herald* present. Or rather, it is part of the tale they tell.

It seems evident that however serenely collegial the effort to record aspects of Gertrude's and especially Mechtild's life and teachings, the process also involved jostling over competing wishes and whispers of secrecy. The *Herald* reports,

> When the *compilatrix* of this book was going to communicate, this [book] was hidden in her tunic under her stole. She proffered the offering to the Lord in eternal praise, without anyone knowing, and according to custom, she inclined deeply on bended knee toward the body of the Lord, [and] the Lord, as if incontinent with a profuse love, was seen by another person . . . to have, on bended knee, embraced her.[78]

The Herald does not say why the *compilatrix* tried to hide the *Herald*—whether her concern with concealment focused on the book per se, or whether she anticipated her meeting with Christ and strained to secure a moment of privacy in which to enjoy it. Her description arouses curiosity, in part, precisely because she does not explain her secretiveness.

Secrecy was central to the composition of the *Book of Special Grace*. Mechtild's editorial participation only occurred during the space of one year. Before this time, a woman to whom the visionary was accustomed to reveal her secrets cultivated Mechtild's intimacy and disclosures, colluding with her fellow writers to keep from Mechtild the end toward which their talk tended. Thus trafficking clandestinely in Mechtild's revelations

---

position of the *Herald* and the *Book of Special Grace*, both impressing these works with her own literary style and in large part determining their content. Ruh has asserted, furthermore, that Sister N.'s own religiosity may have had fundamentally different emphases from Gertrude's (Ruh, "Gertrud von Helfta," 3, 8; Ruh, *Frauenmystik*, esp. 317–20).

[78] *Le Héraut* 5.34 (SCh 331:266–68). Doyère thinks the *compilatrix* made this offering after Gertrude's death, but he provides no evidence for this chronology (*Le Héraut* SCh 331:267, n. 2).

with the aim of bringing them into public light, the writers nursed the desire to keep Mechtild ignorant of their activities, continuing to do so even after she learned about the existence of their work, through some circumstance the *Book of Special Grace* does not disclose.[79] Refusing to speak with her about the book, the visionary writers dismissed the questions Mechtild put to them with the blunt instruction to take her inquiry before God.[80] There seems to be more at work here than a topos of secrecy.[81]

Mechtild is depicted as having been perturbed when she found out about the existence of the *Book of Special Grace* exactly because she was afraid that she might be thought of as its initiator. When she seeks refuge in God after finding out about the book, the comfort he offers her is that the book was composed without her knowledge; he, not she, is responsible for it.[82] This exchange fits snugly within generic conventions of humility. It would not be surprising if Mechtild strove to mold her behavior and attitude in a way she considered compatible with the virtue of humility, so highly prized and regularly cultivated in monastic life. It may be that in this instance, literary convention and assumptions governing attitude and action overlapped. Finally, the authors of the *Book of Special Grace* may have had an additional motive for making much of Mechtild's humility, and, however inadvertently, benefited from interpreting her lack of confidence about the gifts God bestowed on her as an expression of ingratitude. Accentuating Mechtild's humility and ingratitude encourages the reader to meditate on Mechtild's pious but flawed self, and this buffers the authors from accusations of proceeding against Mechtild's will.

[79] *Liber* 2:42–43; 5.24; 5.31 (190–93; 356–58; 370).

[80] *Liber* 2:42 (190).

[81] Siegfried Ringler, *Viten- und Offenbarungsliteratur in Frauenklöster des Mittelalters: Quellen und Studien* (Munich: Artemis Verlag, 1980), 173. On the secrecy topos in the *Book of Special Grace*, see also Haas, "Mechthild," 222; Peters, *Religiöse Erfahrung*, 126; Hubrath, *Schreiben*, 37–38.

[82] *Liber* 2.43 (193).

Collaboration

There is, in any case, reason to suppose that Mechtild and Gertrude shared control over what the literature conveyed about them with the visionary authors. The *Herald* makes evident Gertrude's preoccupation with the work as a whole and her continual involvement with it. She made public the misgivings she had about the *Herald*, alongside her motivations for disclosing her experiences for another (or others) to record. Furthermore, work on the book's second part was a subject that entered repeatedly into her conversations with God, and the prologue implicates her in sewing together the work's two sections. In colloquy with Christ, Gertrude ascertained the titles for each of the *Herald*'s two parts, and at her prompting, God disclosed to her the name the book would carry in its fused form, *The Herald: A Memorial of Abundance of the Divine Loving-Kindness*; they also spoke together about the title's significance. Gertrude also secured Christ's assurance that he had preserved the book from all error.[83] At some point after Mechtild's discovery of their activities, the visionary authors (as they insist) showed Mechtild the *Book of Special Grace* whenever she wished, and Mechtild assumed something akin to editorial oversight over the work, scrutinizing and evaluating its content, instigating revisions, and otherwise guiding it toward completion.[84] Moreover, neither the *Herald* nor the *Book of Special Grace* records Mechtild or Gertrude reproaching their interpreters for inaccuracy in their accounts or otherwise decrying their content.[85]

[83] *Le Héraut* 1 Prol. 2–5; 5.33 (SCh 139:108–15; SCh 331:264–66).

[84] *Liber* 5.31 (370). See also *Liber* 5.31; 5.22 (369, 354), as well as Hubrath, *Schreiben*, 37.

[85] It is not anachronistic to expect that such complaints, had they been expressed, might have been recorded; see Catherine M. Mooney, "The Authorial Role of Brother A in the Composition of Angela of Foligno's Revelations," *Creative Women in Medieval and Early Modern Italy: A Religious and Artistic Renaissance*, ed. E. Ann Matter and John Coakley (Philadelphia: University of Pennsylvania Press, 1994), esp. 51; and Anne L. Clark, *Elisabeth of Schönau:*

Nowhere in the *Herald* or the *Book of Special Grace* do we find the suggestion that the anonymous nuns who worked on these books themselves held positions of authority in the monastery, or that they served as proxies for monastery officials and were thus able to rely on authority to encourage or oblige Mechtild and Gertrude to participate in preparing these testimonies.[86] The authors of the *Book of Special Grace* did work at the behest of Helfta's third abbess, Sophie of Querfort, and with the consent of a man identified as Mechtild's prelate [*praelatus*], perhaps a confessor, provost, or bishop.[87] An anonymous author of the *Herald* acknowledges writing under obedience, and it was in obedience to superiors that Gertrude joined in producing the *Herald*'s second part.[88] It is not clear to whose order Mechtild submitted. It may be that the injunction Abbess Sophia issued to the anonymous authors of the *Book of Special Grace* also compelled Mechtild to cooperate with the writers, but we cannot be certain. When we read in the 1289 approbation in which theologians and friars endorsed the *Herald* that superiors of the monastery examined this work, we cannot discount the possibility that the abbess may have been among those who took on that task and that perhaps other women, such as the prioress, may have done so as well.[89] The directives concerning the creation of the Helfta literature appear to have

---

A Twelfth-Century Visionary (Philadelphia, PA: University of Pennsylvania Press, 1992), esp. 53–54.

[86] If deference was due to any among the principal participants, it was probably most fittingly due Mechtild, who was not only Abbess Gertrude of Hackeborn's sister but also aided the abbess with the monastery's management; see Bynum, "Women Mystics," 220. She was also lead singer in choir (*Le Héraut* 1.11.9 [SCh 139:178]). Moreover, her family were significant benefactors of the monastery.

[87] *Liber* 5:31 (369).

[88] *Le Héraut* 1.4.1–5; 1 Prol. 5–9 (SCh 139:112; SCh 139:12).

[89] *Le Héraut "Approbationes des docteurs"* 1–5 (SCh 139:104). See Ruh, *Frauenmystik*, 6. I know of no literature that addresses the question of why the *Herald* but not the *Book of Special Grace* is accompanied by an approbation. According to book one of the *Herald*, Gertrude's other writings were unanimously approved by theologians. These men remain unidentified. See *Le*

fallen on all parties alike and seem to have been issued by persons whose authority all acknowledged.

The cooperative aspect of the enterprise to create the *Herald* and the *Book of Special Grace* does not mean that the anonymous writers did not recast Mechtild's and Gertrude's words into patterns of meaning they found more to their liking.[90] We should be judicious about tagging this or that devotion, teaching, or revelation to Mechtild's person or to Gertrude's. Those who record have the power to shape, and the visionary writers were impassioned recorders. They exhibit a relentless fascination with their subjects' ecstasies and devotions, they lay bare their own eager attempts to pry into their subjects' lives, and they express the conviction that their literary activities are caught up in a divine plan.[91] They also broadcast their own visions, betraying a heady confidence in their direct relationship with the divine.[92] The visionary writers were far from

---

Héraut "La notice des approbations" (SCh 139:349–50). For the approbation, see chap. 5.

[90] Furthermore, the authors of the *Herald* and the *Book of Special Grace* may have been responsible for several redactions of the writings. Over fifty years ago, Hans Urs von Balthasar (Einführung to *Das Buch*, 17), suggested that a redactor, or redactors, not contemporary with Mechtild were responsible for the book's introductory material and conclusion as well as for some of its biblical references, and Schmidt ("Mechtilde de Hackeborn," DSAM 10:874) has admitted to differences between Mechtild's account of her experiences and what her sisters recorded.

[91] Described this way, the writers bring to mind their male counterparts, who likewise labored in the company of holy women to record aspects of the women's religious lives. A male scribe's enthusiasm for his subject, and his conviction that he worked with her on a common mission, is frequently found in texts that also indicate that the scribe's own interests came to exert a controlling influence over the woman whose experiences he purported to document and thus to compromise her "independence of perspective" (Clark, *Elisabeth of Schönau*, 50–67). And see also Mooney, "Authorial Role," esp. 51–52.

[92] The anonymous authors give voice to none of the deprivation and need that scholarship has found men sometimes expressing in writings they compose with women and in men's hagiographical writings about women. Women's male writing partners often believed that women ought to serve

impartial transcribers. Mechtild and Gertrude, for their part, contributed to the *Book of Special Grace* and the *Herald* far more than raw accounts of their experience. It seems clear that the creative work of all parties overlapped. These works resound with the voices of Gertrude, Mechtild, and the anonymous visionary authors—and of still others.

A Chorus of Voices: Communal Composition

In a variety of ways, the *Book of Special Grace* and the *Herald* bear the imprint of the whole community of religious in whose monastery they took shape. Both books are suffused with representations of the achievements, trials, desires, and devotions of an indeterminate number of nuns—considered both as individuals and as a collective. Often these are tucked into or seem to trigger the visions that come to Gertrude and Mechtild. Sometimes visions attest to Christ's concern for others, as when, for example, Mechtild one day in choir spied Christ in the form of a young man and heard him say to one of her sisters, "I shall follow you wherever you go," holding open for her the book from which she was reading.[93] Visions prompted by those soliciting Gertrude's or Mechtild's mediation periodically break open others' preoccupations. For instance, a woman confided in Gertrude her puzzlement that she received no fruit from the prayers offered on her behalf. Subsequently, God relayed a series of questions to Gertrude, with instructions to put them to her inquiring sister; reflection

---

as conduits of grace to the men in their orbit. Such perceptions gave male confidants the impetus to supplant a woman's own interpretation of her experiences with his own, which included frequently highlighting his importance in her life. See Catherine M. Mooney, *Gendered Voices: Medieval Saints and Their Interpreters* (Philadelphia: University of Pennsylvania Press, 1998), and John Coakley, *Women, Men, and Spiritual Power: Female Saints and Their Male Collaborators* (New York: Columbia University Press, 2006).

[93] *Liber* 4.44 (301).

on them, he said, would illuminate the way of prayer for the nun.[94] Thus edged aside by an emphasis on the content of her revelation or by the person or circumstances that occasioned it, the visionary herself now and then plays a subordinate role in the accounts in which her visions figure.

Furthermore, Mechtild's and Gertrude's revelations frequently concern the larger life of the monastery, as when Gertrude sees Mary sweeping the convent's sins into a corner, tucking them out of sight of her Son's watching, or when Mechtild beholds souls of the monastery's sisters dancing around Abbess Gertrude, who had recently joined them in Paradise.[95] Many of the visions that come to Gertrude and Mechtild, moreover, show their sisters as equal beneficiaries of God's presence. Mechtild beholds Christ in the middle of the choir as the congregation is communicating; rays of light from his face illuminate the faces of her sisters, and Christ's love for them causes the women's hearts to liquefy.[96] In these visions the visionary herself frequently does not act as mediator for the divinity, and Christ's (or his saints' and angels') attentiveness to the nuns often has nothing to do with her solicitude for her sisters. The vision she sees is often prompted (or propelled forward) by the devotions of the sisters who appear in her vision.[97] Moreover, the texts identify nuns in addition to Gertrude, Mechtild, and the anonymous writers as recipients of revelations. Gertrude and Mechtild were not alone in projecting the force of their visionary life onto the household: on one occasion, another woman's revelation resulted in a particular prayer being enjoined on the entire community.[98]

[94] *Le Héraut* 3.79.1 (SCh 143:328–30).

[95] *Le Héraut* 4.48.4 (SCh 255:360–62); *Liber* 6.9 (389).

[96] *Liber* 1.4 (13). See also 1.5 (SCh 139:13, 17); *Le Héraut* 3.17.1; 4.48.4 (SCh 143:72–74; SCh 255:360–62).

[97] See *Le Héraut* 4.2.9–14 (SCh 255:36–44).

[98] *Le Héraut* 1.11.7; 1.16.3; 1.16.5–6 (SCh 139:176–79, 212–14, 216–17).

The Helfta literature also celebrates the efficacy of the nuns' daily public worship, which, it proclaims, redounded to their own benefit as well as to that of the universal church. On one occasion after the sisters finished intoning the psalms,

> Two splendid noble attendants carried a certain golden tablet, which they held out and placed before the Lord. Then the Lord untied the knots that he had collected against his chest; then suddenly, all the words of the psalms and prayers that the convent had spoken were miraculously arranged on the tablet in the likeness of living gems in wondrous diversity, and every little gem spread forth a splendor of wondrous clarity and sounded with an exceedingly sweet clang. The loving play and movement of the light were for the Lord a caress, and the sound moved him so that every fruit would go to the universal church from whatever word [the sisters uttered], and he restored twofold to those who had rendered the same word.[99]

When the *Book of Special Grace* and the *Herald* catalogue the robust devotions and busy productivity that mark the lives of individual sisters and of the monastery as a whole, such accounts do not always depend for their power on Mechtild or Gertrude, who sometimes play only a minor part in them—or no discernible role at all. The *Herald* and the *Book of Special Grace* testify to the potency of the nuns' corporate worship and provide a window into the spiritual lives of many of the individual nuns, as these were interpreted by their sisters.

The variegated content of the two books renders it easy to assume that a protracted tangle of talk among the women in the community, about members of the household in addition to Gertrude and Mechtild, and about lay people and clergy, contributed to fashioning the stream of vignettes concerning family and friends, friars and *conversi*, individual sisters and groups

[99] *Le Héraut* 4.2.11 (SCh 255:38–40). For additional claims to the power of the nuns' devotions, offered collectively, see *Le Héraut* 3.48.1; 5.16.2 (SCh 143:214; SCh 331:178–80); *Liber* 5.17 (345–47).

of nuns. The *Book of Special Grace* was probably composed over a period of about ten years, and more than two decades elapsed between Gertrude's first vision of the beautiful adolescent she recognized as her Lord, the vision that marked her entry into the mystical life, and the completion of the *Herald*'s final books. During this time, it is likely that the nuns who quizzed Gertrude and Mechtild, and other women in whom these two confided, would have spoken with one another about these confidences, and reflected on them together with—as well as in the absence of—the visionaries themselves. Talk with their sisters must have influenced Gertrude's and Mechtild's thought and its expression.[100] Moreover, the structure of the *Book of Special Grace* and that of the *Herald* do not militate against the assumption that multiple discrete writings penned by a number of different hands may have been integrated into each work.[101]

[100] Anne Clark has argued that Gertrude's Marian piety shifted over time in consequence of the questions and concerns her sisters put to her in the course of the *Herald*'s preparation (Clark, "Uneasy Triangle," esp. 44–45, 52–52). Ruh ("Gertrud von Helfta") has concluded that Gertrude may have drawn on the spirituality of an anonymous *compilatrix* of the *Herald*, amalgamating it with her own. Grimes has demonstrated the crucial role of conversation within the cloister in shaping the theology of the entirety of the *Herald*; Laura Marie Grimes, "Writing as Birth: The Composition of Gertrud of Helfta's *Herald of God's Loving-Kindness*," CSQ 42, no. 3 (2007): 329–45.

[101] A little more than a century ago, Dolan contended that fragments of the writings of an untold number of nuns had found their way into the *Herald* (*St. Gertrude*). See *Le Héraut* 1.3; 1.10.4; 1.14.1 (SCh 139:133–42; 168; 196). Köbele, *Bilder*, 105, has highlighted the messiness of the production of the *Book of Special Grace* and concluded that numerous women had a role in writing it. The lack of structure of the *Book of Special Grace* and, even more, the *Herald*, has been observed. John Lansperg, the *Herald*'s sixteenth-century editor, noted that it was difficult to distinguish logical divisions in the work (Doyère, introduction to *Le Héraut*, SCh 139:22–23, 81). See in addition Alexandra Barratt, introduction to *Gertrud the Great of Helfta: The Herald of God's Loving Kindness: Books One and Two*, trans. Alexandra Barratt, CF 35 (Kalamazoo, MI: Cistercian Publications, 1991), 12; Ruh, *Frauenmystik*, 319; Claudia Kolletzki, "'Über die Wahrheit dieses Buches': Die Entstehung des 'Liber Specialis Gratiae Mechthilds von Hackeborn zwischen Wirklichkeit und Fiktion," in *Die Mystik der Frauen von Helfta*, ed. Michael Bangert and

Indeed the author of book one of the *Herald* closes a chapter by informing us that she is offering us a passage written by "a certain person"—"She wrote down what follows as if she had received it from a divine revelation"[102]—and it is unclear whether this is a reference to Gertrude. Like pieces in a patchwork quilt, blocks of text (sometimes organized into discrete chapters, sometimes constructed as part of a chapter) tell stories, offer prayers, or explicate revelations.[103] Such patches of writing are frequently comprehensible in isolation from the others with which they (sometimes) come together to form a larger pattern.

There is, of course, also the thorny question of Mechtild of Magdeburg's influence on the *Herald* and the *Book of Special Grace*. Mechtild had already retired to Helfta when work began on these books. Mechtild of Hackeborn and Gertrude knew the Beguine, and it is striking that the monastery's years of great literary vitality erupted shortly after her arrival there. Although Mechtild of Magdeburg was at the time of her retirement an older woman, who had been persecuted and was perhaps exhausted, it would be remarkable if her vibrant religiosity had not lain hold of some of the household's members. Indeed,

Hildegund Keul (Leipzig: St. Benno Buch- und Zeitschriftenverlagsgesellschaft, 1998), 162–63.

[102] *Le Héraut* 1.7.4 (SCh 139:156).

[103] For the most part, the material internal to each section of both works is organized thematically, and it is not necessary to read in order the sections that comprise either work. Organizing principles are discernible, nonetheless, especially in the *Book of Special Grace*. Thus, for example, the Office and calendar lend structure to the literature: liturgical seasons and individual feasts organize groups of chapters within particular books; certain themes dominate clusters of chapters. With only a few exceptions, neither work proceeds chronologically: *Le Héraut* 1 (SCh 139:118–352); *Liber* 1, *caput praevium*, 5–7; 5.30; 6.1-8; 7.1–22 (363–69, 373–90, 391–421). Both books contain a variety of kinds of writing, and both are crowded with instructions on how one should prepare for communion, chant pleasingly, and fight torpor and other temptations. Each is punctuated by prayers and meditations. A few chapters in each book treat of matter-of-fact concerns, such as "How to Elect an Abbess" (*Liber* 4.14 [270–71]). Entire chapters are given over to commentaries on the liturgy; for example, *Le Héraut* 3.30 (SCh 143:133–64).

at least some of the Helfta nuns felt the pull of her personality and took an interest in her writings, assessing their significance as extraordinary.[104] And yet Gertrude appealed to Christ for a sign in face of the skepticism that an unknown number of members of the community expressed about revelations that appear tagged to Mechtild of Magdeburg.[105] A Sister M., who may be Mechtild of Magdeburg, also appears in a vision that comes to Mechtild of Hackeborn: dancing with Christ and a company of virgins in heaven, Sister M. appeared to Mechtild of Hackeborn shot through with a lance of light from Christ's heart, a sign of his special love for her.[106]

Given the power of conversation to stimulate devotion, reverence, and reflection, it is probably not a coincidence that after the elderly Mechtild's arrival at Helfta Gertrude received the vision she counted as the occasion of her own conversion.[107] The women provided approbation for one another's visions, consulted Christ, carped to him, and responded to the community's concerns about one another, and each one vouched

[104] There is a great deal of speculation about the influence of Mechtild on the sisters and whether the *Flowing Light of the Divinity* was read at Helfta. Thus, for example, Tobin, *Medieval Mystic*, 2–3, thinks the nuns venerated the Beguine, who he believes stimulated the creation of the *Herald* and the *Book of Special Grace*. Peters, *Religiöse Erfahrung*, 64, contends that the monastery's nuns may have played a role in originating and disseminating the *Flowing Light of the Divinity*. Hubrath, *Schreiben*, 36, argues that the nuns may have been preparing a Latin version of the *Flowing Light of the Divinity* even before the older woman came to live among them. Ruh, *Frauenmystik*, 398–99, assumes a courteous distance between Mechtild of Magdeburg and the sisters. Finnegan, *Women of Helfta*, 17, thinks some sisters were skeptical of Mechtild of Magdeburg. According to Barbara Newman, the Beguine's presence in the household energized the nuns, and her dictation to them of the final book of the *Flowing Light of the Divinity* may have inspired them to embark on their own visionary writing program (introduction to *Mechthild of Hackeborn*, 5).

[105] *Le Héraut* 5.7.2 (SCh 331:124).

[106] *Liber* 4.8 (266).

[107] *Le Héraut* 2.1 (SCh 139:228). And see Voaden, "All Girls Together," 71; Alexandra Barratt and Debra L. Stoudt, "Gertrude the Great of Helfta," in *Medieval Holy Women in the Christian Tradition: c. 1100–c. 1500*, ed. Alistair Minnis and Rosalynn Voaden (Turnhout: Brepols, 2010), 460.

for the other's holiness.[108] There is reason to suppose that Gertrude and the two Mechtilds may have consulted one another about their visions and spoken with God on one another's behalf, perhaps each even influencing the content of the others' visions, although we should be cautious about assuming common visionary content on the basis of the evidence; we may, instead or in addition, be reading literary parallels for which the Helfta literature's numerous collaborators are, at least in part, responsible.[109] In the lyrical, nuptial, and courtly imagery of the *Flowing Light of the Divinity*, Mechtild depicts herself as an instrument of God's communication to humankind, evoking the claims associated with Mechtild of Hackeborn and Gertrude. Her sense of God's love and accessibility is also suggestive of the Helfta writings. Barbara Newman attributes a centrally important—indeed, animating and organizing—theme of the *Herald* and the *Book of Special Grace* to Mechtild of Magdeburg, namely Christ's voracious, mutual desire for the soul whom he loves.[110] And there are additional indications of influence, such as the appearance in the *Book of Special Grace* of the *Flowing Light of the Divinity's* allegorical *Frouwe Minne* (Lady Love) and the two Mechtilds' devotion to John the Evangelist, who also figures prominently in Gertrude's piety.[111] The stimulus

[108] *Liber* 4.8 (266).

[109] See, for example, Mechtild of Magdeburg, *Flowing Light* 7.21 (292); Voaden, "All Girls Together," 80.

[110] Newman, introduction to *Mechthild of Hackeborn*, 12. According to Newman, "the beguine's most pervasive influence lies in the intense mutual eroticism of Christ and the Soul" (introduction, 12).

[111] On Lady Love, see *Liber* 1.5; 2.16 (18, 149–50), and see Newman, trans., *Book of Special Grace*, 255, n. 10. For additional instances of borrowings, see Newman, introduction to *Mechthild of Hackeborn*, 11–12. For ways in which John and his gospel figure in the writings associated with Gertrude, see Michael Bangert, "A Mystic Pursues Narrative Theology: Biblical Speculation and Contemporary Imagery in Gertrude of Helfta," *Magistra* 2, no. 2 (Winter 1996): 3–30. On John in the *Book of Special Grace*, see Ann Marie Caron, "Invitations of the Divine Heart: The Mystical Writings of Mechthild of Hackeborn," ABR 45, no. 2 (1994): 325–26. For devotion to John at Helfta, see below, chap. 8.

Mechtild of Magdeburg gave the Helfta nuns is not entirely clear, but the scope of the influence of her *Flowing Light of the Divinity*—in matters relatively minor as well as highly significant—was probably substantial.

In all, we surely hear in the Helfta literature the voices of an unspecified number of women, the nature and extent of whose individual contributions probably varied enormously, and which we cannot, after all, reconstruct. In this cloistered community influence was probably exerted in all manner of directions through a variety of both obvious and subtle means—through talk between and among sisters, the overhearing of bits of conversation, and casual observation, for example. Individual contributors probably disagreed and quarreled with one another and fed on others' experiences and insights, and presumably the emphases of individuals' piety changed over the decades-long creation of these works. The *Book of Special Grace* and the *Herald* are not individualistic works; both are communal collaborative compositions, which drew on the varied and unequal but substantive contributions of an undetermined number of women. There is cause to expect that peeling away the more obvious contributions of the principal writers would reveal not Gertrude's voice or Mechtild's ringing out in splendid isolation but rather densely braided choral strands, so intertwined in the text because the nuns of Helfta were so engaged with one another in life.[112]

Literary Creativity and Spiritual Practice

Scholars have accounted for the involvement of various hands in the *Herald* and the *Book of Special Grace* in a number of ways, including Gertrude's and Mechtild's reticence about

[112] My own study indicates that Doyère, introduction to *Le Héraut*, SCh 139:25, was right when, more than five decades ago, he conceded that while one can discern discrete voices in Helfta's literature, after a point one must be content with speaking about the amalgamated contributions of subject, writer, and other unspecified contributors. And see Jean Leclercq, "Liturgy and Mental Prayer in the Life of Saint Gertrude," *Sponsa Regis* 22 (1960): 1–5.

recording their experiences, their competing preoccupations, and their bouts with illness.[113] A number of factors having to do with the religious and institutional life of the monastery may have facilitated a more clearly collaborative (and not simply communal) process of composition, suggesting at least as much purpose as accident. The sisters who joined in crafting these works probably did so with something like relative parity in education, if not with commensurate intellectual hunger, literary ability, or theological acumen, and their common formation would have contributed to a favorable atmosphere for free and mutual communication.[114]

The majority of scholars have insisted that these writings are far from the isolated or idiosyncratic musings of individual nuns.[115] Kurt Ruh suggests that the involvement of many sisters in instigating, writing, and securing approval for this work was related to a concern to vouchsafe the orthodoxy of the *Herald*.[116] Its multiple authorship is, according to Anne Clark, "symptomatic of its embeddedness in a community," by which she seems to mean that the *Herald* tells of a world in which communal participation in a variety of activities was routine.[117] The teamwork responsible for the creation of the *Book of Special Grace* is indicative, according to Margarete Hubrath, of the

[113] See Grössler, "Die Blützeit," 30; Bynum, "Women Mystics," 179; Jane Klimisch, "Gertrude of Helfta," 250; Finnegan, *Women of Helfta*, 15; Halligan, *Booke*, 37; Carolyne Larrington, ed., *Women and Writing in Medieval Europe: A Sourcebook* (London: Routledge, 1995), 222.

[114] Ruh has argued that among the principal writers and the subjects of the literature, the level of literary skill and theological sophistication was roughly comparable: "Gertrud von Helfta," 3–4. The high level of the nuns' education has received comment in numerous studies. See Paquelin, Praefatio to *Legatus* xii–xiii; Joseph Gottschalk, "Kloster Helfta und Schlesien," *Archiv für schlesische Kirchengeschichte* 13 (1955): 63; Finnegan, *Women of Helfta*, 8–9; Spitzlei, *Erfahrungsraum Herz*, 53–57.

[115] See Doyère, introduction to *Le Héraut*, 72; Schmidt, "Mechtilde de Hackeborn," DSAM 10:875; Bynum, "Women Mystics," 189–90; Hubrath, *Schreiben*, 131–32.

[116] Ruh, "Gertrud von Helfta," 1–20, esp. 5.

[117] Clark, "Uneasy Triangle," 52.

function the text is intended to assume in the life of the monastery, which is to communicate to its Helfta audience a corporate identity.[118]

Such explanations do not exhaust the significance of numerous women's participation in the work. The *Herald* makes clear that all who labor to instruct others in word or writing will receive a reward for the fruit of their books or instructions.[119] For the principal anonymous authors of the *Herald* and the *Book of Special Grace*, this reward was not a distant hope. Their efforts to record Mechtild's and Gertrude's graces as well as those that came to the broader community at Helfta opened up a fertile arena for the authors' own encounters with God. The process of writing about Christ's involvement in the life of the monastery was charged with purpose and conducive to glorious revelation, and it brought with it the sweet sting of awareness that the authors were nourished by Christ's love. Christ's palpable presence in the multifaceted process of the works' production must have rendered the appeal of working on these books enormous. It would have made for a compelling motive for large numbers of nuns to wish to join in these projects. The Helfta writings illuminate, and are the deposit of, a mysticism of literary activity, whose larger context is the wonder evoked by the written word, the value accorded to intellectual engagement, and the connection Abbess Gertrude encouraged between formal education and piety.

We should situate the communal composition practices at Helfta in the broader context of the nuns' acute sensitivity to the power of words to mold the lives of individuals, to foster community, and to please God. Chant was at the core of their activities and was, as the works record, a key means by which the women of Helfta helped one another raise their desires to God.[120] Words voiced in communal song scattered like stars

[118] Hubrath, *Schreiben*.

[119] *Le Héraut* 4.13.2 (SCh 255:146–48).

[120] *Liber* 7.19 (414), for example.

over the dead, providing refreshment to those in purgatory, and "as they reached each of the saints, they adorned them with the wonderful beauty of new glory."[121] Mechtild learned that if a certain sister who was devoted to the holy Catherine chanted for the saint, her song would jog in Catherine memories that would fill her with joy.[122] When Gertrude prayed for a recently deceased sister, all the words she pronounced appeared like writings on Jesus' breast.[123] The words Mechtild offered for her now-deceased sister, the Abbess Gertrude, became roses the abbess offered to her Beloved.[124] The efficacy of words uttered reverently was apparent even to demons: eager to keep tally, one particular demon counted each syllable in every word Gertrude intoned in case she hastily skipped over any part of the psalm.[125] Because they offer proof of devotion to him, words caress Christ.[126] The might of the spoken word meant that even wordlessness was assimilated to speech: greeting the error of one's neighbor with silence was tantamount to voicing the wicked words that Cain spoke.[127] The nuns were alert too to the potential of words to be rendered harmful; Christ instructed Mechtild to close her ears to everything useless and dangerous.[128] She should, he said, circumcise from her lips words that slander, flatter, and judge.[129] The sisters believed that kind words are especially pleasing to God.[130]

The written word held a place of exceptional value at Helfta. The nuns were familiar with works by Jerome, Augustine, Gregory the Great, Benedict, Bede, John of Damascene, Bernard

[121] *Le Héraut* 3.24 (SCh 143:118).

[122] *Liber* 1.32 (111).

[123] *Le Héraut* 5.3.5 (SCh 331:72).

[124] *Liber* 5.2 (319–20).

[125] *Le Héraut* 32.4 (SCh 143:170).

[126] *Liber* 2.20 (75); *Le Héraut* 3.50.2 (SCh 143:220–22).

[127] *Le Héraut* 3.74.2 (SCh 143:314).

[128] *Liber* 4.21 (278). For the damage ugly and untruthful words do, see *Le Héraut* 3.18.9 (SCh 143:88).

[129] *Liber* 1.7 (25–26).

[130] *Liber* 1.26 (94).

of Clairvaux, the Victorines, Elisabeth of Schönau (1129–1164), and more.[131] Talk of writing permeated visions, as when, for example, Gertrude questions John about what he chose to include in his gospel.[132] Gertrude had a special devotion to Bernard of Clairvaux because of his mellifluous words[133] (from whose work Christ himself quotes!).[134] Visions are laced with text: words adorn marble columns that decorate heavenly palaces, are etched on the crowns of saints, and are imprinted on scepters carried by angels.[135] When Mechtild beheld Christ in the company of Saint Agnes, both were clothed in red vestments on which all the virgin martyr's words were inscribed in golden letters.[136] As the bells tolled on his feast day, the Evangelist appeared to Mechtild, while the words he wrote about Christ's divinity, and all the words in all the writings that saints and doctors composed and those they preached concerning the fourth gospel, hung in the air above him, shining like stars.[137] The *Book of Special Grace* declares that through his words God is present to his people, vivifying them.[138] When Gertrude asks Christ where she might obtain pieces of the

[131] For the women's literary leanings, see Barratt and Stoudt, "Gertrude the Great," 461; *Gertrude die Grosse von Helfta, Gesandter der göttlichen Liebe*, trans. Johanna Lanczkowski (Darmstadt: Wissenschaftliche Buchgesellschaft, 1989), 575–76; Minguet, "Théologie spirituelle," esp. 158–61; Newman, introduction to *Mechthild of Hackeborn*, 9. For Gertrude's indebtedness to Bernard and differences from him, see Michael Casey, "Gertrude of Helfta and Bernard of Clairvaux: A Reappraisal," *Tjurunga* 35 (1988): 3–21. For the relationship of the thought of Gertrude to that of Augustine and Bernard, see Bangert, *Demut in Freiheit*. For a consideration of Gertrude's creative indebtedness to Augustine, see Grimes, *Wisdom's Friends*, 44–75. See Newman, introduction to *Mechthild of Hackeborn*, 8, 10, for the influence of Elisabeth of Schönau's *Book of Visions* on the *Book of Special Grace*.

[132] *Le Héraut* 4.4.4 (SCh 255:66).

[133] *Le Héraut* 4.49.1 (SCh 255:396).

[134] *Le Héraut* 3.45.2 (SCh 143:204).

[135] *Liber* 1.8; 1.12 (26, 39).

[136] *Liber* 1.11 (34).

[137] *Liber* 1.6 (22).

[138] *Liber* 3.19 (221).

cross, Christ responds that the most valuable relics he left on earth are his words in Scripture; as he explains, reading about his passion is a central means by which Gertrude can bring to mind the friendship she shares with him.[139]

For Gertrude, the written word was a crucial component of the currency of salvation, and it is apparent that a number of her sisters shared that view.[140] A keen regard for learning and its application to the religious life was alive at Helfta, where literary culture was honored. The nuns studied, taught, and wrote. Gertrude's *Exercises* and the books of revelations are indicative of this climate, in which the author or authors of the first book of the *Herald* unambivalently laud the young Gertrude's precocious intellectual appetite and achievement as well as her later pious scrutiny of obscure scriptural passages.[141] Both the *Book of Special Grace* and the *Herald* single out Abbess Gertrude of Hackeborn as advocating an appreciation for intellectual inquiry among her daughters. The abbess, whose reign stretched over forty years, was convinced that the

[139] *Le Héraut* 4.52.3 (SCh 255:434). See *Liber* 3.19; 4.16 (221, 274). For a fascinating discussion of the *Herald* as "relic" of *Gertrude*, see Grimes, *Wisdom's Friends*, 111–13. The Helfta writings assert the value of Holy Scripture and of books *per se*, and of the *Herald* and the *Book of Special Grace* in particular. For the *Book of Special Grace* itself—as distinct from the holy woman at its center—as a treasure, vested with independent value, see Margarete Hubrath, "The *Liber specialis gratiae* as a Collective Work of Several Nuns," *Jahrbuch der Oswald von Wolkenstein-Gesellschaft* 11 (1999): 241. Christ offers the same benediction to the *Herald*'s content that transforms the bread and the wine into his body and his blood; both the sacrament of the altar and the words of the book have saving power (*Le Héraut* 5.33.1 [SCh 331:264]). Gertrude's heart is like a basket filled with the texts of Scripture (*Le Héraut* 1.1.2 [SCh 139:120]). Christ is reported to have told Gertrude that just as a reader for whom the script of a book is too tiny to read takes up a magnifying glass, Christ—like the magnifying glass—compensates for any failing he finds in Gertrude (*Le Héraut* 1.16.6 [SCh 139:216–18]).

[140] Lewis, *By Women, For Women*, 263–79, remarks on the importance of the written word to the nuns who fashioned the Sister Books and to those whose lives they depict.

[141] *Le Héraut* 1.1.1–2 (SCh 139:118–22).

knowledge acquired through the disciplined study of the liberal arts was a requisite for grasping the significance of the Bible and, therefore, vital to the full flourishing of devotion. For the benefit of all the girls and women in her charge, she cultivated a bookish environment:[142]

> She would read divine Scriptures eagerly and with wondrous delight whenever she was able, requiring her subjects to love holy readings and always recite them from memory. Therefore, she acquired for her church all the good books that she could, or she had the sisters transcribe them. She urged girls to become proficient in the liberal arts, saying that if the pursuit of knowledge were lost, they could no longer understand Scripture, and religious life would go to ruin.[143]

The abbess's enthusiasm for learning fed a hunger for its acquisition. When she neared death, the apostles prepared for her arrival by readying gifts of ornamented books, a sign of the salvific teaching with which she had led those in her charge.[144]

The nuns regarded the monastery's literary excursions as fitting into a long tradition of writing, stretching back to the composition of the Scriptures, that disclosed Christ's merciful dealings with his friends and thus roused readers' devotion.[145]

[142] We are learning more about the value to abbesses of the education of the women for whom they were responsible. See, for example, Fiona J. Griffith, who has shown the importance to Abbess Herrad of Hohenbourg (d. after 1196) of education in the spiritual life of her daughters: *The Garden of Delights: Reform and Renaissance for Women in the Twelfth Century* (Philadelphia: University of Pennsylvania Press, 2007), 19, 214. See also 134–63 for Herrad's understanding of the role knowledge plays in the encounter with God.

[143] *Liber* 6.1 (374–75).

[144] *Liber* 6.1 (377).

[145] The Helfta literature suggests a parallel between the *Herald* and the *Book of Special Grace*, on the one hand, and, on the other, between them and Scripture: reading the *Herald* and the *Book of Special Grace* is a means by which others can learn about the friendship Christ shares with Gertrude and Mechtild.

When Gertrude balked at writing about the gifts he gave her, Christ appeared, recalling to her the efficacy of reading both Scripture and writings penned by holy women and men in the distant past:

> And what utility does there seem to you to come from reading in Catherine's words that when visiting her in prison I said to her, "Hold constant in this, daughter, because I am with you," or from reading that I visited my special friend, John, and said, "Come to me, my beloved," and from reading many other writings concerning these and others, unless the devotion of others is thereby increased and my mercy to humankind is opened up?[146]

Gertrude appears to have been attracted by saintly companions renowned for their spiritual compositions, finding support for her own labor in their friendship and histories. Her conversations with John the Evangelist, Augustine, Gregory, and Bernard (men whose writings she and her sisters knew, with excerpts appearing both in the *Herald* and in the *Book of Special Grace*) about the process of writing and the written word provided her with insights into the significance to the saints, to souls, and to God of the work penned by holy men and women.[147] Bernard responded to Gertrude's queries about his own and Augustine's intentions as writers, and she and he opined on the power of the written word to promote Catholic teaching as well as to excite love of God and love of neighbor.[148]

Gertrude's visions illustrate a conviction that writing is, in addition to confirmation of status, meritorious for the author. They further indicate that associated benefits accrue to the whole of the celestial kingdom in consequence of holy writings, a fact that causes Christ himself to rejoice. A vision of Gregory

[146] *Le Héraut* 1.15 (SCh 139:204).
[147] *Le Héraut* 4.4.4 (SCh 255:66).
[148] *Le Héraut* 4.50.1 (SCh 255:402).

the Great instructed Gertrude that he himself received more glory for his writings than any other prophet.[149] When Gertrude asked Augustine about the merit he received for his *Confessions*, three saints approached him with a large glass filled with delicacies that turned an infinite variety of colors, bringing alternating joys that offered pleasure to each of his senses.[150] Bernard appeared wearing a sparkling crown, a sign of the spiritual progress he had procured for others through the words he spoke and those he wrote.[151] All of heaven was festooned with precious pearls on account of Bernard's words,[152] and Gregory shared with Christ the happiness that came to the saint each time his writing was read in a church.[153]

Recording these encounters with saints of tremendous literary power and prestige must have been intended in part to buttress writing projects underway at Helfta, conveying to the nuns that their various contributions confirmed their own privileged status in relation to God. Mechtild associates John's writing of the Apocalypse with his special friendship with Christ, on account of which Christ revealed mysteries to him.[154] Gertrude beheld the Evangelist so inebriated with the sweet waters of the divinity that through a vein in his heart, they poured onto the earth in the form of his gospel.[155] Writing supposes or confers an enviable status on this author: writing is an overflowing of the divine, which the self, saturated, cannot fully contain.

In the *Herald*, John reclines on Christ's breast, which flows with honey.[156] As medieval Christians did more broadly, the nuns associated John's resting on Christ's breast at the Last

[149] *Le Héraut* 4.10 (SCh 255:120).
[150] *Le Héraut* 4.50 (SCh 255:408).
[151] *Le Héraut* 4.49 (SCh 255:398).
[152] *Liber* 1.28 (98).
[153] *Le Héraut* 4.10.3 (SCh 255:124).
[154] *Liber* 1.6 (23–24).
[155] *Le Héraut* 4.5 (SCh 255:66).
[156] *Le Héraut* 4.4.2 (SCh 255:60).

Supper with his drinking in the wisdom of the divinity, from Christ's heart.[157] Like John, who funneled this wisdom to the whole church through his gospel and the Apocalypse, Gertrude, Mechtild, and the anonymous writers channel this honey-divinity into *their* composite texts. Honey *is* the *Book of Special Grace*. The women who participate in the monastery's composite projects are thus like John in these basic ways: their visions are a sign of closeness to Christ, but they are not private communications but meant for the salvation of the world. Swept up in a vision, Mechtild, like the Evangelist, lay on Christ's breast, listening to the beating of his divine heart,[158] and became God's instrument, distributing his wisdom and grace to others.[159]

The connection between John and Gertrude as writers is explicit, and it is central to the attribution of holiness of both.[160]

[157] Barbara Nolan, *The Gothic Visionary Perspective* (Princeton, NJ: Princeton University Press, 1977), 9; Annette Volfing, "The Authorship of John the Evangelist as Presented in Medieval German Sermons and *Meisterlieder*," *Oxford German Studies* 23 (1994): 8–10; Annette Volfing, *John the Evangelist and Medieval German Writing: Imitating the Inimitable* (Oxford: Oxford University Press, 2001), 11. For the breast as source of revelations, see Carolyn Diskant Muir, *Saintly Brides and Bridegrooms: The Mystic Marriage in Northern Renaissance Art* (London: Harvey Miller, 2012), 68.

[158] *Liber* 2.1 (135–36). Mechtild of Magdeburg talks to John of her experience falling asleep in love on Christ's breast, where she saw and heard marvels (*Flowing Light* 2.24 [90]).

[159] For Christ's side wound as gateway to the divinity in the *Book of Special Grace*, see Caron, "Invitations," 328. And see Christ's crediting to the writer the progress anyone makes on account of her or his writing (*Le Héraut* 4.13 [SCh 255:146–48]).

[160] As Volfing has observed, late medieval German sermon literature and speculative poetry lit upon John's visions as the central feature of his writings, underscoring a direct correlation between them. Volfing argues that late medieval German sermons claim "John's communicativeness as the key to his true greatness, praising the fact that the visions did not remain as 'mere' private experiences" ("Authorship," 2). By the later Middle Ages, John had long been venerated as a visionary writer. Dominican women's houses, especially, celebrated John together with Christ in statuary groups, widespread in these monasteries, and we know that Helfta had some Dominican super-

Regarding Gertrude's expressed hesitance to commit her revelations to writing, it is noteworthy that thirteenth-century German-language sermons proclaim John's generosity in deciding not to hoard but to share in writing the content of his experience with others. John models the writer whom Christ insists that Gertrude become. Her association with John also draws attention to a sense of Gertrude as contemplative theologian, as John was frequently figured in the Middle Ages.[161] The exchanges the two theologians enjoy with each other are based on a shared commitment to writing,[162] their chummy chats resting on a broad sense of identification as visionary writers, beloveds of Christ, and virgins.

John also encourages Gertrude to write. During Mass on the feast of Saint John before the Latin Gate, when thoughts about her own writing intrude into Gertrude's consciousness, she tries to brush them aside, determined to concentrate instead on the words she and her sisters are chanting in John's honor. He forbids her to shift the focus of her attention and in a wondrous way sees to it that exactly while concentrating on her writing, she gains insight into the sequence she is singing.[163] When John confides in Gertrude his pleasures when he reclined on Christ's breast at the Last Supper, he does so expressly so that she may relate what he has divulged to a world grown cold.[164] It is almost as if she were his successor,[165] as if her book were the sequel to his, his the task to communicate the Word and hers to enliven love of the Word by preaching its delights.[166]

---

visors (Volfing, "Authorship," 1–44; Volfing, *John the Evangelist*, esp. 135–36; Jeffrey F. Hamburger, *St. John the Divine: the Deified Evangelist in Medieval Art and Theology* [Berkeley: University of California Press, 2002], 95; Nolan, *Gothic Visionary Perspective*, esp. 55).

[161] Hamburger, *St. John the Divine*, 2.

[162] *Le Héraut* 4.4.4 (SCh 255:64).

[163] *Le Héraut* 4.34.3 (SCh 255:286).

[164] *Le Héraut* 4.4.4 (SCh 255:66).

[165] *Le Héraut* 4.4.4 (SCh 255:66).

[166] See Bangert, "A Mystic," 1.

> It was truly my course to write for the new church a single word about the uncreated Word of God the Father, on which the understanding of the whole human race could chew with satisfaction until the end of the world, although it can be fully understood by no one. But the preaching of the sweetness of these heartbeats was reserved for the modern time, so that the world, whose love of God has waned and become listless, may grow warm again from hearing such things.[167]

Although they do so in different ways, both the *Herald* and *Book of Special Grace* make associations between writing and the saints, associations that express the nuns' sense of community with heaven's inhabitants, a sense of community fortified in recognition of the value of a common, holy enterprise, the production of texts. The nuns perceived that their collective writing endeavors linked them to an ancient and venerable history of those of God's elect whose writing benefited the world, redounded to the glory of the authors, adorned the heavens, and gratified Christ. Such suppositions supported the message the Helfta writings convey by other means: that the writings of the nuns will themselves bear spiritual fruit—for writers as for readers. They may well have encouraged the writing practice and perhaps would have been especially helpful in calming Mechtild's apprehension about the process associated with crafting the *Book of Special Grace*. In addition, the sisters were mindful of the continuing unfolding in their midst of written testimonies to God's graciousness. After the death of Sister M. (probably Mechtild of Magdeburg), Gertrude asks God why he did not perform any miracles through the deceased sister in order to confirm the revelations she had received. In response, God holds up a book, presumably the *Flowing Light of the Divinity*, explaining that he achieved victory not by subduing people and kingdoms through signs and marvels but by converting them through personal experience.[168]

[167] *Le Héraut* 4.4.4 (SCh 255:66).

[168] *Le Héraut* 5.7 (SCh 331:122–24).

The activity of generating the Helfta literature—speaking, overhearing, observing, taking dictation, composing, editing—seems to have been a deliberate, sustained effort, in which the community engaged as a spiritual practice, beneficial to self and to the other who is reader. Thus, my study lends support to the scholarship of the last several decades that has insisted that for many medieval women, writing was both an act of self-integration and a service.[169] The Helfta literature presents us with a sense of medieval visionary women's writing practice that is also somewhat different from that to which such scholarship has accustomed us—with its emphasis on the solitary visionary, driven by divine command and/or internal directive to take up the task of recording her visions and ecstasies (as well as related anxieties) by herself or in collaboration with a male scribe-confidant. Whatever moved Gertrude and Mechtild to participate in crafting the *Herald* and the *Book of Special Grace*, their involvement in the production of these books represents moments in an extended process shared by a whole community. The lone visionary does not bear by herself—or in tandem with any single scribe-confidant—the weight of literary production.

The books give no indication that working collaboratively in community diminished the importance for any individual of her peculiar contribution to the project, or blunted the sense of entitlement she garnered from it. This collaboration seems calculated to advance the participant's spiritual welfare exactly as it integrated her into a broad and pedigreed community of writers, including her own sisters and others living and dead, male and female, among whom were counted the author of the fourth gospel and a persecuted Beguine. The nuns conceived of this practice as offering them the opportunity to

[169] See for example Clark, *Elisabeth of Schönau*, esp. 80–90; Elizabeth Alvilda Petroff, *Medieval Women's Visionary Literature* (New York: Oxford University Press, 1986), 42–44; Caroline Walker Bynum, preface to *Hildegard of Bingen*, trans. Columba Hart and Jane Bishop (New York: Paulist Press, 1990), 1–7.

glorify God and to reach beyond the confines of the monastery to join in the conversation of people outside its walls. Moreover, it opened up the possibility of disclosing God's intervention in the life of the cloister to its members.

Awakening Awareness and Arousing Desire

Although nothing suggests that the intended audience of the *Book of Special Grace* and the *Herald* was only female, it seems clear that both works, and the *Spiritual Exercises* as well, were meant primarily for an audience of enclosed women.[170] The authors of the *Book of Special Grace* and the *Herald* would have perceived their contemporaries, and future nuns, as especially receptive to their sisters' writings, which insist that the diurnal doings of all the women were brilliantly embellished with the divine. The nuns seem to have considered, however, a broader readership, among whom they may have counted male and female laity—including members of the founding family and benefactors, the religious communities with which the monastery shared confraternity, and the houses with which their patrons were connected. Clergy who provided for the sacramental needs of the sisters may have read the women's writings, enlarging their circle of readers further still.

As Laura Grimes points out, the nuns' female relatives outside Helfta might have prayed the *Spiritual Exercises*, in a manner analogous to the way they used books of hours, and the men with whom the nuns were in contact, including the friars

[170] As Laura Grimes observes, the *Exercises*, with its "imaginative spiritual renewals of the rites of clothing with the habit, consecration of virgins, and religious profession," indicates that this work, too, was written with a female religious readership foremost in mind ("Judge Wisdom, Queen Charity: The Feminine Divine in Gertrud of Helfta's *Spiritual Exercises*," *Magistra* 12, no. 2 [Winter 2006]: 77). Hubrath has noticed that the *Book of Special Grace* often refers to the audience as readers, not as listeners (Hubrath, *Liber specialis gratiae*, 241).

to whom the *Herald*'s approbation refers, could have used this work as well.[171] It may be that the nuns' confidence in their fluency in the language of the universal church contributed to the authority and significance with which they invested the *Herald* and the *Book of Special Grace*.[172] They wrote in a language that was to them intelligible, personal, and universal; it was the language in which God revealed himself to the world in his Scriptures and also spoke in plain and intimate conversation.

The Helfta literature has a clear purpose: to shuttle the sinner toward salvation.[173] Although not "how-to" literature, the graphic depiction of visions is calculated, in part, to foster envy in readers of the revelations and ecstasies attributed to Mechtild, Gertrude, and other sisters, thus spurring them on to lay hold for themselves of experiences such as these, a mark of intimacy with Christ, his mother, and his friends—and a source of pleasure for their recipient. Such pleasure gives rise to gratitude, returning the soul to God.[174] The fifth of Gertrude's *Spiritual Exercises* is geared toward stimulating a reciprocal desire for Christ, and Mechtild learns that those who read the *Book of Special Grace* will gain the gifts about which they read.[175] Reading is not merely a means to a far-off end, however, a tantalizing come-hither toward a future satisfaction for which the reader must wait with longing expectancy. According to the *Book of Special Grace*, Mechtild beheld John the Evangelist standing before the bed of a nun who loved him particularly.[176] It is unclear whether the sleeping sister was aware of John's proximity. This is, perhaps and in part, the point. Christ and his friends are nearer than the nuns know.

[171] Grimes, "Judge Wisdom," 77.

[172] For Gertrude's sense that she is speaking for all humanity, see Leclercq, "Liturgy and Mental Prayer," 4; Harrison and Bynum, "Gertrude, Gender."

[173] For example, *Le Héraut* 1 Prol. 6; 5.36 (SCh 139:114; SCh 331:272–74).

[174] *Le Héraut* 5.29 (SCh 331:234).

[175] *Le Héraut* 5 (SCh 331:156–98); for this observation, see Shank, "God of My Life," 260. *Liber* 5.23 (356).

[176] *Liber* 1.6 (21).

These writings describe a monastery in which proximity to God was not the prerogative of a select few, and they make readers the subject of the book they read, since it is revealed that they have been present at many events about which the literature tells: angels dance overhead as the sisters sing the office on the feast of Saint Anna, Christ occupies the abbess's chair at chapter, and the Evangelist reclines on his Savior's breast in the middle of the choir.[177] The reader learns that many fellow nuns (sometimes unbeknownst to themselves) enjoy their own brushes with the saints and angels, and that not a few of her sisters have been recipients of Christ's confidences. She may count herself among these women.[178] A central concern of the Helfta literature is to foster a sensitivity to its environment in its readers, in order to awaken awareness of the reality the visions claim to break open. The reader becomes aware that she has much and should acknowledge this fact. She is urged to want more.[179]

The reader is expected to grow in gratitude as she witnesses the love Christ pours out on Mechtild and Gertrude, for, the authors insist, Christ's love for all humanity is manifested in the gifts he has bestowed on these two women.[180] Christ punctuates his conversations with terms of endearment; he showers them with avowals of love that are virtually endless, and they soar; he bestows glorious compliments on them, and he promises them ever greater delights. Gertrude and Mechtild are not the recipients of God's unconditional praise, however. Gertrude

[177] *Liber* 1.5; 1.6; 1.12 (15, 21–22, 40).

[178] Their revelations allow Mechtild and Gertrude to discern an aspect of Christ's appraisal of a sister of which the woman herself may be unaware, as when Christ discloses to Mechtild that a particular nun is his treasured friend (*Le Héraut* 4.28 [SCh 255:286]) or tells of his history with another: "I elected her freely before the creation of the world" (*Le Héraut* 4.32 [SCh 255:291]).

[179] *Le Héraut* 2.43 (SCh 139:193).

[180] See *Liber* Prol. 2–3; 1, *caput praevium* (1–3, 6); *Le Héraut* 1 Prol. 1; 1 Prol. 6.9–11; 1.2; 1.15 (SCh 139:108, 114, 128, 204).

is unworthy of his graces, Christ concedes, and he readily remarks on Mechtild's lack of gratitude. The visionaries groan, as do their readers, under the burden of sin that is common to all human beings.[181] Their relationship with God is special but not unique. It reflects, in heightened degree, the universal status of creatures in relation to their Creator; it is an exemplary relationship in two senses of the word, both superior and accessible.[182] In becoming part of the story they tell, the visionary writers model for the reader that just as they have become receptive to God's love in the process of creating the *Book of Special Grace* and the *Herald*, so the reader is urged to come alive through her own intimacy with their words. The very act of reading, according to the *Herald*, offers the possibility of immediate closeness to Christ, who vows,

> If anyone desires to advance with devoted spiritual intention to this book, I shall attract him to me in such a way that he shall read it as if it were within my hands, and I shall join myself to him in that work, so that in this way—just as one feels the breathing of the other when two people read from the same page—I shall thus enter the breath of his desires, by which the viscera of my mercy shall be moved over him. On top of him, I shall breathe the breath of my divinity, by which he himself shall be renewed in his interior through my spirit.[183]

Reading is pictured as a companionable activity: the reader and Christ read as if they were one. Christ is a condescending tutor who, drawing his finger over those passages of the book that, written in his heart, are especially suited to his pupil,

[181] *Liber* Prol 2–3; 1, *caput praevium* (6); *Le Héraut* 1 Prol. 1; 1.2; 1.15 (SCh 139:108–114, 128, 204).

[182] See Harrison and Bynum, "Gertrude, Gender"; and Hubrath, *Schreiben*, esp. 47, who makes a similar point.

[183] *Le Héraut* 1 Prol. 2.8–21 (SCh 139:108–10)

points to them.[184] The image of reading the book of Christ's heart as Christ underlines with his finger words most relevant to particular readers attests to the authors' desire to supply the tender presence of him, the work's principal author.[185] Here and now, reading engenders closeness to Christ. The Helfta writings enjoin the reader to strive for what is in some sense already hers.[186] The *Book of Special Grace* and the *Herald* do not shirk from displaying differences among the sisters who both composed the works and were their first and primary readers; they seek to stimulate the readers' yearning to increase their share in the kinds of favors Christ has granted the visionaries (and the visionary writers) and to experience for themselves the exquisite satisfactions that belong to them.[187] The Helfta literature suggests that its cloistered audience had reason to look forward to revelation and to union—if they participated

[184] *Le Héraut* 5.34 (SCh 331:268); see *Le Héraut* 4.5.3 (SCh 255:86–88), and *Liber* 1.19 (156).

[185] The image has roots in 2 Cor 3:2-3, in which Christ is the letter (epistle) written on *our* hearts not in ink but in the spirit. This image was a popular one throughout the later Middle Ages. See Curtius, *European Literature*, 302–47; and Eric Jager, "The Book of the Heart: Reading and Writing the Medieval Subject," *Speculum* 71, no. 1 (1996): 2–3, 11. In the *Book of Special Grace* and the *Herald*, the relationship between the human heart and Christ's heart is a complex one. The two are not always clearly distinct: *Le Héraut* 2.23.8 (SCh 139:336–38); *Liber* 1.1; 1.14 (8–9, 46). On the connection between Gertrude's writings and Christ's heart, see Grimes, *Wisdom's Friends*, 58–75.

[186] Richard Kieckhefer's study of the Sister Books emphasizes the literature's encouraging the reader to see the spiritual attainments about which she reads as being within her reach and argues that it does so, in large part, by eliding differences and underscoring similarities among the sisters (Richard Kieckhefer, "Mystical Communities in the Late Medieval West," Medieval Academy Plenary Address, International Medieval Conference, Leeds, 2007, 6–7).

[187] See for example *Le Héraut* 5.4.10; 5.8.1 (SCh 331:90–92, 128). We know that Gertrude cultivated visions (not always successfully), and it is likely that other women did so as well. For an instance in which meditation and devotion gave rise to vision, see *Le Héraut* 2.6.2 (SCh 139:256–58).

with fervor and devotion in the day-to-day obligations associated with the monastic life.[188]

[188] For a different perspective, see Siegfried Ringler, "Die Rezeption Gertruds von Helfta im Bereich süddeutschen Frauenklöster," in *"Vor dir steht die leere Schale meiner Sehnsucht": Die Mystik der Frauen von Helfta*, ed. Michael Bangert and Hildegund Keul (Leipzig: St. Benno Buch- und Zeitschriftenverlagsgesellschaft, 1998). Scholars have drawn attention to the encouragement about cultivating visions that the Helfta literature gives to its cloistered readership. The *Herald* and the *Book of Special Grace* extol a broad range of routine practices—including corporate prayer, gazing at the elevated Host, and reading Scripture—associated in the medieval monastic milieu, according to Newman, with fostering visionary experience. Barbara Newman, "What Did It Mean to Say 'I Saw'? The Clash between Theory and Practice in Medieval Visionary Culture," *Speculum* 80, no. 1 (2005): 22–25. See also Clark, "Unequal Triangle," 47; Voaden, "Mechtild of Hackeborn," 433. Although they knew that revelation could not be compelled, thirteenth–century nuns and monks regularly encouraged preparedness and the striving after visions. As Jeffrey Hamburger has observed, visionary experience had by the thirteenth century become "a commonplace aspiration" in women's monasteries (Jeffrey F. Hamburger, "The Visual and the Visionary: The Image in Late Medieval Monastic Devotions," in *The Visual and the Visionary: Art and Female Spirituality in Late Medieval Germany* [New York: Zone Books, 1992], 148). For the power of example to induce vision, see Newman, "What Did It Mean to Say 'I Saw'?" 14–15.

Chapter 2

"A Queen Is Magnanimous at Her King's Banquet"

Relationships among the Nuns

For I have given myself most graciously into your power, just as I wholly surrendered on the gibbet of the cross to the command of the Father. Just as I then could not descend from the cross against his wish, so now I can will to do nothing other than what is pleasing to your love. Distribute liberally to whomever you wish, therefore, whatever you desire from the power of my divinity.[1]

The Hush of Monastic Life

At Helfta, the hush of monastic life was laced through and through with a garrulousness that Christ himself condoned when he directed the sisters to create the *Book of Special Grace* and the *Herald* and announced his signal role in their production.[2] The nuns, who knew that trading confidences with Christ

[1] *Le Héraut* 4.35.3 (SCh 255:292).

[2] "The tongue has power over life and death," the Rule of Benedict warns, incorporating the saying from Proverbs, and instructs the monk to exercise restraint of speech for the benefit of his own spiritual advancement (RB 6.21). Everything about the nuns indicates that they emphasized the power of words to give life, to both self and others.

was of invaluable benefit to themselves, were aware that sharing these divine encounters with one another might also be salutary. Helfta's compositions allow us to overhear portions of perhaps hundreds of the sisters' conversations, sometimes at length, sometimes only snatches.[3] We read, for instance, of two sisters debating the relative strength of God's judgment and mercy. In this case, spirited intellectual camaraderie turned contentious, rousing Gertrude's concern. Christ responded to her prayer, saying that when a father sees children squabbling, he holds back as long as their quarrel is playful; if they become rough with each other, the father will insert himself. Just so, Christ, explained, he would intercede with Gertrude's sisters should this become necessary.[4]

In fact, Christ stayed his involvement in the women's conversation, his reserve a tacit endorsement of their discussion. He proceeded with the awareness that conversation might breed disruptive disagreement, leading to disputes worthy of his intervention. Thus, although (as we read in the *Book of Special Grace*) Christ admonished Mechtild to imitate him in never fighting with anyone, he brooked open quarrels.[5] We have here a glimpse into relationships among theologically engaged women—who took up such topics as atonement theory, the pains and gratifications of purgatory, why God answers some prayers and not others, the contribution of manual labor to spiritual progress, the relationship between faith and works—and who were slow to clamp down on discussion and unapologetic about their differences of opinion.

[3] The best work on the role of conversation in the Helfta religiosity is Laura Grimes, *Wisdom's Friends: Gertrud of Helfta's Conversational Theology* (Saarbrücken: VDM Verlag Dr. Müller, 2009). See Gertrud Jaron Lewis, *By Women, for Women, about Women: The Sister-Books of Fourteenth-Century Germany* (Toronto: Pontifical Institute of Mediaeval Studies, 1996) for observations about talk among women religious; and Felicity Riddy, "Women Talking about the Things of God: A Late Medieval Subculture," in *Women and Literature in Britain, 1150–1500*, ed. Carol M. Meal (Cambridge: Cambridge University Press, 1993), for the role of conversation in women's piety.

[4] *Le Hérault* 3.78.2 (SCh 143:328).

[5] *Liber* 3.39 (243).

This was a monastery in which robust intellectual reflection went hand in hand with relishing in sumptuous visions saturated in sensual and sometimes erotic detail:[6] touch (Mary's

[6] Rosalynn Voaden remarks on the intellectual and concrete content of Mechtild's visions ("Mechtild of Hackeborn," *Medieval Holy Women in the Christian Tradition c. 1100–c. 1500*, ed. Alastair Minnis and Rosalynn Voaden [Turnhout: Brepols, 2010], 439, nn. 38 and 44). For a study of the senses in the *Herald*, see Jeffrey F. Hamburger, *St. John the Divine: the Deified Evangelist in Medieval Art and Theology* (Berkeley: University of California Press, 2002), 182; and Ella L. Johnson, *This is My Body: Eucharistic Theology and Anthropology in the Writings of Gertrude the Great of Helfta*, CS 280 (Collegeville, MN: Cistercian Publications, 2020). On Gertrude's *Spiritual Exercises*, see Ella L. Johnson, "Bodily Language in the *Spiritual Exercises* of Gertrud the Great of Helfta," *Magistra* 14, no. 1 (Summer 2008): 79–107. On the sensuality and eroticism of the writings associated with Gertrude, see Alexandra Barratt and Debra L. Stoudt, "Gertrude the Great of Helfta," in *Medieval Holy Women in the Christian Tradition c. 1100–c. 1500*, ed. Alastair Minnis and Rosalynn Voaden (Turnhout: Brepols, 2010), 459. Dyan Elliott points to the heightened eroticism Gertrude associates with consecration of nuns in her *Spiritual Exercises* (*The Bride of Christ Goes to Hell: Metaphor and Embodiment in the Lives of Pious Women, 200–1500* [Philadelphia: University of Pennsylvania Press, 2012], 177–79). See also Alexandra Barratt, "The Woman Who Shares the King's Bed: The Innocent Eroticism of Gertrud the Great of Helfta," in *Intersections of Sexuality and the Divine in Medieval Culture: The Word Made Flesh*, ed. Susannah Mary Chewning (London: Routledge, 2016), 107–19; Colleen McDannell and Bernhard Lang, *Heaven: A History* (New Haven: Yale University Press, 1988), 102–3. To cast the central meaning of the nuns' literary eroticism as a confession of sexual guilt and restriction, as Nancy Partner long ago argued, discounts the meaning the women themselves gave their experience ("Did Mystics Have Sex?" in *Desire and Discipline: Sex and Sexuality in the Premodern West*, ed. Jacqueline Murray and Konrad Eisenbichler [Toronto: University of Toronto Press, 1996], 307–8). In any case, the Helfta nuns offer up no evidence of sexual guilt or frustration, and there is nothing that rings of sublimation in their expressions of desire and delight. Naoë Kukita Yoshikawa argues that key to understanding the somatic quality of Mechtild's visions is Mechtild's assimilation of the larger connection medieval people made between spirituality, wellness, and physical health, and Mechtild's own assimilation of contemporary medical theory ("Heavenly Vision and Psychosomatic Healing: Medical Discourse in Mechtild of Hackeborn's *Booke of Gostlye Grace*," in *Medicine, Religion, and Gender in Medieval Culture*, ed. Naoë Kukita Yoshikawa [Suffolk: D. S. Brewer, 2015], 67–84). For medieval women's preoccupation with embodiment in the religious context, the most convincing study remains Caroline Walker Bynum's *Holy Feast and Holy Fast: The Religious*

hair!),[7] taste (Christ's placing into Gertrude's mouth the stuff of himself from the wound in his side),[8] sound (Christ's heart sounding something like a boiling pot—beating "run, run"—and announcing his relentless need to travel, to preach, to labor),[9] smell (Saint Benedict's fragrant odor filling the whole of heaven),[10] and, of course, sight, dazzling sight—as when Gertrude saw Christ's face pressed up against her own face, his eyes like suns directly opposite her own, and felt the light of his eyes enter hers, until her whole being felt like nothing but divine brightness.[11] The women communicated to one another the pleasure they took in their beloved, a continual source of wonder: the ears that heard the secrets of the faithful,[12] the shoulders that bore the weight of religious life,[13] the whole of the body, wounded and wracked, that hung naked on the cross.[14] And they spoke, too, about bedspreads[15] and the Trinity,[16] their tears,[17] Christ's passion,[18] their headaches,[19] mutual love and longing between themselves and their God,[20] and the experience of growing cool in love of God.[21] They talked with one another about their guilt,[22] annoyances,[23]

Significance of Food to Medieval Women (Berkeley: University of California Press, 1987).

[7] *Liber* 1.29 (100).

[8] *Le Héraut* 3.45.3 (SCh 143:206).

[9] *Liber* 2.7 (142).

[10] *Le Héraut* 4.11.1 (SCh 255:126–28).

[11] *Le Héraut* 2.21.1 (SCh 139:322).

[12] *Le Héraut* 4.4.10 (SCh 255:76–78).

[13] *Le Héraut* 1.7.3 (SCh 139:154).

[14] *Le Héraut* 3.41.3 (SCh 143:190).

[15] *Le Héraut* 5.8.1 (SCh 331:128).

[16] *Liber* 1.24 (84–86).

[17] *Liber* 4.38 (296–97).

[18] *Le Heraut* 1.3.6 (SCh 139:140)

[19] *Liber* 2.26 (168–69).

[20] *Liber* 4.23 (280).

[21] *Le Héraut* 3.16.5 (SCh 143:70–72).

[22] *Le Héraut* 3.62.1 (SCh 143:248).

[23] *Liber* 4.51 (304); *Le Héraut* 3.15.1 (SCh 143:62).

sadness,[24] fears,[25] and jealousies;[26] they wondered aloud why God permits the dying to lose their senses[27] and how a sister's sins influence her course toward death;[28] they spoke of drowsiness during Mass,[29] the steady march of the saints,[30] and the hovering overhead of angels.[31]

They seem to have spoken with God about one another virtually incessantly, sometimes raising hefty theological questions—does soothing another's suffering get in the way of her salvation? How does prayer benefit the one for whom one prays?[32]—in the context of inquiring about one or another of their sisters. Conversation was not only central to the creation of the written legacy the nuns would bequeath to future generations of sisters and to the world outside the walls. It was a crucial component of the religious life to which this literature provides access. Verbal exchange between and among women was valued at Helfta for its power to feed the spiritual life. Among the most significant insights into thirteenth-century monastic spirituality that Helfta's compositions yield is the extent to which talk between, among, and about women played a central role in their religiosity. No relationship is pictured as more talkative, however, than the one Gertrude and Mechtild enjoyed with Christ. These lively encounters provided fodder for their relationships with each other and for those among all the women in their household.

[24] *Liber* 4.23 (280).
[25] *Le Héraut* 4.47; 4.49 (SCh 255:302, 303–4).
[26] *Le Héraut* 3.9.2 (SCh 143:36–38).
[27] *Le Héraut* 5.7.1 (SCh 331:122).
[28] *Le Héraut* 5.6.3; 5.8.1 (SCh 331:120, 128).
[29] *Liber* 3.20 (222).
[30] *Liber* 1.20 (72).
[31] *Liber* 1.1 (9–10).
[32] *Liber* 3.79.1 (328–30).

Gertrude's and Mechtild's Relationship with Christ

At the center of the monastic family, Christ did not occupy one fixed role but was, by turns and simultaneously, daughter,[33] son,[34] mother,[35] father,[36] sister,[37] and brother.[38] He was, in addition, an imposing and magnanimous king,[39] a just judge,[40] the best teacher,[41] a commanding, adoring, and needy spouse,[42] a caring friend,[43] an attentive doctor,[44] a masterful craftsman,[45] a vulnerable baby,[46] a young boy,[47] the soul's guest,[48] and her watchful godmother.[49] Trusting in Christ's words that "whoever does the will of my Father, he is my brother, sister, and mother" (Matt 12:50) and mirroring the many ways Christ related to them, the nuns' sense of who they were in relation

[33] *Liber* 1.22 (81); *Le Héraut* 3.42.2 (SCh 139:194–96). On the simultaneity with which Christ sometimes assumes roles, see Voaden, "Mechtild of Hackeborn," 439, n. 38.

[34] *Liber* 1.11 (35).

[35] See for example *Le Héraut* 4.13.1; 5.8.3; 5.9.1 (SCh 255:146; SCh 331:132, 136); *Liber* 1.11, 18; 2.2; 4.59 (35–36; 53; 137; 178).

[36] *Le Héraut* 4.50.10; 4.13 (SCh 255:416, 145); *Liber* 1.19; 3.5; 4.59 (68, 302, 311).

[37] *Le Héraut* 4.50 (SCh 255:304).

[38] *Le Héraut* 4.54 (SCh 255:450); *Liber* 1.18; 4.50 (55, 304); *Les Exercices* 3.81 (SCh 127:114).

[39] *Liber* 2.14; 4.4; 6.7 (144, 261, 385).

[40] *Liber* 1.1 (7).

[41] *Liber* 3.5 (63), and *Le Héraut* 3.37.1 (SCh 143:178); and see *Liber* 3.41 (244) for Christ as teacher who helps Mechtild understand how to apply a gospel passage to herself.

[42] *Le Héraut* 4.45.2; 4.50.10 (SCh 255:346–48, 416); *Liber* 1.19; 3.5; 6.6 (68, 202, 384); *Les Exercices* 3.1–2, 281 (SCh 127:92, 114).

[43] See for example *Liber* 1.19; 3.5 (68, 202); *Les Exercices* 3.71–72 (SCh 127:98).

[44] *Liber* 1.19 (68). For Mechtild's use of medical imagery, including its relationship with her own experience of illness, see Yoshikawa, "Heavenly Vision."

[45] *Le Héraut* 3.65.3 (SCh 143:264).

[46] *Le Héraut* 2.16 (SCh 139:290–98).

[47] *Liber* 6.3 (380).

[48] *Les Exercices* 1.189 (SCh 127:72).

[49] *Liber* 3.13 (211).

to Christ was also labile. Christ and the nuns frequently swapped roles, or played multiple roles concurrently: the women were Christ's friends;[50] each was his spouse,[51] his sister,[52] his daughter,[53] his son,[54] and his (sometimes loving, sometimes unkind) mother.[55] The roles they assumed do not necessarily align with the characteristics the dominant culture ascribed to them, and the nuns' use of gendered imagery was complex, characterized by fluidity and interchangeability of characteristics.[56]

[50] *Liber* 2.1; 6.7 (135, 372); *Les Exercices* 3.6 (SCh 127:92).

[51] *Liber* 2.1 (135).

[52] *Liber* 2.1 (135); *Le Héraut* 3.23.1 (SCh 143:116).

[53] *Le Héraut* 4.2.3 (SCh 255:26); *Liber* 6.6 (384).

[54] *Liber* 1.19 (68); *Le Héraut* 3.12.2 (SCh 143:52–54).

[55] *Liber* 1.11; 1.22 (35–36, 81); *Le Héraut* 3.42.2 (SCh 143:194–96).

[56] As her mother, he soothes Gertrude with words of love (*Le Héraut* 3.63.1–2 [SCh 143:250–52]). Like a mother who gives her child medicine to make her well, Christ heals the sick soul with a variety of gifts (*Le Héraut* 5.9.1 [SCh 331:136]). As a mother protects her child from the jaws of wolves, so Christ sacrificed himself on the cross (*Liber* 1.18 [53]). The nuns do not associate with Christ as mother solely from a sense of love and succor and sacrifice, however; see Caroline Walker Bynum, "Women Mystics in the Thirteenth Century: The Case of the Nuns of Helfta," in *Jesus as Mother: Studies in the Spirituality of the High Middle Ages* (Berkeley: University of California Press, 1984), 189, 242–43. Gertrude at least once perceived Christ as an exacting mother who trains her child to help with housework, and Christ as mother is sometimes the source of productive pain, or Christ permits pain (*Le Héraut* 3.71.2 [SCh 143:88–90]). Christ was also a gentle (*Le Héraut* 4:50.10 [SCh 255:416]), reliable, and compassionate father (*Le Héraut* 2.18.1 [SCh 139:300]), who on the day of a nun's profession takes her to his paternal breast (*Liber* 4.18 [268]). Sometimes Christ's maternity and paternity are interchangeable. He promises to sequester Gertrude under his "paternal care" just as a mother covers and caresses her child (*Le Héraut* 5.25.3 [SCh 331:206–8]). Thus Gertrude and Mechtild associate with God characteristics that the dominant culture often dichotomized as male and female. What is striking is their attribution to God of such qualities without, apparently, any strong sense that they are dichotomous (see Bynum, "Women Mystics"; Anna Harrison and Caroline Walker Bynum, "Gertrude, Gender, and the Composition of the *Herald of Divine Love*," in *Freiheit des Herzens: Mystik bei Gertrud von He[l]fta*, ed. Michael Bangert [Münster: Lit Verlag, 2004]), and that they sometimes amalgamated the paternal and maternal in Christ.

In these writings, Christ is sometimes the baby the nuns scoop up in their arms. He is affectionate father and demanding mother, and a fresh and caring bridegroom[57]—to many brides. When a virgin enters heaven, Christ greets her, calling to her with loving and regal language lifted from the Song of Songs. "Come to me, my beloved!" he thunders, his voice echoing through the whole of heaven.[58] His is a spring-like, youthful beauty,[59] more radiant than the noonday sun,[60] and he is an eager and demonstrative lover. The pages of the Helfta literature are lush with images of Christ gathering Gertrude and Mechtild into his adult embrace; the visionaries looked forward to union with Christ, their Spouse, in the celestial bridal chamber. If they could not go to him, he came to them: when one was too sick to meet him in communion, Christ, like a king bound by the laws and obligations of marriage, rushed to the bedside of his queen.[61]

This bridal imagery is sometimes suffused with a candid eroticism. In a letter Mechtild wrote to a laywoman, contained in the *Book of Special Grace*, she described the mystical marriage with Christ that awaited the letter's intended recipient: the woman should anticipate a consummating encounter on the bed of the cross. Christ was desirous of her as she was of him, Mechtild assured her without a trace of jealousy or envy.[62]

[57] *Le Héraut* 1.16.1; 2.16.3 (SCh 139:210, 292–94); *Liber* 1.19 (68). For the nuns' bridal mysticism, see, for example, Lillian Thomas Shank, "The God of My Life: St. Gertrude, A Monastic Woman," in *Peaceweavers*, ed. John A. Nichols and Lillian Thomas Shank, vol. 2 of Medieval Religious Women, CS 72 (Kalamazoo, MI: Cistercian Publications, 1987), 243; Miriam Schmitt, "Freed to Run with Expanded Heart: The Writings of Gertrud of Helfta and the Rule of Benedict," CSQ 25, no. 3 (1990): 220; Bernard McGinn, *The Flowering of Mysticism: Men and Women in the New Mysticism—1200–1350* (New York: Crossroad, 1998), 266–82; Elliot, *The Bride of Christ*, 177–79.

[58] *Liber* 2.35 (180).

[59] *Le Héraut* 4.41.1 (SCh 255:326).

[60] *Le Héraut* 5.7.5 (SCh 331:128).

[61] *Le Héraut* 3.39.1 (SCh 143:186).

[62] *Liber* 4.59 (312). For the cross as bridal bed, see *Liber* 3.1 (196).

Descriptions of the soul's union with Christ that joined maternal to nuptial imagery complicated the sisters' sense of themselves and of others as brides of Christ. In the *Book of Special Grace*, Mary's womb is the bridal chamber in which Christ reposed for nine months.[63] Modeled on Mary's relationship with Christ, bridal mysticism (or the literary use of bridal imagery) thus sometimes bleeds into what Rosemary Drage Hale has termed mother-mysticism.[64] On one occasion, Gertrude adored the infant Jesus, savoring the baby's spousal caresses; on another, a twelve-year-old Jesus embraced Abbess Gertrude as his spouse.[65] As Gertrud Jaron Lewis has rightly remarked, the Christ of Helfta is whatever one requires him to be.[66] In the luxurious imagery of the convent's writings, Christ is a downpour of rain, arrows of light,[67] and a warm gust of air;[68] he is experienced as a flower that perfumes the whole world[69] and a devastating coal that softens the hardness of self-will.[70]

[63] *Liber* 1.31 (107). Drawing on Scripture (especially the Song of Songs) and, perhaps, Bernard's sermons on the Song of Songs as well as monastic custom and the larger Marian tradition, the nuns identify Mary as both mother and spouse. In a vision, Mechtild sees Christ emerge from Mary's womb as from a bridal chamber (*Liber* 1.1 [8]). The monastery is also a wedding chamber (*Le Héraut* 1.1.2 [SCh 139:120]). For the confluence of maternal and bridal imagery associated with Mary in late medieval writing, see Marina Warner, *Alone of All Her Sex: The Myth and Cult of the Virgin Mary* (New York: Vintage Books, 1983), 124–30; for the coming together of bridal and maternal "tenderness" in late medieval women's visions of Christ, see Kate Greenspan, "*Matre Donante:* The Embrace of Christ as the Virgin's Gift in the Visions of 13th-Century Italian Women," *Studia Mystica: Women and Mysticism* 13 (Summer/Fall 1990): 26–37, esp. 31.

[64] Rosemary Drage Hale, "*Imitatio Mariae*: Motherhood Motifs in Late Medieval German Spirituality," PhD dissertation, Harvard University, 1992.

[65] *Liber* 6.3 (380).

[66] Gertrud Jaron Lewis, "God and the Human Being in the Writings of Gertrude of Helfta," *Vox Benedictina* 8, no. 2 (1991): 303.

[67] *Le Héraut* 2.5.2 (SCh 139:248–50).

[68] *Liber* 2.3 (140).

[69] *Liber* 1.29 (101).

[70] *Le Héraut* 2.7.2 (SCh 139:260).

The Helfta writings do not detail what constitutes the particular responsibilities and privileges associated with any one type of relationship—spousal, sibling, parental—that evoked Christ's connection with individual nuns. The appeal of the diverse imagery was in part the very spectrum itself. The sisters employed a variety of images in their effort to communicate a sense of the world as saturated with the varied splendor and delicacy of Christ's being. Often, they did so to capture the many expressions of Christ's solicitude, including the consistency and thoroughness with which Christ showers each soul whom he loves with pleasures and satisfactions associated with a number of basic human relationships and with images culled from nature as well.

The ascription to Gertrude and Mechtild of this sense of Christ's pervasive, steady, and multifaceted presence marked the two women as especially sensitive to God's goodness, condescension, and care—as well as to his tolerance. They and their sisters primed themselves to encounter Christ everywhere in everything. He was the attraction in every color, the deliciousness in every taste, the fragrance of every perfume, and the gladness in every sound.[71] "Seek me through your five senses," Christ bade Mechtild, urging her to behave like a host who, waiting for the arrival of a cherished friend, looks through the doors and windows to see if the one whose advent she anticipates has arrived:

> The faithful soul should always search for me through her five senses, which are the soul's windows. Whenever she sees, for example, things that are beautiful or lovable, let her, immediately stretching out to their maker, think how beautiful, lovable, and good is the one who made them. When she hears a sweet melody or something that delights her, let her think, "Oh! how sweet will that voice be that will call me, from which all sweetness of sound proceeds." And when

[71] *Le Héraut* 3.65.3 (SCh 143:264).

> she hears people speaking or reading aloud, let her strive to hear something of her beloved in it.[72]

The nuns' sense of Christ's presence was never so diffuse, however, that it compromised the particularity and poignancy with which he came to them.

Characterized by an easy combination of regal command, parental concern, buttery sweetness, and sometimes romantic, sometimes erotic sensuality, the Helfta spirituality is relatively unencumbered by the overwrought yearnings that we find in a number of other thirteenth-century writings, including those of the nuns' sometime companion, Mechtild of Magdeburg, who appears to have been wracked with back-and-forth bouts of loneliness and experiences of ecstasy.[73] Christ came after Mechtild and Gertrude in hot pursuit, following them even into slumber.[74] One night, greedy for her company, Christ allowed Gertrude only snatches of sleep, and while she slept, infiltrated her dreams.[75] As Gertrude lay in bed, Christ pulled his right arm from the cross, clasped her, and putting his rosy mouth to her ear, repeated, "May my continuous love be your constant languor; may your delicious love be my most pleasing taste."[76]

In spite of Christ's repeated attestations of his commitment to them and the extensive evidence of it, the visionaries did, even so, sometimes ache for even more proof, which from time to time eluded them. Christ now and again seemed to go missing, and the nuns felt his absence keenly. Gertrude recalled

[72] *Liber* 3.44 (246).

[73] See, for example, *Mechthild of Magdeburg: The Flowing Light of the Godhead*, 2.25, trans. Frank Tobin (New York: Paulist Press, 1998), 92–96; and Bynum, "Women Mystics," 230.

[74] *Liber* 3.31 (235).

[75] *Le Héraut* 3.32.3 (SCh 143:168). And for Gertrude's breaking in on Christ's sleep, rousing him with her desire, see *Le Héraut* 3.21.1 (SCh 143:112–14).

[76] *Le Héraut* 3.45.2 (SCh 143:204). This mood is evident in the *Spiritual Exercises* as well (*Les Exercices* 2.72–74 [SCh 127:86]).

that for a period of ten days she forfeited his presence, or, rather, her perception of Christ's nearness. (This was a result, she confessed, "of a worldly conversation." We can only wonder at the cloaked content.)[77] During one of Mechtild's long illnesses, Christ was nowhere to be found: the sounds of Mechtild's sorrow reverberated throughout the monastery; her cries could be heard everywhere.[78] Nonetheless, Gertrude and Mechtild expressed almost-steady satisfaction in their ongoing contact with Christ, treasuring his affectionate companionship.[79]

Convinced of Christ's nearness to their needs, large and small, Mechtild and Gertrude expressed astonishment at his ready responsiveness. The Christ of Helfta was not coy.[80] A single sigh was enough to summon him to her side, Christ told Mechtild.[81] Yearning was sometimes sufficient to activate awareness of Christ's nearness. Some weeks after the vision that occasioned her newfound commitment to the religious life, Gertrude found herself beside the monastery's pond in the morning, contemplating it and desiring "a close friend—loving, capable, and companionable—with whom to share the solitude."[82] That evening, she became aware of Christ's presence in her heart,[83] her wish fulfilled. Christ was a sensitive companion. About Gertrude, he explained,

[77] *Le Héraut* 2.3.3 (SCh 139:238). We learn from the author of book one that on occasions such as these, Gertrude did not become depressed, confident that all was working for the good (*Le Héraut* 1.10.1 [SCh 139:164]).

[78] *Liber* 2.26 (169).

[79] *Le Héraut* 2.3.1 (SCh 139:134–36).

[80] For Christ's accessibility, see Wilhelm Preger, *Geschichte der deutschen Mystik bis zum Tode Meister Eckharts* (Leipzig: Dörffling und Franke, 1874), 116–32; and Bynum, "Women Mystics," 185, 210.

[81] *Liber* 3.35 (235). For Christ's desire for Mechtild, see, for example, *Liber* 2.3 (140); and Voaden, "Mechtild of Hackeborn," 440.

[82] *Le Héraut* 2.3.1 (SCh 139:236).

[83] *Le Héraut* 2.3.2 (SCh 139:236).

> From her infancy, I have carried her and held her in in my arms, keeping her unstained for myself, until the hour when she united herself with me with her entire will, and then I, in turn, gave my whole self, with all my divine power, into her arms. For this reason, her heart's burning love for me continuously caused my inmost being to liquefy into her, so much so that as fat liquefies in the fire, so the sweetness of my divine heart, liquefied by the heat of her heart, is distilled continuously in her soul.[84]

In this vision, thick with sensuality and commitment, Christ asserted that Gertrude has been with him all along, even before she turned to him with love. Now, he welcomed her embrace with all his strength; now, the heat of her heart melted him, and he poured into her. Honey and milk dripped from his mouth into her, Gertrude wrote, calling on the language of the Song of Songs (Song 4:11).[85]

In one of a number of visions that tell of the mutual incorporation of Christ and Mechtild, Christ showed Mechtild an extraordinarily beautiful and spacious house, which she recognized as Christ's heart. Within this house, Mechtild saw another, little, house, and this she recognized as her own soul. Christ sat in the center of this second house, on whose door hung a chain that held the heart of God. And when the door to the smaller house opened, the chain holding God's heart swayed with the door's movement. Here Christ's heart enclosed Mechtild's soul, within which, in turn, Christ sat; furthermore, Mechtild's soul and God's heart were chained to each other, so that when Mechtild's soul moved, so moved the divine heart.[86] Thus, connected soul to heart and mutually incorporated, could Christ say to Mechtild, "wherever you are,

[84] *Le Héraut* 1.3.6 (SCh 139:140).

[85] *Les Exercices* 5.72–73 (SCh 127:162).

[86] *Liber* 1.19 (61–62). Many of Mechtild's visions concern the mutual incorporation of Mechtild's and Christ's hearts; see Voaden, "Mechtild of Hackeborn," 438.

I am."[87] She was his chosen one, his dove, his field of flowers.[88] "Not as I will but as you will" (Luke 22:42), he told Mechtild.[89] "You are my reward," he confessed.[90]

Although Mechtild and Gertrude shared a self-understanding as egregious sinners, unworthy of the gifts God showered on them, they did not express apprehension about their eventual arrival in heaven, and their commitment to self-deprecation was cradled in bold confidence about their relationship with God.[91] They were profoundly hopeful, their optimism grounded in their sense of God's desire for them, his mercy, and his justice. The *Book of Special Grace* on the one hand insists that the more saintly the person, the more she is convinced that she is inferior to all others,[92] and, on the other, calls attention to the hope that characterizes the lives of the holy, who model hopefulness and encourage it in others through their words and example. We read about John the Evangelist's lively hope, which gave him the assurance that Christ would refuse him nothing,[93] about Mechtild's holy audacity that God would remit her sins and make up for all her deficiencies,[94] and about Gertrude's confidence that at her death she would be united with her Beloved.[95]

[87] *Liber* 3.19 (221).

[88] *Liber* 7.2 (392).

[89] *Liber* 2.2 (139).

[90] *Liber* 2.8 (143).

[91] See for example *Liber* 1.1; 1.18 (7, 55–56); *Le Héraut* 1.11.1; 2.6.2 (SCh 139:170–72, 256–58). And see Schmitt, "Freed to Run," 227; Mary Jeremy Finnegan, *The Women of Helfta: Scholars and Mystics* (Athens: University of Georgia Press, 1991), 120. Neither woman associates her sinfulness with her gender: see Bynum, "Women Mystics," for Gertrude and Mechtild, and see Harrison and Bynum, "Gertrude, Gender," for Gertrude.

[92] *Liber* 1.1 (7).

[93] *Le Héraut* 4.4.12 (SCh 255:80).

[94] *Liber* 1.1 (8).

[95] *Le Héraut* 1.4.1 (SCh 139:142).

Mechtild and Gertrude as Mediators

However much Christ dominated their consciousness and ordered their days and nights, Gertrude's and Mechtild's engagement with him was not compensation for absence of fellowship with their sisters. The Helfta literature claims a direct correlation between intimacy with Christ and attentiveness to others. The nuns were, in addition, certain that the communal life they enjoyed was one in which individual relationships with Christ might thrive. The *Herald* and the *Book of Special Grace* underscore that the distinctive role Gertrude and Mechtild played was a consequence of their privileged intimacy with Christ. Within the household, both women acted as counselors, their sisters recognized both as preachers, and the two of them served their sisters as mediators with God and channels to the divinity; Gertrude was a confessor. They were charged and readied for these roles by Christ himself. He told Mechtild and Gertrude that each was the vestment in which he clothed himself.[96] It was Christ himself who executed in each woman all her works for the benefit of others.[97]

However reticent Mechtild may sometimes have been, the *Book of Special Grace* depicts her as earnestly and busily involved in the lives of her sisters. She was to her fellow nuns like the apostles, clinging to Christ day and night.[98] Well before she was fifty and began to reveal encounters with God she had long kept hidden,[99] her sisters looked to her as a mediator who regularly communicated with God on their behalf,[100] and whose encouraging words and instructions for them often came directly from him,[101] even if she did not always divulge the source

[96] *Liber* 3.13 (212); *Le Héraut* 3.18.4 (SCh 143:82).

[97] *Le Héraut* 1.2.1 (SCh 127:128); *Liber* 3.13 (212); *Le Héraut* 3.18.4 (SCh 143:82).

[98] *Liber* 5.30 (366); for an additional comparison of Mechtild to the apostles, see *Liber* 2.26 (170–71).

[99] *Liber* 2.26 (168–69).

[100] *Liber* 4.19; 4.22 (276, 279).

[101] *Liber* 3.38 (242).

of her advice and support. They prized her as kindhearted in her response to their needs,[102] praised her consoling presence,[103] and wondered at her condescension, especially toward those undergoing trials.[104] She was lovable to all.[105]

Offering a governing framework within which to understand Mechtild's person and especially her role in relation to others, the first chapter of the first book of the *Book of Special Grace* describes a vision in which Christ pressed himself against Mechtild's soul. He applied his hands to the hands of Mechtild's soul, his ears to the ears of her soul, his mouth to the mouth of her soul, and his heart to the heart of her soul, liquefying her and incorporating her into himself. In the meeting of their mouths he imparted to her his preaching. The *Book of Special Grace* appears to say here that Christ not only authorized Mechtild to preach but that he conveyed to her what were one and the same: his very words—his very self.[106] Numerous visions find Mechtild channeling the divinity to her sisters. Thus, for example, when Mechtild prayed for those who had commended themselves to her for Christ's fellowship,

> she saw a cord pass from the heart of God into her soul, through which she drew to God all who stood in her presence. Truly, the cord designated love, which God infused abundantly into this blessed soul, through which she drew all by good example and teaching. Then the King extending

[102] *Liber* 4.29 (287).

[103] *Liber* 4.48 (303).

[104] *Liber* 1 (2).

[105] *Liber* 1 (2).

[106] *Liber* 1.1 (8–9). On this passage, see Bruce W. Holsinger, *Music, Body, and Desire in Medieval Culture: Hildegard of Bingen to Chaucer* (Stanford: Stanford University Press, 2001), 243. And see *Liber* 2.34 (179), where Christ gives Mechtild his mouth for all of her utterances, whether speaking, praying, or singing. Bynum, "Women Mystics," 184, observed that Mechtild's and Gertrude's mystical experience allowed them to "serve as counselors, mediators, and channels to the sacraments—roles which the thirteenth-century church in some ways increasingly denied to women and to laity."

> the hand of his omnipotence blessed them, saying, "May the radiance of my face be your eternal happiness."[107]

The *Herald* underscores Gertrude's relentless focus on her sisters' spiritual well-being and ferocious dedication to helping the women pursue God,[108] engrossed in prayer on their behalf and pledged to almost constant contact with them. Drawing on the words of Bede and Bernard, the authors of the *Herald's* first book celebrate Gertrude's commitment and her counsel, although we learn that some of the nuns pressed Gertrude to moderate her investment in her sisters, urging that she disentangle herself from those who would not improve their behavior.[109] Book one of the *Herald* assimilates Gertrude to the prophet Jeremiah,[110] acclaims her wisdom and command of Scripture (so that she could refute almost any kind of error), and provides testimony to Gertrude's divinely ordained command of language as well as the many and varied influences it had on her sisters:

> She possessed a sweet and penetrating eloquence, a clever tongue, and speech so persuasive, efficacious, and gracious that most of those who heard her words testified, by the astonishing softening of their hearts and the change in their will, that God's spirit was speaking in her [Acts 6:10]. . . . Some she prodded by her words to salvation, others she permitted to see God and their own defects; to some she ministered consoling grace, and the hearts of others she caused to burn more radiantly with divine love.[111]

[107] *Liber* 1.10 (33–34).

[108] *Le Héraut* 1.7.1; 1.8.1 (SCh 139:152, 158).

[109] *Le Héraut* 1.7.1 (SCh 139:152).

[110] *Le Héraut* 1 Prol. 3 (SCh 139:110). Christ quotes from Jeremiah 1:9 when he assures Gertrude that all the words she speaks are words he has put in her mouth (*Le Héraut* 1.14.4 [SCh 139:198]).

[111] *Le Héraut* 1.1.3 (SCh 139:124).

Depicted as naturally timid and fighting against modesty for the purpose of helping to secure others' salvation, Gertrude recognized the role in which God cast her[112] and always had her sisters on her mind.[113] She would gladly have exposed herself in the midst of a thousand battle lines[114] in her sometimes caustic zeal to reform her sisters,[115] so we read, and would rather have seen her own mother harmed than to acquiesce to any injustice.[116] As they had with Mechtild, her sisters regarded Gertrude as a preacher. Her incorporation into Christ transformed her into an instrument by which God's grace washed over those whom he selected. "Give me your heart, beloved," Christ insisted to Gertrude on one occasion, and when she had done so, he pressed it to his own heart, which, like a waterpipe, spread streams of his love far and wide.[117]

The *Herald* repeatedly attributes to Gertrude the authority to hear confession, absolve, and assign penance to her sisters. Appearing before her, Christ breathed on Gertrude and said, "Receive the Holy Spirit. Whoever's sins you remit shall be remitted."[118] This passage contains a verbatim reference to a verse in the gospel of John (20:22-23), which, as Gertrude and her sisters would have understood, called the apostles to the priesthood.[119] In response to Gertrude's question, "Lord, how can this be when this power of binding and loosing is given only to priests?"[120] Christ confirmed his authorization so that no doubt about his intentions would remain: "Whomever you, discerning through my spirit, judge to be not guilty will surely

[112] *Le Héraut* 1.11.1 (SCh 139:170).

[113] *Le Héraut* 1.8 (SCh 139:158).

[114] *Le Héraut* 1.6.1 (SCh 139:150).

[115] *Le Héraut* 1.3.6 (SCh 139:140).

[116] *Le Héraut* 1.6.1 (SCh 139:150).

[117] *Le Héraut* 3.66.1 (SCh 143:270). For Gertrude as God's instrument, through whom to make known his loving-kindness, see *Le Héraut* 1.2.2 (SCh 139:128).

[118] *Le Héraut* 4.32.1 (SCh 255:280).

[119] Lewis, "God and the Human Being," 310.

[120] *Le Héraut* 4.32.1 (SCh 255:280).

be counted as blameless before me, and whomever you judge to be guilty will stand accused before me, for I will speak through your mouth."[121] He swept away any of Gertrude's hesitance about her role, filling in the broader outlines of his authorization and reaffirming his animating presence in her pronouncements on others:

> "Does not the church's faith rest universally on the promise I once made to Peter alone when I said, 'all that you shall bind on earth shall be bound in heaven? [Matt 16:19],' and does the church not firmly believe that this has occurred and continues through all the ministers of the church? Why do you, therefore, not believe that I, moved by love, am able and willing to do whatever I promise you with my divine mouth?" And touching her tongue he said, "Behold, I have put my words in your mouth [Jer 1:9], and I confirm in my truth every word that, prompted by my Spirit, you might speak to anyone on my behalf. And if you promise something to anyone on earth on behalf of my goodness, it will be kept in heaven as irrevocably ratified."[122]

Gertrude's own second book confirms that she regarded God as having sanctioned her to evaluate another's sins as trivial or serious, and it points to Gertrude's confidence that God would respect her determination, exercising his judgment in accordance with her own.[123] Her sisters acknowledged that Gertrude enjoyed a form of ordination—associated with a range of clerical privileges, especially preaching and administering the sacrament of penance—conferred directly by God and without intermediary and based not on office but on her union with Christ.[124] We see Gertrude at work in this role in the following account. One Sunday as she was recalling her

[121] *Le Héraut* 4.32.1 (SCh 255:280).

[122] *Le Héraut* 1.14.4 (SCh 139:198).

[123] *Le Héraut* 2.20.2 (SCh 139:310).

[124] Lewis, "God and the Human Being," 314. When Pierre Doyère asserts, "Il ne s'agit pas d'un role sacramentelle, mais de graces de lumière et de persuasion pour mettre au point dans des consciences timorées les problemes

sins, Gertrude fell prostrate at Christ's feet and implored his forgiveness. Christ forgave her, telling her that he would accept in satisfaction any act she offered in memory of his mercy. When she asked Christ to forgive her sisters their sins as well, he pledged that he would do so for all those who wished to share in her satisfaction. The following day, although her sisters were unable to receive the sacrament of penance because their confessor was not present in the monastery, some of the women communicated nonetheless.

During Mass, Gertrude saw her sisters ranged in three groups: those who had learned from her of her initial vision and who had acted on her announcement of forgiveness, those who refrained from communicating because they had not confessed to a priest, and those who communicated, unaware of Gertrude's instruction—but trusting in the goodness of God. If we read a little further into this vision account, we learn that while all the women, those who communicated and those who did not, sat near Christ, the sisters who communicated because they knew of Gertrude's vision were seated closest to him.[125] The documenting of this vision indicates that Gertrude's priestly authority to announce forgiveness was one that her sisters both recognized and celebrated. There is no evidence that any of her sisters questioned the mediating power and authority that Gertrude claimed for herself, even if they did not always take advantage of it.[126]

---

de la culpabilité et du pardon" (*Le Héraut* 2.20 [SCh 139:310–11]), he does not offer textual evidence to support his claim.

[125] *Le Héraut* 4.7.4 (SCh 255:102–4). For a discussion of this vision as authorizing Gertrude to announce forgiveness as would a priest, see Bynum, "Women Mystics," 204–5; and Lewis, "God and the Human Being," 313.

[126] Gertrude does not take up the question of the ordination of women, nor does this question emerge anywhere in the Helfta writings. Her silence is in contrast, for example, to the concern expressed by twelfth-century polymath and fellow nun, Hildegard of Bingen (see Anne L. Clark, "The Priesthood of the Virgin Mary: Gender Trouble in the Twelfth Century," *Journal of Feminist Studies in Religion* 18, no. 1 [Spring 2002]: 5–24; Augustine Thompson, "Hildegard of Bingen on Gender and the Priesthood," *Church History: Studies in Christianity and Culture* 63, no. 3 [1994]: 349–64).

This account acclaims not only Gertrude's desire to communicate to her sisters the forgiveness she has already received but also her ability to instruct them in reception and to absolve them. The literature urges on its readers respect for the varied choices individual sisters make,[127] pointing to the convent's confidence in Christ's recognition of each sister's ability to discern for herself whether she wishes to receive communion in the absence of having confessed to a priest. While the *Herald* lays out a hierarchy among the several available choices, lauding especially those who relied on Gertrude's authority to absolve, it acknowledges that within the community the different decisions others made pulled them also towards Christ, who also commended the humility of those who did not communicate and the confidence in his goodness of those who did.[128]

The *Herald* thus both promotes trust in Gertrude's authority and simultaneously allows sisters to determine a course of action for themselves. In its blithe acceptance of Gertrude's role of confessor, the *Herald* smacks up against the contemporary canon law and scholastic theology that underscored the association of the sacrament of penance with the priesthood. It does not indicate any reluctance among the sisters to confess to a priest, but the special favor accorded to those who believe Gertrude's vision hints at the literature's efforts to buttress the practice of turning to the visionary in lieu of the priest.[129] The

[127] The *Book of Special Grace* conveys the importance of self-examination before communion (*Liber* 1.19 [62–63]).

[128] For the attention in the *Herald* to individual spiritual proclivities and needs, see Alexandra Barratt, introduction to *Gertrude the Great of Helfta: The Herald of God's Loving-Kindness: Book 3*, trans. Alexandra Barratt, CF 63 (Kalamazoo, MI: Cistercian Publications, 1999), 18.

[129] During the eleventh through the thirteenth centuries, first canon lawyers and subsequently theologians and popes strove to consolidate sacramental power into an all-male presbyterate, a power that became gradually understood as having especially the power to consecrate and also to hear confession, absolve, and mete out penance; see Gary Macy, *The Hidden History of Women's Ordination: Female Clergy in the Medieval West* (Oxford: Oxford University Press, 2008), 125. Even into the thirteenth century, the question of who had

whole of the Helfta literature concedes and promotes the sisters' reliance on one another.

Relationships among the Sisters

"Tell her,"[130] Christ directed, with reference to this or that sister who populates the revelations that came to Gertrude and Mechtild or who figured as the principal subjects about whom God and the visionaries conferred. Discrete needs, fears, and questions that bubbled up in the lives of the women with whom they lived captured Gertrude's and Mechtild's attention and drove them into action. The sisters frequently addressed their spiritually adroit companions with queries and anxieties and sought counsel; they were sometimes instructed in dreams to do so.[131] The literature relates Gertrude's and Mechtild's sensitivity to the varied emotions[132] of specific women with whom they lived; the visionaries were accustomed to identifying spiritual maladies among them and responding to them.[133]

---

the authority to perform the ritual of confession and absolution was met with a variety of responses from theologians, however, although the majority of theologians considered that absolution by a priest was requisite; see Bynum, "Women Mystics," 205. For much of the Middle Ages, it was not uncommon for abbesses to hear confessions of the members of their monastic family—and sometimes from others from outside the community—as well as to assign penance; see Macy, *Hidden History*, 51 and 82–83. There is no indication that any of Helfta's abbesses exercised the full scope of the role associated with confessor, however, and Gertrude's and Mechtild's exercise of quasi-priestly authority is not a reversion to an older model of women's liturgical ministry. Instead, the monastery coupled the two visionaries' exercise of quasi-clerical authority with recognition of the abbess's role in meting out penance. And their sisters and the visionaries themselves perceived their authority to be authorized by God through direct contact with him in contrast with the traditional basis of sacramental authority, office; see Lewis, "God and the Human Being," 310.

[130] *Liber* 4.51 (304).

[131] *Le Héraut* 1.2.5 (SCh 139:130), and *Liber* 1.12.2 (188).

[132] See *Liber* 4.50; 4.52; 4.23; 4.24 (304, 305, 280, 281).

[133] See for example *Liber* 4.24; 4.37; 4.38 (281, 295–96, 296–97).

Page after page in the *Book of Special Grace* and the *Herald* brim with accounts that present the two women as problem-solvers, comforters, and instructors, often harnessing their familiarity with Christ to bring before him the troubles of a particular sister and convey his messages to one woman or another.[134]

Both texts are replete with examples of the efficacy of their petitions on behalf of their sisters.[135] After she prayed for a certain nun, Mechtild saw Christ take the woman's hand and lead her into a flower-filled meadow.[136] Her prayer on behalf of a different sister elicited a gloss on a prayer from the Office for Holy Week, which, Christ explained to Mechtild, the woman should offer God, asking for his mercy.[137] When a fellow nun was afraid to receive, Mechtild prayed for her, and Christ told Mechtild, tell her to approach me often, and I promise I will receive her as my queen.[138] When a sister asked what God wanted of her, Mechtild conveyed Christ's message: that she behave toward him as an infant who loves her father tenderly; like a young wife, who is distinguished not by her beauty or nobility or wealth, but by her love; like a friend, who regards everything that pertains to her friend as pertaining to herself.[139] Sometimes we learn of the visionary's own preoccupations regarding a fellow nun without learning what precipitated the concern. Wishing to root out a woman's unspecified worries,

[134] See for example *Le Héraut* 5.3.7 (SCh 331:74).

[135] On the power of Gertrude's prayer, see *Le Héraut* 1.2.2 (SCh 139:128–30).

[136] *Liber* 4.35 (293–94).

[137] *Liber* 4.25 (282–83).

[138] *Liber* 4.48 (303). Reception was a prominent preoccupation among the nuns of Helfta, where frequent expressions of eagerness to communicate were often coupled with apprehensions about doing so. In the visions that come to them, Gertrude and Mechtild routinely urged their sisters to receive with confidence. See for example *Liber* 4.2 (259), and *Le Héraut* 1.14.2 (SCh 139:196–98). They prayed for women who were afraid that they communicated too often, and they spoke with God about their sisters' concerns (see *Liber* 3.26 [229–30]).

[139] *Liber* 4.32 (290–91).

Mechtild carried back to the unsettled sister Christ's assurance of his nearness and commitment to her:

> Why is she disturbed? I created her for myself, and I have given myself to her in everything she desires from me. I am her father in creation, I am her mother in redemption, I am her brother in sharing of my kingdom, and I am her sister in my sweet companionship.[140]

The visionaries' feelings for their sisters were evident in other ways in their mediating interaction with Christ. Gertrude and Mechtild intermittently engaged in a sometimes challenging to-and-fro that highlights their unremitting advocacy on behalf of their companions as well as their strong-mindedness and the straightforwardness that characterized their relationship with Christ. Mechtild once seems almost to have reproached him for allowing one of her sisters to become ill, even though she had served him well in choir; he shot back that it was his prerogative to play with his good friends, and then he explained that when they were ill, he covered his friends in a cloak of glory.[141] Mechtild, apparently satisfied, ceased her questioning. When, on the other hand, Gertrude asked about a sister with whom (she perceived) Christ was displeased, he responded that the woman did not have sufficient trust in him. But Gertrude nudged him, offering an alternate and salutary motive for her sister's attitude: the woman's humility, not a lack of trust, animated her. Gertrude's words had the desired effect: Christ assured her that he would, after all, impart his gifts to the woman.[142] This visionary vignette reveals Gertrude's confidence in her ability to discern the spiritual condition of a sister as well as her eagerness to share her insights with God. As they conceived of themselves, Gertrude and

[140] *Liber* 4.50 (304).
[141] *Liber* 4.30 (287–88).
[142] *Le Héraut* 3.17.2 (SCh 143:217–19).

Mechtild were more than just messengers, facilitating a simple back-and-forth of request and response. Sure in their assessment of their sisters and therefore of their value to Christ, they advocated even when they risked contradicting their divine partner, although the *Book of Special Grace* depicts the older Mechtild as perhaps less inclined to contend with Christ when their perceptions differed.

Mechtild's and Gertrude's sometimes-delicate consideration of individual sisters frequently elicited a communication from Christ that while directed to the particular person on whose behalf he was approached, seems to be for all the women.[143] When Mechtild prayed for someone who was sad, Christ instructed the sister to remember his goodness, a lesson from which everyone could surely benefit.[144] Sensitive to the steady round of disturbances that befell the portress, who was regularly called away from Mass by the arrival of guests, Mechtild shared this concern, then related to the portress words Christ intended for her: "For every step a person takes in obedience, it is as if she were gathering coins in my hand, and they increase her merits."[145] While specifically affirming the value of the portress's workaday responsibilities, Christ's words would have had broad implications: the nuns ought to go about their household tasks obediently, with assurance that Christ understood what was necessary for running the monastery and approved of the nuns' attentiveness to these tasks, even when they conflicted with liturgical commitments. Mechtild's communication may have cooled a concern familiar to many of the nuns, whose daily chores sometimes bumped up against their obligation to attend Mass and Office, making them at least a little anxious about being pulled in two directions at once.[146]

[143] *Liber* 4.31 (289–90).

[144] *Liber* 4.24 (281).

[145] *Liber* 3.45 (248).

[146] See chap. 6 for the relationship between the spiritual meaning of labor in relation to liturgy.

Elsewhere we learn that at the behest of one of her sisters, Mechtild offered to God the woman's act of renunciation, and subsequently during Mass she saw a small child alight from the ciborium. The child was immediately transformed into a lovely young girl, a symbol of the divine will and a confirmation of God's pleasure with the nun. But a demon in the form of a menial kitchen servant simultaneously tried to grab the attention of the other nuns present. Some ignored him, but others smiled and spoke with him in flirtatious whispers. The account forgoes any specificity about the sister or her act of renunciation that would tag the lesson to a certain predicament, and it ends with the warning that if those who follow their own inclinations do not repent, they will suffer eternally—certainly a broadly applicable caution.[147] In this case as in others, the implication is that one woman's need is probably shared among many women, and the exemplary act of one is a model for all.

Throughout the *Herald* and the *Book of Special Grace*, in fact, individual concerns are habitually treated as arising from a shared context, the everyday environment of the monastery, emphasizing commonality among all the nuns.[148] Mechtild's and Gertrude's responses to particular sisters are implicitly presented as having significance for the whole community, whose corporate welfare is never far from their consideration. And yet, even if the counsels, instructions, admonitions, and so forth that Mechtild and Gertrude conveyed were for the most part easily transferable from one woman's quandary to another's and seem, therefore, perhaps not to be firmly anchored in the specificity of any peculiar circumstance, the literature is keen to assert that Gertrude and Mechtild really *are*

[147] *Liber* 4.19 (276).

[148] For a brilliant consideration of individual and community in the Sister Books with particular attention to the cultivation of "inattention" to singularity, see Richard Kieckhefer, "Mystical Communities in the Late Medieval West," Medieval Academy Plenary Address, International Medieval Conference, Leeds, 2007.

mindful of the dilemma that *this* individual sister faces or of *that* particular woman, each of whom, it conveys, they esteem as worthy of their attention and of answers targeted to her malady or tailored to her concern.

A concern to assert and guarantee respect for difference and individuality among sisters is evident in another way in the *Herald*, which relates a conversation in which Gertrude tried to ensure that a particular woman for whom she prayed would share in a special way the benefits God distributed on account of the prayer. The larger context of Gertrude's preoccupation is the conviction that however isolated and discrete a person's good work may be—a single *Our Father*, visiting a sick sister—if performed in union with Christ, it redounds to the benefit of all who will be saved. Exactly on this account Gertrude wondered about the distinctive advantage that might accrue to the person on whose behalf she prayed, how, that is, her gain from Gertrude's prayer would differ from that which the whole church amassed.

When Gertrude queried Christ about the matter, he responded with an analogy: a young woman makes jewelry with which she adorns herself and her sisters—and for which she acquires renown for her mother and father as well as for her entire household. Yet, Christ elaborated, the woman who made and the sister who wears the jewelry stand apart from the others, enjoying greater celebrity than those who are not likewise adorned.[149] Those whom Gertrude loved especially *would* profit in a special way from acts Gertrude performed on their behalf.

It is as if Christ were professing that those who are important to Gertrude mattered to him simply because they were the object of her love. And when he explained that she who has made the offering and she to whom it has been given are both adorned, he reiterated a relationship of reciprocity that the Helfta literature repeatedly underscores, by which, in this

[149] *Le Héraut* 3.75.1 (SCh 143:318–20).

instance, Gertrude and the sister for whom she prayed were bound together through the adornment that prayer confers. Because the benefits that redound to the person for whom one offers a particular work are also credited to the whole church, the intended recipient is likewise integrated into a larger pool of recipients—as is the person who has offered the work, since she has a share in the offering. Thus the intended recipient occupies a singular position, without, however, disinheriting the whole church from participation in the benefits garnered.

Gertrude may not have been alone in struggling to make sense of the implications and mechanism of prayer. Here her message to the reader is clear: Christ will take preferential relationships into account, even as each is drawn together into a larger community—in fact, a much larger community. The nuns taught themselves that the community they joined when they entered the monastery encompassed a far greater population than the women with whom they resided and on whom they focused their attention. Their devotions necessarily spiraled outward, and each prayer they said for one or several among them had implications for all who would be saved. The Helfta literature is unambiguous in asserting that individual binding ties fortify the whole.

One-on-One Relationships

Here and there, we learn a little about those of Gertrude's and Mechtild's relationships with their sisters that assumed a greater degree of familiarity than others. Gertrude remarked on the "sweet society" of a certain Sister E.,[150] and we read about her "special friends"[151] as well as about close friends of Mechtild,[152] while an anonymous nun fears the death of one

[150] *Le Héraut* 5.2.1 (SCh 331:64).

[151] *Le Héraut* 5.4.20 (SCh 331:102). For special friends, see also *Le Héraut* 4.7.2 (SCh 255:100).

[152] *Liber* 1.1; 2.26 (11, 169).

of several intimates.[153] If we wish to consider the place of one-on-one relationships between women in this community, we would do well, however, not to expect the sort of late medieval language of friendship made famous in the letters of Anselm, Bernard, and other twelfth-century male monks, of the hearts of friends melting into each other so as to become one heart, or of lyrical affirmations of friendship as a means of attaining holiness, such as we find in writings of Anselm and Aelred.[154] High-pitched expressions of yearning for the other who is friend and extravagant expressions of the joys of companionship are foreign to the Helfta sensibilities, and the women cast a more delicate light on attachments between the nuns. Friendship in this context is not expressed primarily as a warm bond between two women, capable of bringing intense happiness and satisfaction that solidifies person-to-person connection. It is portrayed as intellectual and spiritual camaraderie, including consultation and advice-giving that may or may not call forth feelings of affection and tender consideration for the other.

We do learn that a principal author of the *Book of Special Grace* was Mechtild's "good friend" (*familiarissimae*);[155] perhaps the reference is to Gertrude. The book makes little of Mechtild's affinity with this particular sister, however, or of sympathetic rapport Mechtild may have had with other women whose wisdom and sensitivity supported her in her spiritual life. For all her expressed sense of humility and diffidence, Mechtild seems to have been more comfortable as counselor than as beneficiary of others' ministrations, less interested in being the

[153] *Le Héraut* 3.85.1 (SCh 147:338). Friendship groups leave a mark in the literature, as when we read that once Gertrude addressed a recently deceased sister because she was goaded on to do so by friends the two had in common, friends who wanted to know the merits the sister had acquired in heaven (*Le Héraut* 5.8.2; 5.10.4 [SCh 331:130, 148]).

[154] See for example Adele Fiske, *Friends and Friendship in the Monastic Tradition*, CIDOC Cuaderno No. 51 (Cuernavaca, Mexico: Centro Intercultural de Documentacion, 1970), 11–15.

[155] *Liber* 5.24 (356–57).

recipient of advice and succor from her sisters than they were in profiting from her insights and care. Everyone wanted to be her friend, we read. What we learn of Mechtild's response is telling: she bore her sisters' desires for her friendship with difficulty.[156] Mechtild seems more reticent than Gertrude about personal relationships within the monastery, the scope of her concern more cosmic.[157]

In any case, Mechtild's status as advisor in the convent, which included being bombarded with the petitions of others, was sometimes spiritually productive. When she prayed for someone who complained of sadness because she felt she loved God too little, the same sentiment overcame Mechtild, and for the same reason, precipitating a conversation with God that paired an audacious claim about his love with an expression of her own worthlessness.[158] Mechtild's prayers on behalf of others regularly resulted in messages from Christ as being as applicable to her as to her sisters.[159] Because her sisters' need for her called on her commitment to Christ, engagement with others seems almost always to have been for her both about the other and about herself, the benefits frequently mutual.

Friendships emerge as of obvious importance to Gertrude, who gauged her relative affection for her friends—some were dearer to her than others,[160] some were her "special" friends[161]—and for those who expressed a longing for companionship.[162] She regularly sought out and received counsel from her sisters and rejoiced in their company.[163] On two occasions she sought out a sister for advice about experiences

[156] *Liber caput praevium* (6).

[157] For a related observation, see Finnegan, *Women of Helfta*, 88. See also Bynum, "Women Mystics," 215.

[158] *Liber* 4.23 (280).

[159] See for example *Liber* 4.32; 4.38 (290–92, 296–97).

[160] *Le Héraut* 1.11.8 (SCh 139:178).

[161] *Le Héraut* 5.4.20 (SCh 331:102).

[162] *Le Héraut* 2.3.1 (SCh 139:236). On Gertrude's need for friendship, see Shank, "God of My Life," 257.

[163] *Le Héraut* 1.3.1; 1.11.12 (SCh 139:132–34, 182).

that seemed especially charged. In one report, Gertrude took up her desire for Christ's wounds with a fellow nun:

> After Vespers during our meal, I was sitting in the refectory next to a certain person to whom I had disclosed part of my secret. I put this here for the salvation of the reader because I often felt the fervor of my devotion increase on such an occasion, and whether your spirit, Lord, incited this, or human affection, is not clear to me, although I have heard from someone accomplished in such matters that a secret like this one may be more usefully revealed to someone who is not only a faithful friend [*fidelitatis familiaris*] on account of her goodness but also a superior by reason of the respect due to greater age.[164]

As Gertrude relates, right relationships (in this case with a good woman who possessed wisdom associated with old age and laced with affection) have the power to kindle love of God and its expressions, including the activating of affective response.[165] Gertrude repeatedly enjoyed exchanges in which she disclosed to some of her sisters aspects of her life that she

[164] *Le Héraut* 2.4.2 (SCh 139:244).

[165] For Gertrude's observations, see Rosalynn Jean Voaden, "All Girls Together: Community, Gender, and Vision at Helfta," in *Medieval Women in Their Communities*, ed. Diane Watt (Buffalo, NY: University of Toronto Press, 1997); Voaden notes that the nuns' emotional connections with one another in the context of common devotional practices built up their spirituality, intensifying their experiences. For a larger context, see Brian Patrick McGuire, *Friendship and Monastic Community, 350–1250*, CS 95 (Kalamazoo, MI: Cistercian Publications, 1988), which examines ways in which "close personal bonds" between and among men were encouraged and discouraged within monastic communities. McGuire largely omits from consideration women's friendship. There is a long history in pre-modern Christian monasticism of the central role of friendship in the journey of self toward God. See for example Brian Patrick McGuire, "The Cistercians and the Transformation of Monastic Friendships," *Analecta Cisterciensia* 37 (1981): 3–65; Jean Leclercq, "L'amitié dans les lettres au Moyen Âge," *Revue du moyen âge latin* 1 (1945): 391–410; Anne Clark Bartlett, "'A Reasonable Affection': Gender and Spiritual Friendship in Middle English Devotional Literature," in *Vox Mystica: Essays on*

more generally kept to herself, indicating a pattern of behavior into which this encounter fit. The author of book one tells us that Gertrude was accustomed to look to those whom she regarded as her spiritual superiors for Christ's testimony concerning her own gifts;[166] for at least the most part, this seems to have meant her sisters.

Gertrude was sensitive to the contours of her relationship with the women with whom she lived and to the meaning of friendship, which she thought worthy of sustained consideration.[167] In the refectory, she expressed curiosity about whether Christ or her affection for her interlocutor was responsible for the increased devotion she felt after speaking with her sister. We have no evidence that she resolved the question—or any indication that she continued to puzzle over it or was made anxious by not knowing. The relationship between friendship, on the one hand, and, on the other, progress in love of God and neighbor was nevertheless a topic that interested her and about which she spoke with others in the household. Her musing suggests that to her mind, there was no sharp divide between the workings of friendship and that of God, but rather an easy congruence:[168]

> If this [increased fervor] was truly incited by human affection, it would be even more fitting that I should sink into the abyss of gratitude, just as your condescension, my God, is greater in condescending to join the gold of your invaluable worth to the mud of my vileness, so that the jewels of your grace might cling to me.[169]

Medieval Mysticism in Honor of Professor Valerie M. Lagorio, ed. Thomas H. Bestul, et al. (Cambridge: Brewer, 1995), 134–45.

[166] *Le Héraut* 1.3.1 (SCh 139:132, 134).

[167] As Shank observed, Gertrude was sensitive to her own moods as well (Shank, "God of My Life," 240).

[168] Voaden has observed that for Gertrude, both human affection and God's spirit "worked in harmony to lead her to heightened spiritual awareness" ("All Girls," 78).

[169] *Le Héraut* 2.4.2 (SCh 139:244).

Emotional affinity with another human being might be a means for cultivating devotion to God, but it is not something about which Gertrude provided additional details. Moreover, we do not learn what effect the refectory conversation might have had on Gertrude's confidante. In describing her talk with her friend and its consequences, Gertrude's attention remained squarely on herself: *she* disclosed *her* secrets to her sister; *her* devotion was increased in consequence of the interchange. We may suppose that to Gertrude, treasured friendship might not have been predicated on mutual give-and-take. That is, friendship might flourish with only one party as obvious beneficiary.[170] On the other hand, perhaps these passages are snapshots of moments in a relationship in which now one party to the friendship, now the other, might receive a hearing from the other and offer counsel.

Several years later, Gertrude asked a sister to include in her daily prayer before the crucifix a petition to Christ to pierce Gertrude's heart with his love. Gertrude attributes a combination of this woman's prayer and her own, as well as the merits and longing of all her sisters, to her subsequent sight of something like a ray of sun coming out of the righthand side of an image of the crucified Christ on the page of a book she held open during Mass.[171] The ray, which had a sharp point like an arrow, pieced Gertrude's heart. Some days later, she heard Christ express the hope that she would anchor in his love all of her emotions, including her pleasure, her hope, her joy, her pain, her fear.[172] Although Gertrude thus credited the

[170] On friendships between monks that did not "necessarily imply equality or even mutuality," see McGuire, *Friendship*, xv.

[171] *Le Héraut* 2.5.1–2 (SCh 139:248, 250). On medieval people's awareness of an image's capacity to provoke imaginative reflections and visions, see Jeffrey Hamburger, "Seeing and Believing: The Suspicion of Sight and Authentication of Vision in Late Medieval Art and Devotion," in *Imagination und Wirklichkeit: zum Verhältnis von mentalen und realen Bildern in der Kunst der frühen Neuzeit*, ed. Klaus Krüger and Alessandro Nova (Mainz: Philipp von Zabern, 2000), 48.

[172] *Le Héraut* 1.5.1 (SCh 139:250).

piercing of her heart to all her sisters, she highlighted the prayer of one particular woman and recounted a related conversation with a fellow nun that took place afterwards. In the following section of book two, we read that Gertrude, recalling that she has heart wounds that need to be washed, anointed, and bandaged, turned to one of her sisters for help in tending to her heart's wound.[173]

Gertrude's description underscores her confidence in this woman's spiritual abilities. The woman was accustomed with greater constancy and delicacy than Gertrude, so we read, to listen to the soft murmurings of God's love.[174] Her sister advised Gertrude to wash away her sins with the water of devotion, apply the salve of thanksgiving in moments of adversity, and bandage herself with the potent power of love.[175] Here revelation gave rise to substantive interchange—and not simply the visionary's recitation to another of the contents of her vision. In this case, it is not the visionary who proffers counsel but the nun in whom she confides. In moments of yearning and delight, Gertrude sought out women who could help her to secure that for which she longed and to calibrate a fitting response to the gifts God gave her, a response that called on her to gather the whole complex of her emotional life and fix it in him and that thus implicated her sisters in the intimate part of herself that God wished her to reserve for himself.

Talking about the revelations that came now to one sister, now to another must have been a means of threading listeners into the life of the speaker, sometimes simply by hearing her out and sometimes by offering her observation or guidance. Gertrude did not indicate whether the women who figure in these two incidents were the same or two different women,

[173] Margaret Winkworth believes that the person in whom Gertrude confided was Mechtild, but the evidence for this view is not clear (*Gertrude of Helfta: The Herald of Divine Love*, trans. Margaret Winkworth [New York: Paulist Press, 1993], 102, n. 31).

[174] *Le Héraut* 2.3 (SCh 139:250).

[175] *Le Héraut* 2.3 (SCh 139.250).

perhaps because her point was not to celebrate a specific friend or friendship, or to champion this or that woman as spiritually astute and companionable. What she seemed to want to point out instead was her own need for her sisters and the advantages that she enjoyed through her friendships. By implication, this acknowledgment both of the need and of such advantages would have encouraged similar relationships among the other nuns. Regarding the first of the two incidents, she wrote, "I put this here for the salvation of the reader."[176]

Friendship and Visions

It seems beside the point to try to categorize the relationships Gertrude and Mechtild enjoy with their sisters as expressions of friendship or of spiritual guardianship. Gertrude's book two and, more broadly, the *Herald* do not distinguish between offering counsel and serving as faithful friend. As the *Herald* makes explicit, true friendship was in any case necessarily predicated on a shared commitment to Christ.[177] If the giving of advice to the one who confides is an act of reciprocity that complements the confidence, then we can suppose friendships were widespread at Helfta, knowing that the giving and receiving of confidences and advice was central to the engagement of members of the community with one another. The Helfta literature lacks extended considerations of what friendship meant to the sisters, along with explicit reflection on the place of friendship in their lives. These silences may not be because friendships were rare there, but because they were largely taken for granted and valued as an arena within which sisters learned about self and God. The narrator of the *Herald's* book one notes casually that Christ conveyed a particular message to Gertrude "through many who were close to her."[178]

[176] *Le Héraut* 2.4.2 (SCh 139:244).

[177] *Liber* 1.6.1 (150–52). For friendship in Christ, see *Liber* 2.42 (192).

[178] *Le Héraut* 1.7.3 (SCh 139:156).

Personal exchanges of the kind I have been describing must have advanced familiarity with modes of visionary experience and sensitivity to visions and therefore facilitated the interlocutors' reception of revelation. One-on-one interactions such as these surely contributed to the production of what appears to be a household of visionaries, confiding in and conferring with one another.[179] God communicated with a number of sisters about Gertrude.[180] The *Herald* recounts one sister's gratefulness for Gertrude's presence in the monastery; it depicts her as roundly caught up in Gertrude's life, privy to her concerns and responsive to them, entering into prayer, marshaling the visions that followed for Gertrude's benefit, and expressing admiration for Gertrude while matter-of-factly conveying God's response to the shortcomings she acknowledged in herself.[181] Book one marshals a wealth of visionary evidence in support of Gertrude's holiness: revelations came to an untold number of people, including women and men both inside and outside the monastery,[182] each of whom received, we read, the whispers of God's communication, which were to them like the sighs of a soft breeze, and which attested to Gertrude's sanctity.[183]

[179] For the cultivation of visions at Helfta, see chap. 1.

[180] *Le Héraut* 1.3; 1.16.3, 1.16.6, 5.29.3 (SCh 139:134–42, 212–14, 216–18; SCh 331:234).

[181] *Liber* 1.3.4 (138).

[182] *Le Héraut* 1.3.1 (SCh 139:132). The waft of Gertrude's sanctity drew at least one woman to Helfta, who, once there, received a divine revelation concerning both Mechtild and Gertrude (*Le Héraut* 1.3.2 [SCh 139:134]). In addition, see *Le Héraut* 1.3.3–7 (SCh 139:136–42). The *Herald*'s Book One tells of an unidentified man to whom Gertrude had commended herself and to whom God spoke about the subject of his petitions (*Le Héraut* 1.5.1–10 [SCh 139:216]). A male religious likewise receives a revelation in which God speaks to him about what he finds pleasing in Gertrude (*Le Héraut* 1.11.7 [SCh 139:176–79]). For the visions that come to the priests in the monastery's employ, see chap. 5.

[183] *Le Héraut* 1.16.3 (SCh 139:212).

God gave other sisters revelations centering on Mechtild.[184] He charged an unnamed nun with informing the bedridden Mechtild when it was time for her to receive holy unction, another sister heard their conversation as she perceived Christ standing before Mechtild when she lay dying, yet another observed Christ summon Mechtild to him as her life ebbed, and three women (all of whom remain anonymous) perceived (perhaps simultaneously) that Christ was present at Mechtild's bedside as she died.[185] Such claims to visionary experience, alighting on one woman's holy life and another's holy death and meant to promote veneration of two esteemed sisters, give us insight into a monastery in which a company of women recorded their own extraordinary sightings and auditions. Visions endowed their recipient's engagement with a particular sister with weighty significance, since they implicated God directly in that relationship.

The revelations that came to the sisters were not always about Gertrude or Mechtild. Christ appeared to the women who crowded around Abbess Gertrude's deathbed,[186] and authorial collaborators on the *Herald* and the *Book of Special Grace* received revelations announcing their own remarkable relationship with God, as did what appear to be numerous other women in the convent.[187] Moreover, it was not solely

[184] See for example *Liber* 1.3.2 (134–36).

[185] *Liber* 7.3; 7.1; 7.2; 7.4 (393–94, 391–92, 392, 394). As Grimes observes, Mechtild is one of several people to whom book one of the *Herald* attributes visions concerning Gertrude, visions that do not differ markedly in content from those attributed to other, anonymous, recipients (*Wisdom's Friends*, 8).

[186] *Liber* 6.4 (381–88).

[187] For the unnamed authors, see chap. 1. For visions not obviously attributable to Gertrude or Mechtild, see for example *Le Héraut* 1.3.3–6; 5.29.3 (SCh 139:136–40; SCh 331:234), which refers to people who communicated to Gertrude God's promises to her. In conversation with a recently deceased nun, Gertrude learned that while she was alive, the woman had received all sorts of gifts from God and did not make them known to her sisters; it seems likely that visionary experiences figured among these gifts (*Le Héraut* 5.10.3 [SCh 331:148]). (It is not always clear who the person is who has a particular vision;

Gertrude and Mechtild who projected the force of their visionary life on the community as a whole.[188] When it was revealed to a sister that Christ would release a great number of souls from purgatory on account of the community's petitions, a special prayer was enjoined on everyone.[189] All the sisters had the potential to instruct the community and to affect its practices. Gertrude casually revealed the apparently many visions her sisters received when she wondered why the content of their revelations was often different from the content of hers. Christ responded that these varied visions helped to shine a brighter light on the depths of his wisdom,[190] allowing us a view into a monastery that sought to make room for its members to share their visionary experience, convinced that a lack of uniformity in each woman's contribution ought not to be feared but celebrated as divinely sanctioned and contributing to knowledge of God. Claims to such experiences may have been quite widespread. We read about a certain woman who sought an answer from God (about what we do not know) and who had to wait a while before God answered her query; God eventually explained that he took a long time in replying because

---

Le Héraut 5.1.20–24; 5.4 [SCh 33:38–46, 78–108].) For a different interpretation, see Siegfried Ringler, who argues that as the Helfta literature portrays it, only a small company of women received visions ("Die Rezeption Gertruds von Helfta im Bereich süddeutschen Frauenklöster," in "*Vor dir steht die leere Schale meiner Sehnsucht": Die Mystik der Frauen von Helfta*, ed. Michael Bangert and Hildegund Keul [Leipzig: St. Benno Buch- und Zeitschriftenverlagsgesellschaft, 1998], esp. 141). Mechtild's and Gertrude's contemporaries at Helfta, Ringler contends, were not obviously interested in cultivating visionary or ecstatic experiences for themselves ("Die Rezeption Gertruds," 135–36).

[188] *Le Héraut* 3.9.2 (SCh 143:36–38). Catherine M. Mooney has suggested that the predominance of visions in writings by women and those about them may be a consequence of male influence ("The Authorial Role of Brother A. in the Composition of Angela of Foligno's Revelations," in *Creative Women in Medieval and Early Modern Italy: A Religious and Artistic Renaissance*, ed. E. Ann Matter and John Coakley [Philadelphia: University of Pennsylvania Press, 1994], 52). The Helfta literature does not support this conclusion.

[189] *Le Héraut* 3.9.1 (SCh 143:34–36).

[190] *Le Héraut* 3.48.2 (SCh 143:214–16).

the inquiring woman, unlike Gertrude, did not trust him.[191] The point of this report is to accentuate the favor Gertrude found with God by contrasting it with his disappointment in one of her sisters. And yet it seems that even sisters with whom God expressed displeasure might be counted among those to whom revelations came.

There is reason, then, to suppose that visions were widely experienced at Helfta and that many women counted themselves, and were acknowledged by their sisters, as recipients of divine insights and sometimes capable of astute counsel on this basis. The visions that came to Mechtild and to Gertrude did not therefore set them entirely apart from their sisters. Spiritual virtuosi though they were, the women at the center of the *Herald* and the *Book of Special Grace* were not perceived as anomalies but as models for the full flowering of the potential of each woman to love God and to enjoy the awareness of his will and presence for the benefit of self and other.

The Relationship between Gertrude and Mechtild

At least since Louis Paquelin, the nineteenth-century editor of the *Herald* and the *Book of Special Grace*, scholars have claimed an abiding friendship between Gertrude and Mechtild of Hackeborn.[192] The assertion is especially attractive in part because there are far fewer medieval texts hailing and surveying

[191] *Le Héraut* 1.10.5 (SCh 139:168–70).

[192] Paquelin, Praefatio to *Liber*, iii. Among the many scholars who have claimed a special friendship between Gertrude and Mechtild, see Hans Urs von Balthasar, Einführung to *Das Buch*, ed. Hans Urs von Balthasar (Einsiedeln: Johannes Verlag, 1955), 12; Lucie Félix-Faure Goyau, *Christianisme et culture féminine* (Paris: Librairie Académique, 1914), 99; Theresa A. Halligan, introduction to *The Booke of Gostlye Grace of Mechtild of Hackeborn*, trans. Theresa A. Halligan (Toronto: Pontifical Institute of Mediaeval Studies, 1979), 36; Alberta Dieker, "Mechtild of Hackeborn: Song of Love," in *Medieval Women Monastics: Wisdom's Wellsprings*, ed. Miriam Schmitt and Linda Kulzer (Collegeville, MN: Liturgical Press, 1996), 232; Shank, "God of My Life," 251; Columba Hart, introduction to *The Exercises of Saint Gertrude*, trans. a Benedictine nun

women's friendships with one another than there are considerations of male friendships.[193] Although the evidence for this friendship and for Gertrude's spiritual apprenticeship to her older sister is less conclusive than is often supposed,[194] the two women do seem to have enjoyed a hearty relationship, chock-full of emotional investment, curiosity about and respect for each other, and the willingness to lob some criticism—at least on Mechtild's part.

One of several passages in book one of the *Herald* that refers to "Sister M., the chantress," depicts Mechtild of Hackeborn receiving a vision that underscored God's pleasure in Gertrude's habits of contemplation and of service. Mechtild asked Christ why Gertrude sometimes judged others' failings severely. Christ responded by accentuating Gertrude's penitent humility: acknowledging with Mechtild that Gertrude could not tolerate any blemish in others, he added in her defense that she also judged herself severely.[195] The author of book one recounts another vision that confirmed to Mechtild the saving power of Gertrude's prayers: Gertrude appeared to Mechtild in the form of a bridge, fortified by Christ's humanity and divinity, and she heard God say, "All those who struggle to come to me over this bridge will never fall or go astray."[196]

---

of Regina Laudis [Columba Hart] (Westminster, MD: The Newman Press, 1956), ix.

[193] There is, in part for this reason, significantly less scholarship on female friendship in the Middle Ages than on male friendship (Karma Lochrie, "Between Women," *The Cambridge Companion to Medieval Women's Writings*, ed. Carolyn Dinshaw and David Wallace [Cambridge: Cambridge University Press, 2003], 74).

[194] Grimes, *Wisdom's Friends*, 6, n. 10, and 8.

[195] *Le Héraut* 1.11.9 (SCh 139:178). When Gertrude's sternness distressed one of her sisters, Christ compared himself to Gertrude; on earth, he like her was moved by strong and passionate feelings; *Le Héraut* 1.12.1 (SCh 139:184–86). Knowing when to be stern with those for whom one is responsible is laudable in a monastic leader; Abbess Gertrude addresses her daughters with severity when the occasion demands (*Liber* 6.1 [376]).

[196] *Le Héraut* 1.14.6 (SCh 139:202).

These accounts of Mechtild's relationship with Gertrude insist on God's high estimation of Gertrude and confirm the efficacy of her counsel, but imply that Mechtild at least sometimes puzzled over the gratification God felt about her sister. And by drawing attention to the interest Mechtild had in her companion, whom she regarded as worthy of discussing with Christ, they suggest Gertrude may have frequently been on Mechtild's mind.

Visions in a hagiographical section of the *Herald* are crowded with Gertrude's testimony to Mechtild's sanctity, the special status she occupies among the saints and angels, and Christ's passion and respect for his beloved, *domna M. cantrix nostra*.[197] Gertrude's revelations broadcast the divine delights Mechtild enjoyed as one of Christ's elect and their universal significance: in her last illness, Christ placed his wound on her mouth, and from his heart, Mechtild drew her breath, her exhalation overflowing onto the whole church, and especially onto those present at her bedside.[198] As Mechtild died, Gertrude heard Christ summon his bride to his kingdom and heard him ask "where is my gift?" so recalling to her the gift of his heart that he had previously given Mechtild. At this moment, Mechtild opened her heart with her hands, Christ opened his, and his heart absorbed her heart.[199]

We have here evidence of two visionaries confirming each other's intimacy with Christ and intercessory powers with him. The relationship was apparently characterized by mutual respect, even if it was asymmetrical, with Gertrude esteeming Mechtild perhaps as her teacher, and Mechtild (probably with some sort of spiritual authority over the younger nun) leveling accusations of severity, a criticism that seems fitting given Gertrude's sometimes-harsh evaluation of her sisters. It is noteworthy that the *Herald* allots far greater space to the dying

[197] *Le Héraut* 5.4.1 (SCh 331:78).

[198] *Le Héraut* 5.4.6–7 (SCh 331:84–86).

[199] *Le Héraut* 5.4.18 (SCh 331:100, 102).

Mechtild than to other sisters whose death it recounts, and Gertrude's visions of Mechtild continued after the older woman died. When Gertrude saw Mechtild in glory, Mechtild's soul is pictured offering the Host with Christ in praise of the Father and on behalf of all souls on earth, in purgatory, and in heaven—yet another in a series of affirmations of Mechtild's holiness.[200] What the authors do not reveal is equally significant. They do not indicate that Mechtild's arrival in heaven benefited Gertrude in a particular way or that sorrow overcame Gertrude when the older nun dies, nor do they relate any other intimacies shared by the two after Mechtild's death. The relationship between the two women is among the most finely drawn in the whole of the Helfta literature and presents some of the strongest evidence for the value and experience of mutual engagement and support at the monastery. But notwithstanding Gertrude's declaration that Mechtild is her special friend and Mechtild's visions heralding Gertrude's sanctity, the women's relationship remains largely hidden.

The Value of Mutual Reliance and the Complexity of the Common Life

With the exception of Gertrude, Mechtild, and Abbess Gertrude of Hackeborn, the sisters in the Helfta literature do not emerge as individuals, one woman different from another woman, and cherished particularly for this or that reason. For the most part the texts do not provide details about prized friendships, and no teacher-student dynamic receives extended treatment. The authors deemed the intricacies of specific relationships unimportant to unfold. The literature does, however, insist on the meaningfulness of the sisters' relationships with one another, in such a way as to imply a quintessentially coenobitic message: the nuns were urged to rely on one another—

[200] *Le Héraut* 5.4.20 (SCh 331:102).

and not to attempt to go it alone.[201] The monastery's writings do not thunder against the danger of individualistic spirituality; they do assert the imperative of mutual dependency. Sociability and friendship between and among women acknowledged need and combated the pursuit of self-sufficiency associated with pride, both fostering and celebrating humility, an especially esteemed virtue at the monastery. A certain Sister G. needed purifying because of her reliance on her own opinion; she was not sufficiently docile in relation to those who taught her.[202] The abbess and the visionaries, in contrast, were models of humility, and each woman repeatedly recommended this virtue, by word and example.[203] The author of book one of the *Herald* attributed Gertrude's consulting with her sisters to her humility and conceived of this practice as pointing to Gertrude's sanctity.[204] She frequently relied on others' guidance (even of those inferior to herself) in determining what course of action to take, and she willingly followed their opinion.[205] Abbess Gertrude was driven by humility to seek advice and comfort from another when she was troubled, and as a reward she received the guidance she sought.[206]

It seems reasonable that Mechtild and both Gertrudes nurtured their sense of dependency on their fellow nuns exactly in part because they were aware of the dangers of pride and trusted in God's presence among their sisters. Mutually depending on one another, furthermore, was an essential means by which the sisters acknowledged, trusted, and praised the

[201] As Bynum has observed, the coenobitic Rule of Benedict does not, however, direct its readers to support the edification of others (Caroline Walker Bynum, "The Cistercian Conception of Community," in *Jesus as Mother: Studies in the Spirituality of the High Middle Ages* [Berkeley: University of California Press, 1982], 76–77).

[202] *Le Héraut* 5.3.2–3 (SCh 331:68–70).

[203] For example, *Le Héraut* 1.16.1 (SCh 139:206); *Liber* 6.1 (373–74).

[204] *Le Héraut* 1.11.12 (SCh 139:182).

[205] See for example, *Le Héraut* 3.54.1 (SCh 143:232–34).

[206] *Le Héraut* 5.1.7 (SCh 331:24).

power of prayer and its centrality in a life dedicated to God and neighbor.[207] Gertrude modeled a sense of interdependency that almost seems to erase boundaries among the sisters when in a bold proprietary sweep she claimed their devotions—only to offer them to Christ; her original spiritual possessions, she concedes, are worth next to nothing. Those of the whole community she takes as her own because of the common life they all share.[208]

For all the illustrations in the Helfta writings and especially in the *Herald* of the value of relationships among the nuns, the women did not portray their dealings with one another in saccharine colors. They allude to a number of nagging irritations associated with living in community,[209] laying bare tensions within the household,[210] and they provide a glimpse of the burdens Mechtild and Gertrude assumed in consequence of their vaunted position in the monastery. Sprinkled throughout the literature are indications of disregard for others' advice,[211] hurt feelings,[212] and annoyances,[213] as well as insinuations and jealousies—as when one woman was disquieted because the sisters gave a fellow nun more attention when

[207] See chap. 4, on the liturgy.

[208] *Le Héraut* 3.9.1 (SCh 143:36).

[209] *Le Héraut* 4.2.1 (SCh 255:22).

[210] The visionaries spoke with Christ about their own and other sisters' ill feelings toward one another. For this observation, see Voaden, "All Girls," 79, who comments on tensions in the Helfta household. The *Herald* especially attests to acrimony within the cloister and irritation among its members with one another, as when Gertrude requested that God moderate the behavior of a particular sister or expressed doubt about the efficacy of the prayers she offered for friends—since the friends never showed improvement. See for example *Le Héraut* 3.33 (SCh 143:170–72). A sister grumbled to God about Gertrude, whom she regarded as obstinate (*Le Héraut* 1.16.2 [SCh 139:210–12]). For a vision that vented tensions in community and provided the visionary with insights meant to help her live peaceably in community, see *Le Héraut* 3.9.4 (SCh 143:15–22, 40).

[211] *Le Héraut* 5.9.7 (SCh 331:142).

[212] See for example *Le Héraut* 3.63.1 (SCh 143:250); *Liber* 4.51 (304).

[213] *Le Héraut* 3.15.1 (SCh 143:62).

both women were ill.[214] And there is carping about others' covetousness[215] and self-congratulatory opining on a sister's eucharistic devotion.[216] Disturbances over the perceived failings of one or another woman dot the *Herald* and the *Book of Special Grace*. A certain nun disapproved of another because of her indulgence in a gold-embroidered bedspread;[217] some women were slow to change their ways for the better.[218] And every so often they undercut each other's sense of purpose: one of Gertrude's friends appealed to Christ, urging him to temper her zeal.[219]

The *Book of Special Grace* indicates that disturbances among the nuns were sometimes the consequence of misapprehensions about one another, to which even the holiest among them could fall prey—as when Mechtild was confronted with the evidence that her unflattering impressions of a certain sister were inaccurate. She prayed for a woman who, because she was lukewarm and frivolous (so Mechtild supposed), frequently neglected to receive communion; she was astonished when at once she heard Christ address her sister sweetly, so that her perception of the woman overturned.[220] On another occasion, seeing Christ recline on a sister's breast and pledge to follow her, Mechtild wondered why he offered the women such a great sign of friendship; it was not obvious to Mechtild what attracted him.[221]

Elsewhere a certain *domna M.* (perhaps Mechtild of Hackeborn) considered that Gertrude sometimes behaved impetuously with her sisters.[222] The authors of the *Herald* may have

[214] *Le Héraut* 5.9.1 (SCh 331:132–34).
[215] *Le Héraut* 5.8.1 (SCh 331:128).
[216] *Le Héraut* 3.18.19 (SCh 143:96).
[217] *Le Héraut* 5.8.1 (SCh 331:128).
[218] *Le Héraut* 3.30.24 (SCh 143:148–50).
[219] *Le Héraut* 1.12.1 (SCh 139:186).
[220] *Liber* 4.47 (302).
[221] *Liber* 4.44 (184).
[222] *Le Héraut* 1.16.2 (SCh 139:210).

included this account of *domna M.*'s ill-humor for a variety of reasons, including to quiet apprehensions about Gertrude's obstinacy that may have been more generally abroad in the monastery: Christ assured the disgruntled *domna M.* that Gertrude followed the impulse of the Spirit—not her own will.[223] As these brief accounts imply, Christ taught the sisters that their notions about one another were sometimes off-target, conceding the important point that he might be pleased with a woman who appeared compromised in her religious commitments. Be cautious in your assessment of one another, the *Book of Special Grace* seems to instruct, fostering forbearance even as—in the case of Christ's conversation with *domna M.*—affirming Gertrude's authority to judge others. In acknowledging sisters' misgivings about one another and portraying Christ as tending to them, the *Book of Special Grace* may in addition have assured the sisters that friction among them is to be expected and does not threaten the fabric of community.

The Helfta literature insists that the sisters could profitably exploit the inevitable rough patches for the spiritual growth of all parties. It offers insights into how the nuns sought to take advantage of tensions that arose within the community for the edification of the individual, coaching readers to admit that one's critical attentiveness to another might provide opportunity for self-discovery.[224] Thus for example we read that during Mass, Mechtild was slothful and sleepy—and that she consequently recognized in herself exactly those faults that she had only just noticed in her sisters.[225] Gertrude knew that turning a sharp eye on another was a roundabout way of learning about reforming the self. As she confessed to Christ,

> By an ingenious device you revealed to me defects in others that were displeasing you. Turning into myself, I found that I was guiltier of the same defects than those other persons

[223] *Le Héraut* 1.16 (SCh 139:210–12).

[224] *Le Héraut* 1.3.7 (SCh 139:140–42).

[225] *Liber* 3.20 (222–23).

> whom you had pointed out to me. But you never gave me the smallest indication that you found any trace of these defects in me.[226]

When Christ moved Gertrude to turn inward in self-examination, he bolstered her in the midst of her damning self-discovery by assuring her that his love for her was alive, unblemished, and unabated. She was mindful that this subtle expression of attentiveness betrayed a mighty desire on his part to shield her from her own discomfort about herself—and to move her toward amending this or that aspect of her life. Thus the nuns knew that their own appraisal of a fellow sister might be yoked to an effort of self-amendment and become an avenue by which to fortify one's relationship with God.[227] They were optimistic about the opportunity community held out for self-scrutiny and the soul's advancement.

This was a household determined to work through complexities in common life, bent on finding something of value in disturbing aspects of every sister and on uncovering something of use to others even (or especially) in unpleasant aspects of a sister's personality. A message that came to a fellow nun whom Gertrude had asked to pray for her conveyed to the sister that what appeared as Gertrude's failings were instead sources of strength: without them, she would be chilled by the wind of vanity.[228] Perhaps many of their sisters, like Mechtild and Gertrude, had entered the monastery when they were little girls. They were bound to one another in shared commitments until death divided them (and even then they perceived continuity in community). All those whom God loves ought to love one another, the nuns insisted, recognizing that they did not always get along. A lifetime of living together is hard work,

[226] *Le Héraut* 2.23.9 (SCh 139:338).

[227] Maureen McCabe, "The Scriptures and Personal Identity: A Study in the *Exercises* of Saint Gertrude," in *Hidden Springs*, ed. John A. Nichols and Lillian Thomas Shank, Medieval Religious Women, vol. 3, book 2, CF 113b (Kalamazoo, MI: Cistercian Publications, 1995), 504.

[228] *Le Héraut* 1.3.7 (SCh 139:140–42).

the women's compositions grant, and perhaps especially so for the visionaries exactly because of the prominent place they held in the community.

Gertrude was aware of the mixed ways the sisters received her interventions in the life of Helfta and voiced her disappointment in this as well as doubt about the effectiveness of the counsel she offered them.[229] "Lord, if you truly speak through my mouth . . . how can it be that my words sometimes have such little effect on people?"[230] She was dogged by a reputation for sternness,[231] knew she needed greater patience,[232] was sometimes ill at ease on account of the approach she had taken with regard to one of her sisters,[233] and sometimes tired of her role among the women with whom she lived.[234] We read of Gertrude's concern for a person who had been troubled because of her. When she became the subject of a talk between the visionary and Christ, Gertrude learned of the larger context of her own role in causing distress:

> "I am using the previous disturbance to expand her bosom, and I have made her hand more able to receive my gifts more abundantly and more fittingly," [said Christ]. Then she said, "Alas, Lord, that wretched I was the whip in your purgation of this friend of yours." And the Lord [said], "Why do you say 'alas'? For anyone who purges my elect without intending to bother them but from the heart sympathizes with them is like a gentle whip in my hand, and her merit will be augmented by the other's purgation."[235]

[229] *Le Héraut* 1.14.2; 3.63.1 (SCh 139:196; SCh 143:250).

[230] *Le Héraut* 1.14.4 (SCh 139:200).

[231] *Le Héraut* 1.12.1 (SCh 139:186).

[232] *Le Héraut* 1.16.4 (SCh 139:214).

[233] *Le Héraut* 3.27.2 (SCh 143:126–28).

[234] *Le Héraut* 3.47.1 (SCh 143:212). Lewis has noticed the burden that the needs of others placed on Gertrude, "God and the Human Being," 316.

[235] *Le Héraut* 4.5.5 (SCh 255:88). Christ elsewhere confirms that Gertrude will be rewarded for her enduring criticisms from her sisters on account of calling her sisters to a more rigorous adherence to the Rule (*Le Héraut* 3.62 [SCh 143:248]).

Hammering home a larger Cistercian preoccupation, the Helfta writings repeatedly insist that the sisters must not dodge their responsibilities for one another,[236] including the obligation to correct one another,[237] a requirement that the *Herald* here acknowledges sometimes reaped disquieting consequences, as Gertrude learned that taking up this task at times brought criticism upon her, and was sometimes trying for her sisters. The nuns knew that right relationships among the sisters did not always produce results free from friction; they did not always and immediately call forth contentment and collegiality.

Gertrude sacrificed sleep, postponed meals, and interrupted contemplation in order to assist the women with whom she lived.[238] Christ once asked her to have pity on *his* exhaustion, and he explained that her work lightened his burdens, in this way toughening her resolve.[239] Gertrude, nonetheless, sometimes expressed a weariness of association with others. "Hide me, most loving Jesus," she pleads,[240] and she sometimes secreted herself in her room after a meal, not because she was tired but to escape company.[241] It was her regular practice to retreat at None so as to gather time in peaceful prayer, far from the busyness that characterized her days.[242] Christ condoned this, giving her leave to allow her sisters to think she was asleep and so not disturb her.[243] Prayer, however, sometimes led to vision, which did not always provide the longed-for shelter from the society of sisters. Indeed, Peter Dinzelbacher

[236] See Bynum, "Cistercian Conception of Community," 68, n. 11, on the duty of correction within the community.

[237] *Le Héraut* 3.74.1–5 (SCh 143:312–18).

[238] *Le Héraut* 1.4.2 (SCh 139:142, 144).

[239] *Le Héraut* 1.7.3 (SCh 139:154).

[240] *Absconde me, amantissime Iesu*; *Les Exercices* 5.42 (SCh 127:190); see also *Les Exercices* 2.46–49 (SCh 127:84). Gertrude encourages others also to hide in Christ: *Les Exercices* 2.41 (SCh 127:84).

[241] *Le Héraut* 4.23.8 (SCh 255:224–26).

[242] *Le Héraut* 5.32 (SCh 331:256); and see *Le Héraut* 3.47.1 (SCh 143:212).

[243] *Le Héraut* 4.23.8 (SCh 255:224–26)

attributes Gertrude's occasional desire for separation from her sisters exactly to her heightened engrossment with the people who populated her visions.[244] Visions that followed prayer for her sisters were at least occasionally enervating, and at least once rushed her right into bed.[245] Moreover, prayer on their behalf carved into the time she might have dedicated to the pleasures of contemplation.[246]

The role Mechtild played in her community was sometimes irksome; she now and then experienced as a trial the attention her care for others drew to herself.[247] It was not always easy for her to determine how much to invest in a particular person. Her engagement with others could gobble up too much of her energy, and deep weariness and brushes with anxiety sometimes overtook her. Once, Christ tried to pry away her apprehension: "Don't worry. All that you do for that person, you do

[244] Peter Dinzelbacher, *Vision und Visionsliteratur im Mittelalter* (Stuttgart: Hiersemann, 1981), 152.

[245] *Le Héraut* 5.27.8 (SCh 331:220): when Gertrude's will joined Christ's will, the tree that sprang from their union produced fruits that fed those for whom Gertrude had previously prayed. At the vision's conclusion, Gertrude was weak and went to bed. See Preger for Gertrude's longing to be alone with Christ (*Geschichte*, 131). Scholars have long pointed to the desire on the part of late medieval religious for, as Penelope Johnson puts it, "respite from total togetherness" (*Equal in Monastic Profession: Religious Women in Medieval France* [Chicago: University of Chicago Press, 1991], 194). A. Mary F. Robinson suggests that the visions that came to Gertrude and Mechtild delivered them from chronic tedium ("The Convent of Helfta," *Fortnightly Review* 40 [1886]: 641–58). Jeffrey Hamburger remarks on nuns' attempts to find arenas of privacy within the communal life ("Art, Enclosure, and the Pastoral Care of Nuns," in *The Visual and the Visionary: Art and Female Spirituality in Late Medieval Germany* [New York: Zone Books, 1992]). Jo Ann Kay McNamara documents sisters' efforts to protect their solitude (*Sisters in Arms: Catholic Nuns Through Two Millennia* [Cambridge: Harvard University Press, 1996], 332). On efforts to combat the oppressive effect of monastic routine more generally, see Joseph Dyer, "The Psalms in Monastic Prayer," in *The Place of the Psalms in the Intellectual Culture of the Middle Ages*, ed. Nancy van Deusen (New York: State University of New York Press, 1999), 64.

[246] *Le Héraut* 4.3 (SCh 255:248–50).

[247] *Liber* 1, *caput praevium* (6).

for me." Then he (we are not told how) charged Mechtild with joy, so that with renewed drive and for love of him, she recommitted herself to the person in need.[248] Christ, furthermore, seemed to want to convince Mechtild that he looked after their relationship, in whatever circumstances she found herself: "You can never be in so large a crowd that you are not alone with me if you turn to me with your whole heart."[249]

Acknowledgment of the visionaries' desire to withdraw at least periodically from encounter and from preoccupation with others may be a literary device, at least in part, intended to assure the reader that however much Gertrude and Mechtild drew others to themselves and offered them counsel and mediation, they were not attention seekers and found their greatest happiness ensconced in Christ's company. It may, on the other hand, or simultaneously, convey the visionaries' authentic sentiments and those of the larger population of sisters as well. The *Herald* and the *Book of Special Grace* indicate that living in a community in which the majority of waking hours was spent in the company of others was draining and fed a longing to seek solace in isolated association with Christ.[250] A low-level apprehension about achieving proper proportionality between more obviously self-centered spiritual pursuits, on the one hand, and, on the other, engagement with individuals and with the community more broadly may have been the penalty Gertrude and Mechtild paid in consequence of their role at Helfta, or may have been a more pervasive disquiet shared among the sisters.[251]

The *Book of Special Grace* alerts its readers that such disequilibrium is just and fitting for all those wishing to please Christ, who observed that when Mechtild was busy with the demands

[248] *Liber* 4.49 (303).

[249] *Liber* 3.10 (209).

[250] See, for example, *Le Héraut* 3.47.1 (SCh 143:212).

[251] My reading in this regard differs Bynum's, who argued that the nuns were not anxious about harmonizing service and contemplation ("Women Mystics," 197–98).

of the community, she was fearful of being disturbed in the spiritual life; when sickness precluded her from addressing household obligations, she was also fearful. Christ approved of this state of affairs, he said, explaining that the just person fears in all he does (Job 9:28).[252] The Helfta writings admit that maneuvering among these sometimes competing obligations and desires was a delicate business, about which the nuns ought not become wholly unworried. Fear of their own faults is appropriate to good souls.[253] Christ seemed to want the nuns always to wonder whether they were in good standing with him. They ought never to become complacent, in relationship to him or to their sisters. Christ was a demanding and vigilant presence at the monastery. And he was firmly invested in the sisters' relationships with one another.

Christ's Support of Friendship and Its Limitations

Gertrude and Mechtild approached Christ regularly and easily, hungry to speak with him about a variety of topics having to do with their sisters and exciting their wonder and worry, giving free rein to their curiosities about the women with whom they lived. Christ took account of their insights and was sometimes responsive to their suggestions, changing his course of action in conversation with the visionaries. There is nowhere any indication that the nuns regarded one sister's reaction to another as too trite or too petty to bring before God, or that Christ on any account distanced himself from the sisters' preoccupations with one another. On the contrary, he involved himself in the particulars of the relationships among

[252] *Liber* 3.45 (248). Compare the nuns' nervousness about how to achieve a proper balance between devotion to the saints and Mary with worship of God, and the sense the literature conveys that one *ought* always to feel some uneasiness about this; see chap. 8.

[253] *Le Héraut* 5.1.11 (SCh 331:30).

the women of Helfta, thus announcing their worth to him. He championed talk between and among the nuns as well as between individual nuns and himself about other women, and he involved himself in the rough details of women's affairs.

As they depicted him, Christ's investment in working through the women's grievances and concerns was extraordinary. He consoled, energized, adjudicated, reminded the sisters of the motivating role of their engagement with each other, and chastised one and confirmed another's point of view. He addressed and sometimes remedied situations that had led to exasperation and fatigue as the nuns contended with one another. He corrected misapprehensions, confirmed laudatory evaluations, and elaborated on his relationship with one or another of the nuns with one or another of her sisters, further confirming the worth of such relationships. When Gertrude prayed for a person who felt guilty because she was annoyed with a sister for having provided a bad example of religious discipline, Christ communicated through Gertrude that the irritated sister ought not to allow herself to become upset by another's faults.[254] When there was acrimony in the cloister, Christ swept in to cheer a dispirited nun.[255] When Mechtild related to God the woman's complaints about a fellow nun, Christ interposed himself, saying, "Tell her to give me her enemies, and I will give her myself and all my saints."[256] Christ burrowed into the particulars of the women's relationships, making clear his commitment to helping them live peaceably in community.

The nuns' relationships were of paramount importance to Christ in other ways. He recognized the emotional hold of friendship by acknowledging the significance of its loss, promising

[254] *Le Héraut* 3.78.1 (SCh 143:22–28).

[255] *Liber* 4.51 (304).

[256] *Liber* 4.51 (304).

to compensate the sister whom death deprived of a friend.[257] While the *Book of Special Grace* focuses less attention on the women's relationships than the *Herald*, it may perhaps picture Christ as implicitly commending particular relationships by using friendship as an analogy to talk about his own associations with the nuns.[258] He told Mechtild that just as the souls of Jonathan and David—those friends famous in the monastic literature of the twelfth century—were glued to each other, so did his and her soul adhere, each to each, seeming to raise up human friendship through the comparison.[259] Moreover, the *Book of Special Grace*, in the context of discussing Christ as friend and family member, tells us that we turn to such people in times of need, danger, and fear, as well as for companionship, elevating the human relationships by enumerating their worth and by comparison with the soul's connection to Christ.[260] In addition, Christ acknowledged to Mechtild the need of friend for friend and the pleasure of affectionate companionship when he responded to her complaint about nuns whom she had accused of being sleepy during Mass. When Mechtild suggested that thinking about the pains of hell or the pleasures of heaven might invigorate her slothful sisters, Christ proposed a different sort of meditation. Her sisters should think about the offer of friendship he extends to them. For "whoever has a beloved friend would suffer at being deprived of his intimacy," and Christ is the most faithful and intimate of friends.[261]

Although they never actually say so, the nuns' goal seems clear: to convert into friendships *all* relationships among those

[257] *Le Héraut* 3.85.1; 5.2.1 (SCh 143:338–40; SCh 331:64).

[258] There are many examples. See for instance *Le Héraut* 3.52.3; 3.54.2 (SCh 143:226–28, 234).

[259] *Liber* 1.23 (82). On Jonathan and David in medieval monastic literature, see, for example, McGuire, *Friendship*, xvii–xix.

[260] *Liber* 1.19 (68).

[261] *Liber* 3.20 (223).

God loved, that is, to try to approximate in loving the other the sort of wildly preferential love they felt from Christ. The nuns recognized, nonetheless, that this was impossible to achieve once and for all in the here and now and that since friendship had the potential to undermine the running of the household and the exercise of virtue, affection must be trained.[262] They sought to ensure that the preferential relationships among them did not compromise commitment to one's fellow sisters considered collectively, or otherwise undermine the common life. Notwithstanding his acknowledgement of the benefits, even the need, for close relationships, the Christ of Helfta also spoke of the limitations of human friendship and love as well as associated risks. He warned that the women ought not to elect their abbess on the basis of personal friendship but in accordance with what would be most pleasing to God, a gloss on the Benedictine Rule.[263]

The Helfta writings have no warnings about special friendships (a phenomenon known to us from the later Middle Ages), however, and no restrictions imposed on the form friendships might take. Nor do they deliver directives on how to balance relationships with friends, on the one hand, and, on the other, commitments to the larger community of women. In the persons of Gertrude the visionary and of Abbess Gertrude, the literature does offer model behavior, praising indifferent affection and detached behavior toward others.[264] The *Book of Special Grace* acclaims the abbess for the impartial sweep of her affection for her daughters, an attitude that, perhaps seeming to some of us paradoxical, produced in her daughters (so we read) a sense of security in their mother's love.[265] According to the *Herald*, the younger Gertrude gave what she did not

[262] See for example *Le Héraut* 1.6.1 (SCh 139:150–52).

[263] *Liber* 4.14 (270–71); RB 64.93–94.

[264] *Liber* 6.1 (373). The abbess is an exemplar of holiness (*Liber* 6.1 [373]).

[265] *Liber* 6.1 (374).

need to those in need, not privileging her best friends in the distribution, not even over her worst enemies. This makes her exemplary in her dispassionate action—and reveals that she did indeed have preferences among her sisters![266] The lessons the Helfta writings transmit are thus familiar from the history of Christian thought on friendship: benevolence must not be predicated on fellow feeling, love must rise to the occasion in the face of enmity, and sober realism must train sometimes feckless emotion, but we can celebrate affection and its ability to stir up and to shape love of God. For the most part, the nuns conceived of personal friendship and community as complementary, secure in their ability to juggle particular friendships with the sort of exemplary indifference associated with the two Gertrudes.

The force of their apprehension about friendship fell not on its danger to the community, but on the fear that it might siphon off affection from Christ, even as friendship seemed to them to hold out the possibility of augmenting devotion toward him.[267] The nuns were attentive to their need to give primacy of place in their affections to Christ,[268] and at Helfta, Christ—that champion of friendship—was also perceived as jealous of those whom he loved: "I'm asking you; answer me, according to the truth of your conscience. Is there anything in the world so dear to you that, if it were in your power, you would not give up for me?" Christ asked Mechtild,[269] demanding that Mechtild seek refuge only in him, confide only in him, just as a spouse confides only in her husband.[270] Carving out a private space between the soul and God, Gertrude disclosed

[266] *Le Héraut* 1.11.8 (SCh 139:178).

[267] See *Liber* 4.59; 6.2 (114–15, 378), for anxiety that affection for people can stifle one's growth in loving God and otherwise impede the soul's closeness to him.

[268] See for example *Le Héraut* 1.6.1 (SCh 139:150–52).

[269] *Liber* 4.60 (315).

[270] *Liber* 4.7 (263–64).

to Christ what she would dare not tell a human friend.[271] Gertrude longed to enter a contract of friendship with Christ, the one and only friend of her intimate thoughts,[272] a friendship that cannot be dissolved.[273] He alone is "the one true friend."[274]

Christ declared himself the Abbess Gertrude's sole consolation, prompting her younger sister to wonder how this could be so, having supposed that the smiles and the joyful gestures with which the abbess had greeted her daughters' attentions in her last illness betrayed the pleasure she took in their presence. Christ set Mechtild straight, urging her to consider that she might have misinterpreted the meaning of the abbess's response to the services her daughters offered her and revealing her to have been so firmly fixed in him that she accepted whatever befell her dispassionately.[275] The abbess's ability to love her daughters with detachment thus spoke not only of her ability to exercise her monastic role expertly but also of a fundamental invulnerability to their presence on account of the fullness of satisfaction she found in her relationship with Christ, and her availability or openness to him and his plans.

Gertrude meditated on the love by which God loves us with reference to human love: pondering how she could please God in spite of her sinfulness, she considered that a person who is ugly is sometimes thought beautiful by the person who loves her and thus came to understand that God's love renders beautiful to him those whom he loves.[276] Love among human beings thus stimulated and formed love of God, and reflection on it was sometimes an illustration of the way in which God loves

[271] *Le Héraut* 2.23.10 (SCh 139:340).

[272] *Le Héraut* 1.7.3 (SCh 139:156).

[273] *Les Exercices* 5 (SCh 127:487–89).

[274] *Le Héraut* 3.68.3 (SCh 143:278). Mechtild and Gertrude cherish Christ as the most faithful of friends (*Liber* 3.6 [202]; *Le Héraut* 3.47.1–2 [SCh 143:212–14]).

[275] *Liber* 6.3 (380).

[276] *Le Héraut* 3.30 (SCh 143:154).

everyone. But the nuns did not confuse the love that flourished in the context of friendship with loving God, and when Mechtild compared love between human beings with the love with which God loves humans, it was not a question of human affection assimilated to divine love or even of human emotion exalted by the comparison. Instead, Mechtild contrasted the *meagerness* of human love with divine love. Once dead, Mechtild continued to communicate with her friend Gertrude, coming to her to say: "Behold, in the light of truth, I now see clearly that all the affection I had for whomever [I had affection for] on earth is like a drop in the sea in comparison with the sweetest affection the divine heart has ineffably for them."[277]

Christ himself seemed sometimes almost to want to wipe away other attachments. The death of a friend was a testing ground for one's reverence for Christ: one should be willing to lose a friend, if this death is God's will.[278] Moreover, Gertrude compared Christ with a mother who so wished to keep her little son close to her that when he prepared to play with his young friends, she put a mask or another frightening object before him so that he became afraid and ran away from his friends—and into her arms.[279] It appeared almost as if Christ from time to time capitulated to cruelty, inflicting the pain associated with death in order to have an occasion to make the mourner's need for him known to her, causing the sorrowful soul to seek succor in him who alone will never abandon her. Then he provided her with that which she knew herself to need and for which she longed.[280] Wishing Gertrude never to be absent from his side, Christ sometimes thwarted her friendships so that she would see there was complete faithfulness in no creature and run to him when a friend injured her.[281] At Helfta,

[277] *Liber* 7.12 (407).
[278] *Le Héraut* 3.85.1 (SCh 143:338–40).
[279] *Le Héraut* 3.63.1 (SCh 143:250).
[280] See in addition *Le Héraut* 3.32.1 (SCh 143:166).
[281] *Le Héraut* 3.63.1 (SCh 143:250).

Christ both vehemently encouraged friendship among the nuns and was compensation for the limitations of friendship, which, as the nuns conceived of it, he helped to promote.

Chapter 3

"Tears and Sighs"

Community in Illness, Death, and Grief

It happened one time that a person was accidentally injured while she was working and suffered with great pain. . . . [Gertrude], feeling compassion, prayed to the Lord for her that he would not permit that a member engaged in honorable work be endangered. The Lord kindly responded, "She will not be endangered, but through that pain she will earn an incomparable reward. And all the members who are motivated to attend to that member to relieve her pain and to cure her will likewise obtain a reward in perpetuity."[1]

Caring for the Sick

"The care of the sick must take precedence over everything else, so that they may be served just like Christ," read the opening lines of chapter 36 of the Rule of Benedict.[2] Indeed, one of the clearest expressions of the commitment of the women of Helfta to one another is the attention they extended to sick and dying sisters in their midst; tending to those with

[1] *Le Héraut* 3.69.1 (SCh 139:280–82).

[2] *The Rule of St. Benedict* 36.1, trans. Carolinne White (London: Penguin Books, 2008), 59 (hereafter RB).

many needs was a demanding activity at the monastery, where illness of one sort or another was never far away.[3] The nuns were one another's primary caregivers, with at least one sister serving as the household nurse;[4] the sometime-presence of doctors complemented their labors.[5] The *Herald* singles out Abbess Gertrude for the great care she took of the sick, fulfilling the obligation the Rule enjoined on her, and the literature documents the warmth with which the nuns sometimes looked after one another, insisting on its importance to both recipient and donor.[6]

The nuns believed that sickness was itself conducive to spiritual growth.[7] There were witnesses to its purgative power: Gertrude saw Mechtild's suffering body emit a vapor that purified her.[8] Pain and illness were especially fortunate when they fell on younger women, who did not otherwise have much opportunity to become purified of their accumulated sins.[9] As Mechtild was dying and Christ made ready to receive her, she asked him to let her live a while longer so that she could continue to suffer and thereby acquit herself of some of the debt she had incurred to him. Pain is a test, and Christ was pleased with Mechtild's choice.[10] He let one of Mechtild's sisters linger a little longer so that her pain might help save her.[11] The nuns acknowledged that pain can be difficult to bear

[3] Thus, for example, Mechtild suffered almost continually from an assortment of aches and pains, and for three continuous years at the end of her life, the Abbess Gertrude suffered from numerous ailments: *Liber* Prol.; 7.1; 6.1 (6, 391, 374).

[4] *Le Héraut* 5.10.2 (SCh 331:144).

[5] *Le Héraut* 5.29.1 (SCh 331:232).

[6] *Liber* 6.1 (373–77); *Le Héraut* 5.9.1 (SCh 331:134).

[7] See for example *Le Héraut* 5.2.1; 5.27.12 (SCh 331:64, 224); *Liber* 4.58 (309–10).

[8] *Le Héraut* 5.4.9 (SCh 331:90) and *Liber* 7.7 (398).

[9] *Le Héraut* 5.2.2 (SCh 331:64).

[10] *Liber* 7.1 (391–92); *Le Héraut* 5.28.1 (SCh 331:230).

[11] *Le Héraut* 5.2.2 (SCh 331:66).

(Mechtild recoiled under its force)[12] but contended, nonetheless, that for the woman whose will is joined to God's, the bitterness of pain becomes sweetness,[13] and suffering suffused with tenderness.[14]

The nuns shared with their contemporaries the late medieval conviction that physical suffering is a form of *imitatio Christi* and assimilation to Christ.[15] On Good Friday, Christ appeared to Mechtild, his body covered with scourge marks; on his head he wore a garland of the most beautiful flowers, which he had woven out of the chantress's headaches.[16] Underscoring the salvific power of pain, Christ said to a certain unnamed sister about Gertrude,

> My soul takes such pleasure in her that often, when others have hurt me, I gently rest in her, by burdening her with a physical or interior trial, which she, in union with my passion, accepts with such gratitude and bears with such patience and humility that I am immediately reconciled by her love and spare countless people.[17]

Although illness and pain as forms of penitential suffering play a relatively minor role in the Helfta writings in comparison with their prominent place in the lives and writings

[12] *Liber* 2.25 (167–68).

[13] *Le Hérault* 5.10.1 (SCh 331:144), and *Liber* 2.25 (167–68).

[14] *Le Hérault* 5.4.2 (SCh 331:80).

[15] *Liber* 7.1 (392). The very position of the body could be a form of imitating Christ: when the convent's nurse asked a young nun in her last illness to try to stretch out her contracted legs, the sister said she wished to offer herself as a sacrifice to God and obliged, and in doing so was understood thereby to assume the position of Christ crucified. She proceeded to devote the whole of her body and each part to God: her eyes, her hands, her ears, her mouth, her heart (*Héraut* 5.10.2 [SCh 331:144]).

[16] *Liber* 1.18 (63–64).

[17] *Le Hérault* 1.3.6 (SCh 139:140). For physical suffering associated with Christ's suffering and with Mary's suffering at the crucifixion, see Ella Johnson, "Reproducing Motherhood: Images of Mary and Maternity in the Writings of Gertrud the Great of Helfta," *Magistra* 18, no. 1 (2012): 12.

of numerous other thirteenth-century women,[18] the nuns, in keeping with larger cultural attitudes and beliefs, did perceive their suffering as a contribution to the salvation of the world.[19] When the Helfta writings focus on illness and physical suffering, they do so for the most part to affirm for the reader that pain is not meaningless but valuable to all souls and to Christ, to draw attention to the compassion animating those sisters who serve the other who is sick, and to affirm that the sick sister may be of service to her fellow nuns in the opportunity she gives them to serve her.

As we read, individual nuns kneaded these notions into their response to their own suffering and that of their sisters. For a while Mechtild resisted taking the medicine her sisters hoped would mitigate her pain.[20] She tried to quiet their concerns when they worried about her enduring, as she neared death, what the authors of the *Herald's* book five describe as intolerable suffering.[21] But she did not always bear with equanimity the pain with which Christ assailed her. Her lifelong headaches were a trial Christ set before her, which she sometimes accepted with joy and which sometimes plunged her into sorrow.[22] Gertrude made clear to Christ that she wanted him to take away a recurring pain in her side.[23] The sisters prayed for others' relief from pain,[24] and they more generally

[18] Caroline Walker Bynum observes that Gertrude placed little emphasis on suffering in comparison with many thirteenth- and fourteenth-century mystics and that suffering is rarely expiation in the *Herald*, even though it is sometimes purgative ("Women Mystics in the Thirteenth Century: The Case of the Nuns of Helfta," in *Jesus as Mother: Studies in the Spirituality of the High Middle Ages* [Berkeley: University of California Press, 1984], 191–92).

[19] *Liber* 2.36; 7.1 (183, 392); *Le Héraut* 5.10.1; 5.27.3 (SCh 331:144, 214).

[20] *Le Héraut* 5.4.3 (SCh 331:80).

[21] *Le Héraut* 5.4.3 (SCh 331.80).

[22] *Liber* 2.26 (168–69). She once suffered for forty days from almost constant headaches: *Liber* 2.30 (175).

[23] *Le Héraut* 3.3.1 (SCh 139:20–22).

[24] See, for example, *Le Héraut* 5.3.1; 5.4.3 (SCh 331:68, 80).

responded to the assorted needs of the sick.[25] They wrestled with the implications of their ministrations for the women whose suffering they sought to soothe.

One account provides an example of the kind of day-to-day incident that raised questions about how the sisters were to look after one another while holding fast to their responsibility to advance one another's spiritual welfare and to their own programmatic commitment to cooperate with Christ in securing the salvation of the world. Feeling compassion for an injured nun, Gertrude prayed that God would not allow the woman to die. Christ assured Gertrude that her sister would live and that he would reward her suffering, adding that anyone who tried to relieve the woman's pain and to cure her would receive an eternal prize: "Just as when one cloth is immersed in saffron, if something else falls in, it will be likewise colored with it, in this way, when one member suffers, all the other members who serve it will be remunerated with it in eternal glory."[26]

Christ's explanation, with its peculiar rewording of the Pauline passage, "If one member suffers, every member suffers with it" (2 Cor 12:26), provoked Gertrude to ask why those who helped to alleviate the woman's suffering were rewarded, since her suffering benefited the woman. This is a question that may have been on the mind of many of the monastery's members; all must have been accustomed to the presence of injured and sick sisters, to tending to them, and to withstanding (or anticipating) suffering themselves, in a community that was, moreover, schooled in the redemptive power of pain. Christ's rejoinder had both practical and theological implications:

> The suffering a person endures patiently out of love for me, and which after the usual remedy for pain she cannot soothe

[25] *Le Héraut* 5.9.1 (SCh 331:134).

[26] *Le Héraut* 3.69.1 (SCh 143:282).

> by her own effort, I sanctify in the words in which, in my extreme need, I prayed to the Father, saying "Father, if it were possible, let this cup pass from me [Matt 26:39]," so that the person gains an incomparable prize and merit through it.[27]

The nuns were to serve the sister in their midst with the aim of lessening her suffering and healing her—Christ himself prayed to evade the suffering he bore on the cross. Again and again, he quieted Mechtild's aches,[28] and Gertrude once sensed that when she had a headache and comforted herself, Christ himself was soothed, her self-care a gift to him.[29] A person should accept what the body needs and what gives her comfort, Christ told a chronically ill woman.[30] Success at soothing suffering did not compromise reward. Moreover, those who tried to help a sister in need shared in her reward not because they suffered with her but because they tried to temper her pain. At the same time, prompted by Gertrude's continued questioning, Christ affirmed the productive power of physical suffering that cannot be assuaged, thus providing the nuns with the opportunity to derive meaning from pain that they could not avoid.

The nuns were sensitive not only to their sisters' physical afflictions but to the sadness or dejection with which some of them struggled, insisting that emotional pain was worthy of attention, too.[31] Psychological suffering also sanctified. From time to time, Gertrude heard screams ringing throughout the cloister as her sisters awakened from nightmares: Christ had

[27] *Le Héraut* 3.69.2 (SCh 143:282).

[28] See for example *Liber* 2.30 (175–76).

[29] *Le Héraut* 1.11.10 (SCh 139:180–82). For a discussion of the role of self-comfort in the *Herald*, see Michael Anthony Abril, "Gertrude of Helfta's Liturgical-Mystical Union," CSQ 43, no. 1 (2008): esp. 87–88.

[30] *Liber* 3.45 (248).

[31] *Le Héraut* 3.73.14 (SCh 143:310–12); *Liber* 2.12 (146). The men the visionaries counseled sometimes also suffered from deep sadness (*Liber* 4.52 [305]).

manipulated their dreams to provoke productive pain.[32] Gertrude prayed for a sister who was depressed, a suffering that, Christ explained, was purgative and that, he assured her, he would measure so as not to overburden her—just as a mother holds her hand between her child and the fire, warming her with its heat while protecting her from the flames. The *Herald* hints, in addition, that her sister's low spirits were a test of Gertrude's own faith, giving us a peek into the ways in which one woman's pain might infiltrate another's life with an empathetic response. In this instance, the visionary's revelation was a comfort, therefore, to both self and other.[33]

On another occasion, when one of Mechtild's sisters cried so profusely that she was at risk of losing her mind, Mechtild calmed her. Mechtild's prayers released her sister from her mental anguish, and Christ transformed the tears she spent into "holy tears": it was as if she had shed them in love, devotion, and contrition.[34] Perhaps this message that Mechtild communicated helped to console her sister. Pain that was meaningful—consecrated by the Savior of the world and significant to *him*—was, maybe, easier to bear. Mechtild here gives a glimpse into a community attentive to the suffering, physical and psychological, of its members, a group of women resolutely invested in easing one another's pain. In doing so, the nuns grappled with the larger cultural belief that pain was redemptive, holding this belief in tension with their desire to heal the hurt. These women had largely grown up with one another and were sure to die in one another's company. They came know and love one another. And they came to the aid of the girls and women in their midst, asserting Christ's approbation of their efforts to relieve the suffering members of their community experienced.

[32] *Le Héraut* 3.32.3 (SCh 143:168–70).

[33] *Le Héraut* 3.83.1 (SCh 143:336).

[34] *Liber* 4.38 (297): *sanctas lacrymas*.

Sickness and Anxiety

It was, however, not always easy for a sick or injured nun to be the beneficiary of her sisters' care.[35] The teaching of the Rule as their household conveyed it was that idleness was an enemy of the soul, a danger to the self and for the example it set for others; anxieties about idleness therefore swept over sisters too ill to carry out their responsibilities.[36] In her *Spiritual Exercises*, Gertrude highlights the danger of unemployment, accenting the value of service as a means of paying the debt each person owes to Christ, a liability the nuns associated with original sin and the series of sins they were sure everyone commits throughout life:

> O dear Truth, O just fairness of God, how will I appear before your face, bearing my wickedness, the debt of my lost life, the weight of my immense carelessness? I did not give to the moneylenders at the table of charity the treasure of Christian faith and of the spiritual life. . . . I have not only spent in indolence the talent of time credited to me, but I have misplaced it, misused it, lost all. Where will I go, where will I turn, and to where will I flee from your face?[37]

In Gertrude's expression of concern about a life misspent, she may reveal a common uneasiness that rested with special power on the sick and the aged. This was a population laboring under the weight of indebtedness and striving to fulfill daily obligations even when rocked with emotional turmoil or physical ailments.

Individually and in groups, the nuns took up a variety of commitments, some assuming the roles of abbess, portress, novice mistress, or choir mistress. They taught girls and boys

[35] See for example *Le Héraut* 1.6.1 (SCh 139:152).

[36] RB 48.1 (72); *Liber* 3.45 (248).

[37] *Les Exercices* 7.79–87 (SCh 127:264).

in the monastery's school.[38] They read and copied manuscripts, and they wrote. Domestic duties included cleaning and spinning.[39] They looked after the disabled, the sick, and the dying. All the women chanted the Office and attended Mass. Each of these activities taxed the body, and the indignities of age and illness may have been particularly trying for those with prominent roles in the community, accustomed to shouldering a broad array of responsibilities necessary for the monastery's full functioning. During one period, Mechtild's physical pain prevented her from going to choir and performing other devotions,[40] and at least from time to time she worried, during her frequent (sometimes incapacitating) illnesses, about uselessness.[41] This was a serious worry for a woman who had been praised in large part because she served everyone exceedingly well[42] and was most useful in the cloister, guiding the nuns in the Divine Office, assisting the abbess in a variety of ways,[43] and counseling her sisters as well as interceding for them with Christ, Mary, and the saints. Gertrude lamented that her own illness limited the attention she could give to the dying Mechtild,[44] dejection overcame an anonymous sister who was too sick to go to choir,[45] and depression submerged a woman whose chores kept her from prayer.[46] When Gertrude was filled with sadness and fearful that she was wasting time when she was ill and unable to join in the choir, Christ reassured her of her worth to him,[47] but there is evidence that the

[38] *Liber* 1.9 (30).

[39] *Le Héraut* 3.32.5 (SCh 143:170).

[40] *Liber* 2.25 (1), and see 2.31 (176).

[41] *Liber* 2.32 (177), and 2.36 (183).

[42] *Liber* 1, *caput praevium* (6).

[43] *Liber* 5.30 (367).

[44] *Le Héraut* 5.4.23 (SCh 331:106).

[45] *Liber* 4.30 (287). Among the evidence for Abbess Gertrude as example to her daughters is her persisting in going to Mass and office even when her health was poor (*Liber* 6.1 [375]).

[46] *Le Héraut* 3.73.14 (SCh 143:310–12).

[47] *Le Héraut* 3.59.1 (SCh 143:242–44). And see *Le Héraut* 3.22.1 (SCh 139:114). For Mechtild's anxiety about wasting time, see for example *Liber* 2.15 (149).

women sometimes perceived Christ to feed such fears: he remarked approvingly on a certain sister who, although suffering weakness associated with a heart condition, did not shirk her regular responsibilities to the community but persevered without complaint.[48]

Abbess Gertrude of Hackeborn was always occupied, either praying or working with her hands or teaching her daughters or reading.[49] It is no surprise that when she was ill, she worried over her inability to execute the tasks for which she was answerable and struggled against exhaustion to make sound judgments about the running of the household and to present herself as a model to her daughters, a mode of behavior that, she was convinced, was crucial to the monastery's well-being after her death.[50] She seems to have wondered about the meaning of any lapses on her part for her own soul, at least as much as the implication for her daughters in need.[51] She tried to manage the limitations of her last illness. For the twenty-six weeks before her death, she lost the full use of her voice and could only repeat *Spiritus meus*,[52] substituting these words for the devotions she was accustomed to make, and when her daughters spoke with her about God, she thanked them by the expression on her face and with the movements of her head. Unable to walk, she insisted on being carried to the bedside of her sick daughters, conveying sympathy and affection through gesture, and eliciting an affective response from them.[53] We may regard this description of Abbess Gertrude's creative fortitude as a hagiographic flourish, meant to underscore the strength and kindness of her character. These accounts may also serve as a testimony to how she and her daughters

[48] *Le Héraut* 5.3.7 (SCh 331:74).

[49] *Liber* 6.1 (376).

[50] *Le Héraut* 5.1.6 (SCh 331:24).

[51] *Le Héraut* 5.1.10 (SCh 331:28): She feared not receiving communion and, on the other hand, feared communicating when illness rendered her incapable of preparing properly for reception.

[52] *Le Héraut* 5.1.13; 5.1.16 (SCh 331:32, 34).

[53] *Liber* 6.1 (374).

tried to compensate for constraints brought on by ailments, suggesting as they do a variety of ways in which the nuns may have tried to adhere to the practices to which each had been committed and to remain connected to their roles in the community as illness and old age threatened ruptures in fellowship along with separation from work.

The nuns were sensitive to the predicament in which sick sisters found themselves. Although the Helfta writings emphasize the importance to one's own salvation of serving the other, they carve out a means by which the woman who is unable to serve—chanting with her sisters in the choir, sweeping the dormitory, instructing the children[54]—need not forfeit spiritual gifts associated with service and so may experience reintegration into the larger cloistered community.[55] Christ told Mechtild that he was closer to her when she was sick than when she was healthy: "When you are sick, I enfold you with my left arm, and when you are well, I embrace you with my right, but know that when I embrace you with my left arm, my heart is much closer to you."[56] When Abbess Gertrude lamented that illness prevented her from serving her sisters and so serving Christ—as Scripture, Rule, and custom compelled—the younger Gertrude sought to comfort the older woman, saying that if Abbess Gertrude could not work on acquiring adornments for her soul through service to her sisters, she might on this account be taken over instead by Christ's embraces simply because of her desire to do his will.[57] Giving her leave from some of her obligations, Christ directed Abbess Gertrude to rest awhile. Just as a king relaxes on his bed, he

[54] *Liber* 1.9 (29).

[55] Richard Kieckhefer has written about the ways in which the women who figure in the Sister Books worked out among themselves the connecting of sick sisters into the community ("Mystical Communities in the Late Medieval West," Medieval Academy Plenary Address, International Medieval Conference, Leeds, 2007, 4–5).

[56] *Liber* 2.32 (177).

[57] *Le Heraut* 5.1.9 (SCh 331:26–28).

said, *she* ought to take a moment to enjoy the delicacies he offered her now, on earth, before he lifted her into heaven.[58]

Gertrude's solicitude toward her abbess, and the words Christ spoke and she related, tell of a community in which paramount importance was placed on responding to the physical and psychological needs of the old and the sick, in easing not just their bodily pain but also the particular spiritual anxieties that aging and illness occasioned or amplified. The transmission of visions was a part of this care. Christ told Gertrude of Helfta,

> When for my praise you are able to overcome something with difficulty that is beyond your ability, I accept it from you as if I needed this to complete my honor. If you abstain from doing this, and you accept comfort for your body with your intention directed at me, I accept this as if I myself were sick and could not do without this comfort. And thus I will remunerate you either way, for the glory of my divine munificence.[59]

These words are about Gertrude, but having been conveyed outwardly, they were surely something like a salve and even an encouragement to her sisters, who might from time to time, or maybe frequently, seek relief from the trying demands of monastic life.

In exchanges they recorded, we catch sight of Gertrude or her collaborators urging the community to make its own what Christ offered Gertrude—acceptance of her need for comfort

[58] *Le Héraut* 5.1.9 (SCh 331:26, 28). Gertrude knew that bedrest might be conducive to encounter with Christ; Ulrike Wiethaus has noticed that Gertrude's bed is among the most spiritually charged locations for her ("Spatial Metaphors, Textual Production, and Spirituality in the Works of Gertrud of Helfta [1256–1301/2]," in *A Place to Believe In: Medieval Landscapes*, ed. Clare A. Lees and Gillian R. Overing [University Park: Pennsylvania State University Press, 2006], 143). The bed is also a frequent site of encounter for Mechtild with Christ; see for example *Liber* 2.32 (177).

[59] *Le Héraut* 3.59.2 (SCh 143:244).

and consideration. Christ was attentive to Mechtild's many moods and her frequent bouts of illness. He helped her to pray when sickness overcame her and she was unable to do so on her own.[60] He seems frequently to have come to her when insomnia hit—sometimes she was kept awake by sorrows rolling in[61]—and revealed that he too did not always sleep through the night.[62] When she exclaimed how wonderful it would be to have him keep her company through the stretch of nighttime silence, Christ assured Mechtild that she was never without him—as long as she wanted him.[63] On one occasion, Mechtild lay on his chest, multiplying testimonies of her love and trading tender words with him.[64] On another, Christ visited Mechtild while she was suffering from a headache that kept her awake. He beckoned her to the wound at his side, through which she entered into his heart. There, Mechtild saw Christ reclining on a bed, covered in a green bedspread and cluttered with as many pillows as she had poundings in her head. She lay down beside Christ and was full of happiness.[65] The nuns carved out the possibility that necessary abstinence from exertion—the daily demands of the Office and of Mass as well as of teaching and maintaining the household and so forth—could itself bring pleasure to Christ and enjoyment to the nun.

Sickness as Service

Moreover, tucking into the comfort of the King's bed or extending him comfort was not, in fact, a retreat from service. A nun's capitulation to the restraining limitations of illness could itself open up an arena in which to serve her sisters.

[60] *Liber* 3.3 (199).
[61] *Liber* 1.15 (47); and see 3.10 (209).
[62] *Liber* 1.14 (46).
[63] *Liber* 3.10 (209).
[64] *Liber* 1.1 (7–8).
[65] *Liber* 2.27 (172).

When Mechtild was troubled to have received more attention from her sisters in her illness than she believed was necessary, Christ waved away her worry, saying,

> Do not be afraid or be troubled [John 14:27], because I truly sustain everything that you suffer, and therefore all the good that people do for you are benefits to me [Matt 25:40], and if they do these things for me, I remunerate them with a worthy reward. And all who come before you in the hour of death with pious compassion will earn my thanks no less than if they were grieving at my passion. Similarly, whoever is present with pious devotion at your funeral will be as welcome to me as if they had given due honor at my sepulcher.[66]

Christ made known to Mechtild that her malady was a form of giving since it afforded her sisters the chance to serve her. Echoing the gospel message "I was sick, and you visited me" (Matt 25:36), and recalling the Rule, the *Book of Special Grace* teaches the reader that Mechtild's sisters served Christ when they served her.[67] When Mechtild prayed for one of the women who was looking after her, she saw the Lord fulfill his promise. Christ showed her his belt, filled with circles, which, he explained, "are the footsteps that she [who served you] trod in your service." He continued, "they shall be before my eyes in eternal memory."[68]

We find the same claim in the *Herald*. When Abbess Gertrude worried that her illness would prevent her from properly guiding her daughters, the younger Gertrude assured her abbess that merit would accrue to all the nuns exactly on account of their attentiveness to their abbess's poor health: Christ would

[66] *Liber* 2.41 (188–89). And for the reward that Christ gives to those who serve the sick, see too *Liber* 3.45 (248), and *Le Héraut* 5.29.4 (SCh 331:234–36).

[67] *Liber* 2.41 (288–89); RB 36.1 (59).

[68] *Liber* 2.41 (289).

regard service to the abbess as service to himself.[69] Gertrude thus provided the abbess with a means of contributing to her daughters' spiritual welfare when she was no longer able to fulfill the everyday tasks of office. Serving was simultaneously a means of imitating Christ. Thus one might imitate Christ both in serving the sick and in offering up one's needy self to one's sisters as an opportunity for service. The nuns could not imagine any individual experience in which meaning and productive power was wholly restricted to the self without the potential to benefit another.

The sick, the aged, and the weak might therefore hold tight to their sense of purposefulness and membership in community at precisely those moments when feelings of isolation and exclusion from the busy, cooperative activities of the household threatened to engulf them. It was easier for the women to conceive of the benefits associated with giving than with receiving, yet their teaching that a sister could help to move her fellow nuns toward salvation just when illness may have seemed to segregate her from them must have gone some distance to remedying the feelings of uselessness associated with limitations in meeting obligations as well as clamping down on anxieties that bloomed when one was the recipient of others' ministrations. Nevertheless, while the individual bed-bound nun may have been taught to be sure of the benefits to the nun who served her, the women expressed little pleasure in being the inheritor of another's gifts of time and attention. Grateful to Christ for his solicitude, the nuns did not express appreciation for the sisters who looked after them, helping them walk about the cloister, and so forth.[70] There is little indication of friendship or even companionability between the sick person and the one who comes to her aid. It seems likely that the women believed they could do without a sense of intimacy and still be sure of reaping the rewards of the relationship.

[69] *Le Héraut* 5.1.11 (SCh 331:30).

[70] *Liber* 1.19 (63).

However sensitive the nuns may have been to the sick in their midst, furthermore, however responsive to their wants and requirements, when they tended to the ill among them, they did so with a purpose that may sometimes have eclipsed the particular person whom they served. On the Monday before the Ascension, we read, Gertrude went before Matins to visit a sick sister and offered her service for all the world's sins. And then it was as if she were encircling with a gold cord a multitude of women and men, whom she led to God, and who received them from her as a king receives from a prince the king's enemies.[71] Although she directed her activity toward one sick woman, the *Herald* does not suggest that the woman at the center of Gertrude's service was of central emotional importance to Gertrude, whose actions were motived by a determination to draw souls to Christ. It is worth noting, furthermore, that we never learn about the effect of Gertrude's service on her sister, suggesting that this detail was unimportant to the writer as well.

The *Herald* instead underscores that it was by means of such acts of charity that Gertrude participated in redeeming souls who had no immediate or obvious connection either to Gertrude or to her sister. Gertrude thought of herself as an ambassador of her convent, marshaling her fellow nuns to participate in making reparation to God for the sins of the world, a world that the *Herald* denounces as opposing God more at the time of its writing than at any other time.[72] The *Herald* graphically represents Gertrude's attachment to those for whom she prayed; the sick woman for whom Gertrude performed pious acts was entangled in this chain of charity, giving redemptive meaning to both her needs and Gertrude's satisfaction of them. Gertrude's tending to this sister with the intention of making reparation for the whole church puts in relief the nuns' sense of the web of interconnectedness between all human beings,

[71] *Le Héraut* 4.35.7 (SCh 255:298).

[72] *Le Héraut* 3.30.4 (SCh 143:136)

just as it diminishes the emotional importance of the particular individual who prompted the engagement while highlighting the same woman's role in the process of redemption, her shared labor with Gertrude. The nuns were convinced that relationships between any two women moved outward, and there were, to them, no exclusive relationships between any two sisters. One-on-one interactions implicated all the sisters, the whole of the congregation, as well as the larger world of the living and the dead.

Death

Over the course of the approximately fifty years Mechtild lived at Helfta and the forty-five or so years that the monastery was Gertrude's home, the two women must have seen many of their sisters, young and old, sicken and die.[73] The presence of death now and then loomed large over the monastery. Out of a population of perhaps a hundred or so girls and women, death once took two sisters in the space of two weeks[74] during the period that Gertrude and Mechtild were at Helfta; at least two additional nuns died within a month of each other,[75] and another, thirty days after the death of her biological sister, both still novices.[76] When, twelve days after the death of Abbess Gertrude, one of her daughters followed her, Gertrude of Helfta noted the swift succession of loss and wondered why Christ had taken her young companion from her so soon after he took her abbess.[77] She felt the pang of death's presence.

The nuns placed a premium on preparing for death, one's own and that of another. "To keep death daily before one's eyes" is one of the instruments of good works the Rule enu-

[73] Death sometimes came for the young; see for example, *Le Héraut* 5.2.2; 5.10.1 (SCh 331:66, 142).

[74] *Le Héraut* 5.2.1 (SCh 331:62).

[75] *Le Héraut* 5.9.1; 5.9.3 (SCh 331:134, 136).

[76] *Le Héraut* 5.5.1 (SCh 331:108).

[77] *Le Héraut* 5.2.1 (SCh 331:62).

merates, and as Gertrud Jaron Lewis has observed, the whole of Gertrude's *Spiritual Exercises* conveys to the reader that she ought to consider her own death all the days of her life.[78] The first of the seven *Exercises* begins by calling the reader to recollect the end of her life,[79] and one's own death is a recurring theme in the *Exercises*.[80] Gertrude may have been the author of a collection of daily meditations designed to help her sisters and other readers take the necessary steps for approaching death.[81] The authors of the *Herald's* book five refer to an exercise (to be completed over the course of five days) that Gertrude composed and that she proposed ought to be read once a month in preparation for death.[82] She followed one of her own exercises in readying herself, perhaps this lost *memento mori*,[83] and a month before Mechtild died, she made a preparatory exercise that Gertrude had composed, whether from this text or another we do not know.[84] Mechtild appears to have interpreted rumination on death as a way of imitating Christ:

[78] Gertrud Jaron Lewis and Jack Lewis, introduction to *Spiritual Exercises*, ed. and intro., Gertrude Jaron Lewis and Jack Lewis, CF 49 (Kalamazoo, MI: Cistercian Publications, 1989), 21; RB 4.47 (18).

[79] *Les Exercices* 1.1 (SCh 127:56).

[80] Mary Jeremy Finnegan, *The Women of Helfta: Scholars and Mystics* (Athens: University of Georgia Press, 1991), 73; Lillian Thomas Shank has counted over sixty-five references to death in the *Spiritual Exercises*; she asserts that death is the *Exercises'* most prominent theme and that this text contains a spirituality and theology of death ("The God of My Life: St. Gertrude, A Monastic Woman," in *Peaceweavers*, ed. John A. Nichols and Lillian Thomas Shank, CS 72 [Kalamazoo, MI: Cistercian Publications, 1987], 256, 264–65).

[81] See for example *Le Héraut* 3.54.2; 2.23 (SCh 143:234; SCh 139:330). Doyère and Columba Hart think the *Herald* refers to a now lost work, to which Hart has given the title *Remembrance of Death* (Doyère, *Le Héraut*, SCh 331:210–11, n. 1; Hart, introduction to *The Exercises of Saint Gertrude*, trans. a Benedictine nun of Regina Laudis [Columba Hart] [Westminster, MD: The Newman Press, 1956], xvi).

[82] *Le Héraut* 5.27.1 (SCh 331:210).

[83] *Le Héraut* 5.27.1 (SCh 331:210). See Eugène Gabriel Ledos, *Sainte Gertrude* (Paris: V. Lecoffre, 1901), 67; and Gilbert Dolan, *St. Gertrude the Great* (London: Sands, 1913), 224.

[84] *Le Héraut* 5.4.1 (SCh 331:78).

the *Book of Special Grace* asserts that from the time he was a young boy, Christ reflected every day on his own death.[85] The call of *memento mori* sounds throughout the Helfta writings, death hovering throughout and always close to the surface of things. From a certain vantage point, this is a literature of consolation and an *ars moriendi*, which seeks to engender in the reader penitence as well as hope in the face of death, offering comfort in times of fear and loss.[86]

This life is vile, an illusion,[87] a prison,[88] exile.[89] Death is a most blessed passage;[90] it is sweetness[91] and sleep,[92] and the object of desire,[93] which Christ excites.[94] Death might be an immediate release into a festival[95] of sheer satisfaction,[96] a wedding[97] that ushers the soul into the bridal chamber in

[85] *Liber* 1.9 (144). When she was sick, Christ advised Gertrude to prepare for her own death: *Le Hérault* 5.23.1 (SCh 331:202). See too *Le Hérault* 5.26.1 (SCh 331:208). On the medieval commitment to preparing for one's own death as a way to mitigate the consequences of a sudden death, see Miri Cowan, *Death, Life, and Religious Change in Scottish Towns, c. 1350–1560* (Manchester: Manchester University Press, 2012), 25.

[86] *Ars moriendi* generally refers to a fifteenth-century phenomenon associated with two related contemporary texts (Nancy Lee Beaty, *The Craft of Dying: A Study in the Literary Tradition of the* Ars Moriendi *in England* [New Haven: Yale University Press, 1970], 2). For a discussion of *ars moriendi* not tied to those texts, within the early Cistercian context and in relation to hagiographic literature, see Ryszard Groń, "Examples of 'Good Death' in Aelred of Rievaulx," CSQ 41, no. 4 (2006): 422–41. See in addition Jean Leclercq, "The Joy of Dying According to St. Bernard," CSQ 25 (1990): 163–75, for twelfth-century Cistercian attitudes toward death.

[87] *Les Exercices* 6.604–8 (SCh 127:244).

[88] *Le Hérault* 5.1.23; 5.9.1 (SCh 331:42–44, 134).

[89] *Le Hérault* 5.27.13 (SCh 331:226).

[90] *Le Hérault* 5.4.7 (SCh 331:86).

[91] *Le Hérault* 5.10.1 (SCh 331:144).

[92] *Le Hérault* 5.10.2 (SCh 331:146).

[93] *Le Hérault* 5.1.20; 5.23.1; 5.23.2–3 (SCh 331:38, 196, 198, 200).

[94] *Le Hérault* 5.29.1 (SCh 331:232).

[95] *Les Exercices* 6.623–25 (SCh 127:244–46).

[96] *Le Hérault* 5.27.9 (SCh 331:220).

[97] *Le Hérault* 5.24.1 (SCh 331:202). Last rites are the soul's wedding ring: *Le Hérault* 5.27.10 (SCh 331:222).

which union with Christ takes place.[98] A chapter in the *Herald*'s book five is dedicated to Gertrude's reflections on her own death, which model meditative flights of the imagination.[99] Gertrude fantasized about dying[100] and about the joys into which death would release her,[101] and she received an anticipatory vision of her own death, in which she disappeared into God like a drop of water evaporated by the sun.[102] As a mark of the wildly optimistic tenor of the whole of the Helfta literature, Christ declared to Mechtild that not one of her sisters would be lost,[103] and both the *Herald* and the *Book of Special Grace* record a number of visions of the magnificent postmortem state of the nuns. Gertrude saw one of her sisters escorted into heaven by angels and welcomed by Christ with the words "You are my glory."[104]

But even the holiest approached death with apprehension, and the very desire to die was sometimes braided with fear.[105] Mechtild wondered to Christ why, when—she supposed—so many anticipated death with joy and longing, she thought of her own impending death with little or no happiness.[106] Catherine of Alexandria may have sought to quell Mechtild's angst when she reminded the visionary that the horror of death had been overcome.[107] Gertrude longed for death, "so that

[98] *Liber* 7.1 (391–92).

[99] *Le Héraut* 5.27.13 (SCh 331:226).

[100] For fantasizing about death, see *Le Héraut* 5.32 (SCh 331:256).

[101] *Le Héraut* 5.27.13; 5.28.1 (SCh 331:226, 228), for example. For Gertrude's longing for death, also see *Le Héraut* 1.10.4 (SCh 139:168).

[102] *Le Héraut* 5.32; 5.7.1 (SCh 331:256, 122). For meditating on the other world as a dimension of *memento mori* see Robert Easting, *Annotated Bibliographies of Old and Middle English Literature*, vol. 3, *Visions of the Other World in Middle English* (Cambridge: D. S. Brewer, 1997), 4.

[103] *Liber* 5.10 (334); and see *Liber* 7.18 (399).

[104] *Le Héraut* 5.10.3 (SCh 331:146): *Tu es gloria mea.*

[105] For the recognition that death is greatly feared, see *Liber* 1.20 (74), and *Le Héraut* 5.28.1 (SCh 331:230).

[106] *Liber* 1.20 (74). Christ was sensitive to Mechtild's fear in this same section of the text.

[107] *Liber* 1.32 (111).

every single hour, it was the same to her whether she lived or died."[108] (She was happy when she slipped on the stairs, hoping that the fall might cause her death.)[109] Yet she too is disquieted, writing in the *Spiritual Exercises* of her anxiety about death's approach,[110] and there are numerous nods in the *Exercises* to the fear that thought of death fans.[111] Although the nuns recognized that freedom from fear of death was a divine gift (one of the changes that came upon the apostles at Pentecost was that they no longer feared death[112]), such fear was not a sign of faithlessness; in this they were in keeping with the broader currents of late medieval piety.[113] "The fear of death distresses me," the nuns would have read in the Office of the Dead,[114] and their depiction of the fear that assaulted Mechtild (and the fear Gertrude may have anticipated would belong to her) seems geared in part to instill a sense of solidarity among the women—and with the saints—by admitting with the psalmist the pervasiveness of fear (Ps 55:4-5), an acknowledgment that perhaps attempts to temper the fear by domesticating it, and universalizing it.

[108] *Le Héraut* 1.10.4 (SCh 139:168).

[109] *Le Héraut* 1.10.4 (SCh 139:168).

[110] *Les Exercices* 7.357–59 (SCh 127:282–84).

[111] See especially *Les Exercices* 7 (SCh 127:258–306), which focuses largely on preparing for one's own death.

[112] *Liber* 1.22 (78).

[113] For the first several centuries of Christianity, fear of death was regarded as betraying a lack of faith in the immortality of the soul and the resurrection of the body as well as injudicious attachment to the flesh. Augustine's concession that fear of death is a constituent component of our humanity marked a decisive change in Western Christian. The nuns are heirs to this tradition. Unlike Augustine, however, they do not explicitly associate fear of death with original sin. Gregory the Great transmitted to the Middle Ages Augustine's teaching on the "naturalness" of fear of death. See Carol Straw, "Timor Mortis," in *Augustine through the Ages: An Encyclopedia*, ed. Allan D. Fitzgerald (Grand Rapids, MI: William B. Eerdmans Publishing, 1999), 838–42.

[114] Cowan, *Death*, 18, on the fear of death and the Office of the Dead. On the Office of the Dead, see also Paul Binski, *Medieval Death: Ritual and Representation* (Ithaca: Cornell University Press, 1996), 53–55.

The nuns wondered, nonetheless, *why* they were so fearful. When Mechtild turned to Christ in bewilderment, he explained that human beings are frightened by death because the soul loves its flesh and cannot bear the bitterness of separation.[115] The nuns did not fasten onto this concern, however. Nor did they boisterously lament a sense of separation from friends or otherwise indulge in the grief of an anticipated distance from confidantes and lifetime companions, although tears of sorrow over separation did fall.[116] By far the most common fear seems to have been not ascending directly to heaven after death, and this basic trepidation precipitated a swarm of worries on the part of the dying individual herself as well as in her sisters on her behalf. The Helfta literature both concedes and inculcates this fear: a company of celestial virgins told Mechtild she was lucky to be alive because she could still acquire merit.[117] One woman was scared because she did not receive absolution on her deathbed—she had pretended to be asleep when the priest came to hear her confession.[118] Another was made afraid by the nearby presence of a demon,[119] and in a vision in which Gertrude perceived herself to be dying, she saw herself protected by the Archangel Michael from pitchfork-bearing devils, who appeared in the form of menacing frogs and snakes.[120] The nuns recorded cries of fright issuing from the dying without the source of the scare evident.[121]

In keeping with the larger medieval assimilation of fear to purgation, the nuns folded into progress toward salvation the terrors that overtook some sisters as death approached; they

[115] *Liber* 1.20 (74). The association of fear of death with the soul's attachment to the body has a long history. See for example Straw, "Timor Mortis."

[116] *Le Héraut* 5.1.20 (SCh 331:40); *Liber* 6.6 (383).

[117] *Liber* 4.9 (267).

[118] *Le Héraut* 5.9.1 (SCh 331:134).

[119] *Le Héraut* 5.9.1 (SCh 331:134).

[120] *Le Héraut* 5.32.3 (SCh 331:258). See for the ancient foe, who sometimes darkens Gertrude's self-restraint, *Les Exercices* 3:231–38 (SCh 127:110).

[121] *Le Héraut* 5.2.2 (SCh 331:64).

did not dismiss them as inconsequential or detrimental.[122] They worried, nevertheless, about the individual sister near death who was frightened, and they showed compassion for one another even while they taught themselves that the very fear associated with dying was purifying.[123] Anticipating the death of one of her sisters and perhaps sensing the woman's distress, Mechtild, apparently wanting to mitigate her sister's hardship, prayed to Christ, "in her last moments, give her a foretaste of eternal life, so that she has assurance she will never be separated from you."[124]

Not only the dying woman herself but also her sympathetic sisters were afraid as death came for one of their own. They were troubled by a perception of the heightened presence of demons near and at the moment of death.[125] A predominant shared worry was the weight of sin a dying woman might carry with her into the afterlife.[126] Gertrude knew that Sister M. B. found joy in superficial things—for example, her bedspread, embroidered with gold images—which Gertrude supposed would be an obstacle to her.[127] They had reason to be concerned: numerous visions Gertrude and Mechtild received confirmed the presence of their sisters in purgatory.[128] The nuns recognized that even the visionaries were in need of prophy-

[122] *Le Héraut* 5.2.2; 5.3.2–3 (SCh 331:66, 68–70).

[123] For the history of the purgative power of fear associated with death, see Straw, "Timor Mortis."

[124] *Liber* 4.35 (294). Mechtild seems to have wanted her sister to believe she would enjoy the sort of intimacy with Christ that Christ promised would be Mechtild's when Mechtild died: *Liber* 2.19 (156).

[125] For demons at the deathbed, see for example, *Le Héraut* 5.5.3; 5.32 (SCh 331:112, 256). This fear purified one young nun, allowing her to enter heaven directly without pausing for a stay in purgatory: *Le Héraut* 5.2.2 (SCh 331:66). For the presence of demons at the monastery, see in addition *Le Héraut* 4.54.6; 4.11.4 (SCh 255:452–54, 130); *Liber* 1.36, 39, 45 (118–19, 123–24, 130).

[126] See for example *Le Héraut* 5.5.3 (SCh 331:112).

[127] *Le Héraut* 5.8.1 (SCh 331:128).

[128] See for example *Le Héraut* 5.5.6 (SCh 331:114, 116).

lactic prayer.[129] Every moment mattered. Gertrude fretted that Mechtild might find occasion to sin between the time she received holy unction and her death.[130]

Yet the sisters perceived that none of their own was destined for hell,[131] all would wend their way to heaven; it was a matter of how expeditious the entry, how painful the wait. There was no temptation to deathbed despair at Helfta. Dying, fear of death, and the promise of heaven were great levelers among the women. All were guaranteed a spot in heaven; all were in danger of postponing their arrival. The nuns thus celebrated each member of the community as holy, even if the holiness of any given nun might during her lifetime be hidden from the view of her sisters, while even the holiest among them was counted as a sinner. All needed to prepare for the final process all the days of their lives;[132] all needed the protective presence of their sisters. No one was exempt from dependence on her community.[133]

Death, the Helfta writings concede, is the one debt that one cannot assume on another's behalf. In spite of this, or perhaps exactly on this account, the literature insists on the nuns' accompanying the dying in their final moments. The nuns assumed a vigilant air around the bedside of the dying, assembling to offer customary prayers[134] and to otherwise look after and meditate on sisters in their last weeks, days, and hours, coming and going at all times of day and night, pausing to eat and then assembling by their sister's side as she received

[129] *Liber* 5.25 (358).

[130] *Le Hérault* 5.4.4 (SCh 331:82).

[131] *Liber* 5.10 (334).

[132] *Le Hérault* 5.27.1 (SCh 331:210), and *Liber* 2 (143–44).

[133] There is a large body of literature on practices surrounding the dying in relation to the creation, sustenance, and celebration of community. See for example Frederick S. Paxton, *Christianizing Death: The Creation of a Ritual Process in Early Medieval Europe* (Ithaca, NY: Cornell University Press, 1990), 5.

[134] See for example *Le Hérault* 5.4.7; 5.7.1; 5.7.3 (SCh 331:88, 122, 124).

last rites.[135] The women's attendance at the deathbed seems to have been driven by rule and custom as well as by the desire to help the soul travel heavenward and to quell the fear they expected would beset its occupant. They were, in addition, aware that merit might accrue to them in consequence of their participation in the period surrounding a sister's death.[136]

Dying was—so the *Herald* and the *Book of Special Grace* wish to convey—an occasion for the individual nun to find herself enveloped in the caring and industrious company of her sisters. All the women congregated around Abbess Gertrude as she received last rites, her Spouse in all his beauty appearing in their midst.[137] As Mechtild died, the whole convent came and went from her bedside repeatedly, interrupting their common prayer in response to fluctuations in her condition, until they were suddenly summoned from choir to recite prayers a final time over her.[138] The process of dying was filled with talk, chant, tears, and kindnesses. One young nun captured the attention of her sisters by saying goodbye to them, promising them her prayers, and then speaking aloud in their presence to her Lord.[139] Once, when the sisters sang *Ad te levavi animam*, the Lord, seemingly roused by their song, leaned over a dying sister and kissed her gently—and then he kissed her again.[140]

As the Abbess Gertrude lay dying, Mechtild contemplated her face, flushed with beauty as her soul shone through: her eyebrows, lightly arched, recalled to Mechtild the care with which the abbess watched over her daughters; her clear eyes, her mercy; her vermillion lips, the compassion that she directed toward those in distress.[141] The *Book of Special Grace* is here

[135] *Liber* 7.7; 7.8 (397–400, 400–402).

[136] *Le Héraut* 5.1.30 (SCh 331:54, 56).

[137] *Le Héraut* 5.1.19 (SCh 331:38). And see for example *Le Héraut* 5.1.21 (SCh 331:40).

[138] *Le Héraut* 5.4.10–12 (SCh 331:90–94).

[139] *Le Héraut* 5.10.1–2 (SCh 331:142–144).

[140] *Le Héraut* 5.7.4 (SCh 331:126).

[141] *Liber* 6.3 (379–80).

intent on intensifying the reader's appreciation for the holy manner in which the abbess fulfilled her office, recounting while retelling her death the extraordinary qualities of her life. The beauty of her face recalls the physical beauty associated with the blessed in the history of Christian literature from late antiquity, a generic convention. We may, in addition, be party to the literary rendering of a prolonged moment when a younger sibling beheld with love the face of her older sister, searching its familiar landscape for markings of a lifetime spent in each other's company, charged with common purpose, and now overcome with gratification, respect, and love at parting. Observing carefully the faces of the dying may have been a regular practice at Helfta: the nuns also read Mechtild's face for signs of her advancement toward death.[142]

On behalf of their sisters, the nuns offered prayers to Christ, Mary, the saints, and the angels, urged on by their conviction that with songs, embraces, and the exchange of gifts heaven's inhabitants accompanied the soul at all stages of dying before ushering her through the permeable membrane separating the living from the dead, caring for her composite self after the death of the body, and never leaving her alone until they escorted her into the welcoming company of Christ.[143] The women assumed a watchfulness among Mary, the saints, and angels that complemented their own:[144] bordering the bed of the abbess were twelve angels who carried reports to Christ about everything that befell her—as well as about the actions of those looking after her.[145] When Mechtild was dying, her sisters recited *Omnes sancti Seraphim et Cherubim, orate pro ea,* angels in a flurry of reverence and joy offered her a place of

[142] *Liber* 7.11 (405).

[143] See for example *Le Héraut* 5.27.9; 5.4.19 (SCh 331:220, 103); *Liber* 7.4 (394–95).

[144] Mary related to Gertrude the words by which anyone can summon her to her side at the moment of death (*Le Héraut* 3.19.3 [SCh 139:108–10]).

[145] *Liber* 6.2 (37–79).

honor before God, and saints summoned one by one through the sisters' prayer appeared, presenting God with gifts to increase Mechtild's glory and her joy.[146] When a young nun died, the prayers the sisters intoned during her requiem Mass beckoned the saints, who deposited their merits with Christ in order to make up for whatever the recently deceased sister had failed to merit all by herself. Confidence in the saints' consoling, protective, and fruitful presence at the hour of death abounded.[147]

The convent's literature emphasizes a sister's movement toward the heavenly nuptial chamber in a crush of Christ's friends and family, sisters and saints working cooperatively toward that end.[148] With her community at her side, Abbess Gertrude entered her last moments,[149] and one of her sisters saw Christ rush to the bedside, as if he were attending a festival. He was accompanied by his mother, the Evangelist, and a multitude of saints, all of whom joined with the sisters, who, overwhelmed with sorrow, remained at the side of the abbess. Approaching the bed of his beloved, the Lord caressed her so that all the bitterness of death was sweetened.[150] Before the day had ended, one of her daughters saw Christ open his heart to the abbess, as if to offer her a garden of exquisite flowers or an apothecary's delightful-smelling spices, and at that moment, celestial spirits inclined from heaven to earth. Inviting her with honeyed melodies, they chanted, "Come, come, come, Lady, because heavenly delicacies await you."[151] The misery

[146] *Le Héraut* 5.4.6 (SCh 331:84–86).

[147] See for example *Le Héraut* 5.28.1 (SCh 331:228).

[148] See for example *Le Héraut* 5.5.27 (SCh 331:220), and *Liber* 6.1 (376).

[149] *Le Héraut* 5.1.21 (SCh 331:40).

[150] *Le Héraut* 5.1.20 (SCh 331:40), and *Liber* 6.5 (382). This combination of anticipatory joy and lamentation for the living is a typical feature of late medieval texts that describe the death of a holy person.

[151] *Le Héraut* 5.1.22 (SCh 331:42). On heaven as a garden, see Binski, *Medieval Death*, 167.

of the deathbed was transformed into the joy of the wedding bed.[152]

For all the anxieties surrounding death, the Helfta literature holds out the potential of a glorious passage, filled with a cornucopia of delights of scent and sound, a courteous summons into a hospitable and convivial community. A sister would know that after death swept in to separate her body from her soul, fellow nuns would carry her body to the chapel, depositing it before the altar, then prostrating themselves in prayer.[153] They would bury her body in the monastery's cemetery, and her sisters would toss earth on her grave,[154] visiting after the burial and participating in commemorative Masses, perhaps on the third, seventh, and thirtieth days after her death.[155] Encircled in the days and nights surrounding death by the women whose company she had kept throughout her life, the dying nun was at the center of a crowd gathered around the bed and, later, at the gravesite.[156]

We are today largely accustomed to think of the moment of death as one of solitude, often terrible, which a person—however deeply and carefully loved, and however well-attended—must face by herself and all alone. The nuns proclaimed the opposite. They did so with the stark admission that dying was a bumpy process, which might fill the soon-to-be deceased and those who accompanied her with a combination of joy and fear as well as with pain. And they did so with the acknowledgment that the dying had basic needs that their sisters were in a position to meet, assuming great responsibility and great

[152] *Le Héraut* 5.30.4 (SCh 331:244). See *Le Héraut* 5.27.9 (SCh 331:220) for illness as the means by which Christ draws his fiancée toward him in anticipation of their wedding. For the deathbed as a bridal bed, see *Liber* 6.6 (383).

[153] *Le Héraut* 5.1.24 (SCh 331:46).

[154] *Le Héraut* 5.1.31 (SCh 331:56).

[155] *Le Héraut* 5.1.34 (SCh 331:59, n. 1); and also see *Le Héraut* 5.10.3; 5.1.31 (SCh 331:146, 56) for the sisters visiting the grave of Abbess Gertrude.

[156] *Le Héraut* 5.30.10 (SCh 331:250).

power at the end of a sister's life and after her death. During Sister M. B.'s funeral Mass, Gertrude saw Christ present to the sister, in the form of various dishes, all the prayers that her sisters had offered for her. At the elevation of the host, Christ held out a cup to her, and when M. B. had drunk only a little, she was penetrated with the sweetness of the divinity. She then joined her hands and prayed for all those who, during her life, had upset her by their ideas, words, and acts, rejoicing now in the merits she had acquired on their account.[157] The text implicitly urges a reappraisal of the value to the self of those with whom one might not get along, a call to allow the more expansive perspective that death will allow each sister to cast a light even now on contemporaneous relationships within the convent. The message is clear: even those whom we do not like may work to our good and be of decisive benefit to us. The deathbed need not be a site of feelings of affection for productivity to inhere in the relationship, and the efficacy of community is, in this case, not dependent on fellow feeling.[158]

The sisters were, indeed, somewhat wary of the emotions that might emerge around the deathbed. The feelings that the sisters who accompanied the dying might elicit in them could pose a threat to them in their last days. Mechtild reproached herself for remaining with the abbess as she neared her end: the younger woman feared that she might be precipitating sin for her sister, hindering her expeditious entry into heaven. The context suggests a concern about the abbess's displeasing Christ by focusing her attention on Mechtild rather than on him. Mechtild was concerned for the state of her own soul, too, and for the same reason.[159] Likewise, the consolation a certain sister received from her friends while she was in the infirmary caused to Gertrude to worry for the woman's soul.[160]

[157] *Le Héraut* 5.8.2 (SCh 331:130).

[158] And see *Le Héraut* 5.9.7 (SCh 331:143).

[159] *Liber* 6.2 (378).

[160] *Le Héraut* 5.9.3 (SCh 331:136).

A Lady S. lingered through five months of purgative pain because she had spoken more than was necessary to another sick person.[161] Even if dying unveiled the value of the community of sisters to each individual sister, and if it was sometimes an occasion for an individual sister to experience the depth of her love for another, it also reinforced apprehensions about the potential of one-on-one relationships to purloin attention properly directed toward Christ.

However necessary the presence of their sisters was to the nuns whose death drew near, passages in the *Book of Special Grace* and the *Herald* highlight the importance of one's dying accompanied by Christ—not by one's sisters. It was Christ whom Mechtild sought as she felt her life draining from her, and it was Christ's face that Abbess Gertrude beheld as she tossed in her last agony.[162] Gertrude meditated on his presence at her deathbed, not that of her sisters.[163] Surely the writings attest to a basic fear of dying alone, being abandoned to traverse a violent crossing without support and companionship. The nuns knew that their sisters were busy, and that they could not always accompany one another in times of illness and need.[164] In underscoring the nuns' desire for Christ to escort them at their death, the *Book of Special Grace* and the *Herald* declare that the sisters would not die alone, seeming with this assertion to try to meet a fundamental need for companionship and attentiveness in the last hours, to keep at bay the loneliness associated with illness and dying.[165]

The Helfta books contain no passage in which a nun nearing death seeks reassurance from her sisters such as that which Mechtild requests of Christ, or in which a sister pledges analogous tender and unequivocal guarantees of companionship as

[161] *Le Héraut* 5.6.1–2 (SCh 331:118, 120).
[162] *Liber* 7.7; 6.4 (397–98, 382).
[163] *Le Héraut* 5.28.1 (SCh 331:228).
[164] *Le Héraut* 2.9.1; 3.3.1 (SCh 139:268; SCh 143:20–22).
[165] *Le Héraut* 3.68.3 (SCh 143:276–78).

does Christ to the dying nun. Nevertheless, the *Herald* does tell of an unnamed sister's expressing pleasure in the pampering and consolation she receives from her friends as she dies,[166] and its authors recount the sadness a sick sister experienced when she thought her sisters paid her insufficient attention, favoring another over her with their company.[167] While the dying did not routinely petition for the presence of their sisters at their deathbeds, they do seem to have depended on it and longed for it.[168] Surely one of the messages the cloistered reader would have received from the Helfta writings was that just as she and her sisters prayed productively for others around the time of death and after death, so her sisters would one day offer supplications on her behalf, and to good effect.

In part through their writings, the women responded to this need for tenderness and assurance, and one of the purposes of the *Book of Special Grace* and the *Herald* is to soothe dying sisters and to quell anxieties abroad about the dying. Christ assured Gertrude that just as a mother tucks her child into the folds of her clothes, holding her against her breasts when they are sailing through a stormy sea, so he would protect her at her death.[169] He comforted Mechtild when she believed that she was dying and asked him to remain with her, promising, "I shall be with you until your final breath."[170] According to a vision attributed to Gertrude, Christ kept his word. For two days after she received last unction, Christ held Mechtild in his arms. The wound in his side pressed up against her mouth, and she seemed to breathe from his heart until she breathed her last.[171] As Abbess Gertrude was dying, Mechtild saw Christ place his face before the abbess's face wherever she turned,

[166] *Le Héraut* 5.9.3 (SCh 331:136).

[167] *Le Héraut* 5.9.1 (SCh 331:136).

[168] See for example *Le Héraut* 5.3.2 (SCh 331:70).

[169] *Le Héraut* 5.25.3 (SCh 331:206–8).

[170] *Liber* 2.39 (187).

[171] *Le Héraut* 5.4.6 (SCh 331:86); *Liber* 7.4 (395).

anticipating the fullness of the embrace her death would bring; then Christ opened up his heart to her, as if he could not contain his love for her, and he enfolded her in it.[172]

Christ promised Mechtild that just as a loving mother receives her son, so at the moment of death he would receive anyone who walked with him in truth,[173] and the authors of the Helfta writings attribute to nameless nuns deathbed joys such as those they claim for the luminaries among them.[174] Gertrude perceived Christ visiting a nun as she was dying—she could tell this from the sister's joy.[175] As a certain Lady S. was dying, Christ nestled her against his chest so that she would not be uncomfortable.[176] As Sister M. (who may be Mechtild of Magdeburg) was dying, Christ drew the breath from her lips, and from this breath, he made a rainbow, whose arch stretched toward the divine heart.[177] Mechtild of Hackeborn saw Christ before a sister's deathbed, and at the moment the priest placed the Host on the woman's lips, Christ offered his bright red mouth to her and took her in his arms. In that instant, Mechtild beheld the sister's soul, in which she could perceive nothing but God.[178] When Mechtild prayed that Christ would be with one of her sisters in the woman's last moments, he assured her that he would do as she asked.[179]

[172] *Liber* 6.5 (382).

[173] *Liber* 4.7 (264).

[174] Gertrude's visionary account of Mechtild's death, as Barbara Newman has observed, clothes the dying woman with "every love-token from God that the sisters desired for themselves" ("*Iam cor meum non sit suum*: Exchanging Hearts, from Heloise to Helfta," in *From Knowledge to Beatitude: St. Victor, Twelfth-Century Scholars, and Beyond, Essays in Honor of Grover A. Zinn, Jr.*, ed. E. Ann Matter and Lesley Smith [Notre Dame, IN: Notre Dame University Press, 2013], 293–94).

[175] *Le Héraut* 5.6.1 (SCh 331:118).

[176] *Le Héraut* 5.6.2 (SCh 331:118).

[177] *Le Héraut* 5.7.4 (SCh 331:126).

[178] *Liber* 4.46 (302).

[179] *Liber* 4.28 (286).

The nuns knew the limits of the comfort the dying could receive from those soon to be left behind, and they taught one another that none of their own would be bereft of Christ's comforting presence at the end. "For," as he told Gertrude, "when a person is approaching her death, destitute of all human support and solace, . . . I, who am the one true friend, come at that moment of anxious need to the desolate soul."[180] Although not so extravagant as the deathbed accounts of Mechtild and Abbess Gertrude, or Gertrude's extended meditation on her own death, the Helfta writings are replete with expressions of Christ's attentive love for a host of unnamed nuns as they approached death. The claim that many among them delighted in Christ's presence as they died must have been a kind of guarantee to all the women that they too could count on Christ's company when death came near. For some, of course, this promise may have become a source of anguish—for those who as the time of death came near may have found their hope lost in disappointment at not finding Christ at their side, and felt all the more alone for the absence of him in whom they had been taught to trust. The Helfta literature does not record such experiences or admit of the possibility. On the contrary, the visions they record showed the sisters that Christ abides not only with the well-known and well-regarded among them but with other, anonymous, nuns.

Dying at Helfta was not a one-way affair. The dying were mindful of their soon-to-be-left-behind sisters. They were sometimes especially chatty.[181] They consoled the soon-to-be bereaved.[182] One young woman, knowing the end was drawing near, said her goodbyes to the women who gathered around her, promising to pray for them when she came before God.[183] The dying otherwise affected their sisters for the good,

[180] *Le Héraut* 3.68.3 (SCh 139:276–78).
[181] *Le Héraut* 5.10.1–2 (SCh 331:142–44).
[182] *Le Héraut* 5.4.3 (SCh 331:80).
[183] *Le Héraut* 5.10.1 (SCh 331:142).

sometimes indirectly, through their exemplary piety. When death loomed over her, a young nun held in her hands an image of the crucified Christ and addressed his wounds with words so tender, and kissed him with such feeling, that those gathered around her were moved to compunction.[184] Her sisters were filled with wonder as they beheld another young woman kiss the figure on the cross, her words to him all wisdom streaked with sweetness.[185] The literature thus does not portray dying as an occasion to cast aside labor and responsibility but as a time of charged activity. In a standard trope of medieval hagiographical literature and *ars moriendi*, the dying listened to their sisters' entreaties and were responsive to them. When Mechtild's sisters came to her on her deathbed to ask for prayers for themselves and for their friends, she, filled with affection for them, acquiesced.[186] And when Gertrude pressed Mechtild to pray for her friends as Mechtild received the last unction, Mechtild responded with a disquisition on why God permits certain faults in those whom he loves.[187] On her deathbed, Gertrude of Hackeborn prayed for all her daughters who had just prayed for her.[188]

The nuns cultivated a generous sense of community at the moment of a sister's death, when her debt was paid and she was united with God. Christ promised that when Sister M. died (probably a reference to Mechtild of Magdeburg), a wave of his honey-blessedness would cover all those whom affection had brought to her side.[189] This promise conveys a sense of community activated by his delectation in receiving the woman he loved, a pleasure that issued in effusive expressions of beneficence: when the abbess died, we read, Christ was liquefied

[184] *Le Héraut* 5.3.1 (SCh 331:66).
[185] *Le Héraut* 5.10.2 (SCh 331:144–146).
[186] *Le Héraut* 5.4.20 (SCh 331:103); *Liber* 7.7 (398).
[187] *Le Héraut* 5.4.20 (SCh 331:102–04).
[188] *Le Héraut* 5.1.24 (SCh 331:46).
[189] *Le Héraut* 5.7.3 (SCh 331:124).

with tenderness and sweetness, so that on the face of the earth there was no just request that he did not at that hour answer.[190] Thus, coupled with the moments of intimacy with the dying that Christ seemed to reserve to himself was an effervescent building and bolstering of community, in which the members of the monastery received special advantages and which also benefited those outside its walls: when Christ opened his heart to a dying Mechtild, grace fell on whole church, although especially on those present.[191]

Grief

Anticipatory grief sometimes shrouded those who clustered before the deathbed,[192] and aching to keep their own among them, the women sometimes worked toward this purpose, reluctant to relinquish a sister into Christ's embrace. On the feast of Saint Lievin, the low-country martyr, the whole community implored him to heal their abbess. The saint instructed them in the error of their appeal: just as a king's family should not disturb a king when he has in his arms one whom he loves, so the nuns ought not to ask for healing for a sister whom their king is caressing.[193] Another passage likewise demonstrates the competing claims the nuns admitted between themselves and God. When her sisters grieved for the death of a fellow nun, Gertrude wondered to Christ why he could not have left the woman among her sisters a little longer, and Christ explained that the woman in question was like a lily that pleased his eyes and that he held in his fingers until her illness made her so fragrant he plucked her, breaking her away from her

[190] *Le Héraut* 5.1.25; 5.29.5 (SCh 331:48, 236).

[191] *Liber* 7.5 (396); *Le Héraut* 5.4.7 (SCh 331:88).

[192] See for example *Le Héraut* 5.1.24 (SCh 331:46), where the daughters of Abbess Gertrude lamented as her death approached. The sisters also mourned *conversi*: *Le Héraut* 5.12.4 (SCh 331:156–58).

[193] *Le Héraut* 5.1.12 (SCh 331:30–32).

sisters, taking her for himself.[194] In this case, Christ bargained with the bereaved women, making the following proposition: he would recompense a hundredfold for the loss of their companion anyone who, recalling the delight of her company, nonetheless abandoned her to his longing.[195]

It was hard for the women to let go of one another. They perceived that Christ allowed for this difficulty, sometimes consoling those left behind. He became to those whom he loved everything they missed about those whom they loved and had lost.[196] He directed those who mourned in a course of contemplation by which they could open themselves up to the comfort he offered them. Promising that no loss they endured was so great that he could not restore it a hundred times in this life, a thousand in the life to come, he both acknowledged the weight of grief and offered the possibility of its relief.[197] He otherwise soothed those whom death had robbed. When Christ swept the abbess into death, an infinite sorrow flooded Mechtild. She confessed, however, that in compensation for her wretchedness, whenever she wished, she was able to see the soul of her sister the abbess and every one of her celestial rewards.[198]

Indeed, thereafter Mechtild saw the abbess repeatedly, in revelations full of conversations with Christ about her and with the abbess herself, who had in the months preceding her death struggled with debilitating illness and who now

[194] *Le Héraut* 5.2.1 (SCh 331:64). For the pleasure that Christ declares himself to take in the sick and failing nun, whom he can keep to himself and away from the crowd, see in addition *Le Héraut* 3.22 (SCh 143:114).

[195] *Le Héraut* 5.2.1 (SCh 331:64). Christ says that he will be to Gertrude all she has lost when her abbess dies: *Le Héraut* 5.25.1 (SCh 331:46–48). Sometimes it is Christ who must suffer, postponing marriage with the ones whom he loves; Gertrude perceived Christ's impatient eagerness to embrace his beloved Abbess Gertrude as she appeared to be dying. As she delayed her passage, he had to wait two months (*Le Héraut* 5.1.19 [SCh 331:38]).

[196] *Le Héraut* 5.1.25 (SCh 331:46).

[197] *Le Héraut* 3.85.1 (SCh 143:338–40).

[198] *Liber* 2.26 (169).

appeared to Mechtild entirely beautiful, so that the very sighting itself was therefore surely a consolation.[199] These visions brought Mechtild respite, integrating Abbess Gertrude into Mechtild's life even in death in a way that may have recalled to the bereaved the regular interactions between the two sisters, who for many years had overseen the household together. Revelations that spoke of immediate or future reunion with the dead may have brought some succor to those in mourning: when Mechtild spied Abbess Gertrude in heaven, hand in hand with their biological sister, Lutgard, who had died in childhood,[200] this vision may have sparked reveries about a time when Mechtild herself might join hands with her sisters—and may have kindled the hope in others for like encounters of their own.

Sadness swept through the monastery as Mechtild died,[201] Abbess Gertrude's daughters wept at her death,[202] and when less than two weeks later death snatched up one of the other nuns, the congregation experienced "sorrow upon sorrow."[203] The dead occupied the nuns' thoughts day and night; the women dreamed about dead sisters.[204] The literature does not, however, plumb the complex or subtle emotions of those left behind. The women noted their grief and accepted it matter of factly, while acknowledging with heavy hearts what they had lost when a friend died.[205] The register of grief's expression was not high-pitched. The literature emphasizes the sorrow of the crowd along with the loss and longing attributed to particular individuals. The enduring connection of the abbess to *all* the sisters is recorded, along with her tie to her blood

[199] See for example *Liber* 5.1; 5.2 (317–20).
[200] *Liber* 1.24 (86).
[201] *Liber* 7.5 (396).
[202] *Liber* 6.6 (383); and see *Le Héraut* 5.1.25 (SCh 331:45).
[203] *Le Héraut* 5.2.1 (SCh 331:62): *dolor super dolorem.*
[204] *Liber* 6.7 (385).
[205] *Le Héraut* 3.85.1 (SCh 143:338–40).

sister Mechtild.[206] Grief was communal, belonging to all, and its weight was democratic.

The nuns' writings contain no reproach of those who grieved for the death of another. Although they document the pain one might cause a friend who remains caught in purgatory by shedding mourning tears,[207] and hint that excessive grief might hinder the soul's heavenward flight,[208] they confront us with the uncomplicated sadness associated with a sense of loss, and they picture a context within which sisters mourned the death of a fellow nun without rebuke. Such passages provide frank and gentle acknowledgements that friends mourn the death of friends.[209] The Helfta writings do recall that grief must be accompanied by an acceptance of God's will,[210] an echo of the familiar Christian anxiety surrounding grief because of its power to lay bare both a lack of faith and hope for the salvation of the deceased. If the nuns found the terms of this condition unpalatable, they give no evidence of it. As the women portray themselves, they had no need to justify sadness associated with bereavement but were self-assured about their ability on the one hand to align their will with God's will and, on the other, to experience sorrow in the face of death and give it expression.[211]

[206] For an example of an individual nun remembering another sister who has died, see *Liber* 5.25 (358).

[207] *Le Héraut* 5.12.4 (SCh 331:156–58).

[208] *Liber* 5.11 (338).

[209] *Le Héraut* 5.12.4 (SCh 331:156–58).

[210] *Le Héraut* 3.85.1 (SCh 147:338–40).

[211] At Helfta we are far from the cries of Bernard, their earlier male counterpart at Clairvaux, and his delicate dissection of the intricacy of his grief over the death of his brother, in which he wrestles with his own apprehension that excessive mourning demonstrates a lack of confidence in Christ's victory over death (Bernard of Clairvaux, *Sermones super cantica canticorum* 26.2.3, SBOp 1:171; Anna Harrison, "'Jesus Wept': Mourning as Imitation of Christ in Bernard's Sermon Twenty-Six on the Song of Songs," CSQ 48, no. 4 [2013]: 433–67).

Moreover, they considered that grief—provided that it was fixed in a foundation of faith—might positively benefit the whole cloistered community. Care for the dead was not a burrowing into a one-on-one relationship exclusive of others but could occasion a capacious sense of community that included but was not limited to the collective of nuns.[212] In recounting her visions of the now deceased abbess, Gertrude shared the fruit of her engagement with their mother with her sisters. Christ received the offering Gertrude made during the abbess's burial Mass under the form of a heart filled with precious gifts, and calling the abbess to him, he instructed her to dispose of these gifts—a trove of various virtues—as she pleased. The abbess distributed these gifts among the women in the monastery, knowing well what each needed and what each desired.[213] This account shows that Gertrude conceived that her relationship with the abbess—mediated in this instance by Christ and expressed as a longing to give—was of immediate advantage to her sisters. We find a similar pattern of commitment to a dead sister fanning outward to include others when Gertrude tried to make up for not having prayed sufficiently for Mechtild when she was dying and after her death. When Gertrude kissed Christ's wounds in compensation for her negligence and in order to increase Mechtild's celestial adornments, flowers blossomed in the wounds, and Mechtild acknowledged the gift, promising that the sweet liquid the flowers distilled would rush over souls in purgatory like a healing balm, a consolation for the just.[214]

In a vision in which Abbess Gertrude appeared to Gertrude of Helfta, the visionary recounted to the abbess the tears her daughters shed in grief over her death and asked the abbess why she did not bring about a cessation of their weeping; she recalled that while the abbess was alive, it had troubled her

[212] *Le Héraut* 5.29.2 (SCh 331:232–34).
[213] *Le Héraut* 5.1.26 (SCh 331:48–50).
[214] *Le Héraut* 5.4.23 (SCh 331:106–8).

that her daughters would grieve needlessly. The abbess explained that the tears Gertrude regarded as being without profit had great worth. It was as if, Abbess Gertrude declared, God allowed her to catch each tear each sister shed in a gold chalice; in exchange for each, a stream of the divinity flowed into her. Drinking happily from the chalice of tears, the abbess sang to Christ a song of thanks for the actions of her daughters.[215]

This vision was surely meant to comfort the reading audience at Helfta as it told of the benefits that accrued to the abbess in heaven in consequence of the sisters' sorrowful remembrance, acclaiming her continual engagement with her daughters. Yet the *Herald*'s description of the tearful sadness that overwhelmed the sisters indicates that they *did* perceive death as introducing a lamentable divide between them and the departed. Even as the vision affirmed Abbess Gertrude's consoling presence among her daughters, it acknowledged the sisters' sense of separation from her; it did not dismiss their sorrow but insisted on its purposefulness.[216] Their grief helped to sustain the nuns' connection to the abbess, joining her perpetually to the convent.

Thus the nuns harnessed grief over the dead to make important claims of continuity in community. The community between the living and the dead in heaven—and in purgatory—was solidified in sorrow and thanksgiving. Mourning for the dead summoned them into conversation with the grief-stricken and affirmed the productivity of sadness. Mourning was otherwise efficacious, according to the women who composed the *Book of Special Grace*, who did not worry that grief for the dead might distract or otherwise detract from their

[215] *Le Héraut* 5.1.1 (SCh 331:52).

[216] Already in the twelfth century, the Cistercian monk Aelred of Rievaulx (1110–1167) proclaimed the productivity for both the living and the dead of grief for the deceased beloved (Anna Harrison, "'Where Have You Vanished?' Aelred of Rievaulx's Lamentation on Simon," *Quidditas* 39 [December 2018], 239–52).

experience of heaven: mourning practices become integrated into the joy of heaven and constitutive of it! These, the literature tells us, stimulated deceased members of the household to channel the sisters' love to God. All the words of every prayer the sisters offered in Masses for their abbess were to her like so many roses, at the center of each of which was a gold petal, a representation of the sisters' love for her. The abbess in turn presented these roses to Christ,[217] directing to him the love that had moved her sisters to pray on her behalf.

The nuns do not depict themselves as needing to work aggressively through their grief. This may be in part because numerous visionaries among them told them that the relationship between the living and the dead perdured. The convent expected revelation to transfer information about deceased sisters back to living sisters. When Gertrude spoke with a recently dead member of the household, the woman knew that their companions would ask Gertrude what she had learned about the woman's heavenly recompense.[218] Moreover, the relationship between the living and the dead resembled that which they had enjoyed while all parties were alive. The nuns expressed no anxiety that the transformation after death would leave behind their former selves or make the living seem unimportant or forgotten.[219] Mourning also occasioned faithful contact with God. If grief at the death of a sister was not wholly mastered at Helfta, it was probably assuaged by promiscuous encounters between the living and the dead and the expressions of love for God they elicited—or so the monastery's writings wish to suggest.[220]

[217] *Liber* 5.2 (319–20).

[218] *Le Héraut* 5.10.3 (SCh 331:148).

[219] See for example *Le Héraut* 5.12.4 (SCh 331:156–58)

[220] Moreover, the sense of relatedness of the saints to the dead may have contributed to creating a sense of relatedness among all parties; living sisters perceived saints singing and moving among both themselves and the happy departed, creating continuity among the living and the recently dead by encompassing both groups in a larger community of shared associates. For the relationship between the sisters and the saints, see chap. 8.

Continuity in Community

Visions of the dead promoted relationships among members of the convent, living and dead. Immediately after her death, one of the nuns took Christ's hand in her own and blessed the community.[221] After Mechtild's death, aspects of her association with her sisters continued as they had before. On the very day of her burial, two of her sisters heard her join the congregation in chanting *Regnum Mundi*, the responsory sung both at sisters' funerals and during the ceremony of the reception of the habit.[222] On this occasion, Mechtild appeared in the choir and proclaimed,

> When I [was alive and] chanted with you in choir with all my desire and strength, I drew your desires upward toward God and in God when the song ascended, [and] when the song descended, . . . I . . . brought down his grace upon you: and I do this now ceaselessly.[223]

Chant was a channel connecting Mechtild to her cloistered community, her ongoing participation in the liturgy in continuity with the role she had occupied while she was alive.[224] Before and after her death, daily devotions expressed in common provided Mechtild with the means to draw her sisters toward God. During Mechtild's requiem Mass, Gertrude saw the older visionary placing golden pipes into Christ's heart for all those who had a special devotion to her, and from Christ's heart each woman took what she desired.[225] After she died, therefore, the *Book of Special Grace* taught its readers that Mechtild served her sisters uninterruptedly as mediator and, in addition, as counselor and teacher, in death as in life, championing devotion to

[221] *Liber* 5.6 (328).
[222] Finnegan, *The Women of Helfta*, 36.
[223] *Liber* 7.19 (414).
[224] Finnegan, *The Women of Helfta*, 34.
[225] *Le Héraut* 5.4.21 (SCh 331:104).

the Sacred Heart.[226] It is easy to suppose that such revelations were an important part of the mourning process, assuring those left behind of the dead's steadfast dedication to the convent, of shared responsibilities and particular obligations, not sloughed off but continuing to be shouldered on the other side of death's divide. Death did not wage a war of attrition on the membership of the monastery and did not dissipate the sisters' connection with one another, the literature relates.

After her entry into heaven, Abbess Gertrude persisted in furnishing spiritual prescriptions, on one occasion instructing her daughters to love God with all their strength[227] and, on another, recalling to them that they ought to be submissive, to love one another, to fix their attention on God in all things, to be merciful to their neighbor, and so forth.[228] Dispensing advice to them, she countered the worry to which her daughters had given voice that without her guidance—to which, during her long forty-year rule, the women had been accustomed—the convent's piety would be put at risk.[229] She gave truth to their hope that she would always be their mother.[230] In a pattern familiar in the Helfta writings, the abbess, installed in heaven, was mindful not only of her daughters considered collectively, praying for the whole community,[231] but sensitive, too, to individual women among them; she communicated to Mechtild, for example, a message for a particular sister about whom Mechtild had inquired.[232] Lodged in her celestial abode, the abbess prayed for the community with which Christ had many years before entrusted her and promised Mechtild that she would never cease to do so.[233] It is almost as if the abbess and

[226] *Liber* 7.12 (406–7).
[227] *Liber* 6.6 (384).
[228] *Liber* 6.9 (390).
[229] *Le Héraut* 5.1.31 (SCh 331:56).
[230] *Le Héraut* 5.1.31 (SCh 331:56).
[231] *Liber* 2.26; 6.6 (171, 384).
[232] *Liber* 6.7 (385–86).
[233] *Liber* 6.8 (387–88).

the individual women in her charge had never parted, or changed the structure and nature of their relationship, a measure of how seriously the women took Gertrude of Hackeborn in her role of abbess.

If we mourn not only the person who is lost but, in addition and simultaneously, the person we were in relationship to that person, it seems that by fixing some among the dead who had played a leading role in the monastery (as chantress, as abbess) in heaven in the same roles they had occupied on earth, the nuns sought to secure the permanency of their own sense of self and interrelatedness. And in part precisely because the nuns conceived of identity as shaped in relation to community, the ties to the dead at Helfta did not get in the way of ties with the living. And yet, such continuing connections may have complicated matters for those who took over the roles previously held by those who had died, although the literature does not concede that this might be so.[234]

It was not only a question of the community's living members' continuing to be connected to dead members of the community. The convent appears to have been in two places at once, or it was as if two convents—earthly and celestial—were integrated, at least in Mechtild's visions. Mechtild saw the abbess in heaven surrounded by all the members of the community, living and dead, who continued to express ready and glad obedience: at her smallest movement, a sweet sound stirred up from the bipartite crowd and, as if in the form of white doves, the flock flew to her.[235] Revelations testified in other ways to the vital interconnectedness among members of the monastery, among those in heaven as well as between those on earth and those in heaven, sounding with assurance the unending value to all of solidarity cultivated in the here and now. At the entrance of a heavenly house constructed from pure gold (a symbol of love), Mechtild beheld all the souls who

[234] I thank Catherine Osbourne for this consideration.

[235] *Liber* 2.26 (171).

had once commended themselves to her and who held in their hands a rope that emerged from Christ's heart, a sign that all those for whom she had prayed shared in God's grace.[236]

Gertrude saw a sister in glory surrounded by kneeling souls whom the sister's prayers had delivered, a sign of the unending gratitude for one another that characterized the experience of heaven. When Gertrude asked whether the community on earth would benefit from the numbers of sisters received into heaven, the sister responded in the affirmative: for each nun in heaven, God multiplied the benefits that their counterparts received while on pilgrimage,[237] a bold assertion that the fate of each woman in the Helfta community had eternal consequence for every other sister. The salvation of one benefited the whole.

On the anniversary of the abbess's death, Mechtild saw the nuns and others associated with the monastery gathered in a circle around the abbess, dancing and singing *O Mater nostra*, and she saw their individual voices enter the heart of Christ, from which they reemerged as a single melody of marvelous beauty.[238] Engagement with the dead, in visions such as this, was at least as much about the unity of community, made more beautiful in Christ, as it was about more obviously personal, one-on-one reunions.

[236] *Liber* 1.13 (45).

[237] *Le Héraut* 5.3.8 (SCh 331:76).

[238] See *Liber* 6.9 (389). And see *Le Héraut* 5.1.32 (SCh 331:56 and 58).

Chapter 4

"I Am Wholly Your Own"

Liturgy and Community

On another night, when the response "the kingdom of the world" was being sung, at the words "for the love of my Lord," she felt and experienced the divine Heart penetrated to its marrow by the devotion of those who chanted this response so that . . . our flesh and our brother, Jesus Christ, exclaimed . . .: "Today I proclaim truly that I am in debt to these women in compensation for their faithful service to me."[1]

Liturgy and Spirituality

Daily Mass and the Divine Office were the sisters' primary prescribed activities and the pivot around which other business of the monastery turned.[2] The sisters sometimes attended

[1] *Le Héraut* 4.54.4 (SCh 331:448–50).

[2] Studies that have commented extensively on the liturgical content of the Helfta spirituality are too numerous to cite. The most comprehensive introduction is Cyprian Vagaggini's richly detailed *Theological Dimensions of the Liturgy*, trans. Leonard J. Doyle and W. A. Jurgen, from the fourth Italian edition, revised and augmented by the author (Collegeville, MN: Liturgical Press, 1976), 741–802, which focuses on the relation between Gertrude's mysticism and her liturgical piety. Although too brief to offer satisfying demonstrations of its many provocative claims, especially insightful is Jean Leclercq's "Liturgy and Mental Prayer in the Life of St. Gertrude," *Sponsa*

Mass twice in one day, and they probably spent the majority of their waking hours chanting the eight canonical hours. Supplementary liturgical observances, such as the Office of the Dead, the Office of the Virgin, and quasi-liturgical gatherings, including chapter—the daily meeting in which the business of the monastery was conducted—further filled their schedule.[3] To the nuns, the liturgy was marked off as an occasion for concentrated praise of God; it was colored through and through with opportunities to move closer to Christ, especially when he was received in communion.[4] During the

---

Regis 31 (1960): 1–5; repr. in "Méditation et célébration: À propos du Mémorial de sainte Gertrude," in *La liturgie et les paradoxes chrétiens* (Paris: Cerf, 1963), 295–300. Bruce Holsinger has examined the creative ways in which the Helfta nuns played with the liturgy (Bruce W. Holsinger, *Music, Body, and Desire in Medieval Culture: Hildegard of Bingen to Chaucer* [Stanford: Stanford University Press, 2001], 240–53), as has Christian Gregory Savage, "Music and the Writings of the Helfta Mystics," MA thesis, Florida State University, 2012. For a consideration of the role of the liturgy in Mechtild's life, see Hans Urs von Balthasar, Einführung to *Das Buch*, ed. Hans Urs von Balthasar (Einsiedeln: Johannes Verlag, 1955), 12.

[3] For the celebration of Mass twice each day, see, for example, *Le Héraut* 5.4.21; *Le Héraut Missa* 1.1–5 (SCh 331:104, 284), and *Liber* 1.26 (94). And see on this point Gilbert Dolan, *St. Gertrude the Great* (London: Sands, 1913), 26. It is unclear how often the nuns received communion. They may have done so more frequently than once a week at Sunday Mass (*Liber* 1.26 [39]); M. Camille Hontoir, "La dévotion au saint sacrement chez les premiers Cisterciens (XIIe–XIIe siècles)," in *Studia eucharistica, DCC anni a condito festo sanctissimi Corpus Christi 1246–1946* (Antwerp: De Nederlandsche Boekhandel, 1946), 146–47. On the Office of the Dead at Helfta, see Vagaggini, *Theological Dimensions*, 797; for its recitation by Cistercian nuns, see Ailbe J. Luddy, *The Cistercian Nuns: A Brief Sketch of the History of the Order from Its Foundations to the Present Day* (Dublin: M. H. Gill and Son, 1931), 15. The nuns may have spent up to eight hours a day carrying out their liturgical commitments; see Marie-Luise Ehrenschwendtner, "'Puellae litteratae': The Use of the Vernacular in the Dominican Convents of Southern Germany," in *Medieval Women in Their Communities*, ed. Diane Watt (Buffalo, NY: University of Toronto Press, 1997), 59.

[4] For both Gertrude and Mechtild, as for thirteenth-century women more generally, receiving the Eucharist and viewing the elevated Host often precipitated union with Christ. For the close connection for thirteenth-century women between Mass and ecstasy, see Roger De Ganck, "The Integration of

liturgy, Christ often came all by himself to Mechtild and to Gertrude; he frequently came with others. Visions interspersed throughout both books indicate that the nuns' liturgical piety, in keeping with broader trends in late medieval religiosity, was undergirded by the conviction that the living, the saints, and the angels are confederates who all together offer praise to God. Mechtild heard all the choirs of angels singing antiphons with the sisters,[5] and as Gertrude commented about a vision

---

Nuns in the Cistercian Order particularly in Belgium," *Cîteaux* 35 (1984): 181; and Caroline Walker Bynum, "Women Mystics and Eucharistic Devotion in the Thirteenth Century," in *Fragmentation and Redemption: Essays on Gender and the Human Body in Medieval Religion* (New York: Zone Books, 1991), esp. 125–29. A great deal of attention has been focused on the Mass and, more specifically, on the place of eucharistic devotion in the Helfta spirituality. See for example Dolan, *St. Gertrude*, esp. 26–27; Hilda Graef, "Gertrude the Great: Mystical Flowering of the Liturgy," *Orate Fratres* 20 (1945/46): 171–74; Vagaggini, *Theological Dimensions*, 774–75; Caroline Walker Bynum, "Women Mystics in the Thirteenth Century: The Case of the Nuns of Helfta," in *Jesus as Mother: Studies in the Spirituality of the High Middle Ages* (Berkeley: University of California Press, 1982), 203–4, 214; Cheryl Clemons, "The Relationship between Devotion to the Eucharist and Devotion to the Humanity of Jesus in the Writings of St. Gertrude of Helfta," PhD dissertation, The Catholic University of America, 1995; Olivier Quenardel, *La communion eucharistique dans le* Héraut de l'amour divin *de Sainte Gertrude d'Helfta: situation, acteurs et mise en scène de la divina pietas* (Turnhout: Brepols/Abbaye de Bellefontaine, 1997); Ella L. Johnson, *This is My Body: Eucharistic Theology and Anthropology in the Writings of Gertrude the Great of Helfta*, CS 280 (Collegeville, MN: Cistercian Publications, 2020). For the relationship of chant to visions in the Helfta literature, see Leclercq, "Liturgy and Mental Prayer," 295–300; and Margot Schmidt,"Mechtilde de Hackeborn," DSAM 10:873–77. Bruce Holsinger points out that the nuns furnished even the melodies they sang with visionary significance (*Music, Body*, 245–46). For more general discussions of the relationship of chant to visionary experience, see Stephanus Hilpisch, "Chorgebet und Frömmigkeit im Spätmittelalter," in *Heilige Überlieferung: Ausschnitte aus der Geschichte des Mönchtums und des heiligen Kultes*, ed. Odo Casel (Münster: Aschendorff, 1938), 263–84; Peter Dinzelbacher, "Die Offenbarungen der hl. Elisabeth von Schönau: Bildwelt, Erlebnisweise und Zeittypisches," *Studien und Mittelungen zur Geschichte des Benediktiner-Orderns* 97 (1985): 462–82; Jeffrey Hamburger, "Art, Enclosure, and the Pastoral Care of Nuns," in *The Visual and the Visionary: Art and Female Spirituality in Late Medieval Germany* (New York: Zone Books, 1992), 80–81.

[5] *Liber* 1.12 (38).

that came to her on the feast of All Saints, in which she beheld a multitude of saints assembled in the monastery's chapel, it was as if God the Father were a powerful *paterfamilias* who gathered into one great banquet all his chosen companions in a festival of praise.[6] The souls in purgatory, frequently on the women's minds, also appeared before their eyes during the liturgy. Ensconced in their choir stalls, the nuns were thus not remote from a larger liturgical community, and the monastery's chapel was far more crowded than might be supposed.

Public common worship was the arena in which the nuns vividly experienced, celebrated, and solidified the bonds linking all the living and the dead, with the exception of those in hell. Theirs was a liturgical sensibility buoyed by confidence in human beings' capacity to provide mutual assistance across death's porous divide. Liturgical observances were flush with opportunities for the sisters to participate in lessening the penalties of purgatory, to facilitate the washing down of God's grace over all the living, and even to augment the joy of the saints themselves.[7] In a variety of ways, therefore, the Helfta literature attests to a generous and coherent sense of liturgical community. This was a community characterized by an almost continual offering of praise to God and by the busy productivity associated with joining Christ in the work of salvation. It was one in which members cultivated the sharing with one another of the spiritual benefits associated with any one group or individual.

The liturgy permeated virtually the whole of the nuns' life.[8] The annual cycles of feasts and seasons, together with the

[6] *Le Héraut* 4.55.2 (SCh 225:454–56).

[7] See, for example, *Le Héraut* 3.18.6 (SCh 143:86). On the purgatorial piety of the nuns, see chap. 7, and on their sense of community with the saints, see chap. 8.

[8] Leclercq has made this observation ("Liturgy and Mental Prayer"). See also Jean Leclercq, "Dévotion privée, piété populaire et liturgie au moyen âge," in *Études de pastorale liturgiques, Vanves, 26–28 janvier 1944*, Lex orandi, vol. 1 (Paris: Éditions du Cerf, 1944), 1948–83.

hours of the Office, provided the basic chronological structure by which the convent ordered and measured the days and the shifting seasons.[9] The authors of the *Herald* and the *Book of Special Grace* mark the day by the introit of the Mass (part of the opening of the celebration of the Eucharist),[10] and theirs was a dense liturgical calendar; the majority of days were feast days. Moreover, the impress of the liturgy is evident everywhere in verbal communication within the cloister.[11] When Christ and the nuns wanted to express their longing and love, or to rejoice in the satisfaction that they brought one another, they called upon the familiar and pliant language of the liturgy. For example, Christ on one occasion avowed his love for Gertrude using language associated with the legend of Saint Agnes, which the sisters may have known as an antiphon sung during the ceremony of a nun's consecration.[12] "Behold," Christ declared, "I see the person whom I have already desired; I hold that person for whom I have hoped; I am joined with her in spirit whom I loved on earth with complete devotion."[13]

The language of the liturgy enabled the nuns to eavesdrop on God's conversations with his friends, the saints and angels, and listen to tales the holy dead told them about earthly encounters and eternal bliss. It was the language of quiet conversation, of homey and erotic intimacy, of awesome reverence, and of joyous cosmic worship. It is not surprising that the

[9] See for example, *Le Héraut* 2.6.2; 2.9.1; 2.23.5 (SCh 139:256–58, 268, 334).

[10] Savage, "Music," 44, makes this point.

[11] See Leclercq, "Liturgy and Mental Prayer," 4, for this observation.

[12] *Le Héraut* (SCh 331:304, n. 14a; 305, n. 1).

[13] *Le Héraut Missa* 14.3–5 (SCh 331:305). As Doyère notes (SCh 331:305, n. 1), the ascription of this language to Christ is noteworthy not least because it attributes to Christ a yearning for union with the soul that parallels the soul's own desire for Christ. On Christ's craving mutuality, see Gertrud Jaron Lewis, "God and the Human Being in the Writings of Gertrude of Helfta," *Vox Benedictina* 8, no. 2 (1991): 303. For the mutuality of desire between Gertrude and Christ, see Colleen McDannel and Bernhard Lang, *Heaven: A History* (New Haven: Yale University Press, 1988), 102–3.

liturgy helped to organize the sisters' thought and provided a governing framework for the convent's literary creations. The *Spiritual Exercises*, the only surviving composition of which Gertrude appears to have been sole author, is saturated with liturgical language, and its basic organization depends on liturgical ritual.[14] The depth and breadth of the liturgy's impress on the form and content of the *Book of Special Grace* and the *Herald* are conspicuous.[15] Cyprian Vagaggini has noticed that when Gertrude quotes verses from Scripture, she tends to quote their liturgically adapted form—not the Vulgate wording.[16]

Just as the liturgy colored the larger life of the cloister, so too a nun's more obviously personal piety came with her when she entered into communal public worship and informed her experience of it, as Jean Leclercq argued over half a century ago and as Jeffrey Hamburger more recently observed regarding Gertrude.[17] The *Herald* describes a vision of Christ's side

[14] The first four of Gertrude's *Spiritual Exercises* draw liberally from the liturgies for baptism, clothing, consecration, and profession, and the final three exercises have the Office as their background. Gertrud Jaron Lewis and Jack Lewis, introduction to *Gertrud the Great of Helfta: Spiritual Exercises*, ed. and intro. Gertrude Jaron Lewis and Jack Lewis, CF 49 (Kalamazoo, MI: Cistercian Publications, 1989), 11. See in addition Columba Hart, Introduction to *The Exercises of Saint Gertrude*, trans. a Benedictine nun of Regina Laudis [Columba Hart] (Westminster, MD: The Newman Press, 1956).

[15] Pierre Doyère, "Gertrude d'Helfta," DSAM 6:334; Pierre Doyère, introduction to *Le Héraut* (SCh 139:25–30); Jean Leclercq, "Exercices spirituels," DSAM 4:1907–8; Bernard McGinn, *The Flowering of Mysticism: Men and Women in the New Mysticism—1200–1350*, vol. 3 of *The Presence of God: A History of Western Mysticism* (New York: Crossroad, 1998), 273; Lewis and Lewis, introduction to *Spiritual Exercises*, esp. 11–12; Hart, introduction to *The Exercises*; Jacques Hourlier and Albert Schmitt, introduction to *Les Exercices*, ed. and trans. Jacques Hourlier and Albert Schmitt, in *Gertrude d'Helfta: Oeuvres spirituelles*, SCh 127 (Paris: Éditions du Cerf, 1967); Vagaggini, *Theological Dimensions*, esp. 742 and 794–96.

[16] Vagaggini, *Theological Dimensions*, 742.

[17] Leclercq, "Liturgy and Mental Prayer"; Jeffrey Hamburger, "The Visual and the Visionary: The Image in Late Medieval Monastic Devotions," in *The Visual and the Visionary: Art and Female Spirituality in Late Medieval Germany* (New York: Zone Books, 1992). Vagaggini, *Theological Dimensions*, has high-

pierced by an arrow of light, a vision that appeared to Gertrude in the chapel as one element in an extended process of supplication, desire, and fulfillment.[18] A few days earlier, Gertrude had asked someone to pray before a crucifix that Gertrude's heart be wounded with the arrow of God's love. Gertrude subsequently received the wound of God's love. We know the experience took place after Gertrude had attended Mass; Mass may have stimulated it. The chapter in which Gertrude describes this interrelated series of events concludes with her admission that she had not been sufficiently grateful for the wound, and she explained that since she had profited little from this and other gifts from God, she felt that she must write about them for the benefit of others. As the *Herald* tells it, God's condescension to her drove her participation in the whole of the literary venture.

Although Christ's merciful gifts were unmerited, he did demand something in return: Gertrude was constrained to share her gifts with others. Her role in the making of the *Herald* was crucial to her endeavor to do so. The brief chapter charting Gertrude's wounding and her response to this gift and others is, therefore, about much more than the satisfaction of one woman's wish. It indicates that multiple discrete expressions of piety—a conversation between sisters, the prayer of a fellow nun, as well as other communal spiritual practices (in this case, the creation of the *Herald*)—were tightly interwoven with the routine of corporate worship. There were easy congress and continuity in the religiosity that thrived inside and outside the confines of the liturgy.

---

lighted the intimate connection between public (liturgical) prayer and Gertrude's private prayer as described in the *Herald*. For a similar assessment of Mechtild's spirituality, see Alberta Dieker, "Mechtild of Hackeborn: Song of Love," in *Medieval Women Monastics: Wisdom's Wellsprings*, ed. Miriam Schmitt and Linda Kulzer (Collegeville, MN: Liturgical Press, 1996), 240.

[18] *Le Héraut* 2.5.2 (SCh 139:248–50). For a discussion, see chap. 2.

However permeable the boundary between the spirituality of corporate religious worship and that which was alive outside the context of the liturgy, there seems to have been something about the liturgy that encouraged intellectual curiosity and creativity, focused reflection on the self, induced vision, and provided a spur to ecstasy.[19] Gertrude herself locates Mass, the elevation of the Host, and the reception of communion as those occasions on which she received extraordinary gifts from God, including his visible presence and union with him. After Mechtild received communion, Christ pressed her heart to his heart so that they became one, and about Gertrude we read,

> When she approached and had received the body of Christ, she recognized that her soul was shining like crystal, bright with sparkling splendor, and that the divinity of Christ that she received in herself shone through the crystal like gold miraculously enclosed.[20]

[19] According to Felix Vernet, few works of mysticism "are more overtly liturgical" than is the Helfta literature (*Medieval Spirituality* [London: Sands, 1930], 220–23, 270). Vagaggini (*Theological Dimensions*, 777) has examined the way Gertrude's mysticism and her liturgical observances influenced each other. Ann Marie Caron has shown that Mechtild's visions are structured according to the cycle of the liturgical year, and she has argued that they should be understood as "visionary commentaries" on the "mystical meaning" of the cycle: "Taste and See the Goodness of the Lord: Mechthild of Hackeborn," in *Hidden Springs: Cistercian Monastic Women*, CS 113 (Kalamazoo, MI: Cistercian Publications, 1995), 512–13. Sabine Spitzlei identifies Gertrude and Mechtild as "liturgical mystics" (*Erfahrungsraum Herz: Zur Mystik des Zisterzienserinnenklosters Helfta im 13 Jahrhundert* [Stuttgart-Bad Cannstatt: Frommann-Holzboog Verlag, 1991], 77); McGinn, *Flowering of Mysticism*, 270, and Hamburger, "Art, Enclosure," 493, n. 221, are in a long line of scholars to have noted the important place of the liturgy in the visionary spirituality ascribed to Mechtild and to Gertrude. For visionary experiences outside of liturgical contexts that are as tender, intimate, and dramatic as any that occur during Mass or Office, see for example *Le Héraut* 2.7.1; 3.45.3; 3.45.2 (SCh 139:260; SCh 143:204–6, 202–4); *Liber* 3.10; 2.26; 3.31 (209–10, 168–71, 235–36).

[20] *Le Héraut* 3.37.1 (SCh 143:180). For the importance to Gertrude's spirituality of the elevation of the host, see Vagaggini, *Theological Dimensions*, 774. For the elevation more generally, see Charles Caspers, "The Western Church

Visions that came during liturgy often included an explosion of synesthetic phenomena, as when during the *Kyrie eleison* Gertrude's guardian angel flew her in his arms to God the Father, and the gems that adorned her dress began to vibrate, producing a delicious melody in God's praise.[21] These visions are awash in images that mingled the domestic and regal with the sensual and the sensible: trees sprouted hearts and hung heavy with soul-satisfying fruit; saints clad in stately robes and jewel-encrusted crowns drank Christ's blood through straws that protruded from a golden chalice held in the hands of a middle-aged nun; Christ's wounds were like blossoming roses whose thorns pricked the soul with love.[22] Objects associated

---

during the Late Middle Ages: *Augenkommunion* or Popular Mysticism," in *Bread of Heaven: Customs and Practices Surrounding Holy Communion*, ed. Charles Caspers, et al. (Kampen: Kok Pharos Publishing House, 1995), 83–97; and Richard Kieckhefer, "Major Currents in Late Medieval Devotion," in *Christian Spirituality: High Middle Ages and Reformation*, ed. Jill Raitt in collaboration with Bernard McGinn and John Meyendorff (New York: Crossroad, 1989), 97.

[21] *Le Héraut* 3.23 (SCh 143:116). The *Kyrie eleison* ("Lord have mercy") is the first of the choral chants of the Ordinary of the Mass (the part of the Mass that is fixed). For the unity of the senses associated with synesthesia and for the role of synesthesia in religious literature, see David Chidester, *Word and Light: Seeing, Hearing, and Religious Discourse* (Chicago: University of Illinois Press, 1992). As Michael Anthony Abril has observed about the Helfta liturgical piety, "everything within the created realm is united in fulfilling their obligation to praise the creator" ("Gertrude of Helfta's Liturgical-Mystical Union," CSQ 43, no. 1 [2008], 91).

[22] The word *straw*—*fistula*—in this context refers to the straws that were sometimes used to receive consecrated wine at communion (Margaret Winkworth, *Gertrude of Helfta: The Herald of Divine Love*, trans. Margaret Winkworth [New York: Paulist Press, 1993], 248, n. 50; Clemons, "Relationship," 544–55). The straw was employed as a protective measure, to prevent the wine from spilling. For a brief discussion and a photograph, see Elizabeth Parker McLachlan, "Liturgical Vessels and Implements," in *The Liturgy of the Medieval Church*, ed. Thomas J. Heffernan and E. Ann Matter (Kalamazoo, MI: Medieval Institute Publications, 2005), 336–67. As Holsinger has observed, the word *fistula* (straw) is ambiguous (*Music, Body*, 398, n. 161); the nuns sometimes used the word *fistula* to mean a musical instrument, a "celestial pipe" (*Music, Body*, 247, 398, n. 161).

with corporate worship also sparked visions and became integrated into their content. One Sunday, Gertrude was in her choir stall when, gazing at a painted image of Christ in a book, she saw a ray of light like an arrow entering and withdrawing from the wound in Christ's side.[23] The words the nuns heard or chanted during liturgical observances also triggered visions. As the sisters processed to chapel singing the responsory *Vidi Dominum facie ad faciem*, the Lord showed his face to Gertrude.[24] When Mechtild sang the verse *Ora pro populo*, Mary got up from her throne, genuflected, and prayed for the congregation; then as the sisters mentioned each choir of saints, they did as Mary had done, offering on bended knee a prayer to Christ on behalf of the community.[25]

Such revelations were sometimes vivid visual manifestations of the nuns' verbal declamations of devotion, and they illustrated (and confirmed)[26] the efficacy of communal song, as when Gertrude saw flames shoot from the wounds of a crucifix held high in the chapel as the nuns' singing moved Christ to demonstrate his uncontrollable love for the Father.[27] To the holiest sisters—as the *Herald* and the *Book of Special Grace* relate—the language of the liturgy was an object of limitless fascination and a regular source of thought about the saints,

[23] *Le Héraut* 2.5.2 (SCh 139:248–50). For a discussion of this event, see chap. 2. Hamburger, "The Visual and the Visionary," 125–27, comments on this passage to draw attention to the way nuns harnessed art to foster visionary experience. For the Helfta nuns' use of hand-held books during liturgical observances, see Holsinger, *Music, Body*, 251. For a general discussion of the thirteenth-century monastic use of art or devotional objects seen or handled in private and in communal settings to induce and focus visionary experience, see Hamburger, "The Visual and the Visionary," 131.

[24] *Le Héraut* 2.21.1 (SCh 143:322).

[25] *Liber* 1.31 (105–6).

[26] See Bynum ("Women Mystics in the Thirteenth Century," 218) on the nuns' assuredness regarding the power and utility of the monastic practices in which they engaged.

[27] See for example *Le Héraut* 3.49.2 (SCh 143:216).

the self, and even the institutional history of religious orders and their place in salvation history. Thus, for example, we read that, on the feast of Saint Bernard, Mechtild reflected on the words *In medio Ecclesia*, and Christ instructed her in the many salutary contributions of Benedictine monasticism.[28]

The Helfta literature suggests that the nuns were quick to embellish liturgical celebrations with questions peculiar to each and to delve into details of any observance that especially intrigued them. When Mechtild heard a priest recite the collect *Infirmitatem nostram respice, quaesumus* and wished to understand it more fully, Christ obliged her, pausing to tease out the meaning of each word and fashioning something like a gloss that might have been lifted from a written document or fitted into one.[29] Mechtild sometimes interpreted her visions as glosses on the liturgy; that is, the direct significance of the vision itself was, at least in part, the laying bare of the meaning of words[30] that might otherwise remain obscure to her and to her sisters, and to which Christ urged her to pay attention.[31] Thus texts heard and declaimed precipitated visions, which sometimes interpreted texts. And so liturgical observance and the visions to which it gave rise offered individual nuns the opportunity for intellectual productivity, perhaps paralleling,

[28] *Liber* 1.28 (97–98). Mechtild's and Gertrude's ruminations on a specific word or series of words routinely ushered in appearances of Christ or compelled the attention of the saints, who provided responses to their questioning thoughts.

[29] *Liber* 1.20 (75–76). And see for example *Liber* 1.1; 2.2 (8, 138–39), and *Le Héraut* 4.27.4 (SCh 255:264–66), an extended gloss on the Alleluia of the Easter Mass. The saints explained the meaning of verses the nuns sang in Office: *Liber* 1.32 (110–11). For the discussion of chants as "vehicles of gnosis," which seems analogous to what I refer to as "glosses," see Savage, "Music," 27, n. 62; see too, for example, Savage, "Music," 41–42.

[30] See for example *Liber* 4.1 (258).

[31] *Liber* 1.16 (48).

supplementing, or fueling the work a contemporary monastic reader might associate with the scriptorium.[32]

Individual responsories might become charged with meaning for the women's own sense of self: the nuns were sure that through the liturgy Christ was speaking not just directly to them but often directly about them. For example, Gertrude assigned to herself words that God spoke to Abraham in the responsory of the Matins service for *Esto mihi*: "Blessing I will bless you," and "and to you and to your seed I shall give these lands,"[33] a bold assimilation of self to Abraham, who was for her a leader of the Christian people. "With these words," Gertrude remarked to Christ, "you touched your venerable hand to your most blessed breast, promising me the land of your unrestrained generosity."[34] The physical objects Mechtild and Gertrude saw and touched, the words they chanted and to which they listened, seeped into their imagination. They occasioned and became the stuff of visions, suffusing communal song, reception, or gospel reading with tangled layers of meaning, charging everyday routine with sometimes exalted, sometimes elaborate, and often hefty intellectual meaning that was not without deeply personal significance. Gertrude and Mechtild emerge as lively and engaged participants in the liturgy, sensitive to the intricacy of the individual components that comprised each observance. As the literature relates, prescribed communal observances were vibrantly

[32] Holsinger has noticed that the "glosses" that the nuns' visions provided were not culled from authoritative texts; the women themselves elaborated them (*Music, Body*, 243). He has argued that whereas women's liturgical practice has often been seen as "inherently conservative," the Helfta mysticism was exceptional for the frequency with which it transformed the structure, practice, and meaning of the liturgy (242). As Clark has observed, "It is clear that the liturgical setting does not determine spiritual experience," and that the women responded creatively to the liturgical context (Anne L. Clark, "An Uneasy Triangle: Jesus, Mary, and Gertrude of Helfta," *Maria: A Journal of Marian Studies* 1 [August 2000]: 55).

[33] *Le Héraut* 2.8.1 (SCh 139:262). Savage makes this observation ("Music," 29).

[34] *Le Héraut* 2.8.1 (SCh 139:262).

supple: both Mechtild and Gertrude were prepared to seek and find in Mass and Office responses to shifting needs and to experience the quickening of intellectual curiosities and of desires as well as their satisfaction.

The Helfta nuns did not discount the practical difficulties of reconciling meditative or mystical delights with the obligation to hold fast to the behavior appropriate to liturgical observances.[35] They certainly did not perceive the extravagant spiritual proclivities of an individual sister and her commitment to rigorous observance of common worship as being in opposition; scholars such as Hilda Graef and Cyprian Vagaggini are right to assert that the literature of Helfta provides relatively little evidence of the visionary's encounters disrupting common religious observances.[36] The visionaries were sometimes aware that instructions Christ gave them might unsettle their fellow worshipers, however. When Christ taught Gertrude to pray with her arms extended in imitation of his passion, she rejoined that she would need to tuck herself into a corner to do so because the posture was not one customarily assumed.[37] Mechtild made astonishing gestures in choir, lifting up and extending her arms, ignorant of what she was doing or of her sisters' response; they sometimes tried to jostle her back to awareness.[38]

Moreover, the nuns knew that an active inner life might draw a sister's concentration from communal worship.[39] They

[35] *Le Héraut* 3.44.1–2 (SCh 143:198–202).

[36] Vagaggini, *Theological Dimensions*, 777–78; Graef, "Gertrude the Great"; and see too Marie-Geneviève Guillous, "La louange à l'école de sainte Gertrude," *Collectanea* 53 (1991): 175. For strategies late medieval nuns used to contend with the potential of mystical experience to disturb communal life as well as with the presence more generally of spiritual virtuosi among them, see Richard Kieckhefer, "Mystical Communities in the Late Medieval West," Medieval Academy Plenary Address, International Medieval Conference, Leeds, 2007.

[37] *Le Héraut* 4.16.4 (SCh 255:180).

[38] *Liber* 5.30 (366).

[39] For example, *Liber* 2.4 (140–41).

were conscious that spiritual ardor might drain a nun of the strength necessary to keep the rigorous schedule of Mass, Office, and supplemental liturgical observances, and that physical fortitude was essential to meet the taxing demands that chant exacted on the body.[40] Participation in the liturgy might itself deplete the visionaries: once, after Gertrude experienced a vision stimulated by the liturgy, she went to bed.[41] The visionaries did not always manage to balance the pull of revelation and ecstasy with the maintenance of public communal worship. On one occasion, the sisters were in choir when the Lord rushed from heaven with arms extended to embrace Mechtild, who became so wholly absorbed in God that members of the congregation were obliged to carry her as if lifeless from her stall.[42]

Revelations also readied their recipient for her liturgical labors and shook her free of thoughts that vied with liturgical services for her attention. When during Vespers Mechtild's clothes were sprinkled with dust—a sign of preoccupation—Mary appeared and with her hand wiped away the dust.[43] The *Book of Special Grace* thus indicates that the content of the vision itself swept away the remnants of what prevented its recipient from fully engaging in the Office, not that the vision itself was a source of Mechtild's distraction. In addition, revelations sometimes supported the visionary when her attention was

[40] See for example *Le Héraut* 3.54.1; 3.59.1–2 (SCh 143:232–34, 242–44). For examples of the physicality of Mechtild's liturgical practice, see *Liber* 3.7; 5.30 (205, 366). For exhaustion associated with spiritual exercises, see, for example, *Liber* 2.30 (175–76). For the toll their common devotions took on the nuns' bodies, see Dolan, *St. Gertrude*, 134.

[41] *Le Héraut* 5.27.8 (SCh 331:220).

[42] *Liber* 2.4 (140–41).

[43] *Liber* 1.13 (42–43). For dust as image of sin in the *Book of Special Grace*, see Rosalynn Jean Voaden, "Articulating Ecstasy: Image and Allegory in *The Booke of Gostlye Grace* of Mechtild of Hackeborn," PhD diss., University of Victoria, 1990, 63.

divided.[44] During Mass, Gertrude was ravished into God and became unaware of whether her sisters in choir were standing or sitting. She lost consciousness of her own actions as well, until someone approached her to say that her behavior was inappropriate. For the remainder of the service, she was able to attend to her exterior deportment while continuing to be rapt into God.[45]

The Helfta literature documents the markedly practical assistance that Christ at times lent the women when their minds wandered from the business of the Office during canonical hours as well as when fatigue or weakness overwhelmed them.[46] When Gertrude fixed her attention on the baby Jesus at each note she chanted in Office, she found she could sing more carefully.[47] As the time for communion approached on the feast of All Saints, Gertrude worried because she had asked no one to help her; for a long time, she had been unable to walk without assistance. Christ brushed away her concerns as he came to her side. Bracing her with the "arm" [*ulna*] of divine grace, he ensured that she was able to receive communion.[48] Exhausted from singing on one occasion, Mechtild felt that God fortified her, so that she drew each breath from the heart of God, and it was as though it was no longer by her own strength but through God's that she was singing.[49] A passage from the *Book of Special Grace* illustrates both that Mechtild's intense commerce with God tired her, compromising her

[44] Mary Jeremy Finnegan observes that, during Office, Gertrude was able to "remain in a state of contemplation while conforming to the actions of the community" (*The Women of Helfta: Scholars and Mystics* [Athens: University of Georgia Press, 1991], 107); and Graef, "Gertrude the Great," 173, remarks that Gertrude received the grace to follow the Office while in ecstasy.

[45] *Le Héraut* 4.15.7 (SCh 255:172–74).

[46] See for example *Liber* 2.6 (141–42).

[47] *Le Héraut* 2.16.2 (SCh 139:290–92).

[48] *Le Héraut* 4.55.6 (SCh 255:460). For Gertrude's concern about her waning physical strength, see for example *Le Héraut* 4.34.1 (SCh 255:284).

[49] *Liber* 3.7 (205).

capacity to join in the Office, and that Christ's presence provided her with the support she needed to assume her liturgical duties. It also suggests that coincidence of this sort formed a common pattern in Mechtild's routine:[50]

> Many times it happened to her that when at Matins she was fully with God in great fruition and sweetness—so that she seemed to have squandered all strength and was unable to read her lesson—the Lord said to her, "Come and read, for I will help you." And beginning the reading in this way, she completed it with great constancy.[51]

Elsewhere as Mechtild read the Gospel during Matins, the Lord so filled her with the sweetness of his grace that she fainted and had to be carried out of the choir to bed. Resting there, she asked Christ to wake her at the appropriate time; at Prime she beheld standing before her a beautiful young man, whose presence charged her with energy.[52]

The nuns regarded a finely focused concentration on the self in relation to God as sometimes compromising one's ability to join in liturgical practices conceived of as beneficial to others. They developed no elaborate or formal rationale reconciling individual religious experience and communal worship. The *Herald* and the *Book of Special Grace* provide evidence of the relative ease with which the nuns reconciled a bustling interior life with the demands of corporate worship. For much of her adult life, Mechtild was the convent's chantress, in charge of liturgical celebration and responsible for leading the nuns in the Divine Office as well as teaching the novices. She seems to have been more fatigued in chapel than Gertrude, perhaps

[50] For this observation, see Finnegan, *Women of Helfta*, 35.

[51] *Liber* 2.5 (141).

[52] *Liber* 2.6 (141–42). For Christ's energizing presence in Gertrude's life, see *Le Héraut* 2.13.1 (SCh 139:282).

because of the demands of her role.[53] Yet there is no indication that her visionary life undermined her execution of her responsibilities.

In the nuns' own depiction of their daily liturgical life, they claimed to have worked out the challenges some of them brought to communal religious observances. Even as the Helfta literature acknowledges disruptions to communal observances that visions, ecstasies, and idiosyncratic physical manifestations of piety might bring about, it gives no indication that Mechtild's and Gertrude's sisters or their abbess regarded such disruptions as irksome. When disruptions did occur, the literature urged its cloistered readers to interpret them not as signs of laxity in observance but as testimonies to holiness: the picture of Mechtild slipping from her liturgical duties and carried as if dead from choir evokes Mary's assumption as related in a vision that came to Mechtild, with the *Book of Special Grace* describing both women as wholly absorbed in God.[54]

It is interesting that Mechtild's swoon both precipitated her removal from communal worship with her sisters and appeared to involve her sisters in her experience. The labor we may ascribe to the sisters (the text says simply that Mechtild was carried out of the choir [*a choro portaretur*][55] but does not specify who carried her) hints at one way in which the women in Mechtild's community may have been integrated into the

[53] As Savage has observed, Gertrude is never described as having been thus physically overwhelmed in choir ("Music," 51). Mechtild's responsibilities as chantress may have been more onerous and so more enervating to her than participation in choir was to Gertrude.

[54] *Liber* 1.26; 2.4 (90, 140). Moreover, her sisters compare her entering into contemplation and being inattentive to her surroundings with the behavior of Bernard of Clairvaux, as Voaden has noticed (*Liber* 5.30 [364]; Rosalynn Voaden, "Mechtild of Hackeborn," in *Medieval Holy Women in the Christian Tradition c. 1100–c. 1500*, ed. Alastair Minnis and Rosalynn Voaden [Turnhout, Belgium: Brepols, 2010], 438).

[55] *Liber* 2.4 (140), and see *Liber* 2.6 (141).

visionary's liturgical life.[56] The *Book of Special Grace*, it is worth observing, does not elaborate on whether her sisters perceived assisting the visionary as an opportunity for grace, as a distraction from their liturgical commitments, as neither, or as both. It is clear that private, intimate encounters with Christ, Mary, and the saints sometimes hindered Gertrude and Mechtild from playing an active role in communal worship; frequently, however, as Vagaggini observed, they provided support that furthered the commitments associated with Mass and Office.[57] They may have integrated the sisters into the visionaries' piety by requiring their involvement in the bodily responses that visions sometimes brought on.

Moreover, non-visionary women were not immune from the toll liturgical participation took, and the nuns expressed solidarity with one another in their shared and arduous duties. When Mechtild prayed for a sister suffering under the combined burden of her unnamed office and choir, Christ appeared to Mechtild with that sister before him, saying, "Whoever sings for my sake in life will sing even more sweetly in heaven everlastingly."[58] For all the ebullient expressions of love and cries of longing that color the *Book of Special Grace* and the *Herald*, certain notes of restraint, in the very midst of extravagant visions, sounded the call for spiritual decorum and sobriety in keeping with the need to uphold common religious observances and basic practices. As historians and theologians have long noted, the Helfta literature aggressively supports and extols the everyday routines of monastic life.[59] The *Book of*

[56] And see *Liber* 2.6 (241–42). I wish to thank Anne Clark for focusing my attention on the sisters' involvement in Mechtild's mystical life in this context.

[57] Vagaggini, *Theological Dimensions*, 77.

[58] *Liber* 1.35 (117).

[59] The clearest and most compelling argument is Bynum, "Women Mystics in the Thirteenth Century." Wilhelm Preger thinks that Gertrude was animated by concerns to uphold monastic Rule and custom but that Christ weaned her from these preoccupations and encouraged her to fall back on her direct (that is, visionary and ecstatic) relationship with him alone (*Geschichte der deutschen Mystik bis zum Tode Meister Eckharts* [Leipzig: Dörffling und Franke, 1874],

Special Grace and the *Herald* are sanguine about reconciling fervent individual piety with conformity to exacting communal standards of behavior. This seems to have been the case at least in part because Mechtild and Gertrude were not alone in sometimes feeling overcome during liturgical obligations and because their sisters themselves detected that advantage flowed both to individuals and to the larger community in consequence of the visionaries' devotion.

The Inward Focus and the Liturgy

For the visionaries, chanting with and to the saints in liturgy moved seamlessly to talking with them. The revelations and ecstasies that came to Gertrude and Mechtild while they were in chapel or chapter involved them in casual encounters and emotionally charged meetings with Christ and his mother as well as the saints and angels. Visionary time flowed differently. Complex discussions and consequential exchanges sometimes occurred within discrete assignations and lingered over a single antiphon, sequence, or alleluia; they sometimes took place over the course of several meetings, extending through many days and a number of liturgical events.

The authors do not hint that heaven's inhabitants are cocooned by the joy of eternity in serene indifference to the little victories, trials, and requests of the living, or their queries, anxieties, and devotions.[60] Bound by an oath of fealty to their Lord, they felt affection for those whom he loved,[61] and, like him, the saints were easily moved by and sensitive to the sisters' desires and requests. During her conversations with John the Evangelist at Matins on his feast day, Gertrude asked

127–29). This interpretation finds little support in the Helfta writings, which insist not that Christ does not demand the women's adherence to monastic observance but that he is exceedingly generous when confronted with lapses in observance.

[60] *Liber* 1.25 (88); *Le Héraut* 4.4.4 (SCh 255:64–65).

[61] *Le Héraut* 3.73.6 (SCh 143:302).

questions about his earthly life and the content of his writings. John responded by relating his experience of the Last Supper, explaining his mission, and divulging aspects of his experience about which he had until then kept silent.[62] At Matins on Saint Benedict's feast day, Gertrude asked Benedict what reward he had received for the way in which he died; he informed her that because he had breathed his last while at prayer, his breath—more delicious than that of all the other saints—charmed heaven's inhabitants with its sweetness.[63] When, singing with her sisters on the feast of Saint Elisabeth of Hungary, Gertrude worried that her attention to God diminished the praise that counted as Elisabeth's own, Elisabeth assured Gertrude that she accepted the nun's song with infinite gratitude.[64]

The nuns believed that to enter into fellowship with the saints was to approximate the closeness with Christ that belonged to Christ's heavenly friends. Thus we read, for example, that during Matins, Gertrude fixed her thoughts on God with more than customary ardor, and John appeared to her and led her before Christ, then placed her on the Lord's right side, where his open wound lay—the wound that provided her with access to Christ's heart, source of all sweetness and gateway to divinity.[65] John placed himself on Christ's left side, mindful that Gertrude could not penetrate so easily as he could—now of one body with Christ—to the inside of Christ's body. John subsequently granted Gertrude a vision in which she saw, enclosed within Christ's heart, "the immense ocean of the divinity," where John swam with delight and freedom.[66] Surely this vision was something like a pledge and a beckoning toward similar heavenly delights that Gertrude hoped would one day be her own.

[62] *Le Héraut* 4.4.4 (SCh 255:64–66).
[63] *Le Héraut* 4.11.4 (SCh 255:130).
[64] *Le Héraut* 4.56 (SCh 255:462).
[65] *Le Héraut* 4.4.3–4 (SCh 255:62–66).
[66] *Le Héraut* 4.4.58–9 (SCh 255:66).

Through accumulated engagements such as these, Mechtild's and Gertrude's relationships with Mary and with a few of the saints—including John the Evangelist, John the Baptist, and Catherine of Alexandria—came to form distinctive patterns and to acquire the patina of a shared history.[67] Christ fostered the women's relationships with the saints, talking with the nuns about the saints' exemplary lives, holy writings, and celestial joys as well as the women's devotion to them. During Mass on the feast of Saint Mary Magdalene, Christ recounted to Mechtild the laudable emotions the Magdalene directed toward him.[68] During Mass on Gregory's feast day, Christ and Gertrude spoke about Gregory's writings, and about the honor he received from his fellow saints because his literary labors had excited others to devotion.[69] On Bernard's feast day, Christ related to Mechtild the glory that now belonged to Bernard, who because he was so filled with love of God had enkindled this love in others.[70]

During other liturgical observances, Christ himself showered Mechtild and Gertrude with his attentions. In such instances, the visionaries fixed their sight on God, who showed them who *they* were and ought to be. When she received Christ in communion, Mechtild heard him say, "I am in you and you are in me, and I will not leave you for eternity."[71] Gertrude relates that on occasion Christ kissed her ten times or more as she chanted a single psalm.[72] Gertrude's and Mechtild's visions witness to the mutuality of emotion that bound each woman with Christ, who repeatedly singled out each with a fierce proprietary love: "Your soul is mine," Christ made known to Mechtild in the middle of Mass.[73] Revelations received during

[67] See for example *Liber* 1.32 (111), and *Le Héraut* 4.42 (SCh 255:332–36).

[68] *Liber* 1.25 (86–87).

[69] *Le Héraut* 4.10.4 (SCh 255:124–26).

[70] *Liber* 1.28 (97–98).

[71] *Liber* 1.1 (10). And see *Liber* 2.24 (166).

[72] *Le Héraut* 2.21.4 (SCh 139:326).

[73] *Liber* 1.23 (82).

liturgy were characterized by the visionary's candid and potent preoccupation with herself in relation to God—cowering before God the Father, luxuriating in Christ's embrace, or comforted by his approbation. On the feast of Saint Matthew, Gertrude reclined on Christ's breast, and as the priest elevated the chalice, she determined that she had contributed little to the offering because she had suffered insufficiently for Christ; she then cast herself on God's mercy as she threw herself on the floor at his feet. Christ immediately lay on the ground by her side and soothed her, saying that without her, he could not live happily. In this moment, Gertrude knew Christ had selected her from among all souls, in heaven and on earth, as uniquely compelling his love.[74]

Visions such as those I have discussed display Mechtild's and Gertrude's steady fascination with their own internal state—with their feelings of remorse, shame, or gratitude. They were convinced that Christ, as well as Mary and the saints, spoke directly to them during the liturgy. They were sure that Christ was desirous of their presence in the liturgy and that he was attentive to their contributions to it: "Lord, what do you do when I pray or recite the psalms?" Mechtild asked Christ. "I listen," he replied.[75] Indeed, the visionaries routinely placed themselves virtually at the center of the liturgy's significance. A sense of the self as singular in the sight of God, singularly adored and singularly unworthy of such adoration, flourished in a corporate setting. In its very promotion of encounter with Christ and its bevy of social relationships with the saints, the liturgy sharpened a sense of self, offering the nuns opportunities to plumb with delicacy and deliberation their own varying inner lives and to wonder about the self in

[74] *Le Héraut* 3.5.1 (SCh 143:26). And see for example *Le Héraut* 3.21; 2.14 (SCh 143:112–14; SCh 139:286). Vagaggini, *Theological Dimensions*, 758, comments on the loving encounters with Christ that Gertrude experienced in a liturgical setting.

[75] *Liber* 3.16 (217).

relation to God and his heavenly friends.[76] Within this context, Mechtild and Gertrude reveled in the sense that they were special—in their peculiar needs and wants and devotions, different from those of others and worthy of their own (and God's) consideration—and they indulged in a relationship with Christ that they believed was, among his many relationships, precious, necessary, and vitalizing for *him*.

Although often stimulated by moments in the Office or Mass, revelations frequently cast members of the congregation outside the visionary's consideration and left her unaware that she was in the choir. Such revelations suggest both that Gertrude and Mechtild may sometimes have longed for distance between themselves and their sisters as well as for privacy, and that they found both in abundance in corporate worship, although neither the *Herald* nor the *Book of Special Grace* describes the individual nun as yearning to tear herself away from the routine rounds of common worship to sequester herself from her sisters so as better to search out God and savor him.[77] It may be that the nuns' intensely corporate life both created individuals' hunger to carve out a world apart from that of their sisters and provided them with numerous occasions to become skilled at obtaining it—that is, of attaining an

[76] The Helfta nuns were not, of course, unique in this regard, as literature on visionaries' establishing relationships with the saints in the monastic context of the liturgy has shown. Scholars such as Barbara Newman and Anne Clark, for example, have drawn attention to the way in which the twelfth-century Benedictine nun Elisabeth of Schönau seems to have drawn on the public communal experience of liturgy to cultivate relationships with the saints and to have mined the liturgy as a source of profoundly personal significance (Anne Clark, *Elisabeth of Schönau: A Twelfth-Century Visionary* [Philadelphia: University of Pennsylvania Press, 1992], 101–11; Barbara Newman, introduction to *Hildegard of Bingen: Scivias*, trans. Columba Hart and Jane Bishop [New York: Paulist Press, 1990], 46–47).

[77] Moved to the point of tears on account of the Good Friday reading, Gertrude expressed a craving for a semblance of privacy during corporate worship. This desire and her concern for discretion prompted her to hold back her tears (*Le Héraut* 4.26.5 [SCh 255:252]).

arena in which the self might enter into solitary reverie and ecstasy as well as into conversation with Christ and his holy friends and family.

Visions may sometimes have offered a welcome and delicious respite from the hubbub of communal life. They may have been a retreat from instances of tedium (which, however vibrant the life of the cloister, must have overcome sisters at least now and then), providing both entry into a larger, more expansive community, crowded with talkative and diverse companions, and moments of peace and insulation from others.[78] Their brushes with Christ, his friends, and his mother were usually winsome and welcoming, although at other times strained; over and over again (so the Helfta literature insists) God and the saints trained their reserves on moving Mechtild and Gertrude toward salvation. They encouraged both women's cultivation of private relationships with them during liturgical observances, and they abetted the visionaries' attention to their inner lives.

Self and Other in Liturgical Observances

Christ and the saints also, however, strove against the women's sometimes inward focus, and of their own accord the visionaries liberally incorporated their sisters into their thoughts and actions. When during a liturgical service Gertrude or Mechtild brought into their exchanges with God a forceful focus on the self—on their feelings of unworthiness before his majesty, their fears about the public exposure of their revelations, their anxieties about not having sufficiently praised him, Mary, or the saints—their heavenly interlocutors from time to time obliged the visionaries to expand the horizon of their concern, so that a reflection or revelation that began

[78] For nuns' manipulation of the liturgy to elevate their mood and lift themselves out of depression, see Anne Bagnall Yardley, *Performing Piety: Musical Culture in Medieval English Nunneries* (New York: Palgrave, 2006), 145.

with a starkly individualistic focus panned out to include other people. A movement from concentrated consideration of the self to a broader perspective including others is evident in one vision Gertrude received during Mass. She was stung with a feeling of unworthiness, so that she dared not look up at the elevation of the Host. Christ acknowledged her lowliness, but he did not permit her to remain in self-referential reflection, however accurate her self-assessment. He urged her to participate in the Mass rather than settle into her humility, insisting that she further the salvation of others by gazing at the elevated Host:

> When a skillful mother wishes something to be worked with silk or pearls, sometimes she places her little child in a higher place, so that the child can hold the thread or the pearl or help in another way. In this way, I have set you in an elevated place so that you take part in this Mass. If truly you apply your will to this task freely, however difficult the labor with which you are willing to serve, so that this oblation will have full effect—in accord with its dignity—in all Christians, those living as well as those dead, in this way you will have helped me in my work.[79]

Gertrude would have refused to raise her eyes to the Host, but Christ had other plans. He did not countenance the sinking into the self that would disassociate a woman from productive devotion that might help Christ in his work on behalf of all Christians.[80]

The revelations that came to Gertrude and Mechtild during Mass, Office, and chapter, and their ruminations on them, contain numerous incidental remarks that indicate that a keen sensitivity to the needs and desires of other individuals as well

[79] *Le Héraut* 3.6.1 (SCh 143:28).

[80] For the notion that viewing the consecrated Host with devotion integrated the viewer more fully into the community of the faithful, see Caspers, "Western Church," 90.

as to the well-being of the nuns as a community was an integral (if not always welcome) component of their liturgical life. They underscored the visionary's attention to the piety of her sisters and her respect for her superiors, as when the *Herald* relates that Gertrude noticed during chapter that, in the person of the prioress, the convent acknowledged its faults before the abbess and subsequently saw that Christ offered absolution,[81] or when during the Vigil of the Nativity Mechtild watched a flood of water (which, like honey, is a sign of divinity) come from Christ, seated on the abbess's throne, and perceived it to wash over each sister's face.[82]

Visions provide snapshots of the way liturgical language prompted the visionaries to reflect on the women with whom they worshiped and commit to prayer on their behalf. At the words *Quem vidi, qum amavi*, Christ came to Gertrude in memory of a person about whom she had often spoken and who was tormented with a desire to see God. Gertrude asked Christ when he would console that soul in such a way that she could sing the response with joy.[83] Visions also drew attention to the benefits to the visionary of her attentiveness to her sisters: on one occasion, Gertrude became aware of Christ's presence in chapter because of the devotion she observed in her fellow nuns.[84]

Visions also convey the visionaries' consciousness of God's gratification in their sympathy for their sisters. When at the introit of Christmas Gertrude held the delicate baby in her arms, she linked her reception of this gift to prayers she had offered before the feast for someone in trouble.[85] An awareness of God's delight in the small favors she performed to further her sisters' liturgical practices intruded into Gertrude's thought: during Mass on another occasion, Gertrude noticed

[81] *Le Héraut* 4.2.13 (SCh 255:42).

[82] *Liber* 1.5 (15).

[83] *Le Héraut* 4.54.3 (SCh 255:448).

[84] *Le Héraut* 4.2.8 (SCh 255:34).

[85] *Le Héraut* 2.16.2 (SCh 139:290–92).

that her soul had been adorned with a garment encrusted with precious stones because at Matins, although illness made her weak, she soldiered on to read a nocturne with another sister for a second time.[86] The nuns' revelations often indicated Christ's (or Mary's or the saints') approbation of the prayers the nuns recited together, and they sometimes contained his (or their) commentaries on such prayers. Thus, for instance, Mary appeared during Mass to Mechtild and conveyed the excellence of the prayer *Ave Maria*, explained the meaning of its words, and related the sweetness that she, Mary, received from this prayer.[87]

In a pattern we find again and again, Mechtild's and Gertrude's visions included prayers for others, and they routinely brought back to individual sisters the messages, pledges, and prayers they collected in the course of their visionary excursions. Thus, for example, when Mechtild prayed to Saint Catherine of Alexandria on behalf of a particular sister, Catherine urged the sister, through Mechtild, to recite an antiphon for the saint.[88] When Mechtild proffered the prayers of another nun to John the Evangelist, John instructed Mechtild to tell the sister, "I shall prepare a feast for all the saints out of all she has offered to me."[89] Mechtild's and Gertrude's revelations frequently concerned the whole of the community, living and dead: at Mass, Gertrude saw Mary sheltering those who had commended themselves to her protection under her mantle.[90] As she and her sisters were chanting, Gertrude offered the devotion of those reciting the canonical hours to

[86] *Le Héraut* 3.61.1 (SCh 143:246–48).

[87] *Liber* 1.42 (126–27). As McGinn has observed, Gertrude's and Mechtild's visions and ecstasies "take place in and for the community" (*Flowering of Mysticism*, 271).

[88] *Liber* 1.32 (111).

[89] *Liber* 1.6 (23).

[90] *Le Héraut* 4.48.43 (SCh 255:360–62). As Doyère points out, the nuns of Helfta may have been aware of visual and literary representations of the Virgin thus depicted, sometimes termed Mother of Mercy (*Le Héraut* [SCh 255:362, n. 1]).

Christ, who in turn presented these offerings to her sisters in the form of a flower for each woman,[91] through Gertrude's mediation, returning a gift to each of them in consequence of their devotion to him.

Visions that highlighted Gertrude's or Mechtild's intimacy with Christ in the liturgy sometimes simultaneously expressed a sense of service. When during the feast of All Saints Christ came to Mechtild and pressed his mouth to the mouth of her soul, his kisses were more than a mark of love, desire, or union. They granted Mechtild the power to praise and pray—and to preach.[92] In a Mass during the Easter octave Gertrude felt the Holy Spirit breathe on her and received the power to bind and loose, conferring on her a quasi-sacerdotal role that confirmed her responsibility to shepherd her sisters and others toward salvation as well as to serve as confessor.[93]

The Helfta literature thus insists that even while in the midst of spiritual adventures wrapping the visionary and Christ in familiarity, a concern for the welfare of others might enter into the visionary's reverie, becoming a central part of the encounter.[94] When Gertrude kissed the wound in Christ's side at each

[91] *Le Héraut* 4.23.3 (SCh 255:216–18).

[92] *Liber* 1.1 (9). On this passage, see Holsinger, *Music, Body*, 243.

[93] *Le Héraut* 4.32 (SCh 255:27–37).

[94] In a vision in which both Gertrude and Mary figure, and which took place during the Christmas liturgy's midnight Mass, Gertrude spied the baby on his Mother's lap and, taking him from Mary, brought him to her own breast. Caressing the infant, Gertrude recalled with contrition a sister for whom she had previously prayed, but, so she reflected, carelessly; she then prayed for sinners and those in purgatory as well as those otherwise troubled. Thus holding God in her arms, her mind turned nevertheless to consider the plight of others and to work, through prayer, on their behalf (*Le Héraut* 2.16.2 [SCh 139:190–92]). We see a movement from description of vision to its implication for all readers in the *Book of Special Grace*, in a section of the book that also offers directions for meditation to the reader. We learn that during Good Friday Vespers, Mechtild saw the Virgin hold her Son in her lap, beckon Mechtild to kiss his wounds, and instruct Mechtild to bury him in her heart; then Mechtild saw a silver sarcophagus with a gold lid, in which Christ was enclosed, and he promised her eternal life—and then he made the same

verse that she and her sisters intoned in chapel, Christ expressed how welcome these kisses were to him. The modern reader may be struck by the graphic nature of the image and miss what came next: Gertrude asked that Christ teach her a short prayer others might recite that would be equally as pleasing to him as her kisses.[95] Christ complied, impressing on her mind three brief verses that, if uttered "in honor of the five wounds and kissing devoutly the same rosy wounds of the Lord," would honor him as greatly as did her kisses.[96] As this example illustrates, the Helfta literature attests to the fluidity with which the visionaries sometimes moved between fierce attentiveness to Christ and purposeful attention to others. As the source of innovative meditation, this vision spoke to Gertrude's desire to help her sisters bring pleasure to Christ, and it valued the day-to-day practices in which all the sisters might engage.

From God's vantage point—as the *Herald* conveys—there was no clear divide between Gertrude's vision and the visualizing meditation Gertrude offers her sisters; if the point was to gratify God, they were analogous.[97] Thus, even as the *Herald*

---

promise to anyone for whom she had prayed. The narrator interrupts the description of the vision and, on the heels of Christ's offer, addresses the reader with a particular directive (echoing Mary's instruction of Mechtild), a directive conducive to her own productive meditation: if the reader wishes to dwell on the passion, the narrator says, she should recite Psalm 29 seven times every Friday and thank God for the bath of salvation that flowed from his wounds. Then Christ interjects to explain to Mechtild that each person who remembers his passion should do so as if he had borne his suffering just for her, shifting the focus from Mechtild onto the reader—each and every one! Thus, the description of this vision contains direct instructions to the intended reader, instructions that are both braided into this vision and central to it, and shrinking the differences between that reader and the visionary (*Liber* 1.18 [57–60]).

[95] *Le Héraut* 3.49.1 (SCh 143:216–18).

[96] *Le Héraut* 3.49.1 (SCh 143:218).

[97] Directions to visualization such as I describe above may have provided a platform from which the meditating nun might soar into visionary flight or enter into ecstasy. The line between vision and visualization is sometimes

does not shirk from documenting differences among the sisters—the Lord, "beautiful and delightful," placed his "sweet wounds" within *Gertrude's* immediate reach, and expressed to *her* the satisfaction he took in her ministrations—it refrained from making a rigid distinction between the anonymous sisters, the intended recipients of the meditation, and the holy woman at its center.[98] It bears witness to an ease in coupling and comparing the visionary forays of one respected sister with the meditative prayers of a collective of anonymous nuns. Emphasizing potential commonality among all the nuns, the *Herald* called attention to Gertrude's exemplary closeness with Christ, signaled her preoccupation with her sisters in a moment of striking intimacy with him, and offered fellow nuns a means to approximate the quality of her relationship with him.

---

a tenuous one. Mechtild receives wounds of love on her soul, and Christ tells her that anyone who sighs for his love in memory of the passion can receive like wounds (*Liber* 1.16 [49]). For what Hamburger calls the leveling of "distinctions between mystical, visionary, and visual experience" in the *Herald*, see Jeffrey F. Hamburger, "Seeing and Believing: The Suspicion of Sight and Authentication of Vision in Late Medieval Art and Devotion," in *Imagination und Wirklichkeit: zum Verhältnis von mentalen und realen Bildern in der Kunst der frühen Neuzeit*, ed. Klaus Krüger and Alessandro Nova (Mainz: Philipp von Zabern, 2000), 60. Richard Kieckhefer has argued that the Sister Books diminish the distinctive nature of the mystical experiences attributed to some among them so as to facilitate attention to similarities among all sisters in an effort to encourage mystical experience in the convent ("Mystical Communities," 6). On the mixing and matching of the experiences recorded in medieval literature of vision, dream, daydream, hallucination, and what Robert Easting calls "waking reality," see Easting, *Annotated Bibliographies of Old and Middle English Literature*, vol. 3, *Visions of the Other World in Middle English* (Cambridge: D. S. Brewer, 1997), 4. See in addition Mary Carruthers, *The Craft of Thought: Meditation, Rhetoric, and the Making of Image, 400–1200* (Cambridge: Cambridge University Press, 1998), 184; Barbara Newman, "What Did It Mean to Say 'I Saw'? The Clash between Theory and Practice in Medieval Visionary Culture," *Speculum* 80, no. 1 (2005): 16.

[98] *Le Héraut* 3.49.1 (SCh 143:216). Such visions seem to have brought enormous pleasure to their recipients, and it seems clear that they were sought after—at least in part—for this reason.

Although the first chapter of the *Herald* insists that Gertrude's many privileges were gratuitous gifts of the Holy Spirit,[99] it is clear that liturgical prayer, meditation, the reception of communion, and gazing at the elevated Host were among a company of regular monastic activities that readied Mechtild and Gertrude to experience union with God. Their visionary lives were the culmination of a consistent and arduous life of prayer and discipline.[100] The connection the Helfta literature makes between the flowering of visionary life and the rush of ecstasy, on the one hand, and, on the other, the devout observance of the day-to-day obligations associated with monastic life suggests that other nuns had reason to look forward to revelation and union as a fruit of their own monastic labors, if executed with care and fervor.

These works also contain a number of direct appeals to the reader that seem calculated to spur her too toward visionary experience, sometimes explicitly instructing the sisters to meditate on the revelations that came to the visionaries among them. In one instance, a narrator summoned readers to concentrate on the contents of a vision that came to Gertrude—in which an angel swept her out of her stall and into the presence of the Trinity—when they found themselves at precisely that moment in the Mass during which Gertrude received this vision.[101] Such calls to reflection and directions for visualization may have provided a platform from which the meditating nun could be lifted into visionary flight. Such visions in turn supported the objective communal observances as well as the individual devotion and mutual reliance that stimulated

[99] *Le Héraut* 1.1.3 (SCh 139:123–24).

[100] Theresa A. Halligan, introduction to *The Booke of Gostlye Grace of Mechtild of Hackeborn*, trans. Theresa A. Halligan (Toronto: Pontifical Institute of Mediaeval Studies, 1979), 39. See Newman's "What Did it Mean," esp. 5 and 14, for the connection between liturgical prayer and visionary experience.

[101] *Le Héraut* 3.23 (SCh 143:116–18).

them.[102] They did so largely by bringing to their recipient consciousness of Christ's love and invigorating her desire to fulfill his expectations of her.

The visions that came to the nuns in public communal worship sometimes highlighted a remarkable coincidence between sublime introversion and conscientious sociability. An account of Gertrude's experience at the elevation of the Host makes clear the fruitfulness for her sisters of Gertrude's own encounter with Christ. At that moment, Gertrude offered her heart to God; then Christ opened his heart and with his two hands placed it against her own. Their hearts were glued together, and a tree of marvelous beauty sprang up at the seam where they joined. The tree's two branches, one of gold and one of silver, entwined, like a vine—a symbol of the union of Christ's will with Gertrude's. And since Gertrude had prayed for those who had recommended themselves to her, she saw the tree produce extremely beautiful fruits, each of which bowed down toward a woman for whom Gertrude had prayed.[103]

During Mass on another occasion, Mechtild peered at her own heart, which had assumed the shape of a house, and she saw this house cupped inside another larger house, which was Christ's heart. Mechtild entered her house (that is, she entered her heart), and there she found Christ, who invited her to enter his divine heart. Mechtild did so, and right away,

> that blessed soul, filled with the Holy Spirit, saw fiery rays go forth from all her limbs, so that each person for whom she had prayed received a ray into herself. And after she communicated, she saw her heart as if liquefied with the

[102] Revelation, the written word (especially Scripture, and including the *Herald* and the *Book of Special Grace*), the multifaceted process of composing the *Herald* and the *Book of Special Grace*, talk among the sisters about matters religious, meditative prayer—all these were vehicles by which the sisters were expected to arrive at a subjective awareness of the extraordinary phenomena their individual and communal devotions precipitated.

[103] *Le Héraut* 5.27.7 (SCh 331:218–20).

> heart of God into one mass of gold, and she heard the Lord say to her, "In this way, your heart shall adhere [to mine] in perpetuity."[104]

Although the larger passage contains among the most vivid and beautiful of descriptions in the Helfta literature of mutual assimilation, there is, from a certain perspective, nothing extraordinary about it. Images of melting and merging appear frequently in the pages of the *Book of Special Grace* and the *Herald*, and both works emphasize a correspondence between the visionaries' hearts and Christ's heart, the exchange of hearts, and the incorporation of the heart of one into the heart of the other.[105]

What is especially noteworthy here is that sandwiched between the threefold nest of hearts and a classical image of mystical union is an expression of concern for others. Twice enclosed and enclosing Christ's heart, Mechtild engulfs and

[104] *Liber* 1.19 (70).

[105] See for example *Liber* 1.1; 1.5; 2.29 (8–11, 18–20, 166–67); *Le Héraut* 2.23.8 (SCh 139:336–38). For the connection in the *Book of Special Grace* between house, heart, and wound, see Voaden, who comments on the intricacy of the passage to which I refer ("Articulating Ecstasy," 44–48, and "All Girls Together: Community, Gender, and Vision at Helfta," in *Medieval Women in Their Communities*, ed. Diane Watt [Buffalo, NY: University of Toronto Press, 1997], 83). Gertrude makes a plea to Christ for mutual incorporation in the *Spiritual Exercises* (*Les Exercices* 2.42–44 [SCh 127:84]). On imagery of the heart in the *Book of Special Grace*, see Voaden, "Articulating Ecstasy," 30–51; and Spitzlei, *Erfahrungsraum Herz*. On the devotion to the Sacred Heart at the monastery and the nuns' contribution to the early modern devotion, see Joseph Stierli, "Devotion to the Sacred Heart from the End of the Patristic Times down to St. Margaret Mary," in *Heart of the Savior*, ed. Joseph Stierli (Freiburg: Herder, 1957), 59–107; Cyprian Vagaggini, "La dévotion au Sacré-Coeur chez Sainte Mechtilde et Sainte Gertrude," in *Cor Jesu: Commentationes in Litteras Encyclicas Pii PP.XII "Haurietis Aquas,"* ed. Augustine Bea, et al., 2 vols. (Rome: Herder, 1957), 2:31–48; Jean Leclercq, "Le Sacré-Coeur dans la tradition bénédictine au Moyen Âge," in *Cor Jesu: Commentationes in Litteras Encyclicas Pii PP.XII "Haurietis Aquas,"* ed. Augustine Bea, et al., 2 vols. (Rome: Herder, 1957), 2:3–28.

is engulfed by the divinity, two hearts become one, and Mechtild's limbs emit rays of light to those for whom she has previously prayed. Even as Mechtild is nestled in Christ, the ties that bind her to others do not dissolve. Those whose needs have at other times pulled her into prayer on their behalf do not fall away from her consciousness. As Giovanna della Croce has observed, Mechtild, when she is absorbed into God, dispenses to others the riches she receives.[106] At the most intimate part of the self, where God and self met and seemed to merge, others had access to concerns of Mechtild, who held herself responsible for her sisters and whose desire to share with others the fruits of her experience remained alive. Thus drawn to others, she drew God to them. Indeed, the *Herald* tells us that God sometimes seeks union with select sisters in order to bring other people to him.[107] Mechtild and Gertrude were thus often acutely aware of their sisters in choir and sensitive to their needs precisely during moments of heightened self-awareness and intimacy with Christ. In such situations, there is no indication that concern for others or activity on their behalf distracted from, diminished, or otherwise undermined the enjoyment of such experiences or detracted from their intimate and unitive aspects.[108]

An attitude of accountability for the sister-other is at play in the numerous visions in which fellow nuns were folded into the revelations Gertrude and Mechtild received, through which they claimed the ability not only to discern phenomena surrounding their sisters, but, in addition, to uncover their sisters'

[106] Giovanna della Croce, *I mistici del nord* (Rome: Edizioni Studium, 1981), 28.

[107] *Le Héraut* 1 Prol. 6 (SCh 139:14). And see *Le Héraut* 3.18.4 (SCh 143:82), in which Christ explains to Gertrude that he dons her like a glove so that he can stretch out his hand among rough sinners.

[108] The coincidence of absorption into Christ and the presence of others makes special sense when we remember that Christ is his members just as they are part of the Body of Christ, as the nuns discuss; for the image of the Body of Christ, see chap. 7.

emotional response to such phenomena. Over and over, within the visions ascribed to both women, Christ, Mary, and the saints are said to have come before a sister other than Mechtild or Gertrude as well as to the congregation as a whole, or they are said to have approached each person in choir,[109] revealing their solicitous presence in the work-a-day doings of the monastery. During the collect, Mechtild heard Christ speaking to the congregation, using words he had addressed to the apostles: "I am in the middle of you. . . . You are those who . . . stayed with me in my trials, and I will prepare the kingdom for you just as my Father prepared it for me, so that you will eat and drink at the table with me in my kingdom."[110]

At another time Christ, Mechtild perceived, walked alongside and approached each of her sisters as they processed from the church after Terce, pronouncing his faithfulness in ministering to the faithful soul.[111] In the form of a beautiful young man, Christ held open a book for a sister who was reciting the collect in choir and, reclining on her breast, said to her, "I will follow you wherever you go; you cannot be taken from me."[112] As the *Herald* and the *Book of Special Grace* depict them, Gertrude and Mechtild were eager that others should share in exactly the kinds of contact with God and his holy companions from which they themselves benefited, and they strove to bring experiences such as their own to their sisters. During Christmas Mass, Mechtild cradled the baby Jesus in her heart, offered the infant to each of her sisters in turn, and saw him kiss and recline on the breast of each one.[113] Now and then, their visions told them, the prayers they offered precipitated Christ's presence among those for whom they prayed.[114] Thus we read

[109] See for example *Liber* 1.10; 1.23 (34, 84).
[110] *Liber* 4.1 (258).
[111] *Liber* 1.19 (64).
[112] *Liber* 4.44 (301).
[113] *Liber* 1.5 (17).
[114] See for example *Liber* 1.4; 1.19 (13, 69).

about Mechtild's experience during Ember Week in Advent, the season in which the nuns readied themselves for Christ's coming and in which images of light figure prominently:

> In the Mass *Veni et ostende*, when she prayed on behalf of all who desired to see God with their whole heart, she saw the Lord standing in the middle of the choir, his face shining as if a thousand suns, enlightening each person with a ray of sun.[115]

The Helfta writings often scarcely distinguish a vision from the setting in which it takes place; the contents of a vision seem like an elaborate transparency to overlay the events and people that swirl around the visionary as she receives a revelation, or to draw these into a vision that is something like a *tableau vivant* in the midst of chapel or chapter. In chapter on the feast of the Annunciation, Gertrude beheld Christ and Mary seated in the abbess's chair. As the community recited the *Miserere*, the Lord placed in his mother's hand each word the sisters uttered under the form of a pearl; Mary mixed these with perfume, sweetening the prayers of the sisters with the troubles each had previously endured and that they had committed to her.[116] Gertrude once saw Christ feeding her liturgical community at the moment each member received the Host from the priest: "when the convent communicated, the Lord showed himself with great condescension to be present, so that he seemed to offer the saving Host with his own venerable hand to each one who was approaching, while the priest nevertheless made the sign of the cross over each Host."[117]

The phenomena attributed to sisters who figured in Mechtild's or Gertrude's revelations often paralleled those associated with the visionaries themselves. Jesus appeared as a boy of about ten years old during Matins on the feast of John

[115] *Liber* 1.4 (13).
[116] *Le Héraut* 4.12 (SCh 255:132–33).
[117] *Le Héraut* 3.38.3 (SCh 143:184).

the Evangelist, and each sister was filled with joy.[118] On the feast of Saint Lawrence, Gertrude saw Christ draw into himself the desire of all those present at Mass and flow into them.[119] As the congregation was communicating on another occasion, Christ stood in the middle of the choir; rays of light from his face illuminated the faces of Mechtild's sisters, and Christ's love for them caused the women's hearts to liquefy.[120] All the sisters interacted with the saints; all received the kinds of favors to which Mechtild and Gertrude were accustomed. The sisters, as they are reported to have done in the vision accounts, responded to Christ when they were in his company. When we read of Christ flowing into the sisters and of the melting of their hearts when they were bathed in the light of his love, or of Mary moving among the nuns and offering her Son to each, we might be reading about one of the many similar phenomena associated with Gertrude or Mechtild. Gertrude's and Mechtild's experience of the liturgy—so the *Herald* and the *Book of Special Grace* relate—thus underscored God's nearness to the whole community of women with whom they worshiped.

Moreover, anonymous sisters making intercessions were sometimes portrayed as just as effective as the holy women themselves. As Gertrude prayed at her request for the hebdomadary who was about to read the psalter for the congregation at Matins, Gertrude saw Christ lead the hebdomadary before the throne of the Father:

> And just as the Son of God stood before the Father, pleading for the church, in this way this person, like Queen Esther, stood before the Lord God the Father, supplicating with the Son for her people, that is, for the congregation. And when in this role she had discharged her responsibility [to recite] the psalter, the Father of heaven accepted each word from

[118] *Liber* 1.6 (21).
[119] *Le Héraut* 3.17.4 (SCh 143:78–80).
[120] *Liber* 1.4 (13).

> her in two ways: that is, just as a lord might accept from a guarantor that [the guarantor] pay debts for the debtors, and just as [the lord] might permit his procurator to offer coins to be distributed to his dearest friends.[121]

Gertrude prayed for the hebdomadary, and the hebdomadary for their sisters, settling their debts with the Father. The hebdomadary is Queen Esther, pleading before God the Father, just as the *Herald* elsewhere calls *Gertrude* Esther.[122]

Thus the Helfta writings proclaimed the presence in the convent of multiple women on whom Christ lavished his attention and affection, whose commitment to their sisters recalled that of Gertrude and Mechtild, and who found in Christ a receptivity to their pleas on behalf of their community. The accumulated accounts served if not to level the status of women within the convent, then to diminish the distance between Gertrude and Mechtild on the one hand, and, on the other, between them and their sisters, and they were an invitation to imitation since they pictured luxurious intimacies and power as belonging not to a fortunate few but to the many, and as being within the reach of still others. It is generally impossible to attach such experiences to a particular nun because the women who figure in these stories remain largely unnamed, an implicit cautioning against the kind of supposition about her sisters of which Mechtild had herself been guilty,[123] inculcating in the reader a respect for the interior life of her sisters, whose reality might be rich but not therefore necessarily discernible to the naked eye.[124]

[121] *Le Héraut* 3.81.1 (SCh 143:332–34).

[122] *Le Héraut* 4.58.4 (SCh 255:470).

[123] *Liber* 4.47 (302).

[124] My findings parallel in this regard what Richard Kieckhefer has noticed about the Sister Books, which indicate to their readers that many of the women who figure in these accounts have been especially favored with mystical experiences and which then suggest that such experiences are available to all ("Mystical Communities," 7).

In the revelations in which the convent's principal visionaries perceived their sisters as equal beneficiaries of God's presence and his response to them, the other nuns remained, for the most part, ignorant of the fullness of the gifts that they themselves—the other nuns—received. In the many visions in which one woman claimed to lay bare events that incorporated another woman, or many women, the boundary between self and other blurred as one woman became privy to the inner world of another. I have found no unambiguous indication that Mechtild or Gertrude, or the anonymous contributors to the *Book of Special Grace* or the *Herald*, believed that the sisters who figured in Mechtild's and Gertrude's visions were themselves conscious of the content of these visions—either of the events Mechtild and Gertrude saw surrounding them or of the events in which they took part (or which took place within them!) as the visions unfolded.[125] It may be helpful to think of visions that came to one woman and whose contents incorporated other women as individual communal visions, not because such visions were revealed simultaneously to more than one woman but because they claimed to capture events of

[125] Newman ("What Did It Mean," 24) calls a "shared vision" a vision that one of the anonymous authors of the *Book of Special Grace* receives (*Liber* 5.24 [356–57]), and that incorporates Mechtild, an anonymous writer of the *Book of Special Grace*, and all the sisters. It is not entirely clear what Newman means by this. This vision appears to have come to one woman alone. Those vision accounts in which one nun's revelations contain many nuns are different from the visions recorded in the Sister Books of the fourteenth-century Rhineland. In the convent chronicles, we find numerous descriptions of visions that come to the nuns as a group as well as reports of sisters individually and one after the other receiving similar visions. See Peter Dinzelbacher, "A Plea for the Study of the Minor Female Mystics of Late Medieval Germany," *Studies in Spirituality* 3 (1993): 91–100; Gertrud Jaron Lewis, *By Women, for Women, about Women: The Sister-Books of Fourteenth-Century Germany* (Toronto: Pontifical Institute of Mediaeval Studies, 1996); Rebecca L. R. Garber, *Feminine Figurae: Representations of Gender in Religious Texts by Medieval German Women Writers, 1100–1375* (New York: Routledge, 2003), 61–104; Anne Winston-Allen, *Convent Chronicles: Women Writing about Women in the Late Middle Ages* (University Park: Pennsylvania State University Press, 2004).

immediate significance to a company of women and in which many women participated.

Sometimes, it is true, what a visionary perceived corresponded to what others observed. We read, for example, that the many revelations that came to Gertrude about Abbess Gertrude accorded with what others saw with their bodily eyes,[126] but this remark speaks to mutual confirmation rather than to shared vision, admitting to different manners of perception at work in the community while asserting shared experience.[127] More often, the literature asserts a difference between participating in the events Gertrude and Mechtild witnessed (such as seeing their sisters holding the baby Jesus or receiving an influx of divinity) and others' being aware of events in which they are seen to participate. The *Book of Special Grace* suggests that what Mechtild saw in visions when she saw her sisters was their souls. We read that after communion, she saw "the Lord was sitting in a throne before the altar, and all the souls of the congregation, in the form of virgins dressed in white robes, were seen as if exiting their bodies; and they went to sit at the Lord's feet."[128] The *Book of Special Grace* does not elaborate on this understanding, however. Nor is the difference between being a participant in an event (within a vision) and being conscious of such participation a topic the *Herald* or the *Book of Special Grace* explicitly takes up.

Yet the *Herald* depicts Gertrude as having been aware of this difference and interested in its implications. The question of

[126] *Le Heraut* 5.1.18 (SCh 331:36).

[127] The phenomenon as described here is similar to what Richard Kieckhefer has found in a vision the Unterlinden Sister Book attributes to one nun, in which she "sees" a dimension of an experience of miraculous communion associated with a second nun, and the second nun herself simultaneously perceives that she has received a "rush of sweetness in her soul" but is unaware of the two angels who delivered the Host to her, the source of the sweetness. The two women are, as Kieckhefer writes, experiencing the same event "from complementary perspectives" ("Mystical Communities," 3).

[128] *Liber* 4.1 (257).

the meaning to her sisters of her visions that included them is one that Gertrude repeatedly entertained when she pondered the significance to her sisters of God's grace flowing among them. When she saw golden tubes emerge from a chalice God offered to those who had commended themselves to her, she observed that the women could neither see nor understand the vision Christ set before her and had no awareness of the fruit her prayers had produced. On this occasion, Christ explained to Gertrude that just as a *paterfamilias* may fill his cellar with wine that will not be enjoyed immediately, so her sisters would not savor his gifts instantaneously.[129] Elsewhere Gertrude broached her subject incidentally, and once again she did so in the context of her concern about the efficacy of prayers she had offered. When Gertrude asked God if he heard her when she prayed for her friends, he affirmed that he did; Gertrude immediately prayed for a particular woman, and this prayer in turn elicited a revelation that was something like a demonstration of God's assurance: "And right away, she saw something like a stream of crystalline purity come forth from the Lord's breast and flow into the innermost part of the person for whom she was praying." This revelation generated additional inquiry, as Gertrude asked about the utility for the person for whom she had prayed of what God had just shown her:

> "Lord, of what benefit is this to the person, since she herself does not feel this influx?" The Lord answered her, "When a doctor administers a medicinal potion to a patient, it is not when he drinks that potion that those around him see the sick person restored to health, nor does the sick person himself feel cured right away. Nonetheless, the doctor who understands the power of the potion knows well how it benefits the sick man."[130]

[129] *Le Héraut* 4.59.4 (SCh 255:480–82).
[130] *Le Héraut* 3.9.4 (SCh 143:38–40).

Christ and Gertrude's conversation and the visionary evidence that Christ offered of the efficacy of Gertrude's prayer was not an analysis of the significance *per se* of visions to those who figure in them. The passage does, however, tell us something about what the nuns of Helfta may have understood about the visions in which sisters other than the visionaries played a part.

Christ proclaimed that something really was happening to the woman for whom Gertrude prayed when Gertrude saw a crystalline stream flow from Christ into her; what Gertrude saw was conducive to promoting change in the person for whom she had prayed. The recognition of Christ's presence may take time—the sick man to whom a doctor administers medicine is not healed right away. Nevertheless, this presence was immediate and at once belonged to the one for whom Gertrude prayed. From the perspective of the authors of the *Herald* and the *Book of Special Grace*, the fact that the sisters who figured in the visions that came to Mechtild and to Gertrude were unaware of the role they played in these visions—of the benefits that the visions documented that they had received—is in some sense irrelevant for the sisters themselves. Yet Christ really was offering himself to those gathered at Mass, and all received him there when Gertrude saw him flowing into each of them and heard him address the congregation and say, "I am wholly your own. Then enjoy me, each according to your desire."[131] *This* is what mattered.

Her sisters may have provoked the questions Gertrude brought before Christ—these women who had probably heard of her visions only to wonder that they felt no personal change despite the influx of grace that Gertrude or Mechtild promised they had received. In any case, the generous distribution of

[131] *Le Héraut* 3.17.4 (SCh 143:80). When they receive him in communion, they do, of course, receive him wholly, whether or not they are aware of it (*Liber* 4.46 [302]). The Holy Spirit's work is not immediately perceptible (*Liber* 2.40 [188]). And see too *Liber* 7.8 (402): grace is like the gift of an orchard, whose recipient cannot eat the fruit until it has ripened.

God's grace among her sisters prompted Gertrude to ask repeatedly about the relationship of individual response to the reception of God's grace.[132] She wondered why, for example, if God heard the prayers she uttered, those for whom she prayed were not comforted.[133] Day-to-day congress among sisters and the concern for others' well-being sometimes occasioned the surfacing of theological questions, which impinged on the nuns' everyday reality; Gertrude aimed to reassure the sisters of their reception of God's grace by recourse to a theological rationale that she supplied in sometimes-domestic images. Those to whom he gives graces have at least *some* awareness of the graces, Christ explained to Gertrude when she wondered to him about those who were ignorant of his gifts about which she knew through revelation.[134]

Moreover, when the souls of her sisters seemed to Mechtild to leave their bodies and approach the altar, the Helfta literature appears to say that the sisters were really drawn to Christ in communion, even if the women remained distanced from a dimension of their engagement with him that Mechtild perceived. Thus one of the purposes of the *Herald* and the *Book of*

[132] When for example Christ promised Gertrude that all the sisters gathered at Mechtild's deathbed would receive an abundant infusion of grace, Gertrude asked how this would affect them if they could not savor it, by which she seemed to imply that they were unaware—because they could not see Christ as she could—of God's grace flowing into them. Christ responded that when someone receives from his sovereign the possession of a field of fruit trees, he cannot know the taste of the fruit, but he has to wait until they are mature. It is, he continued, the same when he gives someone gifts of grace. It is not at that moment that they will perceive the delicious flavor. God's grace will affect the person's behavior, and practicing the virtues that grace supports will later merit her tasting the grace interiorly (*Le Héraut* 5.4.14 [SCh 355:96–98]). See too *Le Héraut* 3.30.32 (SCh 143:154–56), where we learn that God does not always insist that those on whom he confers his grace produce fruit immediately. When another person wonders why her prayers on behalf of others seem not to profit them at all, Christ reassures her, through Gertrude, of their efficacy (*Le Héraut* 3.79.1 [SCh 143:328–30]).

[133] *Le Héraut* 3.72.1 (SCh 143:288).

[134] *Le Héraut* 4.54.5 (SCh 255:450–52).

Special Grace was to teach the nuns that in addition to respecting their fellow nuns, they ought to cultivate a certain reverence for themselves. Revealing a closeness with God about which those who read about themselves were probably not fully aware, the literature almost promised the perception of wonders involving the self to the sister sensitized to her surroundings. Additionally, it communicated to the reader that it might take another to teach her about who she was in relation to God.

Revelations that introduced the visionary's regard for her fellow nuns did not document either that her sympathy for them was unreserved or that she felt related to them in a common movement toward God, however. Remarks scattered throughout the *Book of Special Grace* and the *Herald*, and a number of revelations, call attention to tensions and animosities among the sisters, which sometimes surfaced during liturgical observances. In particular, the opportunity to receive communion seems often to have prompted unkind murmurings and spiritual one-upmanship and to have given rise to disagreement and strife.[135] Although the principal visionaries and Abbess Gertrude encouraged frequent communion, emphasiz-

[135] In the thirteenth century, communion became increasingly regulated by ecclesiastical authorities, and we find a heightened fascination with reception of the Eucharist, buoyed by the notion that reception was a principal occasion for affective response to Christ's self-giving and for union with him. The piety of the period encouraged self-vigilance and self-appraisal as well as deliberate abstention from communion because of the perception of the stringent requirements to communicate and because of the awe in which the host was held; see, for example, Caspers, "Western Church." On thirteenth-century theologians' preoccupation with who might receive the Eucharist, concern for the disposition of the recipient, anxieties related to reception, and pressures exerted on Christians to receive, see Gary Macy, "Reception of the Eucharist According to the Theologians: A Case of Diversity in the 13th and 14th Centuries," in *Treasures from the Storeroom: Medieval Religion and the Eucharist* (Collegeville, MN: Liturgical Press, 1999), 36–58; and Gary Macy, "Commentaries on the Mass During the Early Scholastic Period," in *Treasures*, 142–71.

ing Christ's generosity toward the recipient,[136] the spiritual power associated with communion and the weight of the worry about reception that pressed on the sisters combined to make it an especially compelling topic of conversation.[137] Some trembled with fear that prohibited them from receiving; when they did receive, it was sometimes with trepidation.[138] The nuns were mindful that God would measure the strength of their desire to receive him and assess their worthiness to do so, and they knew that members of the congregation were prepared to arrive at their own estimations of themselves and of their sisters.

The nuns were aware that they communicated under the watchful eyes of others, and so we read, for example, that Mechtild once witnessed a snow-white dove touch with its beak the heart of each person who communicated, lighting a flame within; in some hearts, this flame was extinguished, and in others, it was fanned into a great fire.[139] Sisters were conscious of the care they needed to take to ready themselves for reception and sometimes expressed reluctance about communicating, believing they were unworthy to do so,[140] and they confessed that they were scared of causing scandal when they approached the altar.[141]

[136] See for example *Liber* 3.26; 5.2; 6.3 (229–30, 319, 379–81); *Le Héraut* 1.14.2 (SCh 139:196–98). Saint Catherine of Alexandria told Mechtild that every time a person receives, her soul's beauty is increased and that if she communicates a hundred or a thousand times, she increases her beauty by a hundred or a thousand times (*Liber* 1.32 [110–11]).

[137] See for example *Le Héraut* 1.14.2; 4.7.4–5 (SCh 139:196–97; SCh 143:102–4).

[138] For fear of receiving, see *Liber* 4.48 (303); *Le Héraut* 3.18.20; 5.1.14 (SCh 143:98; SCh 331:32–34). For support for sisters when doubts arise about their preparedness to take communion, see *Le Héraut* 1.14.2 (SCh 139:196–98). Warnings that those who received unworthily courted danger did not perturb Gertrude (*Le Héraut* 1.10.3 [SCh 139:166–68]).

[139] *Liber* 1.23 (82–84).

[140] See for example *Le Héraut* 1.14.2; 2.5.1; 3.18; 3.34.1; 3.38.2 (SCh 139:196–98, 248; SCh 143:80–104, 172–74, 182–84); *Liber* 2.14; 3.6; 3.22 (147, 203, 225–26).

[141] *Le Héraut* 3.18.22 (SCh 143:98–100).

Although Gertrude sometimes entertained scruples about communicating, she nonetheless expressed little patience for the trepidations of others:

> Seeing one of the sisters fearful of approaching the living sacrament, she turned away displeased, as if in indignation, and then the Lord reproved her sweetly, saying, in these words, "Do you not consider that the reverence of honor is no less due to me than the sweetness of love? But because the defect of fragile human nature cannot in one emotion convey both, since you are members of one another [Rom 12:15], it is right that whatever someone lacks in herself, she recuperates through the other. For example, she who with the sweetness of love capitulates to less feeling of reverence should rejoice that another supplies an excess of respect, and should in turn desire that the other obtain the comfort of divine unction."[142]

This vision both acknowledged and helped to resolve a tension at the heart of the Mass. It portrayed Gertrude as fomenting rifts in the liturgical community and, through the medium of revelations that came to her in the context of the liturgy, helping to solder these fractures. Christ's response to Gertrude's brusque dismissal of her sisters' anxieties seems calculated to calm nervous souls, asserting that to approach communion in love and to approach in fear are both courses agreeable to God; it appears intended to temper a tendency—evident in Gertrude's person but perhaps not unique to her—to compare and to compete in assuming the one right attitude toward reception.

This vision contained more than an instruction in tolerance. It taught that God is due both fear, which accompanies rever-

[142] *Le Héraut* 3.18.19 (SCh 143:96). Gertrude's reflections on the attitude the communicant ought to assume while approaching communion is more complex than this particular vision attributes to her. See for example *Le Héraut* 2.19.2 (SCh 139:304–6). On the anxiety Gertrude herself sometimes felt about communicating, see Dolan, *St. Gertrude*, 42–44.

ent acknowledgment of his honor, and love, effected (as the overall context of the Helfta literature suggests) from the sort of familiarity with him to which Gertrude and Mechtild were privy. Because human nature is defective, it shows, one emotion cannot encapsulate the reverence and love to which God is entitled. God placed the onus to address the failings of human nature that come to the fore when each person communicates on the community. The different attitudes with which the sisters approached communion were complementary: the sisters as a collective supplied for one another what each lacked individually. Right worship requires exactly the diversity of attitude that troubled the nuns. God used a cause of conflict in community to create a body of worshipers whose devotion was, from God's perspective, necessarily more complete than that of any one individual.

This vision suggests that Gertrude found theological justification for varying attitudes toward communicating and that she made an effort to rejoice in exactly those that rankled her. Behind the notion that a variety of attitudes was necessary lay an insistence on the frailty of human nature. The nuns did not elaborate on expressions of such frailty evident in any one person. They were more interested in diagnosing weakness as inherent in each individual, in recognizing it as a challenge to contentment in the common life, and in offering a remedy. From the perspective of the nuns, the fragility of each woman cried out for correction in community. As is illustrated in the person of Gertrude, with Christ's intervention, perceiving the failings of one member of the community roused recognition of one's own weakness and the importance of mutual reliance and assistance. Acknowledgment of individual vulnerability was bound up with optimism about the opportunities the liturgical community held out to each of its members. Within this context, Mechtild's and Gertrude's sense of the pious devotion of their sisters flowered. The *Book of Special Grace* trumpeted the eucharistic piety of the convent's nuns as a whole. Drawing special attention to the precocious piety of the novices, Mechtild prayed for her sisters and saw Mary and each of the saints whom she invoked on their behalf kneeling with reverence and praying to the Lord, and while each woman made her profession, Christ received her in his arms and gave each a sweet kiss as she approached communion; each woman thereafter became one in spirit with him.[143] Through the *Herald* and the *Book of Special Grace* such private extraordinary experiences of the Helfta sisters entered the public sphere.

Reading about the visionaries and about themselves, the nuns at Helfta would have been presented with a liturgy in which an absolute sense of interior privacy had no place. They would have been instructed in Gertrude's and Mechtild's attunement to the fervency or tepidity with which their sisters attended Mass or received communion—and engaged in a host of other devotions—as well as the quality of their relationship with Christ, Mary, and the saints, on any given occasion,[144] and they would have learned that anonymous others were likewise sensitive to their interior life, capable of peering in on them, the inside sight itself containing an evaluative declaration. Moreover, the women are often gathered into larger groups, and it is more often groups—not individuals—that are distinguished from one another according to degrees of devotion, quality of intention, and so on. For instance, Mechtild sees not specific people but an anonymous grouping of patient, loving souls gleaming in Christ's heart, while another group of souls shines less beautifully in other parts of his body.[145] Taken up to a heavenly feast, on another occasion, she reports that the bread Christ distributed to the women gathered at his feet tasted delicious to the devout and was without savor to those bereft of devotion.[146]

[143] *Liber* 4.17 (273–74).

[144] For example, *Liber* 1.10 (32–34).

[145] *Liber* 1.20 (72–73).

[146] *Liber* 4.8 (264–65). And see for instance *Le Héraut* 3.18.22; 4.2.9; 4.33.1 (SCh 143:98–100; SCh 255:36–38, 282–84). Examples could be multiplied.

When a virgin appeared during Mass, certain people drew close to her and embraced her, a sign that they conformed their will to God; when a kitchen slave appeared, some kept their back to him, but others turned from the virgin to flirt with him, a sign of their self-will.[147] Gertrude saw Christ offer his heart in the form of a stringed instrument to the Father during Vespers on the feast of the Trinity. The chants of some of the women singing the office sounded in a high register, charming and clear; those who sang out of habit, or because they enjoyed the song for itself, emitted a sound like a murmuring in the background.[148] The anonymity of the sisters who figure in accounts such as these and the frequent representation of collectives rather than individuals protect the sisters' privacy.

The anonymity may not have dulled the reader's perception that there were some within the monastery who were able to spy into the emotions and attitudes of their sisters. It may not have diminished the reader's recognition that she did not therefore exercise sovereignty in determining to whom she would disclose the contents of her inner self. The nuns believed, of course, that God sees into the depths of their hearts and knows about aspects of their selves of which they are ignorant. Friend and lover, he was to them also judge. For these reasons alone, the sisters had reason to be attentive to their interior disposition and to work to mold it into conformity with Christ's will.[149] Their eternal fate depended on this sort of self-vigilance and self-care. But however close the visionaries among them insisted that Christ came to each nun, his final disposition remained at a distance. Mechtild and Gertrude and other women within the community were, however, here and now close by in the flesh, and in a position to cast judgment and make pronouncements with immediate consequences. The accumulated

[147] *Liber* 4.19 (276).

[148] *Le Héraut* 4.41.2 (SCh 255:263). See Therese Schroeder-Sheker, "The Alchemical Harp of Mechthild von Hackeborn," *Vox benedictina* 6, no. 1 (1989): 40–55.

[149] *Liber* 1.18 (52).

visions make clear that the sisters were under continual scrutiny, the community under a sort of self-surveillance. This knowledge may have prompted the individual nun to examine herself more carefully, since she knew that others' eyes might be probing her inner self. In this context, life in community (especially when coupled with reading about life in community) may have facilitated a more attentive—sharper and more sustained—focus on the self.

The relationship between an individual's subjective religious experience and formal prescribed communal worship was a topic that preoccupied medieval nuns in general, as well as the men who had responsibilities for their spiritual care.[150] Numerous scholars such as Cyprian Vagaggini and Jean Leclercq as well as recently, Caroline Walker Bynum, Jeffrey Hamburger, Bruce Holsinger, and Anne Bagnall Yardley have told us much about the spiritual significance to religious women of the Mass and the Divine Office.[151] There has, however, been little sustained examination of the sense of community among nuns as it relates to the liturgy. My study of the convent of Helfta adds to the growing body of research demonstrating that medieval people perceived themselves as thoroughly engaged in liturgical observances and taken up with the corporate implications, as well as purposefully promoting others' active participation in the liturgy.[152]

[150] Hamburger, "Art, Enclosure," 88–89.

[151] Vagaggini, *Theological Dimensions*; Leclercq, "Liturgy and Mental Prayer," 295–300; Caroline Walker Bynum, *Holy Feast and Holy Fast: The Religious Significance of Food to Medieval Women* (Berkeley: University of California Press, 1987); Hamburger, *The Visual and the Visionary*; Holsinger, *Music, Body*; Yardley, *Performing Piety*.

[152] See for example John Bossy, "The Mass as a Social Institution, 1200–1700," *Past and Present* 100 (August 1983): esp. 33, 59–60, 92; Eamon Duffy, *The Stripping of the Altars: Traditional Religion in England 1400–1580* (New Haven: Yale University Press, 1992), esp. 92–154; Caspers, "Western Church," 90; Macy, "Commentaries on the Mass," esp. 158; Jacqueline Jung, "Beyond the Barrier: The Unifying Role of the Choir Screen in Gothic Churches," *Art Bulletin* 82, no. 4 (December 2000): 622–57.

Perhaps nowhere is the Helfta nuns' sense of community felt more intensely than in their liturgical practices. Although modern theologians and historians alike have tended to dismiss non-clerical participants in the medieval Mass and Office both as marginalized spectators and as frankly self-preoccupied,[153] the Helfta literature attests to the sisters' engagement in the liturgy and the complementarity of self-referential experience and attentiveness to others within the liturgical community. All of the Helfta literature showed its sister readers how, through right execution of liturgical responsibilities and through trust in the prayers each nun offered day after day for her sisters, they might please God and achieve the power to advance the salvation of self as well as other.

[153] See, for example Joseph A. Jungmann, *The Mass of the Roman Rite: Its Origins and Development (Missarum Sollemnia)*, 2 vols., trans. Francis A. Brunner (New York: Benzinger Brothers, 1950), 1:117; Theodor Klauser, *A Short History of the Western Liturgy* (London: Oxford University Press, 1969), esp. 98; Dorothy Gillerman, *The Clôture of Notre-Dame and Its Role in the Fourteenth Century Choir Program* (New York: Garland, 1977), 154–55, 194–97; Jef Lamberts, "Liturgie et spiritualité de l'eucharistie au xiiie siècle," in *Actes du Colloque Fête Dieu, 1246–1996* (Louvain-la-Neuve: Institut d'études médiévales de l'Université catholique de Louvain, 1999), 81–95.

PART TWO

Within and Beyond the Cloister

Chapter 5

"A Husband Enjoys His Wife More Freely in Private"

The Nuns and the Clergy

> *While Mass . . . was celebrated and the priest was reading the Gospel, she saw the Lord standing facing the priest, and all the words that the Lord had spoken in the Gospel were like rays of light that passed through the priest himself. And the Lord said, "All the words that I spoke on earth are as efficacious and have the same power as they had when they came from my mouth originally, whoever recites them with devotion."*[1]

Helfta was in the diocese of Halberstadt and would have been under the authority of its bishop.[2] We have minimal documentation about bishops' relationships with the monastery. Nor do its writings reveal what sort of administrative, financial, or other contribution clergy may have given the nuns—or the drain they may have placed on the women's economic resources, as was sometimes the case with a male clerical presence in female houses.[3] The women would have needed a

[1] *Liber* 5.11 (337).

[2] See introduction.

[3] See Ursula Peters, *Religiöse Erfahrung als literarisches Faktum: Zur Vorgeschichte und Genese frauenmystischer Texte des 13. und 14. Jahrhunderts, Gedruckt*

priest for the celebration of daily Mass and for the proliferating Masses offered for the dead, as well as for the ceremonies of Holy Week. Priestly services were essential for confession and absolution, as well as for the performance of deathbed rites.[4] A priest would have preached at the monastery and provided spiritual direction. One person or several might have fulfilled these responsibilities; neither the charters, the chronicles, nor the visionary literature states explicitly who provided the women's pastoral care. It is likely that Dominicans assumed this role, and Franciscans may have also participated.

While no one section of the Helfta writings is dedicated to a consideration of priests or to the priesthood, remarks about individual men figure throughout, suggesting that clergy who tended to the nuns were not far from their thoughts and at least occasionally became objects of curiosity. Friars, confessors, celebrants, canons, and even a bishop figure here and there in the literature. We learn that sisters hungered to confess—and that they dodged their confessors.[5] We read of priests' reciting litanies over the dying and administering holy unction;[6] they celebrated funeral Masses, Masses for feast days, and other daily Masses. Theologians and friars expressed rapt interest in the nuns' revelations, pronounced their fierce admiration for the visionaries, and attested to the transformation they themselves had undergone because of the women's intervention. Friars cried out from purgatory, pulling on the

---

mit Unterstützung der Deutschen Forschungsgemeinshaft (Tübingen: Max Niemeyer Verlag, 1988), esp. 127.

[4] The priest was a usual presence at the deathbed. See, for example, *Liber* 5.6 (326). And see Peter Bowe, "Die Sterbekommunion im Altertum und Mittelalter," *Zeitschrift für katholische Theologie* 60 (1936): 1–54. For women's dependence on the priest for confession, see Penelope Johnson, *Equal in Monastic Profession: Religious Women in Medieval France*, Women in Culture and Society (Chicago: University of Chicago Press, 1991), 260. Female houses also labored under the financial obligation to pay for priests to say Masses for the living and the dead; Johnson, *Equal*, 111 and 260.

[5] *Liber* 2.14 (147); and *Le Héraut* 5.9.1 (SCh 331:134).

[6] *Liber* 5.6 (326).

women's pity and pleading for their intercession. Canons issued an interdict prohibiting the nuns from receiving the Eucharist.[7] And some effort was expended to check the flow of news to the outside world about the nuns' revelations and other extraordinary experiences: one priest tried to halt the spread of Mechtild's visions.[8]

The nuns were alert to the disposition of clergy with whom they came into contact, adducing whether a priest served Mass devoutly or otherwise, for example.[9] Some passages convey the high estimation in which the nuns held priests who faithfully discharged their responsibilities.[10] In one revelation Mechtild received, the words the priest intoned at Mass traveled through him like rays,[11] and now and then she saw Christ in the place of the priest consecrating the Eucharist.[12] Provosts

[7] On the interdict, see for example *Liber* 1.27 (95); *Le Héraut* 3.16.1; 3.17.1 (SCh 143:66, 74).

[8] *Liber* 5.18 (347). On this and related points, see Peters, *Religiöse Erfahrung*, 125–29; Margarete Hubrath, *Schreiben und Erinnern: Zur "memoria" im* Liber specialis gratiae *Mechtilds von Hakeborn* (Paderborn: Ferdinand Schöningh, 1996), 6; Kurt Ruh, *Frauenmystik and Franziskanische Mystik der Frühzeit* (Munich: Verlag C. H. Beck, 1993), 298–99; "Gertrud von Helfta: Ein neues Gertrud-Bild," *Zeitschrift für deutsches Altertum und deutsche Literatur* 121 (1992): 302–3. Caroline Walker Bynum, "Women Mystics in the Thirteenth Century: The Case of the Nuns of Helfta," in *Jesus as Mother: Studies in the Spirituality of the High Middle Ages* (Berkeley, CA: University of California Press, 1984), 176, supposes that the man may have felt threatened by Mechtild's visionary authority. For suspicion and doubt that late medieval priests sometimes expressed about women's spiritual powers, see John Coakley, *Women, Men, and Spiritual Power: Female Saints and Their Male Collaborators* (New York: Columbia University Press, 2006), 211–13. For the broader ambivalence and anxiety in the late Middle Ages about claims associated with the authenticity of experience of those who were championed as holy, see André Vauchez, *Saints, prophètes et visionnaires: le pouvoir surnaturel au Moyen Âge* (Paris: Albin Michel, 1999), 208–19.

[9] *Liber* 5.5 (322–24).

[10] *Liber* 1.30 (103); *Le Héraut* 5.3.6 (SCh 331:74).

[11] *Liber* 5.11 (337).

[12] *Liber* 1.4; 1.30; 5.6 (14, 104, 327). See *Liber* 5.6 (326) for Christ taking the priest's place at the bedside of a dying nun; Christ also took the place of the abbess at chapter: *Liber* 1.5 (15), and *Le Héraut* 4.2.8 (SCh 255:34–36).

and other priests were among the souls adorning the celestial kingdom who danced through the spheres with deceased sisters.[13]

Nuns as Admired Counselors and Mediators to Clergy

The approbation that accompanies the *Herald* tells us that in 1289, distinguished theologians and friars of the Order of Preachers and of the Order of Minors enthusiastically endorsed the whole of this composite work.[14] We do not learn whether one or more of the men who signed the approbation served the nuns as confessor, confidant, celebrant, or preacher, or had some other particular commitment to the house, although its existence supports the likelihood that the monastery was largely served by friars. The approbation enumerates the scholarly acumen of some of its signatories and the praiseworthy spiritual qualities of a few. One is "filled with the Holy Spirit," and another is renowned both for his "literary achievements and for his special gift of spiritual balm."[15]

We learn here of the effect that contact with Gertrude had on a number of the men who approved the *Herald*. On hearing her words, the Dominican Brother Herman of Loweia and "many others . . . witnessed for her on God's behalf."[16] Gertrude's words—whether he heard them, read them, or both—

[13] Provosts were sometimes clerics, and in such cases were responsible for participating in financial as well as pastoral oversight. On sisters and brothers dancing in heaven, see, for example, *Liber* 6.9 (389).

[14] *Le Héraut, "Approbationes des docteurs"* (SCh 139:104–6). The approbation purports to be contemporary with the *Herald*, although Kurt Ruh has raised questions about its authenticity (Ruh, *Frauenmystik*, 317; Ruh, "Gertrud von Helfta," 6). On the purpose of the approbation, see Doyère, who discusses its place in the manuscript tradition ("La notice des approbation," in *Le Héraut*, SCh 143:349–50).

[15] *Le Héraut, "Approbationes des docteurs"* (SCh 139:104).

[16] *Le Héraut, "Approbationes des docteurs"* (SCh 139:106). For clergy as friends, students, and followers of twelfth- and thirteenth-century women whom they perceived as especially holy and possessing spiritual gifts lacking in themselves, see Coakley, *Women, Men*, 2.

so fired up a certain Dom Gotfried Fex that "from then on, he spent his life in wonderful devotion and desire for God."[17] At least one brother, the Dominican Theodore of Apolda (1220/30–1302/3), spoke with Gertrude frequently. The brief approbation (consisting of fewer than two printed pages) closes with fiercely protective words, a stern rebuke to anyone who would challenge the *Herald*, from an anonymous signatory to the document, game to fight to the death with anyone who questions these writings: "I confess in the very truth of the divine light that no one, truly having the holy spirit of God, would rebel with audacious temerity against these writings in any way. In fact, fortified by the spirit of the only lover of humankind, I bind myself to these writings and to fight to the death against any opponent."[18]

Thus a number of clergy, whose high intellectual and spiritual standing the approbation's signatories are themselves keen to credit, regarded Gertrude as source of divine knowledge and recipient of revelations. Expressing no reservations about the authority, power, insights, and teachings the *Herald* attributed to her, they proclaimed the book's orthodoxy. Although only one of these men, Dom Gotfried, testified to Gertrude's having invigorated his own devotional life, she may have offered spiritual and more obviously theological sustenance to someone such as Theodore, about whom we learn only that he spoke with her often. The approbation is evidence that more than half a dozen clergy, at least some of whom knew Gertrude personally, endorsed the entirety of the *Herald*'s content with gusto, brandishing threats, testimony, and their own learning in unequivocal support.

The men associated with the *Herald*'s approbation were not the only clergy who looked to some among the Helfta nuns as especially disposed to receive divine favors and to pass them along to others, including themselves. Gertrude sometimes assumed responsibilities for male superiors who, by behaving

[17] *Le Héraut, "Approbationes des docteurs"* (SCh 139:106).

[18] *Le Héraut, "Approbationes des docteurs"* (SCh 139:106).

badly, became the object of her good works, seeking correction of their faults by commending them to God.[19] A number of clergy had recourse to Mechtild's gift of visions and sought her guidance and succor. The whiff of sanctity seeped out of the convent, attracting laity and religious alike. Thus we read in the *Herald* of a man who consulted with Mechtild about his salvation and who returned the favor by providing her with financial support through a period during which she was ill.[20] Additional economic benefits may have redounded to individual nuns, and perhaps to the monastery as a whole, from people pleased to have access to the sisters' advice and prayer.[21]

A number of male religious also appealed to Gertrude for aid, and she shared with them the blessings she received from God, praying for them, offering divine communications, and otherwise mediating between them and God.[22] She was at ease dispensing advice, sure of the benefit to many men of the guidance solicited by a few.[23] Through Gertrude, Christ beckoned one religious to union with him in love-language such as that associated with Gertrude's and Mechtild's relationship with Christ, and the counsel Gertrude offered the anonymous petitioner is like that which she gave her sisters: the man was to recollect his unworthiness, ponder Christ's mercy, and with wings of desire soar toward his King and into the ecstasy of heavenly joy.[24] About another supplicant we learn that after

[19] *Le Héraut* 3.82.1 (SCh 143:334).

[20] *Le Héraut* 3.75.2 (SCh 143:320–22).

[21] For financial reward associated with women's prayers within the monastery, see Penelope Johnson, *Equal*, 233–34; Jo Ann Kay McNamara, who has written about women's prayers for those in purgatory as a source of economic support for women's houses (*Sisters in Arms: Catholic Nuns Through Two Millennia* [Cambridge: Harvard University Press, 1996], 277, 285, 287, and "The Need to Give: Suffering and Female Sanctity in the Middle Ages," in *Images of Sainthood in Medieval Europe*, ed. Renate Blumenfeld-Kosinski and Timea Szell [Ithaca, NY: Cornell University Press, 1991], 212–21 and 218–19).

[22] See, for example, *Le Héraut* 3.73 (SCh 143:294–308).

[23] *Le Héraut* 3.73.12 (SCh 143:308).

[24] *Le Héraut* 3.73.1 (SCh 143:294–96).

God's grace poured out to him through Gertrude, Christ approached the man and, extending his hand to him, interlaced their fingers, their hands fitting together beautifully.[25] Gertrude directed the men who sought her counsel to find refuge in prayer,[26] balance contemplation and good works,[27] practice self-scrutiny and cultivate contrition,[28] and share God's love with their neighbors.[29]

Both religious and secular clergy associated with the monastery and those who came from a distance to consult with Mechtild attested that she delivered them from their suffering, providing them with consolation they had received from no one else.[30] The matters these men brought before her ranged from queries about the eternal fate of religious and political figures from the distant past to affairs immediately gnawing on their conscience. One brother requested Mechtild to ask the Lord about the state of the souls of Solomon, Samson, Origen, and Trajan.[31] Another brother visited the monastery on at least two occasions and confided in Mechtild that he had hunted for relief from temptations among his fellow friars but with no success; when Mechtild prayed for him, his temptation disappeared.[32] About a certain priest for whom Mechtild prayed, Christ promised, "his soul will adhere to my divine heart."[33]

It may have been a regular occurrence that Mechtild received revelations in response to prayers she offered for particular men and through such visions provided counsel. Christ advised Mechtild about a man overwhelmed with sorrow that

[25] *Le Héraut* 3.73.4 (SCh 143:298).
[26] *Le Héraut* 3.73.7 (SCh 143:302–4).
[27] *Le Héraut* 3.73.9 (SCh 143:304–6).
[28] *Le Héraut* 3.73.11 (SCh 143:306–8).
[29] *Le Héraut* 3.73.5 (SCh 143:298–300).
[30] *Liber* 5.30 (365).
[31] *Liber* 5.16 (344).
[32] *Liber* 4.39 (298).
[33] *Liber* 4.42 (300).

if anyone is so depressed that he would rather die than endure his suffering, he should lay his burden on the Lord.[34] Mechtild expressed a sustained interest in the spiritual state of a number of individual priests and seems routinely to have talked with Christ about them. She was sympathetic:[35] once, inquiring into the state of a priest spiritually spent in God's service, she asked God why he had consumed the man's strength like a bee sucking a flower dry.[36] When she prayed for yet another friar beset by temptations, Christ explained that although he could wave away the man's worries, it was to the brother's benefit that he struggle against the minor temptations that troubled him, so as to become stronger in his ability to direct others facing graver onslaughts.[37]

Mechtild launched into prayer on another occasion for this friar, perhaps, although not necessarily, indicating a long-term commitment to his welfare. Christ subsequently communicated through her a message promising always to protect the man, to guide him, to govern all his works, and to console him. Mechtild's instructions continued, now targeted toward the brother's fellow friars, as she relayed from Christ a series of warnings centering on this command: the friar should not cease to remind his brothers that they should withdraw from earthly goods and honors.[38] If Mechtild's words stuck, she would have served as more than a gentle counselor of this one man; she would have animated him to be a reformer within his household, stirring up his fellow friars to a more perfect life and teaching them to withstand the trials that assaulted them. These accounts show Mechtild assuming responsibility for these men, one that she shouldered with assurance, aware that she was in a position to help them in their own relationship with God and that they, in turn, were responsible for their

[34] *Liber* 4.52 (305).

[35] *Liber* 4.41–43 (299–300), for example.

[36] *Liber* 4.43 (300).

[37] *Liber* 4.40 (298–99).

[38] *Liber* 4.40 (298–99).

brothers' spiritual betterment and (drawing on Christ's aid) would execute their charge. Thus Mechtild's role in the lives of the individual men who sought her out had ramifications for men's religious communities. The *Book of Special Grace* in this way pictures Mechtild introducing herself into a male clerical household—via the disclosure of revelation to individual members—in order to affect that community for the better, an intriguing counterpart to the routine intrusion of male spiritual directors into female households.

The space the *Book of Special Grace* and the *Herald* allot to the piety of individual men and to Mechtild's and Gertrude's prayers and recommendations for the men who sought them out is relatively minimal, however, occupying only several printed pages. And there is little additional evidence suggesting that Mechtild, Gertrude, or any other sisters took on as central to their obligations the role of spiritual muse that is so prominently assigned to holy women in contemporary and near-contemporary writings about women (and sometimes by them), including religious and quasi-religious women.[39] The

[39] For the nuns' relationship as advisors to friars, see Bynum, "Women Mystics," 211. Perceptions about women common among late medieval clerics influenced the content of the hagiographical material about women for which these men were responsible. Late medieval clerics seem to have perceived women as generally more receptive to divine grace than men and to have juxtaposed the power that accrued to the priest through his office with the personal visionary authority associated with holy women. They often shared the attendant belief that women ought to serve as conduits of grace to the men in their orbit, including husbands, confessors, and scribes. Such perceptions gave male confidants the impetus to supplant a woman's own interpretation of her experiences with his, which frequently included highlighting his importance in her life, especially her visionary life, that area that most intrigued and eluded him. See especially Dyan Elliott, "Authorizing a Life: The Collaboration of Dorothea of Montau and John Marienwerder," in *Gendered Voices: Medieval Saints and Their Interpreters*, ed. Catherine M. Mooney (Philadelphia: University of Pennsylvania Press, 1999); Catherine M. Mooney, "The Authorial Role of Brother A. in the Composition of Angela of Foligno's Revelations," in *Creative Women in Medieval and Early Modern Italy: A Religious and Artistic Renaissance*, ed. Ann Matter and John Coakley (Philadelphia:

conspicuous place of male need and the control male confidants often exercised in lives of some twelfth- and thirteenth-century holy women—such as Elisabeth of Schönau (ca. 1129–1164) and Angela of Foligno (1248–1309)—are virtually absent from the Helfta compositions.[40] The concern of the sisters for and with their fellow nuns dwarfed their interest in needy men, however much the nuns may have served as the men's spiritual superintendents. It is evident, nonetheless, that when the occasion arose the women were sure in their ability to guide individual religious men and that they regarded their counsel to be suitable for a larger male audience. Christ made clear to Gertrude the fittingness of the instructions she received for anyone in any religious order.[41]

Indifference to Priests

We learn much less about the role priests occupied in the women's lives as mediators, confidants, or companions in the religious life than we do about the role the women understood themselves to play in the lives of these men. The literature in fact does very little to illuminate the contours of priestly guidance at Helfta. It allots scant space to describing the spiritual or intellectual pull that clerics might have exerted on the nuns.

University of Pennsylvania Press, 1994); John Coakley, "Gender and the Authority of the Friars: The Significance of Holy Women for Thirteenth-Century Franciscans and Dominicans," *Church History* vol. 60, no. 4 (1991): 445–60; Karen Glente, "Mystikerinnenviten aus männlicher und weiblicher Sicht: Ein Vergleich zwischen Thomas von Cantimpré und Katerina von Unterlinden," in *Religiöse Frauenbewegung und mystische Frömmigkeit im Mittelalter*, ed. Peter Dinzelbacher and Dieter R. Bauer (Cologne: Böhlau, 1988), esp. 252–53. For a study of the role certain twelfth- and thirteenth-century holy women played in the lives of their male clerical confidants, see Coakley, *Women, Men*.

[40] This pervasive sense of men's presence comes through both in women's own writing and the writings of men, as in the *Life of Marie of Oignes* that Thomas of Cantimpré (1201–72) composed.

[41] *Le Héraut* 3.73.12 (SCh 143:308).

There is certainly no indication that the women's religiosity was molded by priestly supervision,[42] and the women expressed virtually no concern for the counsel living priests might have for them. As mediators and advice-givers, and as women wise in matters theological and spiritual, Gertrude's and Mechtild's relationship with the priests they knew personally was unequal and not based on a sense of reciprocal need or like ability to shepherd spiritually.[43] Although they do not emphasize it, the women provide illustrations of the men's sometime dependence on them but do not acknowledge a like reliance on their prelates or any other men with whom they may have been in contact.[44]

Thus, for example, when we read about Mechtild in relationship to her two confessors, it is in a passage testifying to her holiness, which tells us nothing about these men's roles in her life.[45] Book one of the *Herald* offers the witness of certain unidentified men, including a religious, who received messages from God about Gertrude's sanctity, but again we do not learn about their relationship to her.[46] We also read in the *Herald* that

[42] Bynum, "Women Mystics," esp. 255–59.

[43] Bynum, "Women Mystics," esp. 255–59. Ella L. Johnson underscores the nuns' sense of equality with men: "Metaphors for Metamorphosis: Mary Daly Meets Gertrud the Great of Helfta," *Magistra* 15, no. 1 (Summer 2009), 30.

[44] Nor do we find in the Helfta writings traces of the sort of relationships between the nuns and their priests that flowered in the free exchange of friendship between men and women in the thirteenth-century Low Countries and that the Cistercian monk Goswin of Villers portrayed in the thirteenth-century *Life of Ida*. Here we find the nun Ida and a clerical friend intimately bound to one another through an experience of ecstasy that she enjoys and that triggers a vision in him that seems to envelop both simultaneously and join them in one spirit, an experience so powerful that it then pulls into their orbit a third woman, Ida's abbess, who witnesses the priest's rapture (Barbara Newman, "Preface: Goswin of Villers," in *Send me God: The Lives of Ida the Compassionate of Nivelles, Nun of La Ramée, Arnulf, Lay Brother of Villers, and Abundus, Monk of Villers,* trans. Martinus Cawley [Turnhout: Brepols, 2003], xxxiv–xxxix).

[45] *Liber* 5.30 (363–64).

[46] *Le Héraut* 1.11.4, 7 (SCh 139:174, 176–78).

Gertrude consulted a trusted elder, presumably a priest, but the point of the account is the man's declaration of her godliness, one among dozens of such attestations threaded throughout the *Herald*, not her reliance on his advice.[47] A reference to the man's wisdom reinforces his pronouncement on Gertrude, and a conversation between holy women occasions it, but neither the man's sagacity nor the content of their talk is the subject of the passage. Although the approbation to the *Herald* similarly discloses that the Dominican friar Theodore of Apolda and Gertrude had frequent exchanges, the substance of their talks remain out of view in this rather perfunctory remark.

Perhaps they spoke about Dominic of Guzman (1170–1221), whose *Life* Theodore composed, or about Elisabeth of Hungary (1207–1231), the royal wonder-worker, of whose *Life* Theodore was also the author.[48] As Willibrord Lampen has shown, language culled from the office of Saint Elisabeth is interwoven with the *Herald*'s long account of the death of Mechtild.[49] Elisabeth is, furthermore, among the identified saints who appear to Gertrude, while most remain anonymous. The vision in which Elisabeth comes to her is also assigned a discrete chapter, a privilege accorded only a minority of the holy dead in Gertrude's revelations, or in Mechtild's.[50]

But if Theodore was a source for Helfta's devotion to Elisabeth, none of the writings acknowledges this, and it may well

[47] *Le Héraut* 1.9.2 (SCh 139:162).

[48] Renate Kroos, "Zu frühen Schrift- und Bildzeugnissen über die heilige Elisabeth als Quellen zur Kunst- und Kulturgeschichte," in *Sankt Elisabeth: Fürstin Dienerin Heilige*, Philipps-Universität Marburg in Verbindung mit dem Hessischen Landesamt für Geschichtliche Landeskunde (Sigmaringen: Jan Thorbecke Verlag, 1982), 215–16; Marie-Hubert Vicaire, *St. Dominic and His Times*, trans. Kathleen Pond (London: Darton, Longman and Todd, 1964), vii, 19; M. Werner, "D. v. Apolda," in *Lexikon des Mittelalters*, ed. Robert Auty, et al. (Munich: Artemis Verlag, 1977–1998), 1032–33.

[49] Willibrord Lampen, "De spiritu S. Francisci in operibus S. Gertrudis Magnae," *Archivum franciscanum historicum* 19 (1926): 736–38.

[50] *Le Héraut* 4.56 (SCh 255:462).

have been the enthusiasm of the convent's founding patron, Elizabeth Mansfeld that drew the nuns to this popular saint.[51] There is no suggestion in the approbation or elsewhere that Gertrude and Theodore spoke to one another as fellow writers.[52] And although Gertrude conversed with dead male authors on the topic of writing and had a keen appreciation for the works men such as Augustine, Gregory the Great, and Bernard of Clairvaux composed, the *Herald* does not recognize the literary achievement of Theodore or of any living man.

Here again, the literature's silences are far more revealing than what it does say. The nuns provide no indication of having benefited in any substantial way from, or having recoiled under the force of, confessors' or other male confidants' guidance. There is no mention of Gertrude, Mechtild, or any of their sisters seeking help from a male spiritual director in interpreting visions, and no evidence that the nuns wanted the guiding presence of a priest in their spiritual lives. We do read that Gertrude at least once confided in an older man about her relationship with God, but when she wondered about the meaning of certain experiences, she seems to have tended to turn to her sisters with her questions.[53] When Mechtild feared her visions might not be divinely inspired, there is no record of her direct appeal to male authority.

A vision of a certain Brother N. of the Order of Preachers is provocative on this account. In life affiliated with the monastery, the dead brother came to Mechtild in a revelation, and she conveyed to him her fear that the vision in which he came to her was a trick of the enemy. In response, he counseled her to wrap herself in the armor of faith and believe that the revelation was a gift from God, an intriguing account in part because there is no analogous instance of the visionaries turning

[51] See introduction.

[52] Joseph Gottschalk calls Theodore Gertrude's friend but does not elaborate ("Kloster Helfta und Schlesien," *Archiv für schlesische Kirchengeschichte* 13 [1955]: 66).

[53] *Le Héraut* 1.9.2 (SCh 139:162).

to a living priest in confidence and receiving like direction. This vision may provide insight into the sort of conversations Mechtild had with a male confidant, just as it underscores the absence of recorded conversations between the nuns and the living men who may have counseled them.

It seems likely that this lack of discernible interest was the case at least in part because priests' guidance was negligible in the nuns' view of things and did not for the most part compel their attention or inform their actions: as Rosalynn Voaden has observed, the priest who directed Mechtild to keep quiet about her revelations seems to have been markedly ineffective.[54] The *Book of Special Grace* follows the account of the priest's instruction several chapters later with the statement that the *Book of Special Grace* was composed with the encouragement of Abbess Sophia and the consent of an (anonymous) prelate.[55] The matter, furthermore, finds no support elsewhere in the text and is eclipsed by reports of her sisters' coaxing Mechtild into speech and of the efficacy of her words for them and others, including clergy. According to Voaden, the *Book of Special Grace*'s lack of acknowledgment of a male confidant is explained by the fact that for contemporary readers, a cleric's spiritual direction would have been assumed. That readers would have made such an assumption is indeed likely. The lack of acknowledgment probably has more to do with another factor, however: the women writers were not interested in exploring one-on-one relationships with a confessor or spiritual director because the men in these roles exerted little influence on their lives that registered as noteworthy.

[54] Rosalynn Jean Voaden, "Women's Words, Men's Language: *Discretio Spirituum* as Discourse in the Writing of Medieval Women Visionaries," in *Proceedings of the International Conference of Conques, 26–29 July 1993*, vol. 5 of *The Medieval Translator*, ed. Roger Ellis and René Tixier (Turnhout: Brepols, 1996), 77.

[55] *Liber* 5.31 (369). Paquelin suggests that the anonymous priest may have been Helfta's provost or the bishop of Halberstadt (*Liber* 5.31 [369, n. 1]). I have found no evidence in the text for either conjecture.

The writings emphasize instead the variety of ways sisters filled for one another the role of spiritual guide. Gertrude even assumed the role of at least a sometime confessor to her sisters. Accounts of Christ's patient and thorough training of this or that nun—as when he coached Mechtild on the meaning of the *Miserere*—and his exquisite counsel, directed now to the visionaries, now to their sisters, may have meant that when it came to understanding the routines and rituals that comprised everyday life and were necessary to their salvation, the women could largely do without recourse to the living men whose job it was to counsel them.[56] This does not, however, mean that the presence of priests at Helfta was an indifferent matter to the nuns.

The Power of Priesthood

The nuns might have had little interest in individual men as confessors and guides, but their recorded revelations proclaim the priest's awesome power as God's instrument in transforming the bread and wine into the Lord's body and blood, making Christ present in the chapel and thus facilitating union with him.[57] During one Mass, Mechtild beheld Mary descending a golden ladder and setting on the altar the Christ Child she had carried in her arms from heaven. When the priest elevated the host, he raised high the baby, whom he offered to the congregation.[58] On another occasion, Mechtild saw that at the moment the priest placed the Host in a sister's mouth, Christ offered his rosy lips to the woman to kiss.[59] Emphasizing the chronological coincidence of Christ's celebration of the Mass in heaven and the priest's celebration in

[56] For Christ's assumption of the role of spiritual father to the nuns, see Christian Gregory Savage, "Music and the Writings of the Helfta Mystics," M.A. thesis, Florida State University, 2012, 42.

[57] *Liber* 4.46 (302).

[58] *Liber* 1.9 (31).

[59] *Liber* 4.46 (302).

the chapel, a vision attributed to Gertrude illustrated the intimacy between the priest's confection of the Eucharist and Christ's self-offering to the Father:

> Truly, in that very same hour in which the Son of God offered his divine heart to God the Father, the bell rang in the church at the elevation of the Host. And thus it happened that at one and the same moment, the Lord in this way performed in heaven what was done on earth through the ministry of the priest.[60]

The connection between Christ and the priest in his sacramental role at the altar, their status as co-workers, was explicit in many visions Mechtild received. On a number of occasions, as the community approached to receive communion, Mechtild saw Christ in the form of a king standing in the place of the priest, indicating, if not an affirmation of any single contemporary theology of the priesthood, that it is Christ who acts in the priest when he serves at the altar.[61] "I do everything the priest does, both with and in him," Christ once declared to Mechtild as he stood by the altar.[62] During a Mass celebrated for the dead, Mechtild saw Christ at the altar clothed in a cloak adorned with grasses, human hair, and animal fur, and shining with the souls of all human beings. A gloss to the vision says that Christ came to Mechtild in this way because these most humble elements of creation burn brightly in the Trinity through the humanity of Christ, because Christ assumed his humanity from this same earth from which these elements come.[63] Endowing the Mass with cosmic significance that highlighted God's embrace of even the most minor details of his creation—fur, hairs, grass—and celebrating the beauty of all

[60] *Le Héraut Missa* 12.1–5 (SCh 331:300–2). For chronological synchronicity between Masses celebrated in heaven and at the chapel at Helfta, see also *Liber* 2.20 (157–58).

[61] *Liber* (14).

[62] *Liber* 2.10 (144).

[63] *Liber* 4.3 (260).

souls, Mechtild beheld Christ cover the priest with this cloak, and when the priest consecrated the Host, Christ assumed the Host into his heart, and it was changed into him.[64] Through the celebrating priest's words, the bread at the altar became Christ, who in his humanity is really in some sense the whole of creation, and who is responsible for the transformation of the bread into himself at the moment of consecration. This is an extraordinary declaration of priests' power, at the same time that it stresses that the true source of this power lies outside the men themselves.

Moreover, the *Book of Special Grace* and the *Herald* call attention to the Mass as the occasion for the liberation of souls from purgatory and the increase of the joy of the saints, sometimes spotlighting the priest as precipitating these feats. Mechtild heard Christ say during Mass to a certain priest, "Your will is my will," and at the *Agnus Dei*, the deceased soul whom the priest wished to deliver from purgatory approached the altar, where Christ kissed her (the soul) sweetly and drew her into heaven.[65] When the priest offered Mass for the deceased Lord C., a priest of Osterhausen, it seemed to Mechtild that the celebrant made offerings of a series of gold chalices, and she understood from this act that he was congratulating the Lord C. on his happiness and praising God for it. Then Mechtild saw Christ open his heart, which exhaled a marvelous perfume, procuring a new ravishment for the soul of Lord C.[66] Here the happiness of one priest (Lord C.) precipitated the praise of another, increasing the heavenly happiness that prompted the

[64] *Liber* 3.4 (260). Mechtild folds the priest into her cosmic vision when she sees that the priest at the altar is clothed in leaves from a tree that grows in the middle of the church, a tree so large that it fills the earth, under which sit sinners and good people, and on whose branches perch souls like birds, and the tree's fragrance refreshes inhabitants of purgatory, while puffs of smoke from heaven chase away demons (*Liber* 1.17 [50–51]). See for example *Liber* 1.16 (49), in which Christ reminds Mechtild that he contains the whole of creation.

[65] *Liber* 5.5 (322–24).

[66] *Liber* 5.10 (334–36).

praise. On another occasion, the role of the priest was highlighted in response to Mechtild's own post-mortem vulnerability. A close friend of hers was concerned that sin might have stained the soul of the recently deceased visionary and saw no better way to ensure compensation for any negligence on Mechtild's part than to have priests celebrate on her behalf as many Masses as years Mechtild was alive.[67]

Priests and Sisters

Similarities between priest and visionary are apparent. Both mediated the divinity to the congregation; both had the power to move souls on earth and in purgatory toward salvation as well as to augment the joy of the saints (a topic I take up in the final chapter of this book); Christ recognizes the alignment to his will of both, and both are the instruments by which he reaches out to others. Insofar as the Helfta literature encourages the nuns to take Gertrude and Mechtild as models for imitation, a consideration of the fundamental parallels between the roles that they enjoyed, on the one hand, and, on the other hand, that which the literature attributes to the priest means that before God, differences among priest, visionary, and anonymous sisters do not collapse, but become far less pronounced than one might suppose.[68]

There are parallels between priest and sisters in addition to those I note above and to which the visionaries bring attention. Evidence scattered throughout the Helfta writings indicates that Mechtild and Gertrude regarded themselves as privy to the inner experience of the priest, just as they understood themselves as seeing into their sisters' souls. The visionaries now and again attributed to a priest the reception of certain

[67] *Liber* 5:25 (358–59).

[68] On the priesthood's belonging to all the faithful, see Gertrud Jaron Lewis, "God and the Human Being in the Writings of Gertrude of Helfta," *Vox benedictina* 8, no. 2 (1991): 309.

gifts—gifts of which the priests, like the anonymous nuns about whom we read, appeared to be largely unaware. As the Helfta literature portrays them, the priests with whom the nuns worshiped in Mass sometimes seemed otherwise to resemble the cloistered women whom they served. Brief shining accounts in the *Book of Special Grace* and the *Herald* attest to the women's confidence that the men in their midst, as individuals and as a group, were worthy of divine communications, could be strengthened and buoyed through the visionaries' prayers and revelations, were in need of Christ's correction, and could have such a forceful desire for God that Christ was compelled to pull them out of life and into death.[69]

In these accounts the clergy recall to us the nuns, who appeared likewise in need of and deserving of Christ's gifts, gifts that sustain and fortify them, and that they sometimes received through the mediation of their visionary sisters, who were also in need of amendment and whose powerful ardor for Christ stimulated his desire for them. The repertoire of images on which the nuns drew in writing about these aspects of the priests' experience is indistinguishable from that they used to communicate the visionaries' exercise of analogous powers. And the kinds of gifts friars and other clergy received are largely impossible to distinguish from the gifts the visionaries perceived their sisters and themselves to receive—although the nuns did receive many more and far more splendid gifts.

Once, for example, Mechtild saw John Evangelist holding open a book for the priest at the altar.[70] On another occasion, the words in the Gospel that Christ spoke and that the priest read flowed through his mouth like rays of light.[71] These gifts and others are strikingly similar to those the women receive. Thus the Evangelist, as we have seen, was a frequent presence in the monastery; we find him sitting at the bedside of and

[69] *Liber* 5.8 (331).
[70] *Liber* 1.6 (24).
[71] *Liber* 1.6 (24).

gazing at an unnamed sleeping nun, talking with Gertrude about his gospel, or relating to Mechtild his familiar relationship to Mary. The words that travel through the priest recall the claim these fiercely bookish nuns made about the words of their own *Book of Special Grace* (the very book in which we read this account): Christ explained to Mechtild that the whole of the *Book of Special Grace* contained his own words—not hers.

In the short narratives of a priest's current or future intimacy with Christ (for example, when Christ shared with Mechtild about a friar that "his soul will adhere to my divine heart") we might be reading of one or another anonymous nun, or perhaps the visionaries themselves, whom Christ offered pledges of his love and glowing attestations of their future with him. Thus, for example, Mechtild gazed favorably at a certain Friar H. of Plauen, whose celestial rewards included a crown with carvings representing Christ's passion, a sign of the friar's devotion. By word and example, the friar's teaching had profited the world so much that Mechtild was moved to ask Christ why he had taken the brother to himself, and she revealed a high estimation of Friar H. when she related Christ's response. "His violent desire constrained me," Christ answered, and then described the brother as having weaned himself from his mother's breast and attached himself to Christ.[72]

Friar H. was in possession of that desire that the *Book of Special Grace* hoped to instill in readers, and he enjoyed the intimacy with Christ associated with Mechtild and other spiritually advanced women in the monastery. And when Christ asserted to the celebrating priest that the man's will was in alignment with Christ's will, we might be reading about Gertrude's or about Mechtild's conformity with Christ, which allowed them to issue judgments and provide guidance to their sisters and others. A number of passages betray the women's admiration for individual clergymen and convey the value of

[72] *Liber* 5.8 (331–32).

the priest's personal religiosity to influence for the better the spirituality of others; in this way, too, they recall powers ascribed to numerous—usually anonymous—nuns in the household in addition to the two principal visionaries. Certain friars, in consequence of their encounters with Mechtild, became reformers in their own community, assuming a role as champions of spiritual integrity and renewal akin to that which Mechtild and Gertrude took up in their monastery.

On one occasion, Mechtild related to a friar these encouraging words from Christ, affirming Christ's support of the man's preaching and teaching, and thus their value: "When he preaches, he can have my heart for a trumpet; when he teaches, he can have my heart for a book."[73] Christ's heart was available to the friar, just as it had become a place of intimacy and a source of sustenance for Gertrude and Mechtild, on account of which they were sometimes said to make the divinity available to others, living and dead. Moreover, it seems as if the friar's powers to teach and preach depended on the sort of personal (we might almost say "mystical") association with Christ that the literature claims as the basis for Mechtild's and Gertrude's quasi-clerical power and authority. Elsewhere Mechtild, dispensing promises from Christ to another brother that resembled those that he made to Mechtild herself and to Gertrude, mediated between Christ and the brother, offering the brother a power of mediation: if it was contrary to the brother's will, Christ would not punish a sinner, and he would pour out his grace on those for whom the friar prayed.[74]

Once again, Mechtild's one-on-one engagement with the priest who sought her counsel primed him to occupy a special place in his own household, authorized by Christ and starkly evocative of Christ's authorization of Mechtild's and Gertrude's interventions in the life of their immediate community. It is unclear whether the anonymous friar whom Christ,

[73] *Liber* 4.40 (299).

[74] *Liber* 4.41 (299).

through Mechtild, authorized to offer God's grace and to stay God's punishment was a priest. If the friar was not a priest, then the conferral speaks to the Helfta nuns' conviction that both they and some of the men in their circle might be counted recipients of divine authorization to take up priestly tasks, bypassing the official priesthood. If he was a priest, Christ's conferral of authority would already have been his by virtue of his office; in this case, the vision may ultimately suggest a similar message, that even when harnessing the power of his office, the priest lacked something the visionary possessed and that God might bestow on him through Mechtild's mediating presence.

When the women's gaze turned heavenward, the saints they beheld seemed further to diminish the difference between nuns and the clergy. The nuns knew that Augustine, Gregory the Great, and Bernard of Clairvaux were priests. As the authors of the *Book of Special Grace* depict Bernard, however, his priesthood is a matter of irrelevance; he is plainly evocative of the holy women at the center of the Helfta writings. Like them, he too was divinely inspired, and everything he knew, he knew through the Holy Spirit.[75] What was important to Christ about the pious priest was not at all different from what was important to Christ about the nuns.

Although the women provide little indication of having turned to priests directly in attitudes of supplication, surrender, or wonder, here and there they made plain their understanding that the priestly office did offer advantages to its occupant. Depictions of such advantages recall experiences attributed to Mechtild and to Gertrude as well as to their sisters. When nuns probed Christ about the benefits that redounded to the priest in consequence of those aspects of his office that most interested them—celebration of Mass and daily

[75] *Liber* 1.28 (98). Barbara Newman has noticed this parallel: introduction to *Mechthild of Hackeborn and the Nuns of Helfta: The Book of Special Grace*, trans. Barbara Newman (New York: Paulist Press, 2017), 260, n. 72.

reception—what came to the fore was both the merit a priest gained in association with his execution of liturgical responsibilities and its increase if the priest distributed the sacrament with devotion and joy.[76]

The priest's liturgical role in Mass was itself meritorious. Christ's response to Gertrude when she asked about the profit to priests of daily communion appears calculated simultaneously to bolster respect for the office of the priest and to temper her envy of the person of the priest for his frequent reception.[77] Christ instructed Gertrude on the great value of frequent communion for furthering union with him, something she knew from her own experience.[78] He cautioned her, nevertheless, not to confuse internal joy with external glory, underlining the difference between the glory the Mass brings to God and the pleasure it may offer to the celebrant.[79] Thus shifting the focus of his conversation with Gertrude from the privilege of the priest's daily reception to the worth of the communicant, Christ redirected Gertrude's attention back to herself, and thus to her sisters: the *Herald* leaves the reader little room to doubt that Gertrude received communion with as much love as any woman or man (we can say the same for Mechtild), and Gertrude's attitude and behavior in reference to reception is presented as a wholly attainable model for her sisters. Moreover, the *Herald* and the *Book of Special Grace*, while alerting the

[76] *Liber* 5.2 (319).

[77] For this observation, see Mary Jeremy Finnegan, *The Women of Helfta: Scholars and Mystics* (Athens: University of Georgia Press, 1991), 120. On the nuns' sense of the dignity of the office of the priest, see for example *Liber* 4.15; 5.2; 5.10 (273, 319, 334–36).

[78] *Le Héraut* 5.38.2 (SCh 331:230).

[79] *Le Héraut* 3.36.1 (SCh 143:176). We read elsewhere that Gertrude asks the soul of a sister with whom she speaks if it is more advantageous than anything to have Mass celebrated for the dead, and the sister responds that it is more fruitful if love animates the priest to help souls rather than simply celebrating another Mass to fulfill his sacerdotal responsibilities. Here it appears that the quality of the priest's heart as he celebrates is relevant for the efficacy for the dead in need of the Mass! (*Le Héraut* 5.3.6 [SCh 331:74]).

reader to individual nuns and groups of sisters who were on occasion wanting in their eucharistic devotion, repeatedly and enthusiastically broadcast approval of the convent's eucharistic piety more generally.

The Helfta writings seem further to undermine differences between sister and priest in that in the nuns' portrayal, the priest was not the only ecclesiastical office-holder whose office Christ animated. Christ appeared to Mechtild to take the place of the Abbess Gertrude during chapter ("*Dominus autem loco Abbatissae in throno eburneo residebat*"),[80] just as Gertrude saw Christ take the place of the priest at the altar. The Rule prescribes that the abbess, like the abbot, is vicar of Christ, his representative.[81] And this notion may hover in the background here. The positions of priest and abbess in the piety of the nuns differ, however, in ways that sometimes underscored the value of the abbess's person by contrast. The Helfta writings laud Abbess Gertrude for fostering the intellectual household that fed the convent's vibrant religiosity, praise her virtues as Christ's own,[82] devote several chapters to a hagiographical account of her death, and identify her as laboring for the good of her daughters (she treats them just as Christ treated his disciples)[83] and all the faithful. "Nowhere is there a place, except the sacrament of the altar, where you will find me more truly and certainly than in her and with her," Christ declares.[84] (He says the same about Gertrude of Helfta.)[85] No priest receives the attention, the affection, or the esteem the nuns heap upon this abbess. Abbess Sophia is credited with initiating work on the *Book of Special Grace*, under obedience to whom

[80] *Liber* 1.5 (15).
[81] RB 2.13.
[82] *Liber* 6.2 (378).
[83] *Liber* 6.2 (378).
[84] *Liber* 6.2 (378).
[85] *Le Héraut* 1.3.3 (SCh 139:136–38).

the work was completed; no priest is centrally important to this or any other of the Helfta writing projects.[86]

The nuns thus attributed to themselves and to the clergy with whom they had contact a range of substantive similarities, at virtually every turn diminishing difference between themselves and their priests, and without hinting at the need to reconcile the priest's institutional role with their own.[87] They did so exactly during a period in Western European history when clerics routinely asserted and roundly accentuated differences between their own caste and all other Christians. As elaborated in twelfth- and thirteenth-century canon law and theology, the role of the priest was associated with teaching, preaching, administering the sacrament of penance, offering counsel, and consecrating the Eucharist, practices increasingly shut off to women, including women religious. Caroline Walker Bynum was right when over thirty years ago she described Gertrude and Mechtild as projecting themselves onto the ecclesiastical structures in their assumption of the mediating role associated with the priesthood, in response to the late medieval clerical insistence on an essential and hard divide between priests, on the one hand, and laity and women religious, on the other.[88] The nuns did not perceive themselves

[86] *Liber* 5.31 (369).

[87] Clerics associated with late medieval holy women seem often to have felt the need to think through the relationship between the two sorts of power and authority. Broadly speaking, and in contrast to the nuns of Helfta, they arrived at the conclusion that each was discrete in its source and without overlap in role. The clerics who wrote about themselves in relation to these women underscored the special access to God the women enjoyed and proclaimed them more virtuous than the men, and these differences (as the men saw it) formed the basis of the partnership the men assumed with the women, a partnership that men cast as basic to the women's holiness (Coakley, *Women, Men*, 212–14, 221). The women of Helfta, on the other hand, do not attend much, explicitly or otherwise, to difference per se, and they do not conceive of their relationship with the men as a partnership.

[88] Bynum, "Women Mystics," 227, 258–59. Bynum argues that the exaltation of the clerical status in the thirteenth century corresponded with a clear defi-

as doing so, however, and there is no indication that they considered their own gifts as in any way mimicking those of the priest. Why would they? Their theological and canonical separation from the priest, joined to their sense of spiritual integrity—insofar as they were for the most part unencumbered by their male confessors, confidants, or spiritual guides—may have helped them sharpen their concentration on themselves and abetted a sense of their own centrality as conduits of the divine. Although from the distance of many hundreds of years, we can, with Bynum, understand aspects of the nuns' experience about which they were themselves unaware, it is striking that the whole of the Helfta literature reads as though the priests were assimilated to Gertrude and Mechtild, rather than the other way around. It is hard not to notice that the nuns fashioned the priest in their own image.

Doing without Priests

Perhaps because of the nuns' sense of the similarities between themselves and the clergy, coupled with their sense of the visionaries' fiercely intimate relationship with Christ, the women of Helfta seem to have been adept at doing without priests when they perceived that it was necessary. When the

---

nition of women's incapacity for that role, generating in women a stronger need for substituting for that role than in the earlier Middle Ages. Raised in an all-female environment with the privileges associated with nobility, the nuns of Helfta were able to elaborate positive roles for themselves, assuming to themselves clerical prerogatives. For the rise of the clerical caste and the setting apart of clergy from the non-clerical population, see R. I. Moore, *The Formation of a Persecuting Society: Authority and Deviance in Western Europe 950–1250* (Oxford: Blackwell, 1987); Gary Macy, "The Invention of the Clergy and Laity in the Twelfth Century," in *A Sacramental Life: A Festschrift for Bernard Cooke*, ed. M. H. Barnes and W. P. Roberts (Milwaukee: Marquette University Press, 2003), 117–35; Robert N. Swanson, "Apostolic Successors: Priests and Priesthood, Bishops, and Episcopacy in Medieval Western Europe," in *A Companion to Priesthood and Holy Orders in the Middle Ages*, ed. Greg Peters and C. Colt Anderson (Leiden: Brill, 2016).

women needed him to do so, Christ could substitute for the priest. Gertrude cried out her longing to join her sisters who were hurrying to hear a sermon at the moment that she was too sick to go, and in response, Christ became a preacher: with Gertrude's head on his chest, Christ spoke to her about the ways his heartbeats worked for salvation of the world.[89] Mechtild was disappointed because she was unable to confess before Mass, and Christ made an allowance for this omission, telling her,

> When a powerful king is coming to visit, one cleans the house hurriedly so that nothing appears that will offend his eyes. But if he is so close that there is no time to get rid of the mess, one sweeps it into the corner until afterward, when one can throw it out. Just so, since you fully will and desire to confess your sins and not to commit them again, they are erased from my sight, and I will not remember them.[90]

The nuns knew the importance of confession.[91] Mechtild's recorded vision may have been a salve to uneasy souls, offering a means by which nuns eager to gain God's forgiveness might conceive of themselves as able to do so when a confessor was unavailable, a reality they experienced periodically.[92] Obviating the immediate need for the priest and placing Mechtild in the company of those theologians who tended to deemphasize the priest's role in remitting the punishment due to sin, the penitent's contrition itself an indication of God's forgiveness—the priest's to declare but not to confer[93]—the vision

[89] *Le Héraut* 3.51.1 (SCh 143:224).

[90] *Liber* 2.14 (147).

[91] See for example *Liber* 1.28; 2.14; 4.30 (99, 147–48, 287–89); *Le Héraut* 3.14.1 (SCh 143:56–60).

[92] *Liber* 4.30 (288–89). And for additional occasions on which a confessor was not available, see *Le Héraut* 3.60.1; 3.61.1 (SCh 143:244–46, 246–48).

[93] Thomas N. Tentler, *Sin and Confession on the Eve of the Reformation* (Princeton, NJ: Princeton University Press, 1977), 23–24; Bynum, "Women Mystics," 205. By the thirteenth century, an earlier preoccupation with contrition was

also speaks to the confidence of this monastic community. It asserted the integrity of its members' consciences and the worth of their self-assessment when it indicated that God might be willing to absolve the contrite sister before she confessed.

When the convent could not rely on priests to facilitate access to Christ in the Mass, the women seem to have found ways around this impediment, too. During a period when the episcopal seat was vacant, canons imposed an interdict on the nuns (perhaps because of unmet financial obligations on the women's part) that prohibited them from receiving communion.[94] The ensuing sadness was short-lived.[95] On the day before the interdict was to take effect, Gertrude asked Christ how he would console her and her sisters for the deprivation they were set to endure, and Christ responded,

> I will increase my delights among you. Just as a husband enjoys his wife more freely in private than in public, so your sighs and desolations shall be my delights. Progress in love

---

muted and associated with a settled recognition that only the individual and God could properly take account of the individual's remorse (Gavin Fort, "Suffering Another's Sin: Proxy Penance in the Thirteenth Century," *Journal of Medieval History* 44, no. 2 [2018], esp. 204–5).

[94] *Liber* 1.27 (95); *Le Héraut* 3.16.1 (SCh 143:66). Thus the *Book of Special Grace* reports that during an episcopal vacancy in the see of Halberstadt, the canons placed an interdict on the community on account of an unspecified financial matter, and the *Herald* testifies to the suspension of divine rites as well (*Liber* 1.27 [95]). And see *Le Héraut* 3.16.1; 3.17.1 (SCh 143:66, 74), in which we learn about the interdict, and *Le Héraut* 3.68.1 (SCh 143:274), in which Gertrude refers to a year during which the monastery strained under debt. The vacancy during which the interdict was issued refers to that brief period that elapsed between the death of Bishop Vulrad and assumption of the bishopric by Herman of Blankenberg (1296–1303) (see Paquelin, Praefatio to *Legatus*, xv; and Raphaela Averkorn, "Die Bischöfe von Halberstadt in ihren kirchlichen und politischen Wirken und in ihren Beziehungen zur Stadt von den Anfängen bis zur Reformation," in *Bürger, Bettelmönche und Bischöfe in Halberstadt*, ed. Dieter Berg (Münster: Werl, 1997), 25.

[95] *Liber* 1.27 (95); *Le Héraut* 3.16.1 (SCh 143:66).

> of me shall increase among you, just as hidden fire spreads more widely. On top of this, just as rising water overflows suddenly with force, just so shall my delights in you and your love in me overflow, both increasing.[96]

The interdict became, rather than a period of absence, the occasion of contact with Christ that carried with it special and delicious pleasures that all parties—Christ and individual sisters—could enjoy.[97]

Moreover, the encounter with Christ during the interdict, although private by analogy with the husband's greater enjoyment of his wife, did not cut off the sisters from the larger community of Christians. Sometime during the period of interdict and on the feast of the Annunciation, Gertrude once again expressed apprehension that Christ would allow nuns to be separated from him, and Christ responded, "If someone can grasp the marrow of my most intimate self, through which you adhere to me, let him cut you off from me." And he added, "The anathema placed on all of you for this reason will hurt you no more than if someone tried to cut something with a wooden knife."[98]

Christ's relation with the sisters was something that the clergy who authorized the interdict did not understand and could not damage.[99] Mechtild received a vision that similarly conveyed the nuns' certainty that the interdict did not prejudice their association with Christ, nor—as Mechtild learned—did it bar their integration into the larger ecclesial community.

[96] *Le Héraut* 3.16.1 (SCh 143:66).

[97] For the nuns' interpretation of the interdict as opportunity rather than punishment, see Bruce W. Holsinger, *Music, Body, and Desire in Medieval Culture: Hildegard of Bingen to Chaucer* (Stanford: Stanford University Press, 2001), 251.

[98] *Le Héraut* 3.16.5 (SCh 143:72).

[99] Holsinger, *Music, Body, Desire*, 251, notes that Christ's intervention in Mass during the interdict, as the visionaries perceived it, "rendered impotent" this particular exercise of clerical authority.

When the priest began the responsory *Vidi speciosam* ("I saw the beautiful one"), Christ, with his mother at his side, both brandishing flags of white and red, led the whole congregation in procession around the monastery's walls. Once inside the chapel, John the Evangelist and Luke ministered with Christ at the altar; the Evangelist read the gospel, and the Baptist the epistle. Christ (vested in a red chasuble and a bishop's miter) sang the preface to the Mass, and at his cry "Sing, all of you! Sing and make melody!" a host of saints chanted "Holy, holy, holy," and Mary's voice, sounding sweet and strong, could be heard over all. When the congregation approached the altar, Christ handed each woman his body, Mary placed a golden chalice at the wound in her Son's side, and each sister drew through a golden straw the sweet liquor that flowed into the cup.[100] When Mass was over, Mechtild saw that gold rings adorned all of Christ's fingers, a sign of her sisters' devotion to his mother and of their betrothal to him.[101]

The encounter between Christ and the soul is one to which no ecclesial authority has access and none can impede, the nuns declared. In light of the close connection between intimacy with Christ and engagement with others, it is therefore not surprising that the sisters, in addition, roundly rejected the notion that the clergy could control their connection to the larger church, which embraces heaven and earth. Indeed, the interdict became the occasion for an acute sense of relationality on the part of the nuns, both with Christ and with all the faithful (including individual and named saints as well as anonymous groups of the holy dead), because it paradoxically

[100] *Liber* 1.27 (95–97). For the presence of three principal ministers in the celebration of Mass (in addition to the celebrant, a deacon and subdeacon) see John Harper, *The Forms and Orders of Western Liturgy from the Tenth to the Eighteenth Century: A Historical Introduction and Guide for Students and Musicians* (Oxford: Clarendon, 1995), 121.

[101] Savage, "Music," 48, remarks on the details that Mechtild offers in her description of this Mass, and he argues that these may have been calculated to support Mechtild and the whole of the convent against the male hierarchy.

offered exceptionally close contact with Christ, in some sense because of and not in spite of the official pronouncements of exclusion. Focusing their attention on Christ as priest and bishop, the women felt themselves far from distant from him and from the communion of saints.

The nuns' attitude toward the clergy responsible for the interdict was fueled by the sort of pragmatism that went hand in hand with the women's admiring appraisal of their own ability to integrate themselves into the heavenly community without the mediation of an officiating priest. The priest might facilitate the women's intensely personal sense of togetherness with Christ during Mass, but he could not control it. It is certain that the nuns believed that their incorporation into the communion of saints was not dependent on their formal reception into the worshiping community that ecclesiastical representatives oversaw and to which they claimed authority to provide or restrict entry.

Joseph Jungmann's long-ago claim that Mass in the late Middle Ages undermined a coherent sense of liturgical community was echoed by liturgical scholars such as Theodor Klauser and John Harper; theologians continue to bemoan the separation of priest and congregation during the medieval Mass and to lament the "mute" presence, as John O'Malley puts it, of the congregation.[102] In the medieval monastic con-

[102] Joseph A. Jungmann, *The Mass of the Roman Rite: Its Origins and Development (Missarum Sollemnia)*, trans. Francis A. Brunner (New York: Benzinger Brothers, 1950), 1:117; Theodor Klauser, *A Short History of the Western Liturgy* (London: Oxford University Press, 1969), 97–98; Harper, *Forms and Orders*, 113–14; Dorothy Gillerman, *The Clôture of Notre-Dame and Its Role in the Fourteenth Century Choir Program* (New York: Garland, 1977), 154–55, 194–97; Barbara Haggh, "Foundations or Institutions? On Bringing the Middle Ages into the History of Medieval Music," *Acta Musicologica* 68 [1996]: 87–128, esp. 89), emphasizes the physical barriers—rood screens, veils, and stone enclosures—that separated the celebrating priest or priests from others present at Mass; Frank C. Senn, *Christian Liturgy: Catholic and Evangelical* (Minneapolis: Fortress Press, 1997), 112, 122–38; Jef Lamberts, "Liturgie et spiritualité de l'eucharistie au xiiie siècle," in *Actes du Colloque Fête Dieu,*

text, scholars have pointed to a lack of synchronicity between the celebration of the Mass in the sanctuary and the chanting of the choir as an illustration of a breach in the communal dimension of the Mass.[103] It is certainly the case that the nuns at Helfta were separated from priests in the chapel and during Mass, theologically, canonically, and spiritually as well as spatially.

Cornelia Oefelein has determined that the choir at Helfta was probably a raised gallery, a common feature of German convents of this period. Developed to maintain claustration in church, the gallery was intended to set the vowed women apart from clergy and from any lay people who may have been present in the monastery chapel, and it undermined visual contact among these groups.[104] It is possible that hung veils or

---

1246–1996 (Louvain-la-Neuve: Institut d'études médiévales de l'Université catholique de Louvain, 1999), 81–95; John O'Malley, *What Happened at Vatican II* (Cambridge, MA: Belknap Press of Harvard University, 2008), 130.

[103] Jungmann, *Mass of the Roman Rite*, 80–81, 88, 103–27; and Harper, *Forms and Orders*, 113–14.

[104] Cornelia Oefelein thinks that the gallery at Helfta may have been separated from the nave with a balustrade or a walled partition, punctuated with latticed windows or other openings that would have enabled the nuns to witness the moment of consecration and to receive the sacrament ("Grundlagen zur Baugeschichte des Klosters Helfta," in *"Vor dir steht die leere Schale meiner Sehnsucht": Die Mystik der Frauen von Helfta*, ed. Michael Bangert and Hildegund Keul [Leipzig: St. Benno Buch- und Zeitschriftenverlagsgesellschaft, 1998], 27). Provisions to provide the nuns with moments of visual access to the sanctuary were standard in women's households (Jeffrey Hamburger, "Art, Enclosure, and the Pastoral Care of Nuns," in *The Visual and the Visionary: Art and Female Spirituality in Late Medieval Germany* [New York: Zone Books, 1992], 47 and 96). The monastery at Helfta was destroyed in 1342, and in part for this reason, the convent's architecture has received little attention, although Oefelein, who has to date most closely considered the architecture at Helfta, has taken steps to remedy this. She offers a speculative "reconstruction" of Helfta based on what we know about women's houses, and, more specifically, Cistercian houses, in Germany in this period; she relies, less heavily, on evidence internal to the Helfta literature. Although little has been written more generally about the nuns' gallery or raised choirs, which emerged as a distinctive feature of German women's houses (Oefelein, "Grundlagen," 27; Hamburger, "Art, Enclosure," 49–50), it is clear that the

tapestries further hindered the women's eyeline to the men serving at the altar. The consequences of this disconnection seem, however, to have been different from what Jungmann described and others have since affirmed. None of the Helfta writings attest to a sense of exclusion on the part of the nuns during the celebration of Masses (including during the period of the interdict) or suggest that the nuns' experience of the Mass was in any way diminished by a lack of the sort of connection with the priest to which studies of the liturgy have drawn our attention.

Mass provided the nuns with the opportunity for intimate engagement with one another, and they believed that the liturgies in which they participated were synchronized with those in heaven. These richly palpable correspondences were what mattered to them. However difficult for us to imagine and, perhaps, however tempting to dismiss (unaccustomed as we are to take seriously claims to routine assignations with the dead), they had a tangible and vibrant sense of community with the saints and the souls in purgatory, one that was full of fellow feeling and perhaps more layered than their sense of community with the priest with whom they worshiped. Moreover, the women did incorporate the clergy who assisted at Mass into their community, and physical separation during Mass did not prevent some among the nuns from claiming access to the priest. On the contrary: the nuns attributed to him a variety of experiences on the basis of revelations that came

---

area nuns occupied in the monastery's church varied according to house, and although legislation offered guidelines for the design of women's houses, the architectural structure of medieval German convents was far from uniform. For the architecture of women's houses in German-speaking areas, see E. Coester, "Die Cistercienserinnenkirchen des 12 bis 14. Jahrhunderts," *Die Cistercienser: Geschichte, Geist, Kunst*, ed. A. Schneider, A. Wienand, and W. Bickel, 3rd rev. ed. (Cologne: Wienand, 1986), 344–57; and Hamburger, "Art, Enclosure," 37–71. Roberta Gilchrist (*Gender and Material Culture: The Archeology of Religious Women* [London: Routledge, 1994], 107–9), discusses the segregation of various groups such as nuns, lay brothers, and lodgers within convent churches; her focus is on women's cloisters in England.

to the cloister's most esteemed visionaries during Mass, visions that indicate that the priests, just like the sisters, enjoyed no perfect privacy when they were in the visionaries' midst, any physical barriers imposed between them proving no match for the women's divinely directed insights. The visions indicate, furthermore, that the nuns recognized that priests might facilitate the connection among all the faithful, on earth, in heaven, and in purgatory, enhancing an expansive sense of community, but could not prevent it.

In her comparative analysis of the sense of self of Gertrude, Mechtild of Hackeborn, and Mechtild of Magdeburg, Bynum taught that the strong sense of self held by Gertrude and Mechtild of Hackeborn, on the one hand, and, on the other, Mechtild of Magdeburg's sometimes lowly self-estimation were attributable at least in part to the varying environments in which the women lived for most of their lives. The all-female context of the monastery supported a robust self-assessment, Bynum argued. In the nuns' confident sense of their similarity to and difference from the priests they routinely encountered, we may see a related dynamic at play. Something about the distancing of the priest from the nuns at Mass may have helped them envision a role for themselves analogous to that which the priest claimed for himself. Energized and emboldened by a highly vaunted sense of themselves, the nuns found in the Mass a context for them to attend to their own gifts alongside or rather than the priest's, gifts that, when offered to their sisters and the dead in purgatory, made them co-redeemers with Christ. Separation from priests was concomitant with a capacious sense of who was present at the Mass and amplified the women's perception of their role in that community.

Clerical Failings and the Limits of Clerical Power

When Gertrude complained to Christ about the men who issued the interdict, he did not align himself with the offending clergy, but neither did he egg her on. Christ tried, instead, to cool her concern, promising to take up the matter at another time.[105] He was far more interested in his and the nuns' mutual need for each other than in the persons or circumstances that temporarily denied the sisters the opportunity to communicate. Confident that they occupied a privileged position in relation to God, the women were determined to find ways to maintain and deepen that relationship, uninterested in thinking through the wider implications of a passing situation that might momentarily compromise their relationship with Christ. To the nuns, the aspect of the priest's role that that principally mattered was that he helped to propel Christ's presence among them, and, in consequence, their connection with Christ and all the faithful. As we have seen, the same women made do without priests when circumstances obliged them to do so, and on such occasions, the priest faded into irrelevance, however temporarily. Among the many remarkable aspects of the nuns' relationship with the priests who served them was the nuns' ability to get along perfectly well without them.

The nuns' direct criticisms of priests were rare; they respected the office,[106] a respect coupled with the unyielding conviction that superiors and the clergy were owed obedience.[107] Mechtild learned from Christ that religious women and men must always willingly subject themselves to their

[105] *Le Hérault* 3.16.3 (SCh 143:70). In the *Book of Special Grace*, we find Christ and Mechtild employing a similar approach when Mechtild is troubled by male ecclesial authority: *Liber* 5.18 (347). A priest prohibits Mechtild from disseminating what she has learned in visions about the fate of certain souls in purgatory, and neither Mechtild nor Christ addresses head on the prohibition but finds a way to skirt it. When Mechtild expresses to Christ concern about the consequences of the proscription of praying for the dead in purgatory, Christ instructs her to pray a certain psalm, assuring her that this will compensate for any donations her acquiescence will cost the monastery.

[106] *Liber* 4.15 (373).

[107] See, for example, *Liber* 1.28; 1.35; 4.6; 4.19 (97, 116–17, 262–63, 276); *Le Hérault* 1 Prol. 4; 1.11.13 (SCh 139:112, 182–84). As Bynum observed, disobedience is the most grievous sin to the Helfta nuns ("Women Mystics," 194 and 239, for example).

superiors, and Christ underscored the magnitude of this obligation when he asserted that chains of obedience bind the soul in love to him, adding that whoever shows contempt for prelates spits in his face.[108] We may suppose that the nuns in this context had in mind both female and male superiors. Using similarly evocative imagery, the *Herald* depicted Christ's body as the victim of callous criticism of superiors: Christ warned Gertrude that those who loved only perfect and devout superiors but scorned those who were wanting brutalized his body with blows.[109]

This reflexive avoidance may explain why, among the comments about priests in the *Book of Special Grace* and the *Herald*, very few are starkly disapproving. Gertrude was perturbed by a certain person, probably a confessor, because he inveighed against those who received communion with what he regarded as inadequate preparation and devotion, frightening away some of the sisters from reception.[110] She put the problem before Christ, who identified the man in question as interfering with Christ's own delights.[111] Christ described the anonymous subject of Gertrude's concern:

> He is like an overly harsh tutor who checks the king's son too harshly or takes him away from the company and games of those his own age who are not nobles or who are poor, whose company the king's son enjoys a lot. And he does this because he regards it as more fitting for the young fellow to enjoy the honor due to royalty than to play in the streets.[112]

Christ was unhappy with the priest because his counsel hurt Christ, who, like a young prince prevented from playing games with his low-born playmates, misses the sisters' company. In spite of the priest's role in depriving Christ of his companions,

[108] *Liber* 1.18 (51).
[109] *Le Héraut* 3.74.5 (SCh 143:316).
[110] Doyère thinks that this man was a confessor (*Le Héraut* 325, n. 1).
[111] *Le Héraut* 3.77.1 (SCh 143:324).
[112] *Le Héraut* 3.77.1 (SCh 143:326).

however, Christ conceded to Gertrude that he would gladly forgive the man if he changed his ways: "Not only would I pardon him, but I would even accept him back, just as the king's son would receive his teacher, if he brought him back to play with his cherished companions, whom he had chased off a little before with dire severity."[113]

Christ's displeasure with the priest was not trivial, but his preoccupation did not lodge in the priest per se; he was intent on securing the companionship of his friends. Christ was willing to forgive, provided the priest returned the nuns to him. The whole account is more about the sisters and Christ than about the cleric, and there is in any case no evidence that the man in question was effective in steering his charges toward less frequent communion. On another occasion, Gertrude questioned how those who had placed the nuns under an interdict could receive Christ's grace.[114] Christ's response to Gertrude was circumspect: "Let it be. I shall deal with them in this matter,"[115] a statement that neither contradicted Gertrude's implicit criticism nor fanned the flames of her indignation. The terse exchange is indicative of a common design in the Helfta religiosity, which now and then vented displeasure with individual priests and groups of clergy, sometimes accompanied by remedies to address the nuns' dissatisfactions and Christ's own, but which did not dwell at length on either the irritation or the remediation in relationship to the clergy. In the case of the interdict, the Helfta writings do not reveal how Christ dealt with the meddlesome clergy. This concern was overshadowed by the nuns' buoyant happiness in Christ's overarching interest in them.

[113] *Le Héraut* 3.77.1 (SCh 143:326).

[114] *Le Héraut* 3.16.3 (SCh 143:70).

[115] *Le Héraut* 3.16.3 (SCh 143:70). Michael Bangert notes that Gertrude's writings are not confrontational to clergy ("A Mystic Pursues Narrative Theology: Biblical Speculation and Contemporary Imagery in Gertrude of Helfta," *Magistra* 2, no. 2 [Winter 1996]: 2).

We do not learn of the response of the clerics who ministered to the women at Helfta to the nuns' sometimes creative bypassing of the priest as celebrant or to their skirting of clerical directives. We may imagine some concern among the canons who imposed the interdict with the visions associated with Gertrude and Mechtild, experiences that claim to allow the sisters to join in a community of worshipers through the mediating presence of Christ, Mary, and the saints. But we have no evidence to indicate that the men familiar with the visions and the writings of the community were ill at ease with their purpose and their claims. This apparent hands-off attitude toward the revelations and literary activity that flowed from Helfta suggests that the men did not regard them as threatening their own authority as instructors in the faith; they may well have shared with the nuns the same basic assessment of their communal compositional enterprises.

Bynum has argued that the Helfta writings would have been especially appealing to contemporary clergy principally because of the centrality of eucharistic piety to the women's own religiosity, a piety that both reinforced clerical power and affirmed the goodness of creation. This reinforcement would have been valuable in the face of the continuing threat from dissenting voices of Catharism, with their bold condemnation of the material world as evil. Given emerging concerns about the Free Spirit, clergy may well have seen the *Herald* and the *Book of Special Grace* as bulwarks against anticlericalism and concomitant rejection of the sacraments, as well as of purgatory.[116] The *Herald* and the *Book of Special Grace* indicate, in addition, that clerical support for these works and the women who wrote them may have been tied to the certainty in the men's sense of the holy power some of the nuns exercised,

[116] For the nuns' support of clergy and support for the sacraments, see Bynum, "Women Mystics," 187 and 256. For Cathar and Waldensian rejection of contemporary teachings on purgatory, see Jacques Le Goff, *The Birth of Purgatory*, trans. Arthur Goldhammer (Chicago: University of Chicago Press, 1984), 239, 278–80.

from which friars and other priests perceived themselves to benefit.[117]

While Laurie Finke has insisted that the nuns' liturgical piety challenged clerical authority, intentionally or otherwise,[118] it is significant that there is no record of the Helfta writings' disturbing contemporary clergy. A fifteenth-century version of the *Herald, ein botte der götlichen miltekeit,* places in relief the attitudes of the thirteenth-century clerics to the nuns' religiosity: Gertrud Jaron Lewis has shown that the person responsible for *ein botte* excised all passages concerning Gertrude's priesthood from the text.[119] In contrast, there is no evidence of the women's male contemporaries interfering in the community's literature. Moreover, the clergy who wrote the *Herald*'s approbation expressed no reservations about the work's content. They offered no cautionary words concerning Gertrude's quasi-clerical role, nor did they gloss that role so as to dull or shape its meaning for the reading audience. Instead the approbation broadcast Gertrude's gifts and heralded the *Herald* with zeal.

[117] The absence of expressed anxiety or ambivalence about the nuns by the men who knew them may indicate these men's confidence in their *own* privileges and sense of security in the rightness of their relationship with the monastery, especially with the visionary women among the nuns. In his study of late medieval male-authored lives of holy women, John Coakley identifies a group of clergy who, he argues, were sufficiently secure in their priestly powers to countenance and even to promote the holy powers of women whom they admired and to whom they sometimes served as confidants (Coakley, *Women, Men,* 212–13). Gavin Fort argues otherwise. The explosion of contemporary hagiographic literature extolling the role of women in successfully taking up the demand to care for souls is evidence of women's stepping in to fulfill priests' central obligations. Male clerical acceptance of women's assumption of these responsibilities was not an expression of male confidence, according to Fort, but a consequence of the fear and shame associated with their doubts about their own ability to fulfill their clerical responsibilities to care for souls (Fort, "Suffering Another's Sin," 202–30).

[118] Laurie A. Finke, *Women's Writing in English: Medieval England* (London: Longman, 1999), 128–29.

[119] Gertrud Jaron Lewis, "Gertrud of Helfta's *Legatus divinae pietatis* and *ein botte der götlichen miltekeit*: A Comparative Study," in *Mysticism: Medieval and Modern*, ed. Valerie M. Lagorio (Salzburg: Institut für Anglistik und Amerikanistik, 1986), 58–71, esp. 67–69.

For their part, despite the nuns' flexible sense of priests' necessity to their lives, as Bynum argued long ago, they also did not wish to undermine the clergy. They made broad and general criticisms of the church[120] and were aware of the failings of priests, about which they wrote plainly, without rancor, and without anxiety, even when the shortcoming had immediate and objectionable consequences for the women themselves.[121] Thus the behavior of a particular priest might not be above reproach, and so he became fair target for the women's criticism. In this, the women acted in conformity with Christ, who acknowledged among the clergy those whose words, actions, and intentions were deficient, even wicked,[122] and who might occasionally voice warning to priests, sometimes oblique, sometimes direct. The nuns expressed hopeful expectation for conciliation with these individual priests. The Helfta literature does not examine systematically or in detail failures or abuses associated with the clergy, and it does not join to the sisters' occasional defiance of the clergy a sustained denunciation of the caste. Problems with clergy were, to the nuns, neither pervasive nor symptomatic of a fundamentally flawed institution or theology of the priesthood. None of the scathing criticism of priests, the thunderous zeal to reform the larger church, such as we find in Hildegard's writing[123] and about which we read in Mechtild of Magdeburg's *Flowing Light*, fueled these nuns' piety.[124]

[120] See for example *Liber* 1.13 (44); *Le Héraut* 3.13.1 (SCh 139:54).

[121] See for example *Liber* 4.1 (258).

[122] *Le Héraut* 3.74.1–2 (SCh 143:312–14).

[123] Barbara Newman, introduction to *Hildegard of Bingen: Scivias* (New York: Paulist Press, 1990), 20–21.

[124] Bynum, "Women Mystics," esp. 240–42; Theresa A. Halligan, introduction to *The Booke of Gostlye Grace of Mechtild of Hackeborn*, trans. Theresa A. Halligan (Toronto: Pontifical Institute of Mediaeval Studies, 1979), 39; and see Voaden, "All Girls," 82. Mechtild of Magdeburg's vulnerability to the power of clergy may have contributed to her suspicion, fear, and general disenchantment; see for example Bynum, "Women Mystics," 246.

The women's resolute sense of the rightness and constancy of their relationship with Christ and their concomitant realization that through him they were necessarily in communion with all the faithful contributed to fostering the serenity governing their attitude toward clergy. Their undercutting of radical differences between themselves and the priest, both in terms of the access of each to Christ and the joy each brought to him, helped them perceive that clerical power over them was frankly limited. Nowhere did they concede that any priest exercised the ability to compromise their contact with God or, therefore, curtail their integration into the larger Christian community. This basic equanimity seems to have allowed the nuns to marry expressions of commitment to obedience to superiors—and repeated calls to their readers for such obedience—with a profoundly independent orientation, without becoming swept up in the complexities of navigating between the two. From their perspective, the words they heard Christ speak to them wiped away any potential impasse. Exceptions to the rule of obedience were ready at hand and built on a secure foundation. Offering obedience was, therefore, neither complicated nor threatening. A number of men close to the convent may have assisted the nuns in arriving at this conclusion.

Chapter 6

"The People Are Also My Members"

Community Within and Beyond the Monastery

When she was praying for a certain person, the King of Glory, the Lord Jesus Christ, appeared to her, showing himself to her in the form of his Body, the mystical body of the church, of which he condescends to be called and to be Spouse and Head. He seemed to be solemnly clothed with royal clothes on the right side of his body, and the left part of his body was naked and full of wounds.[1]

Natal, Connubial, and Monastic Families

For the most part, the monastic family into which the nuns entered as children or as adults probably displaced natal or connubial families as the centerpiece of their personal relationships and formal commitments. The monastery became the principal context within which the nuns exercised their religious and social responsibilities and established ties of affection. The prologue to the *Book of Special Grace* illustrates Mechtild's movement away from her natal family and toward the monastic family by telling of her determination, at the age of seven, to enter the monastery against the objection of her

[1] *Le Héraut* 3.74.1 (SCh 143:312).

parents. We cannot know whether such a conflict of interest between Mechtild and her parents actually occurred. The account may be apocryphal, intended to bolster a narrative of Mechtild's precocious piety.[2]

We do know that children, under the control of their families, exercised little choice about whether or not to enter the cloister.[3] Although there were cases in which girls fought strenuously against their parents' objections to take up the religious life, those who entered were typically still children not yet in their teens, after which it became more difficult for girls to pry themselves from their families.[4] It was customary for families to invest their resources, including their relatives, in a single institution, and a professed family member often exercised a magnetic force, pulling others—mother, daughter, sister—into the monastery where she was established. Biological sisters were the dominant kinship group within female monastic households.[5] Abbess Gertrude of Hackeborn was already at Helfta when her younger sister Mechtild sought entry into the community,[6] and it may well have appealed to Mechtild's family—and to the child herself—to have their little girl join the house of which their teenage daughter was already a member. Additionally, their father Albert had signed the community's foundation charter.[7] Nonetheless, a shifting fidel-

[2] Penelope Johnson, *Equal in Monastic Profession: Religious Women in Medieval France*, Women in Culture and Society (Chicago: University of Chicago Press, 1991), 20–21, hints at this possibility but seems to decide against it.

[3] Johnson, *Equal in Monastic Profession*, 15–27; Anne E. Lester, *Creating Cistercian Nuns: The Women's Religious Movement and Its Reform in Thirteenth-Century Champagne* (Ithaca: Cornell University Press, 2011), 22.

[4] Donald Weinstein and Rudolf M. Bell, *Saints and Society: The Two Worlds of Western Christendom, 1000–1700* (Chicago: University of Chicago Press, 1982), 46.

[5] Johnson, *Equal in Monastic Profession*, 14–15, 18–20.

[6] As Johnson points out, accounts of younger sisters' being attracted to the religious life of older sisters are common in women's Lives (*Equal in Monastic Profession*, 20).

[7] See introduction.

ity is implied in ascribing to Mechtild a blanket rejection of her family's preference, which contrasts with her respectful attention to the wishes of those who would become her sisters in the religious life. According to the Prologue, Mechtild asked the nuns one by one if she might join their community.[8]

The women of Helfta assumed that affections flow naturally toward those to whom one is related and that entrance into the monastic life rechanneled them from their expected course. They taught one another that all their relationships ought to be based on a shared love of Christ, not grounded in pedigree or other familial associations. Christ declared about Gertrude of Helfta (about whose family of origin the literature speaks not at all), "I have exiled from her all her relatives, so that no one would love her because of her family and so that I alone am the reason she is loved by a friend."[9] Within the cloister, however, overlapping relationships between family of origin and monastic family sometimes challenged this basic assumption.[10] In life as in death, the monastic family intertwined with natal and connubial families, and the boundary separating the monastery from the world was fluid and permeable. Thus we read in praise of Abbess Gertrude that she was a mother to all her daughters, not distinguishing between those who were related to her by blood and those who were not.[11]

The nuns evidently expected that the abbess's sympathies would be more attuned to those with whom she had kinship connections. Responding to her care for them with warmth for her, the abbess's daughters, in turn, felt more for her than for their own mothers, fathers, or other relatives, or so the *Book of Special Grace* relates. The comment posits Abbess Gertrude's success at redirecting her emotions toward the community for which she was responsible and with the commendable

[8] *Liber* Prol. (5–6).

[9] *Le Héraut* 1.16.5 (SCh 139:216).

[10] See introduction.

[11] *Liber* 6.1 (374).

consequence of promoting those in her charge to do likewise.[12] When, in the Prologue, we read that Mechtild also became mother to all the nuns,[13] this is likewise a declaration that Mechtild's identity as well as her allegiance had shifted from that of daughter to her biological parents to mother of her cloistered sisters, that the relationships she established with these girls and women were braided with affection, and that she had assumed responsibility for those with whom she had lived since the age of seven.

Such shapeshifting must have been important, especially because numerous nuns were biologically related. Together with the Hackeborns, the founding Mansfeld family figured prominently among those closely associated with the monastery, which claimed members of each family, both as oblates in childhood and, later in life, as widows. Elizabeth Mansfeld herself, having founded the convent near Mansfeld, accompanied the nuns on their move from this location to Rodarsdorf, and two of her granddaughters, Sophia (fl. 13th c.) and Elizabeth (fl. 13th c.), entered the monastery at Helfta. The convent's third abbess, Sophie of Querfort, who ruled the house from 1291 to 1298 or 1301, was a great-granddaughter; Sophie's sister-in-law Irmengard of Schwarzburg (d. after 1301) retired to the convent as a widow.[14] The convent's sixth abbess, Lutgard (1337–1347), also stemmed from the house of Mansfeld, and Oda von Hamersleben, another relative, ruled the convent from 1348–1351. From the monastery's early days, Hackeborn women also populated it. Gertrude and Mechtild were daughters of Albert II of Hackeborn (1209–ca.1250), who signed the monastery's foundation charter in 1229, and two of their nieces became nuns as well.[15]

[12] *Liber* 6.1 (373).

[13] *Liber* 1, *caput praevium* (6).

[14] Sophie was Helfta's third abbess. She resigned because of illness and was succeeded by Jutta around 1303. See introduction.

[15] See introduction.

It is not surprising that expected reorientations in allegiance were neither always easy to achieve nor accomplished once and for all.[16] A revelation that came to Mechtild of her sister the abbess in heaven with their biological sister, Lutgard, who had died when she was a child,[17] suggests that at least some of the nuns continued to expend emotions or reflect on family they might have left long ago and known only briefly. The reunion in heaven of the two biological sisters speaks of a world in which an esteemed abbess, praised for the impartiality of her affections, was not less regarded for continuing nonetheless to feel bound to a young and long-deceased sister even after many years of monastic life. As visionary witness to this reunion, Mechtild may have contemplated a future where she might enjoy the celestial companionship of both her blood sisters.

Although Gertrude of Helfta entered the monastery when she was just a little girl and may not even have known her family of origin, she retained the custom of praying for them. It was only as an adult, sometime after her conversion experience, that she began to pray not for her own relatives but, instead, for Christ's friends, who included all the faithful—or so the *Herald* relates.[18] We may suppose that Gertrude had already long prayed for the universal church; the passage in the *Herald* is didactic. Echoing a Christian tradition more than a millennium old of seeking to pry away the priority of prayer for one's immediate family and friends in favor of the larger

[16] For Cistercian nuns' maintenance of relationships to family and friends outside the monastery, see Lester, *Creating Cistercian Nuns,* 72–73.

[17] *Liber* 1.24 (86).

[18] Elsewhere we read that when Gertrude asked Christ to save sinners, she insisted that she was not asking that he save any of her friends or family members (*Le Héraut* 3.9.5 [SCh 143:40–42]). For a broadening in the later Middle Ages of the population for whose spiritual well-being nuns and monks expressed concern, and for the opening up from a tight focus on religious to include laity, see Brian Patrick McGuire, "Purgatory, the Communion of Saints, and Medieval Change," *Viator* 20 (1989): 82.

Christian community, it cautioned the nuns not to be provincial in their supplications but to include among those counted closest to them those who were dear to Christ. The point is clear: sister readers should not be parochial but far-reaching in the distribution of their care. Christ himself underscored the integration of families of origin and the larger family of the faithful.

At one Mass for the nuns' deceased family members, Gertrude saw souls like sparks shoot into heaven. As she pondered the presence of her relatives among them, Christ explained, "I am your closest relative, father, and brother, and spouse. Those who are special to me are, therefore, very close to you. I cannot, therefore, exclude them from this communal memorial of your family; this is why they are intermixed."[19] The Helfta literature clarified for its readers that ties of kinship, as well as feelings of affection for families of origin, were not to be cast aside for a broad and impartial solidarity but rather amalgamated with a commitment to the larger communion of Christians for whom the nuns cultivated care. The need for such incorporation must have been thrown into relief in the experience and example of those women who had among their cloister companions connubial and natal family members, side by side with their other sisters. The nuns seem to have been sure of their ability to assimilate personal commitments to family into the more capacious sense of community that they perceived Christ urged on them, and they were determined to foster disinterested affection among themselves.

Laborers and Administrators

During Mass on the feast of Saint Lawrence, the chapel at Helfta was crowded. Rays of extraordinary brightness stretched out to all those in attendance when Christ appeared in their

[19] *Le Héraut* 5.17.1 (SCh 331:176).

midst.[20] Exulting in the pleasure Christ's presence gave her, Gertrude reflected on others in her congregation who were absent from Mass and pondered what Christ gave to those who were at that moment "sweating at external labors" and not enjoying similar gratification.[21] It is not immediately evident who Gertrude had in mind: whether, for example, she was thinking of people who were not present on this particular occasion or marking out a category of people whose nonappearance at Mass was habitual.[22] Gertrude considered these people primarily in the context of the labor they performed; they were woman or men (perhaps both) who applied themselves in physical exertion, perhaps on behalf of the monastery. They might have been *conversae* or *conversi*, those who had "converted" from the world. These lay brothers and sisters worked in Cistercian houses, members of an institution the white monks had initiated in the twelfth century as an apostolate to the laity and as a means of securing a reliable labor force to cultivate monastic estates.

Elsewhere in the *Herald*, the expression "those sweating at external labors" is tied to talk about the convent's stewards [*provisores claustri*],[23] men whose duty was to contribute to the monastery's upkeep and who were also probably charged with superintending the house's financial concerns and perhaps its

[20] The rays stretched out *ad personas de Congregatione*: *Le Héraut* 3.17.2 (SCh 143:76).

[21] *Le Héraut* 3.17.2 (SCh 143:76): *exterioribus insudantes*. Elsewhere when Christ tells Gertrude that he is indebted to those women who sing in the choir, Gertrude asks what he has in store for those who are not in attendance: *Le Héraut* 4.54.4 (SCh 255:448–50).

[22] The *Herald* and the *Book of Special Grace* several times refer to individuals and groups of people engaged in physical labor. It is often unclear whether we should count such people as *conversi*, *conversae*, sisters, or laity. See for example *Liber* 4.34 (293).

[23] *Le Héraut* 3.68.1 (SCh 143:274). We know that the abbess shared the handling of financial affairs with stewards: *Le Héraut* 3.68.1 (SCh 143:274). See in addition, *Le Héraut* 5.13.1 (SCh 331:160–62); *Liber* 5.1 (335); Max Krüne, ed., *Urkundenbuch der Klöster der Grafschaft Mansfeld* (Halle: Otto Hendel, 1888), nos. 6, 9, 12, 21–23, 133–36, 140–42.

legal affairs. The nuns might have also numbered these men among the monastery's *conversi*, a word that, at least by the thirteenth century, had become an umbrella term, encompassing laymen engaged in a broad variety of occupations in support of the monastic household, including carpentry, blacksmithing, and farming, as well as administration.[24] Although the use of similar language does not mean that the *Herald* is referring to the same category of people in both contexts, this use of language renders it plausible that Gertrude may have been worrying over those among the monastery's personnel whose responsibilities prevented them from participating regularly in Mass.

The *Herald* characterizes "those sweating at external labors" on the feast of Saint Lawrence in an additional way. In response to her concern about the members of the congregation not at Mass, Christ explained to Gertrude, "I anoint them with balsam":

> When she considered this power, she was greatly astonished at how those who engaged in spiritual exercises and those who did not engage in exercises received an equal benefit: for balsam makes anointed bodies unputrefiable, with little difference whether they are asleep or awake. She also received this more intelligible analogy as an example: when a person eats, the whole body is strengthened in each member, [although] only the mouth delights in the taste of the food.

[24] It is often difficult to determine the canonical category into which monastery personnel fit, and, in any case, their activities failed regularly to mirror what might be elaborated in rules or administrative records. Constance Berman has shown that the words *conversa* and *conversus* may carry a range of meanings in any given medieval document, including but not limited to an agricultural laborer or a knight who converted to the religious life. She has found, furthermore, that the divide between monk or nun on the one hand, and *conversus* or *conversa* on the other, was not always a hard one (Constance H. Berman, "Distinguishing Between the Humble Peasant Lay Brother and Sister, and the Converted Knight in Medieval Southern France," in *Religious and Laity in Western Europe 1000–1400, Interaction, Negotiation, and Power*, ed. Emilia Jamroziak and Janet Burton [Turnhout: Brepols, 2006], 263–81).

> In this way, when a special grace is given to the elect out of the unrestrained goodness of God, merit is also augmented for all members and especially for those belonging to the same congregation.[25]

Thus those who were attending Mass on this feast day did not exhaust Gertrude's notion of who comprised her congregation. Even as she engaged in liturgical devotions in her choir stall, Gertrude wondered about the significance of Mass to those members of the congregation whose primary activities were other than those to which she and her sisters directed themselves, and she was concerned about their welfare.[26] This conversation with Christ suggests that the nuns may have consciously striven to integrate into their sense of liturgical community others whom they acknowledged as members of their congregation but who were not their (regular) companions in the Mass or the many other liturgical devotions that made up their days. But Gertrude's expression of concern and curiosity about these other members is noteworthy in large part because it is exceptional. This is one of the few instances in which we see Gertrude entertaining an extended interest, in the context of the liturgy, in a specified category of fellow monastic personnel other than her sisters.[27]

As the passage above indicates, *congregatio*, whatever else it may mean, seems to include both the "elect" [*electus*] and a group of people about whom Gertrude thought in contrast with them. The word *elect* appears repeatedly in the Helfta literature, taking on different shades of meaning in different contexts.[28] In the above passage, the word *elect* denotes (or

[25] *Le Héraut* 3.17.3 (SCh 143:76–78).

[26] *Le Héraut* 3.17.3 (SCh 143:76).

[27] Cistercian monks often ignored *conversi* when they wrote about their communities; see Martha G. Newman, *The Boundaries of Charity: Cistercian Culture and Ecclesiastical Reform, 1098–1180* (Stanford: Stanford University Press, 1996), 102.

[28] The elect are those who have already won salvation. See for example *Liber* 1.13; 1.28; 1.34; 1.39 (42, 97, 113, 123–24); *Le Héraut* 3.17.1; 4.12.13–15

includes) those who engage in the spiritual exercises associated with Mass. It is apparent from the material I have been discussing that Gertrude counts herself among the elect who engage in these exercises, and this association makes it probable that *the elect* in this context refers to the sisters.[29] Those who are not among the elect are those who are not at Mass and are not, therefore, engaging in liturgical devotions. It seems likely, though not entirely clear, that in this case the division between the two groups—elect and non-elect—is meant to signal a more general distinction between the two groups. The discussion should probably be taken as standing in for a broader understanding the nuns may have had about the monastic personnel with whom they shared their household and their relationship with these members of their congregation. Christ's response to Gertrude indicates that they—the sisters and these other members of the household—constitute one body.

Yet the odd imagery of *bodies*—some awake, others drowsy or asleep—is evocative not so much (or not only) of sameness or unity but of difference and division; the non-elect lumber in a sort of spiritual passivity, reliant for their spiritual well-being on the sisters: they are the body dependent on the mouth.[30]

(SCh 143:72–74; SCh 255:80). The term attaches, in addition, to specific individuals among the living, such as Mechtild and Gertrude, as well as to others for whom God has found favor, the recipients of spiritual secrets, for instance. See for example *Liber* Prol. (1); *Le Héraut* 3.30.14; 4.4.3 (SCh 143:142; SCh 255:62). The term sometimes applies to all the sisters, e.g., *Liber* 1.20 (72). It carries with it the suggestion that such individuals are heaven-bound, and it refers to those people who strive for the salvation of others also on pilgrimage (*Le Héraut* 3.74.1; 3.30.4 [SCh 143:312–14, 136]).

[29] The *Herald* credits Gertrude with distancing herself from association with "the elect" in a context in which the *Herald* refers to "the elect" as those worthy of God's gifts (*Le Héraut* 1.11.1 [SCh 139:170–80]).

[30] For the sense among Cistercian monks that *conversi* occupied a lower spiritual status than they, see Jean Leclercq, "Comment vivaient les frères convers?" 239–59; Newman, *Boundaries of Charity*, 101–6; Megan Cassidy, "'*Non Conversi sed Perversi*': The Use and Marginalization of the Cistercian Lay Brother," in *Deviance & Textual Control*, ed. Megan Cassidy, et al. (University of Melbourne: History Department, 1997), 34–55; Megan Cassidy, *Monastic Spaces and Their Meanings* (Turnhout: Brepols, 2001), 167–93; Brian

All members are part of one body, but the members fulfill different functions. The relationship of the sisters and the other monastic personnel was, from this perspective, unequal. Gertrude's spiritual exercises and those of her sisters sustained the other members of their congregation, who are pictured as passive (asleep) and dependent (the body the mouth feeds), apparently without the resources of their own necessary to acquire spiritual sustenance.

Precisely because of the dissimilar role each group occupies, Gertrude seemed uneasy with the implications of a broadened sense of her liturgical community, consisting in both the elect and those who relied on them. On the one hand, Gertrude was astonished that those who did not labor in spiritual affairs received the same food as those who did;[31] on the other, she communicated no doubt or hesitation about the sisters' power to feed others spiritually—they were the channels through whom God's grace flowed. Gertrude and her sisters may have acknowledged that they, together with their monastic personnel, constituted one body. As the *Herald* portrays her, Gertrude wrestled, nevertheless, with the notion that Christ transfers rewards to those who do not work for them—or at least the *Herald* wanted to highlight this preoccupation, perhaps seeking to satisfy a nagging discomfort among the sisters about this proposition.

Noell, "Expectation and Unrest among Cistercian Lay Brothers in the Twelfth and Thirteenth Centuries," *Journal of Medieval History* 32, no. 3 (2006): 255. We know far less about women's attitudes than we do about men's toward *conversi* and must be careful about mapping onto the female house at Helfta, with its indeterminate affiliation, insights into thirteenth-century Cistercian men's monasteries.

[31] A significant point of the Helfta literature is that grace flows upon those who do not merit it. See for example *Le Héraut* 4.49.1 (SCh 255:396). The community's writings are infused with optimism, which Christ encouraged: whoever believed that Christ would benefit her above what she merited and who praised Christ on this account would receive merit in remuneration. This was so, Christ declared, because it is impossible for a human being not to take possession of those things in which she believes and hopes (*Liber* 3.5 [202]).

The literature's presentation of sisters' attitudes toward members of the congregation whose primary duties were other than the nuns' own was more complicated than this passage suggests, however. Gertrude seems to have assumed that the primary commitments to which she and her sisters were devoted were superior to the activities the stewards were called to perform and so worthy of greater reward.[32] She did not, however, rest easy in this assumption. Elsewhere, the *Herald* depicts Christ pushing Gertrude to enlarge her understanding, not now of the relationship among the various members of her congregation, but of the spiritual significance of labor per se.[33] The *Herald* as well as the *Book of Special Grace* develops the alternative notion that the monastery's members assigned to non-liturgical work might, through their activities, further not only their own salvation but that of others as well.

Once, for example, when Gertrude worried about the convent's stewards, weighed down with financial cares, she prayed that Christ would enable them to pay the household's debts so that the stewards would have fewer distractions and more time for prayer.[34] Christ rejected Gertrude's prioritizing of prayer over administrative duties, recalling to her that he had no need of works, whether obviously spiritual or otherwise: "And how is that beneficial to me? I do not need your good works, and it is the same to me whether you devote yourself to spiritual works or sweat in exterior works provided your will is freely directed toward me."[35] As long as they undertook their tasks with a view toward honoring and loving him, he would reward those who performed the temporal services that

[32] For devaluation of the work in which *conversi* engaged, see Clemens Van Dijk, "L'instruction et la culture des frères convers dans les premiers siècles de l'ordre de Cîteaux," *Collectanea* 24 (1962): 243–58.

[33] For the Cistercian appraisal of the spiritual worth of manual labor, see, among many sources, Leclercq, "Comment vivaient."

[34] *Le Héraut* 3.68.1 (SCh 143:274).

[35] *Le Héraut* 3.68.1 (SCh 143:190). For the *Herald's* emphasis on intention's animating action, see, for example, *Le Héraut* 3.68.3–4 (SCh 143:276–80).

supported the convent, Christ declared. Gertrude then saw one of the stewards offering God a piece of gold set with a precious jewels, and she heard Christ say, "If I alleviated the burden on him for whom you pray, then I would lack that noble jewel in the coin that pleases me, and he would lose remuneration."[36]

The *Book of Special Grace* makes a similar pronouncement about the value of everyday labor to God. When Mechtild prayed for a woman who was zealous in accomplishing her housework, especially the menial tasks to which she was set, she saw the woman before Christ, on her knees, her arms elevated as if in prayer. Christ placed his hands on the woman's hands, balm flowed over her, and Mechtild overheard Christ utter, "Behold, I give you all my works to sanctify your works and to make up for what they lack."[37] Mechtild understood from this that the woman's exertions were exceedingly pleasing to God. It is unclear whether the woman to whom Mechtild refers is one of her own sisters or a *conversa*;[38] the vision under-

[36] *Le Héraut* 3.68.2 (SCh 143:276). For a discussion of passages emphasizing the value God accords the work of administrators at Helfta, see Michael Anthony Abril, "Gertrude of Helfta's Liturgical-Mystical Union," CSQ 43, no. 1 (2008): 77–96, esp. 86–88. Margaret Winkworth (*Gertrude of Helfta: The Herald of Divine Love*, trans. Margaret Winkworth [New York: Paulist Press, 1993], 138, n. 21) and Abril ("Gertrude of Helfta," 87) underscore the complementarity of physical labor and spiritual work in the Helfta writings.

[37] *Liber* 4.34 (293).

[38] I have not found the word *conversa* in any of the Helfta books. *Conversae* can be identified with specificity only rarely in thirteenth-century documents. On *conversae* at Helfta, see Michael Bangert, *Demut in Freiheit* (Würzburg: Echter, 1997), 29–31. For *conversae* in Benedictine and Cistercian convents, see Eileen Power, *Medieval English Nunneries, c. 1275 to 1535* (Cambridge: Cambridge University Press, 1922), 154–55; Philibert Schmitz, *Histoire de l'Ordre de Saint-Benoît*, vol. 7, *Les Moniales* (Liège: Les Éditions de Maredsous, 1956), 227–28; Maren Kuhn-Rehfus, "Cistercian Nuns in Germany in the Thirteenth Century," in *Hidden Springs: Cistercian Monastic Women*, ed. John A. Nichols and Lillian Thomas Shank, CS 113a (Kalamazoo, MI: Cistercian Publications, 1995), 132–33, 155–56; Maren Kuhn-Rehfus, *Die Zisterzienser: Ordensleben zwischen Ideal und Wirklichkeit*, ed. K. [Kaspar] Elm, et al. (Bonn: Rheinland-Verlag, 1980), 132–33; Jean de la Croix Bouton, *Histoire externe:*

scores not the status of its subject but the manual labor in which she is engaged, the omission perhaps a concession to the overlap between sisters who chanted and those who worked in other ways.[39]

Another section of the *Book of Special Grace* tells of Mechtild's compassion for the portress, who was called away regularly from Mass by the arrival of guests. Responding to her concern, Christ assured Mechtild, "Every step a person takes in obedience is like a coin I gather in my hand, augmenting her merit."[40] Christ brought to Gertrude's attention the toll difficult work had taken on the body of one of the monastery's male laborers and proclaimed the value of this to him, Christ.[41] When Gertrude objected that the man in question seemed to her to have mixed motives, Christ agreed that the man could concentrate on his work with greater piety. Nevertheless, he revealed, the man's will was so conformed to Christ's own that Christ was the supreme cause of all the man's actions, an implicit offer of the laborer as a model to Gertrude herself.[42]

These passages illustrate the nuns' determination to attribute spiritual significance to work that called some members of the congregation—male or female, laborers or administrators, sisters or *conversae*—more often than others away from prayer and other more obviously spiritual activities. Christ counted as works worthy of divine recompense the obligations of one of the nuns, the stewards' efforts to contend with the

---

Jusqu'à la fin du XVe siècle, vol. 1 of *Les moniales cisterciennes* (Grignan: Abbaye N. D. d'Aiguebelle, 1986), 21–23; Jean de la Croix Bouton, *Histoire interne: Études sur la vie des moniales* (Grignan: Abbaye N. D. d'Aiguebelle, 1988–89), 3.123–32.

[39] There may be something similar at play in the fourteenth-century sister book from Unterlinden (Richard Kieckhefer, "Mystical Communities in the Late Medieval West," Medieval Academy Plenary Address, International Medieval Conference, Leeds, 2007, 5).

[40] *Liber* 3.45 (248).

[41] *Le Héraut* 3.68.4 (SCh 143:278–80).

[42] *Le Héraut* 3.63.4 (SCh 143:280).

monastery's financial misfortunes, a laborer's physical exertions, and the faith-filled chores of an anonymous woman.[43] In the course of his conversation with Gertrude about Helfta's stewards, Christ declared the worth to self and God of the exertions in which the body joins: "In the future resurrection, when this mortal body will be clothed in incorruption [1 Cor 15:53], then each member will receive a particular reward for each of the works done in my name and for each of the exercises done in love of me."[44]

The sisters admitted, furthermore, that the labor occupying other members of the house, related to both supplying and managing the monastery's resources and housekeeping, contributed to furthering the salvation of the sisters themselves. The *Herald* tells of a woman, identified as illiterate, who was distressed because the cares of her office got in the way of her prayer. She was probably a *conversa*[45] and may have been a cook.[46] Her attenuated participation in the liturgy may be indicative of the practices of the convent's *conversae* more broadly, logging far fewer hours of formal communal prayer than sisters whose primary obligation was to pray in common, but otherwise occupied in the day-to-day maintenance of the household.[47] Christ told Gertrude, about this woman,

[43] See too, *Le Héraut* 5.13.1 (SCh 331:160–62), for the procurator's work making a ladder on which his soul climbed to heaven.

[44] *Le Héraut* 3.68.3 (SCh 143:278).

[45] Martha Newman, "Crucified by the Virtues: Monks, Lay Brothers, and Women in Thirteenth-Century Cistercian Saints' Lives," in *Gender and Difference in the Middle Ages*, ed. Sharon Farmer and Carol Braun Pasternack (Minneapolis: University of Minnesota Press), 185; Noell, "Expectation and Unrest," 256.

[46] *Le Héraut* 3.73.14 (SCh 143:310). The woman seems to have contributed directly to the material welfare of the house and its inhabitants; see SCh 143:310, n. 1; Mary Jeremy Finnegan, *The Women of Helfta: Scholars and Mystics* (Athens: University of Georgia Press, 1991), 93–94.

[47] For the limited participation of *conversi* in the liturgy along with monks, see John Harper, *The Forms and Orders of Western Liturgy from the Tenth to the Eighteenth Century* (Oxford: Clarendon, 1995), 101–2.

> I have not chosen her for this so that she should serve me only one hour of the day but rather so that that she should be with me the whole day, without interruption. That is, so that she should continually carry out all her works to my praise, with the intention with which she would like to pray. And, in addition, she should add this devotion, that in all the works in which she labors in her office, she should always desire that all who make use of her labors are not only refreshed in body but also attracted in spirit to my love and strengthened in all good. And whenever she does [this], it seems to me as though she seasons well with salt each dish of her work and labor.[48]

Proclaiming that he accompanied the woman throughout her work day, not only the one hour each day she dedicated to formal prayer, Christ indicated that what mattered to him was not her activity but her intentions. Her work, moreover, would produce spiritual benefits for those who benefited from it physically (that is, the sisters), just as the sisters' liturgical prayers and other devotions worked for the salvation of many other than themselves. If, as this conversation suggests, some sisters may have been ambivalent about the spiritual significance of the labors of those who also occupied the monastery, others apparently felt called upon to admit their meaning for the salvation of the worker who executed the tasks as well as for the larger community of sisters on whose behalf they toiled. When Mechtild beheld the provost's soul in heaven, it had assumed the form of a cloister in whose windows sat souls in the form of statues—representations of deceased, holy members of the household, imagery that suggests the crediting to the provost of structural support to the monastery conducive to its members' salvation.[49]

[48] *Le Héraut* 3.73.14 (SCh 143:310–12).

[49] *Liber* 5.10 (335). This provost, Otto, is mentioned repeatedly in charters as being occupied with property transactions and implicated in the sending of sisters to the monastery at Hedersleben; see for example, *Urkundenbuch*

The *Herald* and the *Book of Special Grace* thus indicate the sisters' estimation of the faithful discharge of responsibilities to which some other inhabitants of the monastery were principally called, and which intruded into hours that might have profitably been spent in prayer. They understood that postlapsarian human nature required human beings to expend effort on such tasks as securing clothing and food. To them, such physical exertions were not merely a concession to human needs. They knew, in addition, that such activities were pleasing to Christ.[50] He told them so:

> For if I delighted only in spiritual exercises, I would, of course, have reformed human nature after the Fall in such a way that it would not need food or clothing or the other things for which human beings sweat in expending energy to find and gather what is necessary to live. But just as a powerful emperor not only delights in having refined and bejeweled girls in his palace but also retains princes, dukes, knights, and other ministers suitable for various works, thus I delight not only in the interior delicacies of contemplatives but also in the diverse exercises of practical business that are accomplished for my honor and for my love. I am lured to loiter and to remain delightfully among the sons of men, for they exercise greatly love, patience, humility, and the other virtues in such works.[51]

In this unequivocal affirmation of the worth of the work of practical chores and workaday business commitments, and in providing a theological context for the necessity of the bounty

---

der Klöster der Grafschaft Mansfeld, ed. Max Krüne (Halle: Otto Hendel, 1888), nos. 6, 9, 12, 21–23, 133–36, 140–42.

[50] And so were the human needs they aimed to satisfy. For the pleasure Christ took when Gertrude ate and drank, and when anybody sits down to a meal with devotion, see *Le Héraut* 4.23.4–6 (SCh 255:220–22). See Ella L. Johnson, "Bodily Language in the Spiritual Exercises of Gertrud the Great of Helfta," *Magistra* 14, no. 1 (2008): 79–107.

[51] *Le Héraut* 3.68.1 (SCh 143:274–76).

of their labors, Christ recognized, in a litany of virtues, the piety expended in daily chores.[52]

Christ's approbatory words would have been not only meaningful to the nuns' estimation of the men and women whose duty it was to support the sisters, but valuable to the sisters themselves. We know that the abbess shared the handling of financial affairs with stewards, and the *Book of Special Grace* attributes to Mechtild a hand in governing the convent with her sister, in which capacity she also assisted in the house's financial matters. We do not know to what extent other nuns may have engaged in administrative duties. They performed manual labor, including spinning, and they otherwise worked with their hands, copying and perhaps illuminating manuscripts.[53] Periodically, the *Herald* and the *Book of Special Grace* make further incidental references to duties the nuns took up. Thus, for example, we read of the nuns busying themselves in the courtyard and of sisters sweeping and otherwise putting the house in order.[54]

In the convent's hagiographic portrait of Abbess Gertrude of Hackeborn, we learn that she had a knack for juggling prayer with household responsibilities, including seeing to the visitors who must often have demanded her attention, her successful balancing act offered as one of many examples of

[52] The Helfta literature's congratulatory admission of *conversae* into the circle of those who bring great pleasure to Christ casts these women in a more favorable light than that through which Cistercian monks were accustomed to consider the laymen who worked in their monasteries and on their granges. For the difficulties twelfth-century Cistercian monks experienced incorporating *conversi* into their sense of community, see Martha Newman, *Boundaries of Charity*, 101–6.

[53] *Le Héraut* 3.32.5 (SCh 143:170).

[54] *Le Héraut* 5.1.7.3; 3.32.5 (SCh 331:24; SCh 143:170); *Liber* 6.1 (374). While it would be imprudent to take these accounts at face value, they probably do point to activities in which we may assume the nuns took part. There are several other incidental references to manual labor, some of which may concern the nuns (although they may have *conversae* as their subject); see for instance, *Le Héraut* 3.69.1 (SCh 143:280–82).

her holiness.[55] The younger Gertrude of Helfta seems to have remained uncertain about reconciling spiritual and intellectual commitments with manual labor, which Christ revealed to her contributed (if offered with correct intention) to his glory and to the salvation of the neighbor. She concluded that for her part, she could offer God the physical exertions required to hold a book in her hands as she read.[56] The Helfta writings push back strongly against a tendency among the sisters to distinguish sharply between the salvific power associated with the activities to which they were chiefly called (Office and Mass) and those labors (the practical business of cooking, cleaning, and so forth) that tugged at their time and were the central obligations of others in the household, from whom we never hear directly. The nuns were convinced that the importance of widening their sense of the community counted as spiritually productive, which, if not a "glorification of manual labor," is surely an unambiguous recognition of its spiritual potential.[57]

The nuns' recognition of others' ability to promote both their own and the nuns' salvation draws attention to the general deliberateness with which the nuns considered their household companions and, perhaps because of their overlapping commitments, learned something about themselves in the process. The arena in which administrators and *conversi*, male and female, exercised spiritual power differed markedly from that of the nuns; it is probably for this reason that when the nuns fixed their focus on their liturgical community, they did not characterize the relationship between them and other household members with a sense of mutuality. The nuns

[55] *Liber* 6.1 (375). For the larger Cistercian context of monks' seizing on the spiritual value of the physical labors in which they themselves engaged, see Christopher J. Holdsworth, "The Blessings of Work: The Cistercian View," in *Sanctity and Secularity: The Church and the World* (Oxford: Blackwell, 1973).

[56] *Le Héraut* 4.44.1 (SCh 255:342).

[57] Emile Mâle, *The Gothic Image: Religious Art in France of the Thirteenth Century*, trans. Dora Nussey (1958; repr. New York: Harper & Row, 1972), 65.

acknowledged that their own liturgical observations benefited the fellow members of their household, who necessarily depended on them when (or because) work prevented them from attending Mass. The nuns did not, however, explore this dependence extensively. It may be that their recognition of the spiritually productive sphere in which non-religious members of the household labored, and their attribution to them of their own spiritual resources, made it a less pressing concern.

The sisters knew that giving was a privilege; they had it in common with the saints, and they admitted to sharing it with those who did not exert themselves in matters that were—to the sisters—more obviously potent with spiritual power than other works.[58] A recurring concern of the Helfta writings is that the more time one gave over to service, the fewer the hours available for liturgical worship. When Mechtild was sad to have arrived at Mass belatedly, having been occupied with other works that obedience obliged, God did not comfort her by recognizing the value of her labors but instead assured her that he would absolve her of her debt.[59] The nuns remained sure for themselves of the primacy of their own liturgical commitments even as, with Christ's prompting, they found cause to assert unambiguously the spiritual worth of other sorts of work, refusing to rob any activity performed in love and honor of God of significance to him and thus of salvific potency.

The sisters retained for themselves the preeminent role in shoring up the world's salvation, recognizing a hierarchy of importance of members within the monastery.[60] The far greater frequency with which their thoughts alighted on the inhabitants of heaven than on their fellow community members, the strong parallels they perceived between saintly activities and the spiritual practices in which they engaged in common, and

[58] *Liber* 1.11 (35).

[59] *Liber* 1.31 (104–5).

[60] For male Cistercian monks' sense of partnership and hierarchy in relation to *conversi*, see Noelle, "Expectation and Unrest," 257–60.

the ease and enthusiasm with which they moved between heaven and their choir stalls all indicate that the nuns regarded their most important activities as distancing themselves from those members of the congregation whose work tied them more firmly to the mundane needs of fallen humanity, and as lifting them a little closer to the saints and angels. And yet they underscored that they formed one community with all the members of their household—and beyond. During Matins on the feast of the Purification, the sisters sang out *Ora pro populo*, summoning Mary into their midst, and she instructed the angels to defend the monastery from the enemy; they obeyed and, encircling the monastery, interlocked their shields to form a fortification. When Gertrude asked whether only those present in choir benefited from the defense, Mary promised that all members of the community who were dedicated to the religious life or promoted it in others benefited from the protection the Queen of Heaven oversaw.[61]

Laity

Laywomen and men were at least sometimes present in the convent's chapel when Mass was celebrated.[62] Although in the thirteenth century laity were enjoined to attend Mass on the major feasts, including Christmas, Ash Wednesday, and Easter,[63] there is evidence that they came to Mass at Helfta on

[61] *Le Héraut* 4.9.6 (SCh 255:118).

[62] See for example, *Le Héraut* 3.16.5 (SCh 143:70–72). For the presence of laity at the church at Helfta, see Cornelia Oefelein ("Grundlagen zur Baugeschichte des Klosters Helfta," in *"Vor dir steht die leere Schale meiner Sehnsucht": Die Mystik der Frauen von Helfta*, ed. Michael Bangert and Hildegund Keul [Leipzig: St. Benno Buch- und Zeitschriftenverlagsgesellschaft, 1998], 27).

[63] Eamon Duffy, *The Stripping of the Altars: Traditional Religion in England 1400–1580* (New Haven, CT: Yale University Press, 1992), 93 and 95; Gary Macy, "Commentaries on the Mass During the Early Scholastic Period," in *Treasures from the Storeroom: Medieval Religion and the Eucharist* (Collegeville, MN: Liturgical Press, 1999), 142–71. On the participation of laity in the liturgy, see Enrico Cattaneo, "La Partecipazione dei Laici alla Liturgia," *I laici nella*

other occasions as well.[64] Mass thus offered the sisters proximity to people beyond the professed nuns, little girls, noble retirees, laborers, procurators, and priests who made up the monastic family. Interactions among the nuns and laity (as well as the other members of the community) were, however, probably limited or none at all during Mass; the chapel's architecture, including the grill behind which the nuns remained and the balcony where they probably sat, supported and furthered segregation from the laity as well as from the priest. References to the "congregation" [*congregatio*] are peppered throughout the *Book of Special Grace* and the *Herald*, and the term is used variously; it sometimes includes people who came from outside to attend Mass at the convent's church.[65]

There are, however, few explicit references to the presence of laity during the Mass. When we read that during the interdict, the entire congregation [*tota congregatio*] approached the

---

'Societas christiana' dei secoli XI et XII: Atti della terza settimana internazionale di studio, Mendola, 21–27 agosto 1965 (Milan: Vita e Pensiero, 1968), 396–427.

[64] See for example *Le Héraut* 3.16.5 (SCh 143:70–72).

[65] We read again and again of Christ's coming to the monastery's church and moving among the congregation (*congregatio*), and although the contexts in which the word *congregatio* sometimes occurs leaves open the possibility that it attaches to a larger, undefined, community whose lives revolved around the house, when the meaning of *congregatio* is apparent it usually—though not always—seems to be a synonym for the nuns. See for example, *Liber* 2.27; 4.56 (95, 307); *Le Héraut* 3.16.1; 3.16.4 (SCh 143:66, 70). *Congregatio* sometimes incorporates dead members of the monastery: *Liber* 2.26 (171). We read of the congregation's being in debt, in which instance *congregatio* stands for *claustro*, and both words denote the monastery at Helfta as an institution that has corporate financial responsibilities: *Le Héraut* 3.68.1 (SCh 143:274). The writings seem usually to use the word *conventus* with reference to the sisters. See for example: *Liber* 4.2 (259); *Le Héraut* 1.3.6; 1.13.3; 2 Prol.; 2.17.1 (SCh 139:138–40, 192, 226, 298). In the *Herald* 3.16.4 (SCh 143:70), we read that Gertrude offered the Host for God's praise and salvation of whole convent (*totius conventus*); in this case, we know that lay parishioners were present at Mass. It is unclear, however, whether the word *conventus* here is meant to include these lay parishioners. *Conventus* sometimes denotes the physical buildings *and* the sisters; see, for example, *Le Héraut* 4.2.14 (SCh 255:44).

altar at which Gertrude and Mechtild saw Christ serve or that Mechtild saw all the souls of the congregation leave their bodies and approach the altar where Christ awaited them,[66] it is not entirely clear who is part of the group Gertrude and Mechtild had on their minds. There is, however, little reason to suppose that either was thinking of members of the congregation beyond her sisters. When the nuns do name a specific category of people present during Mass, it is almost always themselves they identify. It seems evident that in these instances, as in others like them, the laity did not warrant specific mention, not because the nuns took their presence for granted but because they did not figure significantly in the nuns' sense of who constituted their liturgical community.

Even when we know that laity were present during Mass, the nuns' thoughts did not alight on them for long. During the period of the interdict, when the nuns were prohibited from receiving communion themselves, Mass was still celebrated at the chapel for the benefit of the local population (*civi*).[67] The *Herald* (but not the *Book of Special Grace*) notes the presence of laypeople, although it is unclear why, and it is not evident that they received communion on this occasion. Subsequent to the Fourth Lateran Council in 1215, communion was, for the majority of laywomen and men, an annual event at Easter. Receiving the Eucharist on additional occasions sometimes necessitated special permission, and reception was, in any case, not the primary mode of lay eucharistic devotion; instead, adoring the elevated host was central to lay as well as religious piety.[68] Whatever their form of worship, the laity did not

[66] *Liber* 4.1 (257).

[67] A marginal note in four of Doyère's manuscripts indicates that the interdict did not apply to the parishioners: SCh 143:3, 70, n. 1.

[68] Duffy, *Stripping of the Altars*, 93 and 95; Harper, *Forms and Orders*, 40, for the laity and the elevation of the Host; on the history of the practice of the elevation of the host, see Joseph A. Jungmann, *The Mass of the Roman Rite: Its Origins and Development (Missarum Sollemnia)*, trans. Francis A. Brunner, 2 vols. (New York: Benziger Brothers, 1988), 1:90–92.

impinge on Gertrude's or Mechtild's consciousness. There is certainly no record of the sisters perceiving the laity as contributing to the sisters' own spiritual well-being.

Much has been written in the last decades about the ways in which late medieval laypeople may have felt themselves to be more involved in Mass than used to be supposed.[69] The Helfta literature does not belie this assertion, but neither does it imply that lay participation in the Mass was of much interest to the nuns. There is no compelling evidence that participating with laywomen and laymen in a common Mass furthered the sisters' sense of community with them.

There are a few casual comments in the Helfta literature that make it evident that nuns were clear on the superiority of their state of life to that of lay people. Gertrude's *Exercises* lauds marriage with Christ as suitable for more sublime souls, who despise the coupling of man and women,[70] a narrator remarks on the drunken behavior of laypeople,[71] and the *Book of Special Grace* tosses out a number of disapproving asides, as when we read that Christ criticized the laity to Mechtild for their failure to attend to the word of God and the sacraments.[72] The most dramatic instance of proxy penance in the Helfta literature is associated with lay misbehavior: during Lent, Mechtild scatted bits of broken glass on her bed, a penance on behalf of some people [*populus*] whom she heard singing.[73] But neither reproving textual intrusions about the world beyond the cloister nor

[69] John Bossy, "The Mass as a Social Institution, 1200–1700," *Past and Present* 100 (August 1983): 29–61; Jacqueline Jung, "Beyond the Barrier: The Unifying Role of the Choir Screen in Gothic Churches," *Art Bulletin* 82, no. 4 (December 2000): 626, 629.

[70] *Les Exercices* 3.220–27 (SCh 127:110).

[71] *Le Hérault* 4.14.8 (SCh 255:262).

[72] *Liber* 4.1 (258).

[73] *Liber* 5.30 (365). For the phenomenon in the thirteenth century of one person's paying the penalty for sin of another, see Gavin Fort, "Suffering Another's Sin: Proxy Penance in the Thirteenth Century," *Journal of Medieval History* 44, no. 2 (2018): 202–30.

a frank disregard for the laity in the context of communal public worship tells the full story. As was the case for their consideration of the non-religious members of the household, when the nuns more carefully reflected on the lay exercise of spiritual power, they looked beyond the chapel. And just as the nuns were, however haltingly, confident in their cloister companions' ability to work for both their own salvation and that of others, so too, the Helfta writings suggest, the women trusted in laypeople's ability to do likewise, sometimes but not always leaning on the sisters for support.

As we have seen, the reputation of one or the other principal visionary—and perhaps of others as well—brought priests, religious, and laity to the house, eager to share confidences, make requests for intercession, and receive comfort. Visitors learned there about God and about themselves.[74] Some of them witnessed the women in ecstasy. The nuns depicted themselves as engaged with spiritual needs of the world outside the clois-

[74] *Le Héraut* 1.1.3; 1.3.2; 3.64.1; 5.29.1 (SCh 139:122–24, 134–36; SCh 143:254; SCh 331:232); *Liber* 3.45; 2.26 (248, 169). In most instances, the Helfta writings do not make clear whether these visitors were laypeople, religious, or secular clergy. They allow us merely a peek into the nuns' attitude toward their guests. Their presence might sometimes be irksome, as when the portress was called away from Mass by arrival of visitors, e.g., *Liber* 3.45 (248). Although statutes limited the commerce between the nuns and the laity with whom they attended church, scholars have emphasized the number and variety of encounters that enclosed women had inside and outside the monastery with men and with women who were not their sisters. For these statutes and legislation providing that both groups be able to see or hear Mass and that each was forbidden visual contact with the other, see Jeffrey Hamburger, "Art, Enclosure, and the Pastoral Care of Nuns," in *The Visual and the Visionary: Art and Female Spirituality in Late Medieval Germany* (New York: Zone Books, 1992), 39, 49; J. Hubert, "La Place faite aux laics dans les églises monastiques et dans les cathedrals aux XIe et XIIe siècles," in *I laici nella "Societas christiana" dei secoli XI et XII: Atti della terza settimana internazionale di studio, Mendola, 21–27 agosto 1965* (Milan: Vita e Pensiero, 1968), 470–87. For intercourse between laity and female religious, see Power, *English Nunneries*, 403–35; Johnson, *Profession*, 105–226; Hamburger, "'On the Little Bed of Jesus': Pictorial Piety and Monastic Reform," in *Visual and the Visionary*, 385.

ter in their thoughts, their prayers, and their writings, and they assumed a role in guiding laywomen and laymen.[75] There are hints of a give and take that may have been characteristic of any community's connection with lay people who had financial resources at their disposal.[76] Nowhere is the potential of a layperson to reap spiritual rewards from contributing to monastic life more evident than in a vision attributed to Mechtild in which Count Burchard, who together with his wife, Elizabeth, had founded the monastery, appeared in glory.

As Abbess Sophie's fifteenth-century *Narratio* relates, the providential dream that drove Count Burchard to found the convent was sobering and hopeful, warning him of his wealth's endangerment of his soul and suggesting the means by which he could cooperate with God to secure his salvation.[77] The count sped into action, establishing the monastery near Mansfeld, and just as he had intended, the nuns there now labored at saving souls and, by their own account, were wildly successful. Discounting any participation in winning his own redemption, in Mechtild's vision Burchard insisted on the convent's unique role in catapulting him into heaven. When she asked how he had acquired such a variety of virtues, the names of which were embroidered on his celestial garments, he acknowledged that it was not by his own work but by the goodness of God and the merits of the congregation he loved so dearly.[78]

But the nuns knew otherwise. The *Book of Special Grace* recounts that during his anniversary Mass, Mechtild saw the count before God, flanked by the monastery's first abbess, Cunegund, and Abbess Gertrude, "and on his clothing, souls of the entire congregation that he had founded appeared as beautiful images, both those souls who already reigned in

[75] *Liber* 4.59; 5.30 (310–15, 366–67).

[76] *Le Héraut* 3.75.1 (SCh 143:318–22).

[77] See introduction.

[78] *Liber* 7.20 (416).

heaven and those who would arrive there."[79] From the perspective of the nuns residing at Helfta, Burchard's industriousness had reaped the desired reward. Mechtild's vision emphasized the efficacy of lay donation for the benefactors' own eternal welfare, just as it pointed to the intrinsic connection (underscored throughout the Helfta literature) between fostering another's spiritual well-being and one's own redemption. The gold flowers adorning Burchard's crown mirrored the number of souls that he, as founding patron, had gained for God. The nuns perceived themselves in this instance to work collaboratively with their lay founder on a joint project, whose foundation he had initially secured and to which they, for generations, had contributed their prayers and other good works.

Among the most valuable portions of the Helfta writings that illuminate the convent's attitude toward laity and the nuns' relationship with them is a letter (or a composite of several letters) incorporated into the *Book of Spiritual Grace*, ascribed to Mechtild and addressed to an anonymous woman.[80] We do not know how many such epistles Mechtild wrote, and she may have written prayers for the laity as well; this is the only surviving composition intended for a layperson.[81] Comprising three and a half printed pages, Mechtild's letter provides us with privileged access to what purports to be the visionary's own voice, unfiltered through the scrim of her sisters' questions, prodding, or pen. Perhaps most interesting is that the counsel Mechtild offered is largely the same as that which the

[79] *Liber* 5.10 (334).

[80] *Liber* 4.59 (310–15).

[81] *Liber* 5.30 (365). None of the letters Gertrude may have written is extant. Given what we know about her reputation and confidence in her own spiritual gifts, and the fact that the *Herald* tells us that letter writing was a customary course of action for Gertrude (*Le Héraut* 1.8.1 [SCh 143:158]), it is wise to interpret this lack of evidence as a misfortune of preservation or the result of destruction rather than indicative of a lack of correspondence with laypeople.

Book of Special Grace and the *Herald* offered their monastic readers. This may be, as Barbara Newman supposes, because the intended recipient was a widow newly entered into the religious life, but her state is not obvious from the text.[82] The other possibility is that the nuns believed that laywomen might adopt a spiritual program similar, in important regards, to that which governed their own lives.[83]

Mechtild urged the letter's recipient, in familiar language, to turn to Christ as her mother, lover, spouse, and king.[84] In the erotic language and bridal imagery reminiscent of the larger *Book of Special Grace*, Mechtild counseled her to align her will with God's, to shun pride and cultivate humility, to imitate Christ, to investigate her conscience, to love God, and to praise him. He would protect her from all evil, Mechtild wrote reassuringly, and she must resist all vices. In moments of sadness, take refuge in Christ, who will console you, Mechtild advised; when weariness overcomes you, know that there is a chain of

[82] Barbara Newman, introduction to *Mechthild of Hackeborn and the Nuns of Helfta: The Book of Special Grace*, trans. Barbara Newman (New York: Paulist Press, 2017), 4. The letter is otherwise fascinating for the insight it offers into the way in which Mechtild addressed individuals, instructing them in the spiritual life, and it is evidence for continuity in the piety of the *Book of Special Grace* and the *Herald*, on the one hand, and Mechtild's piety, on the other, underscoring the extent to which the *Book of Special Grace* really does offer us access to Mechtild's religiosity, or else at a minimum attests to the extent to which there was general harmony in the household in the matters the letter addresses.

[83] The *Spiritual Exercises* appears to offer the Virgin Mary as a guide to lay and religious alike: "Pray to the Virgin Mother that she be your guide in the monastic life or in whatever your state of life" [*Ora virginem matrem, ut ipsa sit ductrix tua in religion, aut alio statu tuo*], Gertrude writes, although there is some doubt as to whether *aut alio statu tuo* is original to the *Exercises* and not a later addition (*Les Exercices* 2.66–67 [SCh 127:86]). Hourlier and Schmitt, the editors of the critical edition of the *Exercises*, think that their early modern editor, Lansperg, may have been responsible for the addition of *aut alio statu tuo* but do not explain why they think this to be the case (*Les Exercices* 2.66–67 [SCh 127:87, n. 3]).

[84] *Liber* 4.59 (310–15).

gold that attaches you to the Father and by which he draws you toward his Son. Christ desires to unite himself with you; run to him. A celestial crown, decorated with roses, irises, and pearls, awaits; you should anticipate delicate intimacies with Christ.

There is a slight emphasis on the relinquishment of the so-called "worldly," which the nuns only infrequently recalled to one another, and Mechtild charged her intended recipient with having a cold heart and thoughts that only rarely alighted on Christ: the woman—created to love and to praise God—had distanced herself from him, Mechtild alleged, an accusation she rarely lobbed against her sisters. Yet her correspondent was destined for the delicacies of eternity, Mechtild pronounced, adopting the convent's customarily sunny stance about salvation. Mechtild was uncompromisingly bright about the woman's potential for progress. She scolded, but also soothed and encouraged and guaranteed delights; "He has chosen you for his spouse,"[85] she wrote in a jubilant timbre. Mechtild did not elaborate on the vices the woman was to avoid; we have no information about how these might have been different from those that typically presented themselves to the nuns. Nor did she provide particulars of the practices, attitudes, or emotions the anonymous laywoman could adopt in imitating Christ. What comes to the fore instead is Mechtild's cheering confidence that she was capable of doing so. Christ, Mechtild wrote in the letter's first lines, interlaced his fingers with the woman's fingers. He would not rest until her will rested entirely in him.

If this letter is an indication of the attitudes Mechtild harbored toward the laity, it suggests that she conceived that they could plan a future with Christ as dazzling as any Helfta nun's. Although the path on which they ran to him might be cluttered with greater dangers than the course she herself and her sisters

[85] *Liber* 4.59 (312).

undertook, the letter did not dwell on the perils. If Mechtild wrote this to a laywoman about to enter the monastery or to a recent arrival at Helfta, it suggests the visionary perceived an easy transition from the outside world into the monastery, not a hard divide between the life she and her sisters shared, on the one hand, and the life of her lay correspondent, on the other.

The world outside the cloister did not always shine with promise to the nuns, however, and they did not depict their relationship with laity as uniformly genial. During much of the thirteenth century, the lands surrounding the convent were sites of turbulent partisan jostling, from which the sisters did not remain aloof.[86] This century saw the disintegration of the Hohenstaufen empire, the urbanization of western Germany, and the fight for communal independence in episcopal cities, events that would no doubt have concerned the Mansfelds and Hackeborns. According to Abbess Sophia's *Narratio*, Emperor

[86] For feuds that may have affected the convent during the course of the thirteenth century, see Herman Grössler, "Die Blützeit des Klosters Helfta bei Eisleben," in *Jahres-Bericht über das königliche Gymnasium zu Eisleben* (Easter 1886–Easter 1887), 6; A. Mary F. Robinson, "The Convent of Helfta," *Fortnightly Review* 40 (1886): 641–42. In the seventh book of the *Flowing Light of the Divinity*, which Mechtild of Magdeburg probably wrote after coming to Helfta (see chap. 1), she mentions nearby violence, which may refer to warfare in the environs of the monastery (*Mechthild of Magdeburg: The Flowing Light of the Godhead*, trans. Frank Tobin [New York: Paulist Press, 1998], for example, 7.10 [284], and especially 7.28 [298–99]). For the larger political history of Germany during this period, including the demise of the Hohenstaufens, the interregnum, the conflict between Albert of Saxony and Adolph of Nassau, and the rise of the Habsburgs, see Jean Bérenger, *A History of the Habsburg Empire: 1273–1700*, trans. C. A. Simpson (London: Longman, 1994), 13–19, 54–56; John B. Freed, "Habsburg Dynasty," in *Medieval Germany: An Encyclopedia*, ed. John M. Jeep (New York: Garland, 2001), 41–43; Pierre Gaxotte, *Histoire de l'Allemagne* (Paris: Flammarion, 1963), 1:276–80; Michael Tosh, "Welfs, Hohenstaufen, and Habsburgs," in *The New Cambridge Medieval History*, ed. David Abulafia (Cambridge: Cambridge University Press, 1999), 5:375–404; Adam Wandruszka, *The House of Habsburg: Six Hundred Years of European Dynasty*, trans. Cathleen Epstein and Hans Epstein (New York: Doubleday and Company, 1964), 24–61.

Frederick II (1215–1250) attended the wedding of the convent's founders, Elizabeth and Burchard, and we know that the Hackeborns were allied with the Hohenstaufens. The so-called interregnum (1254–1273), following shortly on the death of Frederick II, was a time of increased regional instability, and the brutality of the German aristocracy during this period has been seen as a motivation for noblewomen in Thuringia and Saxony to take shelter in monasteries. The monastery walls did not, however, insulate the nuns from all depredation. Indeed, among them were women whose elite ancestry probably implicated them in the vicissitudes of local conflict. Proximity to the castle at Mansfeld may have presented dangers, and armed clashes among neighboring lords occurred in the vicinity of the convent's several foundations; violence in the area may have prompted the move to Rodarsdorf.[87]

The nuns were, therefore, not at a distance from incidents that were openly political in nature, from conflicts that rocked the empire during much of the thirteenth century, and from the private injuries inflicted on laypeople by local battles. To some extent, the women insinuated themselves into this maelstrom, and they were sometimes targets.[88] Thus we read that at the death of Emperor Rudolph I (1218–1291), Frederick II's godson, who was elected emperor in 1273, Gertrude and her sisters offered prayers for the election of his successor.[89] Moreover, Gertrude's power of premonition was put into play in this time of heightened political uncertainty. In the final decade of the

[87] Ed. Krüne, *Urkundenbuch der Klöster der Grafschaft Mansfeld*, ed. Max Krüne (Halle: Otto Hendel, 1888), no. 148, 224. And see Manfred Lemmer, "Die Helftaer Nonnen und die Sprache der mittelalterlichen Mystik," in *Protokollband*, 223; Margot Schmidt, "Mechtilde de Hackeborn," in DSAM 10:873. The husband of Elisabeth of Hungary, Ludwig, was in the employ of Frederick II, and he died while on crusade with the Emperor, circumstances that the nuns may have been aware of.

[88] *Le Héraut* 1.2.4 (SCh 139:130).

[89] *Le Héraut* 1.2.3 (SCh 139:130). Lucie Félix-Faure Goyau notes the nuns' concern with the empire and the papacy (*Christianisme et culture féminine* [Paris: Librairie Académique, 1914], 203).

thirteenth century (during the abbacy of Sophia of Mansfeld, which followed that of Gertrude of Hackeborn), a rivalry developed between Duke Albert of Saxony (1255–1308), the eldest son of Rudolph I, and Adolph, count of Nassau (d. 1298), who was supported for a time by electoral princes eager to check the power of the Habsburgs. At the moment of Adolph's election, Gertrude is said to have informed her abbess of the count's triumph, his subsequent death at Duke Albert's hand, and the latter's succession as emperor: "On the very day and, it is believed, even at the hour of the election, which took place in another district, she notified the mother [abbess] that it happened. And she added that this king who was elected on this day would be killed by his successor. The event proved this."[90] It turns out that Albert gained the support of the electors who had previously favored Adolph, and the latter was deposed, after which Adolph was killed, and Albert was subsequently elected king of the Romans. The *Book of Special Grace* hints at the ways the nuns may have been drawn into the sufferings laypeople endured during this chaotic and violent period in the territory's history. One woman twice successfully begged Mechtild for prayers to protect her husband from his many enemies, who were planning to hold him captive until their own prisoners were released. Mechtild's prayers in this case produced a hopeful revelation: Christ promised that no harm would come to the man.[91]

The visionary literature records that groups of armed assailants sometimes ringed the monastery, and the nuns were now and then aware of the nearby presence of menacing political authority and subject to their hostilities. Family relations on either side of the monastery's walls were not always mutually supportive, and from time to time showed signs of strain and antagonism. For reasons that are unclear, Gerhard (d. 1284), great-grandson of the founders and brother of the future Abbess Sophia of Mansfeld, invaded the convent on Good

[90] *Le Héraut* 1.2.3 (SCh 139:130).

[91] *Liber* 5.30 (366–67).

Friday in 1284, ate meat, and committed acts of brutality that go unspecified but for which he was excommunicated by Pope Martin IV (1281–1285). Although the literature does not record the nuns' response to this assault, the *Book of Special Grace* does mention the fear that swept through the monastery when word of an approaching army belonging to an unnamed king rushed the nuns into penitential recitation of the whole of the Psalter, a defensive and apparently successful response:[92]

> When the convent feared the presence of enemies, who, it was said, were strongly armed, moving toward their own monastery, then out of necessity they recited together the Psalter, psalm by psalm, with the verse *O lux beatissima* and the antiphon *Veni Sancte Spiritus*, and this one [Gertrude] gave herself over devoutly in prayer with the others. She understood in spirit that the Lord through this prayer was filling the heart of some [of the sisters] with the Holy Spirit so that they would know their own faults and be penitent, amending themselves with free will and eschewing other faults as far as possible. And when they were thus filled with compunction, she saw the heart of each through the spirit of compunction emit something like a vapor, which wrapped around the monastery and the area. It drove away all the adversaries.[93]

[92] *Liber* 4.11 (268). We do not know the immediate context of the threat to which the women responded. References to war in the convent's literature cannot with any degree of certainty be identified with a particular conflict (Jeanne Ancelet-Hustache, *Mechtilde de Magdebourg [1207–1282]: Étude de psychologie religieuse* [Paris: Librairie Ancienne Honoré Champion, 1926], 48–50), although Preger and Paquelin may be right in their suspicion that the reference is to Adolph of Nassau (Wilhelm Preger, *Geschichte der deutschen Mystik bis zum Tode Meister Eckharts* [Leipzig: Dörffling und Franke, 1874], 83; Paquelin, Praefatio to *Legatus*, xiv–xv; 268, n. 1). We know that Adolph was in the environs of Eisleben in 1294.

[93] *Le Héraut* 3.48.1 (SCh 143:214). Holsinger has observed the "liturgical revisionism" in the above-quoted paragraph, in which the nuns chant the complete cycle of psalms in one sitting (Bruce W. Holsinger, *Music, Body, and Desire in Medieval Culture: Hildegard of Bingen to Chaucer* [Stanford: Stanford University Press, 2001], 240–41). The Cistercians had reduced the number of

The nuns assumed responsibility for the protection of their household in this instance, and took credit for working in tandem with God for the monastery's safety, convinced that right relationships between God and all the sisters were necessary for a divine intervention that would cushion the convent against the blows of aggressors. The nuns perceived that the Holy Spirit moved some of their sisters to compunction as all of the women recited the Psalter in common. This contrite acknowledgement of their sins, coupled with a commitment to avoid these same sins in the future, produced a fortifying vapor from the hearts of these women, a mist that was more effective the greater a sister's remorse, and one that protected all her sisters.

The nuns' account of their response to the threat of attack accentuates their perception of their mutual dependence on one another to secure the integrity of their monastery. They were convinced that guarding the house against outside threats hinged at least in part on the power of common prayer to stimulate the conscience and kindle the spiritual renewal of individual women within the walls. Individual acts of reflective piety had the power to maintain a defensive border between the nuns and the world outside the monastery, isolating the women from menacing forces located beyond the monastery. The nuns believed, in addition, that Christ took advantage of the challenge to their security. As he explained to Gertrude, Christ drew on her sisters' terror of armed assault to draw them to him, that shaken by these troubles and purified through fear, they would run to him in search of comfort and protection. The vision Gertrude received, though prompted by an ominous

---

psalms chanted each week to the original one hundred and fifty prescribed in the Rule. The Helfta nuns may have been assimilating an earlier monastic practice; the monks at Cluny sang approximately two hundred and ten psalms each day (Jean Leclercq, "The Intentions of the Founders of the Cistercian Order," in *The Cistercian Spirit: A Symposium*, ed. M. Basil Pennington [Shannon: Irish University Press, 1970], 100; Louis J. Lekai, *Cistercians: Ideals and Reality* [Kent, OH: Kent State University Press, 1977], 248–49).

external force, turns attention inward to the individual sister and her conscience as well as to her relationship with Christ, whose significance for all the women the vision clarified when it focused on the fortification from assault penance provided.

Another vision prompted by the bellicose environment around Helfta showed up the nuns' sense of difference and separateness from the populations that harassed their household, testing their resolve to integrate foes into their conception of community. A vision Gertrude received while she was praying for an anonymous group who had attacked the monastery and who were continuing to trouble the nuns contained a lesson about the value to Christ of the sisters' recognition of the broad and inclusive community that was Christ's own. When Christ appeared to Gertrude, one of his arms was bent back so far that it was almost torn from its socket. He asked Gertrude to imagine the pain he would endure if someone were to punch this arm, then told her that he was experiencing a similar pain on account of those who were at the same moment decrying the wickedness of the nuns' assailants and hardened to the damnation the men risked because of their violent actions. Those, on the other hand, who offered prayers asking that Christ turn the men from their errors soothed Christ's arm with gentle ointments, while those who guided the aggressors to amend their ways were like expert doctors who gently reset Christ's arm, returning it to its proper place. Christ's words may have contained an implicit approbation of Gertrude's prayer, which we are probably meant to understand as a commitment to the aggressors' welfare as well as a criticism of other sisters. Christ's plea that the women counsel the men to a better way of life[94] is a demanding one, but we should not assume that the nuns did not regard themselves as capable of such an assignment, or that at least some of them were not willing to take up the charge. But none of this is clear in the

[94] *Le Héraut* 3.67.1–2 (SCh 143:272–74).

account of the vision. Instead, the *Herald* draws attention to the fundamental unity between the sisters and the aggressors, a unity that, as the *Herald* relates, the nuns were hard pressed to concede.

The bruised body that Christ presented to Gertrude may have been calculated to stir the sisters into action under such circumstances, in part because it would probably have disturbed them in the arresting contrast it offered to the frequent descriptions of the bodily beauty of their Beloved (so beautiful that the sun and the moon marvel!).[95] These images of beauty, with which the Helfta writings plied their readers, would have been a common component of contemplating Christ. Tall, agile, and handsome,[96] Christ was more typically a glorious king,[97] a beautiful boy,[98] or an eye-catching young man,[99] adorned with flowers, his face gleaming like a thousand suns.[100] Christ's accusation that those who did not pray for their enemies were guilty of torturing him might have aroused a sense of compassion, shame, and remorse in those who were not doing as their Beloved wished. The nuns knew their obligations. When, in another vision, Gertrude saw a kaleidoscope of blue and black bruises covering Christ's face, swollen from knotted scourges hurled at him—the sins of lay and religious—she was moved to compassion for him and for those who were responsible for his suffering, and she prayed for them, according to Christ's instructions.[101] The sisters reminded one another that those who love God love with his love, not their own, so that enemies become friends.[102] In a vision laced with imagery from the Song of Songs, which tells of young lovers and of trees

[95] *Les Exercices* 3.294 (SCh 127:114).
[96] *Liber* 1.4 (13).
[97] *Liber* 4.59 (310–15).
[98] *Liber* 1.9 (29).
[99] *Le Héraut* 5.5.3 (SCh 331:112); *Liber* 1.1 (9–10).
[100] *Liber* 1.4 (13).
[101] *Le Héraut* 4.15.4 (SCh 255:170–72).
[102] *Liber* 1.30 (103).

heavy with nuts and pomegranates, Christ appeared to Gertrude. A gloss on the vision explains their encounter and his request to her: just as nuts and fruit grow together on the same tree, so Gertrude's sweet love for God ought to be mingled with the hard and bitter love of those who persecute her.[103] We read in the *Herald* that a person who loves Christ is necessarily preoccupied with the whole world, a concern that sometimes surfaces with recognition of the wrongs the world has inflicted on Christ, which any person in love with God would wish to redress.[104] Throughout, the writings associated with Gertrude reiterate a yearning to harness the potency of prayer for this reparative purpose.

> . . . from the word that is read in Isaiah, "Arise, arise, rise up, Jerusalem" [Isa 51:17], she understood the profit that accrues to the church militant from the devotion of the elect. For when one loving soul turns with its whole heart to the Lord, with the whole of its will it would, if it had the power, pay for every offence to God's honor, and thus, burning in prayer with the torches of love, it clings caressingly to God. It pleases him so much that at last he is reconciled and spares the whole world.[105]

Yet when the monastery and perhaps even the nuns themselves were threatened, their resolve to love their enemy buckled. Gertrude balked at Christ's claims, reminding him that the assailants had been publicly denounced in consequence of the injuries they visited on the convent, and she fortified her retort by recalling to Christ that the men had been excommu-

[103] *Le Héraut* 3.15.2 (SCh 143:64). See Bossy, "The Mass," 39, for the obligation to pray for one's enemies. There is no evidence in the Helfta writings of the monastic practice to pray for the damnation of one's enemies (Bossy, "The Mass," 41, 45).

[104] *Le Héraut* 4.14.8 (SCh 255:194). And see, for example, *Le Héraut* 4.35.3; 4.39.2 (SCh 255:292, 322).

[105] *Le Héraut* 3.30.4 (SCh 143:136).

nicated, separated from the body of the church.[106] Christ countered that they could still be reconciled to the church: they had not been cut off from *him*. He was still their head. Thus pronouncing the body of the visible church not coextensive with his own body, Christ urged the nuns to be attentive to all who were members of his body, appealing to the nuns (through Gertrude) to cultivate a sense of community with the attackers in conformity with him—and recalling Christ's presence to the nuns themselves when *they* were under interdict.

Christ implied an important distinction between human beings' relationship with the church on earth and the church in heaven when he proclaimed his desire for reconciliation with the menacing men and thus infused his response to Gertrude with eschatological hope. He insisted that she and her sisters take up the same attitude.[107] The notion of the eschatological community in fact imbues the whole of this portion of the *Herald*. What remained unknown to the nuns, as Christ reminded Gertrude, was exactly who the faithful of the community were, although the community's parameters *were* known: they were coextensive with Christ's body, and future glory could still await those who persecuted the monastery. The church was synonymous with all those who might be saved and to whom, therefore, the nuns had an obligation.[108]

The *Herald* reveals that Gertrude and her sisters bumped up against companies of people whom they could not fit without ambivalence within the parameters of the church. The *Herald* does not smooth over acrimony, and however expansive the language the nuns sometimes employed to discuss the community of which they counted themselves as members, when

[106] *Le Héraut* 3.67.1–2 (SCh 143:272–74).

[107] For the eschatological preoccupation woven throughout much of medieval religious literature, which often found expression in what Leclercq calls a "devotion to heaven," see Jean Leclercq, *The Love of Learning and the Desire for God: A Study of Monastic Culture*, trans. Catharine Misrahi (New York: Fordham University Press, 1961), 53–70.

[108] *Liber* 1.30 (103).

confronted with specific groups of people and not the abstract *universa ecclesia*, reservations emerged, and their world seemed on the brink of contracting. It is not surprising that they were more at ease in their role as vanguard in relation to the universal church per se than in relation to some specific groups of individuals. Thus, in the matter of the laborers, the nuns wondered whether the men merited the fruit of the nuns' own labors; in the case of the armed aggressors, they wondered whether their assailants were really members of the church. In both instances, Christ pushed the women to a more generous expression of community, one that included those who had been formally separated from the church. The sense of community that they should strive to embrace, the nuns taught one another, incorporated enormous tension among its members.[109]

The brief account of the sisters' response to armed aggressors ends with a promise and a warning. In this case, Christ associated a threat of violence with the nuns' own spiritual condition. If they acknowledged that they deserved to be attacked as punishment for their sins, Christ would spare the women. If, on the other hand, they hoped or prayed for evil to be done to their assailants, Christ's justice would ensure the women's harm. The consequences of not heeding Christ's directive were brutal, both for the nuns and for Christ, since the sisters were members of the body of the faithful, and had the capacity to injure this body through neglect or ill-will.

[109] The nuns may have been trained to sustain such tensions on the basis of their own family histories. In spite of his destructive trespass, Gerhard, at the request of his widow, Irmengard of Schwarzburg (d. after 1301), was buried at the monastery. Less than a decade after Gerhard's attack, his sister, Sophie, became abbess, and several years later, his widow entered the convent, where she spent the remainder of her life. Gerhard's nephew, Burchard V (1291–1330), bequeathed to Helfta almost thirty acres of land, and with the nuns in procession, Burchard too was laid to rest at the Chapel of Saint John the Baptist and Saint John the Evangelist; see introduction.

Thus the *Herald* illustrates in this account how the women interpreted the meaning for them of the Pauline passage "when one member suffers, all members suffer" (1 Cor 1:26), filtered, that is, through their experience of the damage members of the mystical body can inflict on one another. Here fear of Christ's punishment is meant to coerce their compassion for his wounded arm, the arm that is the men who menaced the convent. The impending punishment that Christ dangled before the nuns was, in their conception, not really a question of retributive justice. It was a guarantee of the reality he urged them to accept: the nuns were members of the body of Christ, which was a body of sinners and also included their enemies. Christ's justice, in this context, was but an expression of the reality on which the nuns insisted: we all constitute one body; we really are one another. When one member suffers, we all really do hurt, whether or not we acknowledge this reality, whether or not we feel it. The *Herald* presents Gertrude as exemplary in conforming to Christ's will when—on what appears to be a different occasion—she scooped grace out of Christ's heart and sprinkled it over enemies who were disturbing the monastic estate, sure that she was offering them salvation by giving them the opportunity to repent.[110] She understood herself to be simultaneously protecting her sisters and herself, surely because of her conviction both that contrition changed people (and thus made armed men less likely to attack vulnerable women religious) and that such change heals the body of Christ and thus all who are among its members.[111]

[110] *Le Héraut* 4.58.4 (SCh 255:470). What we do not find in the *Herald* is the nuns crying out on behalf of a lone sinner or assemblage of sinners born of the nuns' immediate concern for the sinners' particular need. Moreover, for the most part, the nuns expend scant emotion on people for whom they pray. But this lack of emotion for the sinner does not impede the efficacious flow of spiritual fruits produced by the nuns' prayer and other good works.

[111] One should always keep Christ's body in mind, the *Herald* counsels its readers. In one of Gertrude's visions, Christ's right side was adorned with royal garments; his left was naked and pocked with sores. The right side

Despite their vows and cloistered existence, then, the raw woes of a frightened wife and the fate of the empire both impinged on Gertrude and Mechtild, and on their sisters as well, the first claiming the private petitions and prophetic powers of one nun, and the second both literally and figuratively invading the sisters' communal prayer. The capricious political circumstances and the bellicose arena in which their monastery was situated drew the cloister's inhabitants into a host of not entirely external concerns. The women's revelations attest to the interweaving of devotion and defense, of mystical mediation and tender consolation for the war-weary. It was not always easy for nuns to include those who were members of Christ's body in their sense of community. They nevertheless felt themselves pressured by Christ to become more expansive, or to experience immediate consequences that might include assault on their cloister and the wounding of God himself.

---

represented Christ's elect, and the left, souls riddled with faults. The *Herald* insists that all of the elect should attend to those in need of correction. It recognizes that doing so requires commitment, patience, and delicacy, and it warns of the consequences of misbehavior: whoever neglects to give correction applies an ointment to Christ's wounds that infects them; whoever criticizes harshly batters Christ's sores, causing them to sputter with ooze; whoever becomes irritated because those in need do not heed her advice jabs Christ's sores, tearing them (*Le Héraut* 3.74.1–4 [SCh 143:312–16]; Jungmann, *Mass of the Roman Rite*, 90–92).

PART THREE

The Living and the Dead

Chapter 7

"Give Her All That Is Yours"

Community and the Population of Purgatory

Then the Lord, with wondrous tenderness, brought her a multitude of souls released from punishment, saying, "Behold! I have committed all these to your love as a wedding gift, for it will appear eternally in heaven that they are liberated by your prayers, and in the presence of all my saints, this gift will continually contribute to your honor."[1]

Purgatory's Population

A fifth book in the *Herald* and in the *Book of Special Grace* is given over to extended conversations between the visionaries and Christ about those in purgatory. The women expressed concern for the souls languishing at a distance from heaven, and relayed the successful efforts of the sisters in succoring, purging, and rescuing souls from their post-mortem sufferings.[2]

[1] *Le Héraut* 4.27.2 (SCh 255:262).

[2] In keeping with the eschatological emphasis of thirteenth-century theology and religious practice, and as is familiar especially from the purgatorial piety of medieval women, the nuns emphasized the death of the individual as the decisive moment in her existence and focused on the afterlife of the soul before the resurrection of the body. For the purgatorial piety of the nuns, see Gilbert Dolan, *St. Gertrude the Great* (London: Sands, 1913),

Purgatory's inhabitants also figured in numerous revelations, in which they spoke of their woes, told of Christ's merciful condescension, proffered warnings, and gave advice; they offered hope to those they petitioned and presented their lot as an incentive for right behavior. A vigorous and vibrant purgatorial piety was characteristic of the holiness cultivated at Helfta, whose members the convent's writings depict as readily responsive to their fellow faithful among the dead, if sometimes in need of Christ's stimulus and direction. This literature calls attention to the heavy traffic between this world and the next, with the dead seemingly appearing to the spiritual luminaries among the sisters almost relentlessly. In keeping with the larger pattern of Cistercian piety and its well-known preoccupation with the faithful departed and with the centrality of purgatorial piety to the religiosity of medieval women, everything about the monastery's literature tells us that the dead were never very far away.[3]

177–96; Caroline Walker Bynum, "Women Mystics in the Thirteenth Century: The Case of the Nuns of Helfta," in *Jesus as Mother: Studies in the Spirituality of the High Middle Ages* (Berkeley: University of California Press, 1984); Barbara Newman, "On the Threshold of the Dead: Purgatory, Hell, and Religious Women," *From Virile Woman to WomanChrist: Studies in Medieval Religion and Literature* (Philadelphia: University of Pennsylvania Press, 1995), 108–36, 135. See passing references to the place of purgatory in the Helfta mysticism in R. P. Bainvel, *La Dévotion au Sacré Coeur de Jésus, doctrine, histoire* (Paris: Beauchesne, 1931), 218–19; Cyprian Vagaggini, *Theological Dimensions of the Liturgy*, trans. Leonard J. Doyle and W. A. Jurgen from the fourth Italian edition, revised and augmented by the author (Collegeville, MN: Liturgical Press, 1976), 769; Jacques Le Goff, *The Birth of Purgatory*, trans. Arthur Goldhammer (Chicago: University of Chicago Press, 1984), 357; Jo Ann Kay McNamara, "The Need to Give: Suffering and Female Sanctity in the Middle Ages," in *Images of Sainthood in Medieval Europe*, ed. Renate Blumenfeld-Kosinski and Timea Szell (Ithaca: Cornell University Press, 1991), 216. On the development of the doctrine of purgatory and on late medieval purgatorial piety, see Philippe Ariès, *L'Homme devant la mort* (Paris: Seuil, 1977), 109–12; Le Goff, *The Birth of Purgatory;* Brian Patrick McGuire, "Purgatory, the Communion of Saints, and Medieval Change," *Viator* 20 (1989): 61–84.

[3] LeGoff, *Birth of Purgatory*, esp. 295–96, 300–10; McGuire, "Purgatory," 75, 77.

The general impression the literature conveys is of an environment hospitable to the reception of visions of the dead, and for the most part encouraging of their expression. Whether or not the nuns as a whole regularly had the dead on their mind we cannot be sure; however, the convent's literature instructed the reader that the dead in need *should* be on her mind and inform virtually all her actions. The *Book of Special Grace* relates that once Mechtild communicated her anxiety about an anomalous clerical injunction against speaking about her visions of the dead to Christ, remarking that the convent had already accepted money for the prayers to be offered for them. Indeed, the household may have received considerable financial compensation for these kinds of prayers, an economy within which the visions Mechtild (and others) received provided a kind of confirmation, a guarantee of the sisters' success at meeting the needs of the dead.[4]

The visionaries' ability to engage with souls in purgatory also provided a venue for the curiosity of members of the monastic family about the recently deceased and long-ago departed, probably awakening wonder in still others, and perhaps provoking inquisitiveness. On the anniversary of the death of her father, Count Burchard, Abbess Sophia ordered Mechtild to pray for knowledge about his condition.[5] Meanwhile, a certain brother's interest lodged not in the state of near relatives but in the distant past: he wanted to know about the post-mortem condition of Solomon, Samson, Origen, and Trajan. To this query about the reach of God's mercy, Christ responded by emphasizing the depth of his generosity without, however, divulging anything about the fate of these particular souls. It must have been a solace, a scare, and a source of entertainment for sisters to relate to one another, in speech and in writing, what some among them had learned about a population that had already crossed death's divide and who had

[4] *Liber* 5.18 (347).
[5] *Liber* 5.15 (342).

related aspects of their experience that the nuns knew, if they took them to heart, might be salutary.

A spectrum of souls, some freshly dead and some whose bodies had lingered in the grave, came to Gertrude and Mechtild from purgatory. The broad sweep of the population that compelled the nuns' attention, and whose sufferings the sisters labored to assuage, is noteworthy, including nuns and neighbors, knights and *conversi*, patrons and the poor, as well as the women's own family members. Sisters (perhaps including *conversae*—it is often difficult to determine), friars, and *conversi* appear in purgatory more frequently than any other discernible groups of people. The monastery seems to have supported the practice of child oblation,[6] but no children figure among the inhabitants of purgatory.[7] The nuns seem to have assumed that baptized children before a certain age would not have incurred sins that would require the purification and

[6] *Liber* 5.12 (339–40).

[7] Among Mechtild's principal duties as chantress would have been instructing children at the monastery's school. For the education of children at Helfta see Sabine Spitzlei, *Erfahrungsraum Herz: Zur Mystik des Zisterzienserinnenklosters Helfta im 13 Jahrhundert* (Stuttgart-Bad Cannstatt: Frommann-Holzboog Verlag, 1991), 53–55. Furthermore, if Helfta was like other thirteenth-century households, the children who studied there were probably otherwise integrated into the routines of daily life, including joining in the Offices; see Theresa A. Halligan, introduction to *The Booke of Gostlye Grace of Mechtild of Hackeborn*, trans. Theresa A. Halligan (Toronto: Pontifical Institute of Mediaeval Studies, 1979), 36; Mary Jeremy Finnegan, *The Women of Helfta: Scholars and Mystics* (Athens: University of Georgia Press, 1991), 27; Anne Bagnall Yardley, *Performing Piety: Musical Culture in Medieval English Nunneries* (New York: Palgrave, 2006), 36. On the ubiquitous presence of children in thirteenth-century female and male monasteries, and on their integration into the monastic life, see Pierre Riché, "L'enfant dans la société monastique au xiie siècle," in *Pierre Abélard, Pierre le Vénérable: Les courants philosophiques, littéraires et artistiques en occident au milieu du xiie siècle* (Paris: Éditions du Centre National de la Recherche Scientifique, 1975), 689–701. For child oblation in the later Middle Ages, see also Eileen Power, *Medieval English Nunneries, c. 1275 to 1535* (Cambridge: Cambridge University Press, 1922), 262–84; and Mayke de Jong, *In Samuel's Image: Child Oblation in the Early Medieval West* (Leiden: E. J. Brill, 1996).

punishment of purgatory; children do appear in the visions of heaven that the women recorded.[8] Whatever the case, this silence is in keeping with the larger works' overall lack of consideration of children, about whose activities in the monastery, with the exception of some sort of study, we hear virtually nothing.[9]

The nuns appear to have prayed with special fervor for those known to them—for their own relatives or those of their sisters, for those beside whom they had once chanted, or for those who had labored in the monastery's fields or assumed administrative responsibilities alongside the women or on their behalf. They also felt called to pray for a far wider group of people, whom Christ taught them that they must regard as part of their family because they were members of his family and he loved them.[10] There is a long history of Christians encouraging one another not to restrict the prayers and other works offered for the dead to family members and others intimately known and loved.[11] In the visions recounted by the *Book of Special Grace* and the *Herald*, we are witness to the self-directed clamor that the nuns should strive against the occasional stinginess of their devotions, their parochial tendency to pour special attention on those whom they knew

[8] *Liber* 5.12 (339–40).

[9] *Le Héraut* 1.1.14–23 (SCh 139:118–20). Christ tells Mechtild that she should teach the children to do good and to correct them when they err (*Liber* 1.9 [29–30]). A passage in the *Herald* and one in the *Book of Special Grace* celebrating the tenderness Abbess Gertrude exhibited toward children is exceptional for disclosing one woman's attitude toward the children in the community's midst, about which the literature is otherwise reserved (*Le Héraut* 5.1.2 [SCh 331:18]; *Liber* 6.1 [376]).

[10] *Le Héraut* 5.17.1 (SCh 331:176). When Gertrude expanded her prayer to include—in addition to her mother and father—those who were dear to Christ, he was pleased with her (*Le Héraut* 2.16.2 [SCh 139:290–92]).

[11] McGuire, "Purgatory," 70–71, 74, 79. For the primacy of place family members held in the early centuries of Christian purgatorial piety, see Eamon Duffy, *The Stripping of the Altars: Traditional Religion in England 1400–1580* (New Haven, CT: Yale University Press, 1992), 348–54.

when they were alive or to whom they were related. The literature incorporates and reveals the community's demand that the connection between the living and the faithful departed be broadened to include all of the population of purgatory.

The *Herald* holds Gertrude up as a model of this commitment to a more ample sense of community between the living and the dead, although, as ever, in need of Christ's guidance. Once, during a Mass celebrated for the nuns' relatives, Gertrude witnessed numerous souls rise from beneath shadows and then shoot like sparks of fire into the celestial kingdom. When she asked Christ if the sparks represented those for whom she had prayed, Christ explained that he did not exclude from the commemorative Mass for the sisters' relations those who were his special friends.[12] Some of those whom Gertrude saw were her relatives, and some were Christ's. Because his relatives were, as Gertrude learned from him, also her own family, Gertrude subsequently prayed for all those whom he loved.[13] And so we read that the sisters' work was not limited to helping to temper the torments of particular individuals in purgatory, one by one; sometimes the benefits they bestowed washed over purgatory's entire population. Once after she received communion, Gertrude saw herself in the form of a tree whose branches exuded a sap that flowed into purgatory, lessening the tribulations of all those there.[14] Christ on one occasion released a soul for each of the many movements of Gertrude's tongue,[15] and when at the elevation of the Host Gertrude prayed for those in purgatory, she saw Christ extend a long gold rod punctuated by grapples, each of

[12] *Le Héraut* 5.17.1 (SCh 331:176).

[13] *Le Héraut* 5.17.1 (SCh 331:176). His friends are closest to her: *Le Héraut* 4.27.1 (SCh 255:260).

[14] *Le Héraut* 3.18.6 (SCh 143:84–86). For the image of the tree in the Helfta literature, see Finnegan, *Women of Helfta*, 46–47, 85–88; and Mary Forman, "Gertrud of Helfta: Arbor Amoris in Her Heart's Garden," *Mystics Quarterly* 26, no. 4 (December 2000): 163.

[15] *Le Héraut* 5.16.2 (SCh 331:178–80).

which cupped a soul, who by this action was drawn out of pain and into peaceful repose.[16] God released a vast number of souls from purgatory after Mechtild poured out prayers for its inhabitants.[17]

Experience of Purgatory

Souls in purgatory manifested a catalogue of sufferings, physical and psychological. The condition of the deceased corresponded with a geography of the afterlife, although mapping out the purgatorial terrain was not a central concern at Helfta.[18] The location to which souls traveled after death, if they did not depart directly to heaven and were not shut up for an eternity in hell, comprised various regions.[19] In addition to sites of obvious and often gruesome torment, purgatory had pleasant places where souls rested.[20] Its topography included beautiful gardens, raging fires, and pools of water;[21] it was tenanted by angels, who enlightened and consoled, and it was visited by terrorizing demons.[22] A vision that came to Mechtild

[16] *Le Héraut* 4.35.9 (SCh 255:280–300).

[17] *Liber* 5.20 (351).

[18] *Le Héraut* 5.5.2 (SCh 331:108–10).

[19] *Le Héraut* 5.14.2 (SCh 331:164–66); *Liber* 7.14 (409).

[20] *Le Héraut* 5.14.2 (SCh 331:164–66); *Liber* 7.14 (409). These places of rest are perhaps something akin to what is sometimes described as a terrestrial paradise, which may have enjoyed its greatest popularity in the thirteenth century and was associated primarily, at Helfta as elsewhere, with the psychological or emotional pain of separation from God. For the heyday of terrestrial paradise in the thirteenth century, see McGuire, "Purgatory," 81. McGuire also discusses the continuing importance into the later Middle Ages of an older fourfold view of the afterlife (65–66) and its expression in early thirteenth-century Cistercian literature, where it becomes a location of coolness and rest (77). LeGoff identified the Cistercians as central in expressing the idea of purgatory as a place (*Birth of Purgatory*, 168). Doyère considers that Gertrude conceived of the passage through purgatory as consisting in stages or steps (*Le Héraut* 5.12 [SCh 331:152, n. 1]).

[21] *Liber* 5.17 (347).

[22] *Liber* 5.21 (353).

seems to depict purgatory as a mountain.[23] In some scenarios, the physical distance between purgatory and the infernal region below is narrow, as when a knight, sustained by a single joist, dangled precariously over hell's mouth.[24] In others, the bliss of heaven was within reach: Christ stood before a nun who was prevented from falling into his arms only by a nail that cut through her habit, fixing her in place.[25] All inhabitants shared being simultaneously sin-streaked, in need of purgation, and guaranteed salvation. The nuns perceived purgatory as coupling objective experience with a subjective state, with souls' experiences including agony and profound happiness, and sometimes a combination of want and gladness, pain and pleasure. When Gertrude asked Christ about a sister who she perceived was tortured by having to wait to enter Christ's kingdom, Christ assured the visionary that the soul awaited her consummation with joy: she was like a little girl who sees in her mother's hand jewels she will receive the next day.[26] A *conversus* hungers for God and yet enjoys his presence, as if smelling the inviting steam of roasted meat set before him, which, however, he cannot yet eat.[27]

The unfortunates who peopled Gertrude's and Mechtild's visions illustrated the sins for which they were punished or from which they were purified (delineating the two is not a

[23] *Liber* 1.13 (40–45). Some readers have suggested that Mechtild's vision of the mountain of purgatory may have influenced Dante (Newman, *Mechthild of Hackeborn*, 257, n. 34). Barbara Newman claims that the *Book of Special Grace* offered "in embryo, the whole scheme of the *Purgatorio*" (introduction to *Mechthild of Hackeborn*, 29). Duffy contrasts Dante's purgatory as a place that emphasized movement upward and healing ("hope and means of ascent towards heaven")—in this way similar to the *Book of Special Grace*—with a contemporary English conception of purgatory that was less coherent and "grimmer" (*Stripping of the Altars*, 343, 344). Paquelin identified Mechtild with the Matelda who appears in canto 27 of *Purgatorio*, perhaps an acknowledgement of Dante's debt to the Helfta nun (Praefatio to *Liber*).

[24] *Le Héraut* 5.18.1 (SCh 331:180).

[25] *Le Héraut* 5.9.3 (SCh 331:138).

[26] *Le Héraut* 5.9.6 (SCh 331:140–42).

[27] *Le Héraut* 5.12 .1 (SCh 331:152).

major concern of the nuns), the pain they endured, or the torture itself. Gertrude saw a knight fourteen years dead in the form of a beast whose skin was spiked with horns, a sign of his double sins of ambition and pride; vapor from hell's depths carried to him agonies that surpassed the imagination.[28] A certain brother was bound in purgatory by his own sorrow, hindered from gazing at God because in life he had been captivated by his own opinions and had exercised self-will, refusing to heed the advice of others.[29] A *conversus* who assumed the body of a toad endured diverse indescribable torments because he had worked surreptitiously to acquire material goods, secreting away what he gained.[30] It was because one of the souls Gertrude saw had in life spoken disapprovingly about others that that soul was prevented from tasting God.[31]

In keeping with the thirteenth-century penchant for punishments fitting the crime (*contrapasso*), souls announced their dominant vice through their punishments:[32] gluttons and drunks whom post-mortem hunger and thirst had shriveled; those who, having capitulated to fleshy desires, were grilled like meat; a phalanx of the proud, all together tumbling into successive abysses.[33] Sometimes the stuff of the torment is itself underscored, not the pain or the sin for which it is inflicted: once a collection of anonymous souls, some dripping with water in which they had been submerged, some charred from roasting in flames, commanded Mechtild's attention.[34]

[28] *Le Héraut* 5.18.1 (SCh 331:178–80).

[29] *Le Héraut* 5.12.3 (SCh 331:154).

[30] *Le Héraut* 5.15.1 (SCh 331:166–68).

[31] *Le Héraut* 5.22.2 (SCh 331:194–96).

[32] *Liber* 5.20 (351). On this late medieval tendency, familiar to many from Dante's *Inferno* and with roots in the secular legal notion of *contrapasso*, see Paul Binski, *Medieval Death: Ritual and Representation* (Ithaca, NY: Cornell University Press, 1996), 176–77; Victoria Kirkham, "*Contrapasso*: The Long Wait to *Inferno* 28," *Modern Language Notes* 127, no. 1 supp (2012): 1–12.

[33] *Liber* 5.20 (351).

[34] *Liber* 5.17 (347).

The nuns associated purgatory with both liberation from longing for God[35] and frustration of this longing; sometimes the only punishment souls endured was the thwarting of their desire for the divine. When Mechtild quizzed the young Count Burchard, one of the monastery's patrons, about his sojourn in purgatory, the count remarked that he experienced no punishment at all, except that he did not see the Lord, whom he ardently aspired to contemplate.[36] Gertrude saw the soul of a *conversus* seated at a table before all the prayers and good works that had been offered for his release; the man remained dejected, aggrieved that he was not currently sufficiently purified to gaze at his Lord, who sat before him.[37] Graphic physical imagery explicitly conveyed souls' deprivation: Gertrude saw a soul use her nails to scrape off the oozing cartilage that covered her mouth, cartilage continuously cramping her mouth and preventing her from enjoying the deliciousness of the divine.[38]

In a number of revelations that underscored the soul's role in effecting his or her own suffering, the role of conscience emerges as paramount. Blackened from his torments, Brother F., a recently deceased *conversus*, showed himself to Gertrude, consumed by an internal fire—a visual announcement of his soul's sickness and the work of his remorse.[39] Emphasizing that the punishment he endured was self-inflicted, at the sight of yet another brother under the form of a toad—black as carbon—and suffering pain throughout his body, Gertrude looked around and saw no torturer; she realized that the man had turned on himself.[40] A third *conversus*, disciplined by the prick of conscience, exercised self-scrutiny in his post-mortem state, this inward turn itself generating agonies.[41] Yet another

[35] *Liber* 5.11 (338).
[36] *Liber* 5.11 (337).
[37] *Le Héraut* 5.12.1 (SCh 331:152).
[38] *Le Héraut* 5.22.3 (SCh 331:194–96).
[39] *Le Héraut* 5.15.1 (SCh 331:166–68).
[40] *Le Héraut* 5.16. 2 (SCh 331:170).
[41] *Le Héraut* 5.14.1 (SCh 331:162).

lay brother confessed that his own judgment of himself brought upon him so many sorrows that uniting all of the sorrows of all the hearts of human beings would not seem to him as heavy as the woe he bore.[42]

A sister, magnificently adorned and surrounded by glorious light, was too ashamed to lift her eyes to Christ, seated on his throne before her. When Gertrude asked Christ why he did not show her sister tokens of affection but permitted her to stand before him as a stranger, Christ, in answer, extended his hand to the woman, who drew back from his advance. Her sister explained to Gertrude that even if divine justice did not constrain her, she would deprive herself of the favor of Christ's touch; she herself knew she must be purified of her defects.[43] Mechtild saw within the hearts of an undisclosed number of anonymous souls a dog—the soul's conscience and symbol of fidelity—that was tearing at itself with its nails and gnawing on itself, a self-reproach for its ferocious faithlessness.[44]

The experience of purgatory's residents had a democratic cast. Grotesque physical punishment attached to laity and to religious alike: the bodies of religious unfaithful to their rule are bent beneath insupportable burdens,[45] and a nun's mouth seeped gooey stuff, repellant to the saints.[46] Suffering and joy were attributed to both sisters and *conversi*.[47] A nobleman, a *conversus*, and a sister all endured an unfulfilled longing to behold, to taste, to embrace God.[48] Sisters and *conversi* alike withstood the excruciating sting of conscience.[49] The Helfta authors did not clearly assign souls' sins as well as the punishments and cleansing they called forth to lay or religious, man

[42] *Le Héraut* 5.12.3 (SCh 331:154).

[43] *Le Héraut* 5.5.2 (SCh 331:108–10).

[44] *Liber* 5.17 (346).

[45] *Liber* 5.20 (351).

[46] *Le Héraut* 5.22.2–3 (SCh 331:194–96).

[47] *Le Héraut* 5.5.2; 5.6.3; 5.12.1; 5.12.3 (SCh 331:108–10, 120–22, 152, 154).

[48] *Le Héraut* 5.22.2; 5.12.1; 5.9.3 (SCh 331:194–96, 152, 138).

[49] *Le Héraut* 5.15.1; 5.16.2; 5.14.1, 5.12.3; 5.5.2 (SCh 331:166–68, 170, 162, 154, 108–10); *Liber* 5.17 (346).

or woman, and the status of the individual soul at the center of a particular vision and the precise role she or he occupied at the monastery is not always evident.

An attempt to align certain sins and punishments with a precise category of people is complicated by the elasticity of a number of the words the Helfta authors used to identify the people about whom they wrote. Thus, for example, *conversi* in this period were not simply laborers and subordinates but might be charged with financial and other administrative responsibilities.[50] Moreover, in every part of the Helfta writings it is often unclear whether a particular sister (*soror*) about whom we read is a woman who took full vows or a lay sister (*conversa*). Like *conversus*, the meaning of *conversa* varies considerably in the medieval sources. Those lay sisters whose primary charge was to carry out domestic chores would have been expected to undergo a year-long novitiate, and, like their male equivalents, would not have been consecrated but would have taken a vow of obedience to the abbess. The term also sometimes attached to personal servants who worked for wages and may not have lived in the convent.

At Helfta, as elsewhere, the term also identified noble pensioners, such as Elizabeth Mansfeld or Irmengard of Schwarzburg, the widow of Elizabeth's great grandson. Mechtild of Magdeburg is the most famous entrant who came to the convent in her later years and probably did not take full vows. The lack of precision by which the nuns identify this or that inhabitant of purgatory and the parallel experiences attributed to women and men across the lay-religious divide means that death really does appear as the great leveler, at least in purgatory (if not in heaven), occasioning the sloughing off of roles in this life (or better, their bracketing)—*conversus*, domestic laborer, nun, count, poor woman—to reveal no obvious fundamental difference in the sins for which souls were committed to purgatory or in their experience there.

[50] See chap. 6.

The presence in accounts of purgatory of sometimes hard-to-identify women and men may also speak to the nuns' sense of a fluidity between the occupants of various statuses in the monastery's life or to a lack of exacting and hierarchical standards by which they agreed to distinguish one from another and measure their worth, at least in the quasi-equalizing light of eternity. We know that the nuns ruminated on the meaning of the manual and administrative labor to which some members of the household were dedicated and endorsed its salvific potential for both the worker herself or himself and for others, and they wondered about lay contributions to their own redemption, although in more muted tones. Moreover, Gertrude's *Spiritual Exercises* softens the difference between virgin and widow in its treatment of the monastic entrance rites of consecration, investiture, and profession, which offer the opportunity to participate in the chaste love that the Helfta nuns associate with marriage to Christ to both categories of women, not just to virgins.[51]

In light of the larger Cistercian interest in the spiritual well-being of *conversi* as well as of the increasing account religious took of the lives of the non-professed, the Helfta writings make it clear that a range of the women and men who contributed to the monastic household and those beyond its walls occupied the thoughts and feelings of the nuns, figuring in their corporate devotion and private acts of piety and impinging on their consciences.[52] The nuns did not erase differences between

[51] Maria Parousia Clemens, "Gertrude, Spouse of Christ: Espousal with Christ through Liturgies of Entrance into the Monastic Life in the *Spiritual Exercises* of Gertrude of Helfta," unpublished paper presented at the International Congress of Medieval Studies, Western Michigan University, Kalamazoo, MI, 2021, 1–8.

[52] Megan Cassidy has found that monks presented *conversi* as anti-models for the monks themselves, in order to illustrate how disobedience undermined the common life ("'*Non Conversi sed Perversi*': The Use and Marginalization of the Cistercian Lay Brother," in *Deviance & Textual Control: New Perspectives in Medieval Studies*, ed. Megan Cassidy, et al. [University of Melbourne: History Department, 1997], 34–47).

religious and laity, or between themselves and the men and women who labored on their behalf, but they blunted the meaning of difference once souls arrived in purgatory—or rather, purgatorial experience revealed underlying sameness. They seem to have assumed shared values and common fallibilities between them and their lay male cohabiters, knights, and counts, as well as lay women. The visionary writings were meant in part to stimulate and sustain just this capacious sense of community between the nuns, on the one hand, and, on the other, *conversi* (male and female) as well as laity closely associated with the monastery, who, having crossed the threshold of death, as the women saw it, relied on them and also had much to offer the nuns themselves.

Relationship between the Living and the Dead

For all the attention given to elucidating who was in purgatory, the sins for which those there endured punishment and cleansing, and the means of their torment, the *Herald* and the *Book of Special Grace* drive home, more than anything else, the productive nature of the relationships between souls and sisters. Revelations threw into relief and teased out the mutual benefit each group received from the other, lending support to the observation Brian Patrick McGuire made over twenty years ago that what triumphed in late medieval purgatorial piety was a profound "sense of the close bonds existing among the members of the communion of saints."[53] The prologue of the *Herald's* book five, a text jam-packed with accounts of the sisters' success in assisting souls in purgatory, tells us that the very purpose of the revelations it relates is to provide examples to the living of the recompense the dead receive for meritorious works. The dead taught the living to be attentive to the obstacles to celestial felicity they themselves faced.[54] They goaded

[53] McGuire, "Purgatory," 81.

[54] *Le Héraut* 5 Prol. (SCh 331:14).

both by threat and enticement, although Gertrude made known Christ's present-day commitment to leading by fear; Christ commented on the contemporary hardening of hearts, justifying his upping the ante of the torments he revealed to her.[55] Yet the compiled pages, heavy with visions that spoke to the relief the sisters effected for purgatory's inhabitants and that heralded the joys of eternity, belied Christ's pessimistic proclamation.

Sensitive to their physical afflictions, marred consciences, and unmet hungers as well as to their joys, the sisters lent their eyes, ears, tears, silent prayers, and communal song to women and men whom, as the nuns understood it, Christ's Judgment and the souls' own consciences had consigned to purgatory. In celebrating the advantages the nuns were sure they bestowed on the indigent dead, the nuns assumed the common medieval notion that one person can substitute her or his works for those of another. Their perception that the pain associated with purgatory was in continuity with a process of punishment and purification beginning on earth was in keeping with larger trends.[56] Thus one person could make satisfaction for another who was on the other side of the divide between life and death, and a vigilant nun might altogether obviate another's sojourn in purgatory.[57] Without Gertrude's prayers on the morning of the death of Sister M. B., the latter's attachment to a luxurious bedspread and gilded pictures might, Gertrude suspected, have hindered her immediate entry into heaven; after Sister M. B. died, Christ assured Gertrude that the avaricious sister had not, after all, been detained.[58]

[55] *Le Héraut* 5.22.3 (SCh 331:196).

[56] Dolan, *St. Gertrude*, 180, made this observation almost a hundred years ago. See also Le Goff, *Birth of Purgatory*, 241–45.

[57] For a discussion of this notion, see Newman, "On the Threshold of the Dead," 119–21, and for some vivid examples of surrogate payment of debt another has incurred, see Duffy, *Stripping of the Altars*, 352–54.

[58] *Le Héraut* 5.8.1 (SCh 331:128–30).

Notwithstanding the insistence of the Helfta literature that one person could aid another in her journey toward salvation, the nuns communicated to their readership that the contributions of the living built upon groundwork that the soul of the deceased had laid for herself. They proclaimed the transfer of merit (for works accomplished or gifts accepted) from the living to the dead, while never letting go of the notion that the conveyance could occur only if the self had furnished the foundation to receive what another had to give. Thus we read that

> When brother John, procurator of the household, who had presided over the day-to-day work, had died, all of his works of labor appeared in the form of a ladder, on which his soul, leaving its body and needing purgation on account of several faults, climbed, step by step, and the more and more it rose up, the more bearable seemed the punishment. . . . When someone from the congregation by word or thought prayed for the soul, it seemed as though a hand stretched out from above and greatly helped the soul.[59]

In this instructional revelation, Helfta's procurator ascended the ladder rung by rung, pulled upward by the prayers of the sisters. But however much the nuns assisted him in his climb, his ascent began with John himself: his works *were* the ladder. Human beings can rely on one another's aid, this text and others preached, but not exclusively, and one can participate in another's salvation but cannot achieve it for her.[60] Evocative of claims in thirteenth-century scholastic treatises, the nuns

[59] *Le Héraut* 5.13.1 (SCh 331:160–62).

[60] As Christ explained to Gertrude, no soul could after death receive any help that she had not merited in this life (*Le Héraut* 5.16.4 [SCh 331:174]). And see *Le Héraut* 3.65.1–2; 4.49.5 (SCh 143:260–62; SCh 255:400–402) for the relationship between benefiting from another's prayers and merits and building on one's own merits. On the onus that rested with each individual to lay the foundation for her own salvation see Miri Cowan, *Death, Life, and Religious Change in Scottish Towns, c. 1350–1560* (Manchester, UK: Manchester University Press, 2012), 21.

promoted both uncompromising self-reliance and the frank admission of dependence on fellow sinful Christians, all together working with God for one another's good and animated by his grace.[61] They strove to create a sense of community in which dependency did not compromise stringent self-reliance, in which each member carried her own weight even while she both supposed that the others would help bear her burdens and took up responsibility for the others who were also in need.

At the level of the individual, this expectation is optimistic, affirming the ability of human beings to forge their own lives and to contribute to their own salvation.[62] It is also demanding, for the same reason. Relentless appeals to help the dead indicate that the nuns placed enormous pressure on themselves. The commitment to help one another fortified ties of mutual dependency and support among the women, since they pried open the reality of a need on the part of the individual that only another might be able to meet, and as the visions show, the other person in this context was likely to be one's sister. Especially in the face of an unbending call to self-responsibility, the literature offers consolation as it woos the reader into recognizing that the women with whom one lived, sometimes since childhood and, as most must have supposed, until death, were those on whom one should lean. Through their writings, the women of Helfta taught themselves that they *had* to count on one another—and that they could.[63]

[61] Le Goff, *Birth of Purgatory*, 237–88.

[62] McGuire, "Purgatory," 68, 81–82. For a sense of the optimism of the later Middle Ages coupled with a conviction of life "as a seeking and a journeying," see R. W. Southern, *The Making of the Middle Ages* (New Haven: Yale University Press, 1953), 222.

[63] For late medieval people's fear that once dead, they might be forgotten by the living and so bereft of the contributions that family members and others might make to their movement out of purgatory and into heaven, see Duffy, *Stripping of the Altars*, 348–54.

The nuns were, nonetheless, aware of complexities in the economy of salvation, and while setting great store by a world whose governing rules were stable, intelligible, and transparent, and taking comfort that each received reward and punishment commensurate with her merit,[64] the revelations they recorded signal an awareness of the need to work through theological conundrums that had immediate bearing on the sisters' work for the salvation of souls as well as on contemporary relationships among the women in the monastery. When a vision brought to Gertrude's attention the post-mortem rewards that two of her sisters had received, what she learned perplexed her, threatening a simple equation between the merit an individual has acquired by herself (through God's grace) and the recompense she receives in the afterlife. Gertrude learned that although one sister had served longer in religious life than the other and surpassed the other in various virtues, both received the same celestial reward. Wondering about the reason for the difference, Gertrude took up the topic with Christ, who neither contested Gertrude's assessment that each sister had merited a different reward than the other nor contradicted her observation that the two had received the equivalent recompense.

Maintaining that he does judge each person according to her merit, Christ's response to Gertrude nevertheless calls to mind the master's generosity in the parable of the workers in the vineyard (Matt 20:1-13), with Gertrude's puzzlement substituted for the laborers' grumbling about why the one who worked less should receive wages equal to ones who labored longer.[65] As Christ explained to Gertrude, his goodness gratuitously augments merit, sometimes in consideration of the

[64] As Voaden has noticed, the nuns perceived God's justice and predictability as indicative of God's merciful love (Rosalynn Jean Voaden, "Articulating Ecstasy: Image and Allegory in *The Booke of Gostlye Grace* of Mechtild of Hackeborn," PhD diss., University of Victoria, 1990, 49).

[65] *Le Héraut* 5.9.4 (SCh 331:140).

prayers of the faithful. According to this augmentation, he says, he gave "as much good to one as to another."[66] Each individual really was rewarded in proportion to her merit, Christ insisted, explaining that he added to the merit of some souls after death—those souls in need of the meritorious work of others.

The conversation between Christ and Gertrude is probably illustrative of a common curiosity within the monastery about the workings of divine retribution as well as about the relationship of God's justice to his mercy. It was a teaching tool. Relating precisely how they could play a role in effecting change for souls without compromising God's justice, a commonplace concern in contemporary sources from a variety of genres, the women were sure of their ability to tutor one another in the theological underpinnings of the spiritual program central to their common life and their individual spiritual practice, on which each of them had reason to suppose her own future depended. The visionary setpiece may, in addition, witness to a measure of unease about the fairness of a system in which God gave comparable rewards to women whose merit was asymmetrical, a determination on God's part that might, one supposes, have offended this or that sister with resentment upon learning through revelation that a former household companion whom she had regarded as undeserving was, nonetheless, en route to heaven or had arrived.

Not one of the women of Helfta would be lost, Christ declared as a source of solace, promising the sister-reader a rosy future for herself, however bumpy the passage, and it was probably a source of discomfort as well. Yet it may have offered individual sisters a degree of contentment to know that it was sometimes more obviously God's mercy at work (and one's own cooperation with him) that secured a fellow nun's salvation than the woman's own achievements. This would have

[66] *Le Héraut* 5.9.4 (SCh 331:140).

allowed them to praise God for his mercy while holding tight to critical appraisals of some companions. It would probably have promoted recognition that Christ loved and longed for all the sisters, thus offering security that all would bypass eternal punishment while therefore not demanding forgetfulness of the emotion or judgment each sister might have elicited.

The sisters' liturgical life was chock full of activities assisting the population of purgatory. The women kept the Office of the Dead,[67] held Masses on the day of interment[68] as well as anniversary Masses for the deceased,[69] and offered the Host for their deliverance.[70] Before, during, and after Mass as well as in the Office, they prayed for heaven-bound souls.[71] Visions confirmed the efficacy of the women's entreaties. To Brother H., each note the nuns intoned at Mass was like a meal,[72] and when Christ led Mechtild to a garden not far from heaven, she saw a crowd of souls seated at a great table, at which they feasted on food and drink—the words of the vigil the choir

[67] On the Office of the Dead at Helfta, see Vagaggini, *Theological Dimensions*, 797; and Ailbe J. Luddy, *The Cistercian Nuns: A Brief Sketch of the History of the Order from Its Foundations to the Present Day* (Dublin: M. H. Gill and Son, 1931), 15. The Office was a principal means by which the nuns, who were prohibited from celebrating Mass, could remember the dead and honor the requests of their founders and benefactors. By the later Middle Ages, women religious recited this office daily (Yardley, *Performing Piety*, 104).

[68] *Le Héraut* 5.8.2; 5.21.1 (SCh 331:130, 190).

[69] *Le Héraut* 5.8.1–3; 5.17.1; 5.18.1–2 (SCh 331:128–32, 176, 178–80); *Liber* 5.5; 5.17 (322–24, 345–47); see in addition *Liber* 5.1 (317–19). They set aside a certain Sunday each year in memory of the nuns' family members: *Le Héraut* 5.17.1 (SCh 331:176).

[70] See for example *Liber* 5.18 (347). For intercessory prayer during Mass among the nuns of Helfta, see Cheryl Clemons, "The Relationship between Devotion to the Eucharist and Devotion to the Humanity of Jesus in the Writings of St. Gertrude of Helfta," PhD diss., The Catholic University of America, 1995, 548–50.

[71] See for example *Le Héraut* 3.9.5; 3.18.6; 5.18.1 (SCh 143:40, 84–86; SCh 331:178); *Liber* 5.1; 5.2; 5.3; 5.5; 5.7 (317, 319, 320, 322–24, 329).

[72] *Le Héraut* 5.12.3 (SCh 331:156); and see *Liber* 5.11 (339).

recited.[73] The soul of a sister recently dead appeared to Gertrude in the form of a young girl; she darted with joy toward her Spouse only to collapse on his chest, and remained there until her sisters in choir intoned *tibi supplicatio commendet Ecclesiae*, when she began to draw refreshment from Christ's breast, vivified.[74] The nuns supplemented the routine rounds of liturgical devotions with a host of individual and group practices. In solitude or in the company of other women, they may have customarily recited five Our Fathers in honor of the five sacred wounds and on behalf of the dead,[75] and occasional prayers that sisters voiced individually were infused with expressions of desire for the well-being of purgatory's population.[76] Gertrude's prayer worked like a solvent on the animal skin that burdened one soul, and it had related transformative properties: the hide dissolved, revealing the man under the aspect of a little child on whom pain no longer pressed.[77]

The sisters attributed to themselves both the wherewithal to aid souls in tolerating their suffering and the power to ease the pain of purgatory's populace and, for souls' greater good, to intensify it.[78] Gertrude helped but did not wholly heal a certain Brother Th.: her prayer let loose water from Christ's side, which, bubbling with life-giving force, rushed over the *conversus*, strengthening him to endure continuing tortures.[79] The prayers his friends offered for one *conversus* had a gradual effect on him; hour by hour, his pain weighed less on him.[80] Just as, the sisters understand, both freedom from sorrow-filled memories and joyous reminiscences are constitutive of the

[73] For the geography of the garden and its association with heaven, see Binski, *Medieval Death*, 167.

[74] *Le Héraut* 5.6.3 (SCh 331:120–22).

[75] *Liber* 5.18; 5.19 (347, 350); *Le Héraut* 5.14.1 (SCh 331:162).

[76] *Le Héraut* 5.14.1 (SCh 331:162).

[77] *Le Héraut* 5.18.2 (SCh 331:182–84).

[78] See for example *Le Héraut* 14.1 (SCh 331:164).

[79] *Le Héraut* 5.14.1 (SCh 331:165).

[80] *Le Héraut* 5.12.3 (SCh 331:154).

happiness that belongs to the saints,[81] so in purgatory memory hurts, and this hurting heals.[82] The nuns perceived that they were able to insert themselves into this therapeutic process, sometimes by sparking recollection of what needed purging and exciting the conscience of souls. When Gertrude prayed the Our Father for a certain *conversus* and uttered the words "forgive us our trespasses as we forgive those who trespass against us,"[83] she saw the face of the one for whom she prayed become overcast with worry. As the soul explained, these words activated accusatory memories of his own unkind recalcitrance:

> When I was in the world, I did much wrong in that I did not easily forgive those who went against me. On the contrary, I showed severity to them for a long time. And now so that I can experience change, when I hear these words, I am disturbed by an intolerable anxiety and shame.[84]

Sometimes the Helfta writings credit the nuns with otherwise triggering emotional changes in purgatory's residents, boosting them into delight while they remained held in purgatory. When Mechtild prayed on behalf of the young Count Burchard, as the object of her compassion he felt great joy,[85] and when Gertrude expressed her faith in Christ's tenderness, a brother rejoiced.[86] The nuns' writings on purgatory allow us

[81] See for example *Liber* 1.32 (111).

[82] The notion that memory is central to the experience of the self in death runs through the *Book of Special Grace* and the *Herald*. As a soul is released from purgatory, he loses memory of all the sorrow he endured there. Memory can also bring solace in purgatory. Thinking about his fidelity while he was alive, a soul in purgatory was soothed (*Le Héraut* 5.12 [SCh 331:152–54]).

[83] *Le Héraut* 5.12.5 (SCh 331:158).

[84] *Le Héraut* 5.12.5 (SCh 331:158).

[85] *Liber* 5:11 (336).

[86] *Le Héraut* 5.16.2 (SCh 331:172). The prayer Gertrude uttered for the benefit of a certain soul not only pacified his pain; he subsequently became elated (*Le Héraut* 5.18.2 [SCh 331:182–84]).

a glimpse into their perception that a person could impress herself on another's interior life and, in doing so, produce change conducive to salvation.

The implication of the Helfta writings is that the nuns' everyday activities, and all manner of experiences, were at every moment pregnant with the possibility of helping souls in purgatory. One dying nun hoped that the pain of her last illness would contribute to the expiation of these souls' sin,[87] although in distinction to many medieval women, vicarious suffering did not dominate the Helfta piety. Christ promised that at the hour of Gertrude's death, a multitude of souls would pass from purgatory to enter heaven in her company, escorting her to him just as family members accompany the bride as she approaches her bridegroom.[88] Gertrude learned from a *conversus* that if she did not commit the fault for which he was punished (following his will, bucking others' guidance), her upright behavior would relieve his suffering.[89] A day after the death of Count Burchard, Mechtild perceived the liberating power of the tears that she offered on his behalf: the count lingered only a little before entering heaven.[90]

The *Book of Special Grace* notes that giving alms profits souls in purgatory,[91] and the *Herald* reveals that even a single word might be of enormous benefit to a soul languishing there.[92] Physical labor, eating, sleeping, and dying—all of these might be productive avenues for the redemption of souls,[93] whereas

[87] *Le Héraut* 5.10.1 (SCh 331:144). Bynum observes that the central aspect of the growth of purgatory was not so much its creation of a "third place," but its resolution of "the role of suffering in Christianity" (*Holy Feast and Holy Fast: The Religious Significance of Food to Medieval Women* [Berkeley: University of California Press, 1987], 399, n. 4).

[88] *Le Héraut* 5.29.5 (SCh 331:236).

[89] *Le Héraut* 5.12.3 (SCh 331:154).

[90] *Liber* 5.11 (336).

[91] *Liber* 5.11 (339).

[92] *Le Héraut* 5.15.2 (SCh 331:168).

[93] See for example, *Le Héraut* 1.11.10; 5.12.3 (SCh 139:180; SCh 331:156). And see Dolan, *St. Gertrude*, 186–87.

one might easily contribute to their suffering, through a lack of faith, exercise of self-will, and so forth.[94] All of the monastery and its fields became for the nuns sacred spaces in which to work for the benefit of the faithful departed (or to fail to do so, or even to harm them), and it is unclear whether the nuns believed that there was anything they could do that, if executed with right intention, did not contribute to souls' progress. The communities of the living and the dead were in this way inextricably connected, and their sense of this connection probably invigorated association among the women themselves.

Christ fueled the nuns' trust in the power of their devotions. "Ask me with confidence," he persuaded Gertrude when she witnessed a soul in agony and considered whether her petition on the soul's behalf might bump up against the demands of divine justice.[95] He assured Mechtild that he would deliver a thousand souls for each sister's prayer.[96] Crowded with accounts of accomplishment after accomplishment,[97] the nuns' written broadcasting of their successes was surely meant to reinforce to their sister readers the worth of their liturgical observances and individual devotions. A literature *pro domo*,[98] like other late-medieval vision collections, the Helfta writings are an approbation of the whole of the household, especially its public communal worship. As Caroline Walker Bynum

[94] *Le Héraut* 5.12.3 (SCh 331:154).

[95] *Le Héraut* 5.16.2 (SCh 331:170).

[96] *Liber* 1.31 (108).

[97] There are some indications that the sisters wrestled now and then with mitigated success. When Gertrude asked Christ why one woman was delayed even though many friends who loved her greatly had prayed for her, Christ explained that he had in fact answered the prayers favorably; it was on this account that the soul would pass from purgatory to heaven. The implication is that the suffering of the soul in purgatory would have been harsher, or longer, without the nuns' supplications, although they fell short of their desired effect (*Le Héraut* 5.9.4 [SCh 331:138]).

[98] McGuire, "Purgatory," 80, has made this remark about other Cistercian visionary accounts of purgatory.

noticed long ago, they affirmed to their cloistered readership that the system worked.[99]

The sisters may have felt more closely bound to one another in consequence of the significance the convent's writings give to their shared commitment, perhaps narrowing perception of a divide between the household's spiritual luminaries and their fellow nuns, although difference between parties was not erased. One soul was stained with a sin of which the sisters were unaware and about which, therefore, they could not pray. Because Christ revealed only to Gertrude the sin in question, she was able to intercede and relieve the soul.[100] On another occasion, Gertrude's recitation of the Great Psalter freed a soul from the shackles that had prohibited it from receiving the suffrages the church offered on his behalf.[101] In this last instance, special power is attributed to Gertrude's intercession to pry open the possibility of the soul's benefiting from the prayers of the larger community.

However unequal the pleasing power of their work, Gertrude's role was thus sometimes to facilitate the efficacy of her sisters' contributions to suffering souls, and the celebration of her individual and their collective activities may have given the nuns a sense that a common and mighty purpose joined them all. When a recently deceased *conversus* came before her, Gertrude informed him of the sisters' request that God give all the good he accomplished in them to their brother. Then she asked the soul what advantage he had received from the petition. The *Herald*'s reading audience must have been heartened to hear of the brother's reply: that which he lacked he received from Gertrude *and* her fellow nuns.[102] It is worth stressing that

[99] Bynum, "Women Mystics."

[100] *Le Hérault* 5.9.4 (SCh 331:138).

[101] *Le Hérault* 5.18.2 (SCh 331:182–84). On the nuns' recitation of the Great Psalter, a "farced" arrangement of the psalms (with sentences preceding each psalm that generally apply the psalm to Christ) with long prayers after each psalm, see Finnegan, *Women of Helfta*, 8.

[102] *Le Hérault* 5.12.4 (SCh 331:156).

it is exactly the nuns' great success in securing souls' relief and liberation that indicates how much rested on their shoulders, perhaps propelling them into prayer and other works and confronting them with the enormity of any laxity in their labors, an incentive to stay constant in their commitments.

The nuns were not always sanguine about their dealings with the dead, however. Lagging in their enthusiasm, and caught up in competing pleas for attention, they did not at all times succumb to the claims the dead made on their emotions or feel compelled by an attitude of obligation to respond to them. While the convent was reciting the Great Psalter, Gertrude asked Christ why this devotion was of such profit when she found the multiplication of psalms tedious.[103] Mechtild's reaction to requests for prayer was not uniformly prompt: when one friar asked her to pray for the soul of another friar, she neglected to do so, until Christ took her by the hand and swept her into the man's presence, propelling her into service.[104] On the feast of All Souls, Mechtild wished to pray but was hampered by the incessant crashing in of thoughts that funneled her attention to a particular person with whose deplorable post-mortem state she was familiar.

It was not always easy for the nuns to summon up concern for purgatory's inhabitants, especially when the souls in question were, while they were alive, unknown to the nuns. The literature implicitly chided them for their sometimes-perfunctory performance of the prayers they were required to recite for the dead. The women acknowledged that they did not always make offerings with the best of intentions. Whatever conception of community they had with regard to those in purgatory, it did not do away with their need to be reminded of their obligations or to charge their fervor.

The Helfta writings did not dismiss the power of prayer for those in purgatory, however leaden the supplicant might have

[103] *Le Héraut* 5.18 (SCh 331:178–80).

[104] *Liber* 5.8 (331).

been. Rather, they both affirmed the greater efficacy of prayers voiced with right intention and alleged the meaningfulness of those acts performed as a matter of duty. This makes sense; to do otherwise would place in jeopardy the value of much of the nuns' daily activities. The women knew that efficacious relationships between human beings benefited from fellow feeling but maintained that they did not depend on sympathetic sentiments. They insisted, in any case, that God's grace regularly animated Gertrude and Mechtild to feelings of pity for these souls, however checkered with boredom, diminished by distraction, or streaked with indifference their work sometimes was. When Gertrude saw the soul of brother Th. tortured unspeakably by the pangs of conscience, she was moved by compassion to recite five Our Fathers on his behalf and to kiss Christ's five wounds.[105] It was with compassion that Mechtild prayed that the Lord would give to the soul of the nineteen-year-old Count Burchard all the tears she herself had cried for love of God, tears that the young count had himself neglected to shed while he was alive and that now, in purgatory, poured from his eyes.[106] The literature announced the essential importance of compassion or love animating the sisters' intercessions on behalf of the dead.[107] As their exploits showed, obligation and emotion rightly worked in tandem. Cultivating compassion within the context of maintaining formal commitments to those for whom Christ has directed the nuns to offer prayer and other works was in large measure what both the mystical and work-a-day religious life at Helfta was about, a continuing quest for conformity with Christ's own attitude toward sinners.

The literature is otherwise indicative of a household sensitive to the precariousness of emotion as a stable bedrock from which to fix communal commitments and launch devotions,

[105] *Le Héraut* 5.14.1 (SCh 331:162). Gertrude was moved by compassion for the soul of a poor woman: *Le Héraut* 5.21.1 (SCh 331:190).

[106] *Liber* 5.11 (336).

[107] *Le Héraut* 5.16.1 (SCh 331:170).

and thus aware of the need for an alternate foundation into which to sink pledges to aid others in the afterlife. Some of the nun-to-nun appearances obviously built upon already-established relationships, and there are indications of perduring and complex connections between individual women. The following passage and the larger account from which it comes affirmed the advantages to a sister of Gertrude's prayers and also hinted at a turbulent moment in their personal history. After her prayers released a nail that held her sister's habit in place and that had prevented the soul from entering Christ's embrace, Gertrude recalled to her sister that although they had been on good terms before the sister became sick, when she was ill, the soul did not receive Gertrude's advice well:

> the soul gazing at that person [Gertrude] who had poured out prayers on her behalf, gave her thanks with great friendliness. She [Gertrude] said to her, "Although you were always friendly with me, nevertheless, when you were sick you seemed to me not to receive joyfully when I counseled you." And the soul [replied], "Your prayers were of greater profit to me because you poured them out purely in love on account of God."[108]

Continuity of concern of one sister for another after her death was not dependent on there having been unblemished feelings of affection between the two; this passage counsels a commitment to those with whom one may have experienced rocky moments, insisting that love for the other, anchored in love of God, should trump the vicissitudes of friendly feeling. Training themselves in the power of each sister to affect another's post-mortem experience for the better, notwithstanding hard feelings she might have harbored for the now-deceased, would have been a vital message for the well-being of the whole household. With its female membership probably numbering near a hundred during Gertrude's and Mechtild's life-

[108] *Le Héraut* 5.9.7 (SCh 331:142).

times, comprising little girls, middle-aged women, and the old, the convent must have been home to all sorts of relationships—enduring and supportive, and also of uncertain and changing quality, a range that called forth the need to ground solidarity in something that could withstand the ambiguity inherent in human relations.[109] One of the purposes of this literature was to help its monastic readers navigate the demands and challenges of life in community by recalling to them the larger contexts of the relationships formed in the monastery.

The Dead Help the Living

A lay benefactor of the monastery, fellow nuns, a procurator, a poor woman, and *conversi*—the plight of all these souls and of others provides lessons to the living. The very inclusion among purgatory's residents of Helfta nuns makes it plain to the reading community that however holy the household, no nun ought to conceive of herself as exempt from the stains that streaked the souls of all and that landed some in purgatory. The nuns learned, however, that by responding to the plight of the dead, they could immediately affect their own transformation: when Gertrude asked a *conversus* suffering on account of hardened self-will how his pain could be alleviated, he explained that if anyone guilty of the same sin changed her ways, this would soothe him.[110] Her spiritual progress could belong to him.

Souls in purgatory warn and entice, and, offering an account of sin and satisfaction coherent across all states of life, the souls of women and men, lay and religious, laborers and lords, all together taught the nuns who they were and ought to be. The nuns heard from the dead that God was merciful, that he rewarded good acts, and that purgatory was a reward he held

[109] *Liber* 6.1 (376).

[110] *Le Héraut* 5.12.3 (SCh 331:154).

out to the living.[111] The visions were hopeful, emphasizing not purgatory's pains but that its inhabitants would one day wend their way to heaven. There was no sense, however, that sisters were inoculated from the sins to which souls in purgatory, whatever their state in life, fell prey. Speaking with the soul of a knight, Mechtild asked whether he benefited from the merit that accrued to nuns. The knight replied that he did not, because the counsels of merchants inclined his desires and his will toward things of the earth.[112] Although identifying the circumstances of his sin within a thoroughly secular context, the knight's self-indictment involves an accusation general enough that the nuns could apply it to themselves. And the same was the case with regard to Count Burchard, who taught Mechtild that death freed his soul from fetters of the flesh, delivering it from the eating, sleeping, and other constant activities, including engagement with fellow human beings, that sometimes restricted his desire for God.[113]

Revelations pulled from a shared cache of vices and commended a common pool of virtues, accessible to all. Souls educated sisters on the imperative of forgiveness.[114] They offered cautionary tales, urging avoidance of the sins of pride and ambition,[115] for example. The sins of slander and gossip, especially undermining the common life, also figured in these accounts,[116] as did that destabilizing peril to the monastic foundation, disobedience.[117] A toasted toad, the soul of a *conversus*, provides an anti-model: because he had not been docile to his superiors, he was burnt from the inside out, enduring inexpressible sufferings.[118] A troop of religious shuttled across a

[111] *Le Héraut* 5.18.1 (SCh 331:180).
[112] *Liber* 5.11 (338).
[113] *Liber* 5.11 (338).
[114] *Le Héraut* 5.12.5 (SCh 331:158).
[115] *Le Héraut* 5.18.1 (SCh 331:152–54).
[116] *Le Héraut* 5.22.2–3 (SCh 331:194–196).
[117] *Le Héraut* 5.22.1 (SCh 331:192).
[118] *Le Héraut* 5.15.1 (SCh 331:166–68).

wobbly plank; those who submitted to obedience were aided in the crossing by the rails placed on either side of the walkway, keeping them from falling into the clutch of demons waiting below. A heavy load rested on those responsible for maintaining obedience among their charges: those who had neglected to do so walked the plank anxiously because to them the rails on either side were faulty.[119] Visions such as these accentuated the importance of the formal structures of authority governing right relationship within the monastery for all its members. Nothing about the sin of disobedience or the sins of which souls accused themselves introduced a divide among the guilty; familiar charges accrued to all. Moreover, the circumstances in which souls related having sinned did little to reinforce divisions either among the members of the monastery, according to gender or religious status, for example, or between the household's occupants and the population outside the monastery walls.

The dead who came to the nuns served as something like a ghostly assembly of spiritual advisors,[120] a cadre of confidants to whom the women listened trustingly and eagerly, presenting a picture of openness and receptivity that, with the exception of the nuns themselves, no living men or women compelled. If the content of these visions is more than the consequence of idiosyncratic musings, it suggests that women of Helfta believed that they could benefit from the insights of lay brothers,

[119] *Le Héraut* 5.22.2 (SCh 331:194).

[120] For relationships between a *conversus* and women that had a spiritual component and in which the lay brother played the part of spiritual advisor, collaborator, or confidant, see Barbara Newman, "Preface: Goswin of Villers," in *Send me God: The Lives of Ida the Compassionate of Nivelles, Nun of La Ramée, Arnulf, Lay Brother of Villers, and Abundus, Monk of Villers,* trans. Martinus Cawley (Turnhout: Brepols, 2003), xlii–xliii; Jeroen Deploige, "How Gendered Was Clairvoyance in the Thirteenth Century?" in *Speaking to the Eye: Sight and Insight through Text and Image (1150–1650)*, ed. Thérèse de Hemptinne, Veerle Fraeters, and María Eugenia Góngora (Turnhout: Brepols, 2013), 113–14.

a tortured knight, and a longing count, whom, with the power of their pens, the women offered as apt models (and anti-models) to themselves. The literature's encouragement of attentiveness to the perceived needs of the dead and to the lessons they gave did not guarantee responsiveness among those among the living, of course, and it is not evident that the sisters thought they should translate their concern with the deceased to their still-living counterparts. Whether the nuns' receptivity to the trials and teachings of souls in purgatory is compensatory or whether it furthered relationships established while all parties were alive is probably impossible to determine, although Mechtild does seem to have known and interacted with Count Burchard's mother as well as a circle of relatives and friends, or at least we are meant to suppose this, for the soul of the count sent messages via Mechtild thanking them for their prayers.[121]

Matters meaningful between the sisters and souls in purgatory may have been of superficial concern—or none at all—when those now deceased were alive. Yet it is important that the nuns themselves do not minimize their attachment to those dead who appeared in revelations and whose counsels, aches, and susceptibility to the intervention of the sisters made a claim on them. It may be that, as the literature suggests, the nuns found the relationships they cultivated with the dead in purgatory to be no less significant, no less time-consuming, and no less compelling than those they enjoyed with the living.

The purgatorial setpieces featuring *conversi* spotlight intimate dimensions of relationships between them and the nuns about which the literature is otherwise circumspect. Among the most poignant demonstrations of sympathy in the Helfta writings occurs in a conversation between Gertrude and a *conversus*, a dialogue that occupies an entire chapter in the *Herald's* book five, with the revelation occupying a generous

[121] *Liber* 5.11 (338).

four printed pages.[122] Taking up such considerations as sin and punishment, friendship and grief, the chapter raises perhaps unanswerable questions about the nuns' relationship with the men in their midst. Although the familiarity that the sister and brother assume with each other in this context may not have depended on affinities felt in this life, fantasies about the dead are suggestive, and in this instance, they speak of bonds of affection, intellectual camaraderie, and spiritual companionship.[123]

Thus, as Gertrude and the *conversus* spoke together about his death, their talk was thick with conviction of the power of human emotion to move God and an illustration of the nuns' success in doing so. The *conversus* related that as he was dying, he was treated to displays of divine tenderness, expressions of love occasioned by the nuns' plea that God allow him to remain a little longer among the living. And the soul told Gertrude that the tears the sisters had shed on his account now aroused in him an answering sorrow at seeing his friends lamenting on his account. He assured her that once he entered heaven, this sign of their affectionate attachment would become a source of delight to him, an assertion that the living matter to the celestial dead, a ringing note of confidence in the perduring significance of relations—offering, perhaps, the sort of comfort for which the nuns' twelfth-century predecessor, Bernard of Clairvaux, longed when his own brother died.[124] Whatever the contours of the relationship the nuns had with the men who worked at the monastery, their writings suggest

[122] *Le Héraut* 5.12.1–6 (SCh 331:150–60).

[123] On the power of stereotypes associated with the dead to reveal something about attitudes of the living, see Martha G. Newman, *The Boundaries of Charity: Cistercian Culture and Ecclesiastical Reform, 1098–1180* (Stanford: Stanford University Press, 1996), 105–6; and Cassidy, *"Non Conversi sed perversi."*

[124] *Le Héraut* 5.12.4 (SCh 331:156–58). The Helfta literature contains not a hint of anxiety among the nuns of being forgotten by souls upon their arrival in heaven, or of a love that was singular on earth being poured into a pool of indifferent love as souls' love merges with God's love when souls enter.

that they mingled a hope for reunion in heaven with an expectation that friendship would flourish there as well.[125]

The content of some purgatorial visions was calculated to inculcate in the sisters the confidence that their piety was building a corps of colleagues whose liberation they facilitated and who would eventually be in the position to help the sisters themselves cross into bliss. However gradual the journey from purgatory to heaven might be, the nuns were sure that a number of souls caught in punishing pain would travel into heaven during the women's own lifetime. When a sister was dying, those souls whom she had helped to secure a place in heaven sprang into action: they guided the dying nun to confess to God before her death. Although her confession did not obviate a period in purgatory, the words of her prayers for these same souls became jewels that adorned her, presumably hastening her departure from purgatory or making her stay there less painful.[126] It was clear to the nuns that their devotions redounded to the benefit of all who were party to the transaction. They learned to expect an exchange of benefits; experience taught them that they could rely on it.

Thus anticipating a reversal of fortunes, in which those who had once been in a position to extend aid became recipients of relief and vice versa, the nuns and those in purgatory worked in partnership to augment the number of souls in heaven by smoothing the progress of one another's entry into the kingdom.[127] The women underscored a sense of continuity in relationships: ties continued and solidified (or in some cases established) between the sisters and souls in purgatory did not

[125] On hope in purgatory, see Le Goff, *Purgatory*, 306–10.

[126] *Le Héraut* 5.22.1 (SCh 331:196).

[127] When she saw a sister in glory surrounded by kneeling souls whom the sister's prayers had delivered into heaven, Gertrude asked the soul whether the community would benefit from the numbers of sisters received into heaven, and the sister responded in the affirmative. For each sister in heaven, the soul said that God multiplied the benefits that nuns on pilgrimage received (*Le Héraut* 5.3.8 [SCh 331:76]).

dissipate when, in part through the sisters' labors, souls were propelled from purgatory into heaven. Instead, the relationship changed. Guided by an ethic of reciprocity, souls turned back to help those who helped them. There was a flexibility built into the nuns' sense of community that allowed for the shifting of roles and responsibilities between the one in need and the one who answered to that need.

In one vision, such a swapping of roles took place even while souls remained in purgatory. Gertrude saw a soul who had benefited from her prayers offer Christ a silver coin, compensation for the petitions she had poured out on his behalf.[128] This passage suggests that even souls still held in purgatory might appeal to God for his mercy, at least on behalf of the living. By hinting at the efficacy of this soul's offering, this passage perhaps undermines the notion communicated elsewhere in the literature that souls in purgatory have no resources at their disposal other than the foundation they built for themselves while they were alive and on account of which others' offerings on their behalf might be effective. At least, it raises the question of how important to the nuns was the elaboration of a clear and consistent statement with regard to the power of souls in purgatory. The larger context of the Helfta writings suggests that eclipsing any such concern was a far greater one: the nuns' investment in proclaiming the mutual benefits the living and the dead offered one another.[129]

The nuns' piety contributed to cementing the women's sense of community with the saints, since labor on behalf of the languishing dead was a joint venture between saints and sisters, Mary and the angels, in cooperation with God. Thus, for example, a soul feasted on the prayers and other works that Mary and saints (to all of whom the soul while alive had been especially devoted) served, and her feeding gradually cleared the

[128] *Le Héraut* 5.16.5 (SCh 331:174–76).

[129] For the living and the dead in purgatory helping each other toward salvation, see Duffy, *Stripping of the Altars*, 349.

sorrow clouding her mind, enabling her to turn her eyes toward the Lord.[130]

This sense of communion was not without blemish, though. The vile excretion that flowed from the wounds on the mouth of another soul disgusted the saints, and their revulsion had consequences: it prevented the soul from entering God's presence. Thus community between the faithful on earth, in purgatory, and in heaven does not preclude being alienated, in one way or another, by those considered as a member of the larger community of the faithful,[131] though I have found no such expression of revulsion on the part of the sisters with regard to souls in purgatory. The sisters fitted their work into a larger effort among the faithful to help one another.

The angels sometimes facilitated the intermingling of the inhabitants of heaven, purgatory, and earth. In the *Book of Special Grace*, the dead in purgatory, those already citizens of the heavenly Jerusalem, and those who are still alive all drink from the waters of the well of mercy, which the angels proffer.[132] However much they want to insist that a single thread of God's grace heals the soul-sickness that sin causes, grace as it is conveyed to souls in need is a thoroughly social affair.

King, Soldiers, and Knights

The nuns understood their commitment to souls in purgatory to be in conformity with Christ's desires and secured through his mercy.[133] They were not advocates of unreserved compassion for the dead. Accepting the eternal agony of some of God's creatures with equanimity, they did not blanch at the

[130] *Le Héraut* 5.12.2 (SCh 331:152–54).

[131] *Le Héraut* 5.22.2 (SCh 331:194–96).

[132] *Liber* 2.28 (173–74).

[133] The *Herald* makes explicit the correspondence between Gertrude's petitions for souls in purgatory and God's purpose; *Le Héraut* 5.16.2, 5.25.3 (SCh 331:170, 206).

notion of damnation. Hell was a whirlwind of misery for whose unfortunates the nuns expressed not a whiff of compassion, even if there is no indication that they took pleasure in the anguish.[134] The souls of the damned persisted in a horror of darkness.[135] Destitute of every good, they were their own torture.[136] Assuming the shape of dogs, snakes, toads, and lions, they tore at one another.[137] Never having thought sweetly of Christ, not even for one hour, the damned wallowed in infinite despair.[138] In a vision that came to her on Saint Benedict's feast day, Gertrude beheld Benedict carrying a scepter studded with stones. On the side facing him shone rays of happiness from all those who were ever corrected by his Rule; stones on the side turned toward Christ reflected the justice by which some were hurled into eternal torment.[139]

But the plight of the latter did not prompt the nuns to an excursus on divine justice, nor did they explore the reasons that some souls were confined to hell. Christ wanted people to acknowledge both his goodness and his justice, he told Mechtild, explaining that he damned those who did not turn to him in penance; Mechtild did not linger on the remark, and they took up another topic.[140] The women of Helfta rested easy

[134] *Le Héraut* 3.30.4 (SCh 143:136); *Liber* 4.19; 4.20 (276, 277). Bynum has discussed the toughness of the God of these visions and the nuns' notion that God's damnation is just ("Women Mystics," esp. 189, 217, and 254). For an emphasis on the generosity of the nuns' conception of the afterlife, see Newman, introduction to *Mechthild of Hackeborn*. On late medieval notions of hell, see Binski, *Medieval Death*, 166–81; Gérard Le Don, "Structures et significations de l'imagerie médiévale de l'ènfer," *Cahiers de Civilization Médiévale Xe–XIIe Siècles* 22 (1979): 363–72; see also Alan E. Bernstein, *The Formation of Hell: Death and Retribution in the Ancient and Early Christian World* (Ithaca: Cornell University Press, 1993).

[135] *Liber* 5.21 (352).

[136] *Liber* 5.21 (352).

[137] *Liber* 5.20 (351).

[138] *Liber* 5.20; 5.21 (351, 352).

[139] *Le Héraut* 4.11.3 (SCh 255:128–30).

[140] *Liber* 1.13 (44).

with the notion that nothing anyone did was robbed of significance, for no action, however trifling, will fail to be rewarded, and concomitantly no negligence, however minor, will go unpunished.[141]

Awareness of the demands of divine justice was never far from the nuns' consideration, but none of the damned spoke to the nuns; the nuns spied no one among them known to them. Unlike souls in purgatory, hell's residents never did emerge as so many individuals, however despicable, but remained an anonymous mass. Thus no soul confronted the nuns from among the damned, pulling on their pity or challenging the logic of their damnation.[142] The nuns' indifference to this forever-tormented population and to the dynamics of damnation are telltale signs of how utterly foreign the place and the people were to the women; it is as if there were nothing familiar about the damned, nothing recognizable about their fate. Nowhere do we get the sense that the nuns were able even to conceive of any of their own descending to eternal darkness. Christ's promise that no sister would be lost guaranteed that souls in hell would remain forever alien to them. However broad and varied a sense of community for which the nuns rallied, the communion of saints into which they believed they were incorporated was limited by fixed parameters. The boundaries of community were marked by a keen sense of permanent exclusion, and what lay beyond was something about which the nuns seem not to have wondered much at all. It seemed hard for them to even conceive of the damned individuals who made up the population of hell.

Likewise, there were some inflexible restrictions on solidarity among souls. The sisters' suffrages did not challenge God's judgment and were in harmony with his decree. As portrayed

[141] *Le Héraut* 5.10.3; 4.28.2 (SCh 331:146–48; SCh 255:270–72).

[142] It is worth noting in this context that the *Herald* depicts Gertrude as demanding that God's purifying love consume her sins before she dies (*Le Héraut* 3.16.2 [SCh 143:68]). She sounds no analogous insistence that God's love cleanse others whose souls are in jeopardy.

in this literature, the women turned their backs on those whom Christ relegated to eternal damnation, wanting no part of their suffering or its potential alleviation or cessation. This disregard is not surprising. Although questions about everlasting torment and a longing to disbelieve in its existence are evident in writings associated with a few extraordinary female medieval thinkers, they were women who experienced themselves as vulnerable and who were settled outside of the mainstream of society, women such as the Beguine Hadewijch of Brabant (d. 1248) and the fourteenth-century anchorite Julian of Norwich (1342–ca. 1416), and including the Helfta nuns' older contemporary and sometime companion, Mechtild of Magdeburg, who relates in the *Flowing Light of the Divinity* her dying on the cross with Christ and traveling to hell to console souls there.[143] No challenges to the eternity of hell or sustained doubts about damnation come to us from women religious.[144] Perhaps the Helfta nuns' security in the correspondence between their institutional commitments, on the one hand, and, on the other, God's plan for them, their confidence in the central role they played in executing his will to gather into community all those whom he loved, contributed to a hardening of sentiment against those who found themselves outside the communion of saints, set apart from the body of Christ.

The Helfta literature reverberates with the justice and order associated by theologians with atonement theory and by lawyers with the feudal bond. The nuns' God was a God of justice and a God of mercy.[145] When it pertained to the nuns,

[143] Bynum, "Women Mystics," 254; *Mechthild of Magdeburg: The Flowing Light of the Godhead*, 3.10, trans. Frank Tobin, Classics of Western Spirituality (New York: Paulist Press, 1998), 118.

[144] The majority of medieval religious women did not question God's right to punish (see Barbara Newman, "On the Threshold of the Dead," 134).

[145] Bynum has characterized the nuns' spirituality as "balanced" ("Women Mystics," 190–91). Gertrude and Mechtild associate characteristics with Christ that the dominant culture often dichotomized (justice versus mercy, honor and reason versus intimacy and emotionality, and so forth). What is striking is their attribution of such qualities to Christ without apparently any strong

the punishment, temporary or eternal, imposed by God's justice was for the most part not threatening but appealing, not troubling but comforting. Divine justice was frankly beautiful.[146] When in a vision Gertrude learned that human beings cannot do any work with right intention without receiving a particular profit and cannot omit any work without a diminution of merit, she gave no indication that this teaching frightened her.[147] Rather, she appears to have carried from insights such as this the notion that God was merciful exactly because he was just, and in part because his justice provided opportunities to participate in the perfect satisfaction he has made, to share in his superabundant merit.[148] Justice was love to Gertrude,[149] and to the sisters the possibility of benefiting from God's justice was virtually omnipresent.[150] Moreover, the terms of Christ's assessment were fair and evident, and the nuns could count on them. Victory was in their reach.[151] The women were motivated in their piety far more by the expectation of reward—for themselves, for others—than by the fear of punishment. They emphasized Christ's mercy and advocacy, not his severity, underscoring Christ's sweetness and praising him as Defender and Helper, Friend and Lover.[152]

---

sense that they are dichotomous (see Harrison and Bynum, "Gertrude, Gender," 66–68).

[146] *Le Héraut* 3.16.2 (SCh 143:68). They are similar to Anselm in this regard. For both the nuns and Anselm, justice is a "perfectly ordered universe" (Southern, *Saint Anselm*, 212).

[147] *Le Héraut* 4.49.5 (SCh 255:400–402).

[148] The most elaborate and forceful illustration of human beings' opportunity to participate in Christ's satisfaction, which they are obliged to do if they are to achieve salvation, is in the context of Christ's demand that Gertrude write the *Herald* and her response to his demand; see chap. 2. The nuns were obviously confident in their ability to work with Christ, their writings celebrating the monastic life for the incomparable environment it afforded to take full advantage of Christ's merciful offer of cooperation; see *Le Héraut* 4.50.10 (SCh 255:416).

[149] *Le Héraut* 1.6.1 (SCh 139:150).

[150] *Le Héraut* 4.10.2 (SCh 255:122).

[151] *Le Héraut* 5.3.1 (SCh 331:66).

[152] *Le Héraut* 3.65.3 (SCh 143:264).

Although they never fully worked through the paradox of Christ's justice and mercy that they placed in relief, the Helfta literature elaborated an understanding of Christ's justice as infused with a generosity that demonstrated his great mercy. The visionaries themselves experienced Christ's tender mercies as immoderate and sometimes pictured him as so drunk with love as to repudiate his own judgment.[153] The Helfta writings both did and did not insist that Christ in his mercy overlooked the faults of his creatures, some of whom (the literature almost says all of whom) he pursued with loving clemency—even when they spurned his advances.[154] Beguiled by Gertrude, Christ was blind to her guile, charmed by her imperfections, and indulgent of them.[155] He banished into eternal forgetfulness all of Mechtild's crimes, remitted her sins, and supplied his merits for all she lacked.[156]

Echoing the topos of reversal fundamental to Christianity, Gertrude asserted repeatedly that God raised up the weak to confound the strong and turned justice upside down, upsetting the balanced order of things when he made undeserving Gertrude most worthy of his compassion and conferred on her spiritual authority over those worthier than she.[157] The gifts

[153] *Le Héraut* 2.8.3; 5.10.3 (SCh 139:264; SCh 331:146). For the wild optimism about Christ's eagerness to reward souls that infuses the *Book of Special Grace*, see *Liber* 3.5 (202).

[154] *Le Héraut* 2.3.3; 2.20.8; 2.22.1 (SCh 139:238–40, 314–16, 328). Gertrude's explicit preoccupation in book two is more with God's mercy than with his justice. She insists that the tenderness of Christ's friendship moved her more than the punishments she deserved (*Le Héraut* 2.2.2 [SCh 139:234])—punishments that God sometimes, but rarely, meted out (*Le Héraut* 2.3.2 [SCh 139:238]). Mary Jeremy Finnegan, largely on the basis of a reading of book three, has also underscored Gertrude's sense of Christ as merciful ("Idiom of Women Mystics," *Mystics Quarterly* 13, no. 2 [1987]: 65–72, esp. 66).

[155] *Le Héraut* 2.13.1 (SCh 139:284).

[156] *Liber* 1.1 (8).

[157] Inversion is a standard topos in the New Testament; see for example 1 Cor 1:20 and Mark 10:31. For its use by twelfth-century Cistercians, see Bynum, "Jesus as Mother," in *Jesus as Mother*, 127–28. On women's and men's use of this inversion to describe women's spiritual powers, see Peter Dronke, *Women Writers of the Middle Ages: A Critical Study of Texts from Perpetua (d. 203)*

Christ bestowed on human beings—the very offer of salvation he purchased with his blood, his willingness to forgive sins small and large accumulated throughout life's course, and his countless other gifts, including his forthright expressions of longing for souls and delight in them—were gratuitous. They were not, however unconditional.

As did medieval Christians more generally, the Helfta nuns conceived of redemption as a removal of liability to God through payment. Christ paid the debt for original sin on the cross; his blood was an offering to God the Father, mitigating the Father's anger and thus making possible reconciliation between human beings and God.[158] Medieval Christians understood baptism, which washed them clean of the original debt, as participating in this payment. But during the course of a lifetime, the baptized sinner accumulated new debt for sinful works committed and good works omitted, as well as for an assortment of sin-soaked feelings and thoughts. She was responsible for making good on these debts—each and every one!—lest she die with unsettled debt and, therefore, estranged from God.

Life was, from one of the vantage points the Helfta literature offered, perilous because it was an accumulation of debt that none could ever properly repay. Death, at any rate, cut short the reparation process. Because he was just, Christ did not waive the payment due from the soul who died indebted. Because he was merciful, he also did not dispatch all sinners to eternal suffering. To the nuns, God's consigning of souls to purgatory was a clear expression of his justice: the soul tarnished by sin could not accede to heaven. It was also proof of

to Marguerite Porete (d. 1310) (Cambridge, UK: Cambridge University Press, 1984); Dronke, *Women Writers*, 64–79. See also Barbara Newman, "Divine Power Made Perfect in Weakness: St. Hildegard on the Frail Sex," in *Peaceweavers*, ed. Lillian Thomas Shank and John A. Nichols, CS 72 (Kalamazoo, MI: Cistercian Publications, 1987), 103–22.

[158] *Liber* 1.9 (30). Also see *Liber* 1.31; 2.17; 4.5 (104–5, 151–52, 261–62); *Le Héraut* 4.46.2 (SC 255:350).

his mercy: God's offer of salvation extended even to souls who were at their deaths marred by sin. Sinful souls destined for salvation passed through a period in purgatory, while Christ hunted for a pretext to release from their indebtedness those whom he desired, whose entry into heaven would otherwise be prohibitive, an entry for which he had planned in eternity.

This is the context within which Christ intervened by drawing on the merits of the living, who contributed to the expeditious entry into heaven of souls in purgatory by making payment to Christ, substituting their own merit for what these souls owed, souls for whom Christ yearned but who were not yet worthy of entering heaven. Although the Helfta writings spoke to the role of Christ in the work of redemption, the questions to which they responded were not primarily Christological. They addressed the logic of the nuns' partnership with Christ in the processes that governed souls' experience of purgatory and release into heaven, accentuating the role the nuns played in relation to souls on the march. To the women's way of thinking, precisely because God's mercy was not unconditional, cooperation with his grace was both possible and necessary, creating as it did the entry for relationships among human beings, since those who had died could not themselves contribute to their own progress toward salvation.

Caught between his love for souls and the claims of justice, Christ drew on others' participation to satisfy the demands of justice. "Compare me to a king," Christ exhorts Gertrude,

> who detained in captivity some of his most cherished friends. He would release them happily if they were acquitted, if the demands of justice did not prohibit this. They have nothing with which to pay their ransom, but, impelled zealously to redeem them, he would be content if some of his knights placed a payment in the weight in the form of silver or gold, or at least some other thing whose weight is equivalent to their debt, giving him in this way a pretext to free them. And I in this way accept whatever is offered to me for the souls of those who have been redeemed by my precious

> blood and by my death, because in this way I have the opportunity to release them from their punishments and lead them into the joys prepared for them from eternity.[159]

Souls in purgatory were like friends without the means to ransom themselves from the king in whose thrall they were held, who wished to release them, and who would do so gladly, but only if his knights made payment equivalent to what the captives owed and on their behalf. Like this king, Christ, in his zeal to redeem souls, did not care who paid the sinners' debts. What mattered was that the requirements of divine justice be met so that those for whose salvation Christ longed might be liberated. The nuns, like the king's knights, championed his cause; they offered gifts to ransom souls bound in purgatory, who were deprived of the ability to make additional compensatory offerings beyond their suffering.

Although this imagery is evocative of Anselm of Canterbury's argument for the incarnation in *Cur Deus homo*, the nuns' central preoccupation was not, as it was for Anselm, God's honor, the reason for the incarnation, and Christ's role in making good on the service for which human beings defaulted.[160] The nuns assimilated Anselm's theory of atonement, but they shifted focus. They concentrated not on Christ per se, on his singular role in restoring God's honor and the order of the universe, but on the cooperative role of human beings in paying the debt acquired by other human beings—and on their own obligation to Christ, which instigated their assumption of the role of co-redeemer with him. Indebted to Christ, they paid some of what they owed to him by making payment on the debt of others.[161]

[159] *Le Héraut* 5.18.1 (SCh 331:178).

[160] R. W. Southern, *Saint Anselm: A Portrait in a Landscape* (New York: Cambridge University Press, 1990), 197–227.

[161] The whole of the *Herald's* book two elaborates on Gertrude's indebtedness; see also *Liber* 1.18 (51). As Southern argued so elegantly, Anselm's atonement theory displaced the role of the devil in redemption history, putting

Give and You Shall Receive

Christ's gifts were luxurious. Because we are, the nuns insisted, all of us egregious sinners, every gift Christ offers any one of us is in excess of what justice demands; no one has claim to the gifts God confers. God gives with a generosity that is without limit, and the notion of excess gifts colored the whole of the Helfta literary corpus. Christ was the preeminent giver of gifts, and there was no return a soul could make that corresponded, even approximately, with what God had given her. The disparity between the gifts God gave souls and the return souls could make meant that the exchange was always unequal. The reciprocity between God and the soul that God demanded did not, therefore, imply anything like commensurability. Nonetheless, the nuns experienced Christ as exerting a relentless pressure on them *to give* and they conceived of the universe as suffused with possibility for making some return on the gifts they received. The Helfta writings speak to us of a world of plentitude, a lush landscape of possibility, in which every word, every act of kindness, every prayer, and every footstep might be converted into payment to Christ for the debt accumulated, for gifts given: "My kindness will accept it if you take even one footstep with the intention [of laying down your sinfulness], if you pick up a feather from the ground, utter one word, or make one fond gesture, or if you say the *Requiem aeternum* for the dead—or anything at all for sinners or for the just."[162]

Sin spurned could also become a debt payment. In the *Book of Special Grace*, the sins the sisters laid at Christ's feet were

---

human beings (in the person of Christ) face to face with God. In contrast, the Helfta theology places human beings face to face with Christ himself, extolling their everyday intimacies. Sure that right relationships between the individual and God had consequences for right relationships with God for all the faithful, the nuns accented human participation in the economy of salvation, never ceasing to draw attention to God's gracious intervention in each act that each human being contributed to the salvation of his people.

[162] *Le Héraut* 4.7.2 (SCh 255:100).

transformed into gifts of gold, gifts that flowed to her who trusted that Christ would reward her and who would therefore praise him.[163] Gertrude strove to convert virtually all the resources at her disposal into payments to Christ. Because of the close association between Christ and herself, Gertrude gave to Christ some of what she owed him, paradoxically, by giving to herself:

> because whether she slept or ate, or received anything at all that was useful, she rejoiced in giving it to the Lord. She saw herself in him and him in herself because of the Lord's teaching, "whatever you did for one of the least of mine, you did for me." Considering herself in her unworthiness to be the least and most wretched of all creatures, it seemed to her that in giving anything to herself she was giving it to the least of God's creatures.[164]

Thus when Gertrude tried to relieve a headache by chewing aromatic herbs, she perceived that the scent refreshed Christ himself, the present to herself simultaneously a gift to God.[165]

A central lesson of the community's writings was that one could return to Christ some of what one owed to him by giving to another, and reciprocity between self and Christ occurred frequently through the mediation of a third person or persons. Thus when, in Christ's stead, Gertrude or Mechtild pardoned or chastised those who had committed a fault, or offered affectionate counsel to a disconsolate nun, because such works helped to transport others on the way to salvation, they were gifts that Christ received as credit in the accounts of those on whose behalf the visionaries labored. This understanding of gift-giving stimulated reflection on its implications for oneself. Christ explained to Mechtild the peculiar way in which gifts

[163] *Liber* 1.10; 3.50 (32, 202).
[164] *Le Héraut* 1.11.10 (SCh 139:180).
[165] *Le Héraut* 1.11.10 (SCh 139:180–82).

given for the dead multiplied and would be held in reserve for the benefit of the donor:

> Whoever intercedes through compassion or with loving emotion for anyone who is dead will participate in all the good that the church accomplishes for that dead person, and on the day of her departure [from this world], she will discover all that good prepared for her own healing and salvation.[166]

A dominant note echoing throughout the whole of the Helfta literature is the gospel proclamation that to give is really to receive (Luke 6:38). In giving to another what God had given to them, the nuns understood that they would receive yet more gifts, a reward for their generosity. They also knew that each additional gift Christ bestowed—each gentle utterance, each rugged reproach—further increased their indebtedness to him. And the more they gave to others in an effort to alleviate their own debt, the more gifts Christ gave them—gifts of his time, tenderness, mercy, and more—so that any payment they made for the benefit of another soul became a means by which they acquired new gifts, precipitating anew their need to give.[167] And thus a cycle of exchange ensued, binding souls in need to Christ and to one another, diffusing Christ's gifts through their reproduction, while their dispersal itself procured additional gifts for the donor.

These were the ties that interwove to create community beneficial to all parties, between and among donors and recipients. The nuns acknowledged implicitly that one was not strictly obliged to return (or receive) Christ's gifts, all of which were unconditional. Not to reciprocate, however, was a mark of ingratitude. And because the soul's recognition of Christ's liberality was a necessary precondition to her joining Christ,

[166] *Liber* 5.19 (350). And see *Le Héraut* 5.20; 5.21 (SCh 331:188, 190).
[167] See for example *Liber* 1.8 (28).

and because gifts Christ gives are always a self-offering, to reject their offer was to rebuff him, to be deprived of the pleasure of intimacy with him in this life. It was also to be cut off from the community of the faithful, to be excluded from participating in rounds of gift-giving whose source and substance was Christ. It was, in other words, to incur damnation. It is unclear whether in the Helfta imagination any ties bound souls to one another in hell, since where there is no possibility of salvation, there is no exchange, no gift-giving. It is also unclear whether, as the nuns would have thought, there is therefore anything like community among the damned.

The Helfta writings insisted that Christ's mercy alone secured the redemption of all humanity. It was Christ's love that rendered the sisters' works acceptable and potent with salvific force. All gifts originated with Christ; no person was their fabricator; God was their Creator: the gifts that Mechtild, Gertrude, and their sisters gave to Christ and that he distributed among souls were, after all, gifts that he had previously given to them.[168] So, regarding Gertrude,

> When on behalf of a certain dead person she offered to God for the soul of the deceased all the good works that merciful God had ever deigned to operate in her and for her, she saw them before the throne of divine majesty in the form of various beautiful gifts. On account of this, the Lord and all the saints seemed to rejoice in wonder. The Lord received this offering with care, as if he was happy to be able to give

[168] In his late-nineteenth-century account of Gertrude's mysticism, Wilhelm Preger emphasized the role of grace in the theology of the nuns, and because of his understanding of their sense of their utter dependence on God's grace for all the works they accomplished, Preger identified them as forerunners of the reformation (Wilhelm Preger, *Geschichte der deutschen Mystik bis zum Tode Meister Eckharts*, vol. 1 of *Geschichte der deutschen Mystik nach den Quellen untersucht und dargestellt* [Leipzig: Dörffling und Franke, 1874], 120–23). Herman Grössler has made the same point (Herman Grössler, "Die Blützeit des Klosters Helfta bei Eisleben," *Jahres-Bericht über das königliche Gymnasium zu Eisleben* [Easter 1886–Easter 1887], 28).

> something to those in need who did not merit these benefits through their own actions.[169]

What the living offered the dead was nothing other than what Christ had already given the living, who were conduits through whom a circulation of gifts occurred: "I give you each of these [gifts] as if they were yours so that you can give them back to me as if they were yours," he told Mechtild.[170]

Exchange was at the heart of the Helfta piety, where God's gifts came with strings attached.[171] Christ himself modeled a sense of indebtedness. An attitude of obligation and commitment to exchange was at the heart of his relationship with individual nuns and the convent considered collectively. He told Gertrude that he was indebted to her when they spoke together about the songs she had composed out of the sayings of the saints, and he added that he would be indebted to anyone who sang these songs.[172] Once when the sisters were sing-

[169] *Le Héraut* 5.20.1 (SCh 331:188).

[170] *Liber* 1.8 (28).

[171] At least since Marcel Mauss's consideration of gifts that are "in theory voluntary, disinterested and spontaneous, but are in fact obligatory and interested," the notion of "pure gift," one that does not prompt exchange, has engaged anthropologists, historians, theologians, and other scholars; see Jonathan Parry, "*The Gift*, the Indian Gift, and the 'Indian Gift,' " *Man*, New Series 21, no. 3 (1986): 456. Mauss argued that gifts are strictly compulsory, on the pain of private or public warfare, and he discussed the fiction of the free gift (Marcel Mauss, *The Gift: Form and Reason for Exchange in Archaic Societies*, trans. W. D. Halls [New York: Routledge, 2002], 3, 5). As Jacques Derrida put it, the "pure gift" is one that never prompts an exchange, and Mauss thus never discusses the gift at all (Jacques Derrida, *Given Time: I. Counterfeit Money*, trans. Peggy Kamuf [Chicago: University of Chicago Press, 1992], 13). For the theological position on the gratuity of the gift, see for example Kenneth L. Schmitz, *The Gift: Creation* (Milwaukee, WI: Marquette University Press, 1982), 44–45.

[172] *Le Héraut* 3.54.2 (SCh 143:234). For Christ as a model for Gertrude, see *Les Exercises* 2.87–89 (SCh 127:88). There are numerous examples of Christ's ascription to himself of the language of indebtedness. See for example *Le Héraut* 3.54.2 (SCh 143:234).

ing the nocturne *Regnum mundi*, Christ exclaimed before God the Father and all the saints his indebtedness to the women for their service, declaring that they must be recompensed for their service to him.[173] The nuns gloried in the web of exchanges in which they and all the faithful were implicated in relation to one another and to God.[174]

The notion of a God who would not ask for a return on the gifts he distributed was not only foreign to the sisters but would have been deeply troubling, for a number of reasons. It would have undermined their sense of God as just and their recognition of themselves as sinners, obliged to pay what they owed. It would in addition have unraveled the fabric of mutuality in the relationships among those whom God loved, undercutting bonds among all the faithful. In accepting and encouraging as gifts to himself offerings extended to others, Christ prompted and cultivated relationships among those whom he loved. He proceeded as he did, furthermore, because he was desirous of those on earth who, because they benefited from their suffrages on behalf of the population of purgatory, therefore moved closer to his embrace, making good on their own debt to him by helping to settle the accounts of others whom he also loved. There is something about the mutual need associated with sinners who were eager for salvation, among the living and among the dead, that was therefore conducive to creating community, and this mutual need fed the nuns' sense of themselves as co-redeemers with Christ, a self-understanding that Barbara Newman has argued characterized the spirituality of medieval women more broadly.[175]

[173] *Le Héraut* 4.54.4 (SCh 255:450–52).

[174] Thus while Robyn Horner, in a study of the place of "the gift" in modern theology, articulated a common worry when she bemoaned that it is so difficult to give without getting, to avoid what becomes a series of exchanges, the nuns harbored no such concerns (Robyn Horner, *Rethinking God As Gift: Marion, Derrida, and the Limits of Phenomenology* [New York: Fordham University Press, 2001], 5).

[175] Barbara Newman, "On the Threshold of the Dead," 120.

Moreover, Christ's expectation of return had a variety of positive implications for the relationship between the individual soul and Christ. The need to give was a means by which the living acquired positive significance to Christ in the economy of salvation, presupposing that the one to whom Christ gave—including Gertrude, Mechtild, their sisters, everyone—had much to offer *him*. For however much they insisted otherwise, the nuns seem to have experienced Christ as needing them if he was to grasp all those souls whom he loved. The women were flattered by this assessment. However much they sometimes shirked their responsibilities to those in purgatory, however tepid their devotion might sometimes become, they seem not only to have welcomed but to have relished Christ's demand that, cooperating with his grace, they participate through gift-giving in making satisfaction for others. Gertrude and Mechtild were especially powerful members of their community because they and their sisters believed that they had more than ordinary measures to give.

When the sisters aided those in purgatory, their assistance was not motivated either by a selfless regard for those in need or by a noxious concentration on the self. There was no tension between returning to God via another some of what one owed him, because one was indebted to him, and giving compassionately to friends, neighbors, or anonymous souls, seeking to alleviate their suffering out of love for them. Why should it be otherwise? After all, the daily round of monastic life consisted largely in a routine obligation to demonstrate to God one's freely offered love and thanksgiving for him, an offering the nuns regarded as no less authentic for being cultivated within the formal structure of corporate life. The fostering of right attitude and its habitual expression was a safeguard against toiling for the dead with exclusive concentration on the work's significance for oneself, but it was by no means a rebuke to those whose offerings were informed by the recognition of their significance for themselves. In some real sense, one ought to be motivated by a mercenary spirit, that is, driven by desire for the love of God and a craving for him; after all, he was the reward, and the nuns knew that Christ longed for them to be desirous of this reward. He wanted them to want him.

Moreover, in some real sense the souls whom the sisters helped to save were Christ: Christ thrust himself into the center of the nuns' purgatorial piety when he cast himself as its beneficiary, as well as the victim of the souls' sin and as one hungry for souls' salvation. As he explained to Mechtild, appearing to her with hands and feet bound, each time a person sins grievously, that person binds his or her body, and to Gertrude he related that each time she liberated souls, it was Christ himself who was set free.[176] And because all who will be saved are part of the body of Christ, there is no absolute autonomy of the individual, so to participate in the salvation of another is to contribute to setting oneself free. Praying for the dead was not at Helfta a matter of generosity energized by the cries of others (or the cry of Christ), but rather a realization of the benefits to self that giving to another holds out. The plight of another was, in the world of this thirteenth-century monastery, unavoidably about the self.

[176] *Liber* 5.17 (345–47).

Chapter 8

"Unite Yourself with His Family"

Community with Mary and the Saints

She was snatched into God's heart, where she saw and knew all the elect and every creature. And the Lord said to her, "What else could you wish to see or to want? Yours are all good things that heaven and the heaven of heavens rejoice to have. Now share your goods with all of the saints as you please."[1]

Heaven's Inhabitants

At Helfta, the presence of Mary and the saints, while cause for celebration and delight and worthy of documenting, was anything but rare.[2] Heaven's inhabitants were involved in the

[1] *Liber* 1.22 (81).

[2] Barbara Newman has observed that "no other visionary text is so preoccupied with heaven or so convinced of its nearness to earth" (introduction to *Mechthild of Hackeborn and the Nuns of Helfta: The Book of Special Grace*, trans. Barbara Newman [New York: Paulist Press, 2017], 16). On the saints in the *Herald*, see Gilbert Dolan, who remarks on the women's intense interest in the communion of saints (*St. Gertrude the Great* [London: Sands, 1913], 144–53); similarly, see Margot Schmidt, "Mechtilde de Hackeborn," DSAM 10:875. Cypriano Vagaggini notes that saints figure routinely in Gertrude's visions of heaven (*Theological Dimensions of the Liturgy*, trans. Leonard J. Doyle and W. A. Jurgen from the fourth Italian edition, revised and augmented by the author [Collegeville, MN: Liturgical Press, 1976], 769). Gertrude's Marian

nitty-gritty of the nuns' lives. Occupying with the sisters a joint tenancy in the monastery, they habitually moved within and around its walls.[3] Integrating themselves into the choir, the saints chanted praise to God; attending Mass in the chapel, they sometimes concelebrated with Christ.[4] They talked with the women, tending to their spiritual needs and praying for them.[5] They offered solace, as when God's mother gave her baby to Mechtild to comfort her.[6] Revelations sometimes carried with them a rush of gratifying aural, tactile, and visual sensations that brought happiness to their recipients: Mechtild touched Mary's hair, all the saints sang sweetly to Gertrude, and Benedict was, to her, a joy to behold.[7] Such visions tell of a world in which vivid sensual encounter linked the communion of saints, those already in heaven and those on their way. Reading about visions that filled the dormitory, refectory, chapel, and burial grounds with the presence of Mary and the saints may have given hope to some of the nuns that they too might be privy to bursts of beauty and interaction with the

---

piety has generated much interest. See for example Dolan, *St. Gertrude*, 124–43; and Wilhelm Preger, *Geschichte der deutschen Mystik bis zum Tode Meister Eckharts*, vol. 1 of *Geschichte der deutschen Mystik nach den Quellen untersucht und dargestellt* (Leipzig: Dörffling und Franke, 1874); his analysis anticipates claims in Sharon K. Elkins, "Gertrude the Great and the Virgin Mary," *Church History: Studies in Christianity and Culture* 66, no. 4 (1997): 720–34; Gertrud Jaron Lewis, "Maria im mystischen Werk Gertruds von Helfta," in *"Vor dir steht die leere Schale meiner Sehnsucht": Die Mystik der Frauen von Helfta*, ed. Michael Bangert and Hildegund Keul (Leipzig: St. Benno Buch- und Zeitschriftenverlagsgesellschaft, 1998), 81–94; Anne L. Clark, "An Uneasy Triangle: Jesus, Mary, and Gertrude of Helfta," *Maria: A Journal of Marian Studies* 1 (August 2000): 37–56. On Mechtild's Marian piety, which has attracted less attention, see Philibert Schmitz, *Les Moniales*, vol. 7 of *Histoire de l'Ordre de Saint-Benoît* (Liège: Les Éditions de Maredsous, 1956), 300–301.

[3] *Liber* 1.27 (95–97). Mechtild perceives armies of saints processing through the monastery (*Liber* 1.20 [71–76]).

[4] *Liber* 1.19; 1.6; 1.31 (64, 21, 106).

[5] *Liber* 6.8 (387–88).

[6] *Liber* 5.31 (370).

[7] *Liber* 1.29 (100); *Le Héraut* 4.50.9; 4.11.1 (SCh 255:416, 126).

holy in every direction[8]—or perhaps sometimes their reading impressed upon them the absence of such contact in their own lives.

We read reports of the anonymous holy dead, as when Mechtild saw three bodies buried before the altar rise from their tombs, their arms extended as if giving thanks to God; their movements indicated that they were going to play, and they trembled with joy because of their virtues and good works while they were alive.[9] Most frequently, the women wrote about clusters of souls as "the saints," or they told readers of heavenly choirs and identified patriarchs, prophets, apostles, martyrs, confessors, virgins, and so forth.[10] Groups were sometimes marked off from each other by the color of their clothing—white-robed young children, purple-clad laywomen and laymen, scarlet-draped ascetics—and members of one group sometimes banded together around a common celestial residence, a dwelling place of stone or sapphire or silver.[11] "Come,

[8] Ulrike Wiethaus has made this observation ("Spatial Metaphors, Textual Production, and Spirituality in the Works of Gertrud of Helfta [1256–1301/2]," in *A Place to Believe In: Medieval Landscapes*, ed. Clare A. Lees and Gillian R. Overing [University Park, PA: Pennsylvania State University Press, 2006], 136).

[9] *Liber* 5.14 (341).

[10] For example, *Liber* 1.31; 4.8; 6.9 (110, 265–66, 389); *Le Heráut* 5.32.4 (SCh 331:258–60). While visions now and then assert differences among individual saints (see for example *Liber* 1.35 [115–17]), the compositions explore them infrequently, remaining for the most part satisfied with separating out groups of saints from one another. For example, when Mechtild sees in heaven members of her community encircling Abbess Gertrude in dance, each carrying a pyx (a box in which the consecrated Host is reserved, or set aside), some of ivory, some of silver, and others of gold, the varying materials represent souls' purity, service, and love respectively (*Liber* 6.9 [389]). Gertrude learns in conversation with Christ that there is no saint who is like any other saint (*Le Héraut* 4.50.7 (SCh 255:412]), and they leave it at that. About a vision Gertrude receives in which Francis and Dominic figure, we read that they appear as resplendent as Benedict, their differences from each other evident as well: Francis shines with humility and Dominic with fervent desire. We discover nothing more (*Le Héraut* 4.50.8 [SCh 255:414]).

[11] *Liber* 1.13 (44–45).

let's go for a walk," Christ said to Mechtild, extending his hand to her, and in his company she observed that heaven was home to happy children who had died before the age of five, at play without end. She heard married people and widows singing together, and she saw the souls of those who had fought the devil and won.[12]

There is scant indication that the sisters conceived members of one group as aware of another, much less as curious about or anticipating encounter with another group; there is no obvious mingling among them. Heaven seemed not to be a place of enhanced contact with those from whom one remained at a distance in this life. To the contrary, the writings underscored the continuance in heaven of one's inclusion in the company with which one was associated in life, not the breaking down of familiar boundaries to promote intermixing. Among the confessors whom Mechtild saw gathered together in heaven was Saint Benedict, who offered a chalice to the other saints—but only to fellow Benedictines.[13] In this sense, the celestial community appears fragmented rather than complex. These visions reinforced the social and institutional structures that shaped the nuns' lives and those of their readers, asserting their value on earth in proclaiming their permanence in heaven.

Here and there, the reader comes across celestial citizens who upend fixed and familiar categories of holiness. "Come see the least of those who are in heaven," Christ invited Mechtild, and he presented to her a short man with curly hair and sea-green eyes and with an extraordinarily beautiful face. "Who are you?" Mechtild asked, and he said, "In the world, I was a thief and a worthless person, and I never did any good."[14] When she inquired further, he explained that all the bad he did was

[12] *Liber* 1.13 (44–45). Mechtild also saw a baby—who appeared in the form of a virgin—consecrated to God from her mother's womb (*Liber* 4.12 [339–40]).

[13] *Liber* 4.8 (266).

[14] *Liber* 1.33 (112).

out of habit, not out of wickedness. This is what his parents taught him; he had never known better. Moments before dying, he had repented, and through God's mercy, he had endured one hundred years of purgatorial torments before he entered heaven.[15] The Helfta nuns counted among the saints some who were more obviously dependent on God's generosity than others, and the account of the curly-haired crook speaks to the sisters' allowance for the complexity of human sin. Charged with the insight that context informs culpability, the nuns' steady confidence in God's mercy led them to recognize that the reach of redemption was broad, including even those whose lives were spent in crime, provided that they acknowledged their sins and were remorseful.

Christ's phrasing, "the least of those," is one among many indications that the women shared in the dominant medieval concept of rank in heaven, which they conceived of in relation to holiness.[16] They believed that celestial joy did not wash equally over all saints but was a just reward. The soul of one of her sisters revealed to Gertrude that while she was splendidly recompensed in heaven, others were even more richly rewarded, because when they were alive, they had shared with many people the gifts they received from God; this sister, on the other hand, had preferred to be alone with God and secreted away his gifts for herself.[17] Those saints who were privy to greater glory than others gave greater pleasure to others, and they received proportionally more respect from their heavenly companions. John the Evangelist related to Gertrude that he occupied a more eminent rank in heaven than the other

[15] *Liber* 1.33 (112).

[16] See for example *Liber* 6.9 (388–89), and *Le Héraut* 4.50.7 (SCh 255:412). On the maintenance of hierarchy in heaven, see B. Forshaw, "Heaven (Theology of)," *New Catholic*, 6:689; Colleen McDannell and Bernhard Lang, *Heaven: A History* (New Haven: Yale University Press, 1988), 77; Peter Dinzelbacher, "Reflexionen irdischer Socialstruckturen in mittelalterlichen Jenseitsschilderungen," *Archiv für Kulturgeschichte* 61 (1979): 16–34.

[17] *Le Héraut* 5.10.4 (SCh 331:146–48).

saints,[18] and when Mechtild saw him resting on Jesus' breast, she also beheld choirs of saints surrounding the two, dancing and praising Christ for John.[19] In the court of heaven, Pope Gregory shared in the pleasure God received every time one of Gregory's writings pricked with compunction, prompted to devotion, or fired with love anyone reading or hearing them. In the eyes of all the other inhabitants of heaven, it was as if Gregory were a prince or a knight, privileged to wear his king's robe or to feast on the food the king eats, an honor reserved for the doctors of the church on account of their writings.[20]

No heavenly group was happier than the virgins, whom Christ loved and privileged above all others.[21] The moment a virgin arrived in heaven, he greeted her with the welcoming words of the Song of Songs: "Come, my friend, come, my bride, come: you shall be crowned" (Song 4:8).[22] The saints rejoiced and proclaimed, "How beautiful are your footfalls" (Song 7:1).[23] As Christ explained, the relationship of bridegroom to bride in heaven is one of mutual pleasure and mutual incorporation:

> When the virgin comes into my sight, she sees herself in my eyes, and I see myself in hers as in a mirror, and we contemplate each other with great pleasure. Then with the most loving embrace I press myself to her, pouring myself into her with the whole of my divinity and piercing her until she

[18] *Le Héraut* 4.4.7 (SCh 255:70–72).

[19] *Liber* 1.6 (23). Mechtild of Magdeburg's *Flowing Light*, portions at least of which the Helfta nuns probably knew, contains images of saints dancing in heaven (*Mechthild of Magdeburg: The Flowing Light of the Godhead*, trans. Frank Tobin [New York: Paulist Press, 1998], 3.1; 7.37 [104, 308]).

[20] *Le Héraut* 4.10.3 (SCh 255:124).

[21] *Liber* 1.11; 1.24; 1.31; 4.9 (36, 85, 109, 266–67). On the privileged place of virgins in the heaven of Helfta, see for example McDannell and Lang, *Heaven*, esp. 106; and Dyan Elliott, *The Bride of Christ Goes to Hell: Metaphor and Embodiment in the Lives of Pious Women, 200–1500* (Philadelphia: University of Pennsylvania Press, 2012), 178.

[22] *Liber* 2.36 (184).

[23] *Liber* 2.36 (184).

> sees me entirely present in all her limbs, wherever she turns. Then I draw her into myself so that she appears in glory in me, in all my limbs.[24]

In a vision that came to Mechtild, the virgins, together with the Virgin Mary, were joined with Christ in a dancing circle.[25] Mechtild saw a triple gold chain (a symbol of the Trinity) emerge from Christ's heart; this chain looped through the heart of the Virgin Mary and then through the hearts of all the virgin saints, until it returned to enter Christ's heart, uniting the virgins to one another and to Christ, and excluding the multitude of saints dancing outside the ring, those who had not elevated themselves to the gift of virginity.[26]

While it is often the case that the individuals constituting various groupings of saints remain anonymous, the nuns encountered individual holy people on dozens of occasions. Among Christ's contemporaries who figure in the nuns' celestial visions are Mary Magdalene and John the Baptist as well as the apostles James, Bartholomew, Peter, and Paul.[27] Visions were thick with virgin martyrs and popes,[28] and well-known contemporaries and near-contemporaries of the nuns, including Bernard of Clairvaux, Francis and Dominic, Thomas Aquinas and Albert the Great also appeared.[29] The women lifted into heaven others tightly bound to the cloister, such as Saint Elisabeth of Hungary, who was known to relatives of the nuns and

[24] *Liber* 2.36 (184).

[25] *Liber* 1.11 (36).

[26] *Liber* 1.31 (106).

[27] Mary Magdalene (*Le Héraut* 4.46 [SCh 255:348–54], and *Liber* 1.25 [86–88]); John the Baptist (*Le Héraut* 4.42 [SCh 255:132–36]); James (*Le Héraut* 4.47 [SCh 255:354–56]); Bartholomew (*Liber* 1.34 [112–15]); Peter and Paul (*Le Héraut* 4.44 [SCh 255:340–44]).

[28] Catherine of Alexandria (*Liber* 1.32 [110–11]); Agnes and Margaret (*Le Héraut* 4.45 [SCh 255:344–48]); Leo (*Le Héraut* 4.43 [SCh 255:136–41]); Gregory (*Le Héraut* 4.10 [SCh 255:121]).

[29] Bernard (*Le Héraut* 4.49 [SCh 255:396–402]; *Liber* 1.28 [97–98]); Francis of Assisi and Dominic (*Le Héraut* 4.50.8 [SCh 255:414]); Thomas and Albert (*Liber* 5.9 [332–33]).

perhaps to some of the sisters themselves,[30] and we read of the recluse Ysentrude, whom the nuns seem to have known, although we know nothing about the contours of their relationship.[31] The house's first abbess, Cunegard, along with Gertrude and Mechtild of Hackeborn, shone with heavenly splendor, as did another Mechtild, perhaps Mechtild of Magdeburg.[32]

Numerous additional members of the congregation populated the celestial spheres—sisters and *conversi* as well as administrative personnel, such as the provost Otto, named in the act of the foundation of the monastery of Hedersleben under Abbess Gertrude in 1262.[33] Preachers associated with the convent occupied a place in heaven, including a certain Dominican "Brother N.," a man whom the *Book of Special Grace* describes as an intimate and faithful to the convent, whose prayers for her community Mechtild petitioned.[34] The monastery's founders also found their way into heaven. Count Burchard, who with his wife Elizabeth Mansfeld had established the monastery, joins in the celestial joy.[35] There is little evidence of the nuns placing their own family members among the saints, unless they were associated with the monastery as patrons or nuns. When the women fixed their sights on heaven, they were taken especially with saints well known to the wider population as well as those directly associated with the monastery.

Accounts of heavenly visions featuring individuals and gatherings of people whom the nuns knew on earth announced the maintenance of meaningful associations among members of the monastic community who crossed death's divide. When Mechtild observed women and men from her household encircling Abbess Gertrude in dance, one distinguished himself

[30] See introduction and chapter 6.

[31] *Liber* 5.4 (321–22).

[32] Cunegard (*Liber* 5.10 [334]); Gertrude of Helfta (*Liber* 6.9 [388–90]); Mechtild of Magdeburg (*Liber* 4.8 [266]).

[33] *Liber* 5.10 (335; 335, n. 1).

[34] *Liber* 5.7 (329–30).

[35] *Liber* 5.10 (334–36).

from among the crowd, a brother whose marvelously decorated white stole signaled the kindheartedness for which he had been known at Helfta.[36] A vision in which Mechtild extended the chalice to a choir of virgins, recognized one woman among them, and paused to talk with her is another instance of an individual assuming prominence because of her prior familiarity with the visionary.[37]

One of the monastery's *conversi* related to Gertrude his heavenly happiness and the work he had contributed toward his salvation. His joy, the *conversus* divulged, was that of all the hearts he had caused to rejoice: that of the poor person to whom he had given alms, that of the child to whom he had given a gift, that of a sick person to whom he had given fruit.[38] The descriptions both of work and of his happiness buttressed the importance of cultivating right relationships of a variety of sorts—with the poor, the sick, the young—in this life. The source of the *conversus*'s happiness underscored the permeable boundaries between human beings, illustrated by other peoples' emotions flooding into the *conversus*. Piled atop each other, these cases communicated to the monastic reader that harbored within some of the apparently anonymous groupings of saints whom Mechtild and Gertrude beheld were friends and associates, who had much that was meaningful to relate to their own future. The sisters could count on heaven's being crowded with encounters among those who knew them in the here and now.

Membership in the Helfta community was not left behind in heaven. A vision Mechtild received told the reader that saints dancing with Christ sang songs about the congregation.[39] After her death, Abbess Gertrude occupied a superior

[36] *Liber* 6.9 (389).

[37] *Liber* 1.1 (11).

[38] *Le Héraut* 5.11.1 (SCh 331:150). For the heavenly joy of *conversi*, see for example *Le Héraut* 5.14.2 (SCh 331:164–66).

[39] *Liber* 4.8 (266).

rank among the virgins,[40] and Benedict, "father of the order," in a physical demonstration of warm emotion between people rare in the Helfta literature, embraced the abbess, whom he loved and venerated.[41] The sisters thus embedded their own devotion to the saints within the context of the devotion that the saints themselves rendered to their community members. Picturing Benedict enfolding Abbess Gertrude in his arms, they incorporated one of their own into the elite of the heavenly hierarchy and evoked a relationship among heaven's inhabitants characterized by sympathy and mutual reverence. In sharing with the saints a sense of who among them was more deserving and thus aligning themselves with the practices of devotion in heaven, the sisters integrated themselves snugly within the community of saints, all the while underscoring the special status of those they counted among their own, and with whom they perceived that they enjoyed a relationship even now.[42]

Liturgy

The individual and collective presence of saints was nowhere more palpable to the nuns than during a variety of liturgical and quasi-liturgical observances, which they layer

[40] *Liber* 6.1 (377).

[41] *"Patre Ordinis"*; *Liber* 6.6 (384). For a discussion of hugs in heaven, see Manuele Gragnolati, "Nostalgia in Heaven: Embraces, Affection, and Identity in the *Commedia*," in *Dante and the Human Body: Eight Essays*, ed. John C. Barnes and Jennifer Petrie (Dublin: Four Courts Press, 2007), 117–37.

[42] The women were aware of a difference between those whom they located in heaven and whom the church recognized as formally canonized, on the one hand, and, on the other, those who were not canonized. The *Book of Special Grace* authorizes the nuns' devotion to members of their own community when Mechtild brings up her concern with Christ about this difference. In a vision that comes to her while she sleeps, Mechtild sees the soul of her deceased abbess, and Mechtild wonders about her own devotion to her sister, the abbess. Christ dismisses Mechtild's preoccupation, affirming the regard in which he holds the abbess, and he sanctions Mechtild's veneration of her sister (*Liber* 6.7 [385]).

with heavenly souls, who flooded the deathbed precincts, processions, and chapel as a matter of course. Giving sometimes domestic, sometimes dramatic expression to the pervasive medieval belief that monks and nuns sang the Office under the watch of angels and that the Mass offered on earth corresponded with a celestial celebration, chant-filled visions attributed to Gertrude and Mechtild vividly represented heavenly liturgies, and they insisted on the participation of the joyous dead and angelic spirits in the oblations and expressions of praise the sisters offered in their liturgical observances.[43] A mark of the saints' membership in the nuns' everyday routine is the frequency and regularity with which the liturgical calendar seemed to the nuns to summon the saints on their feast days.[44] Agnes appeared in a vision to

[43] The common medieval conception that proximity to God at Mass and at Office brings with it closeness to the saints and angels was not an abstract idea remote from the experience of the Helfta nuns; see, e.g., Jean Leclercq, *The Love of Learning and the Desire for God: A Study of Monastic Culture*, trans. Catharine Misrahi (New York: Fordham University Press, 1961), 55. For joining with the saints and angels to praise and give thanks to God in the *Herald* and the *Spiritual Exercises*, see Miriam Schmitt, "Freed to Run with Expanded Heart: The Writings of Gertrud of Helfta and the Rule of Benedict," CSQ 25, no. 3 (1990): 228–29. On the place of praise in the piety of Helfta, see Vagaggini, *Theological Dimensions*; and Marie-Geneviève Guillous, "La louange à l'école de sainte Gertrude," *Collectanea* 53 (1991): 174–94. For angels' presence during liturgy, see for example *Liber* 1.12; 1.30 (38, 104). Chapter 19 of the Benedictine Rule, which explains how the Divine Office is to be chanted, quotes this text from Ps 137/138:1, "In the sight of the angels" (RB 19.40). See Leclercq, *Love of Learning*, 57–58, for the fellowship religious cultivated with the angels, and see the analysis of the eucharistic prayer (the canon of the Mass) in Enrico Mazza, *The Eucharistic Prayers of the Roman Rite*, trans. Matthew J. O'Connell (New York: Pueblo Publishing, 1986), 6, 48, for the relationship between the praise offered to God by the living and the angels at Mass and participation in Mass on earth as participation in heavenly liturgy.

[44] See for example Augustine (*Le Héraut* 4.50.3 [SCh 255:406]); Bernard of Clairvaux (*Le Héraut* 4.49 [SCh 255:396–402]; *Liber* 1.28 [97–98]); Bartholomew (*Liber* 1.34 [112–15]); Benedict (*Le Héraut* 4.11 [SCh 255:126–30]); Catherine of Alexandria (*Liber* 1.32 [110–11]); Gregory (*Le Héraut* 4.10.4 [SCh 255:120–26]); John the Baptist (*Le Héraut* 4.42 [SCh 255:132–36]); Pope Saint Leo (*Le Héraut*

Mechtild during Matins on Agnes's feast and censed the choir; on his feast day, Bernard came to Mass in the company of a beautiful virgin who represented the love with which he had set so many on fire through his writings.[45]

The saints' appearance was no coincidence; the words the sisters uttered in chant routinely summoned Mary and the saints, who—as the visions confirmed—were responsive to a broad sweep of actions associated with the liturgy and to the particulars of the petitions the sisters made. When the congregation on the feast of the Nativity of Mary sang *Ora, Virgo, nos illo pane coeli dignos effeci*, Mary lifted high the Christ Child, and balsam flowed thickly from the boy, drenching the congregation.[46] As Mechtild consumed the Eucharist, a company of saints sounded in concert, *Panem Angelorum manducavit homo*.[47]

When an interdict prohibited the nuns from receiving communion, and Mechtild was sad to be deprived of the opportunity, Christ appeared to her, wiped the tears from her eyes, and promised, "Today you shall see wonders."[48] She did. From the procession through the monastery and into the chapel that announced the beginning of the Mass to the final priestly blessing, Christ and the saints joined with the sisters in a Mass and offered communion that would otherwise have been denied them. The daily liturgical worship enveloped the nuns in a larger community of praise; Mechtild hears troops of virgins singing with her sisters in choir,[49] and it may have been especially meaningful to Mechtild, since she was the community's chantress, to hear Mary (whose voice Mechtild found particu-

---

4.43.1 [SCh 255:336–40]); John the Evangelist (*Liber* 1.6 [21–24]); Mary (*Liber* 1.26 [88–93]); Mary Magdalene (*Liber* 1.25 [86–88]).

[45] *Liber* 1.11; 1.28 (35–37, 97–98).

[46] *Liber* 1.29 (101).

[47] *Liber* 1.13 (45).

[48] *Liber* 1.27 (95).

[49] *Liber* 1.31 (106).

larly pleasing)[50] joining the women as they sang in choir, day after day. Once Mechtild saw a gold pipe emerge from Christ's heart and heard him sing the antiphon "Give praise to our God all you saints" (Rev 19:5);[51] then the Virgin traversed choirs of angels and saints, each of whom touched a golden symbol that hung from her golden belt, and harmonious sounds burst out in praise of God's graces.[52] The saints and sisters talked with each other about the meaning of the words they sang, unscrolling the significance embedded in their joint enterprise.[53]

The nuns not only perceived that their voices mingled on earth with saintly voices. They recognized in addition that the household's liturgical observances corresponded with heavenly liturgies.[54] When the choir sang the response *Redemptor meus vivit* on the anniversary of the death of Abbess Gertrude, Mechtild saw Christ embrace the abbess and heard her sing the same words her daughters chanted in choir.[55] The record of Mechtild's revelation must have affirmed for the reader the

[50] *Liber* 1.27 (96).

[51] *Liber* 1.1 (8).

[52] *Liber* 1.1 (8–9). In her *Spiritual Exercises*, Gertrude recommends setting aside a day now and then on which to leisurely praise the divine (*Exercices* 6.15 [SCh 127:200]; Schmitt, "Freed to Run," 228, discusses this point). Gertrude regarded private and corporate devotions as a way of inserting herself and her sisters in a catena of praise in which the whole of creation joined and which Mary led; see for example *Exercices* 6 (SCh 127:200–256).

[53] See for example *Liber* 1.32 (110–11).

[54] See for example *Liber* 1.12; 1.27 (39–40, 96). On the intricate details that the *Herald* offers about the liturgy celebrated in heaven, see Hilda Graef, "Gertrude the Great: Mystical Flowering of the Liturgy," *Orate Fratres* 20 (1945/46): 172. See Vagaggini, who considers central to Gertrude's spirituality the tendency to elaborate parallels between the liturgical activities in which her convent engages and liturgical activities in heaven (*Theological Dimensions*, 749, 765, 768). For the medieval conviction that the Mass on earth has its counterpart in heaven, and that the songs of praise the faithful offer on earth mingle with the voices of angels, see Joseph A. Jungmann, *The Mass of the Roman Rite: Its Origins and Development (Missarum Sollemnia)*, trans. Francis A. Brunner, 2 vols. (New York: Benziger Brothers, 1988), 1:126–28, 234–35.

[55] *Liber* 6.9 (388).

triumphal proclamation of the responsory. Her vision, furthermore, underscored the importance of the principal communal activity in which the Helfta nuns engaged and its continuing relevance to the experience of the individual after the death of the body. In offering a glimpse of Abbess Gertrude nestled in the arms of her Redeemer, the vision peeled open the vibrant chant-filled relationships God enjoyed with his heavenly companions, which the nuns regarded as the promise of their own future. This vision is also about community. Offering a window onto the experience of the saints, it demonstrates that the nuns' everyday liturgical observances overlapped in fundamental ways with those of heaven's inhabitants: for souls in the celestial spheres as for the sisters in choir, chant was implicated in close encounters with God.

When Gertrude was unable to attend Mass in the convent's church (probably because she was ill), successive pairs of angels ushered her through heaven and into a Mass at which the assembled congregation she joined was composed entirely of saints and angels, and in which a celestial choir in one harmonious voice sang the sequences, responsories, and offertory the nuns were accustomed to intone on earth.[56] The Mass Gertrude joined in heaven corresponded in time with the Mass in which her sisters at that moment participated in chapel; precisely at the moment of the elevation of the Host, Christ offered his heart to the Father.[57]

[56] The Mass (*De Missa quam Dominus Jesus personaliter decantavit in caelo cuidam virgini adhuc existenti in corpore nomine Truta*) comprises twelve printed pages (*Le Héraut Missa* 5.1–15 [SCh 331:284–308]), for which see Graef, "Gertrude the Great," 172; Vagaggini, *Theological Dimensions*, 765–66; Clemons, *Devotion*, esp. 530–58, who offers a close review.

[57] *Le Héraut Missa* 5.12 (SCh 331:300–302). As Clemons has noticed, Christ offered on this occasion to sing for Gertrude whatever Mass she desired. He provided her the opportunity to select the introit from the midnight Mass of Christmas. Clemons points out that "this is the feast in which is celebrated the union of heaven and earth, God and human beings[, and it] thus provides an appropriate liturgical foundation for a Mass in which Gertrude, though still on earth, participates in a liturgy celebrated in heaven. Nevertheless,

More than chronological synchronicity is implied in this account.[58] In Gertrude, two liturgical communities, of the sisters and of the heavenly court, converged. The text draws attention to this fact when in the company of all the saints and the angels, Gertrude spoke a portion of the creed that was customarily recited by the entire church, and she did so on the community's behalf: "the Lord made a sign to the soul that in the person of the church, she should chant, publicly professing the Catholic faith: *Credo in unum Deum*."[59] As Cheryl Clemons has observed, the call to pray *in persona Ecclesiae* was an obligation for Gertrude as a religious;[60] she thus participated in the heavenly Mass as a member of the monastery and, in some sense, as its representative. Far from her being a lone seer soaring above her sisters in the company of Christ, the saints, and the angels, when revelation lifted Gertrude out of seclusion and into heaven, she drew together heavenly and earthly communions. Reading the *Herald*, her sisters may have understood their own broader liturgical commitments—not simply Gertrude's visionary flight—to be instrumental in bringing together this community of praise.

Gertrude refuses this Mass as she has all others" that Christ has offered. She selected, instead, the introit for the Mass of the day on which the vision comes to her, the third Sunday of Advent. It is unclear why ("Devotion," 530, 532). Perhaps Gertrude underscored the continuity between the liturgy on earth, in which her sisters participated, and that in heaven, in which she joined. Thus both the introit she selected and that which she refused called attention to the union of heaven and earth, the one through its content, the other through replicating the introit sung on the day in question.

[58] For another instance of chronological symmetry between Masses celebrated in heaven and at the chapel at Helfta, see *Liber* 2.20 (157–58).

[59] *Le Héraut Missa* 5.9 (SCh 331:296). Clemons observes, furthermore, that Christ prays the post-communion prayer from the Mass for a confessor, and the text suggests, she says, that it is "Gertrude herself who is the one whose confession of Christ is the source of blessings for others; she is the one remembered and celebrated by the heavenly court assisting Christ the High Priest" ("Devotion," 555).

[60] Clemons, "Devotion," 541.

The heavenly community of saints into which the sisters were integrated stimulated their praise of individual saints and of Mary. Thus, for example, the Helfta literature embeds the convent's special devotions to Mary and John the Evangelist within a larger collective that included all the saints. On one occasion, Mechtild saw an assemblage of saints praise God for John the Evangelist, and this fed Mechtild's own desire to honor him: Mechtild subsequently requested that God instruct her how she should offer praise for John.[61] The recording of Mechtild's desire was probably meant to awaken or reinforce the reader's own desire to venerate John, just as Mechtild's longing was fueled by the saints, suggesting that praising the saints is not only exemplary behavior; it is contagious, or it should be. Mechtild's very desire to praise John in some sense assimilated her to the heavenly community, one of whose principal activities, according to the *Herald* and the *Book of Special Grace*, this was. Venerating Mary also folded the sisters into the activities of the celestial court, as when the congregation together with the apostles sang to congratulate the Virgin on the feast of her Assumption.[62] The nuns emphasized in this regard what they and the saints had in common, not what differentiated each group from the other.

Deathbed Intercessors

The *Book of Special Grace*, the *Herald*, and the *Spiritual Exercises* held out the promise that in the moments surrounding her death, the individual sister would be cocooned by the heavenly companions whom throughout her life she had been accustomed to praise and with whom she had been taught to chant.[63] The writings champion a sense of continuity of community with Mary and the saints, exactly at the moment when death

[61] *Liber* 1.6 (23).

[62] *Le Héraut* 4.58.9 (SCh 255:370).

[63] *Liber* 3.19 (222).

rent a sister from the company of her cloister companions, highlighting her physical nearness to heaven's inhabitants, their gestures, and their song.[64] Dying seems to have brought with it an acute focus on the celestial community cultivated throughout the course of the monastic life—or at the least, the nuns who authored the Helfta writings wished to inculcate belief in this attentiveness in their sisters.

As Mechtild was dying, the whole convent came and went repeatedly, offering their individual supplications for their sister.[65] Called from choir to recite last prayers over her,[66] the women did not come alone: Christ, Mary, the saints, and the angels accompanied them.[67] The saints' attendance at the deathbed was pictured as consoling and protective, providing a sheltering response to varied and diffuse sufferings and to the threats associated with dying. Sometimes the women heralded the saints' role in combating demons who taunted and tempted the dying,[68] and they seem to have felt especially sure of Mary's power to chase demonic creatures from the precincts.[69] Mary instructed Mechtild to relate to a fellow nun that the woman should pray to Mary at the hour of the sister's death,[70] and contained within Gertrude's *Spiritual Exercises* is a prayer that both beseeches and anticipates Mary's facilitating her encounter with Christ at the moment of Gertrude's own

[64] *Le Héraut* 5.32.3 (SCh 331:258–60).

[65] *Le Héraut* 5.4.8 (SCh 331:88–90).

[66] *Le Héraut* 5.4.10 (SCh 331:90–92).

[67] *Le Héraut* 5.4; 5.4.7; 5.4.8 (SCh 331:86, 88, 88–90).

[68] *Le Héraut* 4.11.4 (SCh 255:130).

[69] See for example *Le Héraut* 4.54.6; 5.1.21; 5.3.1 (SCh 255:452–54; SCh 331:40, 66–68); *Liber* 1.26; 1.45; 1.47 (92, 130, 133). See Elizabeth Johnson, "Marian Devotion in the Western Church," in *Christian Spirituality: High Middle Ages and Reformation, World Spirituality*, ed. Jill Raitt, et al. (New York: Crossroad, 1989), 408–9; Rachel Fulton Brown, *Mary and the Art of Prayer: The Hours of the Virgin in Medieval Life and Thought* (New York: Columbia University Press, 2018), 65.

[70] *Liber* 1.45 (130).

death, Mary becoming the light in the darkness that allows Gertrude to see the approaching Sun:

> Oh Jesus, send me when I die the faithful helper, Mary, your lovable Mother, beautiful star of the sea, so that in the sight of the glowing dawn of her glorious face I may recognize you, Sun of Justice, through the clarity of the light as you come toward my soul.[71]

Gertrude fantasized about the comfort she would receive at the moment of her own death from the Queen of Virgins, imagining Mary tenderly holding in her hands Gertrude's head,[72] just as in a revelation Gertrude saw Mary draw close to Mechtild on her deathbed, positioning Mechtild so that she could take her last breaths directly from her Bridegroom's heart.[73]

The literature sometimes celebrated the saints' deathbed presence without elaborating precisely on the value of their nearness. In a passage from the *Book of Special Grace*, we read that when the saints grouped around a dying nun, the song they sang changed suffering into happiness. We do not learn whose suffering (the dying woman's or that of her sisters) or what sort of suffering was at stake. When the Helfta writings shone a spotlight on the death of an individual nun, they typically emphasized this joyful fellowship of the saints and not the worry or sadness associated with the death of the self—or of another. The nuns seem to have enjoyed a sharp sense of the closeness between the living and the holy dead as they joined altogether around the bed of a sister in her last moments, and it is the sense of kindly companionship per se, and the joy of solidarity, at least as much as any one particular benefit to the dying (or recently dead) nun or her mourners

[71] *Exercices* 6.665–70 (SCh 127:248).

[72] *Le Héraut* 5.32.2 (SCh 331:256).

[73] *Le Héraut* 5.7.5 (SCh 331:126–28).

that the writings accentuated. The sisters did not die alone. The saints accompanied the soul at all stages of dying, and they were present at the funeral Mass and the burial, where they hovered in the air around the dead body until the ceremony of interment was complete.[74]

The saints lavished even greater attention on the soul. As the soul left the grieving community of the monastery and entered the celestial kingdom, the saints quivered with joy at her arrival.[75] Once in heaven, the sister who had during her life sung to and with the saints in liturgy found herself honored as the subject of their celestial song, and the holy dead played tambourines and harps in gleeful greeting, welcoming her as they did all newcomers with jewels and dance.[76] Death, which caused the sisters to sob and to sigh, was a time for gladness among the saints; they launched festivities inaugurating the entry of the soul into the society of Christ's friends and family. The saints danced around the bed of a dying nun, and when she left her body, her soul took flight into the arms of the Virgin Mary, who right away delivered the soul into her Son's embrace.[77] At the requiem Mass of another sister, Mary gave wedding gifts to the Trinity, and a company of virgins offered gifts to the Father on behalf of the soul.[78]

The *Book of Special Grace* extolled souls' blissful union with Christ, but when it took up the topic of immediate post-mortem experience, it drew attention to the movement toward the nuptial chamber in a communal crush. The nuns did not neglect to celebrate the wedding festival itself, the exchange of gifts that heralded and facilitated union with Christ, the conviviality and recognition of commonality between the recently

[74] *Liber* 5.6 (328).

[75] *Liber* 5.5 (323).

[76] *Liber* 5.3; 6.6; 6.9 (320–21, 383, 398).

[77] *Liber* 5.6 (383–84). During Abbess Gertrude's funeral Mass, Mary embraced the abbess and led her toward her Spouse (*Le Héraut* 5.1.27 [SCh 331:50–52]).

[78] *Liber* 5.5 (322–24).

deceased and those who preceded her into heaven, and they trumpeted the joy that each new soul in heaven brought others.

Seeing and Speaking with Mary and the Saints

A continual cascade of conversation about mundane matters and urgent concerns joined Mechtild and Gertrude with individual saints, whom the literature pictures as chatty and sociable. The *Herald* and the *Book of Special Grace* are strewn with dialogue.[79] The writings recorded significantly more talk between the sisters and the saints than among the sisters, exchanges initiated by members of both groups, portrayed by the nuns as important to both. Their discussions attest to a mutual engagement and frank enjoyment that, with the exception of Gertrude's and Mechtild's dialogues with Christ and with Mary, is unparalleled in the Helfta literature. These conversations may be indicative of the kind of talk that took place among the women themselves, indulging one another in flights of imagination about what puzzled, delighted, hurt, and otherwise engrossed them, and that they related to one another when speaking about claimed encounters with the saints. Or perhaps they reflect dimensions of the sisters' relationship with confessors. As the writings show, the nuns turned to the saints to grapple with matters of love and loss, to indulge in the pleasures of memory, and to explore the efficacy of pious practices. Contact with the saints fortified the women in their routine religious practices and told them that their work had

[79] Sabine Spitzlei is among those scholars who have drawn attention to the centrality of dialogue to the *Herald* and the *Book of Special Grace* (*Erfahrungsraum Herz: Zur Mystik des Zisterzienserinnenklosters Helfta im 13 Jahrhundert* [Stuttgart-Bad Cannstatt: Frommann-Holzboog, 1991], esp. 75). And see Theresa A. Halligan, who remarks on the dramatic dialogue many of Mechtild's visions contain (introduction to *The Booke of Gostlye Grace of Mechtild of Hackeborn*, trans. Theresa A. Halligan [Toronto: Pontifical Institute of Mediaeval Studies, 1979]).

meaning and power, that the words they declaimed in silence and in song reached into the heavens, while affirming the enduring investment of the recently and long-ago dead in the sisters' daily devotions.

Mechtild and her deceased sister, Abbess Gertrude, talked together about what happens to the prayers a person has uttered once she dies (they become more fruitful),[80] and when Mechtild greeted Catherine on her feast day with the antiphon *Ave speciosa* and asked Catherine to explain its meaning, Catherine obliged.[81] Weaving the stuff of their own now-distant lives into the world the nuns inhabited, Mary and the saints recounted to inquiring nuns aspects of their lives, sometimes alighting on the smallest details of salvation history. Mechtild, more interested in Christ's earthly life than was Gertrude,[82] wondered what Mary offered by way of refreshment to the friends and relatives who visited when Christ was born; the two discussed why Mary did not have a bed in which to give birth, and the foods the mother fed her baby after she weaned him.[83] John and Gertrude conversed as they lay together on Christ's breast: John told Gertrude about the importance he placed during his life on guarding himself from encounters with women not necessitated by material need or the demands of salvation.[84] We may suspect that Gertrude's visionary exchanges with John are an imagined loosening of the constraints between the sexes that the nuns experienced in their routine encounters with men. They may represent freedom from the control a confessor

[80] *Liber* 5.1 (318).

[81] *Liber* 1.32 (110–11).

[82] As scholars such as Bynum and Elkins have observed, the Helfta writings give little attention to the earthly life of Mary or Jesus; see Caroline Walker Bynum, "Women Mystics in the Thirteenth Century: The Case of the Nuns of Helfta," in *Jesus as Mother: Studies in the Spirituality of the High Middle Ages* (Berkeley: University of California Press, 1984), 186–87; and Elkins, "Gertrude the Great," 725, n. 14.

[83] *Liber* 1.5 (20).

[84] *Le Héraut* 4.4.7 (SCh 255:70–72).

tried to exert; in her pious fantasy, Gertrude could shape not only her contribution to the conversations but her interlocutor's as well. Perhaps, on the other hand, the depiction of the visionary's and John's relationship draws on the sorts of relationships the nuns sometimes had with men.

Unleashing their curiosity, the sisters asked probing questions about the saints' recompense and received information about delights in store for the faithful, a provocation and a promise to their readers. While strolling through a celestial palace, Mechtild came across a recently deceased friend and asked whether heaven was as she had supposed; the friend confirmed the truth of all they had been taught.[85] In the company of other saints, Augustine sang sweetly to Gertrude so that she might enjoy for a moment the spiritual delicacies that belonged eternally to heaven's inhabitants, an experience of one woman meant to stimulate the hunger of others.[86] The saints sometimes acted to bolster the nuns' assurance of the brightness of their future. Saint Margaret pledged to Gertrude that her Spouse and Lover would for every hour of every day for thousands and thousands of years give her celestial consolations, filling all her senses and her soul with inconceivable delights.[87]

Now and then dialogue was infused with woe, showing the visionaries' ease in disclosing emotions to the holy dead; Mechtild made known to Mary the sadness that overtook her when she learned about the creation of the *Book of Special Grace*.[88] Sometimes the sisters complained to the saints, as when Gertrude asked Abbess Gertrude why she did not bring about a cessation of the tears of her daughters, who mourned her, with a trace of petulance perhaps lodged in the question.[89] And just as souls caught in purgatory relayed to the sisters

[85] *Liber* 1.1 (11).

[86] *Le Héraut* 4.50.9 (SCh 255:416).

[87] *Le Héraut* 4.45.2 (SCh 255:346–48).

[88] *Liber* 5.31 (370).

[89] *Le Héraut* 5.1.1 (SCh 331:52).

how they might avoid port-mortem suffering, so saints from various states of life dispensed advice, teaching the nuns how to merit heaven.

The visionaries not only talked with the saints; they also eavesdropped on conversations the saints had with one another.[90] When Count Burchard was surrounded by his heirs in heaven, every one of them recited a poem narrating the good each had done while she or he was alive. Burchard was not the only one listening: Mechtild reported what she overheard to her sisters.[91] Simply seeing the saints inspired the sisters, kindled the desire to praise God, and underscored the close bonds among all members of the church.[92] Conveying an astonishing sense of the interconnectedness among human beings, gazing at Pope Leo caused Gertrude to understand that whenever one thanks God for a neighbor's victory or for a favor a neighbor has received, one benefits from the neighbor's merit.[93]

The visual content of visions now and then implicitly urged the nuns to imitate the lives of the saints, long-ago women and men as well as those among the holy dead whom the sisters had known. When Benedict appeared to her, Gertrude saw roses in bloom all over his body, and at the heart of every rose there bloomed another, each surpassing in beauty and scent the rose from which it emerged. The roses signified both the virtuous works Benedict accomplished during his life and the works of those who were stimulated by his example and teaching.[94] Seeing the apostles on the feast of Saint Peter and Saint Paul, Gertrude wondered how she herself might feed Christ's sheep,[95] perhaps fueling her consciousness of her apostolic mission and furthering her commitment to it. Seeing the saints

[90] See for example *Le Héraut* 5.3.5 (SCh 331:73).
[91] *Liber* 5.10 (334–35).
[92] See for example *Liber* 1.34 (113).
[93] *Le Héraut* 4.43.2 (SCh 255:340).
[94] *Le Héraut* 4.11.1 (SCh 255:126).
[95] *Le Héraut* 4.44.1 (SCh 255:340).

sometimes fed fantasies about the self that helped to make them reality.

The visual content of the revelations that came to them prompted the nuns' reflections on who they were and were meant to be. Sightings sometimes sparked imitation and triggered longing, raising questions about the change the visionary wished to see in herself, to which she might aspire, and which the saints sometimes aided in accomplishing. When Agnes appeared to Mechtild, the visionary compared herself unfavorably with the virgin martyr, asking Christ why she, vested in a habit and engaged to him since childhood, did not love him with all her heart, as did Agnes.[96] Such comparison, the overall context of the Helfta literature suggests, did not disquiet or discourage but drove the visionary to new heights of love. Agnes subsequently (and at Christ's command) shared her gifts with Mechtild.[97] The nuns tended to decrease the distance between the celestial spheres and the monastery in emphasizing similarity between the sisters and the saints. The authors of the *Book of Special Grace* described Bernard of Clairvaux—whose exalted status as Doctor of the Church they recalled to the reader—in terms strikingly similar to those associated with Mechtild. The divide between visionary woman and the honey-tongued doctor was resolved in favor of a shared mooring. Like Mechtild, everything Bernard knew, he knew through experience.[98]

Love Makes Debtors of Us All

Whereas the nuns elaborated their relationship with souls in purgatory through a creative appropriation of Anselmian atonement theory, it was their understanding of the indebtedness associated with love between God and the soul that pro-

[96] *Liber* 1.11 (35).

[97] *Liber* 1.11 (35).

[98] *Liber* 1.28 (97–98), and, for relevant comments about Mechtild, see *Liber* Prol. 1 (1–3).

vided the immediate context for their relationships with the saints. The literature coupled images of Christ as scrupulous judge and greedy usurer (and of the self as unworthy and indebted) with those of Christ as loyal friend and demanding lover (and of the self as necessary to God's happiness). The monastery's writings did not overlay the nuns' affective love-mysticism (often but by no means exclusively expressed as bridal- and mother-mysticism) onto a modified Anselmian atonement theory. They underscored instead their complementarity: both love and justice make debtors of us all. Whereas modern minds may worry over the (apparent) tension between love and justice, what captured the nuns' imagination was the soul's indebtedness to Christ to which both sin and love (which constrained the beloved to respond to the lover) gave rise.

Christ—longing lover, loyal friend, sweet spouse, tender mother, delicious baby—elicited the sisters' love for him exactly on account of the love with which he showered them, and he modeled a love in which a sense of reciprocity was integral. "I love those who love me" (Prov 8:17) he announced,[99] evoking the sense of the mutual hunger and the promise of gaining total possession of the beloved that characterized his relationships with the Helfta nuns and that, as we have seen, colors the whole of the Helfta literary corpus. Gertrude was to Christ like his very breath, without which he could not live.[100] She and Christ ran to each other: "Come! Come! Come!" he calls to her. "I come! I come! I come to you!" she answered.[101] Again and again, Christ gave Mechtild his heart,[102] and for his delight, Mechtild once offered him her heart in the form of a rose, and in the form of a goblet from which Christ might drink her, and in the form of a pomegranate, so that Christ might eat her up.[103] In a basic way, what Mechtild and Gertrude gave

[99] *Le Héraut* 4.4.3 (SCh 255:62).

[100] *Le Héraut* 3.26.3 (SCh 143:124–25).

[101] *Exercices* 3.106–7 (SCh 127:100).

[102] See for example *Liber* 1.19; 2.16 (60–71, 149–50).

[103] *Liber* 3.17 (217–18).

Christ was themselves; this was what Christ craved. As Mechtild was dying, Christ asked her, "where is my gift?" She opened her heart with her hands, and placing his heart against hers, Christ joined her to him, absorbing her into himself.[104]

The mutuality of longing carried with it a sense of indenture. Presenting himself as captive to their wishes, Christ offered himself to those whom he loved, cultivating in them attention to his wants, to his desires—and coaxing responsiveness from them. To Mechtild, almost always eager to submit to Christ's will,[105] Christ declared: "Let me be your prisoner," proclaiming his readiness to do her will.[106] When she called to him, he rushed to her more eagerly than a bee seeking to suck the nectar from the green meadow's sweet flowers.[107] He bowed down to her, and Saint Peter was astonished at the condescension.[108] As he beckoned her to him, his voice filled every corner of heaven.[109] "Oh, please me, now, my Lady Queen," Christ implored Gertrude, "as I have so often pleased you."[110] He explained to Mechtild that he was like a mother whose little son, nestled on her lap, learns to address her with the very same words of love she speaks to him.[111] He confided to Gertrude that like a friend who welcomes a friend as a guest into his home, he would give her all that friendship can offer. In such circumstances, he continued, the friend who is guest may wonder how he can fittingly repay the hospitality he has received. Casting himself now as host and now as guest, Christ wondered how he could repay her for all that Gertrude had bestowed on him.[112]

[104] *Liber* 7.11 (405–6).

[105] *Liber* 4.21 (278).

[106] *Liber* 2.31 (176). And see *Liber* 1.18 (55), for another declaration from Christ that her love has made him Mechtild's captive.

[107] *Liber* 2.3 (140).

[108] *Liber* 1.26 (170–71).

[109] *Liber* 2.35 (180).

[110] *Le Héraut* 4.14.6 (SCh 255:160).

[111] *Liber* 3.9 (207–8).

[112] *Le Héraut* 3.47.2 (SCh 143:312–14).

Requests and expressions of commitment such as these are embedded in an expectation of mutuality, in the mutual need and obligation that pervaded the relationship, one of courtship and of surrender (between bride and bridegroom), of mutual hospitality (between friends), of loving response to love that is freely given (between mother and child). Christ's assumption of humans' debt has been brought upon him by his entanglement in love.[113] Like a mother who is moved to increasing displays of affection by her young child's loving response to maternal tenderness, Christ was charged to renewed expressions of love by the soul's loving gestures towards him.[114] Increase of desire on his part was predicated on a loving return to his advances.

This sense of indebtedness to Christ was delightful to the nuns precisely because, as evidence of Christ's continuing love and longing for them, it confirmed and energized their connection with God. They could not conceive of a relationship with Christ that did not entail give and take. A loving relationship requires both parties to honor and affect each other, and to be vulnerable to one another's presence, to want and to expect a ceaseless flow of mutual love. The Helfta writings indicate the community's perception that this privilege was especially evident in the context of Christ's relationship with Mechtild and Gertrude. But Christ proclaimed his indebtedness to all the sisters for their devotion to him. He promised that he would repay them, telling them of his plans, hatched in eternity, to do so.[115] In the convent's optimistic religiosity, infused with a sense of life as progressive movement toward conformity with Christ, human beings became Christ-like to the extent that they wished to give to God what their lover, mother, father, friend, and spouse required of them and to the

[113] *Le Héraut* 2.19.1 (SCh 139:302–4).

[114] *Liber* 3.9 (207–8).

[115] *Le Héraut* 4.54.4 (SCh 255:450–52). Christ is willing to submit to all who love him (*Le Héraut* 5.9.2 [SCh 331:136]).

degree to which they were able to pattern their desire to give themselves to him after his own self-giving, a self-giving that love propelled. In reciprocating, the nuns became more Christ-like. This wishing to give is, the literature implicitly acknowledges, a process associated with spiritual development; desire to give is itself a gift.[116]

Christ's Friends and Family

Intimate encounter with Christ at Helfta was not all high emotion, impassioned desire, and fulfillment. There were formal commitments connected with the love relationship. These are nowhere more apparent than in the imposition Christ made on souls whom he loved to assume the right attitude toward his friends and family. He insisted that those whom he loved ought to have special status among all those who loved him. Thus, a narrator's voice interjects in the *Herald* that John the Evangelist is worthy of being loved by all of Christ's lovers since John was Christ's beloved,[117] and the *Book of Special Grace* shows that just as a husband entrusts his bride to his mother, so Christ delivers the soul whom he loves to Mary, obliging that soul to grow in love for his family and friends.[118] Because each sister, destined to salvation, was Christ's bride, the requirement for saints and sisters to love each other was mutual, the obligation universal.[119] The women conceived of their

[116] *Le Héraut* 5.23.1 (SCh 331:196, 198); *Liber* 2.14 (148).

[117] *Le Héraut* 4.4.3 (SCh 255:62). See too *Liber* 1.6 (23).

[118] *Liber* 1.37 (120–21). As a faithful husband commends his wife to his mother, so Christ commends Gertrude to Mary (*Le Héraut* 2.23.11 [SCh 193:340]). Sarah McNamer writes about the social rewards medieval women religious associated with marriage to Christ, including "fulfilling relationships with others" in heaven (*Affective Meditation and the Invention of Medieval Compassion* [Philadelphia: University of Pennsylvania, 2010], 41).

[119] As Maureen McCabe notes, Gertrude's relationship to Christ incorporates her into the "entire family of God with whom she experienced deep communion" ("The Scriptures and Personal Identity: A Study in the *Exercises* of Saint Gertrude," in *Hidden Springs: Cistercian Monastic Women*, ed. John A.

association with Mary and the saints as fitting into a long history of interconnectedness among the many friends and family members of Christ, a history that traced back to Mary Magdalene and especially to John the Evangelist,[120] both of whom, because they loved Christ, stood by his mother in her time of hardship and suffering and loved her on account of him.[121] Because Christ loved both especially, he instigated a relationship between his mother and John when he entrusted Mary to John's care (John 19:26).[122]

When John appeared to Gertrude on his feast day, his shoulders were decorated with golden lilies on which were written a proclamation of his twin identification as his Lord's beloved disciple and guardian of Christ's mother:

> And on the right-hand one was written in wondrous characters, "The disciple whom Jesus loved" [John 13:23; 21:7], and on the left, "This is the guardian of the Virgin," on account of his special privileges by which he alone deserved to be and was called the disciple whom Jesus loved above all the other apostles and because, as the Lord was about to die on the cross, the Lord judged that he [John] should be entrusted with his lily, that is, his Virgin Mother.[123]

Nichols and Lillian Thomas Shank, CS 113 [Kalamazoo, MI: Cistercian Publications, 1995], 504).

[120] *Liber* 1.26 (89–90).

[121] *Liber* 1.25 (87). A mark of the closeness of the relationship the nuns ascribed to John and Mary is evident in the petition Mechtild made on the feast of the Annunciation: she requested that John, through the love of Christ that allowed John to be deprived of Mary at her assumption, obtain for Mechtild the ability to separate her love from all things and to cleave in love only to Christ (*Liber* 1.26 [89–90]).

[122] *Liber* 1.6 (23); and *Le Héraut* 5.32.4 (SCh 331:260). For the medieval interpretation of Jesus' role in forging the mother-son relationship between Mary and John, see Jeffrey F. Hamburger, "Brother, Bride, and *alter Christus*: The Virginal body of John the Evangelist in Medieval Art, Theology and Literature," in *Text und Kultur: mittelalterliche Literatur 1150–1450* (Stuttgart: Metzler, 2001), 296–327.

[123] *Le Héraut* 4.4.1 (SCh 255:60).

The Helfta writings acclaimed John's respect for Mary and his tender attachment to her. We learn in the *Book of Special Grace* of an experience of Mechtild:

> Once, at the reading of the gospel, . . . she saw the same disciple standing at the altar. . . . And she saw . . . from the eyes of Saint John a ray of wondrous splendor extending to the Virgin's face. As she marveled and wondered what was meant by this, Saint John said, "When I was on earth, I had such reverence and honor for the Mother of my Lord that I did not dare to look at her face." And she asked, "By what name did you call her?" He responded: "*Vrowe mumme*."[124]

The late Middle Ages envisioned an extended family for Jesus, a holy kinship radiating from Anne, mother of Mary, in which John was the son of one of Anne's three daughters, Mary Salome, and thus the Virgin's nephew and Christ's cousin.[125] The vernacular term with which John addresses Mary, "Vrowe mumme" ("Lady Aunt"), conveys a sense of homey familiarity coupled with profound deference,[126] the expression of respectful endearment a gesture toward the type of relationship with his mother to which, the nuns perceived, Christ called each of them.

[124] *Liber* 1.6 (24).

[125] Speaking to Mechtild, Christ identified John as his relative: *Liber* 1.6 (23). The *Book of Special Grace* not only related the familial ties between John and Christ but also drew attention to John's place in Jesus' innermost circle (*Liber* 1.6 [23]); and see Hamburger, "Brother, Bride," 313. For the family tree of Anne and her three daughters, see Pamela Sheingorn, "The Holy Kinship: The Ascendancy of Matriliny in Sacred Genealogy of the Fifteenth Century," *Thought: A Review of Culture and Ideas* 64 (1989): 268–69; and Kathleen Ashley and Pamela Sheingorn, eds., introduction to *Interpreting Cultural Symbols: Saint Anne in Late Medieval Society* (Athens: University of Georgia Press, 1990), esp. 12; Hamburger, "Brother, Bride," 306.

[126] Jeffrey F. Hamburger, *St. John the Divine: The Deified Evangelist in Medieval Art and Theology* (Berkeley: University of California Press, 2002), 177; "Brother, Bride," 313.

The *Book of Special Grace* tells us that Mechtild sought a relationship with Mary analogous to that which John the Evangelist enjoyed. "Entrust me to your mother as you did John the Evangelist, your beloved," she implored Christ.[127] Christ signaled his willingness to do so, and the *Book of Special Grace* indicates that such a relationship was available to all who wished it.[128] On the feast of the Nativity, as the sisters sang *Primogenitus Mariae Virginis*, Gertrude remarked that it would be more appropriate to say "*unigenitus*" than "*primogenitus*" because Mary had conceived no one but Christ, and Mary responded,

> It is by no means *Unigenitus*, but it is most congruous to call my sweetest Jesus *Primogenitus*, whom I procreated first . . . and after him, indeed, through him, I gave birth to all of you who are his siblings and his children by the viscera of maternal charity.[129]

"Woman, behold your son," the nuns intoned during Matins on the feast of the Evangelist, an echo of Christ's words from the cross, and calling to mind for a contemporary readership the custom of linking John to Christ as Mary's other and adopted son.[130] The women of Helfta taught themselves that, like John, they too might become Mary's offspring, and looked to his devotion as exemplifying what they should offer her, also their mother. Desiring to be loved as he loves, Christ loved no creature so much as he loved Mary, because no one loved him so

[127] *Liber* 5.29 (362). For Mechtild's patterning of her relationship with Mary and with Christ after the relationship John enjoyed with each, see *Liber* 1.26 (89–90).

[128] *Liber* 5.29 (362–63).

[129] *Le Héraut* 4.3.7 (SCh 255:56).

[130] Echoing a prevalent medieval notion, founded on John 19:26-27, the nuns coupled Christ's giving over responsibility for his mother to John with the intimacy of John's and Mary's relationship, and they conceived of both in combination as converting nephew and aunt into son and mother. See Hamburger, "Brother, Bride," 306.

much as his mother did, and because he loved her so himself, Christ was extraordinarily pleased with John's love for her. Mary herself insisted that the relationship with her that she made available to the nuns was one that the women must accept if they were to be worthy of her Son,[131] and Christ duly rewarded the sisters for their association with his mother.[132]

As the nuns perceived it, the ties to Mary that they cultivated were illustrative of those that should bind them with all the saints. The Helfta literature as a whole reverberates with the counsel Mary gave Mechtild when she exhorted her, "Attach yourself to his [Christ's] family":

> Unite yourself also with his family, I mean the saints; love them, praise God for them, ask them often to go towards the Beloved to praise him with you. It is in this way that you will be truly holy, as it is written: *With the holy, you shall be holy* [Ps 17:26], as a queen becomes a queen in association with the king.[133]

Christ, Mary, and all the saints conspired to create community on the one hand among the sisters, and on the other, between them and heaven's residents. As John the Evangelist related to Mechtild, he intended to make an offering to all the saints of the prayers he accepted from one of Mechtild's sisters, sure that the heavenly inhabitants would feast on them as if at a banquet, thus facilitating the woman's ability to give pleasure to his celestial companions.[134]

Other individual holy women and men wound together the living and the dead as they spoke with the women about themselves and others of God's holy dead, explaining the significance of their lives and writings.[135] By word and by deed,

[131] *Liber* 1.5 (18).
[132] *Le Héraut* 4.48.6 (SCh 255:364); *Liber* 1.12 (38).
[133] *Liber* 137 (120–21).
[134] *Liber* 1.6 (22).
[135] See for example *Le Héraut* 4.50.1 (SCh 255:404); *Liber* 1.12 (39).

Christ fostered the nuns' reliance on his mother and his celestial friends.[136] He encouraged the sisters to praise the whole company of saints and to praise him for them; he helped the women learn how to do so.[137] Christ appeared to the nuns with the saints over and over.[138] He and the sisters talked about Mary and the saints:[139] he enjoined the nuns to heed their teachings[140] and to meditate on aspects of their lives,[141] and he entertained questions from the visionaries about this or that saint, as when Gertrude asked whether he was as pleased with Bernard as he was with Augustine,[142] or when Mechtild asked whether Christ had baptized John the Baptist.[143]

The Helfta literature both depicted and was a relentless drive to bring together all of those whom Christ loved and who loved him, a fervent enterprise to interweave relationships among Christ's friends and family members.[144] Christ routinely pushed the soul who sought him to do so via intermediaries. When Mechtild longed to unite herself to him, Christ instructed her that she should pray to the saints, and she did, but she first requested Mary's intercession, meeting Christ's instruction and then raising the ante, inserting into her prayer yet one more mediator.[145] On the feast of the Assumption, Gertrude, confined to bed, offered prayers that her sisters had entrusted to her to Mary, who then appeared at

[136] *Liber* 1.31 (104–5).

[137] *Liber* 1.34 (113).

[138] See for example *Liber* 1.25 (86–88).

[139] See for example *Liber* 1.6; 1.25; 1.33; 1.34; 1.44 (22, 86–88, 111–12, 112–15, 128); *Le Héraut* 4.2; 4.47 (SCh 255:62, 354–56). For Christ's encouragement of Gertrude's devotion to his mother, see Elkins, "Gertrude the Great," 724; and see Dolan, *St. Gertrude*, 141, for Christ's instruction that Gertrude honor his mother and for Christ's aiding Gertrude in praising him for Mary's virtues.

[140] See for example *Liber* 1.19 (62).

[141] See for example *Liber* 1.25 (86–87).

[142] *Le Héraut* 4.50.7 (SCh 255:412).

[143] *Liber* 1.8 (27).

[144] Lewis, "Maria," makes this observation.

[145] *Liber* 4.8 (264–66).

Gertrude's bedside, wrapped in a shining green cloak all adorned with golden flowers, each of which represented one of the words from the prayers Gertrude offered on her sisters' behalf. The reflection of these flowers would adorn the soul of the woman who spoke the words they represented, Mary promised Gertrude, explaining, furthermore, that the souls' adornment would bring pleasure to her Son—and to all of the heavenly host.[146] The *Herald* later relates,

> Then, while the sisters were going to communion, the Queen of Glory stood by at the right side of those who approached, covering each with a part of her cloak, which was adorned with the flowers of prayers, and she said, "In memory of me, look to this one, my sweetest Son." At her petition, the Lord, wondrously pleased, lovingly holding and caressing the head of each, extended to each the saving Host. And when she [Gertrude] had similarly communicated, she offered that sacrament to the Lord in eternal praise for the increase of joy, glory, and blessedness of his most blessed Mother, as if in compensation for the offering of her merits by which she had alleviated her [Gertrude's] need. The Lord Jesus, as if offering a gift to this sweetest mother, said, "Behold, Mother, I restore what is yours to you twofold. But I do not take it from this one, to whom you, for love of my love, have deigned to grant it."[147]

As Anne Clark has taught, relationships in the *Herald* are frequently articulated in terms of offerings, the circulation of gifts helping to forge and to strengthen connections with God as well as between and among God's family and friends. This passage, as Clark observes, describes at least six offerings: Gertrude and her sisters offered prayers to Mary, Mary offered Gertrude and her sisters the shelter of her mantle, Mary offered Gertrude and her sisters to Christ, Christ offered Gertrude and

[146] *Le Héraut* 4.48.1 (SCh 255:356–58).
[147] *Le Héraut* 4.48.21 (SCh 255:392).

her sisters the Host, Gertrude offered her communion to Christ in compensation for Mary's offering, and Christ offered a gift to Mary in compensation for her offering to Gertrude. Further, Gertrude facilitated the transfer of prayers to Mary, Mary conveyed these prayers to her Son, Christ returned to his mother on Gertrude's behalf (twofold)[148] the merits Mary had offered for Gertrude, and he offered the Host to each woman whose prayers his Mother presented to him. The passage emphasizes the sequence of exchanges, underscoring the giving and reception of gifts that occurred within encounters. Tucking relationships into other relationships, that is, the introduction of an additional person (or persons) within the context of an already established relationship, was evidently a means by which to multiply the acquisition of gifts for all parties involved, a generous increase of donors and recipients that redounded to everyone's benefit. Because they were associated with bringing pleasure to recipient and donor, and because gift-giving is mutually productive for both, the exchange of gifts builds community, and it does so cumulatively.[149]

At Helfta, the intercession of Mary and the saints was not about fording a gulf between the sisters and Christ. The saints

[148] The passage is an illustration of the Gospel claim that in giving one receives (Luke 6:38), a claim also emphasized elsewhere in the Helfta writings. In this instance, Mary receives twofold what she has given Gertrude. At Helfta, giving generated its own reward—more and more gifts!

[149] It is this basic thrust that helps to account for a fascinating feature in the writings associated with Gertrude over which scholars have puzzled for over a hundred years. At the end of the nineteenth century, Preger observed that Christ mediates between Gertrude and Mary when he offers a gift to Mary to compensate her for the gift of virtues she has bestowed on Gertrude (Preger, *Geschichte*, 129). Sharon Elkins underscored the reversal in Gertrude's religiosity of "the typical medieval pattern in which Mary petitions her son on behalf of her devotees"; this is the case throughout the *Book of Special Grace* as well (Elkins, "Virgin Mary," 725). Clark ("Uneasy Triangle") is correct to suggest that what lies behind this phenomenon is principally the nuns' sense of Christ's ferocious dedication to integrating his family and friends with one another.

were not on this account less vital to the nuns' religiosity.[150] Their sense of Christ's closeness to them and his nearness to their needs, rather than a sense of his distance from them, fueled their familiarity with his other friends and family members, the saints. The women's association with these members of his friends and family fostered happiness for sisters, the saints, and Mary, helped to secure the nuns' salvation, and created community between heaven and earth. Gift-giving bound living individuals to one another, the gifts the living bequeathed to souls in purgatory joined these two populations in community, and as home to a ceaseless series of reciprocal exchanges among the saints, heaven in the Helfta writings is relationality. The unending rounds of gift-giving characteristic of celestial existence meant that the joy the saints conferred on one another via a shared source in God continuously grew anew.[151] The inner life of God in which the saints shared was a serial gift-giving among Father, Son, and Holy Spirit.[152]

However much the nuns used mystical imagery to evoke the assimilation of the soul with God in heaven, they coupled the language of mystical merging with an emphasis on the sharing between and among the saints of the joy that is assimilation to God. The flooding of the self with God was, to the nuns, simultaneously a breaking down of barriers between individual saints, implying the openness of self to other, a boundless reverberation of bliss throughout eternity for saved souls. Thus when the nuns observed that in heaven God becomes the eye by which the soul sees, the light by which she sees, the beauty that she sees,[153] "the soul's life and the movement of all its limbs, so that everything the soul does, God

[150] In a vision that came to Gertrude on the feast of Saints Peter and Paul, Christ explained that rather than coming to her directly, he preferred to attract Gertrude to himself through these saints in order to increase her veneration of them (*Le Héraut* 4.44.2 [SCh 255:342]).

[151] *Liber* 1.34 (114–15).

[152] *Liber* 1.20 (72–73).

[153] *Liber* 5.21 (352).

himself seems to do [within her],"[154] they also noticed that "in this way, it is truly fulfilled in the saints that 'God shall be all in all' [1 Cor 15:28]."[155] This is why the women could write that when the soul enters heaven, "in a wonderous and joyous way, God beholds himself, the soul, and all the saints in and with the soul."[156] When, even before she arrived in heaven, God folded Mechtild into his embrace, pressing her heart to him, this encounter was not just a joining of Mechtild with God but also concurrently a sharing of the joys associated with that encounter with all saints:

> it seemed as though all of her members flowed like streams into all the saints, suffusing them with a new and special joy, holding their hearts in their hands like shining lamps, filled with that gift that God infused into the soul, and giving thanks to the Lord for that soul with great gratitude and happiness.[157]

When the nuns featured the prominent role of Mary and saints in their lives they did so in part as a confirmation and a strengthening of their bond with Christ, elaborating on the coincidence between proximity to Christ and nearness to those whom he loves. The closer one is to Christ, the closer one will be to his friends and family, they understood, and proximity to them will increase intimacy with him, which will in turn fortify one's relationships with those whom he loves. The thoroughly circular pattern to this piety is evident in a revelation found in a short treatise on Mary contained, in eleven chapters and sixteen printed pages, in the first section of the *Book of Special Grace*. Christ answered Mechtild's prayer that he make her serve Mary more diligently when Mechtild saw him seated side by side with Mary on an elevated throne and heard him

[154] *Liber* 5.21 (352).
[155] *Liber* 5.21 (352).
[156] *Liber* 5.21 (352).
[157] *Liber* 2.17 (151).

command his mother to cede her place to the petitioner. Mary obliged, and taking Mechtild into her arms, brought her into her son's embrace.

Then Christ placed Mechtild's lips to his heart, saying, "From now on, you will drink all that you desire to give to my mother from here," and Mechtild felt fall into her soul, like drops of celestial water, words she had never before heard, a prayer in celebration of the Virgin, which the treatise relates in its entirety.[158] The starting point for the revelation was Mechtild's sense of the inadequacy of her devotion to Mary, a recognition that signaled the depth of the holy woman's humility and a commitment to his mother that precipitated Christ's intervention. This intervention, in turn, jumpstarted Mary's engagement with Mechtild, both mother and Son now working cooperatively to secure Mechtild's desire to be joined with Christ.[159] In assuming Mary's position next to Christ, Mechtild achieved her desire to join with her Beloved.

But Mechtild did not leave consideration of Christ's mother behind when she took her place. Instead, Mechtild's devotion to Mary increased, a devotion the authors of the *Book of Special Grace* hoped to multiply when they, on behalf of Mechtild, shared the gift of the prayer Mechtild had received from Christ with their readers. As we have seen in other contexts, therefore, attaching oneself to Christ with love and reverence had the effect of channeling one's love and devotion to others, the self traveling into ever-wider circles of contact. A vision that began with Mechtild's desire for union with Christ concluded with

[158] *Liber* 1.46 (131–32).

[159] *Liber* 1.46 (131–32). For the widespread devotion to Mary in the late Middle Ages, see R. W. Southern, *The Making of the Middle Ages* (New Haven: Yale, 1953); Hilda Graef, *Mary: A History of Doctrine and Devotion*, vol. 1, *From the Beginnings to the Eve of the Reformation* (New York: Sheed and Ward, 1963), 210–321; Claudia Opitz, et al., ed., *Maria in der Welt: Marienverherung im Kontext der Sozialgeschichte 10.–18. Jahrhundert* (Zurich: Chronos Verlag, 1993); Maria Warner, *Alone of All Her Sex: The Myth and Cult of the Virgin Mary* (repr. New York: Vintage Books, 1983); Brown, *Mary*.

a prayer that was a statement simultaneously about her commitment to Mary and to her sisters' lives, a commitment Christ roundly endorsed and rewarded.

The implication of this vision is echoed throughout the monastery's writings: it is only from thorough intimacy with Christ that one can offer those whom he loves the intimate and reverent love that they deserve. Christ himself is the source of the love he enjoins everyone to offer one another. Immediately following the vision above is another that presses home this message. When Mechtild confessed to having neglected to serve Mary properly, Mary gave her son's heart to Mechtild in the form of a lamp and instructed Mechtild to offer this lamp to her with the same love with which Christ loved her, Mary.[160] The point is that without drawing on Christ—the waters of his divinity, the lamp of his heart—no one can properly love and lovingly honor those whom Christ loves. The nuns emphasized that God's love is our love,[161] and their steadfast amplification of this notion is at least in part what animated the emphasis on a lack of absolute boundary in their impulse on the one hand to love and to honor God and, on the other, to love and honor the saints. Thus in choir, the nuns praised the saints, and they praised the Lord in his saints; in keeping with broader currents in medieval theology, the difference and demarcation between the two forms of praise was not always obvious or necessary to them.[162]

The *Book of Special Grace* describes a vision Mechtild received that told of the fruit of her sisters' common worship on the feast of Saint Agnes, a vision that illustrates this happy confusion:

[160] *Liber* 1.46 (132).

[161] *Liber* 1.4; 1.18 (14, 57).

[162] On the close identification between Christ and his saints, whose virtues are a reflection of his and who in heaven share in his glory, see Jaroslav Pelikan, *The Growth of Medieval Theology (600–1300)*, vol. 3, *The Christian Tradition: A History of the Development of Doctrine* (Chicago: University of Chicago Press, 1978), 176.

> When the responsory *Amo Christum* was sung at Matins, the Lord Jesus Christ appeared, embracing holy Agnes with his right arm. . . . From the heart of each person who was devoutly and deliberately chanting the psalms, a ray of light passed into the heart of God, which, furthermore, flowed like delicate liquid into the heart of blessed Agnes. By this, . . . [Mechtild] understood that all the devotion and the fruit of the love, which until now proceeded from . . . [Agnes's] words, and [those that proceeded similarly] from all the saints, flowed back to [their origin], just as when the sun liquefies ice, it makes it flow back to its origin. In this way, all things flow back into God, and the saints delight delicately in these things.[163]

It is not evident from this passage whether the sisters intended their song to connect them with Christ or with his saint. It is not clear that such a distinction mattered or that it even occurred to them. God is the originating source of the love that moved Agnes to confess "*Amo Christum*," and the sisters' chant repeated Agnes's avowal, the basis for their verbal declamation of devotion, which was the fruit of Agnes's love; this fruit flowed back to God, threading through God and then Agnes ribbons of light and liquid, weaving each sister together with Agnes and God.[164] The sisters' song, a labor of love, forged community with the saints and God. Sure that God's love was the source of the love they themselves offered when they praised the saints, they perceived that their love ran a course back through God before it reached his saint, a settled course, in some sense, not entirely dependent on their intentions.[165]

[163] *Liber* 1.11 (34–35).

[164] See in addition *Liber* 2.29 (174). For imagery related to liquid, see for example *Liber* 1.1; 1.22; 2.23; 2.28 (7–11, 77–78, 165–66, 173–74); *Le Héraut* 5.7.1 (SCh 331:122–24). For love flowing from God to the saints and back again to God, see *Liber* 2.23 (110–11).

[165] In the *Book of Special Grace*, love is grace, which flows from God and back into him; Christ is like a bee who sucks his own sweetness, and Mechtild sees something like a bee flying out of God's mouth and then back into it (*Liber* 4.43 [184]).

There was no rigid divide between the nuns' love of God and their love of his mother and the saints.

Although the nuns were certain that a relationship between Christ and the individual, however intoxicating, however satisfying, was incongruous in isolation from others, they were aware that their love for others, or its expression, sometimes faltered. On one occasion, Gertrude confessed to Christ that it would be just for her to be deprived at the hour of her death of the presence of the saints because she did not render them the honor they merited: on the feast of Saint Peter and Saint Paul, she felt remiss: she had meditated on Peter but overlooked Paul.[166] Both Mechtild and Gertrude expressed greater concern about lack of devotion to the Virgin than regarding any saint.[167] This concern makes sense. The monastery was dedicated to Mary[168] and possessed relics of the Virgin with which, together with an image of her, the nuns were accustomed to process.[169] They supposed the importance of Mary's presence at the bedside of the dying.[170] The treatise on Mary we find in the *Book of Special Grace* contains instructions on how to praise Mary intended both to guide and to energize.[171] Marian prayers in the *Spiritual Exercises* insisted on Mary's centrality,[172] and prayers dedicated to her occupied a pivotal place in Gertrude's and Mechtild's piety; Gertrude recited one Hail Mary for each day that Christ had occupied his mother's womb.[173] The dozens of revelations of the Mother of God that the visionaries received, especially when the sisters collectively chanted in her

[166] *Le Héraut* 4.44.2 (SCh 255:342).

[167] Lewis, "Maria," makes this point, 84.

[168] *Exercices* 4.12 (SCh 127:124).

[169] *Le Héraut* 4.2.16 (SCh 255:46). As Lewis, "Maria," has indicated, it is exactly Mary's exalted position in the life of the monastery that accounts for the tension and ambivalence in Gertrude's relationship to her.

[170] For Mary's presence at the deathbed, see for example *Liber* 1.47 (133).

[171] *Liber* 1.36–47 (118–33).

[172] See for example *Exercices* 6 (SCh 127:230–32, lines 421–54); and see Lewis, "Maria," 89.

[173] *Le Héraut* 4.51.1 (SCh 255:418). And see *Liber* 1.43 (127–28).

honor, witnessed to her meaningfulness in their lives and increased their devotion to her.[174]

For the most part, when the literature alights on lapses in Mechtild's or Gertrude's Marian piety, it draws attention to the women's consciousness of their inadequacy and their remorse over their failures to fulfill their duties in relation to Mary.[175] Moreover, expressions of shortcomings were not simply, and sometimes not even chiefly, personal, related to one or another of the two principal visionaries. Such admissions responded to the spiritual exigencies of the larger household. When Mechtild lamented that she was at fault in not serving Mary well, she yoked her carelessness to that of another, unnamed, person, carrying their common burden forward.[176] While it is sometimes the case that the saints, Mary, or Christ sought to quell the visionary's anxieties about the defects of her devotion,[177] Christ did not for the most part brush aside individual or corporate concerns but affirmed the truth of the women's self-assessment. From time to time he intervened when the nuns' desire to honor Mary needed direction and impetus, and he compensated for their lack, the women relying more frequently on his intercession in relation to Mary than to any of the saints.

When Mechtild accused herself of not having loved Mary as much as she ought, Christ advised her how to praise his mother for her role in salvation history.[178] After the sisters

[174] See for example *Liber* 1.39; 1.29; 1.26 (123–24, 99–101, 88); *Le Heraut* 2.1–6 (SCh 139:290–98).

[175] See for example *Le Héraut* 3.37.1; 5.31.1 (SCh 143:176–78; SCh 331:250–52); *Liber* 1.43; 1.46 (127, 131).

[176] *Liber* 1.46 (132).

[177] *Le Héraut* 5.28 (SCh 331:228–30). While singing with her sisters on the feast of Elisabeth of Hungary, Gertrude fretted that her attention to God diminished the praise Elisabeth counted as her own; Elisabeth soothed Gertrude, saying that she accepted Gertrude's song with infinite gratitude (*Le Héraut* 4.56 [SCh 255:462]).

[178] *Liber* 1.44 (128).

chanted the Mass on the vigil of the Assumption, Gertrude prayed to Christ because she had not given Mary her due. Christ immediately embraced Mary, saying "Remember, my Lady, most loving Mother, that I am merciful to sinners because of you, and look upon this one, my elect, with the same affection as if she had pleased you by serving you with the utmost devotion all the days of her life." At these words, Mary became entirely honey, which, as the Helfta literature elsewhere makes evident, is a symbol of the divinity.[179] Scholars have been accustomed to emphasize that in late medieval piety, her Son can refuse Mary nothing.[180] In this instance, it is Mary who melts, softened and sweetened by the embrace and words of her Son.

This passage draws attention to Gertrude's sense of inadequacy in her dealings with Mary, to Christ's solicitude for Gertrude, and to the happy vulnerability of his mother to her Son's words and touch, incited by Gertrude's penitential petition. Gertrude's conscientious recognition of laxity in devotion redounds to Mary's benefit. Christ's intercession benefits Gertrude as well, for it confirms the productivity of her humble self-appraisal. Gertrude, like Mechtild, is a model Marian devotee, sharply aware of her deficiencies and eager that Mary should receive restitution for them.

Indeed, throughout the *Book of Special Grace* and the *Herald*, the women's self-effacement is for the most part to be interpreted as confirmation of their humility and piety, communicating, as it does, their keen awareness of both the depth of devotion that Christ insists his mother and the saints merit and their own limitations in meeting the obligations he imposes on them.[181] Self-accusation is not self-indulgent but productive, speeding the women into action, and in some measure, its purpose is to offer an inducement to greater devotion and

[179] *Le Héraut* 4.48.3 (SCh 255:360).

[180] See for example Graef, *Mary*, 268–69.

[181] Lewis has made a similar observation in "Maria."

not an indictment. When Mechtild acknowledged before God that she had neither loved nor served nor honored his mother as much as was her due, Christ did not dwell on Mechtild's self-denunciation but instructed her to promise to make up for her inattention.[182] When she was unsure whether she had recited the vigil of Compline for Mary, Mechtild's uncertainty became the launching pad for her five-time recitation of the Hail Mary.[183] Likewise, when Gertrude chastised herself for not having prayed to Mary, the Holy Spirit directed her to offer the Virgin the heart of Christ; she did so, and the Virgin accepted the offering joyfully.[184]

It is evident that the nuns shared a basic commitment to establish or to maintain proper balance or relationship between their devotion to Mary, the saints, and all those whom God loves, on the one hand, and, on the other, their love of God.[185] The Helfta nuns' enthusiastic dedication to the communion of saints was coupled with an uncompromising avowal of God's singular and superior place in their life, and they sometimes had difficulty reconciling this double commitment. Thus, for example, when a sermon on the feast of the Annunciation made no mention of Christ, Gertrude found the absence troubling. After the sermon was over, she assumed her habit of fixing her attention on Christ, although called to consider another: walking past the altar of the Virgin, she greeted Mary but noticed herself concentrating less on the mother, more on

[182] *Liber* 1.44 (128).

[183] *Liber* 1.43 (127).

[184] *Le Héraut* 4.2.16 (SCh 255:46).

[185] For Gertrude's difficulty in juggling these obligations, see Elkins, "Gertrude the Great," 724. The tension that Lewis notices in Gertrude's piety—that Gertrude does not wish to praise Mary exclusively and bypass Christ, on the one hand, and, on the other, does not wish to neglect Mary (Lewis, "Maria," 86)—is an observation we should extend to Mechtild as well and to the relationship of both women with all the saints. For concern about balancing devotion to mother with devotion to her Son in the late medieval context, see Brown, *Mary*, 34–35.

the Son. This vignette concludes with Christ reassuring Gertrude of the goodness of her devotion to him while pushing her to compensate for any slight she may have committed against Mary:

> Do not fear, dearest one, that you concentrate more on me in greeting or praise than on my mother, because she delights in this. Since your conscience troubles you on this account, however, be zealous on another occasion to greet the inviolate image of my mother before the altar with more complete devotion and leave off greeting my own image.[186]

Christ's response highlights the nun's motives as impeccable. Gertrude has behaved in the manner of an ardent lover: dazzled by Christ, she directed all that gave her pleasure to him, always on guard for any perceived insults to her beloved and ready in his defense. In spite of this, Christ did not reassure Gertrude with an instruction to rest easy. Calling her to attend to the proddings of her conscience, he directed that she compensate for her preferential consideration of himself by tending at another time to Mary's image and bypassing his.

The larger message implied in the Helfta literature's interplay between expressing devotion to Christ on the one hand and to Mary and the saints on the other is simple, and it is this: Christ wants us to love him and to love one another. The former demands the latter, and yet love of God must always take priority.[187] Putting this double injunction into practice was not always easy for the nuns, and they may have spent a lifetime straining to do so to their satisfaction. This is, perhaps, how they thought it should be. No one ought to become complacent, their writings suggest, in assessing whom and how much to

[186] *Le Héraut* 3.20.1 (SCh 143:110–12). Dolan, *St. Gertrude*, 143, observed that whenever Gertrude read or heard anything in praise of Mary (or the saints), she offered to Christ the pleasure it gave to her.

[187] Lewis has characterized Gertrude's mariology as "sober" in maintaining Christ at the center of her devotions; "Maria," 85–86.

love or and in determining how to express this love. The overall sense the Helfta compositions convey is that the reader ought always to worry about right love relationships—with God, his mother, the saints, and others—but not too much. Gertrude and Mechtild are models of the effort to achieve just the right balance. Their own model was the Virgin Mary herself.

Mary and John: Models and Intercessors

The nuns looked to Mary as model and recognized themselves in her.[188] Gertrude and Mechtild longed to become like

[188] For Mary as model for Gertrude, see Mary Forman, "Visions 'Brimful of Love' During Christmas and Candlemas Liturgies in Gertrude of Helfta's *Legatus* II.16: A Study in *Lectio divina*," *Mystics Quarterly* 32, no. 3/4 (September/December 2006): esp. 7 and 13; Elkins, "Gertrude the Great," 722; Lewis, "Maria," 94; Ella Johnson, "Reproducing Motherhood: Images of Mary and Maternity in the Writings of Gertrud the Great of Helfta," 47th International Medieval Studies Congress, Western Michigan University, 2012; Johnson is correct to argue for the centrality of *imitatio Mariae* in Gertrude's devotional life. On Mechtild of Hackeborn's identification with Mary, see Barbara Newman, "Gender," in *The Blackwell Companion to Mysticism*, ed. Julia A. Lamm (London: Blackwell Publishing, 2013), 45. Mechtild of Magdeburg also identified with Mary (Newman, "Gender," 45). For imitation of Mary in the later Middle Ages, see for example Rosemary Hale, "*Imitatio Mariae*: Motherhood Motifs in Devotional Memoirs," *Mystics Quarterly* 16 (1990): 193–203; Martina Wehrli–Johns, "Haushälterin Gottes: Zur Mariennachfolge der Beginen," in *Mariae, Abbild oder Vorbild? Zur Sozialgeschichte mittelalterlicher Marienverehrung*, ed. Hedwig Röckelein, et al. (Tübingen: Diskord, 1990), 147–67; Jeffrey F. Hamburger, *The Rothschild Canticles: Art and Mysticism in Flanders and the Rhineland circa 1300* (New Haven, CT: Yale University Press, 1990), 88–104. In her groundbreaking *Alone of All Her Sex*, Marina Warner elaborates on the impossibility associated with women's imitation of Mary, an evaluation the nuns of Helfta did not share. More than half a century ago, Simone Roisin argued that in the late Middle Ages devotion to Mary was less attractive to women than it was to men (*L'hagiographie cistercienne dans le diocese de Liège au XIIIe siècle* [Louvain: Bibliothèque de l'Université, 1947], 108, 111–13). Much subsequent scholarship has supported Roisin. On the topic of the imitation of Mary, see Catherine M. Mooney, "*Imitatio Christi or*

Mary, and a web of images portrayed both as successfully following in her footsteps.[189] Mary's prominence in the nuns' piety was anchored in a theology emphasizing the joy she brought Christ and (the two are related) her role in salvation history. *Imitatio Mariae*, at Helfta, was largely about becoming more pleasing to Christ, as Sharon Elkins noticed decades ago.[190] Recalling the power Gertrude and Mechtild exercise over Christ, the literature portrays Mary as the primal instance of a soul captivating Christ through her love for him: Mary captured Christ when, burning with love for her, he quit heaven to enclose himself in her womb.[191] The Helfta compositions emphasized the mutuality of this love as the basis for the incarnation. Once, Gertrude saw flowers covering every part of Christ's adult body, and when Mary embraced her Son, the same flowers overlaid her flesh because it was from Mary that Mary's Son took his flesh.[192] The *Herald* teaches its readers that Christ predestined Mary from all eternity to be his mother;[193] theirs is a love whose scope is boundless.

The Helfta writings are heavy with the praise and expressions of tenderness with which Christ lavished his mother,[194]

---

imitatio Mariae? Clare of Assisi and Her Interpreters," in *Gendered Voices: Medieval Saints and Their Interpreters*, ed. Catherine M. Mooney (Philadelphia: University of Pennsylvania Press, 1998); Kate Greenspan, "*Matre Donante:* The Embrace of Christ as the Virgin's Gift in the Visions of 13th-Century Italian Women," *Studia Mystica: Women and Mysticism* 13 (Summer/Fall 1990): 26–37.

[189] *Liber* 1.13 (40–45). Mary is a model of virginity, and its guardian (*Exercices* 3.341–44 [SCh 127:118]). Christ perfects Gertrude through Mary (*Exercices* 2.69–70 [SCh 127:86]).

[190] For Gertrude's understanding of Mary's place in salvation history, see Lewis, "Maria," 94.

[191] *Liber* 1.11 (36). For Christ's love of Mary as motive for the incarnation, see Mechtild of Magdeburg, *Flowing Light*, 5.23 (198).

[192] *Le Héraut* 4.41.3 (SCh 255:328–30).

[193] *Le Héraut* 5.31.1 (SCh 331:252). Christ chose Mechtild for himself from eternity, too (*Liber* 1.18 [55]).

[194] See for example *Le Héraut* 4.48.11; 5.31.1 (SCh 255:372–74; SCh 331:252); *Liber* 1.39; 1.42; 1.45 (123, 126, 129).

familiar to us from the language of love and longing woven throughout depictions of his association with Gertrude and Mechtild. No one, they say, has achieved a more perfect union with him.[195] As the literature tells it, Mechtild and Gertrude were en route to achieving this assimilation to Christ, who took Mechtild's heart, thrust it into his own, and told her he wished for all her desire to become one with his desire, just as two winds blow together as one, just as a drop of water becomes one with the flood, and just as metals melt together in alloy.[196] Christ compared his indwelling in Gertrude's heart with his presence in the Eucharist: "Nowhere on earth can you find me more surely than in the sacrament of the altar and . . . in the heart and soul of my beloved,"[197] he asserted. Both women were, like Mary, illuminated by Christ with divine wisdom.[198]

Fundamentally, Mechtild and Gertrude were similar to Mary in their sharing of Christ's intimacy with others. Their revelations illustrated Mary's unending dedication to all souls: Mechtild once beheld Mary, her clothes decorated with gold spheres whose continuous spinning signified her ceaseless desire for the well-being of the church.[199] The *Book of Special Grace* taught that the Holy Spirit so filled Mary that whoever sought grace through her would find it[200] and drew attention to the correspondence between Mary as the most grace-filled of all God's creatures and the accessibility to others of God's grace through her. In conversation with Mechtild, Mary put it like this: if a drunk man expresses happiness more freely than a sober man, how could she, Mary, who drinks without pause the wine of the divinity, not be excessively generous with

[195] *Liber* 1.38 (122).

[196] *Liber* 3.27 (230–32).

[197] *Le Héraut* 1.3.3 (SCh 139:136). For a similar pronouncement about Abbess Gertrude, see *Liber* 6.2 (378).

[198] *Liber* 1.42; 1.45 (126, 129); *Le Héraut* 2.23.5; 4.3.1 (SCh 139:334; SCh 255:48).

[199] *Liber* 1.22 (80).

[200] *Liber* 1.42 (126).

others?[201] The *Book of Special Grace* also compared Mechtild to a drunk person when it described God's presence overwhelming her so that she poured out his grace, revealing the secrets he shared with her to others.[202]

We read of both Gertrude and Mary that each contained the divinity within herself, each a crystal in which Christ shone like gold. Carrying Christ within herself, Gertrude, like Mary, delivered him to others.[203] Mary gave Mechtild everything that was hers, including her virginal motherhood,[204] and in a vision that came to Gertrude at Mechtild's deathbed, we learn that Mechtild's desire to become like God's mother was fulfilled. Mechtild gained Mary's crown on account of the nun's fervor for her own spiritual progeny. When Mechtild died, Christ placed one of his mother's necklaces on her because she, like his mother, had given birth to him in many hearts.[205] Gertrude and Mechtild were not alone in imitating Mary successfully. Abbess Gertrude was, like Mary, a loving and protective, stern and demanding mother.[206] The *Herald* assimilates Abbess Gertrude as mother to the Virgin Mother by picturing the younger Gertrude asking Christ to show the abbess, as she approaches

[201] *Liber* 1.38 (122).

[202] *Liber* 2.26 (169).

[203] *Le Héraut* 3.37.1; 4.3.3 (SCh 143:180; SCh 255:50–52). Johnson discusses Gertrude's identification with Mary's womb, observing that a consequence of Gertrude's Marian piety is that, like Mary, she comes to mediate grace ("Reproducing," 12–18). On the image of the womb in medieval religious writings, see Alexandra Barratt, "Context: Some Reflexions on Wombs and Tombs and Inclusive Language," in *Anchorites, Wombs and Tombs: Intersections of Gender and Enclosure in the Middle Ages*, ed. Liz Herbert McAvoy and Mari Hughes-Edwards (Cardiff: University of Wales Press, 2005), 29. Greenspan has observed in the lives of thirteenth-century women saints that the hagiographers depicted holy women as similar to Mary in exactly this way—that they, like her, helped to save through mediation with Christ ("*Matre Donante*," 27).

[204] *Liber* 1.11 (35–36). Mechtild thus became God's mother by grace, just as Mary was his mother by nature.

[205] *Le Héraut* 5.4.11 (SCh 331:92).

[206] For the sternness of medieval Mary, see Brown, *Mary*, 353.

death, the same affection he showed his mother and on account of their analogous roles: the abbess was mother to her daughters, just as Mary was a mother to her Son.[207]

Mary is both "Mother of God and of men," Christ's Mother and our Mother.[208] She who in giving birth to Christ manifested the God-man to the whole world condescended to make special appearances with her Son within the cloister walls. Each day, Mary supported the sisters' requests before the Father and the Son.[209] Mary was a ladder through whom sinners climbed to Christ,[210] a door opening her mercy to whoever presented herself.[211] Her crown dripped drops of grace that God infused in all who served her devoutly.[212] When she appeared to Mechtild, Mary was clothed in a purple vestment covered with gold writing identifying her as "Consolation of all the Afflicted and Refuge of all Sinners."[213] Mechtild relied on Mary for her own well-being, to aid particular sisters,[214] and for the good of the household. She prayed to Mary to obtain from God the forgiveness of her sins,[215] and saw Mary kneel in supplication when she asked her to intercede both for herself and for the convent.[216] On her deathbed, Mechtild commended the house to Mary, perhaps motivated to do so in part because the nuns were in the midst of a five-year interregnum, a consequence of their inability to agree about Abbess Sophia's successor.[217]

[207] *Le Héraut* 5.1.19 (SCh 331:38); see too *Liber* 6.1 (376), for Abbess Gertrude in relation to Mary. Elkins has argued that Gertrude's view of motherhood, associated with her images of both Christ and Mary, may reflect her sense of the abbess (Elkins, "Gertrude the Great," 729).

[208] *Liber* 1.38 (122): "*Mater Dei et Hominis*."

[209] *Liber* 1.39 (123).

[210] *Le Héraut* 4.51.8 (SCh 255:428–30).

[211] *Liber* 1.37 (121).

[212] *Liber* 1.12 (38–39).

[213] *Liber* 1.38 (122).

[214] *Liber* 4.27 (284–85).

[215] *Liber* 1.36 (118).

[216] *Liber* 1.12 (39).

[217] *Liber* 7.6 (397).

Mary was Gertrude's highest consolation after Christ.[218] Gertrude depended on her intervention to soothe her sufferings; she approached Mary when she was weighed down with worry, sure that Mary would bring relief from her troubles.[219] Perceiving Mary as responsive to those in need, Gertrude urged readers of her *Spiritual Exercises* to commend themselves to Mary.[220] In an account of visionary experience that may incorporate Gertrude's encounters with statues and other images of Mary cloaking sinners in her care, Gertrude once detected a bevy of young women huddling under Mary's mantle.[221] When Gertrude beckoned Mary with the verse *Eia ergo advocate nostra*, she was drawn to Gertrude almost as if pulled by ropes, and Gertrude understood that Mary would advocate for anyone who appealed to her in prayer.[222]

Although there was no more powerful advocate before Christ than Mary,[223] the nuns did not count on her indulgence for those whose obedience to her Son was lacking or devotion lackluster; their Mary was both solicitous and unyielding.[224] Mechtild and Gertrude observed that Mary sometimes had the willingness to heal them emotionally and to intercede on their behalf with her Son. They understood, however, that she did so by steering them steadily in the direction he determined. Uneasy on account of someone trying to compel her to reveal a special grace Christ had conferred on her, Gertrude approached Mary; she found disclosure difficult and was fearful

[218] *Exercices* 2.19–22 (SCh 127:82).

[219] *Le Héraut* 3.1 (SCh 143:14).

[220] *Exercices* 3 (SCh 127:118). And see *Exercices* 3.124–26 (SCh 127:102).

[221] *Le Héraut* 4.48.4 (SCh 255:360–62). For the observation about the material images of Mary Gertrude may have seen and that she may have incorporated into this vision, see SCh 255:360, n. 1.

[222] *Le Héraut* 4.51 (SCh 255:428).

[223] *Exercices* 2.20–30 (SCh 127:82).

[224] Brown has shown that medieval Mary was less supple in her intercession than scholars have long argued, more concerned with petitioners' worship of her Son than their devotion to her (*Mary*, 353–413).

that if she refused, she would do so against God's will. Mary did not in response woo Gertrude away from her worries or step in to separate Gertrude from her obligation. Instead, she instructed Gertrude to make good on her debt to Christ. "Pay out what you have,"[225] the Virgin pronounced, underscoring a duty to Christ that he himself had repeatedly brought to Gertrude's attention. Mary in this context acted as an enforcer for Christ, not an advocate before him. When Mechtild was disheartened to learn about the writing of the *Book of Special Grace*, she related to Mary that the two women most responsible for its composition had refused to show it to her. Mary offered the baby Jesus to Mechtild, saying, "Receive my Son, comfort of the afflicted, who can soothe your pain in everything."[226] The infant Christ freed Mechtild from her sorrow. Mary did not, however, intervene to challenge the production of the *Book of Special Grace*, whose creation Christ himself championed.

Thus Mary sometimes lifted emotional loads that pressed on the visionaries, sometimes allowed them, and sometimes guided the women by exhorting them to action they found irksome. Mary's actions signaled her care for Mechtild, Gertrude, and their sisters, as well as her participation in the daily web of their life, coming to them when they were at a rough pass, listening to them and offering ready remedy when they were disappointed or sad, or encouraging them to face and brace for their everyday vicissitudes—all in the service of her Son. Mary, Queen of Heaven,[227] before whom demons quake (they cannot bear even to hear her name),[228] employed her power to buttress her Son's expectations, neither subverting them nor softening them, but campaigning for Christ, proclaiming his justice. Although the *Book of Special Grace* celebrates that

[225] *Le Héraut* 3.1.2 (SCh 143:14).

[226] *Liber* 5.31 (370).

[227] *Liber* 1.42 (126); *Le Héraut* 3.19.1 (SCh 143:106).

[228] *Liber* 1.45 (130).

through the power of her mercy souls destined for eternal suffering are recalled and others snatched from the fires of purgatory,[229] the overall message of the Helfta writings is that Mary's authority, power, and mercy serve Christ's determination. Between mother and Son a spirit of collaboration reigns.[230]

The nuns' description of Mary's intervention is also sometimes cozy and playful. Gertrude once beheld Mary sweeping the convent's sins into a corner to keep them from God's view.[231] In one account, Mary gives dice to one of the nuns, instructing the woman in the game she should play with Mary's Son. Just as when a man plays dice with his wife and takes for himself as part of the game her rings, necklaces, and other jewels, she explains, so should the nun, Christ's spouse, take from her Spouse whatever he has and make it her own.[232] Mary's primary method of mediation opened up to the sisters experiences like her own in relation to her Son and Spouse. She sometimes enlivened Mechtild's affection so that Mechtild became like her: after Mechtild witnessed Mary embrace the child Jesus, Mechtild was moved to express her own love for the baby.[233] Gertrude noticed that when during Mass certain of her sisters advanced toward the altar to offer their prayers to the infant, snug in his mother's arms, Mary, moved by the nuns' devotion, assisted them; it was as if her baby were too frail to receive them without his mother's help.[234] At Matins on the feast of the Nativity, Gertrude saw Mary press the baby to the soul of each sister in turn, each of whom cradled him in

[229] *Liber* 1.44 (128).

[230] As Sharon Elkins has pointed out ("Gertrude the Great"), Christ and Mary tend, in the writings associated with Gertrude, to work cooperatively, and this is true in the *Book of Special Grace* as well. See also Brown, *Mary*, esp. 400–13.

[231] *Le Héraut* 4.9.3 (SCh 255:108).

[232] *Liber* 4.27 (284).

[233] *Liber* 1.5 (15–16).

[234] *Le Héraut* 4.3.7 (SCh 255:56).

the arms of her soul.[235] The *Book of Special Grace* attributes a similar vision to Mechtild,[236] and both works record a number of visions in which Mary offered her baby to the sisters' embrace.[237]

A commitment to *imitatio Mariae* may be at the root of an especially noteworthy series of visions of the Virgin that came to Gertrude on successive days between Christmas and the feast of the Presentation of Christ in the Temple when Christ is proclaimed the Light to the Gentiles. On the feast of Christ's Nativity, Gertrude received the baby Jesus, fresh from his mother's womb, and clasped him to her breast. Some days later, on the feast of the Purification, Gertrude's own desires were seemingly at cross-purposes with Mary's determination to wrest her Son from Gertrude.[238] Addressing herself to Christ, Gertrude writes in book two of the *Herald*,

> while the procession was taking place in which you . . . chose to be carried to the temple during the antiphon *cum inducerent*, your virginal Mother—with a severe expression on her face, as though she were not pleased with the way I was taking care of you, who are the honor and joy of her immaculate virginity—asked me to return you to her, you, the beloved little boy of her womb. And I—remembering that it was because of the grace she found with you that she was given to sinners for their reconciliation and to the desperate for their hope—exclaimed in these words, "O Mother of goodness, was it not for this that the fountain of mercy was given to you as your Son, so that you might obtain grace for those who need it and that you might cover with your copious charity the multitude of our sins and defects [1 Pet 4:8]?" At this, her face took on the expression of serene goodness. It was as if she showed me that although I merited

[235] *Le Héraut* 4.3.6 (SCh 255:52–54).

[236] *Liber* 1.5 (16–17).

[237] See for example *Le Héraut* 4.2 (SCh 255:36–44), and *Liber* 1.20 (72).

[238] *Le Héraut* 2.16 (SCh 139:290–98).

> apparent sternness for my evil deeds, she was nevertheless wholly filled up with internal charity, and she was pervaded to the marrow with divine charity. Her face soon lit up at my humble words, which had driven away all appearance of severity and replaced [it with] the serene sweetness that was natural to her temperament.[239]

At least since the nineteenth century, scholars have argued from this passage that "Gertrude was happiest when she related directly to the Christ-child" and did not have to contend with his mother.[240] There seems to be something else at stake here, however, as Ella Johnson has argued. Gertrude may be drawing on an established literary convention that Kate Greenspan has found in thirteenth-century Italian hagiographic writings, in which through the visionary gift of her Son, Mary facilitated holy women's imitation of her. As Greenspan argues, women in such scenarios became a "second Mary," experiencing the mother's joys and sorrows in their own jubilant reception of the Christ Child and in the suffering they endured when Mary obliged them to return her Son.[241]

Mary facilitated the nuns' imitation of her when she helped join them in marriage with her Son. We read for example of a woman beside whom in her final moments priests recited the litany while sisters encircled her; meanwhile an army of saints moved around them, each kneeling at the invocation of her or his name. Freed from her flesh, the sister's soul flew into the

[239] *Le Héraut* 2.16.3 (SCh 139:292–94).

[240] Preger, *Geschichte*, 129; Elkins, "Gertrude the Great," 724.

[241] Ella Johnson, "Reproducing," 8–9. Kate Greenspan provides several examples from thirteenth-century hagiographies of similar encounters between holy women and Mary ("*Matre Donante*," 26–37). For Gertrude's literary techniques, see Ella Johnson, " 'In mei memoriam facietis': Remembering Ritual and Refiguring 'Woman' in Gertrud the Great of Helfta's *Spiritualia Exercitia*," in *Inventing Identities: Re-examining the Use of Memory, Imitation, and Imagination in the Texts of Medieval Religious Women*, ed. Bradley Herzog and Margaret Cotter-Lynch (Hampshire: Palgrave Macmillan, 2012), 165–86.

arms of Mary, who delivered her into Christ's embrace.[242] During Mass celebrated on the occasion of the interdict, Mechtild saw the congregation at the altar, receiving the Lord's body from his own hand. Through a golden pipe, they sucked sweet liquid that flowed from his chest and into a bowl that Mary held at her Son's side. When Mass was over, each of Christ's fingers bore a gold ring, his pledge to each virgin who was to marry him.[243]

Like Mary, all the saints supported Christ's cause, working under his leadership. They sometimes seemed to pursue their cooperative efforts with a degree of independence, but they were fully coordinated with Christ, and their intercession with him on behalf of the sisters was never characterized as an attempt to override or even to bend his justice.[244] "I love those who love me [Prov 8:17],"[245] John declared, voicing words that the Helfta writings elsewhere attribute to Christ, endowing mutual love with the power to bind him in relationships with others; visions of John made clear his partiality for those disposed toward him. John's preference for those who loved him never compromised his commitment to ascertaining all parties' fealty to Christ, however. Gertrude's and Mechtild's relationship with John—like their relationship with Mary, like their relationship with all saints—is predicated on their collective status: all of them beloved by Christ, sharing love for Christ, and reciprocating love among each other. Thus John kept a

[242] *Liber* 5.6 (325–26).

[243] *Liber* 1.27 (96–97). For the ring as pledge of spiritual espousal, see *Exercices* 3.88–90 (SCh 127:114), and *Le Héraut* 3.2.1 (SCh 143:18–20). Taken from secular marriage ceremonies, the ring long served as a symbol in the consecration of nuns (René Metz, "La Couronne et l'Anneau dans la consecration des vierges: Origine et evolution des deux rites dans la liturgie latine," *Revue des sciences religieuses* 28 [1954]: 113–32).

[244] In contrast, see what Eamon Duffy has found for late medieval England (*The Stripping of the Altars: Traditional Religion in England 1400–1580* [New Haven, CT: Yale University Press, 1992], 186–87).

[245] *Le Héraut* 4.4.3 (SCh 255:62).

ledger in which he accounted for the services the sisters provided Christ, on which he would render judgment after each woman's death.[246]

Generous in sharing their gifts with others, the saints also discriminated in their distribution, reliant on Christ's judgment in electing those to whom to dispense these gifts. When the nuns chanted in Gregory's honor during Mass on his feast, Gertrude saw Gregory kneel and beseech Christ on behalf of the church. Christ opened his heart to Gregory, who placed his hands within Christ's heart and, from this heart, grasped grace to spread over the surface of the earth. At this moment, Gertrude saw a golden belt—symbol of divine justice—delimiting the sweep of grace by preventing it from falling on the unworthy and the ungrateful.[247] Although the saints' presence was ubiquitous, the gifts they channeled flowed in abundance but not to all or to the same purpose. The saints, in conformity with Christ, were both munificent and just. They and Mary modeled for the sisters that one ought to work in unity with Christ, in submission to his wishes, and according to his judgment.

Mary and the saints measured the merit of each woman in relation to the devotion of each to Christ, sometimes accusing the women: Mary complained that Mechtild had been unfaithful to her brother—Mary's Son; virgin saints accused Mechtild of not having loved her bridegroom with her whole self.[248] Mary and the heavenly figures, however, expressed no interest in ascertaining the nuns' veneration of *themselves*, in contrast to other depictions of Mary, popular in contemporary miracle accounts, in which allegiance to Mary sometimes appears to override for Mary any other aspect of the devotee's life.[249] Thus

[246] *Le Héraut* 4.16 (SCh 255:175).

[247] *Le Héraut* 4.10 (SCh 255:126).

[248] *Liber* 1.18 (55).

[249] Southern, *Making of the Middle Ages*, 247–50; Duffy, *Stripping of the Altars*, 187.

we read that from the time she was a child, Gertrude had a particular affection for Catherine (whom she once saw edged around by the fifty philosophers she had guided to heaven[250]), Agnes was especially dear to her,[251] and Bernard of Clairvaux's honey-sweet speech prompted a special devotion to him,[252] but none of these relationships threatened to peel Gertrude away from a connection to Christ. The monastery's writings did little to investigate associations between individual sisters and saints apart from laying bare aspects of Mechtild's and Gertrude's relationship with Christ that the associations implied. Virtually everything about the sisters' relationship to Mary and the saints points to their sense that these relationships drew all parties closer to Christ. This Christocentrism is evident in the sisters' relationship with John the Evangelist, who, after Mary, was the citizen of heaven who figured most prominently in the Helfta writings. And just as the nuns looked to Mary, they looked to John as model and intercessor.[253]

John the Evangelist figures more centrally than any other saint in the Helfta writings. The *Book of Special Grace* dedicates one discrete chapter (four printed pages) to him and the *Herald* two (eleven and two printed pages); he appears elsewhere in both texts more often than any other saint.[254] Both works catalogue reasons that John is superior among the saints, the enumeration in some respects recalling in structure and content the lists that became a basic component of thirteenth- and fourteenth-century Johannine *libelli*, those German-language compilations of devotional texts relating to John, some of which men composed (or translated) for women religious, and

[250] *Le Héraut* 4.54.1 (SCh 255:464).

[251] *Le Héraut* 4.50.8 (SCh 255:412–14).

[252] *Le Héraut* 4.49.1 (SCh 255:396).

[253] It was not uncommon for women religious to identify the two as particularly prized by Christ; see Hamburger, "Brother, Bride," 307–8.

[254] *Liber* 1.6 (21–24); *Le Héraut* 4.4 (SCh 255:58–80).

with which the Helfta nuns may have been familiar.[255] The Helfta writings relate John's and Jesus' love for each other, declaring the Evangelist's singular status as Christ's beloved.[256] In keeping with larger medieval trends, John was to the nuns both virgin and bride, who at the wedding at Cana (John 2:1-12) abandoned his earthly fiancée to follow his heavenly spouse, guarding his chastity in the pursuit.[257] John was a model for many contemporary and near contemporaries of the nuns, with special appeal for women religious, who gravitated toward him at least in part because of the affinity they felt as fellow brides and virgins.[258]

[255] *Liber* 1.6 (23–24). On these lists and the Johannine *libelli* more generally, see Annette Volfing, *John the Evangelist and Medieval German Writing: Imitating the Inimitable* (Oxford: Oxford University Press, 2001), 130–60; Hamburger, *St. John the Divine*, esp. 261, n. 2. In distinction to the *libelli*, the *Book of Special Grace* and the *Herald* encourage imitation of John's mystical experiences rather than expressing anxiety about attempts at imitation; on this aspect of the *libelli*, see Volfing, *John the Evangelist*, 133. Whether this is a gendered response to the matter is worth considering.

[256] *Liber* 1.6 (21–24); *Le Héraut* 4.34.1 (SCh 255:284).

[257] *Liber* 1.6 (23), and see *Le Héraut* 4.4.6; 4.4.7 (SCh 255:68, 70–72). For John as virgin bride of Christ in the later Middle Ages, see Hamburger, "Brother, Bride"; Hamburger, *St. John the Divine*, 159–60; Katherine Ludwig Jansen, *The Making of the Magdalen: Preaching and Popular Devotion in the Later Middle Ages* (Princeton: Princeton University Press, 2001), 150–51; Carolyn Diskant Muir, *Saintly Brides and Bridegrooms: The Mystic Marriage in Northern Renaissance Art* (London: Harvey Miller, 2012), 68. Dominican monasteries especially celebrated John together with Christ in statuary groups, widespread in these monasteries; Hamburger, *St. John the Divine*, 95; Muir, *Saintly Brides*, 79–80. We know that Helfta probably had a number of Dominican supervisors.

[258] On the centrality of John the Evangelist in the devotional literature of the later Middle Ages, see Volfing, *John the Evangelist*, 1. For the particular devotion of religious women to John, see Muir, *Saintly Brides*, 68, 81–85, and 85–86, and Hamburger, *St. John the Divine*, 20, 179–83. McDannell and Lang, *Heaven*, 106, claim that Gertrude believed that only female virgins could be brides of Christ. The case of John the Evangelist indicates otherwise, underscoring a similarity of purpose and achievement between the monastery's luminaries and John, rather than calling attention to differences associated with gender.

Just as they did with Mary, Mechtild and Gertrude taught themselves both to recognize themselves in John and to imitate him. The books mark their relationship as special,[259] one that Christ advanced so that they could become like John through association with him. Christ gave John to Gertrude as her guardian just as at the crucifixion he had commended his mother to John, and he joined them in special friendship like the one he and John enjoyed.[260] Christ spoke with Mechtild about John's compassionate presence at the foot of the cross, intensifying her interest in his beloved, and taught her to praise John, binding her more closely to John in prayer and contemplation.[261] The convent's literature portrayed Mechtild and Gertrude as similar to him in several basic ways. They, like him, were visionaries, recipients of divine insight, and virgin brides of Christ, whom Christ counted among his closest companions and fiercest loves.

In recounting John's and Christ's mutual love for each other, the nuns recalled their description of Mechtild's and Gertrude's own bond with Christ.[262] They pictured John, similar

[259] For Gertrude's devotion to John, see Vagaggini, *Theological Dimensions*, 769; Hamburger, *St. John the Divine*, 179–83; Muir, *Saintly Brides*, 86–87.

[260] *Le Héraut* 4.4.1–2 (SCh 255:60–62). John extends his loyalty to an anonymous sister (*Liber* 1.6 [23]), and Paquelin wonders whether she may be Gertrude of Helfta (*Liber* 1.6 [23, n. 1]).

[261] *Liber* 1.6 (22).

[262] For example, *Liber* 1.6 (21); *Le Héraut* 4.11 (SCh 255:78). Their elaboration of the relationship between the two men is steeped in complex notions of gender largely foreign to a modern sensibility inclined to see an expression of homoeroticism that the nuns (and their medieval counterparts, male and female) would not have supposed (see Hamburger, "Brother, Bride," 302–3). What Alexandra Barratt has written about the language of bridal mysticism that the nuns applied with regard to the image of Christ and Gertrude as bridegroom and bride is, in fact, more applicable to what the nuns write about the relationship between Christ and John: the nuns "tend not to exploit the image's sexual potential but instead stress emotional intimacy, mutual consideration and social niceties" ("The Woman Who Shares the King's Bed: The Innocent Eroticism of Gertrud the Great of Helfta," in *Intersections of Sexuality and the Divine in Medieval Culture: The Word Made Flesh*, ed. Susannah

to Mary in this regard as in others, as facilitating his imitation so as to further his devotees' intimacy with Christ. In the midst of prayer, Gertrude saw John hold Christ tenderly and tightly; she then prostrated herself at Christ's feet, her humility keeping her at a distance from her Lord and his beloved. Just then John called out to her, saying, "Do not let my fellowship [with Christ] cause you to flee. Behold the neck that is enough for the embrace of thousands and thousands of lovers, the mouth that offers sweetness to the kisses of many, and the ears that keep secrets safe from the whispers of all."[263]

John's intimacy with Christ is not a barrier to Gertrude. It is an invitation conducive to imitation, the gateway to Christ's embrace, his kisses, his confidence, and more. John's summons to Gertrude was also extended to all the sisters. John offered the course he ran in life as imitable, telling Gertrude that his celestial joys could belong to others.[264] All those reading this literature, the writings themselves convey, could expect that by cultivating a devotion to John approximating that of Gertrude and Mechtild, they might receive similar gifts from him. There is room for "thousands and thousands of lovers in Christ's embrace," John announced, inviting the reader to join him in Christ's arms.[265]

We read that, on another occasion, John snatched Gertrude up within him into heaven, placing her on the left side of Christ's breast and himself on the right, so that she could more easily drink in the love that through Christ's wound poured out of his heart, filling her with pleasure and, as the *Herald*

Mary Chewning [London: Routledge, 2016], 109). The nuns' relationship with Christ is intensely sensual, and their depiction of John's relationship with Christ is less so.

[263] *Le Héraut* 4.4.10 (SCh 255:76–78).

[264] *Le Héraut* 4.4.6 (SCh 255:68).

[265] *Le Héraut* 4.4.6 (SCh 255:68). John celebrates those who achieve a status analogous to his own in relation to Christ. Thus, for example, he, together with the Virgin Mary, presents the recluse Ysentrude to Christ as his bride (*Liber* 5.4 [321–22]).

suggests, offering her access to the mysteries she would go on to communicate in her writings.[266] Gertrude had in some sense become John,[267] taking up his place reclining on Christ's breast at the Last Supper (John 13:23-25), and imitation of John had become encounter with Christ. Similarly, the *Book of Special Grace* depicts Mechtild lying on Christ's breast, imbibing his teachings through the beating of his heart, just as in the medieval retelling of the biblical account Christ's heart was the source of divine wisdom for John, which he funneled to the church through his gospel.[268] And when Christ explained to Mechtild that John had soared to greater heights into the divine secrets than had any other saint, John's eyes, ears, mouth, and tongue beholding, hearing, and tasting the divine more than those of anyone else,[269] the statement sounds a lot like what book one relates about Mechtild's experience of Christ pressing himself against her soul, hands, ears, mouth, and heart, incorporating her into himself.[270]

Mechtild was another John, her straight-from-the source visionary teachings evocative of the mystical font of the production of his gospel and of Revelation, which medieval people associated with the Last Supper and with visions John received in Patmos.[271] As Annette Volfing has written, me-

[266] *Le Héraut* 4.4.4 (SCh 255:64).

[267] Hamburger, *St. John the Divine*, 180–81.

[268] Mechtild leans on Jesus' breast, and they speak together (*Liber* 1.1 [8]); she leans on his breast and hears his heartbeats inviting her to greater intimacy with him (*Liber* 2.1 [136]). For parallels between Mechtild and John, see Ann Marie Caron, "Invitations of the Divine Heart: The Mystical Writings of Mechthild of Hackeborn," ABR 45, no. 2 (1994): 326. For the late antique association of John's leaning on Christ's breast at the Last Supper with drinking in divine wisdom, see Annette Volfing, "The Authorship of John the Evangelist as Presented in Medieval German Sermons and *Meisterlieder*," *Oxford German Studies* 23 (1994): 8–10, and Volfing, *John the Evangelist*, 11.

[269] *Liber* 6 (23).

[270] *Liber* 1.1 (8–9).

[271] *Liber* 1.6 (23–24). Christ teaches Mechtild that John is especially worthy of praise because in his gospel and the book of Revelation John recorded the

dieval people were accustomed to assert that "nobody else was ever as close to Christ . . .; nobody else had such far-reaching visions; and nobody else wrote such important texts"[272] as did the Evangelist. The confidence with which Gertrude and Mechtild and their sisters conceived of the two holy women as similar to John speaks to a collective sense of the rightness of the monastery's commitment to collaborative- and sole-author writing projects. These projects were to them a reiteration as well as an interpretation of the biblical message, cut-to-the-heart testimonies of who God is and who they were and ought to be in relationship to him.

That the women of Helfta were equally at home in taking Mary and John as models should not be surprising.[273] For the most part, the literature tends to emphasize similarities among all saints, and the difference of gender between Mary and John paled for the nuns in meaning (or mattered not at all!) in comparison to their similarities. Both were virginal brides of Christ who delivered their beloved to others: in the flesh, in the case of Mary; through verbal and written communication, in John's case; and for both, through mystical mediation.[274] There were thus ways in which the nuns could imitate John—through word, written and spoken—in which they could not imitate Mary, although through revelation they inserted themselves into Mary's experiences as joyous and suffering mother. In lauding Mechtild's and Gertrude's successful imitation of John and Mary, the Helfta literature celebrated the achievements of the monastery's most esteemed members and held the two up as themselves admirable and imitable. Because, the writings

---

mysteries Christ had revealed to him (Barbara Nolan, *The Gothic Visionary Perspective* [Princeton: Princeton University Press, 1977], 9). For the breast as source of revelations, see Muir, *Saintly Brides*, 68.

[272] Volfing, *John the Evangelist*, 1.

[273] Ella Johnson, "Reproducing."

[274] Late medieval plastic art and literary works offer parallels between John and Mary as examples, mediators, and intercessors (Hamburger, "Brother, Bride," 296–327, esp. 304; and Hamburger, *St. John the Divine*, 97).

implied, all of its readers could be like the visionaries, all could be like Mary and John, and thus like all the saints.

Attention to imitation would thus have shifted the gaze of contemporary sisters onto themselves. In the optimistic spirituality of the Helfta convent, all members were taught that they could achieve intimacy with Christ and thus make him available to still others. When Mechtild saw Christ embracing Saint Agnes in the vision recounted above, she saw that on their matching red vestments were inscribed in gold Agnes's words that the sisters sang during the responsory, *Amo Christum;* the words on Christ's garment illuminated those on Agnes's, causing hers to shine back onto his with their own splendor. The notion of reciprocity lodged in the image of light opens up their relation to others. For as we read, the light that bounced between the two simultaneously illuminated the choir and all who stood there.[275] In marveling at the devotion of Gertrude and Mechtild, the Helfta writings sought to entice readers to strive after analogous relationships. The world now hidden around and within each nun was pregnant with possibility, and if she became attuned to this reality, each might aspire to have for herself the kind of mutually gratifying and spiritually productive relationships that belonged to Agnes, John, Mary, Mechtild, and Gertrude.[276]

[275] *Liber* 1.11 (57). The *Herald* makes a similar point about Agnes and Christ, identifying the sisters' liturgical song as immediately precipitating these phenomena. Gertrude perceives that the words they sing and attribute to Agnes provoke a stirring in the heart of the sisters who chant in the saint's honor; that Christ adorns Agnes with this devotion, distilling it into her heart; and that she transfers this gift back to the sisters themselves—yet another expression of the value of the circulation of gifts (*Le Héraut* 4.8.2 [SCh 255:106–8]).

[276] Scholars have not failed to notice this centrally important dimension of the literature. McDannell and Lang, for example, recognized in their study of heaven in the Helfta writings the significance in the inclusion in the *Spiritual Exercises* of a liturgy in which the nuns celebrate their union with Christ, connecting it to the literature's overall insistence that the experiences ascribed to Mechtild and Gertrude can belong to others. As the *Spiritual Exercises* instruct,

Coincidence of Opposites: Individuality and Community

In images and declarative statements as well as in silences, the Helfta writings made claims related to their universal invitation to relationship with God. In so doing, they further elucidated the nature of God's love for human beings. The revelations ascribed to Gertrude and Mechtild provided evidence of the broad reach of Christ's affection and documented his love for his many friends and his intimacies and union with them. He was the *paterfamilias* of a large, convivial family, and a sympathetic friend surrounded by an expansive circle of intimates, a king in whose sumptuous court every member was co-consort, a king or queen, with each one of whom he shared not a portion but the whole of his kingdom.[277] Each saint was his lover, his king, his queen.[278] With arms outstretched on the cross, he was ready to hold all who wished for his embrace.[279]

As a further mark of the communal cast of the relationship with Christ that the Helfta literature offers its readers, it contains scant sense of heaven affording its inhabitants pleasures associated with solitude or privacy or the fulfillment of longing for one-on-one intimacy with God in isolation from others'

---

the leader of the prayer intones, "in the kiss of your honeyed mouth take me as your possession into the bridal chamber of your beautiful love" (which McDannell and Lang call "seemingly individualistic"), only to have the whole community answer in unison, "We beseech Thee to hear us" (McDannell and Lang, *Heaven*, 103–4, citing *Les Exercices* 3:170–72 [SCh 127:104]).

[277] *Liber* 1.34 (114). Gertrude sees Christ caressing Saint Margaret with affection (*Le Héraut* 4.45.1 [SCh 255:344–46]), and she sees Jesus holding Mary Magdalene's chin as he embraces her with his words (*Le Héraut* 4.46.1 [SCh 255:348–50]). Mechtild sees Christ holding the Magdalene in his arms (*Liber* 1.25 [86]), and on Catherine's feast day, the saint appeared to Mechtild enveloped in a vestment covered in gold wheels, with two panels of her cloak held together by two hands also cast in gold and signifying the happy and indivisible union of Catherine's soul with God (*Liber* 1.32 [110–11]).

[278] *Liber* 1.34 (113).

[279] *Liber* 1.35 (116).

company. Although Gertrude did see John all alone swimming in the ocean of divinity, a throng of saints surrounded him and his Lord when John was nestled on Christ's breast.[280] When Mechtild similarly received a vision of John lounging with Christ, the two men were not alone: a multitude of dancing saints surrounded them.[281] On the feast of the Assumption, Mechtild saw Mary in bed, with Mary's soul reposing in the arms of her Son, who was filling her with a stream of divine riches; again all the saints encircled mother and Son.[282] Affectionate encounters that Mary and individual saints enjoyed with God took place under the watch of fellow citizens of heaven, with no concern that the quality of the encounter might be diminished by the observing presence of others.[283]

The literature responds to those for whom God's promiscuity might cause concern or confusion. Traveling through the heavens, Mechtild saw God the Father seated at a table with Abbess Gertrude, "caressing her with the sweetest and most loving words and gestures, *as if it were his only joy* [emphasis added] and delight to feast in this way with the soul."[284] The remark seems like an effort to reassure the wary that God's love for the many did not dilute his love for each. Further insistences on the uncompromised nature of God's love appear in a vision that tells of his love's remaining fastened on each nun even as it extended to others. Mechtild saw light pouring out of the Father and entering her heart; this light was the baby Jesus, whom she offered to her sisters in choir, one at a time. The baby clung to the heart of each, the text continues, while remaining with Mechtild.[285] As a narrator elsewhere explains, "God loves each person with the same love, yet he looks

[280] *Le Héraut* 4.4.5 (SCh 255:66–68).
[281] *Liber* 1.6 (23).
[282] *Liber* 1.26 (90).
[283] *Le Héraut* 5.32.2 (SCh 331:3).
[284] *Liber* 6.9 (388–89).
[285] *Liber* 1.5 (16–17).

on each one as if he loved no one else."[286] This was a central matter on which the Helfta writings insisted.

The unyielding repetition with which the *Herald* and the *Book of Special Grace* asserted the passionate, preferential, mutual love Gertrude and Mechtild shared with God—the evidence mounts, examples tossed out one after the other, relentlessly, so as to overwhelm—was calculated to elucidate and make irrefutable just this point: Christ trained a love of spectacular force fully on Mechtild, charged with uncompromising attention to her needs, her desires, her curiosities, and her preoccupations, a love so voluptuous as to seem to banish from his consideration anyone else. And just so he loved Gertrude. Knowing that he loved an unlimited number of creatures on heaven and earth who brought him happiness,[287] Gertrude nevertheless heard Christ say to her, "without you I cannot live happily."[288]

Embracing a sort of coincidence of opposites that gets to the heart of the message they wish to convey, the *Book of Special Grace*, the *Herald*, and the *Spiritual Exercises* taken together announced that the favored love that Christ harbored for Mechtild and for Gertrude was available to all the nuns, that the singular love with which Christ loves those whom he loves is the love he wished all the monastery to desire. Christ insisted over and over that both Mechtild and Gertrude were irreplaceable in his eyes.[289] Especially when the composite writings are read together, therefore, they imply, paradoxically, that this wildly preferential sort of love is precisely the one that the reader should hunger to make her own; it is hers to accept.[290] The fine focus on the principal figure in each book that has seemed to

[286] *Liber* 6.8 (387). As Barbara Newman writes about the *Book of Special Grace*, "since each person knows herself to be infinitely beloved of God, envy never rears its head" (introduction to *Mechtild of Hackeborn*, 9).

[287] Lewis, "God and the Human Being," 306.

[288] *Le Héraut* 3.5.1 (SCh 143:26).

[289] See for example *Le Héraut* 1.7 (SCh 139:156).

[290] See for example *Liber* 1.35 (116).

some commentators small-minded and cloying[291] has as a prime rationale the goal of shifting the reader's attention away from the more obvious subject and onto others, including and especially herself.

The hagiographical account of Abbess Gertrude's life in heaven is evidence of the welcoming call of the celestial spheres, prying open the possibility of an eternity of delight to all readers. Dancing hand in hand with her bridegroom covered with flowers, the abbess offered one of the red gems—symbol of the passion—that adorned her gown to a sister who had served her faithfully; trust in God's mercy, she bade her daughter, instructing her how to make her way toward the celestial dance.[292] In an implied expression of *imitatio Christi* and a dazzlingly risky display of assurance in their monastery's mirroring of the bliss of eternity, Abbess Gertrude, so the authors of the *Book of Special Grace* write, treated all the women in her charge so that each thought herself most loved. In yet another assertion of the proximity of heaven to earth, a foretaste of the experience of preferential love the nuns hungered for from Christ was available to them even now, their literature taught, in the person of their abbess.[293]

Augmenting the Joy of the Saints

The nuns maintained the meaningfulness to Mary and the saints of their intervention in the lives of the sisters. They understood that for heaven's inhabitants, it was a privilege and a pleasure to help and witness the living receive the sorts of gifts that Christ had bestowed on them.[294] When Mechtild,

[291] See introduction.

[292] *Liber* 6.7 (385–86).

[293] *Liber* 6.1 (374).

[294] Mechtild understood that God gave the privilege of giving all that Christ worked in them to those who loved the gifts God had given the saints (*Liber* 1.11 [35]). For the privilege of intercession that Christ conferred on Mary Magdalene, see *Liber* 1.25 (88). It is a privilege in which the saints, as we read, take pleasure (*Le Héraut* 4.4.4; 4.3.8 [SCh 255:64, 56]).

swept up in heaven, leapt with joy, embraced Christ, and feasted with him in the company of the celestial household, the saints themselves rejoiced and thanked God for Mechtild's happiness.[295] In this and in other ways, the Helfta literature drew attention to the sisters' role in fashioning the experience of saved souls in heaven, and it celebrated the sisters' participation in the joy of the saints.[296]

The nuns' ability to affect the holy dead was, they found, nowhere more acute than during liturgical observances. So for example, on one occasion

> when the convent was communicating, . . . [Mechtild] saw the soul of . . . [the abbess] standing with incredible beauty at the right hand of God, and the Lord impressed on her as many sweet kisses as the number of people who communicated; in this way was expressed her special merit, which she has because she so faithfully demanded of the sisters that they take communion often and freely.[297]

Christ's kisses expressed the value of the counsel the abbess gave her daughters; while she was alive, she encouraged their frequent communion. In heaven, the abbess was remunerated for the fruit of her labor, the eucharistic piety of her daughters. It was not, this passage suggests, the abbess's instruction per se (or the intention that infused her deed) that secured the increase of kisses, however. The *Book of Special Grace* drew attention to the significance of the nuns' continuing eucharistic devotion for the abbess: the number of kisses Christ bestowed on her was in proportion to the number of those who communicated. Medieval theologians, mystics, and pious people elaborated the notion that souls' rewards in heaven correspond to degrees of meritorious works. The nuns did not work

[295] *Liber* 1.19 (79).

[296] The idea that the saints rejoice in the right actions of the living is widespread in the Middle Ages. See, for example, Duffy, *Stripping of the Altars*, 160–61.

[297] *Liber* 5.2 (319).

through the dynamics of the instruction, devotion, and kisses, however. They were far more interested in the expression of reward (the kisses) and its relation to *their* labors (the abbess's teachings, the sisters' piety) than on elaborating the theological mechanics of the abbess's remuneration, which neither the *Herald* nor the *Book of Special Grace* explores.

Elsewhere we learn that once during Mass, Mechtild wished she were a queen so that she might make an offering of gold on behalf of her deceased sister, the abbess. Christ right away appeared to Mechtild in the form of a young king, and Mechtild led him before the altar, at which, for the abbess's joy, Christ offered himself with love to God the Father, and the abbess fell into her bridegroom's embrace.[298] In this account, the desire Mechtild directed toward her sister precipitated an expression of Christ's love for Abbess Gertrude. Furthermore, the image of Christ as king and Mechtild as queen evokes a sense of teamwork between the two. This vision suggests that the thoughts the living have about the dead in heaven and the yearning that permeates their musings call forth a cooperative response in Christ, which redounds to the benefit of the holy dead.

Additional instances tell of the sisters' singing the liturgy as augmenting the joy of the saints. In a vision that comes to Gertrude on the feast of the Assumption, she rushes into Christ's arms and strives to sing each word of the antiphon *Tota pulchra est* on the instrument of Christ's heart. Thanks to this act, streams from the divine heart inundate Mary's heart, from which the waters seem to gush, and subsequently all the saints gather with joy around the Lord and are ravished with inexpressible admiration.[299] On the feast of Saint Agnes, Mechtild perceived that each of her sisters, worshiping in com-

[298] *Liber* 6.9 (389–90).

[299] *Le Héraut* 4.8 (SCh 255:366). For an additional example of singing the liturgy as augmenting the joy of the saints, see *Liber* 6.9 (388).

mon, facilitated a flowing out of the divinity into Saint Agnes. Mechtild saw a ray of light proceeding from the heart of each woman who at Matins chanted the responsory *Amo Christum*, a repetition of Agnes's declamation; each ray entered Christ's heart, from where it flowed, like a liquid, into the heart of Agnes.[300] Through the medium of chant, the sisters inserted themselves into Agnes's relationship with Christ, accentuating their own importance to the virgin martyr's experience of heaven. There is no hint in the *Book of Special Grace* that the love between Christ and Agnes is in any way deficient. Mechtild's vision underscores both the long-ago profession of love for Christ that Agnes had made and the mutuality of their love that now joins Agnes with Christ in a heavenly embrace. Nevertheless, the sisters made room for their contribution to the expression of this reciprocal love. The relationship between Christ and Agnes is intimate, but it is nonetheless associated with others. The language of the liturgy provides the nuns with the opportunity to incorporate each member of their monastic community in this relationship and, in doing so, to channel the divinity to one among the saints.

As the Helfta literature relates, the memories the holy dead harbored of sources of satisfaction and delight while they were alive were central to their joy in heaven. A number of passages in the *Book of Special Grace* make evident the nuns' understanding that they might spark merry memories for the saints and for Mary.[301] When Mechtild prayed to Saint Catherine on behalf of a particular sister, Catherine told Mechtild that if the sister chanted, "Come my beloved, come into your spouse's bridal chamber," this antiphon would recall to Catherine the experience of martyrdom, when, upon hearing Christ summon her with these words, Catherine's heart melted with love.[302]

[300] *Liber* 1.11 (34–35).

[301] See for example *Le Héraut* 4.12.4 (SCh 255:136).

[302] *Liber* 1.32 (111).

Let her "remind me of the joy," Catherine directed Mechtild,[303] promising to look favorably on the sister who did so.[304]

Through their devotions, then, the sisters provided an opportunity for the holy dead to reflect on joy-filled experiences with Christ that took place before death rushed them into heaven. Indeed, the sisters attributed to the sung prayer they offered during Mass and Office the jogging of Christ's own memories, to the benefit of Mary and the saints. One passage from the *Herald* relates that a particular responsory the sisters intoned stirred Christ's recollection in such a way as to bring joy to his Mother. When the sisters sang *Descendit de caelis*, a vision came to Gertrude in which the Lord seemed to her to remember the love with which he had entered his mother's womb. Liquefied by love at this recollection, Christ fixed his sight on Mary, causing her to shudder; he kissed her, inducing in her a renewal of the joy of conception; then Gertrude saw that Mary's uterus, transparent as crystal, became wholly filled with the divinity.[305] In this account, the sisters' ability to affect Mary was predicated on Christ's receptive response to their devotions. Christ was susceptible to the nuns' song, which prompted in him a reminiscence that impelled a series of events, all of which had direct bearing on Mary's contemporaneous experience in heaven.

The Helfta writings elsewhere made clear that devotion to Christ brought great happiness to Mary. Thus at the offertory on the feast of the Nativity, Gertrude saw that her sisters' care for Jesus pleased Mary, who helped the women deliver their prayers to him. Sisters reading this account in the *Herald* might

[303] *Liber* 1.32 (111). On the importance of memory, God's and Catherine's, to the saints' joy in heaven, see *Liber* 1.34 (114–15).

[304] *Liber* 1.41 (125). And for indications of the value to Mary of recalling aspects of her experience to her, see *Liber* 1.29; 1.42 (99, 126). For the medieval conviction that Mary rejoiced when the faithful voiced the angelic salutation, see Brown, *Mary*, 63.

[305] *Le Héraut* 4.3.3–4 (SCh 255:50–52). For the gifts that Christ promises those who remind him of his joys, see for example *Liber* 1.19 (65).

have found in it cause for self-satisfaction to mingle with the gratitude for Mary's mediation, gratitude that, it is plain, this revelation sought to elicit in them. They may have considered that their devotion to Christ (aided by Mary) profited not only themselves but Mary as well. In this context, it is not surprising to find in the *Herald* the assertion that Gertrude's union with Christ increased the joy of all the holy dead.[306] Once, we read, Gertrude received the Host and then saw her soul in the form of a tree, whose root was affixed to the wound in Christ's side. She felt Christ's humanity and divinity infuse her, and she prayed that Christ would give to others the favor he had thus bestowed on her. Then, seeing herself, she saw

> [that] each kind [of fruit] in which the fruit of the tree appeared . . . began to exude a most efficacious liquid, some of which, flowing into those [in heaven] . . ., increased their joy; some of which, . . . flowing into purgatory, mitigated the punishments of those there; some of which, . . . flowing onto the earth, augmented the sweetness of the grace of the just and the bitterness of penitence of the sinners.[307]

Gertrude's assimilation to Christ and her plea that he share the benefits of her union with him cause Christ's humanity and divinity to wash over both the souls, living and dead, and the saints, as an expression of solidarity among them. The nuns knew, of course, that Christ was responsible for the expansion of the saints' joy. But the passage highlights Gertrude's union with Christ and her solicitude for the living and the dead as yoking her in a cooperative endeavor with him.

The sisters' understanding of their contribution to the society of saints does not attest to dependency on part of the saints, who were already redeemed, already wholly joyful. Yet the nuns were unequivocal that they were of reliable significance to the saints. Their writings were flush with traces of

[306] *Le Héraut* 4.3.8 (SCh 255:56).
[307] *Le Héraut* 3.18.6 (SCh 143:86).

heady self-importance. They believed that what they did at Mass and in Office, as well as during chapter and in other day-to-day devotions, was meaningful even to those already bathed in the bliss of eternity. Although the Helfta literature again and again praised God as source of all rewards and of all the meritorious works crowned by those rewards, it never compromised the importance of the nuns' contribution to a joint endeavor. The *Book of Special Grace* instructed readers that there is no action, however small, that if performed on earth in God's praise fails to increase the joy and glory of all the saints.[308]

The nuns' confidence in their ability to increase the saints' joy is predicated on the assumption that in heaven, the soul's joy will continue to grow. Increase constituted the very nature of joy, and indeed the joy of heaven consisted in part in the saints' knowing absolutely that their happiness would never level off but forever climb.[309] The nuns even charged themselves with recalling this reality to the saints![310] As depicted in the Helfta writings, the state of saved souls in heaven was characterized by jumps in joy and a variety of experiences that, from the perspective of the sisters, did not depend exclusively on God, who did not demand the undivided attention of the holy dead. The celestial experience was one on which the sis-

[308] *Liber* 1.31 (106).

[309] *Liber* 1.34 (114–15). It may be helpful to consider this understanding within the context of a basic tension in pre-modern Christian conceptions of heaven. On the one hand, medieval people envisaged heaven as stasis, an experience of souls abiding in the stillness of eternal rest (*requies aeterna*), and, on the other hand, they conceived of heaven as both liberating the soul's desire for God from constrictions that in this earthly life weigh it down and as meeting joy's eternal expansion with wave after wave of satisfaction. Most theologians in the thirteenth and fourteenth centuries emphasized heaven as stasis (Caroline Walker Bynum, *The Resurrection of the Body in Western Christianity, 200–1330*, Lectures on the History of Religions, Sponsored by the American Council of Learned Societies, New Series Number 15 [New York: Columbia University Press, 1995], 227–341).

[310] *Liber* 1.34 (114–15).

ters were sure that they, in cooperation with Christ, had direct and substantive effect. Their writings sought to steel and steady contemporary sisters and future generations at Helfta in their monastic commitments by documenting the sisters' efficacy, insisting on the joy with which they colored the heavens, and revealing that in doing so, they—each of them—moved heaven and earth a little closer together.

It may help to make further sense of the Helfta piety to locate the nuns' thought within the context of the widespread medieval conviction that the saints rejoiced in one another's presence, a belief that found clear and clamorous expression in the Helfta literature.[311] A central feature of heaven as the nuns conceived of it was that it abounded in what Colleen McDannell and Bernhard Lang have called "social joys,"[312] joys experienced by this or that saint or by a whole group of saints based in another saint's earthly accomplishments on behalf of the church or the divine delights another saint enjoyed. This joy, the literature suggests, participates in God's joy, whose joy in each saint is as if it were his sole joy, again drawing attention to the importance of sharing in one another's joy.

As the Helfta works depicted this idea, the saints were alert to one another's presence and eager for new membership in their society. Thus the arrival of souls in heaven caused welcoming jubilation on the part of those who had preceded them.[313] The saints were aware of who each soul was when she or he was on earth, and such knowledge gave them pleasure. Mechtild beheld the monastery's founder, Count Burchard,

[311] One of Mary's titles is "Joy of All the Saints" (*Gaudium Omnium Sanctorum*) (*Liber* 1.38 [122]). Saints give joy to one another (*Le Héraut* 4.10 [SCh 255:78]).

[312] McDannell and Lang, *Heaven*, 92. For medieval theologians' notions about the role of the company of the saints in relation to the bliss of heaven, see Forshaw, "Heaven," New Catholic, 6:686.

[313] *Liber* 6.9 (389). For the joy a soul delivered from purgatory brings to the saved, see Le Goff, *Purgatory*, 266.

surrounded by his heirs and deceased members of the monastic household, each of whom recited a poem narrating all the good she or he had accomplished during her or his lifetime. As the count listened to their recitations, his heart filled with happiness.[314] The *Book of Special Grace* and the *Herald* insist, moreover, that the joy and merit that belong to any one of the saints is shared by every other saint,[315] a phenomenon that Barbara Newman has termed a "communism of merits."[316] When Mechtild asked Christ how she should glorify the saints, he responded, providing the most concise statement anywhere in the Helfta literature that the saints participate fully in one another's joy and merit:

> Praise my goodness in the saints, whom I have given bliss so great that they do not only in themselves abound in all good things as individuals. But truly the joy of any one of the saints is augmented by the other saints to such an extent that any one of the saints rejoices from the goods of another saint more than any mother ever could exult in the exaltation of her only child or a father in the glorious triumph of his son. And thus any saint possesses, in extreme jubilant charity, the reward peculiar to each saint.[317]

The nuns' assurance in their ability to affect the society of the saints was interwoven with their supposition that they were themselves in some sense already incorporated into this society. "There is no difference between the way in which the saints enjoy God and my soul's union with him," Mechtild confided in a friend,[318] and in her encounters with the saints,

[314] *Liber* 5.10 (334–36).

[315] *Liber* 1.31 (110).

[316] Newman, introduction to *Mechthild of Hackborn,* 20. The Helfta writings thus insist on both a hierarchy among the saints in heaven and a sharing of each saint's merits and joys with every other saint, so smoothing out differences among the saints that hierarchy reinforces.

[317] *Liber* 1.34 (113).

[318] *Liber* 2.26 (170).

she was not simply a voyeur; as scholars have observed, she participated in the heavenly society.[319] Indeed, so intimate was her affiliation with the saints that she encountered them in her heart, which she entered as if it were a beautiful vineyard and found them there beside a fountain that sprinkled them with waters flowing from Christ's heart. Then she entered Christ's heart, and at his command, she offered the saints everything that was hers, all his heart contained, heaven and earth.[320] On another occasion, Mechtild was so filled with grace that it was as though her body were, like a river, flowing into all the saints, and the saints' hearts were like lamps, alight with the gift that God had suffused into Mechtild's soul.[321]

Elsewhere, when angels carried Gertrude up into a heavenly Mass, she saw Christ withdraw his heart from his body, and it assumed the shape of an altar, on which he placed a chalice into which the angels poured a lifetime of Gertrude's trials and tribulations. Then, "the Lord immediately blessed this chalice with the sign of the holy cross, in the manner of a priest consecrating the Host," the saints raised their own hearts, which took on the form of straws, and inserted these into the chalice.[322] Here the stuff of Gertrude's life, transformed by Christ and into him, became incorporated into the saints. Gertrude was in some sense already in heaven, and through Gertrude's person, a convergence of sorts took place between the communities of the living and the dead. In their ability to affect the saints, the nuns regarded themselves as remarkably like the saints. When the *Herald* and the *Book of Special Grace* voiced the nuns' successful efforts to add to the fund of the saints' happiness, it must

[319] See for example Caron, "Invitations," 335; Barbara Kline, "The Discourse of Heaven in Mechtild of Hackeborn's *Booke of Gostlye Grace*," in *Imagining Heaven in the Middle Ages: A Book of Essays*, ed. Jan S. Emerson and Hugh Feiss (Milton Park, UK: Taylor and Francis, 2000), 83–99.

[320] *Liber* 1.22 (79–81).

[321] *Liber* 2.17 (151).

[322] *Le Héraut Missa*, 9.22–24 (SCh 331:298).

have seemed to their cloistered readers that—however partially and however provisionally—the sisters had even now secured membership in this holy community.

The communion of saints is the larger context within which to situate the nuns' appraisal of their ability to affect the society of saints as well as their integration into this society. As expressed in late medieval thought and practice, the concept was undergirded by the conviction that the living and the dead were friends and confederates, eager to give expression to their solicitude for one another. Colored with confidence in human beings' capacity to offer one another mutual assistance across death's porous divide, the communion of saints cemented links between all the living and all the dead, with the sole exception of those in hell. In the general pattern of late medieval thought, the aid the living and the dead provided one another depended on a tripartite division of those on pilgrimage, the needy dead in purgatory, and the holy dead in heaven. In its basic outlines, the communion of saints implied a universe shot through with reciprocal bonds of obligation: the living helped the dead in purgatory, and the saints in turn rendered assistance to those on earth. It spoke of a chain of interlocking communities, whose members' sympathy for one another, shared interests, and common aspirations bound them in association.

In the claim made by the Helfta literature that the saints were aware of the veneration that the nuns offered them, and in its recognition of the snug bonds between the community of the living and the society of the saints as well as of the routine presence and intervention of the holy dead in the daily lives of those still on the march, it was in keeping with larger currents in thirteenth-century piety. What sets the religiosity of these nuns apart from that of their contemporaries is the unabashed enthusiasm with which they projected themselves onto the particulars of the saints' experience of heaven and their firm trust in the relevance to the saints of their own desires and devotions. The nuns were frankly unable to conceive of a relationship with any group of people that did not credit them with benefiting that community. What may be unexpected is that the sisters' relationship with the saints was to them at least as obviously reciprocal as was their relationship with souls in purgatory. Joined to this attitude and vivifying it was a notion of the Body of Christ in which each member was finely calibrated to every other member or attuned to all others—because all who will be saved in some basic sense really *are* Christ.[323] He is the Head; they are the members, the authors of the *Book of Special Grace* wrote, echoing 1 Corinthians.[324] "The glory of my members is no different from my glory," Christ explained to Mechtild.[325] Thus Christ presented himself before the Father with the souls of all the elect in himself:

> Those who having ascended with him were present as well as all those who would be present in the future, with the works, the sufferings, and the merits of each. Even those who are currently in a state of sin appeared in the way in which they would in the future be in heaven. Truly, loving souls and souls who suffered patiently for Christ glowed in his heart with special splendor, while the rest shimmered in other parts of his body.[326]

[323] Mechtild at least once expressed recognition that her relationship with Christ incorporated all those who were united with him using the image of the harp: Christ is a harp, whose strings are all souls that are united in God (*Liber* 2.2 [139]). Therese Schroeder-Sheker observes that Mechtild's visions ignore the fact that instruments were forbidden within the liturgy ("The Alchemical Harp of Mechthild von Hackeborn," *Vox benedictina* 6, no. 1 [1989]: 49).

[324] *Liber* 1.20 (76).

[325] *Liber* 1.19 (67).

[326] *Liber* 1.20 (72–73).

Epilogue

The Helfta writings present us with a world in which nothing any of us does is empty of meaning, and in which everything each of us does affects every one of us, with the exception of those in hell. Driving home our vulnerability to one another, they accentuate the productive consequences for all parties of this interdependence. Where the literature acknowledges deleterious effects of failing to cultivate mutual reliance, it does so for effect: to combat an individual's pride and inculcate humility; to affirm the power of prayer; to stretch the nuns' (and their larger audiences') recognition of the reach of their community, comprised of all who will be saved; to admit that commitment to the other may require both a nurturing of imagination (of the value of the other) and sustaining certain (apparent and temporary, because not yet swept up and transformed in the glory of eternity) costs to self; and to announce the immediate and profound significance to Christ—and thus to self—of cherishing, or neglecting to cherish, other members of our community.

In the nuns' perception, the individual is forever a member of a larger, expansive, community, her well-being tied uncompromisingly to the spiritual health of the whole, which can be cause for suffering or—as the literature's fervent optimism underscores—for joy. This is because all are one body, a reality the Helfta writings never tire of impressing upon the reader. Sometimes they illustrate the point with graphic immediacy, but more often it hovers in the background, the Pauline insight—"Just as a body, though one, has many parts, but all its many parts form one body, so it is with Christ" (2 Cor 12:12)—

animating virtually every aspect of the relationship between self and other about which the nuns write. The claim (or, as the nuns would prefer, awareness) of interconnectivity is the foundation for their relentless focus on community as well as for their emphasis on human beings' ability to affect Christ himself, whose susceptibility to his devotees' ministrations has consequences for community that, as the nuns saw it, are hard to exaggerate. From a certain vantage point, the Helfta preoccupation with the Pauline imagery is conventional. It stands apart, however, for its centrality to their thought, their eager, go-at-it exploration of the relationship between individual and community, their sunny stance about the possibility of reconciling one woman's desires with those of others and with faithfulness to the whole, their keen sensitivity to the lack of hard boundaries between selves, and their astonishing confidence in the power of the individual to move Christ himself, and thus to affect all.

Joined to the insistence on the meaningfulness of community was an equally deliberate, finely focused, and insistent concern with the individual, cast in terms that recognized each person as different from every other, worthy of Christ's love, discriminating and seeming to be trained exclusively on her. Most important to the nuns was the belief that Christ meets each person with an always-desiring love that attends to her specificity, mindful of her distinctive needs and wants, in this way bringing into view each person's particularity while never closely investigating it. This was in part because the nuns forbore making rigid distinctions among themselves. While they celebrated the spiritual luminaries among them, they laid bare a democratic offer of opportunity and disclosed a basic commonality of experience among the sisters, brightly colored by belief in the potential of each human being to love God and to collaborate in a joint venture to redeem all souls and increase the joy of the saints. The literature depicts the convent as supremely happy, confident in the immensity of its collective contribution to the salvation of the world and unquestioning its value to God, a community he generously judged, comforted, and encouraged, even as he pushed the women to greater displays of love.

An evangelical impulse propelled the nuns' consideration, too, for the world outside their monastery. For although their thoughts were for the most part fairly tightly trained on themselves, they were eager that others should join them in their cooperative work with Christ. Thus while they appear largely at ease in asserting the superiority of their state of life, there are moments in the literature that allow us to see them questioning their own preeminence, suggesting (to themselves) that this was built on a perspectival (and, therefore, limited) consideration of what is pleasing to Christ, whose appraisal of others—subtle, discerning—they determined to take as a model for their own. And, however haltingly, they called themselves to a more considered assessment of the spiritual worth of those who did not share in their monastic life.

It was fundamentally the nuns' notion of love's dynamic that undergirded their conception of community and individuality as mutually complementary. Lavish in documenting the immoderate displays of affection Christ showers on each person whom he loves, the nuns maintained that the delicious reality they described was not only compatible with the far-flung travels of their Beloved's ardor but intensified by it. For they conceived that love—in a single corresponding and harmonious movement—spiraled outward in ever-wider circles, exactly as it seemed to find wholly satisfying shelter in relationship with one person. Perhaps the sisters sought in this way to acknowledge and to still a longing, however muted, for exclusivity, at odds with the Pauline insight and in tension with their sense of God's profligate generosity. But they nowhere confessed to this desire, if indeed it existed. God's condescending indebtedness for their responsive love for him precipitated, they believed, a spilling out from him of more love, triggering a renewal of love's gifts for his beloved—and drenching the cosmos, a self-generating process.

Although accusing themselves of inadequacies in their conception of community, the nuns accepted unassailable boundaries with equanimity: those in hell were permanent outcasts. So fundamental was their sense of community to their perception of reality, however, that they seem almost unable to indulge in giving shape to those individuals forever expelled from the Body of Christ. Images of hell and attestations to its existence pop up here and there, but the nuns did not admit to the notion that God might consign anyone known to them to eternal perdition. Thus it is possible to say that the God of the Helfta nuns was both severe, punishing and damning, *and* wildly generous; the nuns were bewitched by his mercy, palpable in the give-and-take among members of the Body of Christ that he engendered and that bound them all to one another, now and always.

The women of Helfta insisted on the coincidence of opposites between individual and community, frequently exhibiting in moments of contemplation and ecstasy a fluency in directing themselves simultaneously to fellow members of Christ's Body, sure that the spiritual progress and delights of one could belong to another. But they also recognized that they sometimes struggled to manage a one-on-one relationship with Christ along with other-engagement, their relationships with sinners as well as with the saints. They assumed that it would take a lifetime of learning and the promptings of grace to do so well, and the Helfta writings invite the reader to the responsible course of action, to imitating those who love successfully, especially Mary and John the Evangelist. Such imitation is in itself an exercise in living the sort of love of which Mary and John are prime exemplars, they believed, a love that puts God foremost and consequently effortlessly channels his love to others.

The nuns were serene and adamant in their conviction that residues of resistance and of ineptness in loving would fully dissolve in heaven, releasing them into a festival of friends, where—because the love that unites God and saved souls assimilates them to each other—a turning to God is always a flawless movement to all members of his Body. The workings of love in eternity would not, they promised, wash away or dilute the experience of particular love but preserve the integrity of the individual in her relationships. A sister soul rejoicing in the celestial spheres could count on being forever secure in the snug bond of her monastic household, whose vigilant concern with self and other in community had in this life educated her in the power and pleasure of one-on-one engagement, which, notwithstanding its limitations in the here and now, was like a glistening thread, weaving others together in the capacious warp and woof of community. When Mechtild spotted a friend in heaven, she saw her hand in hand with Mechtild of Magdeburg, their cloister companion.[1]

THE END

[1] *Liber* 2.42 (192).

Bibliography

Primary Literature

Editions

Bernard of Clairvaux. *Sermones super cantica canticorum*. Sancti Bernardi opera, 8 vols. in 9. Ed. Jean Leclercq, C. H. Talbot, and H. M. Rochais. Rome: Editiones Cistercienses, 1957–1977.

Gertrude of Helfta. *Le Héraut*. In *Gertrude d'Helfta: Oeuvres spirituelles*, edited and translated by Pierre Doyère, Jean-Marie Clément, the nuns of Wisques, and Bernard de Vregille. SCh 39, 143, 255, 331. Série des texts monastiques d'occident, nos. 25, 27, 48. Paris: Éditions du Cerf, 1968–1986.

Gertrude of Helfta. *Les Exercices*. In *Gertrude d'Helfta: Oeuvres spirituelles*, edited and translated by Jacques Hourlier and Albert Schmitt. SCh 127. Série des texts monastiques d'occident, no. 19. Paris: Éditions du Cerf, 1967.

Mechtild of Hackeborn. *Liber specialis gratiae*. In *Sanctae Mechtildis, virginis ordinis sancti Benedicti: Liber specialis gratiae accedit sororis Mechtildis ejusdem ordinis Lux divinitatis*, edited by the monks of Solesmes [Louis Paquelin]. Vol. 2 of *Revelationes Gertrudianae ac Mechtildianae*. Paris: H. Oudin, 1877.

Mechtild of Magdeburg. *Lux divinitatis*. In *Sanctae Mechtildis, virginis ordinis sancti Benedicti: Liber specialis gratiae accedit sororis Mechtildis ejusdem ordinis Lux divinitatis*, edited by the monks of Solesmes [Louis Paquelin]. Vol. 2 of *Revelationes Gertrudianae ac Mechtildianae*. Paris: H. Oudin, 1877.

Sophia of Stolberg. "Narratio abbatissae Sophiae de Stolberg conscripta anno 1451 de fundatione monasterii novae-Helftae incepti anno 1229." In *Sanctae Mechtildis, virginis ordinis sancti Benedicti: Liber specialis gratiae accedit sororis Mechtildis ejusdem ordinis Lux divinitatis*, edited by the monks of Solesmes [Louis Paquelin].

Vol. 2 of *Revelationes Gertrudianae ac Mechtildianae*. Paris: H. Oudin, 1877.

Urkundenbuch der Klöster der Grafschaft Mansfeld. Ed. Max Krüne. Geschichtsquellen der Provinz Sachsen und angrenzender Gebiete, vol. 20. Halle: Otto Hendel, 1888.

Translations

Barratt, Alexandra, trans. *Gertrud the Great of Helfta: The Herald of God's Loving Kindness: Books One and Two*. CF 35. Kalamazoo, MI: Cistercian Publications, 1991.

Barratt, Alexandra, trans. *Gertrud the Great of Helfta: The Herald of God's Loving Kindness: Book Three*. CF 63. Kalamazoo, MI: Cistercian Publications, 1999.

Barratt, Alexandra, trans. *Gertrud the Great of Helfta: The Herald of God's Loving Kindness: Book Four*. CF 85. Kalamazoo, MI: Cistercian Publications, 2018.

Doyère, Pierre, Jean-Marie Clément, the nuns of Wisques, and Bernard de Vregille, trans. *Le Héraut*. In *Gertrude d'Helfta: Oeuvres spirituelles*. SCh 39, 143, 255, 331. Série des texts monastiques d'occident, nos. 25, 27, 48. Paris: Éditions du Cerf, 1968–86.

Halligan, Theresa A., trans. *The Booke of Gostlye Grace of Mechtild of Hackeborn*. Studies and Texts, vol. 46. Toronto: Pontifical Institute of Mediaeval Studies, 1979.

Hourlier, Jacques, and Albert Schmitt, trans. *Les Exercices*. In *Gertrude d'Helfta: Oeuvres spirituelles*. SCh 127. Série des texts monastiques d'occident, no. 19. Paris: Éditions du Cerf, 1967.

King, Margot. "Letters from Mechthild of Hackeborn to a Friend, A Laywoman in the World, Taken from the *Book of Special Grace*, Book IV, Chapter 59." In Vox mystica: *Essays on Medieval Mysticism in Honor of Professor Valerie M. Lagorio*, edited by Anne Clark Bartlett, Thomas H. Bestul, Janet Goebel, and William F. Pollard. Cambridge, UK: D. S. Brewer, 1995. 173–76.

Lanczkowski, Johanna, trans. *Gertrude die Grosse von Helfta: Gesandter der göttlichen Liebe*. Darmstadt: Wissenschaftliche Buchgesellschaft, 1989.

Lewis, Gertrud Jaron, and Jack Lewis, trans. *Gertrud the Great of Helfta: Spiritual Exercises*. CF 49. Kalamazoo, MI: Cistercian Publications, 1989.

Newman, Barbara, trans. *Mechthild of Hackeborn and the Nuns of Helfta: The Book of Special Grace*. Classics of Western Spirituality. New York: Paulist Press, 2017.

Nuns of Dordogne, trans. *Livre de la grace spéciale: Révélations de sainte Mechtilde, Vierge de l'Ordre de Saint-Benoit*. Paris: Maison Mame, 1920.

Tobin, Frank, trans. *Mechthild of Magdeburg: The Flowing Light of the Godhead*. Classics of Western Spirituality. New York: Paulist Press, 1998.

White, Carolinne, trans. *The Rule of St. Benedict*. London: Penguin Books, 2008.

Winkworth, Margaret, trans. *Gertrude of Helfta: The Herald of Divine Love*. Classics of Western Spirituality. New York: Paulist Press, 1993.

Secondary Literature

Abril, Michael Anthony. "Gertrude of Helfta's Liturgical-Mystical Union." *Cistercian Studies Quarterly* 43, no. 1 (2008): 77–96.

Ahlgren, Gillian T. W. "Visions and Rhetorical Strategy in the Letters of Hildegard of Bingen." In *Dear Sister: Medieval Women and the Epistolary Genre*, edited by Karen Cherewatuk and Ulrike Wiethaus. Middle Ages Series. Philadelphia: University of Pennsylvania Press, 1993. 46–63.

Aigrain, René. *L'hagiographie: ses sources, ses methodes, son histoire*. Mayenne: Bloud and Gay, 1953.

Ancelet-Hustache, Jeanne. *Mechtilde de Magdebourg (1207–1282): Étude de psychologie religieuse*. Paris: Librairie Ancienne Honoré Champion, 1926.

Ankermann, Maren. *Gertrud die Grosse von Helfta: Eine Studie zum Spannungsverhältnis religiöser Erfahrung und literarischer Gestaltung in mystischen Werken*. Göppinger Arbeiten zur Germanistik, no. 640. Göppingen: Kümmerle Verlag, 1997.

Ariès, Philippe. *Le Homme devant la mort*. Paris: Seuil, 1977.

Ashley, Kathleen, and Pamela Sheingorn. Introduction to *Interpreting Cultural Symbols: Saint Anne in Late Medieval Society*, edited by Kathleen Ashley and Pamela Sheingorn. Athens: University of Georgia Press, 1990.

Aubert, R. "Halle." *Dictionnaire d'histoire et de géographie ecclésiastiques*. Ed. R. Aubert and J.-P. Hendrickx. Paris: Letouzey et Ané, 1990. 162–69.

Averkorn, Raphaela. "Die Bischöfe von Halberstadt in ihren kirchlichen und politischen Wirken und in ihren Beziehungen zur Stadt von den Anfängen bis zur Reformation." In *Bürger, Bettelmönche und Bischöfe in Halberstadt: Studien zur Geschichte der Stadt, der Mendikanten und des Bistums vom Mittelalter bis zur Frühen Neuzeit*, edited by Dieter Berg. Münster: Werl, 1997. 1–79.

Bainvel, R. P. *La dévotion au Sacré Coeur de Jésus, doctrine, histoire*. Paris: Beauchesne, 1931.

Bangert, Michael. *Demut in Freiheit: Studien zur geistlichen Lehre im Werk Gertruds von Helfta*. Studien zur systematischen und spirituellen Theologie, vol. 21. Würzburg: Echter, 1997.

Bangert, Michael. "Die sozio-kulturelle Situation des Klosters St Maria in Helfta." In *"Vor dir steht die leere Schale meiner Sehnsucht": Die Mystik der Frauen von Helfta*, edited by Michael Bangert and Hildegund Keul. Leipzig: St. Benno Buch- und Zeitschriftenverlagsgesellschaft, 1998. 29–47.

Bangert, Michael. "A Mystic Pursues Narrative Theology: Biblical Speculation and Contemporary Imagery in Gertrude of Helfta." *Magistra* 2, no. 2 (Winter 1996): 3–30.

Barratt, Alexandra. "Context: Some Reflexions on Wombs and Tombs and Inclusive Language." In *Anchorites, Wombs and Tombs: Intersections of Gender and Enclosure in the Middle Ages*, edited by Liz Herbert McAvoy and Mari Hughes-Edwards. Cardiff: University of Wales Press, 2005. 27–38.

Barratt, Alexandra. Introduction to *Gertrud the Great of Helfta: The Herald of God's Loving Kindness: Books One and Two*. Trans. Alexandra Barratt. CF 35. Kalamazoo, MI: Cistercian Publications, 1991. 7–25.

Barratt, Alexandra. Introduction to *Gertrud the Great of Helfta: The Herald of God's Loving Kindness: Book Three*. Trans. Alexandra Barratt. CF 63. Kalamazoo, MI: Cistercian Publications, 1999. 9–21.

Barratt, Alexandra. "The Woman Who Shares the King's Bed: The Innocent Eroticism of Gertrud the Great of Helfta." In *Intersections of Sexuality and the Divine in Medieval Culture: The Word*

Made Flesh, edited by Susannah Mary Chewning. London: Routledge, 2016. 107–19.

Barratt, Alexandra. *Women's Writing in Middle English*. Longman Annotated Texts. London: Longman, 1992.

Barratt, Alexandra, and Debra L. Stoudt. "Gertrude the Great of Helfta." In *Medieval Holy Women in the Christian Tradition: c. 1100–c. 1500*, edited by Alistair Minnis and Rosalynn Voaden. Brepols Collected Essays in European Culture, 1. Turnhout: Brepols, 2010. 453–74.

Bartlett, Anne Clark. "Miraculous Literacy and Textual Communities in Hildegard of Bingen's *Scivias*." *Mystics Quarterly* 18, no. 2 (1992): 43–52.

Bartlett, Anne Clark. " 'A Reasonable Affection': Gender and Spiritual Friendship in Middle English Devotional Literature." In *Vox Mystica: Essays on Medieval Mysticism in Honor of Professor Valerie M. Lagorio*, edited by Thomas H. Bestul, Janet Goebel, and William F. Pollard. Cambridge: Brewer, 1995. 131–54.

Beach, Alison I. *Women as Scribes: Book Production and Monastic Reform in Twelfth-Century Bavaria*. Cambridge Studies in Palaeography and Codicology, no. 10. Cambridge, UK: Cambridge University Press, 2004.

Beaty, Nancy Lee. *The Craft of Dying: A Study in the Literary Tradition of the* Ars Moriendi *in England*. New Haven: Yale University Press, 1970.

Beckwith, Sara. "Problems with Authority in Late Medieval English Mysticism: Language, Agency, and Authority in the *Book* of Margery Kempe." *Exemplaria* 4, no. 1 (1992): 171–99.

Bérenger, Jean. *A History of the Habsburg Empire: 1273–1700*. Trans. C. A. Simpson. London: Longman, 1994.

Berg, Arnold. "Die Herren von Hackeborn." *Genealogie und Heraldik: Zeitschrift für Familiengeschichtsforschung und Mappenwesen* 5, no. 2 (1950): 65–70.

Berlière, Ursmer D. *La dévotion au Sacré-Coeur dans l'Ordre de S. Benoît*. Collection "Pax," vol. 10. Paris: Abbaye de Maredsous, 1923.

Berlière, Ursmer D. *La familia dans les monastères Bénédictins du moyen âge*. Académie Royale de Belgique, classe des lettres et des science morales et politiques, vol. 29. Brussels: Maurice Lamertin, 1931.

Berlière, Ursmer D. "Sainte Mech[t]ilde et sainte Gertrude la grande, furent-elles Bénédictines?" *Revue Bénédictine* 6 (1899): 457–61.

Berman, Constance H. *The Cistercian Evolution: The Invention of a Religious Order in the Twelfth Century*. Middle Ages Series. Philadelphia: University of Pennsylvania Press, 2000.

Berman, Constance H. "Distinguishing Between the Humble Peasant Lay Brother and Sister, and the Converted Knight in Medieval Southern France." In *Religious and Laity in Western Europe 1000–1400: Interaction, Negotiation, and Power*, edited by Emilia Jamroziak and Janet Burton. Turnhout: Brepols, 2006. 263–83.

Berman, Constance H. "Were There Twelfth-Century Cistercian Nuns?" *Church History: Studies in Christianity and Culture* 68, no. 4 (December 1999): 824–64.

Bernstein, Alan E. *The Formation of Hell: Death and Retribution in the Ancient and Early Christian World*. Ithaca: Cornell University Press, 1993.

Besse, Jean Martial. *Les mystiques bénédictins des origines aux XIIIe siècle*. Collection "Pax," vol. 6. Paris: P. Lethielleux, 1922.

Bihl, Michael. "St. Elizabeth of Hungary." *The Catholic Encyclopedia: An International Work of Reference on the Constitution, Doctrine, Discipline, and History of the Catholic Church*, edited by Charles G. Herbermann, et al. New York: Robert Appleton Company, 1907.

Binski, Paul. *Medieval Death: Ritual and Representation*. Ithaca: Cornell University Press, 1996. 389–91.

Blake, Norman F. Review of *The Booke of Gostlye Grace of Mechtild of Hackeborn*, trans. Theresa A. Halligan. *Speculum* 56, no. 2 (April 1981): 386–89.

Bolton, Brenda. "*Mulieres Sanctae*." In *Sanctity and Secularity: The Church and the World*, edited by Derek Baker. Studies in Church History, vol. 5. Oxford: Basil Blackwell, 1973. 77–95.

Bossy, John. "The Mass as a Social Institution, 1200–1700." *Past and Present* 100 (August 1983): 29–61.

Bouchard, Constance Brittain. *Sword, Miter, and the Cloister: Nobility and the Church in Burgundy, 980–1198*. Ithaca: Cornell University Press, 1987.

Bouton, Jean de la Croix. *Histoire externe: Jusqu'à la fin du XVe siècle*. Vol. 1 of *Les moniales cisterciennes*. Commission pour l'histoire de l'Ordre de Cîteaux. Grignan: Abbaye N. D. d'Aiguebelle, 1986.

Bouton, Jean de la Croix. *Histoire interne: Études sur la vie des moniales*. Vols. 3–4 of *Les moniales cisterciennes*. Commission pour l'histoire de l'Ordre de Cîteaux. Grignan: Abbaye N. D. d'Aiguebelle, 1988–89.

Bouyer, Louis, Jean Leclercq, Francois Vandenbroucke, and Louis Cognet. *La spiritualité du moyen âge*. Vol. 2 of *Histoire de la spiritualité chrétienne*. Aubier: Éditions Montaigne, 1961.

Bowe, Peter. "Die Sterbekommunion im Altertum und Mittelalter." *Zeitschrift für katholische Theologie* 60 (1936): 1–54.

Brown, Rachel Fulton. *Mary and the Art of Prayer: The Hours of the Virgin in Medieval Life and Thought*. New York: Columbia University Press, 2018.

Brunn, Emilie Zum, and Georgette Epiney-Burgard, eds. *Women Mystics in Medieval Europe*. Trans. Sheila Hughes. New York: Paragon House, 1989.

Bynum, Caroline Walker. "The Cistercian Conception of Community." In *Jesus as Mother: Studies in the Spirituality of the High Middle Ages*. Berkeley: University of California Press, 1982. 51–81.

Bynum, Caroline Walker. "Formen weiblicher Frömmigkeiten im späteren Mittelalter." In *Krone und Schleier: Kunst aus mittelalterlichen Frauenklöstern*, edited by Jeffrey Hamburger and Robert Suckale. Bonn and Essen: Kunst- und Ausstellungshalle der Bundesrepublik Deutschland, Bonn; and Ruhrlandmuseum, Essen, 2005. 118–29.

Bynum, Caroline Walker. *Holy Feast and Holy Fast: The Religious Significance of Food to Medieval Women*. Berkeley: University of California Press, 1987.

Bynum, Caroline Walker. "Introduction to the Complexity of Symbols." In *Gender and Religion: On the Complexity of Symbols*, edited by Caroline Walker Bynum, Steven Harrell, and Paula Richman. Boston: Beacon Press, 1986.

Bynum, Caroline Walker. Preface to *Hildegard of Bingen: Scivias*. Trans. Columba Hart and Jane Bishop. New York: Paulist Press, 1990. 1–7.

Bynum, Caroline Walker. "Women Mystics and Eucharistic Devotion in the Thirteenth Century." In *Fragmentation and Redemption: Essays on Gender and the Human Body in Medieval Religion*. New York: Zone Books, 1991. 119–50.

Bynum, Caroline Walker. "Women Mystics in the Thirteenth Century: The Case of the Nuns of Helfta." In *Jesus as Mother: Studies in the Spirituality of the High Middle Ages*. Berkeley: University of California Press, 1982. 170–262.

Caron, Ann Marie. "Invitations of the Divine Heart: The Mystical Writings of Mechthild of Hackeborn." *American Benedictine Review* 45, no. 2 (1994): 321–38.

Caron, Ann Marie. "Taste and See the Goodness of the Lord: Mechthild of Hackeborn." In *Hidden Springs: Cistercian Monastic Women*, edited by John A. Nichols and Lillian Thomas Shank. Vol. 3, book 2 of Medieval Religious Women. CS 113b. Kalamazoo, MI: Cistercian Publications, 1995. 509–24.

Carruthers, Mary. *The Book of Memory: A Study of Memory in Medieval Culture*. Cambridge, UK: Cambridge University Press, 1990.

Carruthers, Mary. *Craft of Thought: Meditation, Rhetoric, and the Making of Images, 400–1200*. Cambridge, UK: Cambridge University Press, 1998.

Carruthers, Mary. "Reading with Attitude, Remembering the Book." In *The Book and the Body*, edited by Dolores Warwick Frese and Katherine O'Brien O'Keefe. South Bend, IN: Notre Dame University Press, 1997. 1–33.

Caspers, Charles. "The Western Church during the Late Middle Ages: *Augenkommunion* or Popular Mysticism." In *Bread of Heaven: Customs and Practices Surrounding Holy Communion*, edited by Charles Caspers, Gerard Lukken, and Gerard Rouwhorst. Essays in the History of Liturgy and Culture. Kampen: Kok Pharos Publishing House, 1995. 83–97.

Cassidy, Megan. *Monastic Spaces and Their Meanings: Thirteenth-Century English Cistercian Monasteries*. Turnhout: Brepols, 2001.

Cassidy, Megan. "'*Non Conversi sed Perversi*': The Use and Marginalization of the Cistercian Lay Brother." In *Deviance & Textual Control: New Perspectives in Medieval Studies*, edited by Megan Cassidy, Helen Hickey, and Meagan Street. Melbourne University Conference Series 2. University of Melbourne: History Department, 1997.

Castel, D. A. *Les belles prières de Ste Mechtilde et Ste Gertrude*. Paris: Desclée de Brouwer-Lethellieux, 1925.

Cattaneo, Enrico. "La Partecipazione dei Laici alla Liturgia." In *I laici nella "Societas christiana" dei secoli XI et XII: Atti della terza settimana internazionale di studio, Mendola, 21–27 agosto 1965*. Miscellanea del Centro di Studi Medioevali V. Milan: Vita e Pensiero, 1968. 396–427.

Cheney, Christopher Robert. *Episcopal Visitation of Monasteries in the Thirteenth Century*. 2nd rev. edition. Manchester: Porcupine Press, 1983.

Cherewatuk, Karen, and Ulrike Wiethaus. "Introduction: Women Writing Letters in the Middle Ages." In *Dear Sister: Medieval Women and the Epistolary Genre*, edited by Karen Cherewatuk and Ulrike Wiethaus. Middle Ages Series. Philadelphia: University of Pennsylvania Press, 1993. 1–19.

Chidester, David. *Word and Light: Seeing, Hearing, and Religious Discourse*. Chicago: University of Illinois Press, 1992.

Clark, Anne L. *Elisabeth of Schönau: A Twelfth-Century Visionary*. Middle Ages Series. Philadelphia: University of Pennsylvania Press, 1992.

Clark, Anne L. "Holy Woman or Unworthy Vessel? Representations of Elisabeth of Schönau." In *Gendered Voices: Medieval Saints and Their Interpreters*. Edited by Catherine M. Mooney. Middle Ages Series. Philadelphia: University of Pennsylvania Press, 1998. 35–51.

Clark, Anne L. "The Priesthood of the Virgin Mary: Gender Trouble in the Twelfth Century." *Journal of Feminist Studies in Religion* 18, no. 1 (Spring 2002): 5–24.

Clark, Anne L. "An Uneasy Triangle: Jesus, Mary, and Gertrude of Helfta." *Maria: A Journal of Marian Studies* 1 (August 2000): 37–56.

Clemons, Cheryl. "The Relationship Between Devotion to the Eucharist and Devotion to the Humanity of Jesus in the Writings of St. Gertrude of Helfta." PhD dissertation, The Catholic University of America, 1995.

Coakley, John. "Gender and the Authority of Friars: The Significance of Holy Women for Thirteenth-Century Franciscans and Dominicans." *Church History: Studies in Christianity and Culture* 60, no. 4 (1991): 445–60.

Coakley, John. *Women, Men, and Spiritual Power: Female Saints and Their Male Collaborators*. New York: Columbia University Press, 2006.

Coester, E. "Die Cistercienserinnenkirchen des 12 bis 14. Jahrhunderts." In *Die Cistercienser: Geschichte, Geist, Kunst*, edited by A. Schneider, A. Wienand, and W. Bickel. 3rd revised edition. Cologne: Wienand, 1986. 363–428.

Coulet, Noël. *Les visites pastorales*. Typologie des sources du moyen âge occident, vol. 23. Turnhout: Brepols, 1977.

Cowan, Miri. *Death, Life, and Religious Change in Scottish Towns, c. 1350–1560*. Manchester: Manchester University Press, 2012.

Curtius, Ernst R. *European Literature and the Latin Middle Ages*. Trans. W. R. Trask. Princeton, NJ: Princeton University Press, 1973.

Curtius, Ernst R. "Poetry and Rhetoric." In *Landmark Essays on Rhetoric and Literature*, edited by Craig Kallendorf. Mahwah, NJ: Hermagoras Press, 1999. 41–61.

De Certeau, Michel. "Hagiographie." *Encyclopaedia Universalis*. Ed. Peter F. Baumberger. Paris: Encyclopaedia Universalis, 1990. 207–9.

De Fontette, Micheline Pontenay. *Les religieuses à l'age classique du droit canon: Recherches sur les structure juridiques des branches féminines des ordres*. Bibliothèque de la société d'histoire ecclésiastique de la France. Paris: Librairie Philosophique J. Vrin, 1967.

De Ganck, Roger. "The Integration of Nuns in the Cistercian Order, Particularly in Belgium." *Cîteaux* 35 (1984): 235–47.

Degler-Spengler, Brigitte. "The Incorporation of Cistercian Nuns into the Order in the Twelfth and Thirteenth Century." Trans. Gabriele R. Hahn. In *Hidden Springs: Cistercian Monastic Women*, edited by John A. Nichols and Lillian Thomas Shank. Vol. 3, book 1 of Medieval Religious Women. CS 113a. Kalamazoo, MI: Cistercian Publications, 1995. 85–134.

De Jong, Mayke. *In Samuel's Image: Child Oblation in the Early Medieval West*. Brill's Studies in Intellectual History. Edited by A. J. Vanderjagt. Leiden: E. J. Brill, 1996.

Della Croce, Giovanna. *I mistici del nord*. Rome: Edizioni Studium, 1981.

Deloffre, Marie-Hélene. "Les Exercices sont-ils l'œuvre de Sainte Gertrude d'Helfta? Approche Stylistique." *Cîteaux* 68, no. 1–4 (2017): 121–91.

Denifle, Henrich. "Uber die Anfänge der Predigtweise der deutschen Mystiker." In *Archiv für Litteratur- und Kirchen-Geschichte des Mittelalters*, edited by Heinrich Denifle and Franz Ehrle. Berlin: Weidmannsche Buchhandlung, 1886.

Deploige, Jeroen. "How Gendered Was Clairvoyance in the Thirteenth Century?" In *Speaking to the Eye: Sight and Insight through Text and Image (1150–1650)*, edited by Thérèse de Hemptinne, Veerle Fraeters, and María Eugenia Góngora. Turnhout: Brepols, 2013. 95–126.

Derrida, Jacques. *Given Time: I. Counterfeit Money*. Trans. Peggy Kamuf. Chicago: University of Chicago Press, 1992.

Dieker, Alberta. "Mechtild of Hackeborn: Song of Love." In *Medieval Women Monastics: Wisdom's Wellsprings*, edited by Miriam Schmitt and Linda Kulzer. Collegeville, MN: Liturgical Press, 1996. 231–42.

Dinzelbacher, Peter. "Die Offenbarungen der hl. Elisabeth von Schönau: Bildwelt, Erlebnisweise und Zeittypisches." *Studien und Mittelungen zur Geschichte des Benediktiner-Ordens* 97 (1985): 462–82.

Dinzelbacher, Peter. "Die 'Vita et Revelationes' der Wiener Begine Agnes Blannbekin (+1315) in Rahmen der Viten- und Offenbarungsliteratur ihrer Zeit." In *Frauenmystik im Mittelalter*, edited by Peter Dinzelbacher and Dieter R. Bauer. Weingarten: Schwabenverlag, 1985. 152–77.

Dinzelbacher, Peter. "A Plea for the Study of the Minor Female Mystics of Late Medieval Germany." *Studies in Spirituality* 3 (1993): 91–100.

Dinzelbacher, Peter. "Reflexionen irdischer Sozialstruckturen in mittelalterlichen Jenseitsschilderungen." *Archiv für Kulturgeschichte* 61 (1979): 16–34.

Dinzelbacher, Peter. *Revelationes*. Typologie des sources du moyen âge occidental, vol. 57. Turnhout: Brepols, 1991.

Dinzelbacher, Peter. *Vision und Visionliteratur im Mittelalter*. Monographien zur Geschichte des Mittelalters 23. Stuttgart: Hiersemann, 1981.

Dinzelbacher, Peter. "Zur Interpretation erlebnismystischer Texte des Mittelalter." *Zeitschrift für deutsches Altertum und deutsche Literatur* 117 (1988): 1–23.

Dolan, Gilbert. *St. Gertrude the Great*. London: Sands, 1913.

Dombi, P. Markus. "Waren die hll. Gertrud und Mechtild Benedikterinnen oder Cistercienserinnen?" *Cistercienser-Chronik* 25 (1913): 257–68.

Donnelly, James S. *Decline of the Medieval Cistercian Laybrotherhood*. New York: Fordham University Press, 1949.

Doyère, Pierre. "Gertrude d'Helfta." *Dictionnaire de spiritualité ascétique et mystique, doctrine et histoire*. Edited by M. Viller, et al. Paris: G. Beauchesne et ses fils, 1967. 331–39.

Doyère, Pierre. Introduction to *Le Héraut*. In *Gertrude d'Helfta: Œuvres spirituelles*, edited and translated by Pierre Doyère, Jean-Marie Clément, the nuns of Wisques, and Bernard de Vregille. SCh 139. Série des texts monastiques d'occident, no. 25. Paris: Éditions du Cerf, 1968. 9–91.

Doyère, Pierre. "Rédaction du Livre II." In *Le Héraut*, in *Gertrude d'Helfta: Oeuvres spirituelles*, edited and translated by Pierre Doyère, Jean-Marie Clément, the nuns of Wisques, and Bernard de Vregille. SCh 143. Série des texts monastiques d'occident, no. 27. Paris: Éditions du Cerf, 1968.

Dronke, Peter. *Women Writers of the Middle Ages: A Critical Study of Texts from Perpetua (d. 203) to Marguerite Porete (d.1310)*. Cambridge, UK: Cambridge University Press, 1984.

Duffy, Eamon. *The Stripping of the Altars: Traditional Religion in England 1400–1580*. New Haven, CT: Yale University Press, 1992.

Dyer, Joseph. "The Psalms in Monastic Prayer." In *The Place of the Psalms in the Intellectual Culture of the Middle Ages*, edited by Nancy van Deusen. New York: State University of New York Press, 1999. 59–89.

Easting, Robert. *Annotated Bibliographies of Old and Middle English Literature*. Vol. 3, *Visions of the Other World in Middle English*. Cambridge: D. S. Brewer, 1997.

Eckenstein, Lina. *Women under Monasticism: Chapters on Saint-Lore and Convent Life Between A.D. 500 and A.D. 1500*. 1896. Repr. New York: Russell and Russell, 1963.

Ehrenschwendtner, Marie-Luise. "'Puellae litteratae': The Use of the Vernacular in the Dominican Convents of Southern Germany." In *Medieval Women in Their Communities*, edited by Diane Watt. Buffalo, NY: University of Toronto Press, 1997. 49–71.

Elkins, Sharon K. "Gertrude the Great and the Virgin Mary." *Church History: Studies in Christianity and Culture* 66, no. 4 (1997): 720–34.

Elliott, Dyan. "Authorizing a Life: The Collaboration of Dorothea of Montau and John Marienwerder." In *Gendered Voices: Medieval Saints and Their Interpreters*, edited by Catherine M. Mooney. Philadelphia: University of Pennsylvania Press, 1999. 168–91.

Elliott, Dyan. *The Bride of Christ Goes to Hell: Metaphor and Embodiment in the Lives of Pious Women, 200–1500*. Philadelphia: University of Pennsylvania Press, 2012.

Erler, Mary C., and Maryanne Kowaleski. Introduction to *Gendering the Master Narrative: Women and Power in the Middle Ages*. Edited by Mary C. Erler and Maryanne Kowaleski. Athens: University of Georgia Press, 1988. 1–16.

Farmer, Sharon A. *Communities of St. Martin: Legend and Ritual in Medieval Tours*. Ithaca: Cornell University Press, 1991.

Ferrante, Joan M. *To the Glory of Her Sex: Women's Roles in the Composition of Medieval Texts*. Women of Letters. Bloomington, IN: Indiana University Press, 1997.

Finke, Laurie A. "Mystical Bodies and The Dialogics of Vision." In *Maps of Flesh and Light: The Religious Experience of Medieval Women Mystics*, edited by Ulrike Wiethaus. Syracuse, NY: Syracuse University Press, 1993. 28–44.

Finke, Laurie A. *Women's Writing in English: Medieval England*. Women's Writing in English. London: Longman, 1999.

Finnegan, Mary Jeremy. "Idiom of Women Mystics." *Mystics Quarterly* 13, no. 2 (1987): 65–72.

Finnegan, Mary Jeremy. "Saint Mechtild of Hackeborn: *Nemo Communior*." In *Peaceweavers*, edited by Lillian Thomas Shank and John A. Nichols. Vol. 2 of Medieval Religious Women. CS 72. Kalamazoo, MI: Cistercian Publications, 1987. 213–21.

Finnegan, Mary Jeremy. *The Women of Helfta: Scholars and Mystics*. 1962. Reprint, with additions from author. Athens: University of Georgia Press, 1991.

Fiske, Adele. *Friends and Friendship in the Monastic Tradition*. CIDOC Cuaderno No. 51. Cuernavaca, Mexico: Centro Intercultural de Documentacion, 1970.

Forastieri, Ana Laura. "Saint Gertrude's Postulation for Doctor of the Church." *Magistra* 24, no. 2 (Winter 2018): 42–45.

Forman, Mary. "Gertrud of Helfta: Arbor Amoris in Her Heart's Garden." *Mystics Quarterly* 26, no. 4 (December 2000): 163–78.

Forman, Mary. "Visions 'Brimful of Love' During Christmas and Candlemas Liturgies in Gertrude of Helfta's *Legatus* II.16: A Study in *Lectio divina*." *Mystics Quarterly* 32, no. 3/4 (September/December 2006): 1–18.

Forshaw, B. "Heaven (Theology of)." *The New Catholic Encyclopedia: An International Work of Reference on the Constitution, Doctrine, Discipline, and History of the Catholic Church*, edited by Bernard L. Marthaler, et al. 2nd ed. Detroit: Gale, 2003. 683–90.

Fort, Gavin. "Suffering Another's Sin: Proxy Penance in the Thirteenth Century." *Journal of Medieval History* 44, no. 2 (2018): 202–30.

Franke, Thomas. "Zur Geschichte der Elisabethreliquien im Mittelalter und in der Frühen Neuzeit." In *Sankt Elisabeth: Fürstin, Dienerin, Heilige*. Philipps-Universität Marburg in Verbindung mit dem Hessischen Landesamt für Geschichtliche Landeskunde. Sigmaringen: Jan Thorbecke Verlag, 1982. 67–79.

Freed, John B. "The Friars and the Delineation of State Boundaries in the Thirteenth Century." In *Order and Innovation in the Middle Ages: Essays in Honor of Joseph R. Strayer*, edited by Bruce McNab, William C. Jordan, and Teófilo F. Ruiz. Princeton, NJ: Princeton University Press, 1976. 31–40.

Freed, John B. *The Friars and German Society in the Thirteenth Century*. Cambridge, MA: Medieval Society of America, 1977.

Freed, John B. "Habsburg Dynasty." In *Medieval Germany: An Encyclopedia*, edited by John M. Jeep. New York: Garland Publishing, 2001. 41–43.

Freeman, Elizabeth. "The Public and Private Functions of Heloise's Letters." *Journal of Medieval History* 23, no. 1 (1997): 15–28.

Fulton, Rachel. *From Judgment to Passion: Devotion to Christ and the Virgin Mary, 800–1200*. New York: Columbia University Press, 2002.

Garber, Rebecca L. R. *Feminine* Figurae*: Representations of Gender in Religious Texts by Medieval German Women Writers, 1100–1375*. Medieval History and Culture, vol. 10. New York: Routledge, 2003.

Gaxotte, Pierre. *Histoire de l'Allemagne*. Vol. 1 of 4. Paris: Flammarion, 1963.

Gehring, Hester. "The Language of Mysticism in South German Convent Chronicles of the Fourteenth Century." PhD dissertation, University of Michigan, 1957.

Gellrich, Jesse M. *The Idea of the Book in the Middle Ages: Language Theory, Mythology, and Fiction*. Ithaca: Cornell University Press, 1985.

Gilchrist, Roberta. *Gender and Material Culture: The Archeology of Religious Women*. London: Routledge, 1994.

Gillerman, Dorothy. *The Clôture of Notre-Dame and Its Role in the Fourteenth Century Choir Program*. New York: Garland, 1977.

Glente, Karen. "Mystikerinnenviten aus männlicher und weiblicher Sicht: Ein Vergleich zwischen Thomas von Cantimpré und Katerina von Unterlinden." In *Religiöse Frauenbewegung und mystische Frömmigkeit im Mittelalter*, edited by Peter Dinzelbacher and Dieter R. Bauer. Cologne: Böhlau, 1988. 251–64.

Gottschalk, Joseph. "Kloster Helfta und Schlesien." *Archiv für schlesische Kirchengeschichte* 13 (1955): 63–82.

Gougaud, Louis. *Devotional and Ascetic Practices in the Middle Ages*. Trans. G. C. Bateman. London: Burns, Oates and Washbourne, 1927.

Goyau, Lucie Félix-Faure. *Christianisme et culture féminine*. Paris: Librairie Académique, 1914.

Graef, Hilda. "Gertrude the Great: Mystical Flowering of the Liturgy." *Orate Fratres* 20 (1945/46): 171–74.

Graef, Hilda. *The Light and the Rainbow: A Study in Christian Spirituality from Its Roots in the Old Testament and Its Development through the New Testament and the Fathers to Recent Times*. Westminster, MD: Newman Press, 1959.

Graef, Hilda. *Mary: A History of Doctrine and Devotion*. Vol. 1, *From the Beginnings to the Eve of the Reformation*. New York: Sheed and Ward, 1963.

Gragnolati, Manuele. "Nostalgia in Heaven: Embraces, Affection, and Identity in the *Commedia*." In *Dante and the Human Body: Eight Essays*, edited by John C. Barnes and Jennifer Petrie. Dublin: Four Courts Press, 2007. 117–37.

Greenspan, Kate. "Autohagiography and Medieval Women's Spiritual Autobiography." In *Gender and Text in the Later Middle Ages*. Edited by Jane Chance. Gainesville, FL: University of Florida Press, 1996. 16–36.

Greenspan, Kate. "*Matre Donante:* The Embrace of Christ as the Virgin's Gift in the Visions of 13th-Century Italian Women." *Studia Mystica: Women and Mysticism* 13 (Summer/Fall 1990): 26–37.

Grimes, Laura Marie. "Judge Wisdom, Queen Charity: The Feminine Divine in Gertrud of Helfta's *Spiritual Exercises*." *Magistra* 12, no. 2 (Winter 2006): 74–89.

Grimes, Laura Marie. "Theology as Conversation: Gertrud of Helfta and Her Sisters as Readers of Augustine." PhD dissertation, University of Notre Dame, 2004.

Grimes, Laura Marie. *Wisdom's Friends: Gertrud of Helfta's Conversational Theology*. Saarbrücken: VDM Verlag Dr. Müller, 2009.

Grimes, Laura Marie. "Writing as Birth: The Composition of Gertrud of Helfta's *Herald of God's Loving-Kindness*." *Cistercian Studies Quarterly* 42, no. 3 (2007): 329–45.

Groń, Ryszard. "Examples of 'Good Death' in Aelred of Rievaulx." *Cistercian Studies Quarterly* 41, no. 4 (2006): 422–41.

Grössler, Herman. "Die Blützeit des Klosters Helfta bei Eisleben." *Jahres-Bericht über das königliche Gymnasium zu Eisleben* (Easter 1886–Easter 1887): 1–38.

Grundmann, Herbert. *Religious Movements in the Middle Ages: The Historical Link Between Heresy, the Mendicant Orders, and the Women's Religious Movement in the Thirteenth Century, with the Historical Foundations of German Mysticism*. Trans. Steven Rowan. Notre Dame, IN: University of Notre Dame Press, 1995.

Guillous, Marie-Geneviève. "La louange à l'école de sainte Gertrude." *Collectanea Cisterciensia* 53 (1991): 174–94.

Haas, Alois Maria. "Die Problematik von Sprache und Erfahrung in der Deutschen Mystik." In *Grundfragen der Mystik*, edited by Werner Beierwaltes. Einsiedeln: Johannes-Verlag, 1974. 73–104.

Haas, Alois Maria. "Mechthild von Hackeborn: Eine Form zisterziensischer Frauenfrömmigkeit." In Haas, *Geistliches Mittelalter*. Freiburg: Universitätsverlag, 1984. 221–39.

Haas, Alois Maria. *Mystik als Aussage: Erfahrungs-, Denk-, und Redeformen christlicher Mystik*. Frankfurt am Main: Suhrkamp, 1996.

Haas, Alois Maria. Sermo Mysticus: *Studien zu Theologie und Sprache der deutschen Mystik*. Unterstützung des Hochschulrates der Universität Freiburg Schweiz und der Stiftung der schweizerischen Landesausstellung 1939 Zürich für Kunst und Forschung. Freiburg: Universitätsverlag Freiburg Schweiz, 1979.

Haggh, Barbara. "Foundations or Institutions? On Bringing the Middle Ages into the History of Medieval Music." *Acta Musicologica* 68 (1996): 87–128.

Hale, Rosemary Drage. "*Imitatio Mariae*: Motherhood Motifs in Devotional Memoirs." *Mystics Quarterly* 16 (1990): 193–203.

Hale, Rosemary Drage. *Imitatio Mariae*: Motherhood Motifs in Late Medieval German Spirituality." PhD dissertation, Harvard University, 1992.

Hallinger, Kassius. "Woher kommen die Laienbrüder?" *Analecta Cisterciensia* 12 (1956): 1–104.

Halter, Annemarie. *Geschichte des Dominikanerinnen-Klosters Oetenbach in Zürich, 1234–1525*. Winterthur: Verlag Keller, 1956.

Hamburger, Jeffrey F. "Art, Enclosure, and the Pastoral Care of Nuns." In *The Visual and the Visionary: Art and Female Spirituality in Late Medieval Germany*. New York: Zone Books, 1992. 35–109.

Hamburger, Jeffrey F. "Brother, Bride, and *alter Christus*: The Virginal Body of John the Evangelist in Medieval Art, Theology and Literature." *Text und Kultur: mittelalterliche Literatur 1150–1450*, Germanistische Symposien, 23. Stuttgart: Metzler, 2001. 296–328.

Hamburger, Jeffrey F. "Introduction: Texts Versus Images." In *The Visual and the Visionary: Art and Female Spirituality in Late Medieval Germany*. New York: Zone Books, 1992. 13–34.

Hamburger, Jeffrey F. *Nuns as Artists: The Visual Culture of a Medieval Monastery*. Studies in the History of Art 37. Berkeley, CA: University of California Press, 1997.

Hamburger, Jeffrey F. *The Rothschild Canticles: Art and Mysticism in Flanders and the Rhineland circa 1300*. New Haven, CT: Yale University Press, 1990.

Hamburger, Jeffrey F. *St. John the Divine: the Deified Evangelist in Medieval Art and Theology*. Berkeley: University of California, 2002.

Hamburger, Jeffrey F. "Seeing and Believing: The Suspicion of Sight and Authentication of Vision in Late Medieval Art and Devotion." In *Imagination und Wirklichkeit: zum Verhältnis von mentalen und realen Bildern in der Kunst der frühen Neuzeit*, edited by Klaus Krüger and Alessandro Nova. Mainz: Philipp von Zabern, 2000.

Hamburger, Jeffrey F. "The Visual and the Visionary: The Image in Late Medieval Monastic Devotions." In *The Visual and the Visionary: Art and Female Spirituality in Late Medieval Germany*. New York: Zone Books, 1992. 131–38.

Hamburger, Jeffrey F., and Robert Suckale, eds. *Krone und Schleier: Kunst aus mittelalterlichen Frauenklöstern*. Bonn and Essen: Kunst- und Ausstellungshalle der Bundesrepublik Deutschland, Bonn; and Ruhrlandmuseum, Essen, 2005.

Harper, John. *The Forms and Orders of Western Liturgy from the Tenth to the Eighteenth Century: A Historical Introduction and Guide for Students and Musicians*. Oxford: Clarendon, 1995.

Harrison, Anna. " 'Jesus Wept': Mourning as Imitation of Christ in Bernard's Sermon Twenty-Six on the Song of Songs." *Cistercian Studies Quarterly* 48, no. 4 (2013): 433–67.

Harrison, Anna. " 'Oh! What Treasure Is in This Book?': Writing, Reading, and Community at the Monastery of Helfta." *Viator* 39, no. 1 (2008): 75–106.

Harrison, Anna. " 'Where Have You Vanished?': Aelred of Rievaulx's Lamentation on Simon." *Quidditas* 39 (December 2018): 239–52.

Harrison, Anna, and Caroline Walker Bynum. "Gertrude, Gender, and the Composition of the *Herald of Divine Love*." In *Freiheit des Herzens: Mystik bei Gertrud von Helfta*, edited by Michael Bangert. Mystik und Mediävistik, vol. 2. Münster: Lit Verlag, 2004. 57–76.

Hart, Columba. Introduction to *The Exercises of Saint Gertrude*. Trans. a Benedictine nun of Regina Laudis [Columba Hart]. Westminster, MD: The Newman Press, 1956. vii–xvii.

Hellgardt, Ernst. "Latin and the Vernacular: Mechthild of Magdeburg – Mechthild of Hackeborn – Gertrude of Helfta." In *A Companion to Mysticism and Devotion in Northern Germany in the Late Middle Ages*, edited by Elizabeth Andersen, Henrike Lähnemann, and Anne Simon. Brill Companions to the Christian Tradition, vol. 44. Leiden: Brill, 2014. 131–56.

Herlihy, David. *Opera muliebria: Women and Work in Medieval Europe*. Philadelphia: Temple University, 1990.

Hilpisch, Stephanus. "Chorgebet und Frömmigkeit im Spätmittelalter." In *Heilige Überlieferung: Ausschnitte aus der Geschichte des Mönchtums und des heiligen Kultes*, edited by Odo Casel. Münster: Aschendorff, 1938. 263–84.

Hindsley, Leonard P. *The Mystics of Engelthal: Writings from a Medieval Monastery*. New York: St. Martins, 1999.

Holdsworth, Christopher J. "The Blessings of Work: The Cistercian View." In *Sanctity and Secularity: The Church and the World*. Oxford: Blackwell, 1973. 59–76.

Hollywood, Amy. "Inside Out: Beatrice of Nazareth and Her Hagiographer." In *Gendered Voices: Medieval Saints and Their Interpreters*, edited by Catherine M. Mooney. Middle Ages Series. Philadelphia: University of Pennsylvania Press, 1998. 78–98.

Hollywood, Amy. *Sensible Ecstasy: Mysticism, Sexual Difference, and the Demands of History*. Chicago: University of Chicago Press, 2002.

Hollywood, Amy. *The Soul as Virgin Wife: Mechthild of Magdeburg, Marguerite Porete, and Meister Eckhart*. Notre Dame, IN: University of Notre Dame Press, 1995.

Hollywood, Amy. "Suffering Transformed: Marguerite Porete, Meister Eckhart, and the Problem of Women's Spirituality." In *Meister Eckhart and the Beguine Mystics*, edited by Bernard McGinn. New York: Continuum, 1994. 87–113.

Holsinger, Bruce W. *Music, Body, and Desire in Medieval Culture: Hildegard of Bingen to Chaucer*. Reading Medieval Culture. Stanford, CA: Stanford University Press, 2001.

Hontoir, M. Camille. "La dévotion au saint sacrement chez les premiers Cisterciens (XIIe –XIIIe siècles)." In *Studia eucharistica, DCC anni a condito festo sanctissimi Corpus Christi 1246–1946*. Antwerp: De Nederlandsche Boekhandle, 1946. 132–56.

Horner, Robyn. *Rethinking God As Gift: Marion, Derrida, and the Limits of Phenomenology*. New York: Fordham University Press, 2001.

Hubert J. "La Place faite aux laics dans les églises monastiques et dans les cathedrals aux XIe et XIIe siècles." In *I laici nella "Societas christiana" dei secoli XI et XII: Atti della terza settimana internazionale di studio Mendola, 21–27 agusto 1965*, edited by Giuseppe Lazzati. Milan: Vita e Pensiero, 1968. 470–87.

Hubrath, Margarete. "The *Liber specialis gratiae* as a Collective Work of Several Nuns." *Jahrbuch der Oswald von Wolkenstein-Gesellschaft* 11 (1999): 233–44.

Hubrath, Margarete. *Schreiben und Erinnern: Zur "memoria" im* Liber specialis gratiae *Mechthilds von Hakeborn*. Paderborn: Ferdinand Schöningh, 1996.

Huemer, Blasius. "Verzeichnis der deutschen Cisterzienserinnenklöster." In *Germania monastica: Klosterverzeichnis der deutschen Benediktiner und Cisterzienser*. Bayerischen Benediktiner-Akademie. Ottobeuren: Kommission Winfried-Werk Augsberg, 1967. 1–47.

Huizinga, Johann. *The Autumn of the Middle Ages*. Translated by Rodney J. Payton and Ulrich Mammitzsch. Chicago: University of Chicago Press, 1996.

Jager, Eric. "The Book of the Heart: Reading and Writing the Medieval Subject." In *Speculum* 71, no. 1 (January 1996): 1–26.

James, William. *Varieties of Religious Experience*. 1902. Reprint, New York: Image Books, 1978.

Jansen, Katherine Ludwig. *The Making of the Magdalen: Preaching and Popular Devotion in the Later Middle Ages*. Princeton, NJ: Princeton University Press, 2001.

Johnson, Elizabeth. "Marian Devotion in the Western Church." In *Christian Spirituality: High Middle Ages and Reformation, World Spirituality: An Encyclopedic History of the Religious Quest*, edited by Jill Raitt, Bernard McGinn, and John Meyendorff. New York: Crossroad, 1989. 392–414.

Johnson, Ella L. "Bodily Language in the Spiritual Exercises of Gertrud the Great of Helfta." *Magistra* 14, no. 1 (2008): 79–107.

Johnson, Ella L. "'In mei memoriam facietis': Remembering Ritual and Refiguring 'Woman' in Gertrud the Great of Helfta's *Spiritualia Exercitia*." In *Inventing Identities: Re-examining the Use of Memory, Imitation, and Imagination in the Texts of Medieval Religious Women*, edited by Bradley Herzog and Margaret Cotter-Lynch. Basingstoke, UK: Palgrave Macmillan, 2012. 165–86.

Johnson, Ella L. "Metaphors for Metamorphosis: Mary Daly Meets Gertrud the Great of Helfta." *Magistra* 15, no. 1 (Summer 2009): 3–31.

Johnson, Ella L. "Reproducing Motherhood: Images of Mary and Maternity in the Writings of Gertrud the Great of Helfta." 47th International Medieval Studies Congress, Western Michigan University, Kalamazoo, MI, 2012.

Johnson, Ella L. *This is My Body: Eucharistic Theology and Anthropology in the Writings of Gertrude the Great of Helfta*. CS 280. Collegeville, MN: Cistercian Publications, 2020.

Johnson, Penelope D. *Equal in Monastic Profession: Religious Women in Medieval France*. Women in Culture and Society. Chicago: University of Chicago Press, 1991.

Jung, Jacqueline E. "Beyond the Barrier: The Unifying Role of the Choir Screen in Gothic Churches." *Art Bulletin* 82, no. 4 (December 2000): 622–57.

Jungmann, Joseph A. *The Mass of the Roman Rite: Its Origins and Development (Missarum Sollemnia)*. 2 vols. Trans. Francis A. Brunner. New York: Benziger Brothers, 1988.

Kieckhefer, Richard. "Major Currents in Late Medieval Devotion." In *Christian Spirituality: High Middle Ages and Reformation*, edited by Jill Raitt in collaboration with Bernard McGinn and John Meyendorff. World Spirituality, vol. 17. New York: Crossroad, 1989. 75–108.

Kieckhefer, Richard. "Mystical Communities in the Late Medieval West." Medieval Academy plenary paper at the International Medieval Conference in Leeds, 10 July 2007.

Kirkham, Victoria. "*Contrapasso*: The Long Wait to *Inferno* 28." *Modern Language Notes* 127, no. 1 supp (2012): 1–12.

Klaniczay, Gábor. *Holy Rulers and Blessed Princesses: Dynastic Cults in Medieval Central Europe*. Trans. Éva Pálmai. Cambridge, UK: Cambridge University Press, 2002.

Klauser, Theodor. *A Short History of the Western Liturgy*. London: Oxford University Press, 1969.

Klimisch, Jane. "Gertrude of Helfta: Woman God-Filled and Free." In *Medieval Women Monastics: Wisdom's Wellsprings*, edited by Miriam Schmitt and Linda Kulzer. Collegeville, MN: Liturgical Press, 1996. 245–59.

Kline, Barbara. "The Discourse of Heaven in Mechthild of Hackeborn's *Booke of Gostlye Grace*." In *Imagining Heaven in the Middle Ages: A Book of Essays*, edited by Jan S. Emerson and Hugh Feiss. Milton Parks, UK: Taylor and Francis, 2000. 83–99.

Knowles, David. *Christian Monasticism*. World University Library. New York: McGraw Hill, 1969.

Köbele, Susanne. *Bilder der Unbegriffenen Wahrheit: Zur Struktur mystischer Rede im Spannungsfeld von Latein und Volkssprache*. Tübingen: Francke, 1993.

Koch, Angela. "Mendikanten in Halberstadt: Ein Beitrag zur Gründung, Etablierung und Auflösung von Bettelordenskonventen im mittelalterlichen und frühneuzeitlichen Halberstadt." In *Bürger, Bettelmönche und Bischöfe in Halberstadt: Studien zur Geschichte der Stadt, der Mendikanten und des Bistums vom Mittelalter bis zur Frühen Neuzeit*, edited by Dieter Berg. Münster: Werl, 1997. 139–211.

Kolletzki, Claudia. "'Über die Wahrheit dieses Buches': Die Entstehung des 'Liber Specialis Gratiae' Mechthilds von Hackeborn zwischen Wirklichkeit und Fiktion." In *"Vor dir steht die leere Schale meiner Sehnsucht": Die Mystik der Frauen von Helfta*, edited by Michael Bangert and Hildegund Keul. Leipzig: St. Benno Buch- und Zeitschriftenverlagsgesellschaft, 1998. 156–79.

Korntner, Beate. *Mystikerinnen im Mittelalter: die drei Frauen von Helfta und Marguerite Porete—zwischen Anerkennung und Verfolgung*. Munich: Akademische Verlagsgemeinschaft München, 2012.

Kroos, Renate. "Zu frühen Schrift- und Bildzeugnissen über die heilige Elisabeth als Quellen zur Kunst- und Kulturgeschichte." In *Sankt Elisabeth: Fürstin, Dienerin, Heilige*, edited by Michel De Waha. Philipps-Universität Marburg in Verbindung mit dem Hessischen Landesamt für Geschichtliche Landeskunde. Sigmaringen: Jan Thorbecke Verlag, 1982. 180–239.

Krüne, Max. Foreword to *Urkundenbuch der Klöster der Grafschaft Mansfeld*. Edited by Max Krüne. Geschichtsquellen der Provinz Sachsen und angrenzender Gebiete, vol. 20. Halle: Otto Hendel, 1888. v–xxiii.

Kuhn-Rehfus, Maren. "Cistercian Nuns in Germany in the Thirteenth Century: Upper-Swabian Cistercian Abbeys under the Paternity of Salem." In *Hidden Springs: Cistercian Monastic Women*, edited by John A. Nichols and Lillian Thomas Shank. Vol. 3, book 1 of Medieval Religious Women. CS 113a. Kalamazoo, MI: Cistercian Publications, 1995. 135–58.

Kuhn-Rehfus, Maren. "Zisterzienserinnen in Deutschland." In *Die Zisterzienser: Ordensleben zwischen Ideal und Wirklichkeit*, edited by K. [Kaspar] Elm, P. Joerissen, H. J. Roth. Bonn: Rheinland-Verlag, 1980. 125–47.

Lachance, Paul. Introduction to *Angela of Foligno: Complete Works*. Translated by Paul Lachance. The Classics of Western Spirituality. New York: Paulist Press, 1993. 15–46.

Lagorio, Valerie M. "Variations on the Theme of God's Motherhood in Medieval English Mystical and Devotional Writings." *Studia Mystica* 8, no. 2 (1985): 15–37.

Lamberts, Jef. "Liturgie et spiritualité de l'eucharistie au xiiie siècle." In *Actes du Colloque Fête Dieu, 1246–1996*. Louvain-la-Neuve: Institut d'études médiévales de l'Université catholique de Louvain, 1999. 81–95.

Lampen, Willibrord. "De spiritu S. Francisci in operibus S. Gertrudis Magnae." *Archivum franciscanum historicum* 19 (1926): 733–53.

Lanczkowsi, Johanna. "Einfluss der Hohe-Lied Bernhards auf die drei Helftaer Mystikerinnen." *Benediktinishe Monatsschrift, Erbe und Auftrag* 66 (1990): 17–28.

Larrington, Carolyne, ed. *Women and Writing in Medieval Europe: A Source Book*. London: Routledge, 1995.

Lawrence, Clifford Hugh. *Medieval Monasticism: Forms of Religious Life in Western Europe in the Middle Ages*. London: Longman, 1989.

Leclercq, Henri. "Oblat." *Dictionnaire d'archéologie chrétienne et de liturgie*. Ed. Fernard Cabrol and Henri Leclercq. Paris: Librairie Letouzey et Ané, 1936. 1857–77.

Leclercq, Jean. "Comment vivaient les frères convers?" *Analecta Cisterciensia* 2 (1955): 239–58.

Leclercq, Jean. "Dévotion privée, piété populaire et liturgie au Moyen Âge." In *Études de pastorale liturgiques, Vanves, 26–28 janvier 1944*. Lex orandi, vol. 1. Paris: Éditions du Cerf, 1944. 149–73.

Leclercq, Jean. "Exercices spirituels." Vol. 4, pt. 2 of *Dictionnaire de spiritualité ascétique et mystique, doctrine et histoire*. Ed. M. Viller, et al. Paris: G. Beauchesne et ses fils, 1961. 1903–8.

Leclercq, Jean. "The Intentions of the Founders of the Cistercian Order." In *The Cistercian Spirit: A Symposium*, edited by M. Basil Pennington. Shannon: Irish University Press, 1970. 88–133.

Leclercq, Jean. "The Joy of Dying According to St. Bernard." *Cistercian Studies Quarterly* 25 (1990): 163–75.

Leclercq, Jean. "L'amitié dans les lettres au Moyen Âge." *Revue du moyen âge latin* 1 (1945): 391–410.

Leclercq, Jean. "Le Sacré-Coeur dans la tradition bénédictine au Moyen Âge." In *Cor Jesu: Commentationes in Litteras Encyclicas Pii PP.XII 'Haurietis Aquas,'* edited by Augustine Bea, et al., vol 1 of 2. Rome: Herder, 1957. 3–28.

Leclercq, Jean. "Liturgy and Mental Prayer in the Life of St. Gertrude." *Sponsa Regis* 31 (1960): 1–5. Repr. in "Méditation et célebration: À propos du Mémorial de sainte Gertrude." In *La liturgie et les paradoxes chrétiens*. Coll. Lex orandi 36. Paris: Les éditions du Cerf, 1963.

Leclercq, Jean. *The Love of Learning and the Desire for God: A Study of Monastic Culture*. Trans. Catharine Misrahi. New York: Fordham University Press, 1961.

Leclercq, Jean. "Ways of Prayer and Contemplation: Western." In *Christian Spirituality: Origins to the Twelfth Century*, edited by Bernard McGinn, John Meyendorff, and Jean Leclercq. World Spirituality: An Encyclopedic History of the Religious Quest. New York: Crossroad, 1989. 415–26.

Le Don, Gérard. "Structures et significations de l'imagerie médiévale de l'enfer." *Cahiers de Civilization Médiévale X^e^–XIIe Siècles* 22 (1979): 363–72.

Ledos, Eugène Gabriel. *Sainte Gertrude*. Paris: V. Lecoffre, 1901.

Le Goff, Jacques. *The Birth of Purgatory*. Trans. Arthur Goldhammer. Chicago: University of Chicago Press, 1984.

Lekai, Louis. *Cistercians: Ideals and Reality*. Kent, OH: Kent State University Press, 1977.

Lemmer, Manfred. "Die Helftaer Nonnen und die Sprache der mittelalterlichen Mystik." In *Protokollband zum Kolloquium anlässlich der ersten urkundlichen Erwähnung Eislebens am 23. November [1]994*. Veröffentlichungen der Lutherstätten Eisleben, vol. 1. Halle: Verlag Janos Stekovics, 1995. 484–96.

Lescher, Bruce. "Laybrothers: Questions Then, Questions Now." *Cistercian Studies Quarterly* 23 (1988): 63–85.

Lester, Anne E. *Creating Cistercian Nuns: The Women's Religious Movement and Its Reform in Thirteenth-Century Champagne*. Ithaca: Cornell University Press, 2011.

Lewis, Gertrud Jaron. *By Women, for Women, about Women: The Sister-Books of Fourteenth-Century Germany*. Toronto: Pontifical Institute of Mediaeval Studies, 1996.

Lewis, Gertrud Jaron. "Gertrud of Helfta's *Legatus divinae pietatis* and *ein bottte der götlichen miltekeit*: A Comparative Study of Major Themes." In *Mysticism Medieval and Modern*, edited by Valerie M. Lagorio. Salzburg Studies in English Literature, Elizabethan and Renaissance Studies, vol. 92, no. 20. Salzburg: Institut für Anglistik und Amerikanistik, University of Salzburg, 1986. 58–71.

Lewis, Gertrud Jaron. "God and the Human Being in the Writings of Gertrude of Helfta." *Vox benedictina* 8, no. 2 (1991): 297–322.

Lewis, Gertrud Jaron. "Maria im mystischen Werk Gertruds von Helfta." In *"Vor dir steht die leere Schale meiner Sehnsucht": Die Mystik der Frauen von Helfta*, edited by Michael Bangert and Hildegund Keul. Leipzig: St. Benno Buch- und Zeitschriftenverlagsgesellschaft, 1998. 81–94.

Lewis, Gertrud Jaron, and Jack Lewis. Introduction to *Gertrud the Great of Helfta: Spiritual Exercises*. Trans. Gertrud Jaron Lewis and Jack Lewis. CS 49. Kalamazoo, MI: Cistercian Publications, 1989. 1–18.

Lifshitz, Felice. "Is Mother Superior? Towards a History of Feminine *'Antecharisma.'*" In *Medieval Mothering*, edited by John Carmi Parsons and Bonnie Wheeler. New York: Garland, 1996. 70–88.

Lochrie, Karma. "Between Women." In *The Cambridge Companion to Medieval Women's Writings*, edited by Carolyn Dinshaw and David Wallace. Cambridge, UK: Cambridge University Press, 2003. 70–88.

Logemann, Silke. "Grundzüge der Geschichte der Stadt Halberstadt vom 13. bis 16. Jahrhundert." In *Bürger, Bettelmönche und Bischöfe in Halberstadt: Studien zur Geschichte der Stadt, der Mendikanten und des Bistums vom Mittelalter bis zur Frühen Neuzeit*, edited by Dieter Berg. Münster: Werl, 1997. 81–138.

Luddy, Ailbe J. *The Cistercian Nuns: A Brief Sketch of the History of the Order from Its Foundations to the Present Day*. Dublin: M. H. Gill and Son, 1931.

Macy, Gary. "Commentaries on the Mass During the Early Scholastic Period." In *Treasures from the Storeroom: Medieval Religion and the Eucharist*. Collegeville, MN: Liturgical Press, 1999. 142–71.

Macy, Gary. *The Hidden History of Women's Ordination: Female Clergy in the Medieval West*. Oxford: Oxford University Press, 2008.

Macy, Gary. "The Invention of the Clergy and Laity in the Twelfth Century." In *A Sacramental Life: a Festschrift for Bernard Cooke*, edited by M. H. Barnes and W. P. Roberts. Marquette Studies in Theology, 37. Milwaukee: Marquette University Press, 2003. 117–36.

Macy, Gary. "Reception of the Eucharist According to the Theologians: A Case of Diversity in the 13th and 14th Centuries." In *Treasures from the Storeroom: Medieval Religion and the Eucharist*. Collegeville, MN: Liturgical Press, 1999. 415–26.

Mâle, Emile. *The Gothic Image: Religious Art in France of the Thirteenth Century*. Trans. Dora Nussey. 1958; repr. New York: Harper & Row, 1972.

Marnau, Maximilian. Introduction to *Gertrude of Helfta: The Herald of Divine Love*. Trans. Margaret Winkworth. Classics of Western Spirituality. New York: Paulist Press, 1993. 5–44.

Mauss, Marcel. *The Gift: Form and Reason for Exchange in Archaic Societies*. Trans. W. D. Halls. New York: Routledge, 2002.

Mazza, Enrico. *The Eucharistic Prayers of the Roman Rite*. Trans. Matthew J. O'Connell. New York: Pueblo Publishing, 1986.

McCabe, Maureen. "The Scriptures and Personal Identity: A Study in the *Exercises* of Saint Gertrude." In *Hidden Springs: Cistercian Monastic Women*, edited by John A. Nichols and Lillian Thomas Shank. Volume 3, book 1 of Medieval Religious Women. CS 113a. Kalamazoo, MI: Cistercian Publications, 1995. 497–508.

McDannel, Colleen, and Bernhard Lang. *Heaven: A History*. New Haven: Yale University Press, 1988.

McDonnell, Ernst W. *The Beguines and Beghards in Medieval Culture, with a Special Emphasis on the Belgian Scene*. New Brunswick, NJ: Rutgers University Press, 1954.

McGinn, Bernard. *The Flowering of Mysticism: Men and Women in the New Mysticism—1200–1350*. Vol. 3 of *The Presence of God: A History of Western Mysticism*. New York: Crossroad, 1998.

McGinn, Bernard. *The Growth of Mysticism: Gregory the Great through the 12th Century*. Vol. 2 of *The Presence of God: A History of Western Christian Mysticism*. New York: Crossroad, 1994.

McGuire, Brian Patrick. "The Cistercians and the Transformation of Monastic Friendships." *Analecta Cisterciensia* 37 (1981): 1–63.

McGuire, Brian Patrick. *Friendship and Monastic Community, 350–1250*. CS 95. Kalamazoo, MI: Cistercian Publications, 1988.

McGuire, Brian Patrick. "Purgatory, the Communion of Saints, and Medieval Change." *Viator* 20 (1989): 61–84.

McLachlan, Elizabeth Parker. "Liturgical Vessels and Implements." In *The Liturgy of the Medieval Church*, edited by Thomas J. Heffernan and E. Ann Matter. TEAMS (The Consortium for the Teaching of the Middle Ages). Kalamazoo, MI: Medieval Institute Publications, 2005. 333–89.

McNamara, Jo Ann Kay. "The Need to Give: Suffering and Female Sanctity in the Middle Ages." In *Images of Sainthood in Medieval Europe*. Edited by Renate Blumenfeld-Kosinski and Timea Szell. Ithaca, NY: Cornell University Press, 1991. 199–221.

McNamara, Jo Ann Kay. "The Rhetoric of Orthodoxy: Clerical Authority and Female Innovation in the Struggle with Heresy." In *Maps of Flesh and Light: The Religious Experience of Medieval Women Mystics*, edited by Ulrike Wiethaus. Syracuse, NY: Syracuse University Press, 1993. 9–27.

McNamara, Jo Ann Kay. *Sisters in Arms: Catholic Nuns through Two Millennia*. Cambridge, MA: Harvard University Press, 1996.

McNamer, Sarah. *Affective Meditation and the Invention of Medieval Compassion*. Philadelphia: University of Pennsylvania Press, 2010.

Menzel, J. J. "Trebnitz." Vol. 8 of *Lexikon des Mittelalters*. Ed. Norbert Angermann, et al. Munich: Lexma Verlag, 1990. 967.

Metz, René. "La Couronne et l'Anneau dans la consecration des vierges. Origine et evolution des deux rites dans la liturgie latine." *Revue des sciences religieuses* 28 (1954): 113–32.

Michael, R. P. Émil. "Die hl. Mechtild und die hl. Gertrud die Grosse Benedictinerinnen?" *Zeitschrift für katholisches Theologie* 23 (1899): 448–552.

Minguet, Hugues. "Théologie spirituelle de sainte Gertrude: le Livre II du *Le Héraut*." Parts 1, 2, and 3. *Collectanea Cisterciensia* 51, nos. 2, 3, and 4 (1989): 147–77.

Minnis, Alistair J. *Medieval Theory of Authorship: Scholastic Literary Attitudes in the Later Middle Ages*. London: Scolar Press, 1984.

Mooney, Catherine M. "The Authorial Role of Brother A. in the Composition of Angela of Foligno's Revelations." In *Creative Women in Medieval and Early Modern Italy: A Religious and Artistic Renaissance*, edited by Ann Matter and John Coakley. Philadelphia: University of Pennsylvania Press, 1994. 34–63.

Mooney, Catherine M., ed. *Gendered Voices: Medieval Saints and Their Interpreters*. Middle Ages Series. Philadelphia: University of Pennsylvania Press, 1998.

Mooney, Catherine M. "*Imitatio Christi or imitatio Mariae?* Clare of Assisi and Her Interpreters." In *Gendered Voices: Medieval Saints and Their Interpreters*, edited by Catherine M. Mooney. Middle Ages Series. Philadelphia: University of Pennsylvania Press, 1998. 52–77.

Moore, R. I. *The Formation of a Persecuting Society: Authority and Deviance in Western Europe 950–1250*. Oxford: Blackwell, 1987.

Muir, Carolyn Diskant. *Saintly Brides and Bridegrooms: The Mystic Marriage in Northern Renaissance Art*. London: Harvey Miller, 2012.

Murray, Jacqueline, and Konrad Eisenbichler, eds. *Desire and Discipline: Sex and Sexuality in the Premodern West*. Buffalo, NY: University of Toronto Press, 1996.

Nemes, Balázs J. "Die 'Geistlichen Übungen' Gertruds von Helfta: Ein vergessenes Zeugnis mittelaltlicher Mystik." In *Gertrud von Helfta: Exercitia spiritualia. Geistliche Übungen. Lateinisch und Deutsch*, edited by Siegfried Ringler. Elberfeld: Burchverlag Oliver Humberg, 2001.

Nemes, Balázs J. "Text Production and Authorship: Gertrude of Helfta's *Legatus Divinae Pietatis*." In *A Companion to Mysticism and Devotion in Northern Germany in the Late Middle Ages*, edited by Elizabeth Andersen, Henrike Lähnemann, and Anne Simon. Brill's Companions to the Christian Tradition, vol. 44. Leiden: Brill, 2014. 103–30.

Nemes, Balázs J. *Von der Schrift zum Buch—vom Ich zum Autor: Zur Text- und Autorkonstitution in Überlieferung und Rezeption des "Fliessenden Lichts der Gottheit" Mechthilds von Magdeburg*. Bern: A. Francke Verlag, 2010.

Newman, Barbara. "Die visionären Texte und visuellen Welten religiöser Frauen." In *Krone und Schleier: Kunst aus mittelalterlichen Frauenklöstern*, edited by Jeffrey Hamburger and Robert Suckale. Bonn and Essen: Kunst- und Ausstellungshalle der Bundesrepublik Deutschland, Bonn; and Ruhrlandmuseum, Essen, 2005. 104–17.

Newman, Barbara. "Divine Power Made Perfect in Weakness: St. Hildegard on the Frail Sex." In *Peaceweavers*, edited by Lillian Thomas Shank and John A. Nichols. Vol. 2 of Medieval Religious Women. CS 72. Kalamazoo, MI: Cistercian Publications, 1987. 103–22.

Newman, Barbara. "Gender." In *The Blackwell Companion to Mysticism*, edited by Julia A. Lamm. London: Blackwell Publishing, 2013. 41–55.

Newman, Barbara. "Hildegard and Her Hagiographers: The Remaking of Female Sainthood." In *Gendered Voices: Medieval Saints and Their Interpreters*, edited by Catherine M. Mooney. Middle Ages Series. Philadelphia: University of Pennsylvania Press, 1998. 16–34.

Newman, Barbara. "*Iam cor meum non sit suum*: Exchanging Hearts, from Heloise to Helfta." In *From Knowledge to Beatitude: St. Victor, Twelfth-Century Scholars, and Beyond: Essays in Honor of Grover A. Zinn, Jr.*, edited by E. Ann Matter and Lesley Smith. Notre Dame, IN: Notre Dame University Press, 2013. 281–99.

Newman, Barbara. Introduction to *Hildegard of Bingen: Scivias*. Classics of Western Spirituality. New York: Paulist Press, 1990. 9–53.

Newman, Barbara. Introduction to *Mechthild of Hackeborn and the Nuns of Helfta: The Book of Special Grace*. Trans. Barbara Newman. Classics of Western Spirituality. New York: Paulist Press, 2017. 1–34.

Newman, Barbara. "On the Threshold of the Dead: Purgatory, Hell, and Religious Women." In *From Virile Woman to WomanChrist: Studies in Medieval Religion and Literature*. Middle Ages Series. Philadelphia, PA: University of Pennsylvania Press, 1995. 108–36.

Newman, Barbara. "Preface: Goswin of Villers and the Visionary Network." In *Send Me God: The Lives of Ida the Compassionate of Nivelles, Nun of Ramée, Arnulf, Lay Brother, and Abundus, Monk of Villers*. Medieval Women: Texts and Contexts. University Park, PA: Pennsylvania State University Press, 2006. xxix–xlix.

Newman, Barbara. Review of *The Women of Helfta: Scholars and Mystics*, by Mary Jeremy Finnegan. *Speculum: A Journal of Medieval Studies* 63, no. 1 (January 1993): 50–56.

Newman, Barbara. *Sister of Wisdom: Hildegard's Theology of the Feminine*. Berkeley: University of California Press, 1987.

Newman, Barbara. "What Did It Mean to Say 'I Saw'? The Clash between Theory and Practice in Medieval Visionary Culture." *Speculum: A Journal of Medieval Studies* 80, no. 1 (2005): 1–143.

Newman, Martha G. *The Boundaries of Charity: Cistercian Culture and Ecclesiastical Reform, 1098–1180*. Stanford, CA: Stanford University Press, 1996.

Newman, Martha G. "Crucified by the Virtues: Monks, Lay Brothers, and Women in Thirteenth-Century Cistercian Saints' Lives." In *Gender and Difference in the Middle Ages*, edited by Sharon Farmer and Carol Braun Pasternack. Minneapolis, MN: University of Minnesota Press, 2003. 182–209.

Noell, Brian. "Expectation and Unrest among Cistercian Lay Brothers in the Twelfth and Thirteenth Centuries." *Journal of History* 32 (2006): 253–74.

Nolan, Barbara. *The Gothic Visionary Perspective*. Princeton, NJ: Princeton University Press, 1977.

Nolan, Edward Peter. *Cry Out and Write: A Feminine Poetics of Revelation*. New York: Continuum, 1994.

Oefelein, Cornelia. "Grundlagen zur Baugeschichte des Klosters Helfta." In *"Vor dir steht die leere Schale meiner Sehnsucht": Die Mystik der Frauen von Helfta*, edited by Michael Bangert and Hildegund Keul. Leipzig: St. Benno Buch- und Zeitschriftenverlagsgesellschaft, 1998. 12–28.

O'Malley, John. *What happened at Vatican II*. Cambridge, MA: Belknap Press of Harvard University, 2008.

Opitz, Claudia, et al., eds. *Maria in der Welt: Marienverehrung im Kontext der Sozialgeschichte 10.–18. Jahrhundert*. Zurich: Chronos Verlag, 1993.

Ortner, Sherry. "Resistance: Some Theoretical Problems in Anthropological History and Historical Anthropology." *Comparative Studies in Society and History* 37 (1995): 173–91.

Oury, Guy-Marie. "Oblats (Institute religieux)." *Dictionnaire de spiritualité, ascétique et mystique, doctrine et histoire*. Ed. M. Viller, et al. Paris: Beauchesne et ses fils, 1982.

Paquelin, Louis. Praefatio to *Sanctae Gertrudis Magnae, virginis ordinis sancti Benedicti: Legatus divinae pietatis accedunt ejusdem Exercitia spiritualia*. Ed. the monks of Solesmes [Louis Paquelin]. Vol. 1 of *Revelationes Gertrudianae ac Mechtildianae*. Paris: H. Oudin, 1875. i–lxii.

Paquelin, Louis. Praefatio to *Sanctae Mechtildis, virginis ordinis sancti Benedicti: Liber specialis gratiae accedit sororis Mechtildis ejusdem ordinis Lux divinitatis*. Ed. the monks of Solesmes [Louis Paquelin]. Vol. 2 of *Revelationes Gertrudianae ac Mechtildianae*. Paris: H. Oudin, 1877. i–xvi

Parisse, Michel. *Nonnes au moyen âge*. Le Puy: Christine Bonneton, 1983.

Parry, Jonathan. "The Gift, the Indian Gift and the 'Indian Gift.'" *Man*, New Series, 21, no. 3 (1986): 453–73.

Partner, Nancy. "Did Mystics Have Sex?" In *Desire and Discipline: Sex and Sexuality in the Premodern West*, edited by Jacqueline Murray and Konrad Eisenbichler. Toronto and Buffalo: University of Toronto Press, 1996. 296–312.

Paxton, Frederick S. *Christianizing Death: The Creation of a Ritual Process in Early Medieval Europe*. Ithaca, NY: Cornell University Press, 1990.

Pelikan, Jaroslav. *The Growth of Medieval Theology (600–1300)*. Vol. 3, *The Christian Tradition: A History of the Development of Doctrine*. Chicago: University of Chicago Press, 1978.

Peters, Ursula. "Frauenliteratur im Mittelalter? Überlegungen zur Trobiaritzpoesie, zur Frauenmystik und zur feministischen Literaturbetrachtung." *Germanisch-Romanische Monatsschrift* 38 (1988): 35–56.

Peters, Ursula. *Religiöse Erfahrung als literarisches Faktum: Zur Vorgeschichte und Genese frauenmystischer Texte des 13. und 14. Jahrhunderts, Gedruck mit Unterstützung der Deutschen Forschungsgemeinschaft*. Tübingen: Max Niemeyer Verlag, 1988.

Peters, Ursula. "Vita religiosa und spirituelles Erleben: Frauenmystik und frauenmystiche Literatur im 13. und 14. Jahrhundert." In *Deutsche Literatur von Frauen, vom Mittelalter bis zum Ende des 18. Jahrhundert*, edited by Gisela Brinker-Gabler. Vol. 1 of *Deutsche Literatur von Frauen*. Munich: Beck, 1988. 88–112.

Petroff, Elizabeth Alvilda. *Medieval Women's Visionary Literature*. New York: Oxford University Press, 1986.

Petroff, Elizabeth Alvilda. "The Spirituality of Medieval Holy Women." *Vox benedictina* 6, no. 1 (1989): 14–39.

Poor, Sara S. "Cloaking the Body in Text: The Question of Female Authorship in the Writings of Mechthild von Magdeburg." *Exemplaria* 12, no. 2 (Fall 2000): 417–53.

Poor, Sara S. *Mechthild of Magdeburg and Her Book: Gender and the Making of Textual Authority*. Middle Ages Series. Philadelphia: University of Pennsylvania Press, 2004.

Poor, Sara S. "Mechthild von Magdeburg, Gender, and the 'Unlearned Tongue.'" *Journal of Medieval and Early Modern Studies* 31, no. 2 (Spring 2001): 213–49.

Pourrat, Pierre. *La spiritualité chrétienne*. 4 vols. Paris: Librairie Lecoffre, 1951.

Power, Eileen. *Medieval English Nunneries, c. 1275 to 1535*. Cambridge Studies in Medieval Life and Thought. Cambridge: Cambridge University Press, 1922.

Preger, Wilhelm. *Geschichte der deutschen Mystik bis zum Tode Meister Eckharts*. Vol. 1 of *Geschichte der deutschen Mystik nach den Quellen untersucht und dargestellt*. Leipzig: Dörffling und Franke, 1874.

Quenardel, Olivier. *La communion eucharistique dans le* Héraut de l'amour divin *de saint Gertrud d'Helfta*. Monastica, vol. 2. Turnhout: Brepols, 1997.

Rahner, Hugo. "Grundzüge einer Geschichte der Herz-Iezu-Verehrung." *Zeitschrift für Askese und Mystik* 18 (1943): 61–83.

Rayez, André. "Direction spirituelle en occident." Vol. 3 of *Dictionnaire de spiritualité ascétique et mystique, doctrine et histoire*. Ed. M. Viller, et al. Paris: G. Beauchesne et ses fils, 1957. 1099–1108.

Riché, Pierre. "L'enfant dans la société monastique au xiie siècle." In *Pierre Abélard, Pierre le Vénérable: Les courants philosophiques, littéraires et artistiques en occident au milieu du xii siècle*. Colloques internationaux du Centre National de la Recherche Scientifique, no. 546. Paris: Éditions du Centre National de la Recherche Scientifique, 1975. 689–701.

Richstätter, Karl. *Die Herz-Jesu-Verhrung des deutschen Mittelalters*. Regensburg: J. Kosel and F. Pustet, 1924.

Riddy, Felicity. "Women Talking about the Things of God: A Late Medieval Subculture." In *Women and Literature in Britain, 1150–1500*, edited by Carol M. Meale. Cambridge Studies in Medieval Literature, vol. 17. Cambridge: Cambridge University Press, 1993. 104–27.

Ringler, Siegfried. "Die Rezeption Gertruds von Helfta im Bereich süddeutschen Frauenklöster." In *"Vor dir steht die leere Schale meiner Sehnsucht": Die Mystik der Frauen von Helfta*, edited by Michael Bangert and Hildegund Keul. Leipzig: St. Benno Buch- und Zeitschriftenverlagsgesellschaft, 1998. 134–55.

Ringler, Siegfried. "Gnadenviten aus süddeutschen Frauenklöstern des 14. Jahrhunderts: Vitenschreibung als mystische Lehre." In *Minnichlichiu Gotes Erkennusse Studien zur frühen abendländischen Mystikinterpretation*, edited by Dietrich Schmidtke. Mystik in Geschichte und Gegenwart, Texte und Untersuchungen, pt. 1, Christliche Mystik, vol. 7. Stuttgart-Bad Cannstatt: Frommann Holzbogg, 1990. 89–104.

Ringler, Siegfried. *Viten- und Offenbarungsliteratur in Frauenklöster des Mittelalters: Quellen und Studien*. Münchener Texte und Untersuchungen zur deutschen Literatur des Mittelalters, Kommission für deutsche Literatur des Mittelalters der Bayerischen Akademie der Wissenschaften, vol. 72. Munich: Artemis Verlag, 1980.

Robinson, A. Mary F. "The Convent of Helfta." *Fortnightly Review* 40 (1886): 64–158.

Roisin, Simone. "L'Efflorescence cistercienne et le courant féminin de piété au xiiie siècle." *Revue d'histoire ecclésiastique* 39 (1943): 342–78.

Roisin, Simone. *L'hagiographie cistercinne dans le diocese de Liège au XIIIe siècle*. Recueil de travaux d'historie et de philologie, vol. 3. Louvain: Bibliothèque de l'Université, 1947.

Rubin, Miri. "Small Groups: Identity and Solidarity in the Late Middle Ages." In *Enterprise and Individuals in Fifteenth-Century England*. Stroud: Alan Sutton Publishers, 1991. 132–50.

Ruh, Kurt. *Frauenmystik und Franziskanische Mystik der Frühzeit*. Vol. 2 of *Geschichte der abendlandischen Mystik*. Munich: Verlag C. H. Beck, 1993.

Ruh, Kurt. "Gertrud von Helfta: Ein neues Gertrud-Bild." *Zeitschrift für deutsches Altertum und deutsche Literatur* 121 (1992): 1–20.

Savage, Christian Gregory. "Music and the Writings of the Helfta Mystics." M.A. thesis, Florida State University, 2012.

Schindele, Pia. "Elemente der Benediktinerregel in den Offenbarungen der heiligen Gertrud von Helfta." In *Und sie folgten der Regel St. Benedikts: Die Cistercienser und das benediktinische Monchtum: eine Würdigung des abendländischen Mönchsvaters als Nachlese zum Benediktusjubiläum 1980*, edited by Ambrosius Schneider with Adam Wienand. Cologne: Wienand, 1981. 156–68.

Schlenker, Gerlinde. "1000 Jahre Eisleben – Zentum des Mansfelder Landes." In *Protokollband zum Kolloquium anlässlich der ersten urkundlichen Erwähnung Eislebens am 23. November [1]994*. Veröffentlichungen der Lutherstätten Eisleben, vol. 1. Halle: Verlag Janos Stekovics, 1995. 13–32.

Schmidt, Margot. "Mechtilde de Hackeborn." *Dictionnaire de spiritualité ascétique et mystique, doctrine et histoire*. Edited by M. Viller, et al. Paris: G. Beauchesne et ses fils, 1980. 873–77.

Schmitt, Miriam. "Freed to Run with Expanded Heart: The Writings of Gertrud of Helfta and the Rule of Benedict." *Cistercian Studies Quarterly* 25, no. 3 (1990): 219–32.

Schmitz, Kenneth L. *The Gift: Creation*. The Aquinas Lecture. Milwaukee, WI: Marquette University Press, 1982.

Schmitz, Philibert. *Les Moniales*. Vol. 7 of *Histoire de l'Ordre de Saint-Benoît*. Liège: Les Éditions de Maredsous, 1956.

Schroeder-Sheker, Therese. "The Alchemical Harp of Mechthild von Hackeborn." *Vox benedictina* 6, no. 1 (1989): 40–55.

Schulenburg, Jane Tibbetts. "Saints' Lives as a Source for the History of Women, 500–1000." In *Medieval Women and the Sources of Medieval History*, edited by Joel T. Rosenthal. Athens: University of Georgia Press, 1990.

Schwietering, Julius. "The Origins of the Humility Formula." *Modern Language Journal* 69 (1954): 1279–91.

Scott, Karen. "Mystical Death, Bodily Death: Catherine of Siena and Raymond of Capua on the Mystic's Encounter with God." In *Gendered Voices: Medieval Saints and Their Interpreters*, edited by Catherine M. Mooney. Middle Ages Series. Philadelphia: University of Pennsylvania Press, 1998. 136–67.

Senn, Frank C. *Christian Liturgy: Catholic and Evangelical*. Minneapolis: Fortress Press, 1997.

Shahar, Shulamith. *The Fourth Estate: A History of Women in the Middle Ages*. Trans. Chaya Galai. London: Methuen, 1983.

Shank, Lillian Thomas. "The God of My Life: St. Gertrude, A Monastic Woman." In *Peaceweavers*, edited by Lillian Thomas Shank and John A. Nichols. Vol. 2 of Medieval Religious Women. CS 72. Kalamazoo, MI: Cistercian Publications, 1987. 239–73.

Sheingorn, Pamela. "The Holy Kinship: The Ascendancy of Matriliny in Sacred Genealogy of the Fifteenth Century." *Thought: A Review of Culture and Ideas* 64 (1989): 268–86.

Southern, R. W. *The Making of the Middle Ages*. New Haven, CT: Yale University Press, 1953.

Southern, R. W. *Saint Anselm: A Portrait in a Landscape*. New York: Cambridge University Press, 1990.

Southern, R. W. *Western Society and the Church in the Middle Ages*. The Penguin History of the Church, vol. 2. London: Penguin Books, 1970.

Spearing, A. C. "Secrecy, Listening, and Telling in *The Squyr of Lowe Degre*." *The Journal of Medieval and Early Modern Studies* 20, no. 2 (1990): 273–92.

Spearing, Elizabeth. *Visionary Literature; Medieval Writings on Female Spirituality*. New York: Penguin Books, 2002.

Spitzlei, Sabine B. *Erfahrungsraum Herz: Zur Mystik des Zisterzienserinnenklosters Helfta im 13 Jahrhundert*. Mystik in Geschichte und Gegenwart, Texte und Untersuchungen, vol. 9. Christliche Mystik, no. 1. Stuttgart-Bad Cannstatt: Frommann-Holzboog, 1991.

Standaerts, M. "Helfta." Vol. 23 of *Dictionnaire d'histoire et de géographie ecclésiastiques*. Ed. R. Aubert and J.-P. Hendrickx. Paris: Letouzey et Ané, 1990. 894–96.

Stierli, Joseph. "Devotion to the Sacred Heart from the End of the Patristic Times down to St. Margaret Mary." In *Heart of the Savior: A Symposium on Devotion to the Sacred Heart*, edited by Joseph Stierli. Freiburg: Herder, 1957. 59–107.

Stock, Brian. *The Implications of Literacy: Written Language and Models of Interpretation in the Eleventh and Twelfth Centuries*. Princeton, NJ: Princeton University Press, 1983.

Stock, Brian. "The Self and Literary Experience in Late Antiquity and the Middle Ages." *New Literary History* 25, no. 4 (Autumn 1994): 839–52.

Straw, Carol. "Timor Mortis." In *Augustine through the Ages: An Encyclopedia*, edited by Allan D. Fitzgerald. Grand Rapids, MI: William B. Eerdmans Publishing, 1999. 838–42.

Swanson, Robert N. "Apostolic Successors: Priests and Priesthood, Bishops, and Episcopacy in Medieval Western Europe." In *A Companion to Priesthood and Holy Orders in the Middle Ages*, edited by Greg Peters and C. Colt Anderson. Brill's Companions to the Christian Tradition, vol. 62. Leiden: Brill, 2016. 4–42.

Tapié, Victor-Lucien. *The Rise and Fall of the Habsburg Monarchy*. Trans. Stephen Hardman. New York: Praeger Publishers, 1971.

Tentler, Thomas N. *Sin and Confession on the Eve of the Reformation*. Princeton, NJ: Princeton University Press, 1977.

Thompson, Augustine. "Hildegard of Bingen on Gender and the Priesthood." *Church History: Studies in Christianity and Culture* 63, no. 3 (1994): 349–64.

Thompson, Sally. "The Problem of Cistercian Nuns in the Twelfth and Early Thirteenth Centuries." In *Medieval Women: Dedicated and Presented to Professor Rosalind M. T. Hill on the Occasion of Her 70th Birthday*, edited by Derek Baker. Oxford: Blackwell, 1978. 227–52.

Tobin, Frank. "Henry Suso and Elsbeth Stagel: Was the *Vita* a Cooperative Effort?" In *Gendered Voices: Medieval Saints and Their Interpreters*, edited by Catherine M. Mooney. Middle Ages Series. Philadelphia: University of Pennsylvania Press, 1998. 118–35.

Tobin, Frank. Introduction to *Mechthild of Magdeburg: The Flowing Light of the Godhead*. Trans. Frank Tobin. Classics of Western Spirituality. New York: Paulist Press, 1998.

Tobin, Frank. *Mechthild von Magdeburg: A Medieval Mystic in Modern Eyes*. Columbia, SC: Camden House, 1995.

Tobin, Frank. Review of *Mystische Erfahrung und spirituelle Theologie: Zu Meister Eckharts Auseinandersetzung mit der Frauenfrommigkeit seiner Zeit*, by Otto Langer. *Speculum* 64, no. 4 (October 1989): 996–97.

Toepfer, Michael. *Die Konversen der Zisterzienser: Untersuchungen über ihren Beitrag zur mittelalterlichen Blüte des Ordens*. Berliner historische Studien, vol. 10. Berlin: Duncker and Humblot, 1983.

Tosh, Michael. "Welfs, Hohenstaufen, and Habsburgs." *The New Cambridge Medieval History*, edited by David Abulafia. Cambridge, UK: Cambridge University Press, 1999. 375–404.

Ulpts, Ingo. "Geschichte des Franziskanerkonvents in Halberstadt vom 13. bis zum 16. Jahrhundert." In *Bürger, Bettelmönche und Bischöfe in Halberstadt: Studien zur Geschichte der Stadt, der Mendikanten und des Bistums vom Mittelalter bis zur Frühen Neuzeit*, edited by Dieter Berg. Münster: Werl, 1997. 213–52.

Underhill, Evelyn. *Mysticism: A Study in the Nature and Development of Man's Spiritual Consciousness*. 1901. Repr. New York: E. P. Dutton, 1930.

Unger, Helga. "Interaktion von Gott und Mensch im *Legatus divinae pietatis* (Buch II) Gertruds der Großen von Helfta. Liturgie—mystische Erfahrung—Seelsorge." In *Liturgie und Literatur: Historische Fallstudien*, edited by Cornelia Herberichs, Norbert Kössinger, and Stephanie Seidl. Lingua Historica Germanica, 10. Berlin: De Gruyter, 2015. 213–52.

Vagaggini, Cyprian. "La dévotion au Sacré-Coeur chez Sainte Mechtilde et Sainte Gertrude." In *Cor Jesu: Commentationes in Litteras Encyclicas Pii PP.XII "Haurietis Aquas,"* edited by Augustine Bea, et al. Vol. 1 of 2. Rome: Herder, 1957. 31–48.

Vagaggini, Cyprian. *Theological Dimensions of the Liturgy: A General Treatise on the Theology of the Liturgy*. Translated by Leonard J. Doyle and W. A. Jurgens from the fourth Italian edition, revised and augmented by author. Collegeville, MN: Liturgical Press, 1976.

Van Dijk, Clemens. "L'instruction et la culture des frères convers dans les premiers siècles de l'ordre de Cîteaux." *Collectanea Cisterciensia* 24 (1962): 243–58.

Vauchez, André. *Saints, prophètes et visionnaires: le pouvoir surnaturel au Moyen Âge*. Paris: Albin Michel, 1999.

Vernet, Felix. *Medieval Spirituality*. London: Sands, 1930.

Vicaire, Marie-Hubert. *St. Dominic and His Times*. Translated by Kathleen Pond. London: Darton, Longman and Todd, 1964.

Viola, C. "Jugement de Dieu et jugement dernier: Saint Augustin et la scholastique naissante fin xie–mileu xiiie siècles." In *The Use and Abuse of Eschatology in the Middle Ages*, edited by W. Verbeke, et al. Louvain: Leuven University Press, 1988. 242–98.

Voaden, Rosalynn Jean. "All Girls Together: Community, Gender, and Vision at Helfta." In *Medieval Women in Their Communities*, edited by Diane Watt. Buffalo, NY: University of Toronto Press, 1997. 72–91.

Voaden, Rosalynn Jean. "Articulating Ecstasy: Image and Allegory in *The Booke of Gostlye Grace* of Mechtild of Hackeborn." PhD dissertation, University of Victoria, 1990.

Voaden, Rosalynn Jean. "The Company She Keeps: Mechthild of Hackeborn in Late-Medieval Devotional Compilations." In *Prophets Abroad: The Reception of Continental Holy Women in Late-Medieval England*, edited by Rosalynn [Jean] Voaden. Woodbridge: Boydell and Brewer, 1996. 51–69.

Voaden, Rosalynn Jean. "Mechtild of Hackeborn." In *Medieval Holy Women in the Christian Tradition, c. 1100–c. 1500*, edited by Alastair Minnis and Rosalynn Voaden. Turnhout: Brepols, 2010. 431–51.

Voaden, Rosalynn Jean. "Women's Words, Men's Language: *Discretio Spirituum* as Discourse in the Writing of Medieval Women Visionaries." In *Proceedings of the International Conference of Conques, 26–29 July 1993*, edited by Roger Ellis and René Tixier. Vol. 5 of *The Medieval Translator*. Turnhout: Brepols, 1996. 64–83.

Volfing, Annette. "The Authorship of John the Evangelist as Presented in Medieval German Sermons and *Meisterlieder*." *Oxford German Studies* 23 (1994): 1–44.

Volfing, Annette. *John the Evangelist and Medieval German Writing: Imitating the Inimitable*. Oxford: Oxford University Press, 2001.

Von Balthasar, Hans Urs. Einführung to *Das Buch vom strömenden Lob*. Einsiedeln: Johannes Verlag, 1956. 7–18.

Wandruszka, Adam. *The House of Habsburg: Six Hundred Years of European Dynasty*. Translated by Cathleen Epstein and Hans Epstein. New York: Doubleday and Company, 1964.

Ward, Benedicta. Introduction to *The Prayers and Meditations of St. Anselm with the Proslogion*. Trans. Benedicta Ward. London: Penguin Books, 1973.

Warner, Marina. *Alone of All Her Sex: The Myth and Cult of the Virgin Mary*. New York: Vintage Books, 1983.

Watson, Nicholas, and Jacqueline Jenkins, eds. The *Writings of Julian of Norwich: A Vision Showed to a Devout Woman and A Revelation of Love*. Turnhout: Brepols, 2006.

Weeks, Andrew. *German Mysticism: From Hildegard of Bingen to Ludwig Wittgenstein: A Literary and Intellectual History*. Albany: State University of New York Press, 1993.

Wehr, Gerhard. *Die deutsche Mystik: Gestalten und Zeugnisse religiöser Erfahrung von Meister Eckhart bis zur Reformationszeit*. Gütersloher Taschenbücher/Siebenstern. Gütersloh: Gütersloher Verlagshaus Gerd Mohn, 1980.

Wehrli-Johns, Martina. "Haushälterin Gottes: Zur Mariennachfolge der Beginen." In *Mariae, Abbild oder Vorbild? Zur Sozialgeschichte mittelalterlicher Marienverehrung*, edited by Hedwig Röckelein, Claudia Opitz, and Dieter R. Bauer. Tübingen: Diskord, 1990. 147–67.

Weinstein, Donald, and Rudolph Bell. *Saints and Society: Christendom, 1000–1700*. Chicago: University of Chicago Press, 1982.

Werner, M. "D. v. Apolda." *Lexikon des Mittelalters*, edited by Robert-Henri Bautier. Munich: Artemis Verlag, 1986. 1032–33.

Werner, M. "E. v. Thüringen." *Lexikon des Mittelalters*, edited by Robert-Henri Bautier. Munich: Artemis Verlag, 1986. 1032–33.

Wiberg, Else Marie. "Image of God—Image of Mary—Image of Woman: On the Theology and Spirituality of Beatrice of Nazareth." *Cistercian Studies Quarterly* 29, no. 2 (1994): 209–20.

Wiethaus, Ulrike. Review of *Die Vita der Heiligen Elisabeth des Dietrich von Apolda*, edited by Monika Rener. *Speculum* 71, no. 1 (January 1996): 152–53.

Wiethaus, Ulrike. "Spatial Metaphors, Textual Production, and Spirituality in the Works of Gertrud of Helfta (1256–1301/2)." In *A*

Place to Believe In: Medieval Landscapes, edited by Clare A. Lees and Gillian R. Overing. University Park: Pennsylvania State University Press, 2006. 132–49.

Williams-Krapp, Werner. "Thierry d'Apolda." *Dictionnaire de spiritualité ascétique et mystique, doctrine et histoire*. Ed. M. Viller, et al. Paris: G. Beauchesne et ses fils, 1980. 691–93.

Winston-Allen, Anne. *Convent Chronicles: Women Writing about Women in the Late Middle Ages*. University Park: Pennsylvania State University Press, 2004.

Wogan-Browne, Jocelyn. "Powers of Record, Powers of Example: Hagiography and Women's History." In *Gendering the Master Narrative: Women and Power in the Middle Ages*, edited by Mary C. Erler and Mayanne Kowaleski. Ithaca, NY: Cornell University Press, 2003.

Wogan-Browne, Jocelyn, and Nicholas Watson, Andrew Taylor, Ruth Evans, eds. *The Idea of the Vernacular: An Anthology of Middle English Literary Theory, 1280–1520*. University Park: The Pennsylvania State University Press, 1999. 71–93.

Yardley, Anne Bagnall. *Performing Piety: Musical Culture in Medieval English Nunneries*. New York: Palgrave, 2006.

Yoshikawa, Naoë Kukita. "Heavenly Vision and Psychosomatic Healing: Medical Discourse in Mechtild of Hackeborn's *Booke of Gostlye Grace*." In *Medicine, Religion, and Gender in Medieval Culture*, edited by Naoë Kukita Yoshikawa. Suffolk: D. S. Brewer, 2015. 67–84.

Index